BUSINESS DATA COMMUNICATIONS: INFRASTRUCTURE, NETWORKING AND SECURITY

SEVENTH EDITION

William Stallings

Thomas Case

Georgia Southern University

International Edition contributions by
Arup Kumar Bhattacharjee
RCC Institute of Information Technology, Kolkata

Soumen Mukherjee
RCC Institute of Information Technology, Kolkata

PEARSON

Boston   Columbus   Indianapolis   New York   San Francisco   Upper Saddle River
Amsterdam   Cape Town   Dubai   London   Madrid   Milan   Munich   Paris   Montréal   Toronto
Delhi   Mexico City   São Paulo   Sydney   Hong Kong   Seoul   Singapore   Taipei   Tokyo

Editorial Director: Marcia Horton
Executive Editor: Tracy Johnson
Associate Editor: Carole Snyder
Director of Marketing: Christy Lesko
Marketing Manager: Yez Alayan
Marketing Coordinator: Kathryn Ferranti
Director of Production: Erin Gregg
Managing Editor: Jeff Holcomb
Production Project Manager: Kayla Smith-Tarbox
Publisher, International Edition: Angshuman Chakraborty
Publishing Administrator and Business Analyst, International Edition: Shokhi Shah Khandelwal
Senior Print and Media Editor, International Edition: Ashwitha Jayakumar

Acquisitions Editor, International Edition: Sandhya Ghoshal
Publishing Administrator, International Edition: Hema Mehta
Project Editor, International Edition: Karthik Subramanian
Senior Manufacturing Controller, Production, International Editions: Trudy Kimber
Manufacturing Buyer: Pat Brown
Creative Director: Jayne Conte
Manager, Rights and Permissions: Michael Joyce
Text Permission Coordinator: Zachary Galaboff
Lead Media Project Manager: Daniel Sandin
Full-Service Project Management/Composition: Shiny Rajesh/Integra Software Services Pvt. Ltd.
Cover Printer: Courier Westford

Pearson Education Limited
Edinburgh Gate
Harlow
Essex CM20 2JE
England

and Associated Companies throughout the world

Visit us on the World Wide Web at:
www.pearsoninternationaleditions.com

© Pearson Education Limited 2013

British Library Cataloguing-in-Publication Data
A catalogue record for this book is available from the British Library

10 9 8 7 6 5 4 3 2 1
14 13 12 11 10

Typeset in 10/12 Times Ten Roman by Shiny Rajesh/Integra Software Services Pvt. Ltd.

Printed and bound by Courier Westford in The United States of America

The publisher's policy is to use paper manufactured from sustainable forests.

PEARSON

ISBN 10: 0-273-76916-2
ISBN 13: 978-0-273-76916-3

For my loving wife Tricia

—WS

To Carol, Ethan, and Maryn for their continuous inspiration and love

—TC

CONTENTS

ONLINE CHAPTERS AND APPENDICES[1]

---

[1]Online chapters, appendices, and other documents are Premium Content, available via the access card at the front of this book.

ONLINE RESOURCES

Site	Location	Description
Companion Web site	WilliamStallings.com/BusinessDataComm	*Student Resources* link: Useful links and documents for students *Instructor Resources* link: Useful links and documents for instructors
Premium Content	Click on *Premium Content* link at www.pearsoninternationaleditions.com/stallings and enter the student access code found on the card in the front of the book	Online chapters, appendices, and other documents that supplement the book
Instructor Resource Center (IRC)	Click on *Instructor Resource* link at www.pearsoninternationaleditions.com/stallings	Solutions manual, projects manual, slides, and other useful documents
Computer Science Student Resource Site	ComputerScienceStudent.com	Useful links and documents for computer science students

PREFACE

In the four years since the sixth edition of this book was published, the field has seen continued innovations and improvements. In this new edition, we try to capture these changes while maintaining a broad and comprehensive coverage of the entire field. To begin the process of revision, the sixth edition of this book was extensively reviewed by a number of professors who teach the subject and by professionals working in the field. The result is that, in many places, the narrative has been clarified and tightened, and illustrations have been improved. One noteworthy result of this review process, is that the chapter order has been restructured; see Chapter 0 for a discussion.

Beyond these refinements to improve pedagogy and user-friendliness, there have been substantive changes throughout the book. Much of the material has been revised and new material has been added. The most noteworthy changes are as follows:

- **Cloud computing:** Cloud computing has become a vital and essential tool in business IT. Cloud computing concepts are covered in a number of chapters throughout the book.
- **Big data:** A new section examines the creation, manipulation, and management of very large data sets (measured in terabytes, petabytes, exabytes, etc.) and the facilities in which these are stored.
- **Fourth-generation (4G) mobile networks:** 4G networks continue to expand worldwide and a section covering this recent technology has been added.
- **Dynamic Host Configuration Protocol (DHCP):** DHCP is a widely used protocol that enables dynamic IP address assignment. A new section covers this protocol.
- **MPLS:** New to this edition is a section devoted to Multiprotocol Label Switching (MPLS), which is becoming increasingly important on the Internet and other IP-based networks, as well as in telecommunications networks.
- **Evolution of Ethernet:** The book covers new developments in Ethernet technology and application, including Power over Ethernet (PoE) and Wide Area Ethernet (WAE).
- **Virtual LANs (VLANs):** VLAN technology is covered, as well is the IEEE 802.1Q standard.
- **Electronic mail:** The section on e-mail in Chapter 10 has been expanded to include a discussion of the standard Internet mail architecture.
- **Multimedia applications:** A new discussion of this topic is in Chapter 10.
- **Acceptable use policies:** A new section on acceptable use policies for e-mail, Web, and Internet applications is in Chapter 10.
- **Internet addressing:** The section on Internet addressing has been updated and expanded to include CIDR and IPv6 addresses.
- **Multicasting:** A new section on multicasting, which is increasingly important in the business environment, has been added.
- **VoIP:** Voice over IP (VoIP) is increasingly replacing traditional voice services. A new section in Chapter 15 discusses technology and service aspects.

- **Presence information and services:** The increased use of instant messaging and VoIP, plus the increased use of collaboration services, is supported by presence services now becoming available. A new section in Chapter 15 explores presence information and services.

With each new edition it is a struggle to maintain a reasonable page count while adding new material. In part, this objective is realized by eliminating obsolete material and tightening the narrative. For this edition, chapters and appendices that are of less general interest have been moved online, as individual PDF files. This has allowed an expansion of material without the corresponding increase in size and price.

Finally, the number of authors of this book has doubled! Our backgrounds and experience are complementary in many respects and we are confident that the partnership has produced a book that is even more useful to the business student than the preceding edition.

BACKGROUND

Technological developments and the widespread acceptance of standards are transforming the ways in which information is used to support the business function. In addition to the traditional communications requirements for voice and data (meaning text and numerical data), there is now the need to deal with pictorial images and video information. These four types of information (voice, data, image, and video) are essential to the survival of any business in today's competitive international environment. What is needed in a business data communications book is a treatment not just of **data communications** but also of **information communications** for the business environment.

Information communications and computer networking have become essential to the functioning of today's businesses, large and small. Furthermore, they have become a major and growing cost to organizations. Management and staff need a thorough understanding of information communications in order to assess needs; plan for the introduction of products, services, and systems; and manage the systems and technical personnel that operate them. This understanding must comprise the following:

- **Technology:** The underlying technology of information communications facilities, networking systems, and communications software
- **Architecture:** The way in which hardware, software, and services can be organized to provide computer and terminal interconnection
- **Applications:** How information communications and networking systems can meet the requirements of today's businesses

APPROACH

The purpose of this text is to present the concepts of information communications in a way that relates specifically to the business environment and to the concerns of business management and staff. To this end, the book takes an approach based on requirements, ingredients, and applications:

- **Requirements:** The need to provide services that enable businesses to utilize information is the driving force behind data and information communications technology. The text outlines the specific requirements that this technology is intended to address. This linkage between requirements and technology is essential to motivate a text of this nature.

- **Ingredients:** The technology of information communications includes the hardware, software, and communications services available to support distributed systems. An understanding of this technology is essential for a manager to make intelligent choices among the many alternatives.
- **Applications:** Management and staff must understand not only the technology but also the way in which that technology can be applied to satisfy business requirements.

These three concepts structure the presentation. They provide a way for the student to understand the context of what is being discussed at any point in the text, and they motivate the material. Thus, the student will gain a *practical* understanding of business information communications.

An important theme throughout the book is the essential role of standards. The proliferation of personal computers and other computer systems inevitably means that the manager will be faced with the need to integrate equipment from a variety of vendors. The only way to manage this requirement effectively is through standards. And, indeed, increasingly vendors are offering products and services that conform to international standards. This text addresses some of the key groupings of standards that are shaping the marketplace and that define the choices available to the decision maker.

INTENDED AUDIENCE

This book is addressed to students and professionals who now have or expect to have some information technology management responsibility. As a full-time job, some readers may have or plan to have responsibility for management of the company's telecommunications function. But virtually all managers and many staff personnel will need to have a basic understanding of business information communications to perform their tasks effectively.

The new edition should be especially appealing to universities seeking alignment with the ACM/AIS IS 2010 curriculum model. This text covers all the recommended topics for IS 2010.5 IT Infrastructure, one of the core courses in the model curriculum. It also addresses multiple topics recommended for the IS 2010.3 Enterprise Architecture course including virtualization, business continuity, software as a service (SaaS), enterprise data models, network management, and emerging technologies.

For students, this text is intended as an introductory course in information communications for business and information management students. It does not assume any background in data communications but does assume a basic knowledge of data processing. By focusing on the business factors driving the evolution of network infrastructures and the metrics used to measure network performance, the content of this text will be especially appealing to MIS and business majors. Students will better understand why businesses are investing in communication technologies and the benefits they expect to realize from making these investments.

The book is also intended for self-study and is designed for use as both a tutorial and a reference book for those already involved in business information communications.

PLAN OF THE TEXT

The book is divided into six parts, which are described in Chapter 0:

- **Requirements**
- **Data communications**
- **The Internet and distributed applications**
- **Local area networks**
- **Wide area networks**
- **Management issues**

The book includes a number of pedagogic features, including the use of animations and numerous figures and tables to clarify the discussions. Each chapter includes a list of key words, review questions, homework problems, suggestions for further reading, and recommended Web sites. The book also includes an extensive glossary, a list of frequently used acronyms, and a reference list. In addition, a test bank is available to instructors.

INSTRUCTOR SUPPORT MATERIALS

The major goal of this text is to make it as effective a teaching tool for this exciting and fast-moving subject as possible. This goal is reflected both in the structure of the book and in the supporting material. The text is accompanied by the following supplementary material that will aid the instructor:

- **Solutions manual:** Solutions to all end-of-chapter review questions and problems.
- **Projects manual:** Suggested project assignments for all of the project categories listed below.
- **PowerPoint slides:** A set of slides covering all chapters, suitable for use in lecturing.
- **PDF files:** Reproductions of all figures and tables from the book.
- **Test bank:** A chapter-by-chapter set of questions with a separate file of answers.

All of these support materials are available at the **Instructor Resource Center (IRC)** for this textbook, which can be reached through the Publisher's Web site www.pearsoninternationaleditions.com/stallings. To gain access to the IRC, please contact your local Pearson sales representative.

The **Companion Web site**, at WilliamStallings.com/BusinessDataComm (click on *Instructor Resources* link), includes the following:

- Links to Web sites for other courses being taught using this book
- Sign-up information for an Internet mailing list for instructors using this book to exchange information, suggestions, and questions with each other and with the author

ONLINE CASE STUDIES

The book also includes a number of case studies. These are not "made-up" or "toy" cases but actual cases reported in the literature. Each case is chosen to reinforce or extend concepts introduced in the book. For this edition, a number of new case studies have been created

Table P.1 Case Study Key

Case	Reference Chapter	Major Concepts Addressed in Case	Other Relevant Chapters
Unified Communications at Boeing	Chapter 1	Unified communications; converged IP networks	Chapter 17
CORE Credit Union	Chapter 2	Voice and data networks; virtual private networks (VPNs); cloud services	Chapter 3; Chapter 9; Chapter 10; Chapter 12; Chapter 13; Chapter 19
MasterCard	Chapter 3	Data warehouses; massive storage systems; "big data"	Chapter 2; Chapter 19; Chapter 21
Broadband Access	Chapter 6	Broadband Internet access options; "wired communities" and nations; digital divide	Chapter 7; Chapter 8; Chapter 10; Chapter 17
Net Neutrality	Chapter 7	Internet traffic growth; business use of the Internet	Chapter 9; Chapter 10; Chapter 11; Chapter 17
Chevron	Chapter 9	Cloud computing; Web services	Chapter 3; Chapter 10; Chapter 17; Chapter 21
Guardian Life	Chapter 10	E business/digital commerce; Web portals	Chapter 10; Chapter 17; Chapter 19
Carlson Companies	Chapter 12	Mass storage systems; storage area networks; backend networks	Chapter 3; Chapter 13
St. Luke's Health Care System	Chapter 14	Wireless LANs; mobile applications	Chapter 17; Chapter 19; Chapter 21
Choice Hotels	Chapter 17	Satellite-based communications; wireless WANs	Chapter 2; Chapter 3; Chapter 21
Cloud Computing (In)Security	Chapter 19	Cloud computing; network security; network design	Chapter 3; Chapter 9; Chapter 10; Chapter 17; Chapter 21

and several case studies from the previous edition have been updated. Table P.1 indicates the point in the book at which each case study can be read.

These case studies are available at www.pearsoninternationaleditions.com/stallings

PROJECTS AND OTHER STUDENT EXERCISES

For many instructors, an important component of a Business Data Communications course is a project or set of projects by which the student gets hands-on experience to reinforce concepts from the text. This book provides an unparalleled degree of support for including a projects component in the course. The IRC not only includes guidance on how to assign and structure the projects but also includes a set of User's Manuals for various project types plus specific assignments, all written especially for this book. Instructors can assign work in the following areas:

- **Animation assignments:** Described in the following section.
- **Practical exercises:** Using network commands, the student gains experience in network connectivity.

- **Wireshark projects:** Wireshark, formerly known as Ethereal, is a protocol analyzer that enables students to study the behavior of protocols.

- **Research projects:** A series of research assignments that instruct the student to research a particular topic on the Internet and write a report.

- **Security case studies:** A set of real-world security-related case studies, including learning objectives, case description, and a series of case discussion questions.

- **Reading/report assignments:** A list of papers that can be assigned for reading and writing a report, plus suggested assignment wording.

- **Writing assignments:** A list of writing assignments to facilitate learning the material.

This diverse set of projects and other student exercises enables the instructor to use the book as one component in a rich and varied learning experience and to tailor a course plan to meet the specific needs of the instructor and students. See Appendix A in this book for details.

ANIMATIONS

This edition incorporates an expanded set of animations, building on those provided in the previous edition. Animations provide a powerful tool for understanding the complex mechanisms of network protocols. A total of 17 Web-based animations are used to illustrate protocol behavior. Appendix A provides a key that maps animations to the appropriate point in the book where the concept is illustrated. Each animation allows the users to step through the operation of the protocol by selecting the next step at each point in the protocol exchange. The entire protocol exchange is illustrated by an animated diagram as the exchange proceeds. The animations can be used in two ways. In a **passive mode**, the student can click more or less randomly on the next step at each point in the animation and watch as the given concept or principle is illustrated. In an **active mode**, the user can be given a specific set of steps to invoke and watch the animation, or be given a specific endpoint and required to devise a sequence of steps that achieve the desired result. Thus, the animations can serve as the basis for student assignments. The instructor's supplement includes a set of assignments for each of the animations, plus suggested solutions so that instructors can assess the student's work.

For access to the animations, click on the rotating globe at this book's Companion Web site.

STUDENT RESOURCES

For this new edition, a tremendous amount of original supporting material for students has been made available online, at two Web locations. The **Companion Web site**, at WilliamStallings .com/BusinessDataComm (click on *Student Resources* link), includes a Recommended Reading list, a list of relevant links organized by chapter and an errata sheet for the book.

Purchasing this textbook new also grants the reader six months of access to the **Premium Content site**, which includes the following materials:

- **Online chapters:** To limit the size and cost of the book, two chapters of the book are provided in PDF format. The chapters are listed in this book's table of contents.

- **Online appendices:** There are numerous interesting topics that support material found in the text but whose inclusion is not warranted in the printed text. Twelve appendices cover these topics for the interested student. The appendices are listed in this book's table of contents.

- **Homework problems and solutions:** To aid the student in understanding the material, a separate set of homework problems with solutions are available. These enable the students to test their understanding of the text.

- **Key papers:** Several dozen papers from the professional literature, many hard to find, are provided for further reading.

- **Supporting documents:** A variety of other useful documents are referenced in the text and provided online.

To access the Premium Content site, click on the *Premium Content* link at www .pearsoninternationaleditions.com/stallings enter the student access code found on the card in the front of the book.

ACKNOWLEDGMENTS

This new edition has benefited from review by a number of people, who gave generously of their time and expertise. The following people reviewed the manuscript: Khaled Kamel (Texas Southern University), Barbara Holt (Northern Virginia Community College), Kenny Jih (Middle Tennessee State University), Asim Roy (Arizona State University), Michael Chilton (Kansas State University), Dave Croasdell (University of Nevada), Brad Prince (University of West Georgia), Bin Wang (Wright State University), Zchai Zhou (University of Houston), Glen Sagers (Illinois State University), Manoel Oliveira (Florida International University), Annette Kerwin (College of Dupage), Angela Clark (University of South Alabama), Mark Harris (University of South Carolina), Randall Boyle (University of Utah), Kuan Chen (Purdue University), Jeffrey Kane (Nova Southeastern University), Robert Folden (Texas A&M University), and Brian West (University of Louisiana).

Thanks also to the people who provided detailed technical reviews of one or more chapters: Nikhil Bhargava (Hughes Systique, India), John South (University of Dallas), Paul Pot, Vance Shipley, Jennifer Jabbusch, and Peter Tregunno.

Larry Tan of the University of Stirling in Scotland developed the animation assignments. Michael Harris of Indiana University initially developed the Wireshark exercises and user's guide. Dave Bremer, a principal lecturer at Otago Polytechnic in New Zealand, updated the material for the most recent Wireshark release; he also developed an online video tutorial for using Wireshark.

Finally, we would like to thank the many people responsible for the publication of the book, all of whom did their usual excellent job. This includes the staff at Prentice Hall, particularly our editor Tracy Johnson, her assistant Carole Snyder, production supervisor Kayla Smith-Tarbox, and production project manager Pat Brown. We also thank Shiny Rajesh and the production staff at Integra for another excellent and rapid job. Thanks also to the marketing and sales staffs at Pearson, without whose efforts this book would not be in your hands.

The publishers would like to thank Debraj Ghoshal for reviewing the content of the International Edition.

ABOUT THE AUTHORS

Dr. William Stallings has authored 17 titles, and counting revised editions, over 40 books on computer security, computer networking, and computer architecture. His writings have appeared in numerous ACM and IEEE publications, including the *Proceedings of the IEEE and ACM Computing Reviews*. He has 10 times received the award for the best Computer Science textbook of the year from the Text and Academic Authors Association.

In over 30 years in the field, he has been a technical contributor, technical manager, and an executive with several high-technology firms. He has designed and implemented both TCP/IP-based and OSI-based protocol suites on a variety of computers and operating systems, ranging from microcomputers to mainframes. As a consultant, he has advised government agencies, computer and software vendors, and major users on the design, selection, and use of networking software and products.

He created and maintains the *Computer Science Student Resource Site* at WilliamStallings .com/StudentSupport.html. This site provides documents and links on a variety of subjects of general interest to computer science students (and professionals). He is a member of the editorial board of *Cryptologia*, a scholarly journal devoted to all aspects of cryptology.

Dr. Stallings holds a PhD from MIT in computer science and a BS from Notre Dame in electrical engineering.

Dr. Thomas Case is Professor and Chair of the Department of Information Systems at Georgia Southern University, where he teaches graduate and undergraduate courses in business data communications, network design, digital commerce, enterprise resource planning (ERP) systems, human resource information systems (HRIS), IT management, and IT strategy. He joined the Georgia Southern faculty in 1981 after completing a PhD at the University of Georgia.

In the early 1980s, Dr. Case taught management. He transitioned to teaching networking and information systems during the mid-1980s commensurate with the growing importance of business data communications. This background has helped his students appreciate the evolution of computer networks from a business perspective.

Dr. Case has held numerous leadership roles in professional associations and he was one of the founding fathers of the Southern Association of Information Systems (SAIS). He is an Associate Editor for the *Communications of the AIS* and serves on the editorial boards of multiple IS journals. Prior to *Business Data Communications 7e*, he authored three textbooks on computer networking and management information systems. He has published more than 30 journal articles and has won numerous Best Paper awards at professional conferences.

He serves on advisory boards for educational institutions, financial institutions, and technology associations and is an active participant in the SAP University Alliances and multiple Americas SAP Users Group chapters. Across his career he has received numerous accolades including his university's Excellence in Contributions to Instruction Award and its Excellence in Service Award.

READER'S AND INSTRUCTOR'S GUIDE

This book, with its accompanying Web sites, covers a lot of material. In this chapter, we give the reader an overview.

0.1 OUTLINE OF THIS BOOK

Following an introductory chapter, the book is organized into six parts:

Part One Requirements: Defines the needs for information communications in the business environment. Discusses the way in which various forms of information are used and the need for interconnection and networking facilities. An examination of the nature and role of distributed data processing is the highlight of this part.

Part Two Data Communications: Deals with the basic technology of information communication. The emphasis is on digital communications techniques, since these are rapidly displacing analog techniques for all products and services related to information communications. Key topics include transmission media, data link control protocols, and multiplexing.

Part Three The Internet and Distributed Applications: Provides an overview of the Internet and the basic protocols that are the foundation of the Internet and addresses the critical issue of quality of service (QoS). It also deals with the specific business applications that require information communications facilities and networks. This part presents key applications, such as electronic mail and the World Wide Web, and includes a discussion of client/server computing and intranets.

Part Four Local Area Networks: Explores the technologies and architectures that have been developed for networking over shorter distances. The transmission media, topologies, and medium access control protocols that are the key ingredients of a local area network (LAN) design are explored and specific standardized LAN systems are examined.

Part Five Wide Area Networks: Examines the internal mechanisms and user-network interfaces that have been developed to support voice, data, and multimedia communications over long-distance networks. The traditional technologies of packet switching and circuit switching are examined, as well as the more recent Multiprotocol Label Switching (MPLS) and wireless wide area networks (WANs).

Part Six Management Issues: Deals with two key areas: network security and network management.

A number of online appendices at this book's Web site cover additional topics relevant to the book.

0.2 TOPIC ORDERING

The book has been restructured from the sixth edition to more closely match the needs of the student. The business/IS/IT student wants, and rightly so, to see the technical material in the context of the needs of the business and the ways in which communications and networking technology support desired business functions. Thus, this book begins by defining the requirements for information communications in business. The types of information and their utility are examined first. The book then examines fundamental communications technologies. These two sections set the stage to discuss the applications that can meet those requirements and the role of the Internet in supporting the applications. We are then in a position to examine the communications networks, both LANs and WANs, that form the infrastructure for distributed applications and the network. Finally, security and network management issues are discussed. It is hoped that this strategy will make the material more comprehensible and provide a structure that is more natural to a reader with a business orientation.

Some readers, and some instructors, are more comfortable with a bottom-up approach. With this approach, each part builds on the material in the previous part, so that it is always clear how a given layer of functionality is supported from below. Accordingly, the book is organized in a modular fashion. After reading Part One, the other parts can be read in a number of possible sequences.

0.3 INTERNET AND WEB RESOURCES

There are a number of resources available on the Internet and the Web that support this book and help readers keep up with developments in this field.

Web Sites for This Book

We maintain a **Companion Web site** for this book at http://williamstallings.com/BusinessDataComm. For students, this Web site includes a list of relevant links, organized by chapter, and an errata list for the book. For instructors, this Web site provides links to course pages by professors teaching from this book.

There is also an access-controlled **Premium Content Web site** that provides a wealth of supporting material, including additional online chapters, additional online appendices, a set of homework problems with solutions, copies of a number of key papers in this field, and a number of other supporting documents. See the card at the front of this book for access information.

Finally, additional material for instructors, including a solutions manual and a projects manual, is available at the **Instructor Resource Center (IRC)** for this book. See Preface for details and access information.

Computer Science Student Resource Site

Bill Stallings also maintains the **Computer Science Student Resource Site**, at ComputerScienceStudent.com. The purpose of this site is to provide documents, information, and links for computer science students and professionals. Links and documents are organized into six categories:

- **Math:** Includes a basic math refresher, a queuing analysis primer, a number system primer, and links to numerous math sites.
- **How-to:** Advice and guidance for solving homework problems, writing technical reports, and preparing technical presentations.

- **Research resources:** Links to important collections of papers, technical reports, and bibliographies.
- **Miscellaneous:** A variety of other useful documents and links.
- **Computer science careers:** Useful links and documents for those considering a career in computer science.
- **Humor and other diversions:** You have to take your mind off your work once in a while.

Other Web Sites

Numerous Web sites provide information related to the topics of this book. The Companion Website provides links to these sites, organized by chapter.

0.4 USEFUL PUBLICATIONS

This book serves as a tutorial for learning about the field of business data communications and a reference that can be turned to for help on a specific topic. However, with the rapid changes taking place in this field, no book can hope to stand alone for very long. If you are truly interested in this field, you will need to invest some of your time keeping up with new developments, and the best way to do that is by reading a few relevant periodicals. The list of publications that could be recommended is huge. Included here is a small, select list of publications that will repay the time that you devote to them. All of these publications have Web sites (Table 0.1).

Network World, a weekly newsmagazine, is an excellent source of information about the industry and market for information communications products and services.

Table 0.1   Useful Periodicals

Name	Web Site
Network World	The best Web site on this list. Contains a well-organized archive of the paper's contents. Also contains links to sites related to current news stories, sites related to various technical topics covered in the paper, and vendor information.
Network Computing	Articles from the magazine available plus pointers to advertisers. Site also includes a hypertext network design manual with useful practical tips for end-user network design.
Performance Edge Journal	Archive of all past issues.
Telecommunications	Articles and new product information from past issues, plus an extensive international listing of industry trade shows. Product listings include a brief description plus the ability to request product information from the vendor. A useful search capability can be used to search articles and product listing by keyword.
IT Professional	Includes career resources and links related to information technology.
ACM Networker	Includes online copies of magazine articles.

The coverage is thorough and includes buyers' guides on products and services. Each week, there are one or more in-depth articles that touch upon a single area, such as network management. The treatment is from a management rather than a technical orientation. The newsmagazine also provides product comparisons. *Network Computing* not only focuses on networking products but also has some technical articles. This magazine provides an excellent means for tracking new product releases and for obtaining comparative analyses of product offerings.

Performance Edge Journal focuses on network performance management issues. This is a free online magazine. *Telecommunications* is a monthly magazine that contains both industry-related and technical articles. The magazine concentrates heavily on long-distance networking topics, such as telephone, telecommunications, and regulatory issues.

IT Professional, published by IEEE (Institute of Electrical and Electronics Engineers), is intended for developers and managers of enterprise information systems. The magazine is good at explaining technology to help you build and manage your information systems today, and provides advance notice of trends that may shape your business in the next few years. *Networker* published by ACM (Association for Computing Machinery), is another good source of information for developers and managers of enterprise information systems, but with more emphasis on networking and data communications than *IT Professional*.

CHAPTER 1

INTRODUCTION

Learning Objectives

After reading this chapter, you should be able to:

♦ Identify the major forces shaping the evolution of enterprise networks and their business drivers.

♦ See the "big picture" of the major topics discussed in the book.

♦ Describe the importance of the Internet and wireless communications in business planning.

♦ Understand the central role of standards in data communications and networking.

This introductory chapter begins with an overview of the role of data communications and networking in the enterprise. Then a brief discussion introduces each of the parts of this book.

1.1 INFORMATION AND COMMUNICATION

Computers and communication technologies are woven into the fabric of business enterprises and continue to transform competition in the global marketplace. The generation, storage, and movement of information are central to managing an enterprise's business processes and for ensuring long-term profitability and competitiveness. As a result, businesses must be vigilant about ensuring that they are using information and communication technologies (ICTs) that best satisfy their information management needs.

We are unquestionably dependent on computers and the communication devices and services that connect them. The number of computers, terminals, and mobile devices used by workers around the world is in the billions. Connectivity, integration, and ease of access to information are essential for effective communication among workers and business partners. Many enterprises are assimilating social media, such as Twitter and Facebook, to enhance communication and business processes. So fundamental is information communication technology to business success that it is emerging as the foundation for new business models and strategies. This is perhaps most evident in enterprises that have embraced cloud computing to provide competitive products such as infrastructure as a service (IaaS), platform as a service (PaaS), and software as a service (SaaS).

As businesses continue to be tested by such forces as global competition, mergers, and acquisitions, traditional organizational structures with divisional walls and top-heavy management pyramids are giving way to new corporate structures that are flatter, leaner, more agile and responsive to innovation. Traditional boundaries between enterprises and their business partners (suppliers, customers, service providers, etc.) are being blurred by closely intertwined partnerships that make it difficult to determine where one organization's processes end and another's begin. At the same time, *networking* technology is making inter-organizational business processes more transparent by facilitating the flow of information needed to coordinate activities among business partners. Today, networking technology does much more than just support a business's internal processes, it also serves as a linchpin in supply chain management (SCM), customer relationship management (CRM), and other enterprise-wide applications that are transforming business networks.

Communication technology helps companies in numerous ways. For example, good networks make it easier to manage geographically dispersed operating locations. They also help organizations deliver information to workers in a timely manner, including anytime-anywhere access on a mobile device if necessary. Perhaps most importantly, good networks improve communication and information management within and between business organizations. Good networks also bring business partners closer together in ways that improve efficiency, customer service, agility, and innovation. As we examine the technology and applications throughout this book, we will see the many ways in which information communication technology contributes to business success.

1.2   DATA COMMUNICATIONS AND NETWORKING FOR TODAY'S ENTERPRISE

Effective and efficient data communication and networking facilities are vital to any enterprise. In this section, we first look at trends that are increasing the challenge for the business manager in planning and managing such facilities. Next, we introduce the concept of business drivers that guide the enterprise in developing an overall data communications and networking plan.

Trends

Three different forces have consistently driven the architecture and evolution of data communications and networking facilities: traffic growth, development of new services, and advances in technology.

Communication **traffic**, both local (within a building or business campus) and long distance, has been growing at a high and steady rate for decades. Network traffic is no longer limited to voice and data and increasingly includes image and video. Increasing business emphasis on Web services, remote access, online transactions, and social networking means that this trend is likely to continue. Thus, business managers are constantly pressured to increase communication capacity in cost-effective ways.

As businesses rely more and more on information technology, the range of **services** that business users desire to consume is expanding. For example, mobile broadband traffic growth is exploding as is the amount of data being pushed over mobile networks by business users' smartphones and tablets. In addition, mobile users are increasingly demanding high-quality services to support their high-resolution camera phones, favorite video streams, and high-end audio. To keep up with mushrooming traffic generated by both consumers and business users, mobile service providers have to keep investing in high-capacity networking and transmission facilities. In turn, the growth in high-speed network offerings at competitive price points encourages the expansion of mobile applications and services. Thus, growth in services and growth in traffic capacity go hand in hand. Figure 1.1 gives some examples of information-based services and the data rates needed to support them [ELSA02].

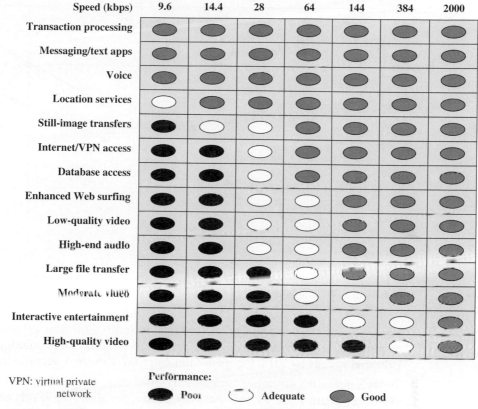

Figure 1.1 Services versus Throughput Rates

Finally, trends in **technology** enable the provision of increasing traffic capacity and the support of a wide range of services. Four technology trends are particularly notable and need to be understood by business information technology managers:

1. The trend toward faster and cheaper services, in both computing and communications, continues. In terms of computing, this means more powerful computers and clusters of computers capable of supporting more demanding applications, such as multimedia applications. In terms of communications, the increasing use of optical fiber and high-speed wireless has brought transmission prices down and greatly increased capacity. For example, for long-distance telecommunication and data network links, dense wavelength division multiplexing (DWDM) enables communication traffic to be carried by fiber-optic cables at rates of multiple terabits per second. For local area networks (LANs), many enterprises now have Gigabit Ethernet or 10-Gbps Ethernet backbone networks.[1] Further, the need for the next-generation

---

[1]See Appendix 1A for an explanation of numerical prefixes, such as *tera* and *giga*.

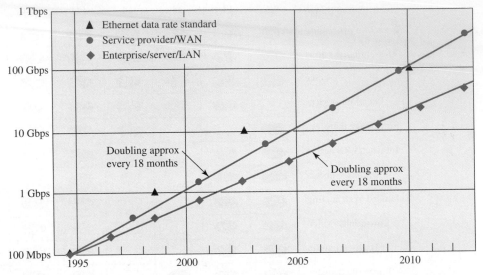

Figure 1.2 Past and Projected Growth in Ethernet Bandwidth Compared to Existing Ethernet Data Rate Standards

100-Gpbs Ethernet is pressing. Forty Gigabit and 100 Gigabit Ethernet products have started to hit the market and some pundits are predicting terabit Ethernet speeds by 2015. Figure 1.2 indicates the Ethernet demand trend.

2. Today's networks are more "intelligent" than ever. Two areas of intelligence are noteworthy. First, today's networks can offer differing levels of quality of service (QoS), which include specifications for maximum delay, minimum throughput, and so on to ensure high-quality support for applications and services. Second, today's networks provide a variety of customizable services in the areas of network management and security.

3. The Internet, the Web, and associated applications have emerged as dominant features for both business and personal network landscapes. The migration to "everything over IP" continues and has created many opportunities and challenges for ICT managers. In addition to exploiting the Internet and the Web to reach customers, suppliers, and partners, enterprises have implemented intranets and extranets[2] to isolate proprietary information and keep it free from unwanted access.

4. Mobility is the newest frontier for ICT managers, and popular consumer devices such as the iPhone, Droid, and iPad have become drivers of the evolution of business networks and their use. While there has been a trend toward mobility for decades, the mobility explosion has occurred and has liberated workers from the confines of the physical enterprise. Enterprise applications traditionally supported on terminals and office desktop computers are now

---

[2]Briefly, an intranet uses Internet and Web technology in an isolated facility internal to an enterprise; an extranet extends a company's intranet out onto the Internet to allow selected customers, suppliers, and mobile workers to access the company's private data and applications. See Chapter 6 for a discussion.

routinely delivered on mobile devices. Cloud computing is being embraced by all major business software vendors including SAP, Oracle, and Microsoft and this ensures that further mobility innovations will be forthcoming. Industry experts predict that mobile devices will become the dominant business computing platform by 2015 and that enhanced ability to use enterprise information resources and services anywhere-anytime will be a dominant trend for the remainder of the decade.

Business Drivers

The trends discussed in the preceding subsection are facilitating the development of enterprise network and communications infrastructures that are closely integrated with the information base on which the enterprise runs. Enterprise network management and operation depend on key organization-specific information, such as names, network addresses, security capabilities, end-user groupings, priority designations, mailboxes, and application attributes. With the increasing capacity and functionality of enterprise networks, this information can be unified with the enterprise information base to ensure that the information is correct, consistent, and available across all business applications.

The nature of the enterprise networking and communications infrastructure depends on the applications that support the business processes. [MILO04] lists four main application areas that continue to drive the design and makeup of today's enterprise networks. These are illustrated in Figure 1.3. Orange Business Services [ORAN12] identifies five additional application areas that will be shaping the design and infrastructure of future enterprise networks. These are summarized in Table 1.1 along with their business drivers and examples of typical uses.

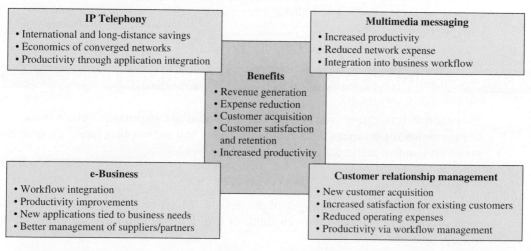

IP = Internet Protocol
e-Business = Enterprise activities based on mobile, global access to enterprise networks

Figure 1.3   Applications Driving Enterprise Networks

Table 1.1   Emerging Enterprise Network Applications

Application	Typical Uses/Examples	Business Rationale
Telepresence	Videoconferencing	Reduced travel expenses Reduced energy costs Reduced carbon footprint Increased executive productivity Increased sales success rates Increased sales cycle times
Video broadcasting and e-learning	Marketing Training Surveillance	Better informed customers Increased worker competency Deployment of company YouTube channel Reduced training-related travel expenses
Video enriched collaboration	Video chat Unified communications Intercompany collaboration	Better management of virtual teams Improved business process execution Increased individual productivity Enhanced team communication Increased business use of social media
Smart objects	Machine-to-machine communication "Internet of things" Vehicle tracking	Maturing RFID applications Falling costs of sensors, actuators, and modems Better equipment monitoring and troubleshooting Migration to IPv6
Cloud computing	Anytime-anywhere access to applications, services, storage Software as a service (SaaS) Platform as a service (PaaS)	Pay-as-you-grow computing Third-party data centers Increasing variety of cloud-based services and on-demand solutions Reduced on-premises network expenses Enhanced support for mobility Increased agility and flexibility

1.3   CONVERGENCE AND UNIFIED COMMUNICATIONS

This section introduces two related concepts that are important determinants of requirements for business data communications and networking facilities: convergence and unified communications.

Convergence

Convergence refers to the merger of previously distinct telephony and information technologies and markets. We can think of this in terms of a three-layer model of enterprise communications:

- **Applications:** These are seen by the end users of a business. Convergence integrates communications applications, such as voice calling (telephone), voice mail, e-mail, and instant messaging, with business applications, such as workgroup collaboration, customer relationship management, and back-office functions. With convergence, applications provide rich features that incorporate voice, data, and video in a seamless, organized, and value-added manner. One example is multimedia messaging, which enables a user to employ a single interface to access messages from a variety of sources (e.g., office voice mail, e-mail, SMS, and mobile voice mail).

- **Enterprise services:** At this level, the manager deals with the information network in terms of the services that must be available to ensure that users can take full advantage of the applications that they use. For example, network managers need to make sure that appropriate privacy mechanisms and authentication services are in place to support convergence-based applications. They may also be able to track user locations to support remote print services and network storage facilities for mobile workers. Enterprise network management services may also include setting up collaborative environments for various users, groups, and applications and QoS provision.

- **Infrastructure:** The network and communications infrastructure consists of the communication links, LANs, WANs, and Internet connections available to the enterprise. Increasingly, enterprise network infrastructure also includes private and/or public cloud connections to data centers which host high-volume data storage and Web services. A key aspect of convergence at this level is the ability to carry voice, image, and video over networks that were originally designed to carry data traffic. Infrastructure convergence has also occurred for networks that were designed for voice traffic. For example, video, image, text, and data are routinely delivered to smartphone users over cell phone networks.

Figure 1.4 illustrates the major attributes of the three-layer model of enterprise communications. In simple terms, convergence involves moving an organization's

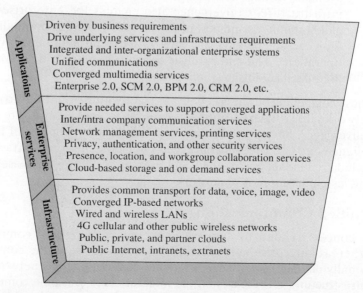

Figure 1.4   Business-Driven Convergence

voice, video, and image traffic to a single network infrastructure. This often involves integrating distinct voice and data networks into a single network infrastructure and extending the infrastructure to support mobile users. The foundation of this convergence is packet-based transmission using the Internet Protocol (IP). Using IP packets to deliver all varieties of communications traffic, sometimes referred to as "everything over IP," enables the underlying infrastructure to deliver a wide range of useful applications to business users.

Convergence brings many benefits, including simplified network management, increased efficiency, and greater flexibility at the application level. For example, a converged network infrastructure provides a predictable platform on which to build new applications that combine video, data, and voice. This makes it easier for developers to create innovative mashups and other value-added business applications and services. Three key benefits of IP network convergence are summarized below:

- **Cost savings:** A converged network can provide significant reductions in network administration, maintenance, and operating costs. Converging legacy networks onto a single IP network enables better use of existing resources, and implementation of centralized capacity planning, asset management, and policy management.

- **Effectiveness:** The converged environment has the potential to provide users with great flexibility, irrespective of where they are. IP convergence allows companies to create a more mobile workforce. Mobile workers can use a virtual private network (VPN) to remotely access business applications and communication services on the corporate network. A VPN helps maintain enterprise network security by separating business traffic from other Internet traffic.

- **Transformation:** Because they are modifiable and interoperable, converged IP networks can easily adapt to new functions and features as they become available through technological advancements without having to install new infrastructure. Convergence also enables the enterprise-wide adoption of global standards and best practices, thus providing better data, enhanced real-time decision making, and improved execution of key business processes and operations. The end result is enhanced agility and responsiveness, the key ingredients of business innovation.

These compelling business benefits are motivating companies to invest in converged network infrastructures. Businesses, however, are keenly aware of the downside of convergence: having a single network means a single point of failure. Given their reliance on ICT, today's converged enterprise network infrastructures typically include redundant components and back-up systems to increase network resiliency and lessen the severity of network outages.

Unified Communications

A concept related to network convergence is unified communications (UC). Whereas enterprise network convergence focuses on the consolidation of traditionally distinct voice, video, and data communications networks into a common infrastructure, UC focuses on the integration of real-time communication services to optimize business processes. And like converged enterprise networks, Internet

Protocol is the cornerstone on which UC systems are built. Key elements of UC include the following:

1. UC systems typically provide a unified user interface and consistent user experience across multiple devices and media.

2. UC merges real-time communications services with non-real-time services and business process applications.

Figure 1.5, based on [LAZA07], shows the typical components of a UC architecture and how they relate to one another. The key elements of this architecture are as follows:

- **Real-time communications (RTC) dashboard:** A RTC dashboard is a key component of UC architecture. This is the element that provides UC users with a unified user interface across communication devices. Ideally, the user has a consistent interface no matter what communication device he or she is currently using whether it is a cell phone, wireless tablet computer, desktop system, or office telephone attached to the corporate private branch exchange (PBX). As may be observed in Figure 1.5, RTC dashboards provide access to real-time communication services such as instant messaging, audio- and video conferencing, and interactive whiteboards; RTC dashboards also provide access to non-real-time services such as unified messaging (e-mail, voice mail, fax, and SMS) in unified view. The RTC dashboard includes presence information about co-workers and partners so that users can know on the fly which colleagues are available to communicate or join a collaborative communication session. RTC dashboards have become necessities in organizations that require high levels of communication and collaboration to support business processes.

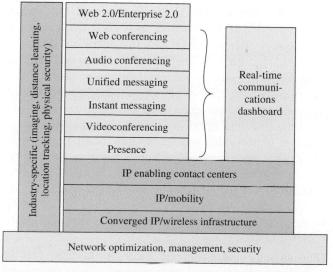

Figure 1.5   Elements of Unified Communications Architecture

- **Web conferencing:** Refers to live meetings or presentations in which participants access the meeting or presentation via a mobile device or the Web, either over the Internet or corporate intranet. Web conferences often include data sharing through Web-connected interactive whiteboards (IWBs).

- **Audio conferencing:** Also called conference calling, audio conferencing refers to a live meeting in which participants are linked together for audio transmission and reception. A participant may be on a landline or mobile phone, or at a "softphone"—a computer equipped with microphone and speaker.

- **Unified messaging:** Unified messaging systems provide a common repository for messages from multiple sources. It allows users to retrieve saved e-mail, voice mail, and fax messages from a computer, telephone, or mobile device. Computer users can select and play voice-mail recordings that appear in their unified messaging in-boxes. Telephone users can both retrieve voice mail and hear text-to-voice translations of e-mail messages. Messages of any type can be saved, answered, filed, sorted, and forwarded. Unified messaging systems relieve business users from having to monitor multiple voice-mail boxes by enabling voice-mail messages received by both office phones and cell phones to be saved to the same mailbox. With UC, users can use any device at any time to retrieve e-mail or voice mail from unified messaging mailboxes.

- **Instant messaging (IM):** Real-time text-based messaging between two or more participants. IM is similar to online chat because it is text-based and exchanged bidirectionally in real time. IM is distinct from chat in that IM clients use contact (or buddy) lists to facilitate connections between known users whereas online chat can include text-based exchanges between anonymous users.

- **Video teleconferencing (VTC):** Videoconferencing allows users in two or more locations to interact simultaneously via two-way video and audio transmission. UC systems enable users to participate in videoconferences via desktop computers, smartphones, and mobile devices.

- **Presence:** The ability to determine, in real time, where someone is, how he or she prefers to be reached, and even what he or she is currently doing. Presence information shows the individual's availability state before co-workers attempt to contact them. It was once considered simply an underlying technology to instant messaging (e.g., "available to chat" or "busy") but has been broadened to include whether co-workers are currently on office or mobile phones, logged in to a computer, involved in a video call or in a meeting, or out of the office for lunch or vacation. A co-worker's geographic location is becoming more common as an element in presence information for a number of business reasons including the ability to quickly respond to customer emergencies. Business has embraced presence information because it facilitates more efficient and effective communication. It helps eliminate inefficiencies associated with "phone tag" or composing and sending e-mails to someone who could more quickly answer a question over the phone or with a quick meeting.

- **IP enabling contact centers:** Refers to the use of IP-based unified communications to enhance customer contact center functionality and performance.

Employee profiles	At desk	Somewhere on site	On the move
Desk soldier Accountant	90%	10%	
On-site rover Assistant	70%	30%	
Home worker Tele-agent	100% (Home)		
Road warrior Salesperson	10%	10%	80%
Off-site rover Consultant	30%		70%
Global hopper Corporate executive marketing, pre-sales	25%	25%	50%

Figure 1.6   Three Main Profiles for Mobile Employees

The unified communications infrastructure makes use of presence technology to enable customers and internal enterprise employees to be quickly connected to the required expert or support person. Additionally, this technology supports mobility, so that call center personnel need not be located at a particular office or remain in a particular place. Finally, the unified communications infrastructure enables the call center employee to quickly access other employees and information assets, including data, video, image, and audio resources.

- **IP/mobility:** Refers to the delivery of information to and collection of information from enterprise personnel who are usually mobile, using an IP network infrastructure. In a typical enterprise, upward of 30% of employees use some form of weekly remote access technology in the performance of their jobs. Industry researchers indicate that the number of mobile workers and telecommuters is increasing and will exceed more than 60 million U.S. workers by 2016. Figure 1.6, from [SENS02], illustrates the typical breakdown of usage profiles for mobile employees.

- **Converged IP/wireless infrastructure:** A unified networking and communications base uses IP packet transfer to support voice, data, and video transmission and can be extended to include local and wide area wireless communications. UC-enabled mobile devices are able to switch between Wi-Fi and cellular systems in the middle of a communication session. For example, a UC user could receive a co-worker's call via a smartphone connected to Wi-Fi network at home, continue the conversation while driving to work over a cellular network connection, and could end the call at the office while connected to the business's Wi-Fi network. Both hand-offs (home Wi-Fi to cellular and cellular to office Wi-Fi) would take place seamlessly and transparently without dropping the call.

The importance of unified communications is not only that it integrates communication channels but also that it offers a way to integrate communication functions and business applications. Table 1.2 summarizes some of the major benefits of

Table 1.2 Business Benefits of Unified Communications

Level	Business Benefits
Individual worker	Enhanced communication with co-workers Increased responsiveness to customers and partners Improved productivity Remote/mobile access to UC system Improved access to all message forms (voice mail, e-mail, text messages)
Workgroup	Increased collaboration among team members Real-time idea exchange and problem-solving Group calendaring facilitates meeting scheduling Ability to escalate IM session to conference call Better management/coordination of work team activities Improved project management Improved incident management
Enterprise	Improved business process execution via communication-enabled business processes (CEBP) Improved continuity across business processes Ability to provide UC interface to ERP, CRM, SCM, and other enterprise systems Reduced telephony costs Enhanced customer service Increased customer retention Reduced sales cycle time Revenue acceleration from faster sales closure

unified communications. Three major categories of benefits are typically realized by organizations that use UC:

- **Personal productivity gains:** Presence information helps employees find each other and choose the most effective way to communicate in real time. Less time is wasted calling multiple numbers to locate co-workers or checking multiple work-related voice mailboxes. Calls from VIP contacts can be routed simultaneously to all of a UC user's phone devices (office phone, softphone, smartphone, home phone) to ensure faster responsiveness to customers, partners, and co-workers. With mobile presence information capabilities, employees who are geographically closest can be dispatched to address a problem.

- **Workgroup performance gains:** UC systems support real-time collaboration among team members which facilitates workgroup performance improvements. Examples include the use of presence information to speed identification of an available individual with the right skills a work team needs to address a problem. Enhanced conferencing capabilities with desktop VTC and interactive whiteboards and automated business rules to route or escalate communications also help to increase workgroup performance.

- **Enterprise-level process improvements:** IP convergence enables UC to be integrated with enterprise-wide and departmental-level applications, business processes, and workflows. UC-enabled enhanced communications with customers, suppliers, and business partners are redefining best practices for CRM, SCM, and other enterprise-wide applications and are transforming relationships among members of business networks. Communication-enabled business processes (CEBP) are fueling competition in several industries including financial services, health care, and retail.

Enterprises are increasingly migrating to unified communications, and industry experts estimate that as many as 50 million U.S. workers will be UC users by 2015. This growth is somewhat surprising because currently, there are no internationally recognized standards in place to ensure interoperability among the systems being sold by Avaya, Cisco, ShoreTel, Siemans, and other major UC vendors. New UC capabilities resulting from the evolution of IP-based Session Initiation Protocol (SIP) seem to be overcoming traditional corporate aversion to proprietary solutions, at least for now. The benefits that businesses can realize from unified communications and converged network infrastructures are driving change at all three layers of the enterprise communications model illustrated in Figure 1.4 and secm destined to do so for the foreseeable future.

1.4 THE NATURE OF BUSINESS INFORMATION REQUIREMENTS

A business survives and thrives on information: information within the organization and information exchanged with suppliers, customers, and regulators. Moreover, the information needs to be consistent, accessible, and delivered to the right location. In Part One, Chapters 2 and 3, we consider the four major types of information carried over business networks (voice, data, image, and video) and the infrastructures needed to support distributed data storage and processing.

In this book, the term **voice communications** primarily refers to telephone-related communications. The telephone conversation continues to be the most common form of communication in businesses and other organizations. The telephone has been a basic business tool for decades and for some organizations, it continues to be the primary communication technology. Telephone communication has been enhanced by a variety of computer-based services, including voice mail and computerized telephone exchange systems. Voice mail provides the ability to send, forward, and reply to voice messages nonsimultaneously, and it is deployed across organizations of all sizes. Advances have also been made in computerized telephone exchange systems, including in-house digital private branch exchanges and Centrex systems provided by the local telephone company. These new systems provide a wide range of features, including caller identification, call forwarding, camp-on call waiting, least-cost routing of long-distance calls, and a variety of accounting and auditing features. More recently, the merger of voice and Internet technologies, based on the voice over IP (VoIP) protocol, has resulted in both on-premises and hosted IP-PBX offerings that provide full Internet support.

The term **data communications** is frequently used to refer to virtually any form of information transfer other than voice. It is sometimes convenient to limit this term to information in the form of text (such as reports, memos, and other documents) and numerical data (such as accounting files). The rapid changes in technology have created fresh challenges for business managers who want to make effective use of data communications. Later in this chapter, we briefly outline the major changes in transmission technologies, networks, and communications software that are bringing new and powerful business tools to the table and making it more challenging for managers to choose among competing alternatives.

Image communications is an increasingly important component of the office environment. The best-known example of this technology is facsimile (fax). Facsimile machines continue to be a common method of sending documents between locations, especially over long distances. With fax, the document can have any content, including text, graphics, signatures, and even photographs and documents can be transmitted over telephone networks in seconds. Fax capabilities are often bundled with network-attached office copiers as well as with multiple-function printers that are common in small office/home office (SOHO) networks. In larger organizations, copiers are often attached to an Ethernet or IP-network which enables fax images to be transmitted to other locations over the Internet. In addition, images are often attached or embedded in e-mail messages. Thus, all sorts of images, including engineering and design specifications, mixed documents (text, graphs, signatures, etc.), presentation material, and so on, are being moved quickly within and between offices by business users. Image communications are also impacting mobile communications. Today's smartphones routinely enable users to take and send high-resolution digital images across mobile networks. Enterprises are being challenged to capture, transmit, and store the images being created by business users. This creates a demand for high-capacity networks and is one of the driving forces in the development of new networking technologies.

Video communications is also becoming important in the office environment. Traditionally, this technology has been used as a one-way delivery system of entertainment programs. Now, with the availability of high-capacity transmission links and networks, videoconferencing—or video teleconferencing—has emerged as an important business application. The time and money saved on travel, food, and lodging make videoconferencing a powerful tool for increasing efficiency and productivity. The evolution of videoconferencing includes the emergence of high-resolution telepresence systems that enable geographically dispersed users to conduct planning sessions, contract negotiations, and project reviews in real time as if they were physically present in the same room. And, as noted previously, videoconferencing is supported by unified communication systems which enable business users to participate in videoconferences using desktop computers and smartphones. Video over IP (and TV over IP—TVoIP) is also being used by businesses to deliver high-definition live and on-demand employee training programs, video signage, security and surveillance, and customer sales presentations. It is also being used more widely in health care for remote patient monitoring and diagnosis. IPTV (Internet Protocol Television) is being increasingly used in education and the hospitality industry and is expected to become a very popular way of delivering television content to the digital entertainment systems in consumers' homes.

All these forms of information communications play a key role in today's businesses. Chapter 2 more closely examines the business uses of these four types of information and the communications requirements that must be met to ensure adequate transmission rates over enterprise networks.

1.5 THE TRANSMISSION OF INFORMATION

The basic building block of any enterprise network infrastructure is the transmission line. Much of the technical detail of how information is encoded and transmitted across a line is of no real interest to the business manager. Instead, business managers are more concerned with whether the network has the required capacity to handle its voice, data, image, and video traffic, with acceptable reliability, at an affordable cost. However, there are certain aspects of transmission technology that business managers must understand to ask the right questions and make informed decisions.

One of the basic choices for business network users is the transmission medium. For on-premise networks, this choice is generally completely up to the business. For interconnecting geographically dispersed business locations, the choice is generally limited to what is available from Internet service providers (ISPs) and/or long-distance carriers. In either case, the evolution of transmission media is changing the mix of media used in enterprise networks. For example, fiber-optic transmission and wireless transmission media are now driving the evolution of data communications transmission.

The ever-increasing availability of fiber-optic communication circuits is making channel capacity a virtually free resource. Since the early 1980s, the growth of the market for optical fiber transmission systems is without precedent. During the past 10 years, the cost of fiber-optic transmission has dropped by more than an order of magnitude, and the capacity of such systems has grown at almost as rapid a rate. Almost all of the long-distance telephone communications trunks within the United States and the highest speed links on the Internet consist of fiber-optic cable. Because of its high capacity and its security characteristics (fiber is difficult to tap), it is becoming increasingly used within office buildings and local area networks to carry the growing load of business information. The spreading use of fiber-optic cable is also spurring advancements in communication switching technologies and network management architectures.

The increasing use of a second medium, wireless transmission, is a result of the trend toward universal personal telecommunications and universal access to communications. Universal personal telecommunications refers to the ability of a person to a single account to use any communication system anytime/anywhere, ideally globally. Universal access to communications refers to the ability to use one's preferred computing device in a wide variety of environments to connect to information services (e.g., to have a laptop, smartphone, or tablet that will work equally well in the office, on the street, and on an airplane, bus, or train). Today, both concepts are subsumed under the business push to support mobility. Wireless LANs have become common components of enterprise networks as well as SOHO networks, and smartphones and tablets with wireless capabilities are rapidly becoming mainstream business user communications devices. As mentioned in our previous discussion of UC, mobility has the potential to unleash higher performance at all business levels: personal, workgroup, and enterprise-wide. This provides compelling rationale for further business investment in wireless technologies.

Despite the growth in the capacity and a drop in the cost of transmission media, transmitting voice, data, image, and video traffic across enterprise networks continues to consume a major chunk of the communications budget for most businesses. To ensure that the enterprise is getting the biggest bang for the buck, business managers need to understand how to make the most efficient use of transmission media within the enterprise network infrastructure. The two major approaches to more efficient use of communication circuits are multiplexing and compression. *Multiplexing* refers to the ability of a number of devices to share a transmission line. The sharing arrangement allows the cost of the transmission link to be spread over many users and helps ensure that the total capacity of the transmission link is used. *Compression*, as the name indicates, involves squeezing the data into a smaller form so that a lower-capacity, cheaper transmission line can be used to transfer it between computing devices. These two techniques may be used separately or in combination to ensure efficient use of transmission media within enterprise networks and both are supported in a number of types of communications equipment. Knowing when and where to use these techniques can help businesses minimize or reduce their data communication costs.

Chapters 5 and 6, in Part Two, examine the key issues and technologies related to information transmission. Chapter 6 describes the major types of multiplexing in use today—frequency division, time division, and wavelength division—as well as the types of circuits on which these are used.

Transmission and Transmission Media

Information can be communicated by converting it into an electromagnetic signal and transmitting that signal over some medium, such as a twisted-pair cabling. The most commonly used transmission media are twisted-pair cable, coaxial cable, optical fiber cable, and terrestrial and satellite microwave. The data transmission rates that can be achieved and the rate at which transmission errors can occur depend on the nature of the signal and the type of medium. Chapter 4 examines the significant properties of electromagnetic signals. Chapters 12, 14, and 17 discuss the various transmission media used in today's enterprise networks.

Communication Techniques

The transmission of information across a transmission medium involves more than simply inserting a signal on the medium. The technique used to encode the information into an electromagnetic signal must be determined. There are various ways in which the encoding can be done, and the choice affects performance and reliability. Furthermore, the successful transmission of information involves a high degree of cooperation between senders and receivers. Some means of controlling the flow of information and recovering from its loss or corruption during transmission must be used. Many of these functions may be performed by a data link control protocol. These fundamental data transmission issues are examined in Chapters 5 and 6.

1.6 DISTRIBUTED DATA PROCESSING

The steady drop over many years in the cost of data processing equipment, coupled with an increase in the capability of such equipment, has led to the proliferation of small- and medium-size computers within businesses. Desktop systems are standard equipment in business offices and these are typically interconnected to data communication equipment, servers, storage technologies in communication closets, server rooms or data centers depending on the size of the organization and the complexity of the network needed to support the enterprise. Local area networks are the basic building block for any enterprise networks and these support the distributed data processing configurations that dominate the computing landscape in today's organizations. Distributed data processing capabilities have been extended within many businesses as a result of implementing wireless local area networks. The push to support mobile workers is also making distributed data processing more common.

In the early days of business networks, the data processing function was centrally organized around a mainframe computer. Today, however, it is much more common to find a distributed data processing configuration where computers and/or terminals are linked together by networks. This does not mean that centralized data processing configurations no longer exist. Virtualization, data center consolidation, shared service centers, third-party data centers, and cloud computing are causing many observers to claim that centralized data processing is resurging. Chapter 3 examines the business issues that surround centralized and distributed data processing and discusses the various forms that each type of configuration may take.

1.7   THE INTERNET AND DISTRIBUTED APPLICATIONS

Businesses need to be concerned with two dimensions of computer communications software: the application software that is provided to business users' computing devices over enterprise networks, and the underlying interconnection (networking) software that allows these computing devices to work together cooperatively.

The mere existence of a large population of computing devices among business users creates the need for these devices to work together. For example, when most employees in an organization have access to a laptop personal computer (PC) or smartphone, one of the most effective means of communication within the organization is electronic mail (e-mail). When an employee needs to communicate with a co-worker, a message sent by e-mail can be far more effective than hit-or-miss attempts to reach the person by telephone. A detailed e-mail message can be left in the recipient's "electronic mailbox," to be read and answered later when the recipient is available. The proliferation of computing devices among business users creates demand for a wide range of applications geared for a network environment including collaboration, document and data sharing, and workflow applications.

The key to the success of these applications is that all computing devices "speak" the same language. This is the role of the underlying interconnection software. This software must ensure that all the devices transmit messages in such a way that they can be understood by the other devices they want to communicate with. In the early days of business networks, the only way to guarantee communication among computing devices was through proprietary network solutions such as IBM's Systems Network Architecture (SNA). SNA was introduced in the 1970s and worked only with IBM equipment. Other vendors followed IBM's lead with their own proprietary communications architectures to tie together their equipment. Although an enterprise-wide network could be created using a single vendor's architecture and equipment, interconnecting locations or organizations with different communications architectures was nearly impossible. Happily, that situation has changed radically as the result of the adoption of standards for interconnection software that enables equipment from multiple vendors to be used in a single network. By understanding the scope and status of these standards, today's business managers can build robust multiple-vendor, network infrastructures tailored for their enterprises.

Modern data communications and microelectronics are radically changing the architecture of modern information systems. Most business software applications no longer require large, general-purpose mainframe computers to run, and centralized computing architectures have given way to *distributed computing* which shares the processing load with user computing devices. Business user devices are supported by specialized servers which perform functions such as printing, storing files, or supporting database activities and user devices are typically connected to the servers by high-speed LANs. This approach, called *client/server architecture*, requires sophisticated, reliable, and secure data communications, but its inherent flexibility and responsiveness have made it a common element in today's enterprise networks.

Part Three of this book takes a closer look at a number of topics that deal with the infrastructure for supporting distributed applications.

The Internet

Businesses of all sizes are competitively exploiting the Internet and the Web. The Web provides a myriad of ways for businesses to communicate with consumers and to market their products and services. It has become an important sales channel and the dollar volume of e-commerce transactions continues to increase. Search engine and social media marketing are gobbling up an increasing percentage of business advertising budgets, often at the expense of print (magazine and newspaper) advertising. Internet technology, in the form of intranets and extranets, enables secure communication both within an enterprise and with customers, suppliers, and partners. Chapter 7 in Part 3 provides important background on the Internet and why it has emerged as a critical aspect of most enterprise networks.

TCP/IP

One of the most difficult problems that has traditionally inhibited the development of agile enterprise networks stems from the proprietary architectures developed by different data communication equipment vendors. The emergence of the Internet and its use of standardized communications protocols has facilitated the ability of enterprises to integrate diverse equipment from different vendors within their network infrastructures. In Chapter 8, the focus is on the TCP/IP (Transmission Control Protocol/Internet Protocol) protocol suite, which is now universally used for the communications software function across multiple-vendor equipment and is the basis for the operation of the Internet.

Client/Server Architectures, Intranets, Extranets, and SOA

In Chapter 9, the characteristics of client/server architectures are discussed along with the reasons why these have evolved as the dominant distributed computing architecture in today's enterprise networks. In the **client/server** model, separate computers (servers) provide specialized services such as database functions, file storage, printing, and other functions on a shared basis for many users (clients). These servers, which can offer enhanced performance and cost savings through specialization, are accessed over LANs and other communications networks.

Intranets have also gained widespread support within business organizations. An intranet provides the same sort of applications and interfaces as found on the Internet and World Wide Web. The difference is that an intranet is confined to authorized users within the organization, with no access to outsiders. The intranet is a flexible, easy-to-use, and easy-to-implement approach for supporting many business applications. Examples include employee self-service (ESS) and management self-service (MSS) portals used for human resource management purposes such as training and development, time and attendance, requesting/approving time off, and benefits administration.

In addition to examining client/server computing and intranets, Chapter 9 also discusses extranets and Service-Oriented Architecture (SOA). Like intranets, extranets rely on TCP/IP protocols and applications. Extranets enable outside clients and business partners to access corporate computing resources and are among the major approaches used to support inter-organizational business processes such as supply chain management (SCM) and just-in-time (JIT) manufacturing. SOA is another type of client/server architecture that has been widely adopted by enterprise systems' software vendors to enable customers to get access to their business software products at hosted sites. Because of SOA, medium and small enterprises (MSEs) can use ERP, CRM, and other enterprise systems software to run their businesses without having to install it on premises. Gaining an understanding about SOA is fundamental to understanding Web services, SaaS (software as a service), PaaS (platform as a service), and the other cloud-based computing services that are being increasingly used by today's businesses.

Distributed Applications

Distributed information processing is essential in virtually all businesses. There is a growing use of applications that are commonly used by distributed computing devices for both intracompany and intercompany information exchange. These include SMTP, HTTP, and other widely used TCP/IP-based applications. Chapter 10 examines some of the key applications used in enterprise networks and also examines Session Initiation Protocol (SIP), the protocol that is driving business adoption of unified communications.

1.8 NETWORKS

The number of computers in use worldwide is in the billions. Moreover, the expanding memory and processing power of all types of computing devices, including smartphones, means that many workers can use their preferred devices for all types of work-related applications and functions. Accordingly, the pressure from users to be able to use their favorite computing devices for all types of business and personal applications is irresistible. It is changing the way communication equipment vendors think and the way all communications infrastructure products and services are sold.

This demand for connectivity is manifested in two specific requirements: the need for communications software, which is previewed in the next section, and the need for robust networks capable of supporting voice, data, image, and video traffic.

One type of network that has become commonplace is the local area network (LAN). Indeed, LANs are found in virtually all medium- and large-size office buildings. LANs, especially Wi-Fi LANs, are also increasingly used for small office and home networks. As the number and power of computing devices have grown, so have the number and capacity of LANs be found in business networks. The development of internationally recognized standards for LANs has contributed to their proliferation in enterprises. Although Ethernet has emerged as the dominant LAN architecture, business managers still have choices to make about transmission rates (e.g., 100 Mbps vs. Gigabit vs. 10 Gbps Ethernet) and the degree to which both wired and wireless LANs will be combined within the enterprise network. Interconnecting and managing a diverse collection of local area networks and computing devices within today's business networks presents ongoing challenges for networking professionals.

A business's need for a robust network to support voice, data, image, and video traffic is not confined to a single office building or LAN; today, it is an enterprise-wide communication requirement. Advances in LAN switches and other data communication technologies have led to greatly increased LAN transmission capacities and the concept of integration. *Integration* means that the communication equipment and networks can deal simultaneously with voice, data, image, and even video. Thus, a memo or report can be accompanied by voice commentary, presentation graphics, and perhaps even a short video introduction, demonstration, or summary. Image and video services that perform adequately within LANs often impose large demands on WAN transmission and can be costly. Moreover, as LANs become ubiquitous and as their transmission rates increase, the need for enterprise networks to support interconnections among geographically dispersed areas has increased. This, in turn, has forced businesses to increase WAN transmission and switching capacity. Fortunately, the enormous and ever-increasing capacity of fiber optic and wireless transmission services provides ample resources to meet these business data communication needs. However, the development of switching systems that are capable of responding to the increasing capacities of transmission links and business communication traffic requirements is an ongoing challenge not yet conquered.

The opportunities for a business to use its enterprise network as an aggressive competitive tool and as a means of enhancing productivity and slashing costs are great. When business managers understand these technologies, they can deal effectively with data communication equipment vendors and service providers to enhance the company's competitive position.

In the remainder of this section, we provide a brief overview of various types of networks included in enterprise network architectures. Parts Four and Five of this book cover these topics in greater detail.

Wide Area Networks

Wide area networks generally cover a large geographical area. They often require the crossing of public right-of-ways, and typically rely at least in part on circuits provided by one or more *common carriers*—communications companies that offer communication services to the general public. Typically, a WAN consists of a number of interconnected switching nodes. A transmission from any network-attached device is routed through these nodes to the specified destination device. These nodes are not concerned with the content of the data; rather, their purpose is to provide a switching facility that will move the data from node to node until they reach their destination.

Traditionally, WANs have been implemented using one of two technologies: circuit switching and packet switching. More recently, frame relay and cell relay networks have assumed major roles. Chapter 16 looks more closely at frame relay and ATM (Asynchronous Transfer Mode), the most widely used cell relay technology; multiple protocol label switching (MPLS) and wide area Ethernet (WAE) are also considered.

CIRCUIT SWITCHING In a circuit-switching network, a dedicated communications path is established between senders and receivers through the network's switching nodes. That path is a connected sequence of physical links between nodes. On each link, a logical channel is dedicated to the connection between the sender and receiver. Data generated by the sending device are transmitted along the dedicated path as rapidly as possible. At each switching node, incoming data are routed or switched to the appropriate outgoing channel without delay. The classic example of circuit switching is the telephone network. When you call someone and they answer, a circuit connection is established over which a steady stream of data can be passed. The circuit functions the same way no matter how many switching nodes are needed to establish the connection with the person you called. The circuit is yours to use for as long as you need it and is terminated when you hang up.

PACKET SWITCHING A different approach is used in a packet-switching network. In this case, it is not necessary to dedicate transmission capacity along a path through the network. Rather, data are transmitted in a sequence of small chunks, called packets. Each packet is passed through the network from switching node to switching node along some path leading from source to destination. At each switching node, the entire packet is received, may be stored briefly, and then transmitted to the next node. Traditionally, packet-switching networks have been most commonly used for terminal-to-computer and computer-to-computer data communications; today, they are also used to carry time-sensitive voice and video traffic. Packet switching and circuit switching are examined in greater detail in Chapter 15.

FRAME RELAY Packet switching was developed at a time when digital long-distance transmission facilities exhibited a relatively high error rate compared to those that are available today. As a result, there is a considerable amount of overhead built into packet-switching schemes to compensate for errors. The overhead includes additional bits added to each packet to facilitate error checking and additional processing at destination devices and intermediate switching nodes to detect and recover from errors.

With modern high-speed telecommunications systems, this overhead is unnecessary and counterproductive. Error rates have been dramatically lowered and the few errors that remain can easily be caught and addressed by destination devices. This means that it is no longer necessary to carry out error-checking activities at switching nodes. The elimination of node-to-node error checking and error recovery also means that circuit capacity can be more productively used to carry data rather than error control information.

Frame relay was developed to take advantage of the higher data rates and low error rates that are available to implement WANs. Whereas the original packet-switching networks were designed to support per user data rates of about 64 Kbps, frame relay networks are designed to operate efficiently at user data rates of 2 Mbps or more. The key to achieving these high data rates is using less error-prone circuits and stripping out most of the overhead involved with error control.

ATM   **Asynchronous Transfer Mode (ATM),** which is also commonly referred to as cell relay, is a culmination of advancements in both circuit switching and packet switching. However, ATM is widely viewed as an evolution from frame relay. The most obvious difference between frame relay and ATM is that frame relay uses variable-length packets, called frames, and ATM uses fixed-length packets, called cells. As with frame relay, ATM provides little overhead for error control, depending on the inherent reliability of the transmission system and using destination devices to catch and correct errors. By using a fixed packet length, the processing overhead associated with moving data across the network can be reduced even further for ATM compared to frame relay. The result is that ATM is designed for data rates of 100s of Mbps, and in the Gbps range.

ATM can also be viewed as an evolution from circuit switching. With circuit switching, only fixed-data-rate circuits are available to sending and receiving devices. ATM allows senders and receivers to establish multiple virtual channels with data rates that are dynamically defined at the time each virtual channel is created. Each channel can be used to carry a different type of data (e.g., voice, data, image, or video) making ATM ideal for supporting videoconferencing and other time-sensitive multimedia applications. By using small, fixed-size cells, ATM is so efficient that it can offer logical, dedicated constant-data-rate channels even though it is using a packet-switching technique. Thus, ATM extends circuit switching to allow multiple channels with the data rate on each channel dynamically set on demand. Both ATM and frame relay are examined more fully in Chapter 16.

Local Area Networks

As with WANs, a LAN is a communications network that interconnects a variety of devices and provides a means for information exchange among those devices. There are several key distinctions between LANs and WANs:

1. The geographic scope of the LAN is small, typically a single building or a cluster of buildings. This difference in geographic scope leads to different technical solutions, as we shall see.

2. It is usually the case that switches and communication equipment used to implement the LAN is owned by the same organization that owns the LAN-attached computing devices. For WANs, this is less often the case, with all or at least a significant fraction of the WAN circuits and switching nodes not owned by the business. This has two implications. First, care must be taken by business managers when choosing LANs because the choices can translate into substantial capital investment in network equipment purchases and ongoing

network maintenance. Second, the network management responsibility for a LAN falls solely on the owner.

3. The internal data rates of LANs are typically much greater than those of WANs. Data rates of 100 Mbps or exceeding 1 Gbps can be cost-effectively achieved within LANs but interconnecting LANs across WANs at comparable data transmission rates can be costly.

LANs come in a number of different configurations. The most common are switched LANs and wireless LANs. The most common switched LAN is a switched Ethernet LAN and the most common type of wireless LANs are Wi-Fi LANs.

Part Four of the book covers LANs. Chapter 12 covers the various types of LANs found in enterprise networks—including storage area networks (SANs), backbone networks, tiered-LANs—and the media, structured cabling infrastructures, and media access control architectures used to implement LANs. Ethernet LANs are the focus of Chapter 13, and Wi-Fi networks are examined in greater detail in Chapter 14.

Wireless Networks

As was just mentioned, wireless LANs are common and are becoming standard features in business networks. The business push for mobility means that enterprise networks commonly include wireless technology to support wide-area voice and data networks. Chapter 17 focuses on wireless WANs and includes sections on cellular networks, third-generation (3G) and fourth-generation (4G) wireless services, and satellite-based communications.

Metropolitan Area Networks

As the name suggests, a metropolitan area network (MAN) occupies a middle ground between LANs and WANs. Business interest in MANs has been driven by a growing awareness that traditional point-to-point and switched network techniques used in WANs may be inadequate to satisfy communication traffic increases needed within enterprise networks. While frame relay and ATM continue to be used to satisfy a wide range of high-speed needs, there is an expanding need for both private and public networks capable of providing high capacity at low costs over a large metropolitan area. A number of approaches have been implemented, including wireless networks (e.g., WiMax and Wi-Fi clouds) and metropolitan extensions to Ethernet—Metro Ethernet.

The primary market for MANs is the business customer that has high-capacity needs in a metropolitan area. A MAN is intended to provide the required capacity at lower cost and greater efficiency than obtaining an equivalent service from a local telephone company or an Internet service provider.

An Example Configuration

To give some feel for the scope of concerns of Parts Three through Five, Figure 1.7 illustrates some of the typical communications and network elements in use today. In the upper-left-hand portion of the figure, we see an individual residential user connected to an Internet service provider through some sort of subscriber connection. Common examples of such a connection are a digital subscriber line (DSL), which

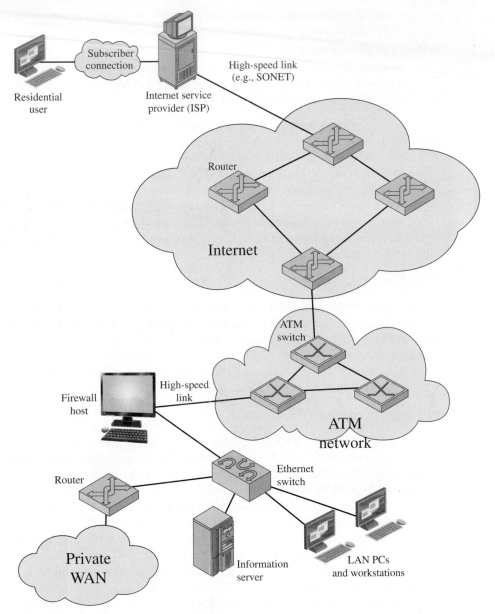

Figure 1.7 A Networking Configuration

provides a high-speed link over telephone lines or fiber-optic cable and requires a special DSL modem, or connecting to a cable TV service provider, which requires a cable modem. In each case, there are separate issues concerning signal encoding, error control, and the internal structure of the network that the residential user connects to.

Typically, an ISP's network consists of a number of interconnected servers (although only a single server is shown in Figure 1.7) connected to the Internet through a high-speed link. One example of such a link is a SONET (synchronous optical network) line, described in Chapter 6. The Internet consists of a sizable number of interconnected routers that span the globe. These routers forward packets of data from source to destination through the Internet.

The lower portion of the figure shows a LAN implemented using a single Ethernet switch. This is a common configuration at small businesses and other small organizations. The LAN is connected to the Internet through a firewall that provides security services. In this example, the firewall connects to the Internet through an ATM network. There is also a router off of the LAN hooked into a private WAN, which might be a private ATM or frame relay network.

A variety of design issues, such as signal encoding and error control, relate to the links between adjacent elements. Examples are links between routers on the Internet, between switches in the ATM network, and between a residential or business subscriber and an ISP. The internal structure of the various networks (telephone, ATM, Ethernet) raises additional issues. The design features suggested by Figure 1.7 are discussed in Parts Three through Five.

1.9 MANAGEMENT ISSUES

Part Six concludes the book by examining key management issues related to business data communications.

Network Security

As companies rely increasingly on networks and as access by outsiders via the Internet and other links grows, the vexing question of security becomes ever more important. Companies are at risk for the disclosure of confidential information and for the unauthorized altering of corporate data. Chapters 18 and 19 look at the basic tools for achieving network security and discuss how they can be adapted to meet a company's needs.

Since network security is a topic that cannot and should not be isolated from other data communication and networking concepts in this book, no attempt is made to confine and limit its discussion to only Chapters 18 and 19. Instead, these two chapters examine numerous network security concepts that do not readily lend themselves to detailed discussion in relation to important concepts addressed in previous chapters. For example, in this chapter, intranets, extranets, and VPNs are introduced. These typically include security mechanisms such as access controls, encrypted messages, and firewalls and their associated security controls are among the reasons why they are used by businesses.

Security is referenced as an issue throughout this book whenever it should be identified as an important business consideration. For example, as mobile and wireless computing, cloud computing, and third-party data centers become increasingly important components of enterprise network infrastructures, the security issues associated with them also increase in importance. We would be remiss if we failed to mention security concerns while discussing these technologies. Hence, you will see that security is an important theme throughout the book and that the topics addressed in Chapters 18 and 19 supplement or provide a more in-depth look at security concepts identified in previous chapters.

Network Management

In the early years of data communications, the key focus was the functionality and performance of the technology. The key questions were, What could the technology do? How fast? For which transactions? As computer-based information systems became part of the basic fabric of many businesses, managers discovered that the operation of their businesses had become dependent on their information systems and that the economic performance of their firms depended on the cost-effective use of the technology. That is, like any business resource, information technology had to be managed. For example, today, data communications managers are often most concerned about network reliability and availability. Many required network management functions are common to other aspects of business management, but the following requirements are special to enterprise networks:

- Networks have evolved from an easily controlled client/server (i.e., mainframe/ dumb terminal) approach into peer-to-peer interconnections among highly distributed systems.
- Peer-to-peer networks have grown larger and larger—some have tens or hundreds of thousands of attached devices—so that managing, monitoring, and maintaining them has become very complex.
- In many business sectors, such as banking, retailing, and other service industries, networks of computing devices constitute a critical strategic resource that cannot be allowed to fail.
- Communications costs continue to be an important business issue and there is a shortage of skilled personnel to staff network command centers and to handle network management. The desire to contain communication costs is contributing to increasing business adoption of virtualization and cloud computing.
- Mobile computing is exploding with smartphones and tablets becoming preferred computing devices among business users. The proliferation of Web-based mobile applications has the potential to transform the way work is performed. Corporate IT departments must address the management, support, and security challenges that come with mobile computing.

In large businesses, network management must provide global visibility on corporate information flow. Sophisticated network management systems are needed that provide remote monitoring and control, rapid notification of failures, and automatic invocation of recovery measures. On-the-fly analysis of network performance and dynamic adjustment of network parameters are needed to provide adaptation to varying cycles of business activity. Today, network management is a complex discipline, particularly in a multivendor environment. Business managers must understand the requirements for network management and the tools and technologies available to plan and effectively implement an appropriate network management strategy.

Chapters 20 and 21 focus on network management, but as the previous paragraphs in this section suggest, some network management topics are not easy to confine to specific sections of a data communications textbook. This is especially true for topics related to the evolution of enterprise network infrastructures. Most business managers recognize their organizations' critical reliance on networks to operate and compete and this elevates the importance of effectively managing network resources. Many industry experts think that cloud computing and mobility will bring changes to enterprise network infrastructures comparable to those associated moving from centralized, mainframe-centric networks to client/server architectures. If mobility and cloud computing spur equally monumental changes in enterprise network architectures, all aspects of business will be affected.

Like security, network infrastructure is running theme that must be emphasized at numerous points throughout the book. It is especially evident in Parts Three, Four, Five, and Six. Part Three's discussion of the Internet, client/server architectures, intranets, extranets, Service-Oriented Architecture (SOA), and Internet applications provide insight into how the public Internet and IP-based applications are used in enterprise networks. Part Four discusses both wired and wireless LANs, central building blocks in on-premise networks, and Part Five discusses how WANs are used to interconnect geographically dispersed business units. Part Six discusses how network management systems are used to maximize enterprise network availability and performance by monitoring business communication traffic and alerting network managers about problems. It also discusses how networks can be designed to ensure adequate performance of mission-critical business applications. Network infrastructure is also a theme in Part One's discussion of distributed data processing. Chapter 3 provides insight into why storage area networks (SANs) have become important components in many enterprise networks and why "big data" is expected to become key basis for competition, business growth, and innovation.

1.10 STANDARDS

Standards are a very important part of the data communications landscape. Virtually all vendors of data communications products and services are committed to supporting international standards. Throughout this book, we describe the most important standards in use, or are being developed for various aspects of data communications and networking. Numerous organizations have been involved in the development or promotion of these standards. Several of the most important standard-setting organizations are:

- **Internet Society:** ISOC provides leadership in addressing issues that confront the future of the Internet and is the organization home for the groups responsible for Internet infrastructure standards, including the Internet Engineering Task Force (IETF) and the Internet Architecture Board (IAB). These organizations develop Internet standards and related specifications, all of which are published as Requests for Comments (RFCs).
- **ITU-T:** The International Telecommunication Union (ITU) is an international organization within the United Nations System in which governments and the private sector coordinate global telecom networks and services. The ITU Telecommunication Standardization Sector (ITU-T) is one of the three sectors of the ITU. ITU-T's mission is the production of standards

covering all fields of telecommunications. ITU-T standards are referred to as Recommendations. ITU-T standards are typically depicted with a capital letter followed by a period (.) and number. Examples include H.263 (video encoding), V.90 (dial-up modems), and X.25 (packet switching).

- **ISO:** The International Organization for Standardization (ISO)[3] is a world-wide federation of national standards bodies from more than 140 countries, one from each country. ISO is a nongovernmental organization that promotes the development of standardization and related activities with a view to facilitating the international exchange of goods and services, and to developing cooperation in the spheres of intellectual, scientific, technological, and economic activity. ISO's work results in international agreements that are published as *International Standards.*

- **IEEE 802:** The IEEE (Institute of Electrical and Electronics Engineers) 802 LAN/MAN Standards Committee develops local area network standards and metropolitan area network standards. The most widely used standards are for the Ethernet family (802.3), wireless LAN (802.11), and virtual LANs (802.1q). An individual working group provides the focus for each area.

- **National Institute of Standards and Technology:** NIST is a U.S. federal agency that deals with measurement science, standards, and technology related to U.S. government use and to the promotion of U.S. private-sector innovation. Despite its national scope, NIST Federal Information Processing Standards (FIPS) and Special Publications (SP) have a worldwide impact.

A more detailed discussion of these organizations is included in Appendix B.

Case Study I: Unified Communications at Boeing

The major concepts addressed in this case study include Unified communications and converged IP networks. **This case study and more are available at www.pearsoninternationaleditions.com/stallings**

1.11 KEY TERMS, REVIEW QUESTIONS, AND PROBLEMS

Key Terms

asynchronous transfer mode (ATM)	frame relay	TCP/IP
circuit switching	image communications	unified communications
client/server	Internet	video communications
convergence	local area network (LAN)	voice communications
data communications	metropolitan area network (MAN)	wide area network (WAN)
distributed applications	packet switching	wireless network

---

[3]ISO is not an acronym (in which case it would be IOS), but a word, derived from the Greek, meaning *equal.*

Review Questions

1.1 Identify and list some uses of at least three emerging enterprise network applications.

1.2 Briefly describe a real-time communications (RTC) dashboard.

1.3 Briefly define convergence and describe the major business benefits of convergence.

1.4 Briefly describe the characteristics of *unified communications (UC)* and describe how UC contributes to personal, workgroup, and enterprise-wide performance gains.

1.5 Identify and briefly describe the four types of communication traffic carried by business networks.

1.6 Why has optical fiber cabling become common in enterprise network infrastructures?

1.7 Why is wireless transmission becoming more widely used by businesses?

1.8 Why is network security required in business data communication?

1.9 Name some of the most important standard-setting organizations and explain their functions.

1.10 Contrast the major characteristics of WANs with those of LANs and MANs.

Problems

1.1 Do some online research on the characteristics of software as a service (SaaS), platform as a service (PaaS), and infrastructure as a service (IaaS). Write a short paper describing the differences between these services and identifying some of the major providers of each type.

1.2 Find and view several YouTube videos on unified communications. Identify the URLs for three that you think do a particularly good job illustrating the characteristics and capabilities of UC systems. Select the one that you think is best and briefly justify your selection.

1.3 Do some online research to find information on several businesses that have benefited from implementing unified communications. Write a short paper describing how/why they are using unified communications and the business benefits that they have realized.

1.4 Do some online research to find information on several businesses that have implemented IPTV. Write a short paper describing how/why they are using IPTV and the business benefits that they have realized.

1.5 Do some online research on MANs and Metro Ethernet. Write a short paper comparing Metro Ethernet to other MAN alternatives that are available for business use.

1.6 Use Skype, Yahoo Instant Messenger, or a similar tool that combines real-time voice, video (Webcam), and chat to establish a communication session with a friend or family member. Use one or more screen captures to document the convergence of voice, video, and chat for the communication session and paste these to a word processing document in a format (such as .rtf or .docx) that can be opened by your instructor. Your screen capture(s) should include Webcam windows for yourself and your friend/family member and a window illustrating your real-time chat.

APPENDIX 1A PREFIXES FOR NUMERICAL UNITS

The **bit** (b) is the fundamental unit of discrete information. It represents the outcome of one choice: 1 or 0, yes or no, on or off. One bit represents two potential outcomes. So, for example, one bit can represent the on/off state of a switch. Two bits can represent four outcomes: 00, 01, 10, 11. Three bits represent eight outcomes: 000, 001, 010, 011, 100, 101, 110, 111. Each time another bit is added, the numbers of outcomes double (Table 1.3). A **byte** (or **octet**, usually abbreviated as B) is the name given to

Table 1.3   Bits and Outcomes

Number of Bits (x)	Number of Outcomes (2^x)	Typical Use
1	2	Basic unit of information
4	16	Hexadecimal digit
7	128	IRA (International Reference Alphabet) character without parity bit
8	256	Byte; character with parity bit
10	1024	Number of bytes in a kilobyte of storage
13	8192	Number of bits in a kilobyte of storage
16	65,536	Address size in older computers
20	1,048,576	Number of bytes in a megabyte of storage
23	8,388,608	Number of bits in a megabyte of storage
32	4.3×10^9	Common memory address size
64	1.84×10^{19}	Memory address size on newer computers

8 bits (e.g., 8 b = 1 B). The number of potential outcomes a byte represents is $2 \times 2 \times 2 \times 2 \times 2 \times 2 \times 2 \times 2 = 2^8 = 256$. Bytes are usually used in representing quantities of storage in computers. Bits are traditionally used in describing communications rates.

In the computer science literature, the prefixes kilo, mega, and so forth are often used on numerical units. These have two different interpretations (Table 1.4):

- **Data transmission:** For data transmission, the prefixes used are those defined for the International System of Units (SI), the international standard. In this scheme, prefixes are used as a shorthand method of expressing powers of 10. For example, one kilobit per second (1 Kbps) = 10^3 bps = 1000 bps.

- **Computer storage:** The amount of data in computer memory, in a file, or a message that is transmitted is typically measured in bytes. Because memory is indicated by binary addresses, the size of memory is expressed as powers of 2. The same prefixes are used in a way that approximates their use in the SI scheme. For example, one kilobyte (1 kB) = 2^{10} bytes = 1024 bytes.

Table 1.4   Numerical Prefixes

Prefix Name	Prefix Symbol	Factor SI	Factor Computer Storage
tera	T	10^{12}	2^{40}
giga	G	10^9	$2^{30} = 1,073,741,824$
mega	M	10^6	$2^{20} = 1,048,576$
kilo	k	10^3	$2^{10} = 1024$
milli	m	10^{-3}	
micro	μ	10^{-6}	
nano	n	10^{-9}	

BUSINESS INFORMATION

CHAPTER

2

Learning Objectives

After reading this chapter, you should be able to:

♦ Distinguish between digital and analog information sources.

♦ Characterize business information types into one of four categories: audio, data, image, and video.

♦ Estimate quantitatively the communication resources required by the four types of information sources.

♦ Explain why system response time is a critical factor in user productivity.

The volume of communications traffic being transported over business networks is increasing. This is due in part to growing business reliance on networks to compete and operate. It is also the result of the evolution of the types of information being carried by enterprise networks. Video and image traffic growth is driving businesses toward more robust enterprise network infrastructures.

It is important to understand how information communication relates to business requirements. A first step in this understanding is to examine the various forms of business information at an elemental level. There is a wide variety of business applications, each with its own information characteristics. For the analysis and design of enterprise networks, however, the kinds of communication traffic associated with business applications usually can be categorized as requiring one (or a combination) of a small number of basic information sources: **audio**, **data**, **image**, and **video**.

Our examination covers the following topics:

- How the impact of information sources on communications systems is measured

- The nature of the four basic forms of business information: audio, data, image, and video

- The major business uses of each of these forms of information

- An introductory look at the network infrastructure implications of these business uses from the point of view of the communications requirements that are necessary to adequately support them.

Business information can be transmitted in **digital** or **analog** form. A *digital* system uses a sequence of discrete, discontinuous values or symbols to represent information. Discrete information has a finite "alphabet." Examples include letters, numbers, icons, and binary data (which represent one of two states as "on or off," "yes or no," etc.). In digital systems, the information rate and the capacity of a digital channel are measured in bits per second (bps).

Nondigital *analog* systems use a continuous range of values to represent information. Analog information sources include sounds, music, and video. Humans primarily experience the world in an analog fashion. This is especially evident in hearing and vision. For example, we visually experience the world as being made up of gradations of shapes and colors and when we listen to a symphony orchestra, we experience a wide range of tempos, pitches, and loudness. Similarly, we experience temperature as continuous gradations of warm from very cold, through cool, lukewarm, warm, to hot, and not as discrete "hot" or "cold" values.

Analog communication systems use a continuous signal to represent either continuous or discrete information sources. Voltage may be used because it can take on a continuum of values to represent information. An analog microphone, for example, produces an analog electrical signal when someone speaks into it. In this case, the analog electrical signal represents the continuous acoustic changes in air pressure that make up the sounds produced by the human speaking into the microphone. For analog communication systems, information rate and channel capacity are measured in hertz (Hz) of bandwidth (1 Hz = 1 cycle per second). Virtually any communication signal, from either discrete or analog sources, can be expressed as a combination of pure oscillations of various frequencies. In analog systems, bandwidth measures the limits (range) of the frequencies that can be used to represent the information. The higher the range of frequencies allowed, the higher the bandwidth and the more accurately a complex information source can be represented.

It is important to understand that both analog and discrete information systems can be transmitted over either digital or analog transmission systems. For example, today we routinely "digitize" analog information sources such as voice and video to enable *digital audio* or *digital video* transmission over digital communication systems. It is also possible to represent discrete data as continuous signals for transmission over analog communication systems. Because businesses are not limited to using only digital transmission for discrete information sources and to using only analog systems for transmitting information from analog sources, managers need to understand which transmission systems are capable of satisfying their information requirements.

2.1 AUDIO

Audio communication services support applications based on sound, especially the human voice. Traditionally, telephony (telephone communication) has been the primary business application of audio services. Other applications include telemarketing, voice mail, audio conferencing (conference calls), interactive voice response (IVR) systems, call centers, podcasting, and commercial radio. The quality of sound associated with audio applications is characterized mainly by the bandwidth used (Figure 2.1). On traditional analog circuits, voice on a telephone is limited to about

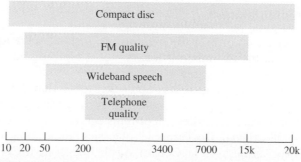

Figure 2.1 Signal Frequency and Bandwidth (Hz)

3400 Hz of bandwidth, which provides a moderate level of quality. For audio teleconferencing, about 7000 Hz of bandwidth is needed. For high-fidelity sound of reasonable quality, about 15,000 Hz (approximately the range of the human ear) is needed. For compact discs, 20,000 Hz is supported for each of two channels for stereo.

Audio information can also be represented digitally. A more detailed discussion of the analog-to-digital conversion (digitization) process used to do this is provided in Chapter 4. We give an abbreviated discussion here. To get a good representation of sound in digital format, we need to sample its amplitude at a rate (samples per second, or smp/s) equal to at least twice the maximum frequency (in Hz) range of the analog signal. For voice of telephone quality, one usually samples at a rate of 8000 samples per second (smp/s); this is twice the average range of frequencies for human speech (about 4000 Hz). For high-quality sound on compact discs, 44,100 smp/s is the sampling rate used for each channel. After sampling, the signal amplitudes must be put in digital form, a process referred to as **quantization**. Eight bits per sample are usually used for telephone voice and 16 bits per sample for each channel for stereophonic compact disc. In the first case, 256 levels of amplitude can be distinguished, and in the second, 65,536 levels. Thus, without compression, digital voice requires 8 bits/sample (b/smp) $\times$ 8000 smp/s = 64,000 bps. In the case of CDs, a straightforward multiplication of the foregoing parameters (16 b/smp $\times$ 44,100 smp/s $\times$ 2 channels) leads to a data rate of about 1.41 Mbps for both channels. A CD with a capacity of about 600 megabytes (MB) can therefore hold about one hour of stereo sound.

Typical telephone conversations have an average length in the range of one to five minutes. For ordinary voice telephone communication, information in either direction is transmitted less than half the time; otherwise, the two parties would be talking at once [SRIR88].

Audio compression algorithms can be used to reduce the bandwidth requirements for transmitting digital audio streams over communication lines. They can also be used to reduce the storage size of audio files. Both "lossy" and "lossless" audio compression algorithms exist and these are implemented in audio codecs (coder/decoders) and computer software in digital transmission systems. Lossy algorithms provide greater compression ratios than lossless algorithms and are used in numerous consumer audio devices.

There are important differences between lossy and lossless compression algorithms. With **lossless compression**, receivers can reproduce an exact digital duplicate of the original audio stream transmitted by the sender by expanding/decompressing the file that is received. When **lossy compression** is used, irreversible changes are made to original file that diminishes the quality of the original audio stream when the receiver decompresses the file. In some instances, the loss in sound quality may not be noticeable to human listeners, but it typically becomes more evident with higher levels of compression.

Lossy algorithms can reduce audio files to less than 20% of their original size with 5–20% being the average reduction of the original file. Examples of lossy algorithms are MP3 and Vorbis. Lossless algorithms can reduce an audio file to approximately 50–60% of its original size. Examples of lossless audio compression algorithms include FLAC (Free Lossless Audio Codec), Apple Lossless, MPEG-4 ALS (MPEG-4 Audio Lossless Coding), and WMA Lossless (Windows Media Audio Lossless).

Networking Implications

Because telephony continues to be a primary business application of audio services, powerful and flexible access to telephone services are considered to be essential in today's enterprise networks. Outside services may be provided by public telephone networks, including the local telephone company, competitive local exchange services (CLECs) that provide voice services, and long-distance carriers such as AT&T or a national PTT (postal, telegraph, and telephone) authority. In addition, various private networking facilities and leased line arrangements are possible and cloud-computing alternatives are increasingly available for audio-oriented business applications. Needless to say, the business push for mobility means that cellular telephone service providers have become an important part of the enterprise network landscape. Traditional telephony options are discussed in Chapter 15. Cellular networks are discussed in Chapter 17.

Businesses have traditionally thought that the most effective way to manage voice requirements at a particular location is to tie all of the phones into a single system. There are two main alternatives for this: the private branch exchange and hosted services such as Centrex. The **private branch exchange (PBX)** is an on-premise telephone switch, owned or leased by an organization, that interconnects the telephones at that location and provides outside access to the public telephone system and other voice services (Figure 2.2a). Typically, PBX and Centrex services enable a telephone user at a business location to reach another on-site co worker by dialing a three- or four-digit number; to get an outside line, the user dials a one-digit (usually 8 or 9) number and then the rest of the call recipient's telephone number.

One of the latest developments in the evolution of PBXs is the use of Internet Protocol (IP) to carry phone calls. A PBX that supports voice over IP (VoIP)

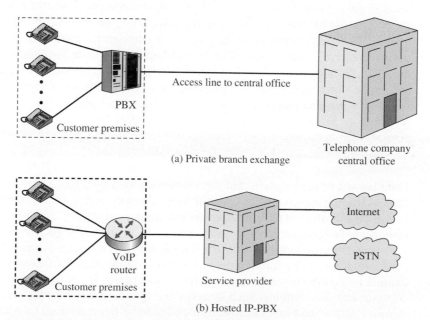

(a) Private branch exchange

(b) Hosted IP-PBX

Figure 2.2 Business Telephone Configurations

is called a VoIP PBX or **IP-PBX**. A hosted IP-PBX provides the same types of services as a PBX as well as additional features that are available through IP communications including unified messaging services that extend user access to voice mail via Web portals, or as e-mail .WAV files. A hosted IP-PBX is physically located at the premises of the provider and the only equipment at the customer's site are IP handsets that communicate with the PBX via IP telephony (see Figure 2.2b). Hosted IP-PBXs have largely replaced *Centrex*, which is a service offered by telephone companies, and some CLECs, that provides the same sort of services as a PBX but performs the switching function in equipment located in the telephone company's central office.

Today's PBXs and hosted IP-PBX services can support a wide variety of voice-related services including voice mail and audio conference calls. To remain viable as business communication services, PBX and hosted IP-PBX services are adapting to support collaboration among on-premise and mobile business users such as that made possible by unified communications (UC) systems. Hosted, cloud-based, and on-premises PBXs that support unified communications are becoming common elements in enterprise network infrastructures.

The increasing use of digital transmission to carry audio over business networks requires network managers to monitor the quality of the audio that is being delivered to users. Appropriate choices must be made about the types of audio compression algorithms used to increase the efficiency of audio traffic. Needless to say, businesses do not want to compress audio files so much that user, customer, or partner experience is significantly degraded.

Another important audio communication issue for business network managers is that telephony is integrated with enterprise systems applications such as CRM (customer relationship management). To realize their business potential, CRM systems must log every customer contact with the company whether it is via e-mail, the Web, text message, office or home telephone, or mobile phone. Such logging enables business users to instantly access a customer's contact history to know if questions have been answered or if problems have been resolved. CRM systems are also typically integrated with other enterprise systems such as ERP (enterprise resources planning) and have capabilities that surpass those of computer-integrated telephony applications that are widely used in call centers.

2.2 DATA

Data consist of information that can be represented by a finite alphabet of symbols, such as the numbers 0 through 9 or the symbols represented on a computer keyboard. Common examples of data include text and numerical information. Symbols are often represented in computers or for transmission by groups of 8 bits (octets or bytes).

A familiar example of digital data is *text* or character strings. While textual data are convenient for human beings to communicate with one another, they cannot be easily stored or transmitted in character form by data processing and communications systems. Such systems are designed for binary data, 0s and 1s. A number of text-to-binary conversion codes have been devised in which text characters are represented by a sequence of binary digits (bits). Perhaps the earliest common example of this is the Morse code. Historically, the most commonly used text code has been the **International Reference Alphabet (IRA)**.[1] Each character in this code is represented by a unique 7-bit pattern; thus 128 different characters can be represented. This is a larger number than is necessary to represent all the symbols on a computer keyboard, and some of the patterns represent invisible, non-printable *control characters*. IRA-encoded characters are almost always stored and transmitted using 8 bits per character. The eighth bit is a parity bit used for error detection. This bit is set such that the total number of binary 1s in each octet is always odd (*odd parity*) or always even (*even parity*). Thus a transmission error that changes a single bit, or any odd number of bits, can be detected.

After text-to-binary conversion has taken place, each of the characters or symbols is represented as a string of bits (0s and 1s). These bits can be transmitted using either analog or digital transmission.

The ACSII (IRA) character set is the most common format for English-language text files. Text files, files saved with a .txt extension, contain very little formatting and do not support formatting such as boldface, italics, or underline. Because files with a .txt extension can be opened and read by any program that reads text, they are considered to be platform independent.

Another important text-to-binary encoding scheme is **UTF-8** (the UCS [Universal Character Set] Transformation Format)-8. As an 8 bit code that is backward compatible with the IRA, you might think that UTF-8 is limited to representing 256 characters and symbols. However, because it supports variable-length encoding, which allows multiple bytes to be used to represent characters in an alphabet or character set, UTF-8 is capable of representing symbols and characters used in all the major languages spoken around the world. UTF-8 allows characters and symbols to be represented by one, two, three, or four bytes and is therefore capable of representing more than a million different characters or symbols. In 2007, UTF-8 became the dominant character-encoding scheme on the World Wide Web when the total number of Web pages using UTF-8 encoding surpassed more than 50%.

Unicode is another important character-encoding scheme that is supported in numerous programming languages, including Java, Microsoft's .NET Framework, and XML. It is also supported by the operating systems used on most computing and communication devices. Unicode is a 16-bit code that is backward compatible with IRA/ASCII and UTF-8 is essentially an 8-bit version of Unicode. Like UTF-8, recent revisions of Unicode, including Unicode 6.0, enable symbols in some languages to be represented by more than one byte thereby enabling it to be used to represent characters for most of the writing systems used worldwide.

Businesses typically organize text, numerical data, and other types of data, including image and video, into one or more databases. Industry experts estimate that the 15 petabytes (15,000 gigabytes) of new electronic data are created every day, much of this is the result of huge growth in video, image, audio, and social media data. The growing appetite for creating, gathering, and storing data are ongoing

---

[1]IRA is defined in ITU-T Recommendation T.50 and was formerly known as International Alphabet Number 5 (IA5). The U.S. national version of IRA is referred to as the American Standard Code for Information Interchange (**ASCII**). A description and table of the IRA code is contained in Appendix D.

challenges for business and have significant communication and networking infrastructure implications. The networking implications associated with the deployment and use of business databases is explored in Chapter 3.

To provide a better understanding of the communication implications of the text-to-binary conversion concepts discussed in this section, let us estimate approximately how many bits are required to transmit a single typewritten page. Commonly, a letter of the alphabet or a typographical symbol is represented by a *byte*, or 8 bits; this is definitely the case for written English using ASCII-8 or UTF-8. Let us consider an 8.5-by-11-inch sheet of paper, with a 1-inch margin on all sides. This leaves a 6.5-by-9 inch space in which to type characters. A double-spaced page ordinarily has three lines to the inch, or 27 lines for the page. In a common typeface, there are 10 characters per inch, or 65 characters per line. This gives us a total $8 \times 27 \times 65 = 14{,}040$ bits if full use of the message space within the margins is used. This overstates the number of characters on a page because not all lines include the same number of characters, especially those at the beginning and end of paragraphs. In addition, not all pages of a document are full. So, as round number, 10,000 bits per page (or 1250 characters per page) is probably a fair estimate. If Unicode was used in place of ASCII-8 or UTF-8, 20,000 bits (1250 characters $\times$ 16 bits/character) is a reasonable per page estimate.

For a residential customer with a dial-up connection over a telephone line using a relatively slow modem, a typical channel capacity is 56,000 bps. Thus, it would take about 0.18 seconds to transmit a page encoded in ASCII-8 or UTF-8. It would take approximately 0.36 seconds to transmit a Unicode encoded page. If the residential user had a DSL connection with an average transmission rate of 400,000 bps (400 Kbps), it would only take 0.025 seconds to transmit an ASCII-8 encoded page and 0.050 seconds to transmit a Unicode encoded page. If the residential customer had a cable modem with an average transmission rate of 750 Kbps, it would take just 0.013 seconds to transmit an ACSII encoded page and 0.026 seconds to transmit a Unicode encoded page. As you can see, both the text-to-binary conversion scheme and connection transmission speed determine how long it takes to transmit a fixed-size data file over communication lines. Businesses must be able to estimate the total amount of data that needs to be transmitted within a particular time period (e.g., per second, minute, hour, etc.) to know how much communication line capacity is needed.

This is by no means the whole story. For example, data compression techniques can be employed to use fewer bits than would be required to transmit the data in its original form. Lossless compression algorithms are used for data compression because it is critical for destination devices to receive exact duplicates of the characters and symbols transmitted by senders. **Lempel-Ziv** encoding algorithms are the most widely used lossless data compression schemes for both data storage and data communication over networks. For example, Lempel-Ziv algorithms are employed to "zip" files into compressed files/folders with .zip extensions that can be sent as attachments to e-mail messages. Data compression algorithms are supported by most types of modems, including dial-up. For example, **V.44** is an ISO standard for data compression that uses Lempel-Ziv encoding to compress a data stream being transmitted across a communication line. The number of "compressed" bits needed to represent the original data depends on the content of the data being sent, but reductions of 6:1 can be achieved on average when V.44 is used.

Using data compression algorithms can help businesses make efficient use of communication lines; however, another important issue that must be considered for many data-oriented information sources is the response time required. In some instances, it is critical for businesses to be able to react quickly to data changes. When quick reactions are needed, lengthy delays in data transmission and receipt are not acceptable and enterprise network infrastructure must provide sufficient capacity and transmission speed to ensure adequate response times. Response time and its associated data communication issues are discussed in greater detail later in this chapter.

Networking Implications

The networking and infrastructure requirements for supporting data-oriented business applications vary widely depending largely on the types and volumes of data that need to be generated, transmitted, and stored. We begin a consideration of these requirements in Chapter 3. In many instances, it is also important to ensure that the data are transferred and stored securely. Encryption is widely used to protect data while it is being transmitted and important business files are often stored in encrypted form. Encryption is discussed in Appendix J.

2.3 IMAGE

The **image** service supports the communication of individual pictures, charts, or drawings. Image-based applications used by businesses include facsimile, computer-aided design (CAD), electronic publishing (e-publishing), online (Web) publishing, and medical imaging. Many information workers and consumers have smartphones that are equipped with cameras that can be used to take and transmit pictures using text messaging services or as attachments to e-mail messages. Photos taken with camera phones may also be uploaded to social media sites such as Facebook. As enterprise networks are increasingly required to handle growing volumes of image traffic, appropriate decisions must be made to ensure that sufficient infrastructure is in place to efficiently handle these types of files.

As an example of the types of demands that can be placed by imaging systems, consider medical image transmission requirements. Table 2.1 summarizes the communication impact of various medical image types [DWYE92]. In addition, giving the bits per image and the number of images per exam, the table gives the transmission time per exam for three standard digital transmission rates: DS–0 = 56 Kbps, DS–1 = 1.544 Mbps, and DS–3 = 44.736 Mbps.

Again, compression can be used. If we allow some barely perceivable loss of information, we can use "lossy" compression, which might reduce the data by factors of roughly 10:1 to 20:1. On the other hand, for medical imaging lossy compression usually is not acceptable. Using lossless compression, ratios for these applications run below 5:1. PNG (Portable Network Graphics) and GIF (Graphics Interchange Format) are examples of image file formats that only use lossless image compression algorithms. TIFF (Tagged Image File Format) and MNG (Multiple-image Network Graphics) support both lossy and lossless image compression.

Table 2.1 Transfer Time for Digital Radiology Images

Image Type	Mbytes per Image	Images per Exam	DS-0 Time/Exam (seconds)	DS-1 Time/Exam (seconds)	DS-3 Time/Exam (seconds)
Computerized tomography (CT)	0.52	30	2247	81	3
Magnetic resonance imagery (MRI)	0.13	50	928	34	1
Digital angiography	1	20	2857	104	4
Digital fluorography	1	15	2142	78	3
Ultrasound	0.26	36	1337	48	2
Nuclear medicine	0.016	26	59	2	0.1
Computerized radiography	8	4	4571	166	6
Digitized film	8	4	4571	166	6

Note: DS–0 = 56 Kbps; DS–1 = 1.544 Mbps; DS–3 = 44.736 Mbps

Image Representation

There are a variety of techniques used to represent image information. These fall into two main categories:

- **Vector graphics**: An image is represented as a collection of straight and curved line segments. Simple objects, such as rectangles and ovals, and more complex objects are defined by the grouping of line segments.

- **Raster graphics**: An image is represented as a two-dimensional array of spots, called pixels.[2] A pixel is the smallest single component of a digital image. In the simplest form, each pixel is either black or white. This approach is used not only for computer image processing but also for facsimile.

All of the figures in this book were prepared with a graphics package (Adobe Illustrator) that makes use of vector graphics. Vector graphics involves the use of binary codes to represent object type, size, and orientation. In all these cases, the image is represented and stored as a set of binary digits and can be transmitted using digital signals.

Figure 2.3 shows a simple 10 × 10 representation of an image using raster graphics. This could be a facsimile or raster-scan computer graphics image. The

---

[2]A pixel, or picture element, is the smallest element of a digital image that can be assigned a gray level. Equivalently, a pixel is an individual dot in a dot-matrix representation of a picture.

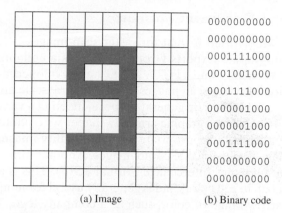

(a) Image	(b) Binary code

Figure 2.3   A 100-Pixel Image and Its Binary Code

10 × 10 representation is easily converted to a 100-bit code for the image. In this example, each pixel is represented by a single bit that indicates black or white. A *grayscale image* is produced if each pixel is defined by more than 1 bit, representing shades of gray. Figure 2.4 shows the use of a 3-bit grayscale to produce eight shades of gray, ranging from white to black. Grayscale can also be used in vector graphics to define the grayscale of line segments or the interior of closed objects such as rectangles.

Images can also be defined in color. There are a number of schemes in use for this purpose. One example is the RGB (red-green-blue) scheme, in which each pixel or image area is defined by three values, one for each of the three colors. The RGB scheme exploits the fact that a large percentage of the visible spectrum can be represented by mixing red, green, and blue in various proportions and intensities. The relative magnitude of each color value determines the actual color.

Color images are the most common type of image being transmitted over today's enterprise networks and the number of distinct colors that can be represented in an image file depends on the number of bits used to represent each pixel, or bits per pixel (bpp). A 1 bpp image using a single bit to represent each pixel is limited to two colors such as black and white. A 2 bpp image could display four colors and a 3 bpp image could support 8 colors. An 8 bpp image can support 256 distinct colors and a 24 bpp image can support 16.8 million colors.

The resolution of transmitted images is also related to the number of pixels used to display the image. Today, digital cameras, including those in smartphones, are capable of taking pictures represented by millions of pixels. A megapixel (MP) is one million pixels and numerous cameras have resolutions of 3.1 MP or more; 3.1 MP is the equivalent of a 2048 × 1536 array of pixels. If 3 bytes (24 bits) are used to represent each pixel, then more than 18.3 million bits are needed to digitize 3.1 MP color images or photographs.

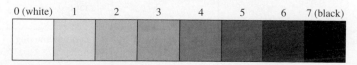

Figure 2.4   An Eight-Level Grayscale

Image and Document Formats

The most widely used format for raster-scan images is referred to as JPEG. The Joint Photographic Experts Group (JPEG) is a collaborative standards-making effort between ISO and ITU-T. JPEG has developed a set of standards for the compression of raster-scan images, both 8-bit grayscale and 24-bit color. The JPEG standard is designed to be general purpose, meeting a variety of needs in such areas as desktop publishing, graphic arts, newspaper wire photo transmission, and medical imaging. JPEG is appropriate for high-quality images, including photographs and is widely used to encode photo images. Another format that is often seen on the Web is the Graphics Interchange Format (GIF). This is an 8-bit color format that can display up to 256 colors and is generally useful for nonphotographic images with a fairly narrow range of color, such as a company logo. Table 2.2 compares these and other popular formats.

TIFF (.TIF) files are widely used by commercial printers and publishers. It is a format of choice for storing/archiving important documents and is excellent for high-resolution photographs and high-quality graphics, logos, line art, and documents when its lossless compression option is used. It supports 24-bit or 48-bit color and 8- or 16-bit grayscale. Relative to other image formats, TIFF files are very large and this essentially rules them out for use on Web pages because of their potential to slow the download process.

PNG (Portable Network Graphics) support the same color and grayscale ranges as TIFF. It uses lossless ZIP compression and like TIFF, it can be used to store or archive high-quality images of photographs, logos, graphics, documents, and master copies of data. PNG files on average are 25% smaller than TIF files and 10–30% smaller than GIF files.

There are also two popular document formats that are suitable for documents that include text and images. The Portable Document Format (PDF) is widely

Table 2.2   Comparison of Common Graphics File Formats

Type	File Extension	Compression Methods	Principal Application/Usage	Originated by
Graphics Interchange Format	.gif	Lempel-Ziv-Welch (LZW) algorithm	Flat-color graphics, animation	CompuServe
Joint Photographic Experts Group	.jpg	Various lossy	Photographic images	Joint Photographic Experts Group
Portable Network Graphics	.png	Lossless	Replacement for GIF	World Wide Web Consortium
Raw negative	Various	None	High-end digital camera	Individual equipment makers
Tagged Image File Format	.tif	Various or none	Document imaging, scanning	Adobe Systems, Inc.
Windows bit map	.bmp	None	On-screen display	Microsoft Corp.

used on the Web, and PDF readers are available for virtually all operating systems. Postscript is a page-description language that is built into many desktop printers and virtually all high-end printing systems.

Networking Implications

The various configurations by which image information is used and communicated do not fundamentally differ from the configurations used for text and numerical data. The key difference is in the volume of data. As was mentioned, a page of text contains about 10,000 bits of 8-bit character data. The bit image of a good-quality personal computer screen requires over two million bits (i.e., for the $640 \times 480 \times 256$ video mode). A facsimile page with a resolution of 200 dots per inch (which is an adequate but not unnecessarily high resolution) would generate about four million bits for a simple black-and-white image and considerably more bits for grayscale or color images. Thus, for image information, a tremendous number of bits is needed for representation in the computer.

The number of bits needed to represent an image can be reduced by the use of image compression techniques. In a typical document, whether it contains text or pictorial information, the black-and-white areas of the image tend to cluster. This property can be exploited to describe the patterns of black and white in a manner that is more concise than simply providing a listing of black-and-white values, one for each point in the image. Compression ratios (the ratio of the size of the uncompressed image, in bits, to the size of the compressed image) from 8 to 16 are readily achievable.

Even with compression, the number of bits to be transmitted for image information is large, especially for color images. As usual, there are two concerns: response time and throughput. In some cases, such as a CAD/CAM (computer-aided design/computer-aided manufacturing) application, the user may interactively manipulate an image over communication lines in real time. If the user's computing device is geographically separated from the CAD/CAM server, the WAN link(s) must have sufficient capacity to ensure adequate response time. For other business applications, such as facsimile, a delay of a few seconds or even a few minutes is usually of no consequence. However, the business's communications infrastructure must still have a capacity great enough to keep up with the average rate of facsimile transmission. Otherwise, delays on the facility grow over time as a backlog develops.

Security is an important issue for some types of image transmissions. For example, in the United States, the transmission of medical images must comply with HIPPA (Health Insurance Portability and Accountability Act) requirements. This typically means that inter-facility image transfers must take place over secure links; encrypting the images prior to transmission is typically required. Encrypting and decrypting files are additional processing steps at sender and destination locations and that can have negative effects on response time. Encryption is also required for numerous types of financial transactions including those carried out at bank ATM (automatic teller machines) terminals. Some ATM machines support check deposits and the check images stored on and transmitted from these machines must be encrypted to comply with banking laws and regulations.

2.4 VIDEO

Video applications carry sequences of pictures in time. In essence, video makes use of a sequence of raster-scan images. Here it is easier to characterize the data in terms of the viewer's (destination's) television or computer display monitor rather than the original scene (source) that is recorded by the video camera.

Video can be captured by either analog or digital video recorders. The video that is captured can be transmitted using continuous (analog) or discrete (digital) signals, can be received by either analog or digital display devices, and can be stored in either analog or digital file formats. Needless to say, all of the possibilities associated with video capture, transfer, display, and storage can be confusing. For examples, consumers who think that all high-definition television (HDTV) systems are digital may be surprised to learn that Japanese HDTV is broadcast using analog signals.

The first televisions and computer monitors used cathode-ray-tube (CRT) technology; there are still plenty of CRT display devices in use and will be for some time to come. CRT monitors are inherently analog devices that use an electron gun to "paint" pictures on the screen. The gun emits an electron beam that scans across the surface of the screen from left to right and top to bottom. For black-and-white television, the amount of illumination produced (on a scale from black to white) at any point is proportional to the intensity of the beam as it passes that point. Thus at any instant in time the beam takes on an analog value of intensity to produce the desired brightness at that point on the screen. Further, as the beam scans, the analog value changes. Thus the video image can be thought of as a time-varying analog signal.

Figure 2.5 depicts the scanning process. At the end of each scan line, the beam is swept rapidly back to the left (horizontal retrace). When the beam reaches the bottom, it is swept rapidly back to the top (vertical retrace). The beam is turned off (blanked out) during the retrace intervals.

To achieve adequate resolution, the beam produces a total of 483 horizontal lines at a rate of 30 complete scans of the screen per second. Tests have shown that this rate produces a sensation of flicker rather than smooth motion. To provide a flicker-free image without increasing the bandwidth requirement, a technique known as **interlacing** is used. As Figure 2.5 shows, the odd-numbered scan lines and the even-numbered scan lines are scanned separately, with odd and even fields alternating on successive scans. The odd field is the scan from A to B and the even field is the scan from C to D. The beam reaches the middle of the screen's lowest line after 241.5 lines. At this point, the beam is quickly repositioned at the top of the screen and recommences in the middle of the screen's top-most visible line to produce an additional 241.5 lines interlaced with the original set. Thus the screen is refreshed 60 times per second rather than 30, and flicker is avoided.

While only a single electron gun is needed for black-and-white CRT televisions and display monitors, three are needed for color CRTs. One is used to hit red phosphor dots on the screen, a second only hits green phosphors, and the third only hits the screen's blue phosphor dots. The guns use essentially the same scanning process described above. In computer monitors, color image resolution can be changed by controlling the positions of the beams and how fast they turn on or off. This enables the CRT to create pixels that vary in size. A computer uses a video card

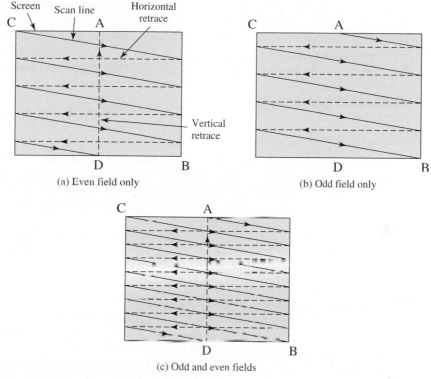

(a) Even field only

(b) Odd field only

(c) Odd and even fields

Figure 2.5 Video Interlaced Scanning

(also called graphics card) to convert the computer's digital signal into an analog signal that can be used by the CRT's electronic guns to create images.

Digital Video

The term *digital video* refers to the capture, manipulation, and storage of video in digital formats. If an analog video camera signal is digitized and then transmitted or stored in a digital format, it may be considered digital video. However, the term is more typically applied to video content that is initially captured with a digital video device.

Digital video cameras capture moving images digitally. In essence, this is done by taking a series of digital photographs, at a rate of at least 30 frames per second. Typically, the resolution is considerably less than that of a digital still camera, more in line with a typical PC screen. At the low end of digital video cameras are Web cameras (Webcams). Their low resolution is tailored to match the needs of Webcasting and video messaging.

Digital video cameras use either the interlaced technique discussed previously or progressive scan, in which all the lines of each frame are drawn in sequence. Progressive scan is used for computer monitors and most HDTV schemes.

Liquid-crystal display (LCD) televisions and computer monitors, better known as flat panel or flat screen monitors, are inherently digital devices. These screens use thin sandwiches of glass containing a liquid-crystal material to display images.

Electric current causes the molecules of the liquid-crystal material to change their alignment to either block or transmit light and create images. Each pixel in LCD displays is composed of red, green, and blue subpixels. Because LCDs are digital devices, they fit well with digital video sources and transmission by helping to ensure that captured and transmitted images are received with no signal loss or corruption.

Networking Implications

Video traffic on business networks is expanding at dramatic rates in step with growing use of video for e-learning, online advertising, videoconferencing, surveillance, social media marketing, and a variety of multimedia applications. As noted in Chapter 1, videoconferencing capabilities are being extended to mobile business users via unified communications and other real-time collaboration systems. In addition, telesurgery and other telepresence applications are being used more widely by health care organizations.

As noted previously, image files are very large and video can be viewed as a sequence of images. This means that unless it is compressed, real-time video traffic requires extensive bandwidth to ensure an adequate user experience.

For example, a black-and-white TV signal for videoconferencing might have a frame resolution of 360 by 280 pixels sent every 1/30 second with an intensity ranging from black through gray to white represented by 8 bits. This would correspond to a raw data rate, without compression, of about 25 Mbps. To add color, the bit rate may go up by 50% or more. Table 2.3 gives the sampling rate for three common types of video. The table gives only the rates for luminance, because color is treated differently in the three formats. At the extreme, uncompressed high-definition color television would require more than a gigabit per second to transmit.

As with images, lossy compression can be used. Moreover, use can be made of the fact that video scenes in adjacent frames are usually very similar. At a basic level, lossy video compression algorithms analyze the video stream and discards information that is indiscernible to the viewer. Reasonable quality can be achieved using compression ratios from about 20:1 to 100:1.

Discrete cosine transform (DCT) is the video compression algorithm that underlies JPEG, MPEG, and H.263 video file formats. It samples an image at regular intervals, analyzes the image's frequency components, and discards the frequencies that do not affect how the human eye would perceive the image. JPEG was introduced in the previous section since it is also used for image files. MPEG (Motion Pictures Expert Group) is an ISO/IEC working group that develops standards for digital audio and video formats and several MPEG standards are widely

Table 2.3   Digital Television Formats

Format	Spatio-Temporal Resolution	Sampling Rate (MHz)
CIF	360 × 288 × 30	3
CCIR	720 × 576 × 30	12
HDTV	1280 × 720 × 60	60
HDTV RGB	1920 × 1080 × 60	60

used including: MPEG-1 (for moving pictures and audio), MPEG-2 (for digital television set-top boxes and DVD compression), MPEG-4 (for multimedia and Web compression). *H.263* is an ITU standard for two-way video communication (videoconferencing); it is arguably the most important VTC standard and is widely supported in unified communications systems.

The transmission of video over IP-based networks, including the Internet and private intranets, is increasingly important to businesses. This type of transmission is known as video streaming or TVoIP (television over IP). TVoIP places substantial burdens on enterprise networks but brings substantial benefits. As a free or subscription cloud-based television service, it offers an alternative to IPTV (pay TV) services that are driving providers like AT&T to invest in infrastructure upgrades. Both IPTV and TVoIP demonstrate that routing video traffic over IP networks is the wave of the future. Thus, a key challenge for enterprise networks is scaling up IP networks to effectively support video transmission while also providing adequate quality of service to other business transmission requirements.

2.5 PERFORMANCE MEASURES

A 2011 study conducted by ABI Research suggests that data traffic will grow at a compound rate of 50% each year between 2012 and 2016 with robust growth in video traffic being a driving factor [NG11]. The total annual volume is expected to exceed 60,000 petabytes by 2016 with video and TV streaming exceeding all other forms of Web and Internet traffic. Wireless traffic for mobile connections is expected to grow at nearly the same annual rate during this time frame. Businesses will continue to be challenged to accommodate traffic increases on their networks to be able to meet the needs of workers, customers, and business partners. This section considers three key parameters related to the performance of business applications on enterprise networks: response time, quality of experience, and throughput.

Response Time

A user's ability to productively use a business application is often dictated by the rapidity of the interaction between the application and the user. Today's business users increasingly multitask and work simultaneously on more than one task. For example, a knowledge worker may take phone calls while composing e-mail message and retrieving database records. If the responsiveness of one computer application is slow, a multitasking business user may focus attention on a second application rather than concentrating on the one that is slow. There is growing evidence that user impatience with slow computer applications is rising. Users increasingly expect interactive applications to provide instantaneous responses and have difficulty tolerating those which do not. Meeting such user expectations is an ongoing challenge for business network managers.

Response time is the time it takes for a system to react to a given input. In an interactive transaction, it may be defined as the time between the last keystroke by the user and the beginning of the display of a result by the computer. For some types of business applications, a slightly different definition is needed. In general, it is the time it takes for the system to respond to a user's request to perform a particular task.

Ideally, one would like the response time for any application to be short. However, it is almost invariably the case that shorter response time is accompanied by greater cost. This cost comes from two sources:

- **Computer processing power:** The faster the computer, the shorter will be the response time. Of course, increased processing power typically means increased cost.
- **Competing requirements:** Providing rapid response time for some applications may penalize other applications.

Thus the business value of a given level of response time for an application must be assessed versus the cost of achieving that response time.

In client/server network architectures, computing processing power can be an issue at both ends of the network connection between servers and client computing devices. The evolution of both servers and clients is toward faster processing power and as both servers and client devices become faster it is often the ability of the network to handle the demands imposed by multiple applications that is the primary determinant of a given business application's response time.

Table 2.4, based on [MART88], lists six general ranges of response times. Network design difficulties may be faced when a response time of less than one second is required. It is often not feasible for a business to provide a network infrastructure that is capable of ensuring that all applications have a response time of one second or less. The cost of doing so can be prohibitive. As a result, business network designers often prioritize applications by importance and design enterprise networks in a way that ensures rapid response times for mission critical applications even if this means that response times for less important applications are sacrificed. *Quality of service (QoS)* mechanisms are often used to support adequate performance of important business applications, especially real-time video and voice applications.

That rapid response time is the key to the productivity of workers using interactive applications has been confirmed in a number of studies [THAD81; SHNE84; GUYN88; SEVC03]. These studies show that when a computer and a worker interact at a pace that ensures that neither has to wait on the other, productivity increases significantly, and the quality of the work that is performed tends to improve. Increased worker productivity and efficiency means that the overall business cost of the work done on computers is reduced.

It used to be widely accepted that a relatively slow response, up to two seconds, was acceptable for most interactive applications because the person was thinking about the next task. However, it now appears that productivity increases as rapid response times are achieved. Normally, the response time for a business application should be as fast as possible. However, it is also important to ensure that the system does not react so fast that the user cannot keep up. For example, if the response to a user action is not displayed long enough for the user to read or react to, potential productivity gains from rapid response times cannot be realized.

Today, if the application reacts in a tenth of a second (0.1 s) or less, the user perceives the system as reacting instantaneously. Users notice a delay of 1.0 second,

Table 2.4 Response Time Ranges

Greater than 15 seconds
This rules out conversational interaction. For certain types of applications, certain types of users may be content to sit at a terminal for more than 15 seconds waiting for the answer to a single simple inquiry. However, for a busy person, captivity for more than 15 seconds seems intolerable. If such delays will occur, the system should be designed so that the user can turn to other activities and request the response at some later time.
Greater than four seconds
These are generally too long for a conversation requiring the user to retain information in short-term memory (the user's memory, not the computer's). Such delays would be very inhibiting in problem-solving activity and frustrating in data entry activity. However, after completing a lengthy entry, delays from 4 to 15 seconds may be tolerated.
Two to four seconds
A delay longer than two seconds can be inhibiting to users performing tasks that demand a high level of concentration. A wait of two to four seconds can seem surprisingly long when the user is absorbed and emotionally committed to completing what he or she is doing. Again, a delay in this range may be acceptable between interactive actions.
Less than two seconds
When the user has to remember information throughout several responses, the response time must be short. The more detailed the information that must be remembered, the greater the need for responses of less than two seconds. For elaborate interactive activities, two seconds represents an important response-time limit.
Subsecond response time
Certain types of thought-intensive work, especially with graphics applications, require very short response times to maintain the user's interest and attention for long periods of time.
Decisecond response time
A response to pressing a key and seeing the character displayed on the screen or clicking a screen object with a mouse needs to be almost instantaneous—less than 0.1 second after the action. Interaction with a mouse requires extremely fast interaction if the designer is to avoid the inclusion of alien syntax (one with commands, mnemonics, punctuation, etc.) in the application.

but it is not enough to interrupt their flow of thought. Hence, response times between 0.1 and 1.0 second are good for interactive business applications. Workers start losing focus when delays exceed 10 seconds and often want to perform other tasks while waiting for the system to finish. In such instances, it is advisable for the application to include a percent-done or progress indicator to give the user a sense of how long they have to wait (and to make the wait less painful).

Response time is an important determinant of the productivity of workers who perform online transactions. A transaction consists of a user command from a computing device and the system's reply and is the fundamental unit of work for online system users. It can be divided into two time sequences:

- **User response time:** The time span between the moment a user receives a complete reply to one command and enters the next command. People often refer to this as *think time*.

- **System response time:** The time span between the moment the user enters a command and the moment a complete response is displayed on the computing device.

As an example of the effect of reduced system response time on worker productivity, Figure 2.6 shows the results of a study carried out on engineers using

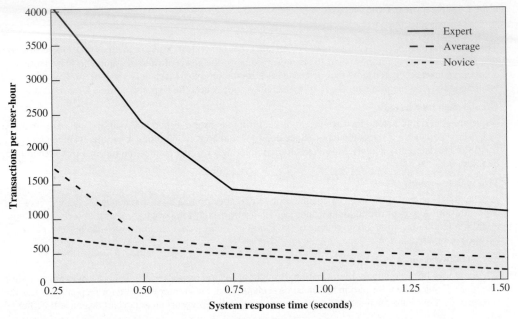

Figure 2.6 Response Time Results for High-Function Graphics

a CAD graphics program for the design of integrated circuit chips and boards [SMIT88]. Each transaction consists of a command by the engineer that alters in some way the graphic image being displayed on the screen. The results show that the number of transactions performed by the engineers rises dramatically once system response time falls below one second. What is happening is that as the system response time falls, so does the user response time. This has to do with the effects of short-term memory and human attention span.

Rapid response time is more important for some types of business information systems than for others. It is especially critical for transaction processing systems. The output of management information systems and decision support systems is generally a report or the results of some modeling exercise. In these cases, rapid turnaround is desirable, but not essential.

Today, enterprise resource planning (ERP) systems are the core transaction processing systems for large businesses and they are becoming more prevalent in medium and small enterprises (MSEs). ERP users require rapid response times for transactions whether the systems they interact with are on premises or cloud-based. Rapid response times are also needed whether they are interacting with the ERP system from the desktop in their office or from a mobile device. Business users expect rapid response times for any integrated enterprise systems including customer relationship management (CRM) systems and supply chain management (SCM) applications.

While business users show more patience for applications such as electronic mail and video teleconferencing, the general trend is toward rapid response time for most, if not all, business applications. The business network implications of this trend is quite clear: if a network connects the interactive user's computing device to the application server and the application requires a rapid response time, then the network must be designed in a manner that is compatible with the response time requirement. Thus, if a transaction processing application requires a response time of 1 second and the average time it takes the application server to generate a response to a user request is 0.75 second, then the network must be designed in a way that ensures the transmission of the user request and delivery of the server's response to the user takes no more than 0.25 second.

Another area where response time has become critical is the delivery of applications to business users via IP networks including the Internet, an extranet, or a corporate intranet.[3] The time it takes for a Web page to download and display on a user's screen can vary greatly. As is true for other business applications, user engagement with interactive Web-based applications is affected by response times; in particular, Web-based applications with very fast response times tend to command more user attention.

As Figure 2.7 indicates, Web systems with a three-second or better response time maintain a high level of user attention [SEVC96]. With a response time of between 3 and 10 seconds, some user concentration is lost, and response times above 10 seconds discourage the user, who may simply abort the session. For an organization that maintains an Internet Web site, much of the response time is determined by forces beyond the organization's control, such as Internet throughput, Internet congestion, and the end user's access speed. In such circumstances, the organization may consider keeping the image content of each page low and relying heavily on text, to promote rapid response time.

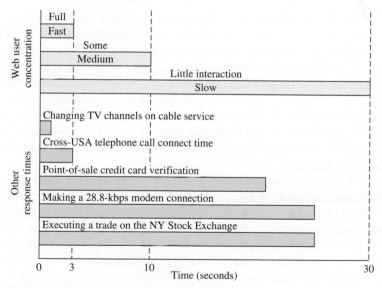

Figure 2.7   Response Time Requirements

---

[3]*Intranet* is a term used to refer to the implementation of Internet technologies within a corporate organization, rather than for external connection to the global Internet; this topic is explored in Chapter 9.

Quality of Experience

Response time is an important contributor to users' overall experiences with network applications and services, their **Quality of Experience (QoE)**. QoE is a subjective measure of the user's perception of the overall value of the network application or service. QoE is not the same as QoS, however, it can be affected by the extent to which QoS is used to improve the performance and user engagement with the application or service. QoE is measured at end-user computing devices and there are many network elements that can degrade the quality of the service as it is experienced by the end user including encoding processes, WAN infrastructure components, the business LAN or home network, and the user's computing device. Network elements that facilitate flexibility, security, cost, mobility, and personalization may contribute positively to QoE for users of a particular network application or service.

The increasing use of converged IP networks to deliver all types of traffic (voice, data, image, and video) has increased the importance of QoE and other measures of user experience with network applications and services. Adequate QoE is especially important for real-time applications such as voice and video. Users are particularly sensitive to jittery, blurry, or distorted video and audio because they degrade their experience with the application or service. With video, audio, and multimedia content on the rise and soon to surpass all other types of network traffic in volume, QoE will become an increasingly important factor in the design of business networks.

Throughput

The trend toward higher and higher transmission speeds makes possible increased support for different services (e.g., broadband multimedia services) that once seemed too demanding for digital communications. To make effective use of these new capabilities, it is essential for businesses to have a sense of the demands each service puts on the storage and communications requirements of converged enterprise networks. As you have seen in this chapter, network applications and services can be grouped into data, audio, image, and video categories that place widely varying demands on the networks over which they are carried. Figure 2.8 gives an indication of the data rates required to provide acceptable performance and user QoE [TEGE95].

Throughput has numerous meanings within the business context including the productivity of a machine, process, system, or procedure over a given time period. In business networks, throughput is the average rate of message delivery over a communication channel or the network as a whole. It can be thought of as the total bandwidth capacity of a communications channel or network and can be measured in various ways including bits per second, bytes per second, or packets per second. In subsequent chapters in this textbook, you will learn that throughput can be affected by numerous factors including communication media, media access control protocols, switch and router capabilities, security mechanisms, network congestion, the configuration of end devices, and appropriate use of QoS mechanisms.

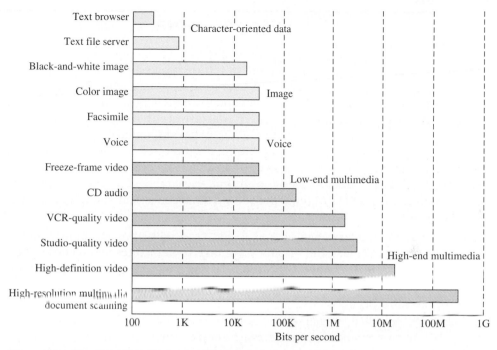

Figure 2.8   Required Data Rates for Various Information Types

Growing reliance on converged networks to carry all categories of business applications (voice, data, image, and video) has made throughput an increasingly important factor in enterprise network design. Investment in network infrastructure and business software upgrades is often driven by the need for greater throughput, improved QoS, and perceived QoS (or QoE). Increased throughput can contribute to improved response times and enhanced worker productivity. Hence, there are multiple reasons why business managers should be concerned with ensuring that enterprise networks provide adequate throughput to support current and planned applications and services.

Increased use of video, image, and other bandwidth-hogging applications can make it difficult for companies to invest in infrastructure upgrades fast enough to satisfy their users' desires. In such instances, it is important for a business to prioritize its network traffic requirements to ensure that mission critical applications and services are provided with sufficient throughput to perform at adequate levels. QoS mechanisms are used to identify and tag high-priority traffic so that it can be delivered rapidly over the network, even if this results in delays for less important applications or services. Appropriate use of audio, data, image, and video compression algorithms and file formats can also contribute to adequate performance of network services and applications.

Throughput, response time, and QoE are important factors associated with the end-to-end delivery of network applications and services. These are concepts that all business managers need to be familiar because of their potential to contribute to worker productivity and the efficiency of business processes.

APPLICATION NOTE

File Sizes

Image file sizes are based on the amount of information on the page and the color content. High-resolution color images can take up a very large amount of storage space. Sound and video files can be larger still. Though audio files do not contain data or color they extend over a period of time. The characteristics that change audio file sizes are length, sampling rate, and bits per sample. The better the sound quality, the larger the file and the greater the bandwidth required to transmit the sounds. For example, CD quality sound takes up much more storage space than a basic recording of the same music. Video is essentially a series of color pictures over time and so these files can be immense. Frame rate describes the number of times per second an image is sent and this value can drastically change the file size or bandwidth required for transmission.

The popularity of digital cameras has exploded, especially since becoming a common feature in most smartphones. Because they can take both pictures and record video, a little understanding of file sizes and types can help users understand why digital photos can rapidly fill up hard drive and removable media storage space.

To start, we must decide on the quality required. Higher quality reduces our options for reducing file size. Next, we will select the appropriate file type. Depending on the application, this can be an important choice. For example, using very high quality, large images, and video on a Web page can have a negative impact on how rapidly it will download, especially over slower communication lines. It is for this reason that so much thought goes in to optimizing content on business Web sites. By adjusting the image size, color content, or file type we can dramatically reduce the file size and the page loading time.

As an example, the following is a table of various image file sizes based on the type of information.

Information	File Type	Size
640 × 480 pixel picture	24-bit bitmap	900 KB
640 × 480 pixel picture	256 color (8 bit) bitmap	300 KB
640 × 480 pixel picture	16 color (4 bit) bitmap	150 KB
640 × 480 pixel picture	GIF	58 KB
640 × 480 pixel picture	JPEG	45 KB

As you can see, changing the file type used and the color content can have a tremendous affect on the size of the file. It is no wonder that a digital camera taking high-resolution pictures can run out of memory so quickly. The downside of modifying an image or stream with lossy compression in order to reduce the size is that you usually sacrifice some amount of quality. Once the quality is gone it cannot be recovered without the original file. For applications like spreadsheets and word processing, lossy compression is not an option because exact duplicates must be transmitted or stored. Fortunately, files of this type, with text only, do not take up much room.

The network is often on the receiving end of this shift to digital images and video streams. As more information is sent via the network, links can become overutilized and response times can be slow. Voice over IP, streaming media, and videoconferencing all contribute to performance problems. It is for this reason that businesses are redesigning and upgrading their networks to accommodate these changes and are putting pressure on network administrators to supply sufficient network storage and bandwidth. However, there is not much that network managers can do to change information once it has been transmitted. By using appropriate compression algorithms and file formats before data are transmitted, some network utilization and storage problems can be alleviated before they even start.

2.6 SUMMARY

Today's enterprise networks carry a variety of types of information, which can be conveniently categorized as audio (voice), data, image, and video. The growing prevalence of converged networks means that each of these types of network traffic are sharing communication lines and network resources despite requiring varying levels of bandwidth, throughput, and response time to ensure adequate quality of experience for users. Priorities may be assigned to applications and services to ensure adequate performance levels for those that are most important to the business. Growing volumes of video and multimedia traffic are causing businesses to redesign their networks and invest in infrastructure upgrades. Appropriate use of compression algorithms, file formats, and quality of service mechanisms are increasingly important for ensuring acceptable performance levels for business applications, especially Web-based, interactive applications.

Case Study II: CORE Credit Union

The major concepts addressed in this case study include voice and data networks; virtual private networks (VPNs) and cloud services. **This case study and more are available at www.pearsoninternationaleditions.com/stallings**

2.7 KEY TERMS, REVIEW QUESTIONS, AND PROBLEMS

Key Terms

analog	IRA	raster graphics
ASCII	Lempel-Ziv	response time
audio	lossless compression	throughput
Centrex	lossy compression	Unicode
data	private branch exchange	UTF-8
digital	(PBX)	vector graphics
image	Quality of Experience	video
interlacing	(QoE)	voice
IP-PBX	quantization	V.44

Review Questions

2.1   Differentiate between Quality of Experience (QoE) and Quality of Service (QoS).

2.2   What are the differences between discrete and continuous information sources? Provide examples of each.

2.3   Briefly describe what will happen if a higher range of frequencies is allowed for an analog communication.

2.4   Contrast lossless and lossy compression.

2.5   What is the difference between PBX and hosted IP-PBX?

2.6   Briefly describe the characteristics of each of the following: IRA, UTF-8, and Unicode.

2.7   Briefly explain why lossless compression is used to compress data (symbols, numbers, and characters) for storage or transmission.

2.8   Define bits per pixel (bpp).

2.9   What is the difference between an 8 bpp image and a 24 bpp image?

2.10   Briefly explain the difference between PNG and MNG image formats.

2.11   Differentiate between user response time and system response time.

2.12   Describe interlacing and its role in preventing flicker in a video screen.

2.13   Contrast CRT and LCD display monitors.

2.14   What is digital video?

2.15   What are the video file formats that the discrete cosine transform underlies?

2.16   What is the difference between MPEG-2 and MPEG-4 standards?

2.17   What are the uses of Centrex?

2.18   Define quantization.

2.19   How is response time related to worker productivity?

2.20   What are the different forms of transmission of business information?

2.21   What are the different factors associated with the end-to-end delivery of network applications and services?

2.22   What is Quality of Experience (QoE)? List several factors that affect QoE.

2.23   What does throughput mean in the context of business networks?

2.24   Explain why throughput is an increasingly important issue for enterprise networks.

Problems

2.1   Do some online research on how organizations are using interactive voice response systems (IVRs) to improve business processes. Write a short paper that illustrates the patterns of IVR use by businesses, business reasons for implementing IVRs, and benefits realized from IVR deployment. Include several case examples.

2.2   Do some online research on the capabilities of IP-PBX systems. Write a short paper explaining how businesses are benefiting from the capabilities of the current generation of IP-PBX systems and new capabilities that are likely to be added in the future.

2.3   A company's telephone exchange (PBX or hosted IP-PBX) digitizes telephone channels at 8000 smp/s, using 8 bits for quantization. The telephone exchange transmits simultaneously on 24 telephone channels over the same communications link.
   a.   What's the required per channel data rate?
   b.   What is the combined data rate for the 24 channels over the communications link?
   c.   In order to provide voice-mail service, the telephone exchange can store three-minute audio messages using the same digitizing process used for a telephone channel. How many megabytes of data storage space are needed to store a three-minute voice-mail message?

2.4   How many quantization levels are needed to represent each of the following sets of symbols, characters, or states?
  a. The uppercase alphabet A, B,..., Z
  b. The digits 0, 1,..., 9
  c. 256 different colors
  d. 10,000 Han characters
  e. four billion computing devices

2.5   Review the IRA code in Appendix D (mercury.webster.edu/aleshunas/COSC% 205130/Q-IRA.pdf)
  a. Indicate the 7-bit code for the following letters: B, D, C, 7, e.
  b. Repeat part (a), but this time show the 8-bit code that includes an odd parity bit.

2.6   The text of the *Encyclopaedia Britannica* is about 44 million words. An average word length is 6.3 characters per word (this includes both the letters in the word and the spacing and punctuation between words).
  a. Approximately how many characters are there in the encyclopedia?
  b. How long would it take to transmit encyclopedia over a T-1 line at 1,544 Mbps? Over a fiber-optic link at 51.84 Mbps? Over a 40-Gbps Ethernet link?

2.7   A drawing in an 8.5-by-11-inch sheet is digitized by means of a 300 dpi (dots per inch) scanner.
  a. What is the visual resolution of the resulting image (number of dots in each dimension)?
  b. If 8 bits are used for the quantization of each pixel, how much data storage space is needed to store the image in uncompressed form?

2.8   When examining X-rays, radiologists often deal with four to six images at a time. For a faithful digital representation of an X ray photograph, a pixel array of 2048 by 2048 is typically used with a grayscale of intensity for each pixel of 12 bits. As you would hope, radiologists do not look kindly on compression that degrades quality.
  a. How many levels of grayscale are represented by 12 bits?
  b. How many bits does it take to represent a single X-ray photograph?
  c. Suppose five X-rays have to be sent to another site over a T-1 line (1.544 Mbps). How long would it take, ignoring overhead?
  d. Suppose now that we wish to build a communications system that provides the five X-rays of part (c) upon demand; that is, from the time the X-rays are requested we want them available within 2 seconds. What is the lowest channel rate that can support this demand?
  e. The next generation of displays for X-rays is planned for 4096 by 4096 pixels with a 12-bit grayscale. What does the answer to part (d) become when using this resolution?

2.9   Commonly, medical digital radiology ultrasound studies consist of about 25 images extracted from a full-motion ultrasound examination. Each image consists of 512 by 512 pixels, each with 8 bits of intensity information.
  a. How many bits are there in the 25 images?
  b. Ideally, however, doctors would like to use $512 \times 512 \times 8$ bit frames at 30 fps (frames per second). Ignoring possible compression and overhead factors, what is the minimum channel capacity required to sustain this full-motion ultrasound?
  c. Suppose each full-motion study consists of 25 seconds of frames. How many bytes of storage would be needed to store a single study in uncompressed form?

2.10 An 800×600 image with 24-bit color depth needs to be stored on disc. Even though the image might contain 2^{24} different colors, only 256 colors are actually present. This image could be encoded by means of a table (palette) of 256 24-bit elements and, for each pixel, an index of its RGB value in the table. This type of encoding is usually called Color Look-Up Table (CLUT) encoding.
  a. How many bytes are needed to store the image as raw information?
  b. How many bytes are needed to store the image using CLUT encoding?
  c. What's the compression ratio achieved by using this simple encoding method?

2.11 A digital video camera provides an uncompressed output video stream with a resolution of 320 × 240 pixels, a frame rate of 30 fps, and 8 bits for quantization of each pixel.

    a. What's the required bandwidth for the transmission of the uncompressed video stream?

    b. How much data storage space is needed to store two minutes of the video stream?

2.12 Do some online research on how businesses are using TVoIP to support their business processes. Write a short paper that summarizes patterns of business use of TVoIP and the characteristics of the network infrastructure that is needed to ensure acceptable performance. Include case examples.

DISTRIBUTED DATA PROCESSING

Learning Objectives

After reading this chapter, you should be able to:

♦ Describe the communications and infrastructure issues associated with "big data."

♦ Describe the differences between centralized and distributed data processing and discuss the pros and cons of each approach.

♦ Identify and briefly describe the characteristics of data centers and the technologies that have shaped data center evolution.

♦ Identify and briefly describe the characteristics of client/server architectures.

♦ Describe the role of application service providers and cloud computing in enterprise networks.

♦ Describe the different forms of distributing applications and application processing.

♦ Describe the different forms of distributed databases.

♦ Discuss the networking and communications implications of distributed data processing.

In Chapter 2, we looked at the overall requirements for information in an organization and found that four types of information are vital to the competitive health of any business: data, voice, image, and video. Today's organizations are capturing, transmitting, storing, and mining each of these types of information.

For much of the history of data communications, it was data (as it was defined in Chapter 2) that shaped corporate strategy. Voice was treated as an entirely separate requirement, and is still treated that way in some organizations. The migration to digital transmission, networking equipment, and storage, plus the use of flexible transmission protocols such as IP (Internet Protocol), has made it feasible for businesses to integrate voice, data, image, and video to provide cost-effective networking solutions.

As discussed in Chapter 2, voice, image, and video have each created transmission and storage challenges for enterprise networks. Today, each of these types of information may be transmitted and stored over the same converged network. Traditional definitions of business data, which at one time were restricted to alphanumeric characters and symbols, have had to expand to include audio (voice), image, and video. Most recently, a new term has become commonplace in conversations among business professionals and IT and software vendors: "big data."

In simple terms, **big data** refers to everything that enables an organization to create, manipulate, and manage very large data sets (measured in terabytes, petabytes, exabytes, etc.) and the facilities in which these are stored. Distributed data centers, data warehouses, and cloud-based storage are common aspects of today's enterprise networks. Many factors have contributed to the merging of "big data" and business networks including continuing declines in storage costs, the maturation of data mining and business intelligence (BI) tools, and government regulations and court cases that have caused organizations to stockpile large masses of structured and unstructured data including documents, e-mail messages, voice-mail messages, text messages, and social media data. Other data sources being captured, transmitted, and stored include Web logs, Internet documents, Internet search indexing, call detail records, scientific research data and results, military surveillance, medical records, video archives, and e-commerce transactions.

Data sets continue to grow as more and more data are gathered by remote sensors, mobile devices, cameras, microphones, radio frequency identification (RFID) readers, and similar technologies. Some experts estimate that more than 2.5 quintillion bytes of data are created each day and most industry experts agree that data variety, volume, and velocity will continue to grow [DOOL11].

Converged networks and big data are transforming businesses and understanding how and why begins with taking a closer look at the different data processing systems that businesses may deploy. We begin with a look at the two extremes in organization of the computing function: centralized and distributed data processing. The computing function in most businesses typically lies somewhere along a spectrum between these two extremes. By examining this spectrum, including the advantages of distributed data processing and the evolution of data center technologies, we can get a clearer picture of the communications and networking requirements for today's businesses. We consider how application processing and data can be distributed within enterprise networks and how client/server architectures opened the door for cloud-computing services to become common components in many business networks. Big data and the evolution of data processing and communications technologies continue to reshape the balance of centralized and distributed processing within enterprise networks.

3.1 CENTRALIZED VERSUS DISTRIBUTED PROCESSING

Centralized and Distributed Organization

Data centers are important components in enterprise networks. A **data center** is a facility that houses computer systems and their associated components including storage and telecommunication systems. A data center can occupy a single room in a building, one or more floors, or an entire building. Much of the equipment inside a data center consists of servers mounted in rack cabinets that are placed in rows that form corridors (aisles) that enable access to both the front and the rear of each cabinet. Because mainframe computers and storage devices can be comparable in size to the rack cabinets, they are placed alongside the racks. To ensure proper performance of the servers and computing equipment, air-conditioning is used to control temperature and humidity in the data center.

Today's data centers are descendants of the huge computer rooms/centers that characterized the early days of computing. Because early computing systems were complex to maintain and use and because they needed a climate-controlled environment in which to operate, they were typically housed in controlled access computer rooms staffed by specially trained computer center operators and managers. It was only when computers got smaller and easier to use and combine into networks that they moved out of the central data center into other buildings and individual offices. Today, a number of factors have combined to bring a resurgence in centralized data centers that are reminiscent of early computing centers and their centralized data processing architectures.

In a **centralized data processing** architecture, data processing is done on one or a cluster of computers, generally powerful and/or physically large computers, located in a central data processing facility. Some business processing tasks, such as payroll updates, may be performed in their entirety, from start to finish, by personnel at the central data center. Other tasks may require interactive access by personnel who are not physically located in the data processing center. For example, a data entry function, such as an inventory update, may be done by personnel at sites throughout the organization and transmitted to the data center where the actual database updates are performed by data center computers. Hence, in a centralized architecture, the data processing for an application does not take place on the user's computing device. Instead, users transmit data to the centralized data processing facility where it is processed by applications running on the computers that are located there.

A fully centralized data processing facility is centralized in many senses of the word. It may include:

- **Centralized computers:** One or more computers are located in a central facility. Historically, large organizations had one or more large mainframe computers which required special facilities such as air-conditioning and a raised floor. In a smaller organization, the central computer or computers may be high-performance servers or midrange systems. The Power Systems server line from IBM includes midrange systems.

- **Centralized processing:** All applications are run on computers in the central data processing facility. This includes applications that are clearly central or organization-wide in nature, such as payroll, as well as applications that support the specialized needs of users in a particular business unit. For example, users in the product design department may interact with a computer-aided design (CAD) graphics application that runs on servers at the central facility.

- **Centralized data:** Most data are stored in files and databases at the central facility. This includes data used by many business units in the organization, such as inventory figures, as well as data that are only used by particular business units. For example, the marketing unit may maintain a database located at the data center that is populated with results of customer surveys.

- **Centralized control:** The central facility is managed by a data processing or information systems manager. Depending on the size and importance of the facility, the data center manager may be either a mid-level (middle) manager or hold an executive level position. It is quite common for the data center manager to report to a vice-president (e.g., VP of IT Services) or chief information officer (CIO) who has authority at the board level. In some instances, the data center manager may report to a chief security officer (CSO) or chief technology officer (CTO) who has broader authority in matters related to corporate acquisition, use, and protection of information.

- **Centralized support staff:** A centralized data processing facility must include a technical support staff to operate and maintain the data center hardware. In addition, programming and application development services that support both organization-wide and unit-specific applications may be associated with the centralized facility.

A centralized data processing architecture has a number of attractive aspects. There may be economies of scale in the purchase and operation of equipment and software. A centralized IT services organization is often better able to attract and retain the highly paid professional programmers needed to support enterprise-wide systems and/or the specialized needs of strategic business units. Data center managers can maintain control over data center hardware procurement, enforce standards for data quality, and design and implement appropriate security policies.

Figure 3.1 illustrates, in general terms, the centralized data processing facility that has been implemented by Dallas County [CLAR03]. The county's information technology (IT) infrastructure is fairly typical of government entities of its size. The bulk of the county's applications and databases are housed in the data center. The data center includes several mainframes and a number of high-end servers. The mainframe runs customized applications that support the court and justice system requirements. The servers support a variety of database applications needed by county employees to perform their jobs.

The networking architecture is an example of a *hub-and-spoke* configuration. Some sites have direct high-speed leased lines connecting to the data center's base router. Other sites are connected by means of private frame relay wide-area network services. This arrangement minimizes transmission costs and the amount of network equipment needed to handle the communications traffic among locations. Finally, the data center provides an Internet connection that is protected by a firewall.

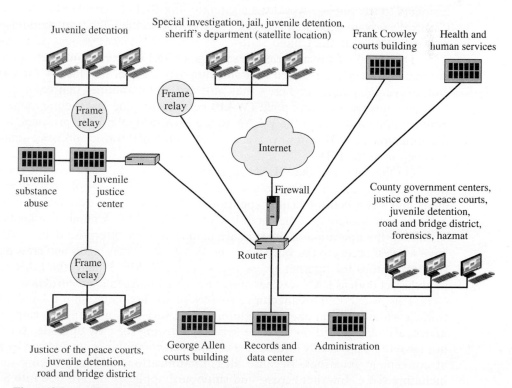

Figure 3.1 Dallas County Information Systems Architecture

This centralized configuration meets a number of objectives for Dallas County. To meet security and privacy requirements, Dallas County has found that the centralized database and applications are more easily protected than if these resources were geographically distributed. County employees have access to the data and applications they need to do their jobs and the network architecture that ties everything together has simplified network management.

A data processing facility may depart in varying degrees from the centralized data processing organization by implementing a **distributed data processing (DDP)** strategy. When a distributed data processing strategy is followed, computers (usually smaller computers) are dispersed throughout an organization. The objective of such dispersion is to process information in a way that is most effective based on operational, economic, and/or geographic considerations, or all three. A DDP facility may include a central data center plus satellite data centers, or it may more nearly resemble a community of peer computing facilities. In either case, some form of interconnection is usually needed; that is, the various computers in the system must be connected to one another. As may be expected, given the characterization of centralized data processing that we have provided, a DDP facility involves the distribution of computers, processing, and data.

A simple example of a distributed data processing architecture is that implemented on the cruise ship *Carnival Valor*, owned by Florida-based Carnival Cruise Lines [KNAU05]. The on-board network (Figure 3.2) is a wireless local area network (WLAN) that supports both data traffic and voice over IP (VoIP). The WLAN connects to the outside world via a satellite link that connects to the Internet, to Carnival's private wide area network (WAN), and to the public switched telephone network (PSTN) in the United States.

The on-board private branch exchange (PBX) supports a number of business telephones directly connected to it and supports a voice-mail facility for Carnival employees. Passengers and crew may also use mobile phones that connect to the WLAN via wireless access point (WAP) equipment. The WAP equipment routes mobile phone traffic over the WLAN to the PBX using the VoIP protocol. Routers that function as VoIP gateways convert between VoIP traffic and voice signals for connection to the PBX.

On the data side, the WLAN supports a distributed data processing configuration based on application. Separate servers handle call management, network management, and access control/security applications. These servers are directly connected to switches that interconnect the wired LAN and the WAPs. A number of applications specific to the operation of the ship are managed from enterprise data servers that have wireless access to the WLAN via the WAPs. Both passengers and crew may use wireless laptops for Internet access, again via the WAPs. Finally, the LAN services modules act both as LAN switches and as network management control points.

This distributed architecture provides great flexibility. Ship-related applications, such as entertainment scheduling, food serv.ices, and engineering/maintenance, are maintained on separate servers, allowing for easy upgrade. Servers do not have to be physically located in a centralized computer room and can be placed at convenient locations. Because all communications and networking services, including voice, Internet access, and shipboard applications, are tied into a single LAN, network management and network security are more easily managed.

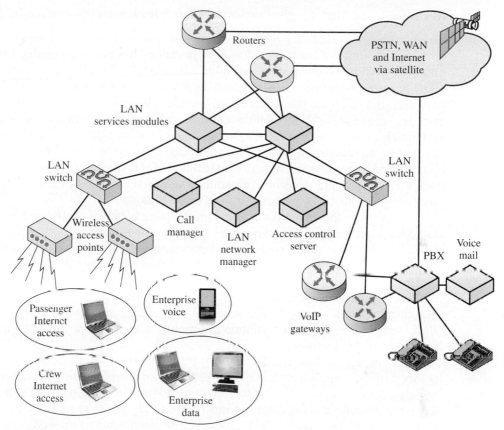

Figure 3.2   Carnival Valor Wireless LAN

Technical Trends Leading to Distributed Data Processing

Until the early 1970s, the centralized data processing approach enjoyed near-universal use in businesses. Since that time, there has been a steady evolution to distributed processing. We can address this trend from two points of view: means and motive. First, let us look at the changes in the data processing industry that have given companies the means to choose distributed processing. We then turn to the question of why distributed data processing is preferred over centralized data processing.

The key factor that has made DDP an attractive option for businesses is the dramatic and continuing decrease in cost of computer hardware, accompanied by an increase in its capabilities. Today's personal computers have processing capabilities that exceed those of the midrange systems and even some of the mainframes used by businesses just a few years ago. Equally important has been the evolution of graphical user interfaces (GUIs) that provide unprecedented ease of use and responsiveness. With very powerful and easy-to-use computing devices at the fingertips of business users, it is easy to understand why computing capabilities are no longer limited to centralized data centers.

Management and Organizational Considerations

The increasing availability of inexpensive yet powerful systems coupled with a growing repertoire of business software applications has made it possible for organizations to disperse computing capabilities throughout their business units. While many businesses continue to have centralized data centers, today, this is more likely to be a matter of choice than a necessity. Some organizations have opted for distributed data centers to address their computing needs, but the centralized option is still very much available to businesses even though, in some instances, the data center may not be on premises and may be owned and operated by a third-party firm. The evolution of computing and networking technologies continues to present IT executives with challenging decisions regarding whether centralized or distributed data processing architectures are best for their organizations.

To examine the issues associated with choosing between centralized or distributed data processing, let us first consider the requirements for corporate computing. Table 3.1 summarizes nine goals that corporations commonly establish for their IT departments. A compelling case can be made that requirements 1, 3, 7, 8, and 9 can be satisfied with a distributed arrangement of low-cost servers and end-user computing devices. For example, distributing adequately powerful but inexpensive computing systems among business units can provide highly personalized service, allow users to establish and maintain autonomy in their operations, and improve departmental productivity.

Two aspects of user needs demonstrate the truth of the preceding statement: the need for new applications and the need for short response time. First, consider the need for new applications. For any organization to remain competitive, each department within the organization must continually strive to improve productivity and effectiveness. Increasingly, these outcomes are best achieved by using IT to improve business processes. However, even in the most well-managed organizations, the demand for new user applications is greater than the IT staff's ability to roll them out. This creates a backlog of needed applications and in many businesses, the backlog is growing. The adoption of a distributed data processing strategy that

Table 3.1   Requirements for the Corporate Computing Function

1. Provide computing capabilities to all organizational units that need them.
2. Contain the capital and operations costs associated with provisioning computing services within the organization.
3. Assist in satisfying the special computing needs of user departments.
4. Provide equitable support for all business units whose operations are dependent on computing (i.e., avoid mismatches in the level of support provided to business units).
5. Ensure that managers have the information needed to manage business units and the overall organization.
6. Provide computing services in a reliable, professional, and technically competent manner.
7. Allow business units sufficient autonomy in their use of technology to optimize creativity, innovation, and performance.
8. Deploy computing services in ways that preserve the autonomy of business units while also increasing the importance and influence of their operations to the larger organization.
9. Deploy technology in ways that make the work of employees enjoyable as well as productive.

gives business units control over their computing destinies may help to alleviate application backlogs. Allowing business units to increase the technical skills of its workers and/or implementing productivity-improving off-the-shelf applications can make a business unit less reliant on the IT department. Backlogs may also be addressed by allowing business units to use contract programmers to develop the new applications that they need.

The second need for short response times may also favor a distributed data processing architecture. As described in Chapter 2, for many business applications, worker productivity levels are directly tied to response time. Locating adequately powerful application servers close to business units is one way to ensure acceptable response times. This is a reason why new office and academic buildings often have distributed communication closets and server rooms.

We can see, then, that an argument can be made that when distributed small systems are both physically close to the user and dedicated to the user's particular applications, user productivity and business unit effectiveness may be improved. However, today's IT managers should not move too quickly to adopt a distributed strategy, especially if the potential exists for a loss of centralized control over the proliferation of computing systems. Individual departments may adopt incompatible systems, making interdepartmental coordination and integration difficult. Procurement decisions may be made without systematic forecasts of requirements and cost and without enforcement of standards for hardware, software, or communications. These effects jeopardize the achievement of goals 4 and 6 of Table 3.1 and may also limit the organization's ability to achieve objective 5.

Tables 3.2 and 3.3 summarize additional potential benefits and drawbacks of distributed data processing.

Data Center Evolution

It is important to note that the achievement of corporate computing goals summarized in Table 3.1 do not require the adoption of a DDP strategy. Achieving these goals is and should be independent of the organization's decision to centralize or distribute its computing resources. While compelling arguments can be made in favor of DDP, the evolution of data communication technologies, data center technologies, and data centers themselves has strengthened the case for centralized facilities. This has led some businesses consolidate their distributed data processing facilities and in some instances the end result has been a return to a centralized data processing facility. In this section, we examine some of the major drivers of the renewed interest in centralized facilities.

DATA CENTERS   As noted previously, a data center is a facility that houses computer systems and their associated components in storage systems and networking equipment. Redundant/backup power supplies, environmental controls (e.g., heating/air-conditioning and fire suppression), and data communication connections are common in today's data centers. Redundant computing systems (e.g., mirrored or duplexed servers) and storage systems are also common and sophisticated security mechanisms may be used to protect the data and equipment within the data center. These redundancies are designed to minimize the chances of the business systems

Table 3.2 Potential Benefits of Distributed Data Processing

Responsiveness

Distributed computing facilities can often be managed in such a way that they can more directly satisfy the needs of a local business unit than can a central facility which is responsible for satisfying the needs of the total organization.

Availability

With multiple interconnected systems, the loss of any one system should have minimal impact on a business's ability to operate. Key systems and components (e.g., servers running critical applications, storage technologies that store mission critical data) can be replicated so that a backup system can quickly take up the load after a failure.

Correspondence to Organizational Structure

Many organizations employ a decentralized organizational structure with corresponding policies and operational procedures. Data and application requirements may differ among decentralized business units and may be best addressed by distributed systems.

Resource Sharing

Distributed systems enable expensive hardware, such as a wide-body color plotter, to be shared by multiple users. Data files can be centrally managed and maintained, but with organization-wide access. Services, applications, and databases developed to support the entire organization can be distributed to dispersed facilities.

Incremental Growth

In a centralized data center, an increased workload or the need for new capabilities often involves major equipment purchases and/or major software upgrades and potential disruptions to operations organization-wide when these are installed. With a distributed system, it may be possible to gradually replace applications or systems in locations where these are most needed. This may be more affordable and less disruptive than making "all-or-nothing" upgrades in a centralized data center that effect all locations.

Increased User Involvement and Control

When computing equipment is physically located close to users, users have a greater opportunity to affect system design, operation, and use.

Decentralized Operation and Centralized Control

Decentralized applications and facilities can be tailored to the individual organizational unit's requirements and enhanced by centralized services and databases that have centralized control.

End-User Productivity

Distributed systems may provide better response time for user interactions with applications. Also, the applications and their user interfaces may be more easily customized to meet the needs of the organizational unit. Unit managers may be in a better position to assess the effectiveness of the distributed system and to make the appropriate local changes.

Distance and Location Independence

Distributed systems can provide users with access to organization-wide applications, data, and services. When properly configured, users are unable to distinguish the performance of distributed systems from on-premises systems.

Privacy and Security

With a distributed system, it may be easier to assign responsibility for security and integrity of data and other resources to the owners and users of those resources.

Vendor Independence

When properly implemented, a distributed system can accommodate equipment and software from a variety of suppliers. This provides greater competition and enhanced bargaining power on the part of the buyer. The organization is less likely to become dependent on a single vendor with the risks that that position entails.

Flexibility

Users may be in a position to adapt their application software to changing circumstances. They may be able to change the configuration of their systems without affecting the systems used at other locations.

Table 3.3 Potential Drawbacks of Distributed Data Processing

More Challenging Failure Diagnosis

When there is a high degree of interaction between elements of a distributed system, it can be more difficult to determine the cause of failure or performance degradation.

More Dependence on Communications Technology

To be effective, a distributed system must be interconnected by communication and networking technologies. Networking and communications become critical to the day-to-day operation of the organization.

Incompatibility among Equipment

Equipment from different vendors may not easily connect and communicate. To minimize this problem, businesses often restrict investments in computing resources to those for which standards exist.

Incompatibility among Data

In distributed environments, especially those with decentralized organization structures, data generated by an application at one location may not be usable in the generated form by applications at other locations. The use of organization-wide data dictionaries and database standards such as ODBC (Open Database Connectivity) can help to minimize data incompatibilities.

Network Management and Control

Because equipment is physically dispersed, may involve multiple vendors, and may be maintained and controlled by various organizational units, it can be difficult to effectively manage and control the entire network. If standards for software and data are inconsistently followed or enforced across business units, data processing facilities and services may evolve in an uncontrolled fashion.

Difficulty in Control of Corporate Information Resources

Data may be dispersed or, if not, at least access to data is dispersed. If distributed users can perform update functions (essential in many applications), it becomes challenging to control the integrity and security of the data needed at the corporate level. In some cases, it may even be difficult to gather information required by management from the dispersed and dissimilar databases.

Suboptimization

With the dispersal of computer equipment and the ease of incrementally adding new equipment and applications, it becomes easier for managers to justify procuring new computing resources for their business units. Although each purchase may be individually justifiable, the totality of procurements throughout an organization may exceed the total requirement.

Duplication of Effort

Distributed systems and data centers require appropriately skilled support personnel. Without appropriate oversight and coordination, distributed environments may have unnecessary and costly duplication of effort.

Data Integrity

With distributed access to distributed data, it may be more difficult to ensure that overlapping requests do not corrupt databases. If data files are duplicated to provide more efficient access, this requirement can be even more difficult to satisfy.

Security

Enforcing security policies and authenticating users can be more complex in a distributed environment.

---

being unavailable. Business operations can be severely impaired if the systems in the data center become unavailable. As a result, it is easy to justify business investment in redundant equipment for the data center.

As may be observed in Table 3.4, data center tiers are primarily defined by the extent to which redundancies are in place in the data center. Tier 1 data centers are the most basic and have few redundant components. In Tier 4 data centers, most major components have a redundant backup; even the HVAC equipment has dual

Table 3.4   Major Characteristics of Data Center Tiers

Tier Level	Characteristics
Tier 1	No redundancy guarantees for servers, storage systems, network equipment, and communication connections to Internet or other networks.
	Single path for power and cooling distribution; no redundant components.
	Availability: 99.671%
Tier 2	Meets or exceeds all Tier 1 requirements.
	Single, nonredundant connection to Internet and/or other networks.
	Redundant capacity components (servers, storage systems, network equipment).
	Includes raised floor, UPS (uninterruptible power supply), and on-site generator.
	Availability: 99.741%
Tier 3	Meets or exceeds all Tier 2 requirements.
	Dual-power sources for all IT equipment.
	Multiple independent distribution links between IT equipment and network switches.
	Provides multiple (redundant) links to the Internet and/or other networks.
	Includes sufficient capacity to carry load on one distribution path while doing maintenance on the other.
	Availability: 99.882%
Tier 4	Meets or exceeds all Tier 3 requirements.
	All components have redundant backups to ensure that they are fault-tolerant. This includes storage systems, HVAC (heating, ventilation, and air conditioning) systems, servers, etc.
	Includes on-site electrical power storage and distribution facilities.
	Typically includes compartmentalized security zones controlled by biometric access controls.
	Availability: 99.995%

power sources to eliminate the possibility of power failure. Power and communications failures are the major threat to data center operations, especially if the business has a single centralized facility.

To ensure business continuity, many organizations with central data centers have contracts with third-party companies to ensure that redundant data and processing equipment is available off-site should the data center be hit by a catastrophic event. The third-party firm's data center houses backup servers that the businesses can use should their data center fail as well as backup copies of the businesses' databases.

The availability of third-party data centers has motivated some businesses to move most or all of their data and computing out of on-premise data centers. Moving the bulk of data processing activities to the third-party data center enables the business to significantly reduce, or close down, its on-premises data center. Hence, considerable cost savings may be realized by using third-party data centers to satisfy business data processing needs. The number of third-party data centers competing to attract business customers is increasing and this is motivating many third-party firms to invest in Tier 3 and Tier 4 data centers to draw the interest of bigger companies.

DATA CENTER COMPUTING AND STORAGE TECHNOLOGIES Centralized data centers remain viable in part because of the renaissance of mainframes. Like other types of computers, powerful mainframes found in data centers have dropped in price and increased in power. Mainframe sales continue to be strong and they are increasingly being used as a hub for enterprise infrastructure because of their potential to enhance security, ensure availability, and improve manageability. As noted in our discussion of virtualization, a mainframe can host multiple operating systems and this means that they are capable of running all major business software packages.

Another important technical development related to renewed interest in centralized data centers is **in-memory computing** systems. In-memory processors include terabyte-plus RAM capable of storing large data sets. By keeping data close to the processor, computations on big data sets can be performed much faster than is possible with traditional server processors where data has to be sent back and forth to storage devices because of limited RAM. In-memory computing has the potential to revolutionize business intelligence (BI) by making it possible to bring the data warehouse into memory to enable real-time data mining and business analytics. SAP's in-memory computing system is called HANA (High performance Analytic Appliance). It looks like other high-end servers that can be installed in regular-sized data center server racks, but is equipped with Intel in-memory processors [HARD1?] HANA boxes are pricey, but the performance gains that businesses may realize from in-memory computing have resulted in rapid adoption of HANA by companies that use SAP. SAP has fueled demand for HANA by tweaking its ERP and Business Suite software applications to enable them to run on HANA boxes.

The increasing popularity of in-memory processing enables companies with distributed data centers to reconsider their DDP strategy and consolidate their high-performance computing resources into a centralized data center. Businesses that moved away from mainframe-centric computing and centralized data processing facilities now have a compelling reason to migrate back to a central data center. This has invigorated business investment in data center technologies and has increased the importance of data centers as components of enterprise network infrastructures.

Data storage hardware has also evolved and continues to drive the cost of storing data to unprecedented low levels. In 2000, the average cost to store a gigabyte of data was approximately $10; by 2004, the average cost had declined to $1 and by 2010 the average cost had sunk to $0.10 [BUSH11]. This decline, however, has been offset by businesses' increased appetite for storing all types of data including voice and video. As a result, businesses continue to invest in storage technologies of all types including storage area networks (SANs) and network-attached storage (NAS). When all expenses are considered (including backup storage devices, support staff, server infrastructure, electrical power, cooling, etc.), the real cost of data storage for a business is closer to $25 per gigabyte per month [VERT09].

VIRTUALIZATION Virtualization is another important computer hardware trend that is shaping the evolution of data centers and their role in enterprise networks. **Virtualization** is the creation of a virtual (rather than actual) version of something and in computing, this means creating virtual versions of operating systems, servers, storage devices, and networks. Partitioning a hard drive to create, in effect, two different hard drives is an example of virtualization. In reality, the second hard drive does not exist, but it shows up in your computer directory just as it would if you had installed a second hard drive in your computer.

Four categories of virtualization are pertinent to the current discussion: operating system virtualization, server virtualization, storage virtualization, and network virtualization. A brief description of each follows.

With operating system virtualization, software is used to allow a piece of computer hardware to simultaneously run multiple operating system images. This was first used on mainframes several decades ago to ensure that expensive processing power was not being wasted.

Server virtualization masks the details of physical servers from the users of those servers. Users see one server rather than the details of the actual collection of physical servers, processors, and operating systems that they are interacting with.

Storage virtualization is widely used in SANs. It pools the physical storage from multiple storage devices into what appears to be a single storage device that can be managed from a central console.

Network virtualization disguises the complexity of the underlying communications network. It enables the network bandwidth to be split into independent channels that can be assigned to particular servers or devices.

Virtualization has contributed to business interest in "computing on demand" and "utility computing." In virtualized environments, users often think that the organization's computing resources are limitless. When more bandwidth is needed to support network applications, channels can be reassigned. If more servers are needed to support users, these can be added to the data center infrastructure without changing users' directories. If more storage devices are needed to support the businesses' insatiable demand for data, these too can be added without changing user interfaces. Virtualization contributes to creating the impression of an infinitely scalable network. The ability to centrally monitor and administer a virtualized computing environment in which computing devices and data storage devices are geographically separated from user locations has provided additional fuel for business interest in cloud computing.

Client/Server Architecture

The widely used client/server (C/S) architecture is intended to provide the best aspects of both distributed and centralized computing. Users work on PCs, laptops, tablets, and mobile devices, collectively known as *clients* which are supported by specialized *servers*. Servers are specialized computers that provide services for clients such as database services, printing services, and communication services. Server names in C/S architectures follow the functions they carry out for clients. A server that provides database services is often called a database server. Print servers, fax servers, communication servers, and application servers are other widely used server types. The C/S architecture has gained widespread acceptance as the result of the evolution of high-speed local area networks (LANs), WAN/LAN integration technologies, and sophisticated systems software that provides intermachine processing.

Client/server architecture is attractive to businesses for several reasons. First, it is cost-effective and achieves economies of scale by centralizing support for specialized functions. File servers and database servers also make it easier to provide universal access to information by authorized users and to maintain consistency and security of files and data. The physical architecture of servers used can be customized to best support the services they provide to clients.

Another reason for the popularity of the C/S architecture is its flexibility. Flexibility is provided by the fact that the functional services provided by servers are not necessarily in a one-to-one relation with physical computers. For example, file services and print services could both be provided on the same server instead of having a separate server for each service. At an opposite extreme, database services could be provided to clients by multiple geographically dispersed machines. Services can share a processor within a server for information systems in smaller organizations, or they can be split among multiple processors in several servers in larger organizations to increase availability, capacity, and responsiveness. This popular approach is examined in more detail in Chapter 9.

During the 1990s, corporate interest in client/server architecture increased when this architecture was embraced by enterprise systems software vendors such as SAP. These business software vendors developed three-tier versions of their products similar to that illustrated in Figure 3.3. Separating the user interface (client) from the application (e.g., an ERP system) and the enterprise system's database helped to convince business executives that computing resources could be distributed across locations. Users no longer had to be physically close to application servers and application servers no longer had to be in the same location as the organization's data storage systems. This realization fueled business interest in DDP.

An example of a client/server architecture in business is that used by MasterCard International. It is described in the online case study.

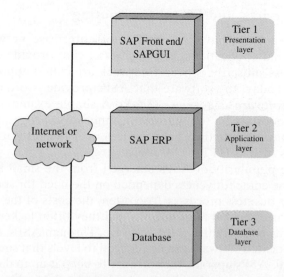

Figure 3.3   Three-Tier Enterprise System Architecture

Intranets and Extranets

Intranets and extranets have also played a role in the evolution of distributed data processing in businesses. Many experts describe the Internet, intranets, and extranets as examples or extensions of the client/server model. In essence, an intranet provides users of client devices with applications associated with the Internet but isolated within the organization. Key features of an intranet are as follows:

- Uses Internet-based standards, such as the HyperText Markup Language (HTML) and the Simple Mail Transfer Protocol (SMTP)
- Uses the TCP/IP protocol suite applications and services
- Includes wholly owned content that is not accessible to external users over the public Internet. Such content can also be accessed by authorized internal users even though the corporation has Internet connections and runs a Web server on the Internet

The advantages of the intranet approach include ease of implementation and ease of use. Intranets are examined in detail in Chapter 9.

Similar to an intranet, an extranet makes use of TCP/IP protocols and applications, especially the Web. The distinguishing feature of the extranet is that it provides access to corporate resources by authorized outside clients, typically suppliers and customers of the organization. This outside access can be provided via the company's connections to the Internet or through other data communications networks. An extranet provides more than access to the organization's public Web site. It also enables authorized outside clients with fairly extensive access to corporate resources, usually in a fashion that enforces a security policy. As with an intranet, the typical model of operation for the extranet is client/server. Extranets are also examined in more detail in Chapter 9.

Web Services and Cloud Computing

Many businesses have extended their enterprise networks to include hosted services and applications. The businesses that provide computer-based services to business subscribers over a network are called **application service providers (ASPs)**. Today, the software that ASPs provide is often called *on-demand software* or *software as a service (SaaS)*. A simple example of an ASP is a business that provides access to a particular application program (such as a time and attendance electronic timesheet service) over the Internet using standard TCP/IP protocols such as HTTP.

The popularity of ASPs emerged from the small and medium-size companies whose competitiveness depended on the need for specialized software to support their business processes. Too often, the costs of the specialized software they needed far exceeded their budgets and they often lacked the expertise needed to support the complexities of the software. Through ASPs, the costs and complexities of sophisticated software can be reduced to levels that small and medium-size firms can afford. ASPs upgrade the software to keep it up to date, provide $24 \times 7 \times 365$ technical support, and handle the physical and electronic security to ensure business continuity for subscribers.

The application software that is accessible to ASP subscribers resides on the vendor's system and is accessed by users through a Web browser or by using special-purpose client software provided by the vendor. The ASP owns, operates, and maintains the application software and the servers on which it runs. ASP subscribers pay to use the software on a per-use basis or a monthly or annual fee and ASPs often offer a *service-level agreement* that guarantees certain levels of service, such as availability.

The opportunities for subscribers to customize ASP software may be limited and in general, they have to accept the application as is. If the ASP's software is used to perform critical business functions, the subscriber may have limited control over that function and its ability to operate may be in jeopardy if the ASP experiences a major failure.

Despite these limitations, ASP services come in many forms and continue to thrive. There are several categories of ASP business including:

- Functional/specialist ASPs provide single application such as credit card processing or payroll processing;
- Vertical market ASPs provide solution packages for specific typon of cusﬆomers, such as a doctor's office;
- Enterprise ASPs provide a wide range of enterprise system solutions.

As mentioned previously, ASP services have been traditionally targeted to small and medium-size businesses. Today, software is just one of the services that are available to business subscribers through what is called "cloud computing." In its most general sense, **cloud computing** encompasses any subscription-based or pay-per-use service that extends an organization's existing IT capabilities over the Internet in real time. Cloud-computing service providers enable businesses to increase capabilities or capacity without investing in new infrastructure, licensing new software, or training new personnel. As noted by [KNOR12], cloud computing continues to evolve and has taken on many forms including:

- **Software as a service (SaaS):** Delivers a single application through a Web browser to subscribers via a multitenant architecture;
- **Infrastructure as a service (IaaS):** Provides storage and virtual servers (virtual data centers) and networking services to subscribers;
- **Platform as a service (PaaS):** Provides subscribers with a development environment that can be used to create applications that run on the provider's infrastructures and are delivered to the subscriber's customers over the Internet using the provider's servers.
- **Managed service providers (MSP):** Provides subscribers with specialized services that augment its existing IT services such as e-mail virus scanning, application monitoring, anti-spam services, desktop management services, and security management services.

Cloud-computing services are often *device agnostic* because they can be delivered to any end-user computing device including a PC, laptop, tablet, or smartphone. The ability to support mobile users is another reason why cloud computing is increasing in popularity among businesses.

Cloud computing is discussed in more detail in Chapter 9, but it is appropriate to mention it here as well because it has become a component in many organizations' DDP architecture.

3.2 FORMS OF DISTRIBUTED DATA PROCESSING

We have defined a DDP system as a computing architecture in which interconnected computers are dispersed within an organization. DDP systems have been implemented in a wide variety of forms that conform to this general definition. One way to gain an appreciation of this variety is to consider in more detail how the following functions or objects may be distributed within the network:

- Applications
- Devices
- Network management
- Data

It is often the case that two or more of these functions or objects are distributed in a DDP system. For our purposes, however, it is sufficient to examine them one at a time to gain insight into DDP implementation configurations. We examine the first three topics in this section and the last topic in the next section.

Distributed Applications

Two dimensions characterize the distribution of applications. First, there is the allocation of application functions within the network:

- One application may be split up into components that are dispersed among multiple computers
- One application may be replicated on different computers
- Different applications may be distributed among different computers.

Distributed application processing can also be characterized by whether the distribution of the application is vertical or horizontal. In general, vertical partitioning involves one application split up into components that are dispersed among a number of machines, whereas horizontal partitioning involves either one application replicated on a number of machines or a number of different applications distributed among a number of machines.

With **vertical partitioning**, data processing is distributed in a hierarchical fashion. This distribution may reflect organizational structure, or it may simply be the most appropriate for the application. Examples include the following:

- **Insurance:** Data processing distribution is often a two-level hierarchy in insurance companies. Typically, each branch office has a computer system that it uses for preparing new contracts and for processing claims. In most cases, these types of transactions can be handled directly by the local office. Summary information is sent to a head office. The head office uses contract and claim information to perform risk analysis and actuarial calculations. On the basis of the company's financial position and current exposure, the head office can adjust rates for customer groups and individual customers and communicate the changes to the branches.

- **Retail chains:** Retail stores typically include point-of-sale terminals and other computers for use by sales and office personnel. Frequently, a single server houses all the information used at the store. The nature of the POS (point-of-sale) application lends itself more readily to such an arrangement. Point-of-sale terminals make use of pricing information stored in the server. Sales transactions are recorded as are changes in inventory and accounts receivable as goods are sold. Sales and office personnel can use client devices to display summary sales information, inventory levels, accounts receivable, and customer transaction summaries. Store management can access reports on total sales performance, goods aging, and other analyses. Store-level data and information can also be transmitted to a head office within the retail chain.

- **Process control:** The process-control function in a factory adapts readily to a vertical DDP system. Each major operational area is controlled by a console or workstation, which is fed information from distributed process-control microprocessors. These microprocessors are responsible for the automated control of sensors and robots or other effector devices on the shop floor. The operations control workstation scans sensor readings, looking for exceptions or analyzing trends. It may also control part of the work operation to vary the rate or mix of production. These distributed workstations ensure rapid response to changing conditions at the work process level. All the workstations are linked to a powerful server or mainframe computer where management applications such as operations planning, optimization, business analytics, and general corporate data processing are run.

- **Web mashups:** Web-based mashups have enjoyed widespread popularity. These are frequently created by integrating data from multiple sources to create a new application in a manner that hides the details of the data sources in order to provide a seamless experience for users. Major Web services companies like Google, eBay, and Amazon have made it relatively easy for developers to create new mashups by providing application programming interfaces (APIs) to many of their services at little or no cost. The APIs that underlie mashups are arranged in tiers and the mashups themselves are often formed by combining APIs across tiers. The data sources associated with the Web services used in mashups are typically housed in distributed data centers. In essence, many Web mashups are examples of a vertically partitioned DDP that is experienced by users in real time. Additional insight into Web services is provided in Chapter 9's discussion of Service-Oriented Architecture.

As these examples illustrate, a vertically partitioned DDP system generally consists of a central computer system (server or mainframe) with one or more levels of satellite systems. The nature of the partition reflects organizational structure or the structure of the work tasks that are performed, or both. The objective is to assign the application's processing load to the level of the hierarchy at which it is most cost-effective. Such an arrangement combines some of the best features of both centralized and distributed data processing and conforms to the client/server framework.

With **horizontal partitioning**, data processing is distributed among a number of computers that have a peer relationship. That is, there is no concept of client/server separation. Computers in a horizontal configuration normally operate autonomously, although in some cases this configuration is used for load balancing. In many cases, horizontal partitioning reflects organizational decentralization. Two examples follow:

- **Small Office/Home Office (SOHO) peer-to-peer networks:** In small office or home office networks, users may be linked together in peer-to-peer LANs. Within peer-to-peer MS Windows networks, SOHO computing devices are members of the same "workgroup" and each device can be configured to share files, printers, and other services with other devices in the workgroup. In this arrangement, each computing device may be both a client and a server. There is no special network operating system residing on one of the computers in the network that provides server-side applications (such as directory services) for the other devices in the network. In peer-to-peer LANs, access rights to sharable resources are governed by setting sharing permissions on the individual machines. For example, if one user has an attached printer that a second user wants to access, he or she must set his or her machine to allow (share) access to the printer. Similarly, if one user wants to have access to a folder or file stored in a folder on another user's machine, the other user must enable file sharing on his or her computer. Security options are limited in peer-to-peer networks, but access to shared folders and printers can be controlled by assigning passwords to those resources.

- **Air traffic control system:** Each regional center for air traffic control operates autonomously of the other centers, performing the same set of applications. Within each center, several computers are used to process radar and radio data and to provide a visual status to the air traffic controllers.

It is more often the case that an organization's computing function includes both horizontal and vertical partitioning of business applications. Corporate headquarters may maintain a centralized data center where a mainframe's applications provide the primary corporate management information systems and decision support systems. Other central functions, such as public relations, strategic planning, and corporate finance and accounting, may be supported here. A vertical partition is created by providing subordinate computing facilities at branch offices. Within each branch office, a horizontal partition provides office automation support.

Other Forms of DDP

DPP environments may also include distributed device controllers and/or distributed network management. Let us briefly examine each of these possibilities.

DISTRIBUTED DEVICES   One natural use of DDP in enterprise networks is to support a distributed set of business devices such as automatic teller machines. Another common application of this approach is in factory automation. A factory may contain a number of sensors, programmable controllers, and robots that are used to automate the manufacturing process. Such systems involve the distribution of computing technology to the manufacturing process at various locations in the work centers.

NETWORK MANAGEMENT   Any distributed system requires some form of management and control, including monitoring of the status of various components of the distributed system, and management of the communications network that interconnects the distributed components to ensure its availability and responsiveness. In many instances, some sort of central network management system is needed. However, such a system needs to obtain status information from various devices in the distributed system, and may need to issue commands to those devices to avoid disruptions in performance. Thus, at least some computers in the distributed system must include some management and control logic to enable them to interact with the central network management system. A more detailed look at these issues is included in Chapter 20.

3.3 DISTRIBUTED DATA

Before beginning our discussion of distributed data, it is necessary to say something about the nature of the organization of data in a computer system. We first provide a brief overview of some of the fundamental concepts of databases and database management system, and then look at the various ways in which an enterprise may choose to distribute its data.

Database Management Systems

In some cases, a business can function with a relatively simple collection of files of data. Each file may contain text (e.g., copies of memos and reports) or numerical data (e.g., spreadsheets). A more complex file consists of a set of transaction records. While small businesses may be able to get along with by having only files and spreadsheets, larger businesses need more complex data organization schemes which are most commonly called databases. A **database** is a structured collection of data stored for use in one or more applications. In addition to data, a database contains the relationships between data items and groups of data items. As an example of the distinction between data files and a database, consider the following. A simple personnel file might consist of a set of records, one for each employee. Each record gives the employee's name, address, date of birth, position, salary, and other details needed by the personnel department. A personnel database includes a personnel file, as just described. It may also include a time and attendance file, showing for each week the hours worked by each employee. With a database organization, these two files are tied together so that a payroll program can extract the information about time worked and salary for each employee to generate paychecks.

Accompanying the database is a **database management system (DBMS)**, which is a suite of programs for constructing and maintaining the database and for offering ad hoc query capabilities to multiple users and applications. A **query language** provides a uniform interface to the database for users and applications.

Figure 3.4 provides a simplified diagram of a DBMS architecture. Developers make use of a data definition language (DDL) to define the database's logical structure and procedural properties, which are represented by a set of database description tables. A data manipulation language (DML) provides another powerful set

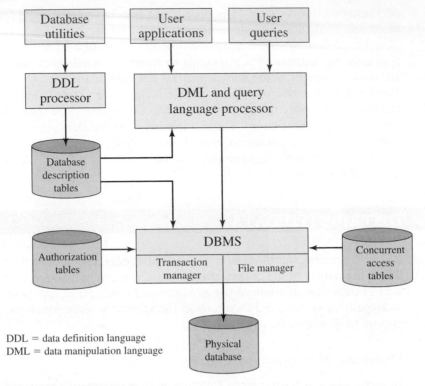

Figure 3.4 DBMS Architecture

of tools for application developers. Query languages are declarative languages designed to enable end users to access specific subsets of data within the database. The database management system makes use of the database description tables to manage the physical database. The file manager module and a transaction manager module provide interfaces to the database. In addition to the database description table, two other tables support the DBMS. The DBMS uses authorization tables to ensure the user has permission to execute the query language statement on the database. The concurrent access table prevents conflicts when simultaneous, conflicting commands are executed by database users.

Database systems provide efficient access to large volumes of data and are vital to the operation of many organizations. As illustrated in Figure 3.3, databases play a critical role in enterprise systems and serve as the central repository for all data associated with an enterprise system's integrated business processes.

A **distributed database** is a collection of several different databases, distributed among multiple computers, that looks like a single database to the user. The computers may be located within a centralized data center or in different, geographically dispersed data centers. The DBMS controls access to the distributed database and enables the user to treat the distributed database as if it was a single database. The DBMS must include a directory that identifies the physical location of each data element in the database whether these are on different machines within the same data center or on machines in distributed data centers.

In general terms, we can distinguish three ways of organizing data for use by an organization: centralized, replicated, and partitioned.

Centralized Versus Distributed Databases

A centralized database is housed in a central computer facility. However, the users and application programs that rely on the database can be at remote locations and still have access to the centralized database. A centralized database is often used with a vertical DDP organization. It is desirable when the security and integrity of the data are paramount, because a central data center is often more easily controlled than is a dispersed collection of data and computing technologies. On the other hand, there are a number of reasons why a distributed data organization might be attractive, including the following:

1. A distributed design can reflect an organization's structure or function. This makes the design of the data organization and the use of the data more understandable and easier to implement and maintain.

2. Data can be stored locally, under local control. Local storage often decreases response times and communications costs and increases data availability.

3. Distributing data across multiple autonomous sites confines the effects of a computer breakdown to its point of occurrence; the data on the surviving computers can still be accessed and processed.

4. The size of the total collection of data and the number of users of those data need not be limited by a single computer's size and processing power.

Replicated Databases

When data are distributed, one of two overall strategies may be adopted: replicated or partitioned. In a **replicated database**, all or part of the database is copied at two or more computers. Before looking at the general principles of this important strategy, we briefly describe two examples from [CONN99].

The first example is Golden Gate Financial Group, which makes about $1 billion in trades per month. The trades are recorded at their system in San Francisco and, as each trade is made, it is also recorded in a remote office in San Jose. Golden Gate makes use of a leased line to transfer about 6.6 gigabytes of data each month to achieve replication. The company recouped its investment in replication software as well as a year's worth of leased line charges when San Francisco was hit by a daylong power outage. Employees traveled to San Jose, set up shop, and used current replicated data to do their work. As a result, trading at the financial firm was down only for half an hour.

A different strategy is used by Merrill Lynch, which must distribute 2 gigabytes of critical financial information to three remote offices daily for use by staff. Previously, information systems (IS) staff copied the entire database to remote offices once per week by manual command. Now, data are updated twice per day to servers in each remote location. Only changed data, amounting to about 200 megabytes, is sent, thus saving bandwidth and time. Now users have access to the latest data, and the data are local, avoiding the need to use long-distance hookups.

Table 3.5 Replication Strategy Variants

	Real Time	Near-Real Time	Deferred
Design Architecture	Two-phase commit	Cascade or broadcast distribution	Messaging and queuing
Benefits	Tight data synchronization Distributed transactions Data currency	Data consolidation Data distribution Improved response time Less WAN loading	Heterogeneous database updates Guaranteed delivery across any network Multiple network protocol support
Drawbacks	Longer response time Difficult to implement Two-phase commit does not always work	Lack of data currency Single-vendor solution	Time delay in updates More programming work required

Data replication has become increasingly popular. Numerous vendors offer data replication technology for Windows and UNIX platforms for backing up mainframe-based data. Its use is virtually mandated in the banking industry to ensure protection for the accounts of their customers. The key advantage of data replication is that it provides backup and recovery from both network and server failure.

Three variants of data replication are in common use: real time, near-real time, and deferred, as shown in Table 3.5 (based on [GOLI99]). **Real-time replication** is often used in transactional systems, such as order fulfillment processes in ERP system, where all copies of data must be synchronized immediately. Updates typically involve the use of an algorithm called the two-phase commit, which attempts to avoid inconsistencies in the two databases (primary and backup) by adding a confirmation step to each update. This operation decreases the total response time for database updates and may not always succeed.

Near-real-time replication is also an option. In this case backups occur in batches, with a small amount of lag time (e.g., 10–30 minutes). This is adequate for many business applications.

Deferred replication involves bulk transfer of a large number of changes at longer intervals than near-real-time replication, such as once or twice a day. The transfer may be a bulk file transfer involving a large amount of data. This approach minimizes network resource requirements needed to synchronize replicates, but it does not ensure the same levels of consistency between replicates that a business would have with real-time and near-real-time replications.

Partitioned Databases

In a partitioned database, the database exists as distinct and nonoverlapping segments that are dispersed among multiple computer systems. In general, there is no duplication of data among the segments of a partitioned database, that is, each partition stores a nonoverlapping subset of the total database. This strategy can be used with either a horizontal or vertical DDP organization.

The main advantage of this approach is that it disperses the data storage and updating load and it eliminates a single point of failure. This approach can

Table 3.6   Advantages and Disadvantages of Database Distribution Methods

Type of Distribution	Advantages	Disadvantages
Common database accessed by users at all user locations (**Centralized**).	No duplication of data, little reorganization required.	Contention among multiple users attempting to access the same data simultaneously. If the database is large, response time may be slow. During storage system failures, all users may lose access to data.
Copy of the common central database stored at each user location (**Replicated**).	Reduces contention among users for data in the database. Short response times. During failure, new copy can be obtained from another location.	Higher storage requirements and costs due to extensive duplication of data. Updates of one copy of the database must subsequently be made to all other copies.
Individual database for each user location (**Partitioned**).	Not duplicating the entire database at each location can minimize total data storage costs. Size of database at each location is determined by local use and can be incrementally increased. Short response time.	It may be challenging to develop corporate-level ad hoc or management reports that must obtain data from the different databases at distributed locations.

be counterproductive if the typical database request involves data from multiple partitions.

Table 3.6 provides a simplified comparison of these three approaches to database organization. In practice, a mixture of strategies is common. A more detailed look at strategies for database organization is provided in Table 3.7 (based on [HOFF02]). For replicated databases, two strategies are possible. First, a central database is maintained, and copies of portions of the database are extracted for local use. Typically, such systems lock the affected portion of the central database if the remote computer has the authority to update. If this is the case, the remote computer transmits the updates back to the central database upon completion of the transaction. Alternatively, a more elaborate synchronization technique can be employed so that updates to one copy of a replicated database are automatically propagated throughout the DDP system to update all copies of the replicate. This strategy requires considerably more processing and communications loads within the enterprise network but provides the business with a more flexible system.

The simplest partitioned strategy is one in which there are a number of independently operated databases that each allow remote access. In effect, we have a collection of centralized databases, with more than one center. A more complex system is one in which the database partitions are integrated so that a single query by the user may require access to any of the partitions. In a sophisticated system, this access is invisible to users, who need not specify where the data are located and need not use different commands to access data in different partitions of the distributed database.

Thus, we can see that a variety of strategies is possible. In designing a distributed database, two sets of objectives are paramount: database objectives and communications objectives. *Database objectives* include accessibility of the data,

Table 3.7 Strategies for Database Organization

Strategy	Reliability	Expandability	Communications Overhead	Manageability	Data Consistency or Integrity
Centralized					
Centralized database Database resides in one location; data values may be distributed to geographically dispersed users for local processing	**Poor to Good** Highly dependent on redundancies in central data center	**Poor to Good** Virtualization may overcome memory limitations that constrain performance in traditional systems	**Very high** High traffic to one site; redundant load-carrying links to central data center be used to address higher traffic loads	**Very good** One monolithic site facilitates coordination	**Excellent** All users always have same data
Replicated					
Distributed snapshot databases Copy of portion of the central database created by extraction and replication for use at remote sites	**Good** Redundancy and tolerated delays	**Very good** Cost of additional copies may be less than linear	**Low to medium** Periodic snapshots exchanged between locations can cause bursts of network traffic	**Very good** All copies are identical	**Medium** Fine as long as delays are tolerated by business needs
Replicated, distributed database Data are replicated and synchronized at multiple sites	**Excellent** Redundancy and minimal delays	**Very good** Cost of additional copies may be low	**Medium** Messages are constant, but some delays are tolerated	**Medium** Synchronization adds some complexity to manageability	**Medium to very good** Close to precise consistency
Partitioned					
Distributed, nonintegrated databases Independent databases that can be accessed by applications on remote computers	**Good** Depends on local database availability	**Good** New sites independent of existing ones	**Low** Little if any need to pass data or queries across a network	**Very good** Easy for each site, until there is a need to share data across sites	**Low** No guarantees of consistency
Distributed, integrated database Data span multiple computers and software	**Very good** Effective use of partitioning	**Very good** New nodes get only data they need without changes in overall database design	**Low to medium** Most queries are local but queries that require data from multiple sites can cause temporary load increases	**Difficult** Especially difficult for queries that need data from distributed tables, and updates must be tightly coordinated	**Very poor** Considerable effort and inconsistencies not tolerated

security and privacy, and completeness and integrity of the data. *Communications objectives* are to minimize the communications load and response times for users' requests for data stored at other locations.

We can characterize the requirements for communications and networking generated by the use of distributed data processing as falling into three key areas: connectivity, availability, and performance.

The **connectivity** of a distributed system refers to the ability of components in the system to exchange data. In a vertically partitioned DDP system, components of the system generally need links only to components above and below them in the hierarchical structure. Such a requirement can often be met with simple direct links between systems. In a horizontally partitioned system, it may be necessary to allow data exchange between any two systems. For example, in SOHO peer-to-peer network, it may be advantageous to allow any user to share some files with any other user in the workgroup.

In a system requiring high connectivity, some sort of network may be preferable to a large number of direct links. To see this, consider Figure 3.5. If we have a distributed system requiring full connectivity and use a direct link between each pair of systems or locations, the number of links and the communication interfaces

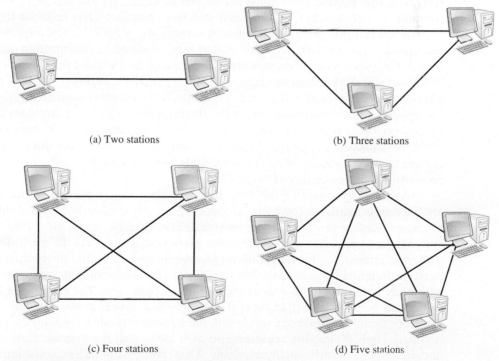

(a) Two stations   (b) Three stations

(c) Four stations   (d) Five stations

Figure 3.5 Full Connectivity Using Direct Links

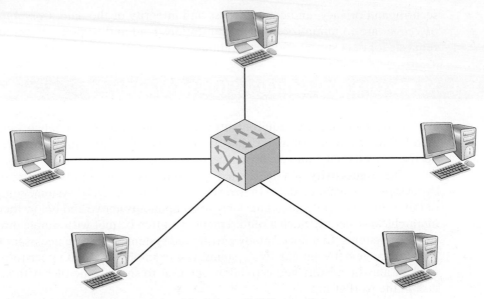

Figure 3.6   The Use of a Central Switch for Full Connectivity

needed grows rapidly with the number of systems or locations. With four computers, six links are required; with five computers, ten links are required. Instead, suppose we create a network by providing a central switch connecting each computer
system to that switch. The results are shown in Figure 3.6. In this case, with four
computers, four links are required, and with five computers, five links are required.

If the components of a distributed system are geographically dispersed, the
requirement for connectivity dictates that some method of transmitting data over
long distances is needed. This may involve the use of the ISPs and the public Internet,
WAN services/links from telecommunications carriers, or investing in a private
infrastructure. As noted in Section 3.1, third-party data centers are increasingly being
incorporated into enterprise networks. Business uses of third-party data centers
range from being backup and recovery sites that store database replicates to serving
as the organization's centralized data processing site. Today, many third-party data
centers provide a variety of "cloud computing" services for their subscribers. Cloud
computing is discussed more fully in Chapter 9.

Availability refers to the percentage of time that a particular function or
application is available for users. Depending on the application, availability may
be merely desirable or it may be essential. For example, in an air traffic control
system, the availability of the computer system that supports the air traffic controllers is critical. High availability requirements mean that the distributed system
must be designed in such a way that the failure of a single computer or other device
within the network does not deny access to the application. For example, a backup
server can be installed for any server that provides critical applications or services
for users. Should the primary server fail, the backup is ready to pick up the processing load. High availability requirements also mean that the communications links
and equipment must be highly available. Thus, some form of link and communication equipment redundancy and backup is needed.

Finally, the **performance** of the communications network providing interconnections for the applications that run on the DDP system must be considered. For highly interactive applications, such as a data entry system or a graphics design application, response time is critically important. It is not just the computer processors that execute the applications must be fast, but the network connections must also be fast. The network must have sufficient capacity and flexibility to provide the required response time. On the other hand, if the application moves a lot of data around but without the time being critical, the major network performance concern may be throughput. In this case, the network must be designed to handle large volumes of data.

Once we have examined the details of the data communications techniques and facilities that businesses can use in enterprise networks, we reexamine strategies for communications and network planning including those that best fit DDP.

3.5 BIG DATA INFRASTRUCTURE CONSIDERATIONS

We began this chapter by noting that businesses are storing more types of data in greater volumes than ever before. Growing appetites for data have made virtualized storage systems in centralized data centers more popular and these systems are often described as "private clouds." The ability to expand storage capacities with storage services in the public cloud is also becoming more popular among businesses.

Traditional business data storage and management technologies include relational database management systems (RDBMS), network attached storage (NAS), storage area networks (SAN), data warehouses (DWs), and business intelligence (BI) analytics. The characteristics of these technologies are summarized in Table 3.8.

Traditional data warehouse and BI analytics systems tend to be highly centralized within an enterprise infrastructure. These often include a central data repository with a RDBMS, high performance storage, and analytics software, such as online analytical processing (OLAP) tools for mining and visualizing data.

Big data may include these technologies but often requires others as well. To process large quantities of data within tolerable time periods, big data may need distributed file systems, distributed databases, cloud-computing platforms, Internet storage, and other scalable storage technologies. The size of the data sets often makes it challenging to rely solely on relational databases and shared storage systems such as NAS and SAN may be too slow for big data applications. The desktop statistics and data visualization software used in big data analytics is spawning new forms of massively parallel processing that enables faster searching, sharing, analyzing, and visualizing. Real- or near-real-time information delivery is one of the goals of big data analytics, and this increasing business appetites for in-memory processing systems which enable real-time analytics by bringing large data sets into memory.

Big data applications are becoming a source of competitive value for businesses, especially those that aspire to build data products and services to profit from the huge volumes of data that they capture and store. There is every indication that the exploitation of data will become increasingly important to enterprises in the years ahead as more and more businesses reap the benefits of big data applications.

Table 3.8   Traditional Data Storage/Management Technologies

Data Storage/Management Technology	Major Characteristics
Relational Database Management System (RDBMS)	A database management system (DBMS) that is based on the relational model. In a RDBMS, data is stored in tables; relationships among data are also stored in tables. This allows stored data to be accessed or reassembled in different ways without having the change to data tables.
	Users access and manipulate data in RDBMS using query languages such as Structured Query Language (SQL).
	Most popular databases currently in use are based on the relational database model.
Network Attached Storage (NAS)	Network attached storage systems are networked appliances which contain one or more hard drives that can be shared with multiple, heterogeneous computers. Their specialized role within networks is to store and serve files.
	NAS disk drives typically support built-in data protection mechanisms including redundant storage containers or redundant arrays of independent disks (RAID).
	NAS enables file-serving responsibilities to be separated from other servers on the network and typically provide faster data access than traditional file servers.
Storage Area Networks (SAN)	A SAN is a dedicated network that provides access to various types of storage devices including tape libraries, optical jukeboxes, and disk arrays.
	To servers and other devices in the network, a SAN's storage devices look like locally attached devices.
	Because it is specifically designed for storage communications, Fibre Channel is often used for SAN interconnections.
	SANs can be centralized or distributed within enterprise networks depending on computing requirements.
Data Warehouse (DW)	A DW is a database used for reporting and analysis. The data in a DW is uploaded from other operational systems. Metadata, data about the data, is also stored in the DW.
	Data warehouses can be subdivided into data marts which store subsets of data from the DW. A data mart is similar to a partition in a traditional database.
	DW data is cleaned, transformed, catalogued, and made available for use by managers and other business professionals for decision support, market research, data mining, online analytical processing (OLAP), and other forms of business intelligence.
Business Intelligence (BI)	BI technologies provide current, predictive, and historical views of business operations. Because BI aims to improve business decision making, BI systems are often classified as decision support systems (DSS).
	Technologies often identified as BI technologies include benchmarking, business analytics, business performance management, data mining, event processing, predictive analytics, and text mining.

APPLICATION NOTE

Distributed Computing Support

It is difficult to imagine running a business without a large number of desktop computers. Today, the same can be said for laptop computers and handheld devices. Supporting such a collection of powerful appliances, some of which are mobile, can present an organization with unprecedented challenges. Using the appropriate strategy can be the difference between an efficiently run shop and one that is not only less efficient, but much more costly.

One of the largest of these challenges is the maintenance demands on an already overworked support staff. Perhaps the single most important approach that a business can take in order to save money, time, and energy when dealing with computers and data networks is to standardize on a set of applications, computing platforms, and networking hardware. While there are always a few exceptions, where possible, the choices should be minimal. By selecting a single set of applications for desktop and laptop use, licensing and software fees can be reduced by buying in bulk. Licenses can be very expensive on a per seat basis but site licensing can be much more cost-effective. In addition, the maintenance of the software becomes easier as technicians have fewer variables to contend with in their troubleshooting and updates.

The same is true of hardware. With a single manufacturer to deal with, fewer spares need to be kept on hand, technicians become very familiar with the equipment and the vendors are known and have a vested interest in keeping their customer happy. It can be a troubleshooting nightmare moving from one machine equipped with Windows to an Apple computer or a Linux machine.

Security has become one of the primary concerns for network and systems administrators, particularly when dealing with so many machines. In addition to patches, spyware, adware, and viruses, we must battle regular attacks from outside. In many cases, an attack can have consequences beyond the initial problem. As an example, when a virus is downloaded, it is often shared between users. Most viruses come through e-mail downloads, but today we can add USB memory sticks as an ideal way to spread viruses between autonomous systems. In the case of a fully distributed environment, the best cure for this eventuality is prevention. A good antivirus package on all machines and the server is critical.

Once the virus has been contracted by the network and by the machines, a virus removal process must be initiated immediately. Standard scans may not be enough to eradicate the virus. In some cases, scanning from removable media and an inoculation procedure must be followed to remove the virus. Worse yet, the infected machine(s) may be backed up to the network resulting in infected servers and potential large-scale loss of the organizations' data. If this occurs, it is possible that the data cannot be recovered. Any removable media that was in use at the time of the infection must also be considered at risk.

Understanding all of the security measures necessary to protect a modern communications network is a difficult, full-time job. If we add the mobile and handheld devices, we can see what a truly daunting task security can become, so training is very important. It must also be continuing, for administrators and end users alike, as the environment is constantly changing.

(Continued)

Many problems like this can be resolved quickly and easily if the computing staff is skilled and has a solid support structure. Often, IT departments are not considered part of the core business and so receive secondary consideration for budgets, personnel, and equipment. There are dozens of stories in which computing departments receive little support but all of the blame for problems. Because personal computers are inexpensive and have a reduced complexity when compared to mainframes, organizations may staff themselves with personnel having a corresponding level of training and skill. While this may be an attempt at cost-effectiveness, it is inappropriate for long-range planning.

Often underestimated is the helpdesk or trouble call center. Staffing and reliability are important aspects of this particular area. For large organizations, the number of trouble calls can be staggering. An ineffective or understaffed group answering the telephones or handling the troubleshooting can slow the primary business functions down and have a significant effect on the bottom line due to excessive man-hours spent and downtime. Additionally, the software used to support such a system should be simple and also have functions such as trend analysis, searching, categorizing, and various reporting capabilities.

Decentralized or distributed systems can pose unique problems not experienced by fully centralized systems. With large numbers of autonomous nodes, an understanding of the issues, proper training, and appropriate resources can minimize the financial impact of problems and reduce downtime of the communications system.

3.6 SUMMARY

With the increasing availability of inexpensive yet powerful personal computers and mobile devices, there has been an increasing trend toward distributed data processing (DDP). With DDP, processors, data, and other aspects of an organization's data processing system may be dispersed. This provides businesses with a communications network that is responsive to user needs, is able to provide better response times, and is cost-effective. A DDP system involves either the horizontal or vertical partitioning of the computing function and may also involve a distributed organization of databases, device control, and interaction (network) control. This trend has been facilitated by the advent of client/server architectures and the emergence of cloud computing.

At this stage, we are not yet ready to translate our description of DDP characteristics into an analysis of the needed data communications and networking facilities. In general terms, we can say that a DDP system involves business requirements in the areas of connectivity, availability, and performance. These requirements, in turn, dictate the type of data communications or networking approach that is appropriate for a given DDP system.

**Case Study III: Managing Massive Data Warehouses
                 at MasterCard International**

The major concepts addressed in this case study include data warehouses; massive storage systems; "big data". **This case study and more are available at www.pearsoninternationaleditions.com/stallings**

3.7 KEY TERMS, REVIEW QUESTIONS, AND PROBLEMS

Key Terms

application service provider (ASP) availability big data centralized data processing client/server architecture connectivity	database data center distributed database distributed data processing (DDP) extranet horizontal partitioning	Intranet partitioned database performance peer-to-peer network replicated database vertical partitioning

Review Questions

3.1 Define business data.

3.2 Briefly describe how data grows among present business sectors.

3.3 Briefly describe the major characteristics of data centers.

3.4 What is the use of centralized control?

3.5 What are the key characteristics of centralized data processing facilities?

3.6 What are some advantages of a centralized data processing facility?

3.7 What is a distributed data processing (DDP) strategy?

3.8 What are the requirements for the Corporate Computing Function?

3.9 What is the key factor that has made distributed data processing an attractive option for businesses?

3.10 How can the responsiveness of data centers be increased by distributed data processing?

3.11 How does incompatibility among data become a drawback for distributed data processing?

3.12 What are the differences among Tier 1, Tier 2, Tier 3, and Tier 4 data centers?

3.13 Why do businesses partner with third-party data centers?

3.14 What is an in-memory processor?

3.15 What is HANA?

3.16 How is virtualization shaping the evolution of data centers and their role in enterprise networks?

3.17 Briefly describe the differences between storage area networks (SANs) and network attached storage (NAS) systems.

3.18 What is "utility computing"?

3.19 Why is client/server architecture attractive to businesses?

3.20 What role have intranets and extranets played in the evolution of distributed data processing in businesses?

3.21 What are the categories of ASP businesses?

3.22 Why are cloud-computing services often device agnostic?

3.23 What is a query language? Briefly describe the DBMS architecture.

3.24 What is a distributed database?

3.25 What are the differences among replicated and partitioned databases? Identify the major advantages and disadvantages of each.

3.26 Identify and briefly describe each of the following DDP networking implications: connectivity, availability, and performance.

3.27 Identify some uses of real-time replications.

Problems

3.1 Do some Internet research on big data best practices. Identify several good sources of information related to how businesses are managing their growing volumes of data and using the data that they are amassing for competitive advantage. Summarize your findings in a 500–1000 word paper or 8–12 slide PowerPoint presentation.

3.2 You have just accepted the position as CIO for Holiday Inn (Figure 3.7). As your first official act, the CEO has asked you to assess the corporation's computer operations and report back to her with your recommendation on whether to remain with the status quo (i.e., a centralized IS architecture similar to that depicted in Figure 3.1), migrate to a distributed architecture, or create a hybrid solution using aspects from both general architectures and possibly includes ASPs and cloud-computing services. Prepare a compelling 8–12 slide case in PowerPoint for presentation at the next staff meeting.

3.3 The Internet, if viewed from a global client/server perspective, generally consists of Web servers and their associated databases and other data repositories on the server side and various Web browser applications and associated plug-ins on the client side. Is a system of this sort best described as vertically distributed application processing, horizontally distributed application processing, or some hybrid of these two characterizations?

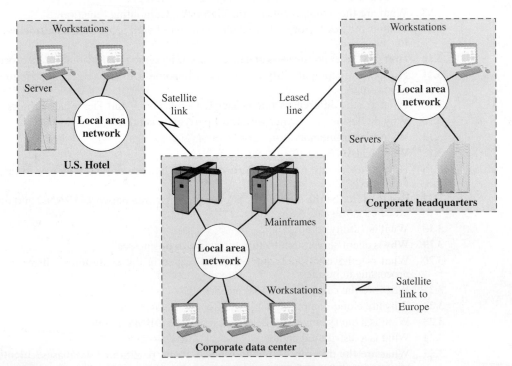

Figure 3.7 Holiday Inn Information Systems Architecture

3.4 Do some Internet research on in-memory computing systems and why they are being adopted by businesses. Compose a 500–1000 word paper (or 8–12 slide PowerPoint presentation) that summarizes the major reasons why businesses are investing in in-memory computing systems and how these systems are being used by business enterprises.

3.5 Do some Internet research on virtualization and the major vendors that are driving the evolution of virtualization. Compose a 500–1000 word paper (or 8–12 slide PowerPoint presentation) that summarizes the factors that drive business interest in virtualization and identifies the major vendors that are providing businesses with virtualization technologies and services.

3.6 Do some Internet research on application service providers and the types of services that are most popular among business subscribers. Also find information on the ASPs that have done the best job of attracting business subscribers. Compose a 500–1000 word paper (or 8–12 slide PowerPoint presentation) that summarizes the most popular types of applications that businesses access via ASPs and specific examples of ASPs that have attracted the most business subscribers.

3.7 Do some Internet research on third-party data centers and how they are being used within business networks. Compose a 500–1000 word paper (or 8–12 slide PowerPoint presentation) that summarizes the major reasons why businesses are partnering with third-party data centers and the major ways that third-party data centers are being used within enterprise networks.

3.8 Two data centers used for retail credit authorization are located in two different major population centers, which are separated from each other by a large zone of very little population. Each data center is intended to cover a particular geographical area and thus contains data that reflect the account status of the cardholders in that area only. Communication between both data centers occurs only in case a cardholder from one geographical area shops in a retail credit establishment of the geographical area covered by the other data center.
  a. Classify the relationship between the data centers as either client/server or peer to peer.
  b. Classify the database of the retail credit system as either partitioned or replicated.
  c. Should the two data centers be consolidated into a single, centralized, cloud-based facility? Why or why not?

3.9 Retail was one of the first areas to adopt distributed data processing. Instead of centralizing the POS systems, retailers deploy distributed databases, so all of their POS systems are local, but linked to a central system. Prices for all merchandise are determined and maintained at the central system. Each day, before stores open, relevant prices are downloaded to the POS system at each store, replicating the data of the central system. Analyze the economic advantages of this form of distributed data processing in the retail area.

3.10 Napster was a famous music exchange system that additionally offered many add-on services. It was sentenced to go out of business due to copyright infringement. The system worked as follows. The Napster server held a database of all music files offered by the participating users. Users had to login to the Napster server, and send the list of files they offered. Each user could then send search requests to the Napster server, in order to receive a list of the users that offered files that matched the query. The requester could then choose a user from that list, establish a direct connection with him, and request a download of the file.
  a. Categorize the relationship between the Napster server and the users of the system as either client/server or peer to peer.
  b. Categorize the relationship between the users of the system as either client/server or peer to peer.
  c. Categorize the database of music files as centralized, decentralized, or distributed.
  d. Categorize the database containing the list of available music files as either centralized or distributed.

3.11   A company plans to deploy a credit-sales system that will provide service to ten large population centers. A database will be used to store user information and record credit transactions. The IT department is considering two choices:
   a. A centralized database, where a single copy of the data is stored in one datacenter and used from all population centers.
   b. A replicated database, where one copy of the data is stored at multiple data centers (one in each population center) and all copies of the data are synchronized.
   Prepare a compelling 8–12 slide PowerPoint presentation for the next IT staff meeting that summarizes the pros and cons of each approach and recommends the one that should be deployed.

3.12   Do some Internet research on solid-state storage technologies and the reasons behind their popularity in data centers and "big data" environments. Find several images of widely used high-capacity solid-state storage equipment. Develop an 8–12 slide PowerPoint presentation that describes the connection between solid-state storage and "big data" management; include the images found when researching the topic in the presentation.

DATA TRANSMISSION

CHAPTER

4

Learning Objectives

After reading this chapter, you should be able to:

♦ Explain the various ways in which audio, data, image, and video can be represented by electromagnetic signals.

♦ Discuss the characteristics of analog and digital waveforms.

♦ Discuss the various transmission impairments that affect signal quality and information transfer over communication media.

♦ Identify the factors that affect channel capacity.

Data and signals are two of the fundamental building blocks of any computer network. In the previous two chapters, we considered the major types of data captured, stored, and transmitted within business networks. In this chapter, we address some of the fundamental concepts associated with signals.

In order to transmit data between devices attached to a computer network, the data must be converted to appropriate signals. In this chapter, we primarily focus on one particular type of signal that is used to transmit data: electromagnetic waves. All of the forms of information that we have discussed (audio, data, image, and video) can be represented by electromagnetic signals and transmitted over a suitable transmission medium.

We first look at the types of electromagnetic signals that are used to convey information and their fundamental characteristics. In doing so, we describe the most straightforward way in which each of the four types of information can be represented. Then we discuss the impairments that can introduce errors and inefficiencies when electromagnetic signals are used to transmit data. In the final section of the chapter, we discuss how channel capacity is related to both signal characteristics and signal impairments.

Individuals interested in the business aspects of computer networks benefit from mastering the concepts discussed in this chapter in several ways. Most importantly, knowing the fundamentals of computer networks provides the foundation for understanding more advanced computer network topics discussed in subsequent chapters. This chapter introduces multiple terms that will help you interact in a knowledgeable manner with network professionals. It also helps you understand the factors that limit the data transmission capacity of communication channels and provides some insight into why all forms of communication (voice, data, image, and video) are migrating from analog to digital transmission systems.

4.1 SIGNALS FOR CONVEYING INFORMATION

Electromagnetic Signals

Nearly all signals used for communications are part of the electromagnetic spectrum. Electromagnetic energy travels in waves that radiate outward from its source. In computer network, the source is generically called a transmitter and the electromagnetic energy that is created by the transmitter is carried over transmission media in the form of electromagnetic waves. Common examples of the propagation of electromagnetic energy include the transmission of electrical energy over wires and the broadcasting of radio signals. Visible light is another example of the propagation of electromagnetic energy.

As noted in Chapter 2, data can exist in either analog or digital form. Analog data are represented as continuous waveforms that, at any given point in time, can be at an infinite number of points between a maximum and minimum value. Music and video, in their natural states, are examples of analog data. So is the human voice. When a person speaks into the mouthpiece of a traditional telephone, the receiver in the mouthpiece converts the air-born speech waveforms into analog electromagnetic waves that have maximum and minimum voltage levels.

There are several fundamental characteristics of electromagnetic signals that are important to understanding how data are transmitted in computer networks. First, time and time intervals are components of the definitions of most fundamental electromagnetic signal concepts. When expressed mathematically, an electromagnetic signal is a function of time. However, an electromagnetic signal can also be expressed as a function of frequency; that is, the transmitted signal consists of components of different frequencies. Most signals, including voice, video and audio signals, are actually composed of multiple frequencies. It is the presence of multiple frequencies that enable us to distinguish one musical instrument from another, or one person's voice from another's. While it is important to understand that electromagnetic signals can be viewed from either the time or frequency perspective, at the end of the day, the frequency view of a signal is most important for understanding data transmission. The reasons will become clear when we talk about signal impairments, such as noise, and how their effects can be minimized in computer networks.

Both the time and frequency views of electromagnetic signals are introduced here.

TIME PERSPECTIVE CONCEPTS   Viewed as a function of time, an electromagnetic signal can be either analog or digital. An **analog signal** is one in which the signal intensity varies in a smooth fashion over time. In other words, there are no breaks or discontinuities in the signal. A **digital signal** is one in which the signal intensity maintains a constant level for some period of time and then changes to another constant level. Figure 4.1 shows examples of both kinds of signals. The analog signal might represent speech, music, or video, and the digital signal might represent binary 1s and 0s.

The simplest sort of signal is a **periodic signal**, in which the same signal pattern repeats over time. Figure 4.2 shows an example of a periodic analog signal (sine wave) and a periodic digital signal (square wave). The sine wave is the fundamental analog signal. A general sine wave can be represented by three basic components: peak amplitude (A), frequency (f), and phase (ϕ). The **peak amplitude** is the maximum height of the wave above or below a given reference point. It represents the strength of the signal over time; typically, this value is measured in volts. In some cases, the amplitude can denote the power level of signal measure in watts, or the current level of the signal measured in amps, but most frequently, it represents the voltage level of the signal.

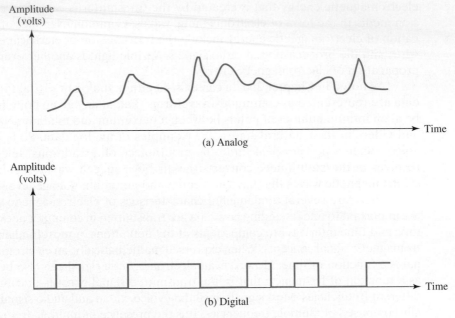

Amplitude (volts)

Time

(a) Analog

Amplitude (volts)

Time

(b) Digital

Figure 4.1 Analog and Digital Waveforms

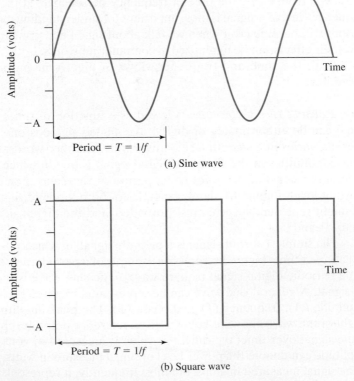

Amplitude (volts)

A

0

Time

$-A$

Period $= T = 1/f$

(a) Sine wave

Amplitude (volts)

A

0

Time

$-A$

Period $= T = 1/f$

(b) Square wave

Figure 4.2 Examples of Periodic Signals

The **frequency** is the number of times the signal makes a complete cycle within a given time frame. The number of complete signal repetitions per second is typically expressed in cycles per second, or hertz (Hz). The length, or time interval, for one cycle is called the signal's **period** (T). The period can be calculated as the reciprocal of the frequency (f), that is, the period is equal to 1/frequency (or $T = 1/f$). **Phase** is a measure of the position of the waveform relative to a given moment of time within the period of a signal. It is illustrated more fully later in the chapter.

The general sine wave can be mathematically expressed as follows:

$$s(t) = A \sin(2\pi ft + \phi)$$

Figure 4.3 shows the effect of varying each of the three components (amplitude, frequency, and phase). In part (a) of the figure, the frequency is 1 Hz; thus the period is $T = 1$ second. Part (b) illustrates a sine wave that has the same frequency and phase as that in part (a) but only has a peak amplitude of 0.5. Part (c) illustrates a sine wave that has the same peak amplitude and phase as that in part (a) but its frequency per second is 2 ($f = 2$); this means that the period for the wave in part (c) is half the size of that for the wave in part (a); that is, $T - 1/2$.

Part (d) of Figure 4.3 illustrates a 45-degree phase shift for the sine wave depicted in part (a). In part (a), the waveform oscillates up and down in a repeating pattern and never makes an abrupt change. A phase shift (change) involves jumping forward (or backward) in the waveform at a given point in time. Jumping forward by one half of the signal's complete cycle represents a 180-degree phase shift; jumping forward by one quarter of the cycle produces a 90 degree phase change. In part (d) of Figure 4.3, the phase shift is 45-degrees, the equivalent of jumping ahead in the waveform

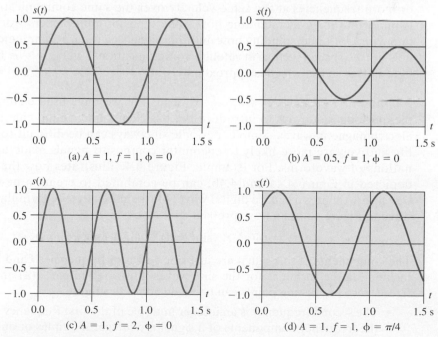

(a) $A = 1$, $f = 1$, $\phi = 0$

(b) $A = 0.5$, $f = 1$, $\phi = 0$

(c) $A = 1$, $f = 2$, $\phi = 0$

(d) $A = 1$, $f = 1$, $\phi = \pi/4$

Figure 4.3 $s(t) = A \sin(2\pi ft + \Phi)$

by one eighth of the cycle. (A 45-degree shift can be represented mathematically as $\pi/4$ radians; mathematically, a complete cycle of the waveform is 2π radians $= 360° = 1$ period.) Phase shifts of 45, 135, 225, and 315 degrees are quite common in analog data communication systems.

In Figure 4.3 the horizontal axis is time; the graphs display the value of a signal at a given point in space as a function of time. These same graphs, with a change of scale, can be used to display the value of a signal at a given point in time as a function of distance. For example, for a sinusoidal transmission (say, an electromagnetic radio wave some distance from a radio antenna or a sound some distance from loudspeaker) at a particular instant of time, the intensity of the signal varies in a sinusoidal way as a function of distance from the source. Another way of saying this is that signal becomes less intense as it gets further from the source.

Wavelength is the concept that helps us understand why the same sine way can be expressed as a function of time or space. The **wavelength** (λ) of a signal is defined as the distance occupied by a single cycle, or put another way, the distance between two points of corresponding phase of two consecutive cycles, such as maximum amplitudes or where the wave crosses zero. Wavelength is often measured in meters. Wavelength may be easiest to understand by considering a situation in which two sine waves with different frequencies are transmitted by the same source and travel at the same velocity v. The wavelength of each wave is related to its period as follows: $\lambda = vT$ (wavelength $=$ velocity $\times$ spatial period). Mathematically, this means that $\lambda f = v$ (wavelength $\times$ frequency $=$ velocity). For two waveforms traveling at the same velocity, the one with the lower frequency has the greater wavelength.

As is shown in Chapter 6, understanding how it is possible to transmit two or more frequencies at the same velocity over the same communication medium is important for understanding how some types of multiplexers work. It is also important for understanding how multiple signals can share communication channels in free space (such as in satellite communications) where $v = c$, the speed of light in free space, which is approximately 3×10^8 m/s.

FREQUENCY PERSPECTIVE CONCEPTS   Thus far, we have used examples of simple, periodic sine ways to introduce the basic components and characteristics of electromagnetic waves. Simple, periodic sine ways can be difficult to find in real life and you are more likely to encounter composite signals made up of combinations of waveforms. For example, Figure 4.4c illustrates how the sine waves depicted in Figure 4.4a and 4.4b, can be combined to create a new sine wave that approximates a square digital wave. Mathematically, the formula for the sine wave in Figure 4.4c can be expressed as:

$$s(t) = (4/\pi) \times (\sin(2\pi f t) + (1/3)\sin(2\pi(3f)t))$$

The components of this signal are just sine waves of frequencies f and $3f$ which are included in the formulas for the sine waves illustrated in parts (a) and (b) of the figure. Two interesting points can be made about this figure:

- The second frequency is an integer multiple of the first frequency. When all of the frequency components of a signal are integer multiples of one frequency, the latter frequency is referred to as the **fundamental frequency**.

- The period of the total signal is equal to the period of the fundamental frequency. This can be seen in Figure 4.4c (the period of the component $\sin(2\pi ft)$ is $T = 1/f$, and the period of s(t) is also T).

By adding together enough sinusoidal signals, each with the appropriate amplitude, frequency, and phase, any electromagnetic signal can be constructed. Put another way, any electromagnetic signal can be shown to consist of a collection of periodic analog signals (sine waves) at different amplitudes, frequencies, and phases.

Figures 4.4 and 4.5 illustrate that multiple analog signals can be combined to produce a digital signal. The process for doing so is best explained in a branch of mathematics known as Fourier analysis, which shows that any complex, periodic waveform (including a digital signal) is a composite of simpler periodic waveforms. By adding more waveforms (that are integer multiples of the fundamental frequency) to the composite waveform illustrated in Figure 4.4c, the more closely it would resemble the square digital signal in Figure 4.5c. This composite signal would increasingly both look and behave like a digital signal. Although digital signals are often described as having nothing in common with analog signals, they are, in fact, composed of a combination of sine ways.

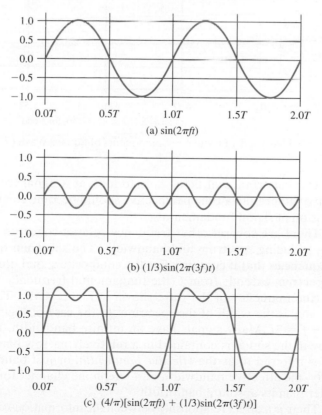

(a) $\sin(2\pi ft)$

(b) $(1/3)\sin(2\pi(3f)t)$

(c) $(4/\pi)[\sin(2\pi ft) + (1/3)\sin(2\pi(3f)t)]$

Figure 4.4 Addition of Frequency Components ($T = 1/f$)

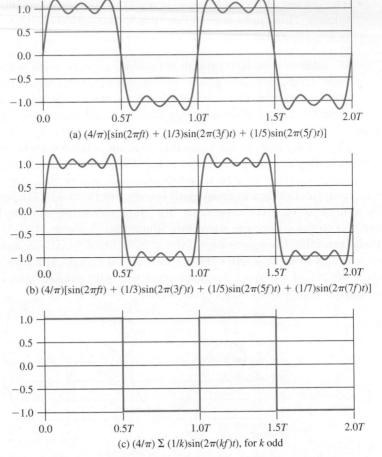

(a) $(4/\pi)[\sin(2\pi ft) + (1/3)\sin(2\pi(3f)t) + (1/5)\sin(2\pi(5f)t)]$

(b) $(4/\pi)[\sin(2\pi ft) + (1/3)\sin(2\pi(3f)t) + (1/5)\sin(2\pi(5f)t) + (1/7)\sin(2\pi(7f)t)]$

(c) $(4/\pi) \Sigma (1/k)\sin(2\pi(kf)t)$, for k odd

Figure 4.5   Frequency Components of Square Wave ($T = 1/f$)

The importance of being able to look at a signal from the frequency perspective rather than a time perspective should become clearer as we continue our discussion of signal fundamentals.

There are several other frequency-related concepts that are important to know, including spectrum and bandwidth. The **spectrum** of a signal is the range of frequencies that it contains. For the composite signal illustrated in Figure 4.4c, the spectrum extends from f (the fundamental frequency shown in Figure 4.4a) to $3f$ (the frequency of the wave shown in Figure 4.4b). The *absolute bandwidth* of a signal is the width of the spectrum. In the case of Figure 4.4c, the bandwidth is $3f - f = 2f$. Many signals have an infinite bandwidth. However, most of the energy in the signal is contained in a relatively narrow band of frequencies. This band is referred to as the *effective bandwidth*, or just **bandwidth**. As we will see shortly, the effective bandwidth of a telephone channel for human voice is much smaller than its absolute bandwidth.

There is a direct relationship between the information-carrying capacity of a signal and its bandwidth: The greater the bandwidth, the higher the information-carrying capacity. As a very simple example, consider the square wave of Figure 4.2b. Suppose that we let a positive pulse (at level A) represent the binary digit 0 and a negative pulse (level −A) represent the binary digit 1. This means that the waveform represents a stream of binary digits 0101.... The duration (time interval) of each pulse is one half of the signal's period ($[1/2]T$ or $1/[2f]$); thus the data rate is two pulses per period T or $2f$ bits per second (bps).

What are the frequency components of the signal in Figure 4.2b? To answer this question, consider again Figure 4.4. By adding together sine waves at frequencies f and $3f$, we get a waveform that begins to resemble the original square wave. Let us continue this process by adding a sine wave of frequency $5f$, as shown in Figure 4.5a, and then adding a sine wave of frequency $7f$, as shown in Figure 4.5b. As we add additional odd multiples of f, suitably scaled, the resulting waveform approaches that of a square wave more and more closely.[1]

What happens if we limit the bandwidth to just the first three frequency components? We have already seen the answer, in Figure 4.5a. As we can see, the shape of the resulting waveform is reasonably close to that of the original square wave.

We can also use Figures 4.4 and 4.5 to illustrate the relationship between data rate and bandwidth. Suppose that we are using a digital transmission system that is capable of transmitting signals with a bandwidth of 4 MHz. Let us attempt to transmit a sequence of alternating 1s and 0s as the square wave of Figure 4.5c. What data rate can be achieved? We look at three cases.

Case I. Let us approximate our square wave with the waveform of Figure 4.5a. Although this waveform is a "distorted" square wave, it is sufficiently close to the square wave that a receiver should be able to discriminate between a binary 0 and a binary 1.[2] In this case, for a bandwidth of 4 MHz, a data rate of 2 Mbps is achieved.

Case II. Now suppose that we have a bandwidth of 8 MHz. Let us look again at Figure 4.5a, but now with $f = 2$ MHz; in this case, the effective data rate is 4 Mbps.[3] Thus, other things being equal, by doubling the bandwidth, we double the potential data rate.

---

[1]Indeed, it can be shown that the frequency components of the square wave with amplitudes A and $−A$ can be expressed as follows:

$$s(t) = A \times \frac{4}{\pi} \times \sum_{k\,\text{odd},\,k=1}^{\infty} \frac{\sin(2\pi kft)}{k}$$

Thus, this waveform has an infinite number of frequency components and hence an infinite bandwidth. However, the peak amplitude of the kth frequency component, kf, is only $1/k$, so most of the energy in this waveform is in the first few frequency components.

[2]If we let $f = 10^6$ cycles/second = 1 MHz, then the bandwidth of the signal

$$s(t) = \frac{4}{\pi} \times \left[\sin\big((2\pi \times 10^6)t\big) + \frac{1}{3} \sin\big((2\pi \times 3 \times 10^6)t\big) + \frac{1}{5} \sin\big((2\pi \times 5 \times 10^6)t\big) \right]$$

is $(5 \times 10^6) − 10^6 = 4$ MHz. Note that for $f = 1$ MHz, the period of the fundamental frequency is $T = 1/10^6 = 10^{-6} = 1$ μs. If we treat this waveform as a bit string of 1s and 0s, one bit occurs every 0.5 μs, for a data rate of $2 \times 10^6 = 2$ Mbps.

[3]Using the same line of reasoning as before, the bandwidth of the signal is $(5 \times 2 \times 10^6) − (2 \times 10^6) = 8$ MHz. But in this case $T = 1/f = 0.5$ μs. As a result, one bit occurs every 0.25 μs for a data rate of 4 Mbps.

Case III. Now suppose that the waveform of Figure 4.4c is considered adequate for approximating a square wave. That is, the difference between a positive and negative pulse in Figure 4.4c is sufficiently distinct that the waveform can be successfully used to represent a sequence of 1s and 0s; in this case, the bandwidth and data rate are the same, 4 Mbps.[4]

To summarize,

- **Case I:** Bandwidth = 4 MHz; data rate = 2 Mbps
- **Case II:** Bandwidth = 8 MHz; data rate = 4 Mbps
- **Case III:** Bandwidth = 4 MHz; data rate = 4 Mbps

Thus, a given bandwidth can support various data rates depending on the ability of the receiver to discern the difference between 0 and 1 in the presence of noise and other impairments.

Let us summarize the major points that we can take away from the preceding discussion. First, a digital signal is an electromagnetic signal that is a composite of many analog sine waves. The more components it includes, the closer it gets to a perfectly square waveform such as that depicted in Figure 4.2b. Second, any perfectly square waveform has infinite bandwidth. This means that digital signals have, in theory, infinite information-carrying capacity. For example, by reducing the duration of the pulses used to represent binary 0s and 1s, we can transmit proportionately more information in a given time period. This leads to the third major point: when digital signals are transmitted over a communication medium, the transmission system that is used limits the amount of information that can be transmitted. For any given medium, greater bandwidth is associated with greater cost; if a business wants to transmit greater volumes of data over the same medium, it has to invest more in the transmission system to make this possible. This causes businesses to seek an acceptable balance between bandwidth and communication cost by pushing as much information as possible across the medium even if this means using a less than ideal waveform to carry data. Hence, given a choice between Case II and Case III, businesses may be motivated to choose Case III, especially if there is more cost associated with acquiring the additional bandwidth associated with Case II.

As we discuss in Section 4.2, limiting bandwidth increases the possibility that signal impairments create distortions that make it more difficult for receivers to properly interpret the signals that they receive. The more limited the bandwidth, the greater the distortion and the greater the potential for error by the receiver.

Analog Signals

AUDIO SIGNALS   Just as an analog signal is one whose value varies in a continuous fashion, analog information is information that takes on continuous values. Analog information was introduced in Chapter 2.

---

[4]Assume as in Case II that $f = 2$ MHz and $T = 1/f = 0.5$ μs, so that one bit occurs every 0.25 μs for a data rate of 4 Mbps. Using the waveform of Figure 4.4c, the bandwidth of the signal is $(3 \times 2 \times 10^6) - (2 \times 10^6) = 4$ MHz.

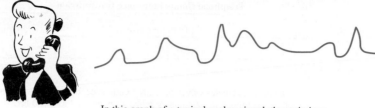

In this graph of a typical analog signal, the variations
in amplitude and frequency convey the gradations
of loudness and pitch in speech or music. Similar
signals are used to transmit television pictures, but
at much higher frequencies.

Figure 4.6   Conversion of Voice Input to Analog Signal

The most familiar example of analog information is audio, or acoustic, information, which, in the form of sound waves, can be perceived directly by human
beings. One form of acoustic information, of course, is human speech, which has
frequency components in the range 20 Hz to 20 kHz (20,000 Hz). Human speech
and other acoustic information are easily converted to an electromagnetic signal
for transmission (Figure 4.6). The conversion process involves converting the sound
frequencies, whose amplitude is measured in terms of loudness, into electromagnetic frequencies, whose amplitude is measured in volts. The traditional analog telephone handset contains a simple mechanism (a sound transducer) for making such
a conversion.

Thus, in analog telephone systems, voice sound waves are represented and
transmitted as electromagnetic signals. In order to transmit the full range of frequencies of human speech, telephone circuits with a bandwidth of 20 kHz would be
necessary. However, in practice, the bandwidth of analog voice channels in traditional telephone networks is much smaller.

The decision to compromise the fidelity (accuracy) of the sound was inten-
tional. Using a smaller bandwidth helps keep voice transmission costs reasonable;
the cost of transmission increases with increasing bandwidth. In addition, even
though human speech has a spectrum of 20 Hz to 20 kHz, tests have shown that
a much narrower bandwidth, the range 300–3400 Hz, produces acceptable voice
reproduction. That is, when frequency components of human speech that are outside that range are subtracted, the remainder sounds quite natural. For this reason,
telephone networks are able to use communication facilities that limit the transmission of sound to that narrower bandwidth (Figure 4.7).

As you can see in Figure 4.7, the actual size of a telephone channel for voice
transmission is 4 kHz, not 3.1 kHz. The extra bandwidth serves the purpose of isolating the signal transmitted in the voice channel from interference from signals in
adjacent voice channels.[5] For transmission, then, the sound transducer in the telephone handset converts the incoming voice-produced sound wave into an analog

---

[5]We show in Chapter 6 that it is common to have a number of signals occupy the same transmission
medium at different portions of the spectrum, a process known as multiplexing. The extra bandwidth, or
guardbands, prevents adjacent signals from interfering with one another.

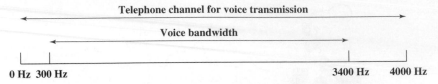

The human voice creates waves of many frequencies, but natural-sounding speech can be limited to a frequency range, or band, of 300–3400 Hz. Telephone equipment allows voice a bandwidth of 4000 Hz, which includes a guardband at each end of the frequency range to prevent interference from adjacent voice channels when a number of voice channels are multiplexed.

Figure 4.7   The Voice Band

electromagnetic signal over the range 300–3400 Hz. This signal is then transmitted over the telephone network to a telephone receiver, which reproduces a sound wave from the incoming electromagnetic signal.

VIDEO SIGNALS   A TV (television) camera functions similar to those of telephone handsets to produce a video signal to transmit to receiving TVs. One component of the camera is a photosensitive plate, upon which a scene is optically focused. An electron beam sweeps across the plate from left to right and top to bottom, in the same fashion as depicted in Figure 2.5 (which illustrates the video scanning process used in the receiver of an analog video signal). As the beam sweeps, an analog electric signal is developed proportional to the brightness of the scene at a particular spot. A total of 483 lines are scanned at a rate of 30 complete scans per second.[6]

To transmit analog video information at the necessary rate, a bandwidth of about 4 MHz is needed. As with voice transmission over the telephone network, video signaling over cable TV or via broadcast involves the use of extra bandwidth or guardbands to isolate video signals. With these guardbands, the standard bandwidth for color video signaling is 6 MHz.

Digital Signals

The term *digital signaling* usually refers to the transmission of electromagnetic pulses that represent the two binary digits, 1 and 0. For example, a constant positive voltage pulse could represent binary 0 and a constant negative voltage pulse could represent binary 1. Another alternative is to have one binary digit represented by a constant-voltage pulse and the other represented by the absence of any voltage. In either case, what is being represented is binary information. Binary information is generated by computers, terminals, and other data processing equipment and then converted into digital voltage pulses

---

[6]This is an approximate number taking into account the time lost during the vertical retrace interval. The actual U.S. standard is 525 lines, but of these, about 42 are lost during vertical retrace. Thus the horizontal scanning frequency is (525 lines) × (30 scan/s) = 15,750 lines per second, or 63.5 μs/line. Of this 63.5 μs, about 11 μs are allowed for horizontal retrace, leaving a total of 52.5 μs per video line.

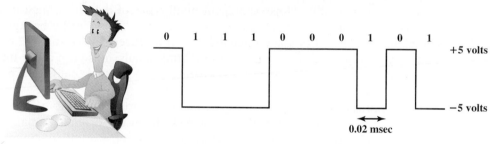

User input at a PC is converted into a stream of binary digits (1s and 0s). In this graph of a typical digital signal, binary 1 is represented by −5 volts and binary 0 is represented by +5 volts. The signal for each bit has a duration of 0.02 msec, giving a data rate of 50,000 bits per second (50 kbps).

Figure 4.8   Conversion of PC Input to Digital Signal

for transmission. This is illustrated in Figure 4.8. As mentioned in Chapter 2, numbers[7] or text is often converted into binary strings using encoding schemes such as ASCII or UTF-8. After being converted into binary form, the information can be converted into a digital signal.

It was also noted in Chapter 2 that all types of data can be represented by digital signals. The process for converting analog data, such as music, video, and voice, into binary form involves sampling and quantization. Digital encoding of analog information is discussed in Chapter 5.

4.2 TRANSMISSION IMPAIRMENTS AND CHANNEL CAPACITY

With any communications system, the signal that is received differs from the signal that is transmitted, due to various transmission impairments. Collectively, these impairments are called noise. **Noise** is electromagnetic or electrical energy that

---

[7]For humans, numbers are represented in decimal form. In the decimal system, 10 different digits are used to represent numbers. The position of each digit in a number determines its value. Thus, the decimal number 83 means eight tens plus three:

$$83 = (8 \times 10 + 3)$$

and the number 4728 means

$$4728 = (4 \times 1000) + (7 \times 100) + (2 \times 10) + 8$$

The decimal system is said to have a base of 10. This means that each digit in the number is multiplied by 10 raised to a power corresponding to that digit's position. Thus,

$$83 = (8 \times 10^1) + 3$$
$$4728 = (4 \times 10^3) + (7 \times 10^2) + (2 \times 10^1) + 8$$

In the binary system, we have only two digits, 1 and 0. Thus, numbers in the binary system are represented to the base 2. As with decimal notation, each digit in a binary number has a value depending on its position. For example,

$$10 = (1 \times 2) + 0 = \text{decimal } 2$$
$$11 = (1 \times 2) + 1 = \text{decimal } 3$$
$$100 = (1 \times 2^2) + (0 \times 2) + 0 = \text{decimal } 4$$

The binary notation can be extended to represent fractional values and negative numbers but the details for doing so are beyond the scope of this book.

degrades signal quality. Noise is present in all types of data transmission systems and its effects range from an almost imperceptible "hiss" in the background to complete signal loss. For analog signals, noise introduces various random modifications that degrade the signal quality. For digital signals, noise can cause bit errors: the signal that represents a binary 1 is distorted into a signal that is interpreted by receivers as a binary 0, and vice versa.

One of the major shortcomings of analog information and analog signals is the difficulty associated with separating noise from the original signal. Because noise occurs as an analog waveform, when it occurs, it has additive impacts on the original analog signals that can result in composite signals that distort the transmitted signal. Because noise can have debilitating impacts on signal quality, most data transmission systems attempt to reduce noise as much as possible.

In this section, we examine the major causes of noise in data transmission systems and how they impair signal quality and the information-carrying capacity of communications links. Chapter 5 looks at measures that can be taken to compensate for these impairments.

For guided media such as twisted pair, coaxial cable, and optical fiber, the most significant sources of signal quality impairments are:

- Attenuation and attenuation distortion
- Delay distortion
- Noise

With wireless transmission, signal impairments are most likely to result from:

- Free-space loss
- Atmospheric absorption
- Multipath
- Refraction
- Thermal noise

Guided Media

ATTENUATION   When an electromagnetic signal is transmitted along any medium, it gradually becomes weaker at greater distances; this is referred to as attenuation. Attenuation introduces three considerations that cannot be overlooked by network professionals:

1. A received signal must have sufficient strength so that the electronic circuitry in the receiver can properly detect and interpret the signal.
2. The signal must maintain a level sufficiently higher than noise to be received without error.
3. Attenuation is greater at higher frequencies, and this causes distortion.

The first and second considerations are dealt with by attention to signal strength and the use of amplifiers or repeaters. In computer networks, data transmission occurs between a *transmitter* and a *receiver* over a *transmission medium*.

In a very simple network, there may be a direct link between the transmitter and receiver. If the link is very short with little distance between transmitter and receiver, no measures may need to be taken to compensate for attenuation. For greater distances, attenuation becomes significant, and one or more intermediate devices are placed between the transmitter and receiver to compensate for attenuation. In the case of analog signals, an amplifier is used; the amplifier boosts the amplitude, or strength, of the signal. In the ideal case, the amplifier does not alter the information content of the signal. In practice, however, the amplifier introduces some distortion to the signal. This distortion is cumulative if multiple amplifiers are used along the path between the transmitter and receiver. In the case of digital signals, the intermediate devices used to compensate for attenuation are repeaters. The repeater receives the incoming signal on one side, recovers the original binary waveform, and transmits a new digital signal on the other side (Figure 4.9). With repeaters, there is no accumulation of distortion. However, any error made during the process used by the repeater to recover the binary waveform from the incoming signal persists for the remainder of the transmission path to the receiver.

The third consideration, known as *attenuation distortion*, is particularly noticeable for analog signals. Because attenuation is different for different frequencies, and because most analog signals are composite signals made up of a number of components at different frequencies, the received signal is not only reduced in strength but is also distorted. To overcome this problem, techniques are available for equalizing attenuation across a band of frequencies. This is commonly done for telephone lines by using loading coils that change the electrical properties of the line to smooth out attenuation effects. The types of equipment used to achieve equalization of frequency components in electronic signals are called *equalizers*.

As noted previously, digital signals are also made up of a number of frequencies. However, most of the energy in a digital signal is concentrated in a reasonably narrow band. Hence, attenuation distortion is less of a problem than it is for analog signals.

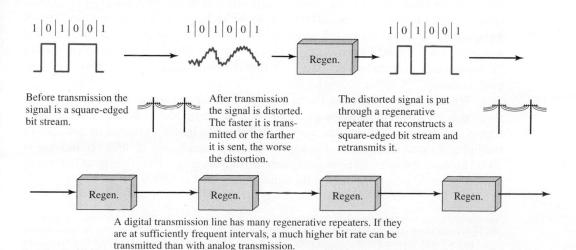

Before transmission the signal is a square-edged bit stream.

After transmission the signal is distorted. The faster it is transmitted or the farther it is sent, the worse the distortion.

The distorted signal is put through a regenerative repeater that reconstructs a square-edged bit stream and retransmits it.

A digital transmission line has many regenerative repeaters. If they are at sufficiently frequent intervals, a much higher bit rate can be transmitted than with analog transmission.

Figure 4.9 Regenerative Repeaters

DELAY DISTORTION   Delay distortion is a phenomenon that occurs in transmission cables (such as twisted pair, coaxial cable, and optical fiber); it does not occur when signals are transmitted through the air by means of antennas. Delay distortion is caused by the fact that the velocity of propagation of a signal through a cable is different for different frequencies. For a signal with a given bandwidth, the velocity tends to be highest near the center frequency of the signal and to fall off toward the two edges of the band. Thus, various components of a signal arrive at the receiver at different times.

This effect is referred to as delay distortion because the received signal is distorted due to a variable delay in its frequency components. Delay distortion is particularly critical for digital data. Because of delay distortion, some of the signal energy in one bit position spills over into other bit positions, which may cause signal interpretation errors in receivers; this is a major limitation to the data rate for digital data.

NOISE   When information is transmitted in the form of an electromagnetic signal, the received signal consists of the transmitted signal, modified by attenuation and various distortions imposed by the transmission system, plus the addition of unwanted electromagnetic energy that is inserted somewhere between transmitter and receiver. The latter, undesired signals are referred to as noise. Noise is the major limiting factor in communications system performance.

Noise may be divided into four categories:

- Thermal noise
- Intermodulation noise
- Crosstalk
- Impulse noise

Thermal noise is due to thermal agitation of electrons in a conductor. Thermal noise is always present to some degree in data communication media and is dependent on the medium's temperature. When the temperature increases, the activity level of the electrons in the medium increases and this in turn increases the level of noise on the medium. Thermal noise is uniformly distributed across the frequency spectrum and hence is often referred to as **white noise**. It is a continuous type of noise similar to the static heard between two stations when tuning a radio. Thermal noise can be reduced by passing the signal through filters, but because it cannot be completely eliminated, it places an upper bound on communications system performance.

When signals of different frequencies share the same transmission medium, the result may be *intermodulation noise*.[8] The effect of intermodulation noise is to produce signals at a frequency that is the sum or difference of the two original frequencies or multiples of those frequencies. For example, if two signals, one at 4000 Hz and one at 8000 Hz, share the same transmission medium, they might produce energy at 12,000 Hz. This noise could interfere with a third signal transmitted at 12,000 Hz.

---

[8]Intermodulation noise is produced when there is some nonlinearity in the transmitter, receiver, or intervening transmission system. Normally, these components behave as linear systems; that is, the output is equal to the input times a constant. In a nonlinear system, the output is a more complex function of the input. Such nonlinearity can be caused by component malfunction or the use of excessive signal strength. It is under these circumstances that the sum and difference terms occur.

Crosstalk has been experienced by anyone who, while having a telephone conversation, has been able to hear another telephone conversation; it is an unwanted coupling between signal paths. It can occur by electrical coupling between nearby cables (such as two sets of twisted-pair wires in a telephone line) or by the overlap of signals transmitted by antennas. Typically, crosstalk does not have a debilitating effect on signal quality. Its impact on data transmission is equivalent to, or less than, that for thermal noise.

All of the types of noise discussed so far have reasonably predictable and reasonably constant impacts on signal distortion. Thus, it is possible to engineer a transmission system to cope with them. *Impulse noise*, however, is noncontinuous, consisting of irregular pulses or noise spikes of short duration and of relatively high amplitude. Typically, it is an analog burst of energy that interferes with transmitted analog signals. It is generated from a variety of causes, including external electromagnetic disturbances, such as lightning, and faults and flaws in the communications system.

Impulse noise is generally only a minor annoyance for analog data. For example, voice transmission may be corrupted by short clicks and crackles with no loss of intelligibility. However, impulse noise is the primary source of error in digital data communication. For example, a sharp spike of energy of 0.01 s duration would not destroy any voice information but would wash out about 500 bits of data being transmitted at 56 Kbps. Figure 4.10 is an example of the effect on a digital signal.

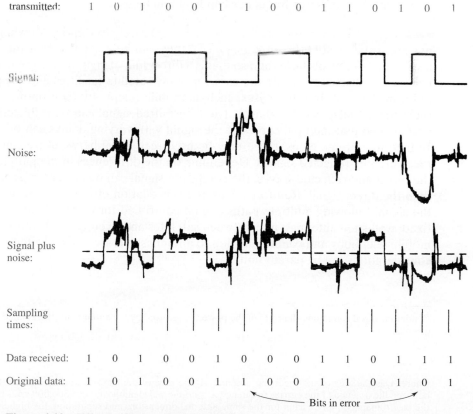

Figure 4.10   Effect of Noise on Digital Signal

Here the noise consists of a relatively modest level of thermal noise plus occasional spikes of impulse noise. The digital data are recovered from the signal by sampling the received waveform once per bit time. As can be seen, the noise is occasionally sufficient to change a 1 to a 0 or a 0 to a 1; this would cause errors during the digital waveform recovery process.

Unguided Media

FREE-SPACE LOSS   For any type of wireless communication, the signal disperses with distance. Therefore, an antenna with a fixed area receives less signal power the farther it is from the transmitting antenna. For satellite communication this is the primary mode of signal loss.[9]

ATMOSPHERIC ABSORPTION   An additional loss between the transmitting and receiving antennas is atmospheric absorption. Water vapor and oxygen contribute most to attenuation. Peak attenuation occurs in the vicinity of 22 GHz due to water vapor. At frequencies below 15 GHz, the attenuation is less. The presence of oxygen results in an absorption peak in the vicinity of 60 GHz but contributes less at frequencies below 30 GHz. Rain and fog (suspended water droplets) cause scattering of radio waves that results in attenuation. This can be a major cause of signal loss. Thus, in areas of significant precipitation, either the distance between transmitters and receivers have to be kept short or lower-frequency bands should be used.

MULTIPATH   For wireless facilities, there is a relatively free choice of where antennas are to be located. In some instances, they can be placed so that there are no nearby interfering obstacles and so that is a direct line-of-sight path from transmitter to receiver. This is generally the case for many satellite facilities and for point-to-point microwave. In other cases, such as mobile telephony (cell phone systems), there are obstacles in abundance. The transmitted signal can be reflected by such obstacles so that multiple copies of the signal with varying delays can be received. In fact, in extreme cases, there may be no direct signal between transmitter and receiver, only reflected signals. Depending on the differences in the path lengths of the direct and reflected waves, the composite signal can be either larger or smaller than the direct signal. Reinforcement and cancellation of the signal resulting from the signal following multiple paths can be controlled for communication between fixed, well-sited antennas, and between satellites and fixed ground stations, but for mobile telephony and communication to antennas that are not well sited, multipath considerations can be paramount.

----

[9]Under idealized conditions, the ratio of the power P_r received by the antenna to the radiated power P_t is given by

$$\frac{P_r}{P_t} = \frac{A_r A_t f^2}{(cd)^2}$$

where A_r is the area of the receiving antenna, A_t the area of the transmitting antenna, d the distance between the antennas, f the carrier frequency, $\lambda = c/f$ the wavelength, and c = 300,000 km/s the speed of the electromagnetic wave. Thus, for the same antenna dimensions and separation, the higher the carrier frequency f, the lower is the free-space path loss.

REFRACTION Radio waves are refracted (or bent) when they propagate through the atmosphere. The refraction is caused by changes in the speed of the signal with altitude or by other spatial changes in the atmospheric conditions. Normally, the speed of the signal increases with altitude, causing radio waves to bend downward. However, on occasion, weather conditions may lead to variations in speed with height that differ significantly from the typical variations. This may result in a situation in which only a fraction or no part of the line-of-sight wave reaches the receiving antenna.

THERMAL NOISE As noted previously, thermal or white noise is inescapable. It arises from the thermal activity of the devices and media in the communication system. Because of the weakness of the signal received by satellite earth stations, thermal noise is particularly important for satellite communication. If thermal noise at the satellite earth station is not controlled for, it could overwhelm the signal being received from the satellite.

Channel Capacity

We have seen that there are a variety of impairments that can distort or corrupt a signal. For digital data, the question that then arises is to what extent these impairments limit the data rate that can be achieved. The rate at which data can be transmitted over a given communication path, or channel, under given conditions, is referred to as the **channel capacity**.

There are four major interrelated concepts that determine channel capacity:

- **Data rate:** This is the rate, in bits per second (bps), at which data can be communicated.
- **Bandwidth:** This is the bandwidth of the transmitted signal as constrained by the transmitter and the nature of the transmission medium, expressed in cycles per second, or Hertz.
- **Noise:** This is the average level of noise over the communications path.
- **Error rate:** This is the rate at which errors occur, where an error is the reception of a 1 when a 0 was transmitted or the reception of a 0 when a 1 was transmitted.

The problem we are addressing is this: Communications systems are expensive, and, in general, the greater the bandwidth that is needed in the computer network, the greater the cost. Furthermore, almost all transmission channels that businesses are likely to consider to be affordable have limited bandwidth. Reducing noise, preventing interference, and other error prevention approaches also increase data transmission costs. Accordingly, businesses like to make as efficient use as possible of limited bandwidth channels. For digital data, this means that we would like to get as high a data rate as possible at a tolerable error rate for a given bandwidth. The main constraint on achieving desired levels of efficiency is noise.

We have already illustrated the relationship between bandwidth and data rate in Figure 4.4. All other things being equal, doubling the bandwidth doubles the data rate. Now consider the relationship among data rate, noise, and error rate. This can be explained intuitively by again considering Figure 4.10. The presence of noise can corrupt one or more bits. If the data rate is increased, the bits become "shorter," so that more bits are affected by a given pattern of noise of any duration. Thus, at a given noise level, the higher the data rate, the higher the error rate.

All of these concepts can be tied together neatly in a formula developed by the mathematician Claude Shannon. As we have just illustrated, the higher the data rate, the more damage that unwanted noise can do. For a given level of noise, we would expect that a greater signal strength would improve the ability to receive data correctly in the presence of noise. The key parameter involved in this reasoning is the *signal-to-noise ratio* (SNR, or S/N), which is the ratio of the power in a signal to the power contained in the noise that is present at a particular point in the transmission. Typically, this ratio is measured at a receiver, because it is at this point that an attempt is made to process the signal and eliminate the unwanted noise. The signal-to-noise ratio is important in the transmission of digital data because it sets the upper bound on the achievable data rate. Shannon's result is that the maximum channel capacity, in bits per second, obeys the equation

$$C = B \log_2(1 + \text{SNR})$$

where C is the capacity of the channel in bits per second and B is the bandwidth of the channel in Hertz. The Shannon formula represents the theoretical maximum that can be achieved. In practice, however, lower rates are achieved. One reason for this is that the formula assumes white noise (thermal noise). Impulse noise is not accounted for, neither are attenuation distortion or delay distortion.

Several observations concerning the Shannon equation can be made. The measure of efficiency of a digital transmission is the ratio C/B, which is the bps per Hertz value that is achieved. For a given level of noise, it would appear that the data rate could be increased by increasing the signal strength or bandwidth. However, as the signal strength increases, so do nonlinearities in the system, leading to an increase in intermodulation noise. Note also that because noise is assumed to be white, the wider the bandwidth, the more noise is admitted to the system. Thus, as B increases, SNR decreases.

APPLICATION NOTE

Analog Signals

We are surrounded by signals from a wide variety of sources. Understanding these signals can often help us get through basic problems with communications equipment. For example, cellular telephone users often learn to stand by windows to improve their reception. When we are responsible for communications systems, understanding the signals around us can be the difference between reliable and spotty connectivity.

It is interesting to note the differences between digital and analog signals. Analog communications, based largely on the modulation of a sine wave, have certainly been around for a much longer period of time. With the digital revolution in the 1970s and 1980s, analog systems were believed to be inferior. And now with advances in cellular technology and other communications systems, we all want digital communication. What is interesting is that all communication is, in fact, still analog. What is really meant by the terms *digital cellular communication* or *digital subscriber lines* is that we are converting digital information for conveyance over an analog network.

Communication in many systems, and especially communication through the air, requires an analog carrier. Even high-speed communications over fiber optics use analog-based signals. Digital cellular phones still use an analog carrier to carry the digitally encoded messages from one place to another. Even digital local area network signals can be broken down into their component analog parts.

For this reason, understanding analog signals, environmental effects, and the infrastructure type can be extremely beneficial to business organizations. Appreciation for the issues makes us better able to make appropriate choices during design phases and facilitates troubleshooting should problems occur after installation.

For guided media, problems are easier to track down and eliminate. As we discuss in Part Four's chapters, the best defense against communication problems in guided media systems is a solid installation. This is true not only for copper-based systems like Ethernet over UTP, but for fiber as well. For wireless systems, even the finest quality system can be rendered inoperable by uncontrollable, outside forces. These forces do not have to be significant events like hurricanes. Even small changes to the environment can create problems. Cellular telephone providers know this only too well as they have experienced the difference even a tree can make depending on whether or not it is wet. Local construction of a new building or fountain can create reflections or even eliminate line of sight between source and destination.

In addition to obvious problems like skyscrapers are unseen obstacles such as other sources of electromagnetic radiation. Cellular towers, radio stations, police and fire channels, Sirius XM radio, and many others can, individually or together, create problems for a local wireless system. In the case of wireless optical communications, radio interference is not a problem, but line of sight and weather conditions certainly are. Probably the worst problem in terms of weather is mist or fog, but other problems, such as heating/cooling of the transceiver platform, wind, dust, and even large trucks, can cause misalignment problems or reduce performance.

Sirius XM radio presents an interesting case of radio interference. Sirius XM radio is a satellite-based service offering primarily music and news channels over the satellite frequencies. The frequencies happen to be very close to those used by WiFi or wireless local area networks. Wireless "hotspots" have been installed in increasing numbers and these hotspots cause interference with the Sirius XM radio receivers. Because the Sirius XM radio providers paid for the license to operate in this portion of the spectrum, it was felt that their signals were improperly interfered with from an unlicensed source. Unfortunately, the vast proliferation of wireless networking equipment makes the problem difficult to fix.

The problems experienced by wired and wireless analog systems are many and varied. Even though people clamor for digital information, the reality is that we continue to rely heavily on analog transmission. Understanding how analog signals propagate, their interaction and the effect of local conditions can vastly improve our chances for successful and robust communications. It is intriguing that what we are learning about analog wired and wireless communications, amateur radio operators have known for years.

4.3 SUMMARY

All of the forms of information that are discussed in this book (audio, data, image, and video) can be represented by electromagnetic signals and transmitted over a suitable transmission medium. Depending on the transmission medium and the communications environment, either analog or digital signals can be used to convey information. Any electromagnetic signal, analog or digital, is made up of a number of constituent frequencies. A key parameter that characterizes the signal is bandwidth, which is the width of the range of frequencies that comprise the signal. Generally speaking, as the bandwidth of the signal increases so does its information-carrying capacity.

A major problem in designing a communications facility is transmission impairment. The most significant impairments are attenuation, attenuation distortion, delay distortion, and the various types of noise. The various forms of noise include thermal noise, intermodulation noise, crosstalk, and impulse noise. For analog signals, transmission impairments introduce random modifications that degrade the quality of the received information and may affect intelligibility. For digital signals, transmission impairments may cause bit errors.

The designer of a communications facility must deal with four factors: the bandwidth of the signal, the data rate that is used for digital information, the amount of noise and other impairments, and the level of error rate that is acceptable. The bandwidth is limited by the transmission medium and the desire to avoid interference with other nearby signals. Because bandwidth is a scarce resource, we would like to maximize the data rate that is achieved in a given bandwidth. The data rate is limited by the bandwidth, the presence of impairments, and the error rate that is acceptable. The efficiency of a transmission system is measured by the ratio of data rate (in bps) to bandwidth (in Hz). Efficiencies of between 1 and 5 bps/Hz are considered good.

4.4 KEY TERMS, REVIEW QUESTIONS, AND PROBLEMS

Key Terms

amplitude	frequency	phase
analog signal	fundamental frequency	radian
attenuation	Hertz	sine wave
bandwidth	noise	spectrum
channel capacity	peak amplitude	square wave
delay distortion	period	wavelength
digital signal	periodic signal	white noise

Review Questions

4.1 What is the difference between an analog electromagnetic signal and a digital electromagnetic signal?

4.2 What is peak amplitude?

4.3   Give three examples of the propagation of electromagnetic energy.

4.4   What is the period of a signal? How is it measured?

4.5   What is the complete cycle of a waveform?

4.6   When is a frequency called a fundamental frequency?

4.7   What is the phase of a signal?

4.8   What is a square wave?

4.9   What is the relationship between a signal's spectrum and its bandwidth?

4.10 Why do telephone networks have voice channels with a bandwidth that is much narrower than the spectrum of the human voice?

4.11 What is free-space loss?

4.12 How can atmospheric absorption be reduced in areas of significant precipitation?

4.13 Define error rate.

4.14 What is thermal noise?

4.15 What are the different sources of signal quality impairments for guided media?

4.16 What is intermodulation noise?

4.17 What is crosstalk and how does it affect a signal?

4.18 Briefly describe the limitations of analog signals.

4.19 Define absolute bandwidth.

4.20 How can the efficiency of a transmission system be measured?

Problems

4.1   A signal has a fundamental frequency of 1000 Hz. What is its period?

4.2   What is the bandwidth of a signal composed of frequencies from 50 Hz to 5000 Hz?

4.3   Find and view several YouTube videos that focus on describing the fundamental characteristics of sine waves: amplitude, frequency, wavelength, and period. Provide the URLs for the three that you think do the best job explaining these concepts. If you could only recommend one video to others, which would you pick? Why?

4.4   Explain why data transmission costs increase as bandwidth increases.

4.5   What type of noise is most difficult to remove from a digital signal? Why?

4.6   What type of noise is most difficult to remove from an analog signal? Why?

4.7   What types of signals are susceptible to intermodulation distortion?

4.8   Do some Internet research on Shannon's theorem. Identify several references that you think do a good job explaining the relationships among the components of the equation. Summarize that guidance that Shannon's theorem provides network planners.

4.9   Why can noise reduction in computer networks be costly?

DATA COMMUNICATION FUNDAMENTALS

CHAPTER 5

The transmission of data across a transmission medium in a business network involves more than simply inserting a signal on the medium. A considerable degree of cooperation between devices at either end of the medium is needed. This chapter and the next discuss the essential mechanisms involved in the successful transmission of data between two devices across a transmission medium. First, we discuss the distinction between analog and digital transmission. Then we discuss the ways in which signals can be encoded for effective and efficient communication. Next, we look at the issue of synchronization: in order to correctly decode the incoming signal, the receiver must know when each arriving bit begins and ends so that it can keep pace with the transmitter. Several common techniques for synchronizing the receiver with the transmitter are described. Finally, this chapter introduces the concept of error detection.

5.1 ANALOG AND DIGITAL DATA COMMUNICATIONS

Electromagnetic signals, which are capable of propagation on a variety of transmission media, can be used to convey data. The exact way in which these signals are encoded to convey data determines the efficiency and reliability of the transmission. This section introduces some basic concepts that are essential to understanding how data are passed from sender to receiver over a transmission medium.

The terms *analog* and *digital* correspond, roughly, to *continuous* and *discrete*, respectively. These two terms are frequently used in data communications in at least three contexts: data, signaling, and transmission.

Signals and data are fundamental components in computer networks and it is important to understand how they differ. Signals are used to represent data that is passed across a computer network and data must be converted into appropriate signals by transmitters that can be correctly interpreted by receivers.

The use of these terms in different contexts is often the source of confusion in articles and books. In this section, we clarify the various uses of these two terms. Briefly, we define **data** as entities that convey meaning, or information. **Signals** are electric or electromagnetic representations of data. **Signaling** is the physical propagation of the signal along a communication medium. **Transmission** is the communication of data across a computer network by the propagation and processing of signals.

Many different types of data are captured, transmitted, and stored in business networks. As we have seen in the previous chapters, audio, video, and image have joined text and numbers as important types of business data. We have also observed that some forms of data are analog while others are digital.

Analog data take on continuous values on some interval. For example, voice and video are continuously varying patterns of intensity. Most data collected by sensors, such as temperature and pressure, also have continuous values. **Digital data** take on discrete values; examples are text, integers, and binary data. To transmit either type of data from one point to another over a wired or wireless medium, the data has to be converted into signals. Hence, signals are used to encode and transmit data and different types of equipment are used to convert data into signals, and vice versa, depending on the type of data (analog or digital) and the type of transmission facilities (analog or digital) in the network.

One of the major takeaways from Chapter 4 is that electromagnetic signals are the basis of data transmission in business and other communication systems. An **analog signal** is a continuously varying electromagnetic wave that may be transmitted over both guided and unguided media. The components of analog (sine) waveforms, amplitude, frequency, and phase can be used to convey data. A **digital signal** is a sequence of voltage pulses that may be transmitted over a wired medium; for example, a constant positive voltage may represent binary 0, and a constant negative value may represent binary 1. The principal advantages of digital signaling are that it is generally cheaper than analog signaling and is less susceptible to noise interference. The principal disadvantage is that digital signals suffer more from attenuation than do analog signals. Note that digital signaling is possible only on copper media and cannot be used on optical fiber or wireless media.

Both analog and digital data can be represented by either analog or digital signals; this is illustrated in Figure 5.1. The trend today is decidedly toward digital transmission, wherever this can be used. Local area networks, which are designed for transmitting computer data, have always supported digital signals. LANs have made the use of digital signals to transmit both digital and analog data commonplace in businesses of all sizes. However, there is still a lot of communications equipment in place that is only capable of transmitting data as analog signals so it remains important to have a fundamental understanding about both analog and digital data transmission.

Converting analog data to analog signals is quite common. Transmitter technologies in traditional telephones, broadcast television, analog cable television, and AM and FM radio use modulation techniques that enable sound and/or video waveforms to be conveyed as electromagnetic waveforms over wires or airwaves. In some instances, the electromagnetic waves that are transmitted are nearly identical to the waveforms for the original analog waveforms; the transmitted frequency range (spectrum) may be the same and in most respects, these are electromagnetic equivalents of the original analog waveform. This is essentially what happens when transducers in analog telephone handsets convert voice sounds to electromagnetic sine waves that are carried over the telephone network. In other instances,

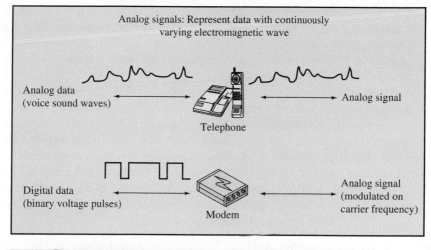

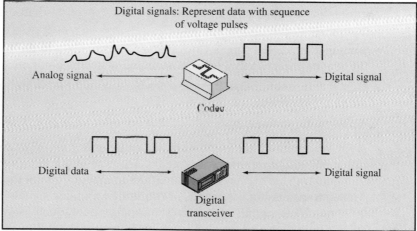

Figure 5.1   Analog and Digital Signaling of Analog and Digital Data

the analog data are converted into an analog signal whose frequency range is different from that for the original data. An example is the transmission of an FM radio broadcast over an analog cable TV channel.

Converting digital data to analog signals involves the use of a **modem** (modulator/demodulator). The modem converts a series of incoming binary voltage pulses, which represent binary 0s and 1s, into an analog signal by modulating a *carrier frequency*. The resulting signal occupies a certain spectrum of frequency centered about the carrier. The most common modems, dial-up modems, represent digital data in the voice spectrum and hence enable digital data to be propagated over ordinary voice-grade telephone lines. At the other end of the line, a modem demodulates the signal to recover the original data. The major varieties of modulation techniques used by modems are discussed later in this section.

In an operation very similar to that performed by a modem, analog data can be represented by a digital signal. The device that performs this function is a

codec (coder/decoder). In essence, the codec takes an analog signal that directly represents voice, audio, or video data and approximates that signal by a bit stream. At the other end of a line, the bit stream is used to reconstruct the analog data. The basic process used by codecs to perform this conversion is discussed in Section 5.2.

Finally, digital data can be represented directly, in binary form, by two voltage levels, one to represent a binary 1 and the other to represent a binary 0. To improve propagation characteristics and synchronization between transmitters and receivers, however, the binary data may be encoded into digital signals that use voltage-level transitions, rather than constant-voltage levels, to represent the binary data. The major types of digital data encoding are outlined in Section 5.2.

Each of the four combinations just described is in widespread use. The reasons why businesses choose a particular combination for any given communications task vary. Some of the representative reasons include:

- **Digital data, digital signal:** In general, the equipment for encoding digital data into a digital signal is less complex and less expensive than digital-to-analog equipment.

- **Analog data, digital signal:** Conversion of analog data to digital form permits the use of modern digital transmission and switching equipment.

- **Digital data, analog signal:** Some transmission media, such as optical fiber and satellite, only propagate analog signals.

- **Analog data, analog signal:** Analog data are easily converted to an analog signal.

A final distinction remains to be made. Both analog and digital signals may be transmitted on suitable transmission media. The way these signals are treated is a function of the transmission system. Table 5.1 summarizes the methods of transmission. **Analog transmission** is a means of transmitting analog signals without regard to their content; the signals may represent analog data (such as voice) or digital data (such as data that pass through a modem). In either case, the analog signal suffers attenuation, which limits the length of the transmission link. To achieve longer distances, the analog transmission system includes amplifiers that boost the energy in the signal. Unfortunately, the amplifier also boosts the noise components of any signal. With amplifiers cascaded to achieve long distance, the signal has the potential to become more and more distorted. For analog data, such as voice, quite a bit of distortion can be tolerated and the data (spoken words) remain intelligible. However, for digital data transmitted as analog signals, cascaded amplifiers are likely to increase the number of errors.

Digital transmission, by contrast, is concerned with the content of the signal. In general, a digital signal can be propagated only a limited distance before attenuation endangers the integrity of the data represented by the signal. To achieve greater distances, repeaters are used. A repeater receives the digital signal, recovers the pattern of ones and zeros, and retransmits a new signal. Thus the attenuation is overcome.

The same technique may be used with an analog signal if it is assumed that the signal carries digital data. At appropriately spaced points, the transmission system has retransmission devices rather than amplifiers. The retransmission device

Table 5.1   Analog and Digital Transmission

(a) Data and Signals

	Analog Signal	Digital Signal
Analog Data	Two alternatives: (1) signal occupies the same spectrum as the analog data; (2) analog data are encoded to occupy a different portion of spectrum.	Analog data are encoded using a codec to produce a digital bit stream.
Digital Data	Digital data are encoded using a modem to produce analog signal.	Two alternatives: (1) signal consists of two voltage levels to represent the two binary values; (2) digital data are encoded to produce a digital signal with desired properties.

(b) Treatment of Signals

	Analog Transmission	Digital Transmission
Analog Signal	Is propagated through amplifiers; same treatment whether signal is used to represent analog data or digital data.	Assumes that the analog signal represents digital data. Signal is propagated through repeaters; at each repeater, digital data are recovered from inbound signal and is used to generate a new analog outbound signal.
Digital Signal	Not used	A digital signal represents a stream of 1s and 0s, which may represent digital data or may be an encoding of analog data. The signal is propagated through repeaters; at each repeater, stream of 1s and 0s is recovered from inbound signal and is used to generate a new digital outbound signal.

recovers the digital data from the analog signal and generates a new, clean analog signal. Thus noise is not cumulative. This process is illustrated in Figure 4.9.

The question naturally arises as to which is the preferred method of transmission of business data. The answer being supplied by the telecommunications industry and its business customers is digital, despite the enormous investments that were made in analog communications facilities during the last century. Today, both long-haul and intrabuilding networks are being converted to digital transmission and, where possible, digital signaling techniques. The most important reasons for this are summarized in Table 5.2.

We now turn to an examination of each of the major forms of signal encoding. We consider analog encoding of digital data, digital encoding of analog data, digital encoding of digital data, and analog encoding of analog data.

5.2   DATA ENCODING TECHNIQUES

As we have pointed out, data, either analog or digital, must be converted into a signal for purposes of transmission.

In the case of digital data, different signal elements are used to represent binary 1 and binary 0. The mapping from binary digits to signal elements is the *encoding scheme* for transmission. Encoding schemes are designed to minimize

Table 5.2   Advantages of Digital Transmission

Cost

The evolution of digital circuitry has resulted in a continuing drop in the cost and size of digital circuitry. Analog equipment has not shown similar declines. Further, maintenance costs for digital circuits are often a fraction of those for analog circuits.

Fewer Errors: Higher Integrity of Transmitted Data

Because transmitted data is binary, it is easier to detect and correct errors. With the use of digital repeaters rather than analog amplifiers, the effects of noise and other signal impairments are not cumulative. This makes it possible to transmit data over longer distances with fewer errors thereby maintaining the integrity of the transmitted data.

Greater Efficiency and Capacity Utilization

It is possible to send more data through digital circuits. It has become economical to build transmission links of very high bandwidth, including optical fiber and satellite channels. A high degree of multiplexing is needed to effectively utilize such capacity, and this is more easily and cheaply achieved with digital (time division) rather than analog (frequency division) techniques (see Chapter 6).

Security and Privacy

Encryption techniques can be readily applied to digital data and to analog data that have been digitized.

Simpler Integration of Voice, Data, and Video

By treating both analog and digital information digitally, all signals have the same form and can be treated similarly. This makes them easier to combine on the same circuit. Economies of scale, convenience, and convergence of voice, video, image, and data traffic can be realized.

---

errors in determining the start and end of each bit and errors in determining whether each bit is a 1 or a 0.

For analog data, the encoding scheme is designed to enhance the quality, or fidelity, of transmission. That is, we would like the received analog data to be an accurate and exact reproduction of the transmitted data.

Analog Encoding of Digital Information

The basis for analog encoding is a continuous constant-frequency signal known as the *carrier signal*. Digital information is encoded by means of a **modem** that modulates one of the three characteristics of the carrier: amplitude, frequency, or phase, or some combination of these. Figure 5.2 illustrates the three basic forms of modulation of analog signals for digital data:

- Amplitude-shift keying
- Frequency-shift keying
- Phase-shift keying

In all these cases, the resulting signal contains a range of frequencies on both sides of the carrier frequency; this range is the bandwidth of the transmitted signal.

In **amplitude-shift keying (ASK)**, digital data are represented as variations in the different amplitudes of the carrier wave. In its most simple form, one binary digit (typically a 1) is represented by the presence of the carrier wave, the other (typically a 0) by the absence of the carrier. This is illustrated in Figure 5.2a. In other cases, one amplitude shift represents a binary 1 and a second amplitude shift

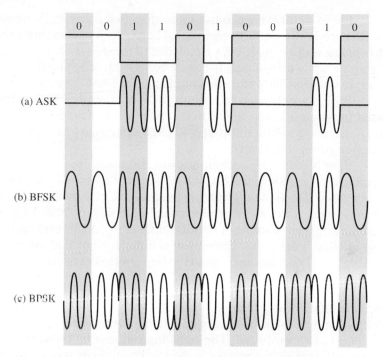

Figure 5.2   Modulation of Analog Signals for Digital Data

represents a binary 0. ASK is susceptible to sudden gain changes from noise, distortions, and other signal impairments. This makes it a rather inefficient modulation technique. However, ASK modulation and demodulation techniques are inexpensive and this can increase its attractiveness for business networks.

The ASK technique is also commonly used to transmit digital data over optical fiber. For LED transmitters, binary 1 is represented by a short pulse of light and binary 0 by the absence of light. Laser transmitters normally have a fixed "bias" current that causes the device to emit a low light level. This low level represents binary 0, while a higher-amplitude lightwave represents binary 1.

In **frequency-shift keying (FSK)**, digital information is transmitted through discrete frequency changes of the carrier wave. The simplest form of FSK is called binary FSK (BFSK), in which the two binary values are represented by two different frequencies near the carrier frequency. BSFK is illustrated in Figure 5.2b. FSK is less susceptible to noise and other error sources than ASK; it is easy to decode and often has a better signal-to-noise ratio than ASK. FSK is a signaling option supported by most dial-up modems. It is also commonly used for high-frequency (4–30 MHz) radio transmission.

In **phase-shift keying (PSK)**, the phase of the carrier signal is shifted to encode data. Figure 5.2c is an example of a two-phase system. In this system, a 0 is represented by sending a signal burst of the same phase as the preceding signal burst sent. A 1 is represented by sending a signal burst of opposite phase to the preceding one. Figure 5.2c represents binary phase-shift keying (BPSK) which uses two shifts separated by 180°.

Phase-shift keying can use more than two phase shifts. A four-phase system could encode two bits with each signal burst. Such systems are examples of *quadrature phase-shift keying (QPSK)*. Relative to BFSK, QFSK can be used to double the data rate while maintaining the same bandwidth. The phase-shift keying technique is more noise resistant and efficient than either ASK or FSK.

PSK is widely used in business networks, especially wireless networks. It is used in wireless LANs and RFID (radio frequency identification) applications. It is also used in Bluetooth and ZigBee systems as well as in modems used for satellite communications.

Finally, the basic techniques just discussed may be combined. A common combination is PSK and ASK, where some or all of the phase shifts may occur at one or two amplitudes. These techniques are referred to as *multilevel* signaling because each signal element represents multiple bits. Note that four-phase phase-shift keying is an example of multilevel signaling. Multilevel signaling is in common use in today's networks. Examples include 56 Kbps dial-up modems, digital subscriber line (DSL) modems, and Gigabit Ethernet networks.

DATA RATE AND SIGNALING RATE   With multilevel signaling, we must distinguish between data rate, which is the rate, in bits per second, at which bits are transmitted, and modulation rate, or signaling rate, which is the rate at which signal elements are transmitted. The signaling rate can be thought of as the number of times different signal pulses can be transmitted per second by the transmitter. It can also be thought of as the number of different amplitude, frequency, or phase changes that can be transmitted per second. This rate is expressed in *baud*, or signal elements per second.

Four-phase PSK helps to illustrate the difference between the data rate R (in bps) and the modulation rate D (in baud) of a signal. Let us assume that this scheme is being employed with digital input in which each bit is represented by a constant-voltage pulse, one level for binary 1 and one level for binary 0. Let us also assume that the four-phase PSK being used has 16 different combinations of amplitude and phase, that is, 16 distinct signal elements. With 16 signal elements, each transmitted signal represents four bits ($L = 4$). Hence, if the modem has a baud rate of 2400 (can transmit 2400 signal elements per second), and each signal element represents 4 bits, the modem's data rate is 9600 bps ($R = D \times L$). This example shows that higher bit rates can be achieved over voice-grade lines by employing more complex modulation schemes, including multilevel signaling.[1]

---

[1]In general,

$$D = \frac{R}{L} = \frac{R}{\log_2 M}$$

where
D = modulation rate, baud
R = data rate, bps
M = number of different signal elements = 2^L
L = number of bits per signal element

MODEMS   Although both public and private telecommunications facilities are becoming increasingly digital, the use of analog transmission is still widespread. Thus, the modem continues to be one of the most widely used pieces of communications gear. A modem is essentially a device that modulates an analog carrier wave to encode digital information; it also demodulates the signals it receives to decode transmitted information.

Modems are offered in several different forms for use in different applications. Standalone modems, for instance, are self-contained, with internal power supplies, and are used with separate information products. Where a number of circuits come together—such as at the interface to an Internet service provider's computer system—rack-mounted modems are often used, sharing power supplies and packaging. Modems can also be packaged inside another system (such as personal computer). Such integrated modems usually lower overall cost but increase the complexity of the computing device and the cost of designing it. Integrated modems are usually offered as an option, because to standardize on a particular modem type with a product might restrict the usefulness of the product.

Modems are pervasive in today's computer networks. For example, direct broadcast satellite, Wi-Fi, and mobile phones use modems to communicate. Modems are also found in WiMax systems and some home networking systems. In this subsection, we provide a brief introduction to three popular types of modems: voice-grade, cable, and ADSL.

Voice-grade modems are designed for the transmission of digital data over ordinary telephone lines. Thus, the modems make use of the same 4-kHz bandwidth available for voice signals. Because modems are used in pairs for communications, and because this use often occurs over the public telephone network, standards are essential to allow different voice-grade modems to be paired. Table 5.3 lists the most popular voice-grade modem types, as designated by the ITU-T Recommendation that defines them.[2]

Table 5.3   Modem Specifications

ITU-T Recommendation	Data Rate (bps)	Dial-Up	Half-Duplex	Full-Duplex
V.29	9600		X	X
V.32	9600	X		X
V.32 bis	14,400	X		X
V.33	14,400			X
V.34	33,600	X	X	X
V.90	33,600 (send) 56,000 (receive)	X	X	X
V.92	48,000 (send) 56,000 (receive)	X	X	X

---

[2]A discussion of ITU-T and other standards bodies is contained in a supporting document at this book's Web site.

A **cable modem** permits Internet access over cable television networks. The cable television industry has been an early leader in providing high-speed Internet access to the home. Figure 5.3 shows a typical layout for cable delivery. At the cable central location, or linked by a high-speed line, is the Internet service provider (ISP). Typically, the cable company is an ISP but it may also provide links to other ISPs. From the central location, the cable company lays out a network of above or underground fiber and coaxial cable lines that can reach every home and office in its region of operation. Traditionally, this system has been used to deliver one-way transmission of television channels, using 6 MHz per channel. The same cable layout, with appropriate electronics at both ends, can also be used to deliver a data channel to the subscriber and to provide a reverse channel from subscriber to the central location. Both upstream and downstream channels used for data transmission are shared among a number of subscribers, using time-division mul- tiplexing a line-sharing technique described in Chapter 6. Within the subscriber's home or office, a splitter is employed to direct ordinary television signals to a tele- vision and the data channel to a cable modem, which can serve one or a network of PCs. Because cable modems enable data and television transmission to occur simultaneously over the same cable, they are an example of a broadband modem.

Some cable TV companies offer VoIP telephone service. This enables cable TV customers to eliminate connections to the public telephone network should they

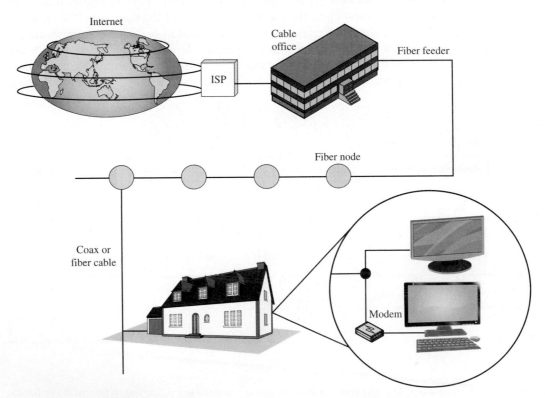

Figure 5.3   Cable Modem Application

choose to do so. Bundled voice, TV, and Internet services are often very competitively priced. This makes them attractive to consumers and small businesses.

In the implementation and deployment of a high-speed wide area public digital network, the most challenging part is the link between subscriber and network: the digital subscriber line. With billions of potential endpoints worldwide, the prospect of installing new cable for each new customer is daunting. Instead, network designers have sought ways of exploiting the installed base of twisted-pair wire that links virtually all residential and business customers to telephone networks. These links were installed to carry voice-grade signals in a bandwidth from 0 to 4 kHz. However, the wires are capable of transmitting signals over a far broader spectrum—1 MHz or more. The **asymmetric digital subscriber line (ADSL)** is the most widely publicized of a family of modem technologies designed to provide high-speed digital data transmission over ordinary telephone wire. ADSL is available from most carriers in the U.S. and is supported by ISPs in most countries around the world.

Figure 5.4 depicts the ADSL configuration for Internet access. The telephone central office can provide support for a number of ISPs, each of which must support the ADSL modem technology. At the central office, the ISP data signal is combined with a voice signal from the ordinary telephone voice switch. The combined signal can then be transmitted to/from a local subscriber over the subscriber line. At the subscriber's site, the twisted pair is split and routed to both a PC and a telephone. At the PC, an ADSL modem demodulates the data signal for the PC. At the telephone, a microfilter passes the 4-kHz voice signal. The data and voice

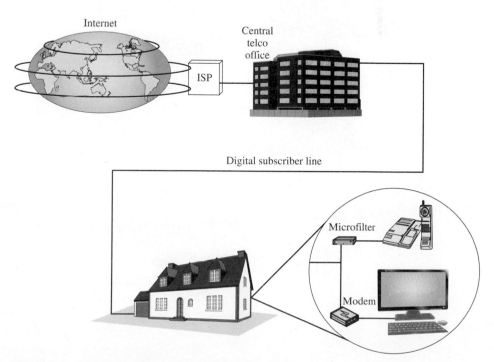

Figure 5.4   ADSL Modem Application

signals are combined on the twisted-pair line using frequency-division multiplexing techniques, as described in Chapter 6. Because they enable both voice and data to be transmitted simultaneously over the same link, ADSL modems are a type of broadband modem.

Currently, the best performance is available with the use of optical fiber from the carrier directly to the home or business premises, referred to as fiber to the home (FTTH) or fiber to the premises (FTTP). FTTH/FTTP has become a feasible alternative to cable and DSL technologies for residential and small business customers. Figure 5.5 depicts a typical configuration for residential service. An optical fiber cable runs from the central office to a neighborhood. The cable's bandwidth is shared by up to 32 end users by splitting the signal at the neighborhood end. The central office provides a broadcast service in one frequency band for television and video on demand service. Other frequency bands are assigned separately to each end user for two-way Internet access and two-way voice service to the ordinary public telephone network. Thus, unlike cable, with FTTH, each subscriber has dedicated channels for data and voice transmission. At the end user, a modem converts the optical signal to an electrical signal for access by devices such as computers, telephones, and televisions.

Table 5.4 compares the performance of the various modems we have discussed and with ISDN (integrated services digital network) access, which uses a digital signaling technique.

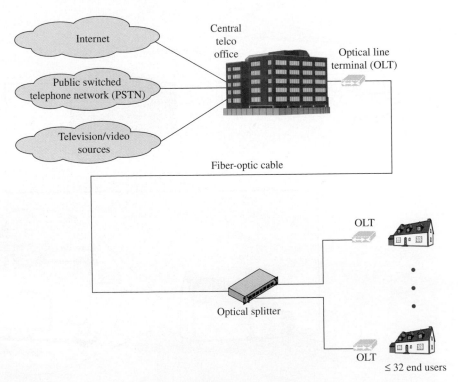

Figure 5.5   Fiber to the Home Configuration

Table 5.4   Speeds for Internet Access Methods

Access Method	Upload Speed	Download Speed	Download Time (10 megabit file)
Dial-up modem	48 Kbps	56 Kbps	3 minutes
ISDN basic rate (two channels)	128 Kbps	128 Kbps	1.3 minutes
ADSL	16–740 Kbps	1.5–11 Mbps	0.9–6.7 seconds
FTTH	2–60 Mbps	10–147 Mbps	0.07–1 second
Cable modem	20 Mbps	30–100 Mbps	0.1–0.3 second

Digital Encoding of Analog Information

The evolution of public telecommunications networks and private branch exchanges to digital transmission and switching requires that voice data be represented in digital form. The best-known technique for voice digitization is **pulse code modulation (PCM)**. PCM is based on the sampling theorem, which states that if a signal is sampled at regular intervals of time and at a rate higher than twice the highest significant signal frequency, then the samples contain all the information of the original signal.

If voice data were limited to frequencies below 4000 Hz, as is done in the analog telephone network, then 8000 samples per second would be sufficient to characterize completely the voice signal. Note, however, that these are analog samples. To convert to digital, each of these analog samples must be assigned a binary code. Figure 5.6 shows an example in which the original signal is assumed to be bandlimited

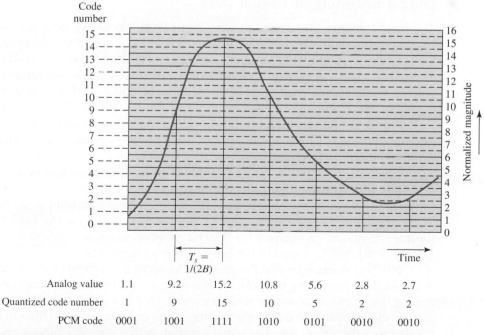

Figure 5.6   Pulse Code Modulation Example

with a bandwidth of B. Analog samples are taken at a rate of $2B$, or once every $Ts = 1/2B$ seconds. Each analog sample is approximated by being *quantized* into one of 16 different levels. Each sample can then be represented by 4 bits, ranging from 0000 (to represent 0) to 1111 (to represent 15). But because the quantized values are only approximations, it is impossible to recover the original signal exactly. By using an 8-bit sample, which allows 256 quantizing levels, the quality of the recovered voice signal is comparable with that achieved via analog transmission. Note that this implies that a data rate of 8000 samples per second $\times$ 8 bits per sample $= 64$ kbps is needed to represent the voice data as a digital signal.

PCM can, of course, be used for applications other than voice signals. For example, a color TV signal has a useful bandwidth of 4.6 MHz. According to the sampling theorem, its analog waveform would have to be sampled 9.2 million times per second to reasonably approximate the original signal. With this sampling rate and the use of 10-bit samples (representing 1024 quantization levels), the data rate would be 92 Mbps.

In recent times, variations on the PCM technique, as well as other encoding techniques, have been used to reduce the digital data rate required to carry voice. By using compression techniques, such as those discussed in Chapter 2, good-quality voice transmission can be achieved with a data rate as low as 8 Kbps. With video, advantage can be taken of the fact that from frame to frame most picture elements do not change. Interframe coding techniques low the video requirement to be reduced to about 15 Mbps, and for slowly changing scenes, such as those in a video teleconference, down to 1.5 Mbps or less. Indeed, recent advances have resulted in commercial videoconference products with data rates as low as 64 Kbps.

Digital Encoding of Digital Data

The most common, and easiest, way to transmit digital signals is to use two different voltage levels for the two binary digits. Typically, a negative voltage represents binary 1 and a positive voltage represents binary 0 (Figure 5.7a). This code is known as **Nonreturn-to-Zero-Level (NRZ-L)** (meaning the signal never returns to zero voltage, and a constant-voltage level is used for the duration of the signal pulse that represents the binary digit). The amount of time a digital signal is left at a particular voltage level to indicate a binary value is called a *bit interval* or *bit time*. NRZ-L is often used for very short connections, such as between a personal computer and an external modem or a terminal and a nearby host computer.

A variation of NRZ is **NRZI (NRZ, Invert on Ones)**. As with NRZ-L, NRZI maintains a constant-voltage pulse for the duration of a bit interval. The data themselves are encoded as the presence or absence of a signal transition at the beginning of the bit interval. A transition (low to high or high to low) at the beginning of a bit interval denotes a binary 1 for that bit time; no transition indicates a binary 0 (Figure 5.7b). NRZI is used in 100 Mbps Ethernet networks.

NRZI is an example of *differential encoding*. In differential encoding, the signal is decoded by comparing the polarity of adjacent signal elements rather than determining the absolute value of a signal element. One benefit of this scheme is that it may be more reliable to detect a transition in the presence of noise than to compare a value to a threshold. Another benefit is that, with a complex cabling layout, it is easy to lose the sense of the polarity of the signal. For example, if the leads from an

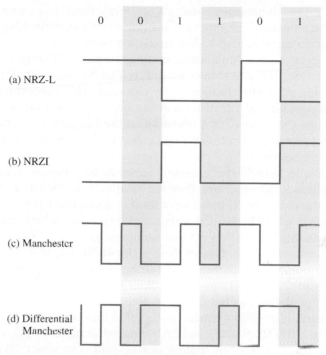

Figure 5.7 Example of Digital Signal Encoding Schemes

attached device to a twisted-pair cable are accidentally inverted, all ones and zeros are inverted for NRZ-L. This does not happen with differential encoding.

A significant disadvantage of NRZ transmission is that it is difficult to determine where one bit ends and another begins. To picture the problem, consider that with a long string of ones or zeros for NRZ-L, the output is a constant voltage over a long period of time. Under these circumstances, any drift between the timing of transmitter and receiver results in the loss of synchronization between the two.

There is a set of alternative coding techniques, grouped under the term *biphase*, that overcomes this problem. Two of these techniques, Manchester and differential Manchester, are the most well-known. All of the biphase techniques require at least one transition per bit time and may have as many as two transitions. Thus, the maximum modulation rate is twice that for NRZ; this means that the bandwidth required is correspondingly greater. Because a transition between two voltage levels is required to represent each bit, twice as many voltage pulses are needed to transmit a given number of bits in comparison to NRZ. However, biphase schemes have two major advantages:

- **Synchronization:** Because there is a predictable transition during each bit time, the receiver can synchronize on that transition. For this reason, the biphase codes are known as self-clocking codes.

- **Error detection:** The absence of an expected transition can be used to detect errors. Noise on the line would have to invert both the signal before and after the expected transition to cause an undetected error.

In the **Manchester** code (Figure 5.7c), there is a transition at the middle of each bit interval. The midbit transition serves as a clocking mechanism and also represents data: A high-to-low transition represents a 0, and a low-to-high transition represents a 1. Manchester coding is used in 10 Mbps Ethernet and a number of other local area networks. In **differential Manchester** (Figure 5.7d), the midbit transition is used only to provide clocking. The encoding of a 0 is represented by the presence of a transition at the beginning of a bit period, and a 1 is represented by the absence of a transition at the beginning of a bit period. Differential Manchester is used in token ring LANs and in some types of magnetic and optical storage systems.

While Manchester encoding schemes help ensure synchronization between transmitters and receivers, they are relatively inefficient because the baud rate is twice the data rate. If these were used in a Gigabit Ethernet LAN, a baud rate of two billion would be needed. Other digital encoding schemes have been developed to maintain synchronization without having to have a baud rate which is twice the data (bits per second) rate. One of these is the 4B/5B encoding scheme. In **4B/5B** encoding, the transmitter takes each 4-bit string of data and converts it into a 5-bit sequence that ensures frequent signal transitions (for synchronization). This is illustrated in Table 5.5. 4B/5B uses NRZI signals. Receivers take the 5-bit codes and convert them back into the original 4-bit data strings that they represent.

In a 100 Mbps Ethernet LAN running at full capacity, each 100 million transmitted bits "carries" 80 million bits of data. The other 20 million bits are those added by 4B/5B encoding to ensure synchronization. This makes 4B/5B only 80% efficient. Higher speed Ethernet networks use digital encoding schemes that operate in a manner that is similar to 4B/5B. Gigabit Ethernet, for example, uses 8B/10B encoding. 8B/10B encoding is also used in Firewire (IEEE 1394), Fibre Channel, InfiniBand, and USB 3.0. 64B/66B encoding is used in 10 Gigabit Ethernet, 10 Gigabit Fibre Channel, and InfiniBand.

Table 5.5   4B/5B Digital Encoding

4-Bit Data String (Original)	5-Bit Code (Converted)	Unused 5-Bit Codes
0000	11110	00001
0001	01001	00010
0010	10100	00011
0011	10101	01000
0100	01010	10000
0101	01011	
0110	01110	
0111	01111	
1000	10010	
1001	10011	
1010	10110	
1011	10111	
1100	11010	
1101	11011	
1110	11100	
1111	11101	

Analog Encoding of Analog Information

In some instances, analog information can be converted directly into an analog signal that occupies the same bandwidth. The best example of this is voice. A voice-generated sound wave in the range of 300–3400 Hz can be represented by an electromagnetic signal with the same frequency components. This signal can then be directly transmitted on a voice-grade telephone line.

It is also possible to use an analog signal to modulate a carrier to produce a new analog signal that conveys the same information but occupies a different frequency band. There are two principal reasons for doing this:

- A higher frequency may be needed for effective transmission. For unguided media, it is virtually impossible to transmit low-frequency signals; the required antennas would have to be many kilometers in diameter. Guided media also have constraints on frequency range. Optical fiber, for example, requires that the frequency be on the order of 10^{14} Hz.

- Analog-to-analog modulation permits frequency division multiplexing, an important technique explored in Chapter 6.

As with digital-to-analog modulation, analog-to-analog modulation involves an information source that is used to modulate one of the three principal characteristics of a carrier signal: amplitude, frequency, or phase.

Figure 5.8 illustrates the three possibilities. With amplitude modulation (AM), the amplitude of the carrier varies with the pattern of the modulating signal. Similarly, frequency modulation (FM) and phase modulation (PM) modulate the frequency and phase of a carrier, respectively.

5.3 ASYNCHRONOUS AND SYNCHRONOUS TRANSMISSION

Recall from Figure 4.10 that the reception of digital data involves sampling the incoming signal once per bit time to determine the binary value. One of the difficulties encountered in such a process is that various transmission impairments corrupt the signal so that occasional errors occur. This problem is compounded by a timing difficulty: in order for the receiver to sample the incoming bits properly, it must know the arrival time and duration of each bit that it receives.

Suppose that the sender simply transmits a stream of data bits. The sender has a clock that governs the timing of the transmitted bits. For example, if data are to be transmitted at one million bits per second (1 Mbps), then one bit is to be transmitted every $1/10^6 = 1$ microsecond (µs), as measured by the sender's clock. Typically, the receiver attempts to sample the medium at the center of each bit time. The receiver times its samples at intervals of one bit time. In our example, the sampling occurs once every 1 µs. If the receiver times its samples based on its own clock, then there is a problem if the transmitter's and receiver's clocks are not precisely aligned. If there is a drift of 1% (the receiver's clock is 1% faster or slower than the transmitter's clock), then the first sampling is 0.01 of a bit time (0.01 µs) away from the center of the bit (center of bit is 0.5 µs from beginning and end of bit). After 50 or more samples, the receiver may be in error because it is sampling in the wrong bit time ($50 \times 0.01 = 0.5$ µs).

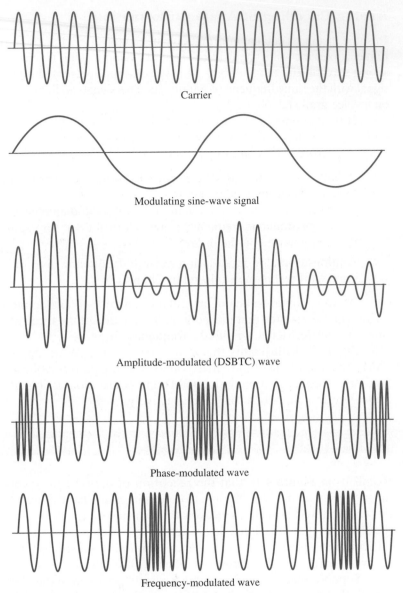

Figure 5.8 Amplitude, Phase, and Frequency Modulation of a Sine-Wave Carrier by a Sine-Wave Signal

For smaller timing differences, the error would occur later, but eventually the receiver will be out of step with the transmitter if the transmitter sends a sufficiently long stream of bits and if no steps are taken to synchronize the transmitter and receiver.

Asynchronous Transmission

Two approaches are common for achieving the desired synchronization. The first is called, oddly enough, **asynchronous transmission**. The strategy with this scheme is to avoid the timing problem by not sending long, uninterrupted streams of bits.

Instead, data are transmitted one character at a time, where each character is 5 to 8 bits in length.[3] Timing or synchronization must only be maintained within each character; the receiver has the opportunity to resynchronize at the beginning of each new character.

Figure 5.9 illustrates this technique. When no character is being transmitted, the line between transmitter and receiver is in an *idle* state. The definition of *idle* is equivalent to the signaling element for binary 1. Thus, for NRZ-L signaling (see Figure 5.7), which is common for asynchronous transmission, idle would be the presence of a negative voltage on the line. The beginning of a character is signaled by a *start bit* with a value of binary 0. This is followed by the 5 to 8 bits that actually make up the character. The bits of the character are transmitted beginning with the least significant bit. For example, for IRA characters, the data bits are usually followed by a parity bit, which therefore is in the most significant bit position. The parity bit is set by the transmitter such that the total number of ones in the character, including the parity bit, is even (even parity) or odd (odd parity), depending

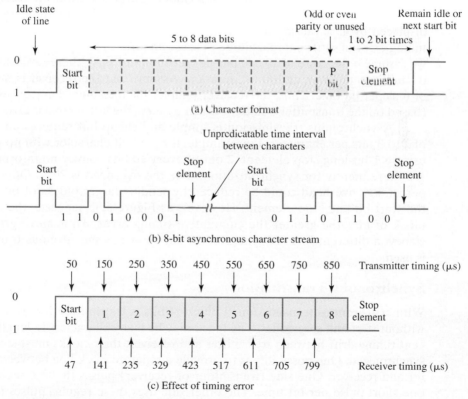

Figure 5.9   Asynchronous Transmission

---

[3]The number of bits that comprise a character depends on the code used. We have already seen one common example, the IRA code, which uses 7 bits per character (Chapter 2). Another common code is the Extended Binary Coded Decimal Interchange Code (EBCDIC), which is an 8-bit character code used primarily on IBM mainframe and midrange systems.

on the convention being used. This bit is used by the receiver for error detection, as discussed in Section 5.4. The final element is a *stop element*, which is a binary 1. A minimum length for the stop element is specified, and this is usually 1, 1.5, or 2 times the duration of an ordinary bit. No maximum value is specified. Because the stop element is the same as the idle state, the transmitter continues to transmit the stop element until it is ready to send the next character.

If a steady stream of characters is sent, the interval between two characters is uniform and equal to the stop element. For example, if the stop element is one bit time and the IRA characters ABC are sent (with even parity bit), the pattern is 01000001010010000010101011000011111...111.[4] The start bit (0) starts the timing sequence for the next nine elements, which are the 7-bit IRA code, the parity bit, and the stop element. In the idle state, the receiver looks for a transition from 1 to 0 to signal the beginning of the next character and then samples the input signal at 1-bit intervals for seven intervals. It then looks for the next 1-to-0 transition, which will occur no sooner than one more bit time.

The timing requirements for this scheme are modest. For example, IRA characters are typically sent as 8-bit units, including the parity bit. If the receiver is 5% slower or faster than the transmitter, the sampling of the eighth character bit is displaced by 45% but is still correctly sampled. Figure 5.9c shows the effects of a timing error of sufficient magnitude to cause an error in reception. In this example, we assume a data rate of 10,000 bits per second (10 Kbps); therefore, each bit is of 0.1 millisecond (ms), or 100 μs, duration. Assume that the receiver is fast by 6%, or 6 μs per bit time. Thus, the receiver samples the incoming character every 94 μs (based on the transmitter's clock). As can be seen, the last sample is erroneous.

Asynchronous transmission is simple and cheap but requires an overhead of 2 to 3 bits per character. For example, for an 8-bit character with no parity bit, using a 1-bit-long stop element, 2 out of every 10 bits convey no information but are there merely for synchronization; thus the overhead is 20%. Of course, the percentage overhead could be reduced by sending larger blocks of bits between the start bit and stop element. However, as Figure 5.9c suggests, the larger the block of bits, the greater the cumulative timing error. To achieve greater efficiency, a different form of synchronization, known as synchronous transmission, is used.

Synchronous Transmission

With **synchronous transmission**, a block of bits is transmitted in a steady stream without start and stop codes. The block may be many characters in length. To prevent timing drift between transmitter and receiver, their clocks must somehow be synchronized. One possibility is to provide a separate clock line between transmitter and receiver. One side (transmitter or receiver) pulses the line regularly with one short pulse per bit time. The other side uses these regular pulses as a clock. This technique works well over short distances, but over longer distances the clock pulses are subject to the same impairments as the data signal, and timing errors can occur. The other alternative is to embed the clocking information in the data signal.

---

[4]In the text, the transmission is shown from left (first bit transmitted) to right (last bit transmitted).

For digital signals, this can be accomplished with Manchester, differential Manchester encoding, or 4B/5B encoding, as explained in Section 5.2. For analog signals, a number of techniques can be used; for example, the carrier frequency itself can be used to synchronize the receiver based on the phase of the carrier.

With synchronous transmission, there is another level of synchronization required to allow the receiver to determine the beginning and end of a block of data. To achieve this, each block begins with a *preamble* bit pattern and generally ends with a *postamble* bit pattern. In addition, other bits added to the block convey control information used in the data link control procedures, discussed in Chapter 6. The data plus preamble, postamble, and control information are called a **frame**. The exact format of the frame depends on which data link control procedure is being used.

For sizable blocks of data, synchronous transmission is far more efficient than asynchronous. Asynchronous transmission requires 20% or more overhead. The control information, preamble, and postamble in synchronous transmission are typically less than 100 bits. For example, one of the more common schemes, HDLC, contains 48 bits of control, preamble, and postamble. Thus, for a 1000 character block of data, each frame consists of 48 bits of overhead and $1000 \times 8 = 8000$ bits of data, for a percentage overhead of only $48/8048 \times 100\% = 0.6\%$.

For applications involving low-speed terminals or personal computers, asynchronous transmission may be used. The technique is inexpensive, and its inefficiency is not a problem in most interactive applications, where more time is spent in looking at the screen and thinking than in transmission. However, the overhead of asynchronous transmission can be a heavy price to pay in more communications-intensive applications.

For large systems and computer networks, the efficiency of synchronous transmission is needed, even though it introduces the technical problem of synchronizing the clocks of transmitter and receiver.

In addition to the requirement for efficiency, large data transfers introduce a requirement for error checking. While the interactive application user often checks his or her own input and output for errors by looking at the screen and rekeying portions that contain errors, such a procedure is clearly impractical for long file transfers that occur at fast rates and often without an operator present. As we shall see, synchronous transmission involves the use of a data link control procedure, which automatically detects transmission errors and causes a frame in error to be retransmitted.

5.4   ERROR DETECTION

The Need for Error Control

As discussed in Chapter 4, noise and other signal impairments have the potential to cause data communication errors. The ability to detect and recover from errors has always been an important aspect of computer networks and its importance has grown over time. This is partly because data integrity is increasingly important to business operations. No business needs a network that captures, transmits, and stores data that is deficient in quality. It is important to detect data that has been corrupted in transit before it is stored or used for database updates. Certain data simply cannot be wrong; for example, consider the effect of an undetected data error on an electronic funds transfer. Businesses have become less tolerant of errors in communication and mass storage systems as bandwidths and volumes of data have increased. In general, uncorrected and undetected errors can degrade performance and response times in any system that handles large volumes of data.

The process of **error control** involves two elements:

- **Error detection**: Redundancy is introduced into the data stream so that the occurrence of an error is detected.
- **Error correction**: Once an error is detected by the receiver, the receiver and the transmitter cooperate to cause the frames in error to be retransmitted.

In this section, we look at the error detection process. We examine error correction in Chapter 6.

Parity Checks

The simplest approach to error detection is to append a parity bit to the end of a block of data. A typical example is asynchronous transmission of IRA characters, in which a parity bit is attached to each 7-bit character. The value of this bit is selected so that the character has an even number of 1s (even parity) or an odd number of 1s (odd parity). So, for example, if the transmitter is transmitting the character G (1110001) and using odd parity, it appends a 1 and transmits 11100011. The receiver examines the received character and, if the total number of 1s is odd, assumes that no error has occurred. If one bit (or an odd number of bits) is errone-ously inverted during transmission (e.g., 11000011), then the receiver detects an error. Note, however, that if two (or any even number of) bits are inverted due to error, an undetected error occurs. Hence, the use of the parity bit is not a foolproof data detection scheme.

In practice, noise impulses are often long enough in duration to destroy more than one bit, particularly at high data rates. Impulse noises can corrupt parity bits in addition to data bits. The ability of parity checking to detect errors is therefore dependent on the total number of bits corrupted by noise impulses (odd or even) and the parity convention that is used (odd or even). Typically, even parity is used for synchronous transmission and odd parity for asynchro-nous transmission.

Cyclic Redundancy Check

When synchronous transmission is used, it is possible to employ an error detection technique that is both more efficient (lower percentage of overhead bits) and more powerful (more errors detected) than the simple parity bit. This technique requires the addition of a **frame check sequence (FCS)**, or **error-detecting code**, to each syn-chronous frame. The use of an FCS is illustrated in Figure 5.10, using the cycli-cal redundancy check (CRC) code described in this subsection. On transmission,

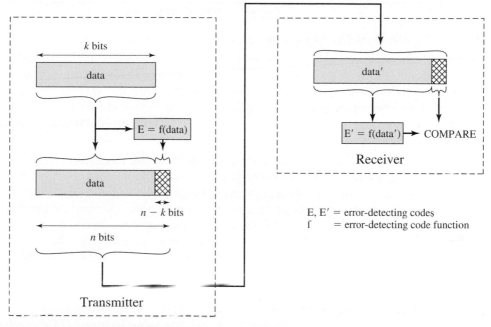

Figure 5.10 Error Detection Process

a calculation is performed on the bits of the frame to be transmitted; the result is inserted as an additional field in the frame. On reception, the same calculation is performed on the received bits and the calculated result is compared to the value stored in the incoming frame. If there is a discrepancy, the receiver assumes that an error has occurred.

One of the most common and powerful error-detecting codes is the **cyclic redundancy check (CRC)**. For this technique, the message to be transmitted is treated as one long binary number. This number is divided by a unique prime binary number (a number divisible only by itself and 1), and the remainder is attached to the frame to be transmitted. When the frame is received, the receiver performs the same division, using the same divisor, and compares the calculated remainder with the remainder received in the frame. The most commonly used divisors are a 17-bit divisor, which produces a 16-bit remainder, and a 33-bit divisor, which produces a 32-bit remainder. Respectively, these are called CRC-16 and CRC-32; the numbers 16 and 32 represent the size, in bits, of the FCS appended to each transmitted frame.

The measure of effectiveness of any error-detecting code is what percentage of errors it detects. For a CRC of length N, the rate of undetected errors is on the order of 2^{-N} (see [STAL04] for details). This means that CRC-16 detects 99.998% of communication errors while CRC-32 detects nearly 99.9999998%. In summary, the CRC is a very powerful means of error detection and requires very little overhead. As an example, if a 16-bit FCS is used with frames of 1000 bits, then the overhead is only 1.6%. With a 32-bit FCS, the overhead is 3.2%.

APPLICATION NOTE

Devices, Encoding, Communication Parameters, and Protocols

Encoding schemes, protocols, and errors are not normally a part of our everyday networking experience. From an end-user perspective, all we know is whether or not the network (or computer) is working. Even if we directly interact with the various communication systems, we do not often have to give these things much thought. However, during network installation, maintenance, and troubleshooting, insight into the mechanisms used by data transmission equipment and the standards involved can make a big difference.

Today's computers have a number of methods they can use to communicate with other machines. USB, EIA232 (a.k.a. COM or serial port), Firewire, network cards, video, and interfaces for mice and keyboards all represent some form of data transmission. What adds to the confusion is that organizations often wind up with several different computing platforms. As a result, the protocols and encoding schemes used by one device can be markedly different from the next. As an example, a company may have a variety of Macintosh computers alongside Windows-based machines. This can create an environment wherein peripherals, such as printers, must be purchased for both Firewire and USB. In addition, the network protocols can be different or require additional support.

Terminal emulation programs can also be a source of difficulty. Computers connected via a serial connection must be configured to "speak the same language." This amounts to determining the speed of the link, the number of data bits used, and the parity. This is a manual configuration that must be done on both ends of the link. The most common application for these programs is to configure routers and access points via a console port. However, networking protocols such as those connecting us to the WAN may require some additional serial-based configuration. If any one of these is incorrect, the communication cannot proceed.

Operating systems and device drivers can create problems because they expose settings that users can change. An example can be found in Ethernet-speed configurations. Ports on network equipment and the network interface card can be configured for a particular speed and full or half duplex. While normally left to "auto sense" the network, manually changing these can limit or even stop network connectivity. In this case, different settings will make it impossible for the two ends to understand each other because not only are the speeds different, but the encoding schemes have completely changed. Another example is the type of wireless network that you are connecting to. Simply changing from one 802.11 standard to another can disconnect you from the network.

Part of every successful transmission is error control. Error control can mean error detection or error detection *and* correction. Contemporary networks have extremely low error rates. Having a single bit in error for a billion bits transmitted would be excessive. The most common forms of error detection today are single parity bits, cyclical redundancy checks, and checksums. These are used primarily by lower-layer protocols and file systems. Some lower-layer protocols have many error checking and testing functions built in. Protocols like the Point-to-Point Protocol (PPP) have provided extra tools, although they are not often used today. Supplementing these mechanisms are those used in the upper-layer protocols such as the sequence numbers and retransmission in TCP.

With the advent of wireless networks, the error rates have increased and additional problems such as lost connections can occur. Generally, the throughput of wireless local area networks is less than that of wired networks. This is because the wireless network is a shared medium and the nodes must contend with each other for bandwidth. The access method used is similar to Ethernet but can take even longer. Finally, each frame in a wireless LAN is typically acknowledged (ACK), which further slows things down. While some of this delay will be alleviated with the newer, faster wireless standards, the media will remain shared and still require ACKs. For these reasons, it may be necessary to modify communication parameters (e.g., preamble length, load sharing, channels) to ensure the successful completion of wireless transmissions.

End users or network administrators cannot modify all of the parameters in a communication system. For example, no one will change the 4B/5B encoding used by 100baseT Ethernet. However, understanding the interrelated nature of encoding schemes, settings, and protocol operation can help improve efficiency, speed troubleshooting efforts, and assist in the design phases so that many problems can be avoided. It is the wise network administrator who understands what settings end users can (and will) change. In many cases, getting back to basics is the only way to solve a communications problem.

5.5 SUMMARY

Both analog and digital information can be encoded as either analog or digital signals. The particular encoding that is chosen depends on the specific requirements to be met and the media and communications facilities available. For example, to transmit digital information over an analog telephone line, a modem is used to convert the digital data into analog form. Similarly, there is an increasing use of digital facilities, and voice information must be encoded in digital form to be transmitted on these digital facilities. The various combinations of data and signals found in today's networks are summarized in Table 5.6.

Table 5.6 Data and Signal Combinations

Data	Signal	Encoding Scheme	Conversion Device(s)	Examples
Digital	Analog	Amplitude-shift keying (ASK) Frequency-shift keying (FSK) Phase-shift keying (PSK)	Modem	Cable modems DSL modems Dial-up modems
Analog	Digital	Pulse code modulation (PCM)	Codec	Digital telephones
Digital	Digital	4B/5B Differential Manchester Manchester NRZI NRZ-L	Digital transceiver	Local area networks ISDN PC to external modem
Analog	Analog	Amplitude modulation (AM) Frequency modulation (FM) Phase modulation (PM)	Transducer	Telephone Cable TV AM and FM radio

The transmission of a stream of bits from one device to another across a transmission link involves a great deal of cooperation and agreement between the two sides. One of the most fundamental requirements is synchronization. The receiver must know the rate at which bits are being received so that it can sample the line at regular intervals to determine the value of each received bit. Two techniques are in common use for this purpose. In asynchronous transmission, each character of data is treated independently. Each byte begins with a start bit that alerts the receiver that a character is arriving. The receiver samples each bit in the character and then looks for the beginning of the next character. This technique would not work well for long blocks of data because the receiver's clock might eventually drift out of synchronization with the transmitter's clock. However, sending data in large blocks is more efficient than sending data one character at a time. For large blocks, synchronous transmission is used. Each block of data is formatted as a frame that includes a starting and ending flag. Some form of synchronization, such as the use of Manchester encoding, is employed to maintain synchronization.

Error detection techniques are an important part of data transmission. The most widely used algorithm for error detection is the cyclic redundancy check.

5.6 KEY TERMS, REVIEW QUESTIONS, AND PROBLEMS

Key Terms

amplitude-shift keying (ASK) analog data analog signal analog transmission asynchronous transmission codec	cyclic redundancy check (CRC) digital data digital signal digital transmission error-detecting code error detection	4B/5B frequency-shift keying (FSK) modem phase-shift keying (PSK) pulse code modulation (PCM) synchronous transmission

Review Questions

5.1 What is transmission?

5.2 Distinguish among analog data, analog signaling, and analog transmission.

5.3 Distinguish among digital data, digital signaling, and digital transmission.

5.4 What function does a modem perform?

5.5 What function does a codec perform?

5.6 Identify the major reasons why digital transmission is preferred over analog transmission in business networks.

5.7 Identify and briefly describe the three fundamental ways in which digital data are encoded as analog signals.

5.8 What is the meaning of "baud rate"?

5.9 What is amplitude-shift keying (ASK)?

5.10 Describe the differences among the following types of modems: voice-grade, cable, ADSL.

5.11 What is pulse code modulation? How does it work?

5.12 What is NRZ-L? How does NRZI differ from NRZ-L?

5.13 What are the two major advantages of biphase schemes?

Device/System	Data/Signal
Modem transmissions	A. Digital data/digital encoding
Ethernet	B. Digital data/analog encoding
AM/FM radio	C. Analog data/digital encoding
PCM	D. Analog data/analog encoding

5.14 Match the device or system with the correct type of signal and data.

5.15 What are the primary differences between asynchronous and synchronous transmission?

5.16 What additional bits are added to each character in asynchronous transmission? Briefly explain why each is added.

5.17 Why is synchronous transmission typically more efficient than asynchronous transmission?

5.18 What is differential Manchester encoding?

5.19 What are the two major components of error control?

5.20 How does parity checking work?

5.21 What types of errors does parity checking miss?

5.22 How does cyclical redundancy checking work?

Problems

5.1 Given the bit pattern 01100, encode this data using ASK, BFSK, and BPSK.

5.2 Using Manchester encoding, encode the bit pattern 01001110.

5.3 What is the baud rate of a digital signal that employs differential Manchester encoding and has a data transfer rate of 4 Mbps.

5.4 What 4B/5B code would be used for each of the following 4-bit data strings: 1011, 0011, 1101, 1001?

5.5 Given the character 1010010, what bit would be added to support even parity?

5.6 Two communicating devices are using a single-bit even parity check for error detection. The transmitter sends the byte 10101010 and, because of channel noise, the receiver gets the byte 10011010. Will the receiver detect the error? Why or why not?

5.7 Locate and view several YouTube videos about the advantages of digital transmission. Identify the URLs of three that you would recommend for viewing by other business data communication students. If you could only recommend one, which would it be? Why?

5.8 Do some Internet research on the evolution of dial-up, cable, and DSL modems. In an 8–12 slide PowerPoint presentation, summarize how the capabilities and transmission speeds of each of these types of modems are increasing and the major reasons behind these improvements. Also summarize how these technologies are expected to change in the years ahead.

5.9 Do some online research to find several images that you think do an excellent job communicating how pulse code modulation is used to digitize analog waveforms. Also find information about common examples of PCM applications. Include your images in an 8–12 slide PowerPoint presentation that examines the fundamental PCM process and its widespread use.

5.10 Suppose that a pulse code modulated signal results in a not so good representation of the original data when it is decoded by receivers. Briefly describe two ways to improve the accuracy of the modulated signal.

5.11 What is the data rate of a pulse code modulated signal that samples the analog data 8000 times per second and converts each sample into an 8-bit value?

5.12 Suppose you need to download a file that is 400,000 bytes in size. Assume that control characters involved in the download increase the total number of downloaded bytes by 10% (to 440,000 bytes). Calculate how long it would take you (in seconds) to download the file using each of the following types of modems:
a. 56 Kbps dial-up modem.
b. 1.5 Mbps ADSL modem
c. 10 Mbps cable modem

DATA LINK CONTROL AND MULTIPLEXING

CHAPTER
6

Learning Objectives

After reading this chapter, you should be able to:

♦ Explain the need for flow control and error control.

♦ Explain the need for transmission efficiency and list the two major approaches used to achieve efficiency.

♦ Discuss the use of frequency-division multiplexing in video distribution and voice networks.

♦ Describe the use of multiplexing in digital carrier systems.

♦ Discuss T-1 service and describe its importance and the applications that may use it.

♦ Discuss the SONET standard and its significance for wide area networking.

This chapter examines two important data communications concepts: data link control and multiplexing.

A data link control protocol includes techniques for regulating the flow of data over a communications link and for compensating for transmission errors. Data link control protocols are found in all types of business computer networks including Ethernet LANs, Wi-Fi networks, and private WANs. We first examine the concepts of flow control and error control and then turn our attention to multiplexing and the types of links on which multiplexing is commonly used. The appendix at the end of this chapter illustrates flow and error control in the data link control protocol HDLC.

This chapter provides insight into why multiplexing is widely deployed in both public and private data communication networks. A major source of expense in any business distributed data processing (DDP) environment is transmission cost. Businesses must purchase or lease communication lines to connect their geographically dispersed operating locations and there may be considerable cost associated with either approach for acquiring transmission lines.

In early business computer networks, communication lines were primarily provided by telephone companies. Business data was frequently conveyed over voice channels by using modems to modulate analog carrier signals. In these instances, the data followed existing telephone lines from business premises to switches in the telephone company's central office. From there, the data flowed through the telephone company's circuit-switched network and was delivered to the business's other operating locations. Businesses that did not want their data routed over the public switched telephone network (PSTN) could lease communication lines to provide point-to-point connections between operating locations.

Today, telephone companies compete with competitive local access carriers (CLECs) and other companies that are Internet service providers (ISPs), such as cable television companies, to provide communication lines for business subscribers and consumers. Dial-up connections, leased lines, and various broadband services are often available from multiple vendors competing in local markets. Such local competition helps businesses keep a lid on their data communication costs, but requires them to monitor pricing and service offering to ensure that they are getting the most value from their communication investments.

In order to achieve the greatest return on their data communication investments, it is important for businesses to maximize the amount of information carried over their transmission lines. This means coming as close as possible to using the full capacity of the links in their networks. It does not make business sense to invest in additional capacity if you are not making full use of the capacity that is already available. It also does not make business sense to invest in excess communication capacity that is not needed. Why rent a 1.5 Mbps communication line if you can get by with a less expensive 56 Kbps line? Finding the sweet spot that balances communication cost and data transmission requirements is an ongoing challenge for business computer network managers.

In a general sense, the business decision is a matter of data transmission efficiency. It is driven by the desire to transmit the organization's data among its operating locations as cost-effectively as possible. The transmission facilities that you use must have the capacity to handle the volume of data traffic that must be communicated. However, the organization sacrifices efficiency when it wastes money on communication lines with capacities that are much higher than it needs. Hence, most of this chapter is devoted to one of the major approaches used to achieve transmission efficiency: multiplexing.

6.1 FLOW CONTROL AND ERROR CONTROL

Physical interface standards provide a means by which a stream of data can be transmitted, either synchronously or asynchronously, onto a transmission medium. However, these interfaces do not include all of the required functions for data communication. Among the most important items lacking are flow control and error control.

To provide these needed functions, a data link control protocol is used. Such protocols are generally only used for synchronous transmission. The basic scheme is as follows. The data to be transmitted by an application are sent to the data link module, which organizes the data into a set of frames. Each frame is supplemented with control bits that allow the two sides to cooperate to deliver the data reliably. The control bits are added by the sender of the frame. When the frame arrives, the receiver examines the control bits and, if the data arrive successfully, strips off the control bits and then delivers the pure data to the intended destination point within the system. Figure 6.1 illustrates the process. With the use of control bits, a number of functions can be performed, including flow control and error control.

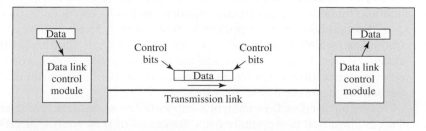

Figure 6.1 Operation of a Data Link Control Module

Flow Control

Suppose that we wish to write a program, called a printer driver, to pass data from a computer to a printer. We connect the printer with an appropriate cable to a communications port on the computer. The communications port is programmable to match the peripheral device. In this case, let us say that the printer is set up for IRA (ASCII) 7-bit characters, odd parity, a stop of 1-bit length, and a data rate of 9600 bps. We use these parameters to program the communications port, and try to send a page of text to the printer. The result is that, after the first few lines of text, there are a number of missing characters, in fact more characters are missing than are printed.

What is the problem? First, let's calculate the character transfer rate. We have 7 bits for the character, 1 for the start bit, 1 for parity, and 1 for stop, for a total of 10 bits per character. Because the computer is transmitting at 9600 bps, the character rate is 960 characters per second. Checking the printer manual, we find that the printer can print at a maximum rate of 80 characters per second. This means that we are sending 12 times as much data as the printer can accept. No wonder that data are lost.

It may seem odd that the printer is equipped with a higher data reception rate capability than its printing capability, but this is common. The printer includes a small buffer (perhaps 200 characters) so that it can accept characters in a burst of speed, print those characters, and then accept another burst. This allows the printer to be used on a shared line that is running at a sufficiently high speed to service a number of printers and computers. For example, a 9600-bps line could easily accommodate 5 or 10 such printers. However, because the data rate is higher than the printing rate, it is possible for the overrun condition previously described to occur.

Flow control is a technique for assuring that a transmitting entity does not overwhelm a receiving entity with data. Many devices attached to business networks, such as printers or disk drives, have fixed-size buffers for receiving data. When data is transmitted to a computer, it is typically destined for some application or system program. The receiving computer allocates a data buffer of some maximum length for that application or system program. When data are received, the computer must do a certain amount of processing before passing the data to the higher-level software. In the absence of flow control, the receiver's buffer may fill up and overflow while it is processing previously received data.

Flow control is one of the primary functions performed at the data link layer (layer 2) of Open Systems Interconnection (OSI) reference model for network communication. The data link layer is immediately above the physical layer at which signals are transmitted that convey data. The data link layer is responsible for providing reliable data transfer across physical links (telecommunications paths) within the network. In addition to flow control, the data link layer's primary functions include defining frames and, performing error detection and control on those frames.

For data link control protocols, flow control is achieved by numbering each frame sequentially (e.g., 0, 1, 2, ...). Initially, a buffer is allocated at the receiver of an agreed size. As frames arrive and are processed, the receiver returns an acknowledgment indicating which frames have been received and an implicit indication to the sender that more frames may be sent.

Sliding window flow control is supported by many data link control protocols. This is illustrated in Appendix 6A's discussion of flow control in HDLC. It is also discussed in more detail in online Appendix K.

Error Control

In Chapter 5, we discussed techniques that enable a receiver to detect errors that occur in the transmission and reception process. To correct these errors, data link control protocols provide mechanisms by which the two sides cooperate in the retransmission of frames that are detected to include errors. These mechanisms extend the flow control techniques discussed previously. Again, data are sent as a numbered sequence of frames. In addition, we consider two types of errors:

- **Lost frame:** A frame fails to arrive at the other side. In type of network error, the network may simply fail to deliver a frame. In the case of a direct point-to-point data link, a noise burst may damage a frame to the extent that the receiver is not aware that a frame has been transmitted.

- **Damaged frame:** A recognizable frame does arrive, but some of the bits are in error (have been altered during transmission).

The most common techniques for error control are based on some or all of the following ingredients:

- **Error detection:** The destination detects frames that are in error-using techniques such as CRC, described in Chapter 5, and discards those frames.

- **Positive acknowledgment:** The destination returns a positive acknowledgment (ACK) to successfully received, error-free frames.

- **Retransmission after timeout:** The source retransmits a frame that has not been acknowledged after a predetermined amount of time.

- **Negative acknowledgment and retransmission:** The destination returns a negative acknowledgment (NAK) to frames in which an error is detected. The source retransmits such frames.

Collectively, these mechanisms are referred to as **automatic repeat request (ARQ)**. The effect of ARQ is to turn a potentially unreliable data link into a reliable one. ARQ processes are further described in Appendix 6A as part of our discussion of HDLC.

6.2 MOTIVATION FOR MULTIPLEXING

Typically, two communicating stations do not utilize the full capacity of the data link(s) that connect them. For efficiency and increased capacity utilization, it should be possible to share that capacity with other communication devices. A generic term for such sharing is *multiplexing*.

A common application of multiplexing is in long-haul communications. Trunks on long-haul networks are typically high-capacity fiber, coaxial, or microwave links. These links can carry large numbers of voice and data transmissions simultaneously using multiplexing.

Figure 6.2 depicts the multiplexing function in its simplest form. There are n inputs to a multiplexer. The multiplexer is connected by a single data link to a demultiplexer. The link is able to carry n separate channels of data. The multiplexer combines (multiplexes) data from the n slower speed input lines and transmits over

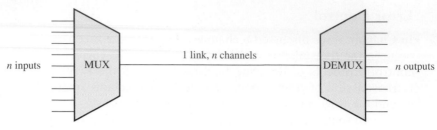

Figure 6.2   Multiplexing

a higher-capacity data link. The demultiplexer accepts the multiplexed data stream, separates (demultiplexes) the data according to channel, and delivers them to the appropriate output lines.

The widespread use of multiplexing in data communications can be explained by the following:

- The higher the data rate, the more cost-effective the transmission facility. That is, for a given application and over a given distance, the cost per Mbps declines with an increase in the data rate of the transmission facility. Similarly, the cost of transmission and receiving equipment, per Mbps, declines with increasing data rate.

- Most individual data communication devices require relatively modest data rate support. For example, for many personal computer and mobile device applications that do not involve Web access or intensive graphics, a data rate of between 9600 bps and 64 Kbps is generally adequate.

The preceding statements were phrased in terms of data transmission. Similar statements apply to voice communications. That is, the greater the capacity of a transmission facility, in terms of voice channels, the less the cost per individual voice channel.

The remainder of this chapter concentrates on two types of multiplexing techniques. The first, frequency-division multiplexing (FDM), is the most heavily used and is familiar to anyone who has ever used a radio or television set. The second is a particular case of time-division multiplexing (TDM) known as synchronous TDM. This is commonly used for multiplexing digitized voice streams and data streams.

6.3   FREQUENCY-DIVISION MULTIPLEXING

Frequency-division multiplexing (FDM) is a familiar and widely used form of multiplexing. A simple example is its use in cable TV systems, which carry multiple video channels on a single cable. FDM is possible when the useful bandwidth of the transmission medium exceeds the required bandwidth of signals to be transmitted. A number of signals can be carried simultaneously if each signal is modulated onto a different carrier frequency and the carrier frequencies are sufficiently separated that the bandwidths of the signals do not overlap. A general case of FDM is shown in Figure 6.3a. Six signal sources are fed into a multiplexer that modulates each signal onto a different frequency ($f_1, \ldots, f_6$). Each modulated signal requires a

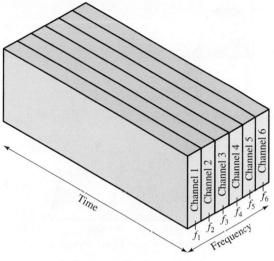

(a) Frequency-division multiplexing

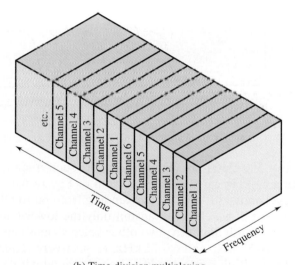

(b) Time-division multiplexing

Figure 6.3   FDM and TDM

certain bandwidth centered on its carrier frequency, referred to as a *channel*. To prevent interference, the channels are separated by guardbands, which are unused portions of the spectrum.

The composite signal transmitted across the medium is analog. Note, however, that the input signals may be either digital or analog. In the case of digital input, the input signals must be passed through modems to be converted to analog. In either case, each analog input signal must then be modulated to move it to the appropriate frequency band.

A simple example of FDM is illustrated in Figure 6.4, which shows the transmission of three voice signals simultaneously over a transmission medium. As was mentioned, the bandwidth of a voice signal is generally 4 kHz, with an effective

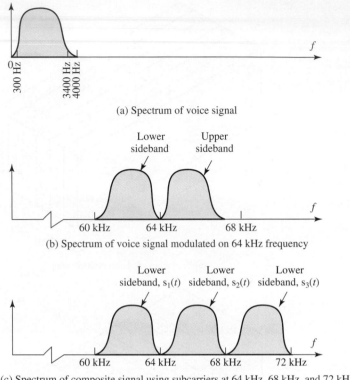

(a) Spectrum of voice signal

(b) Spectrum of voice signal modulated on 64 kHz frequency

(c) Spectrum of composite signal using subcarriers at 64 kHz, 68 kHz, and 72 kHz

Figure 6.4   FDM of Three Voiceband Signals

spectrum of 300–3400 Hz (Figure 6.4a). If such a signal is used to amplitude-modulate a 64-kHz carrier, the spectrum of Figure 6.4b results. The modulated signal has a bandwidth of 8 kHz, extending from 60 to 68 kHz. To make efficient use of bandwidth, we elect to transmit only the lower half of the spectrum, called the lower sideband. Similarly, two other voice signals can be modulated to fit into the ranges 64–68 kHz and 68–72 kHz, respectively. These signals are then combined in the multiplexer to produce a single signal with a range of 60–72 kHz. At the receiving end, the demultiplexing process involves splitting the received signal into three frequency bands and then demodulating each signal back to the original voice band (0–4 kHz). Note that there is only a minor amount of overlap between the multiplexed signals. Because the effective bandwidth of each signal is actually less than 4 kHz with guardbands on either side of the effective spectrum, no noticeable interference results.

FDM was the mainstay of telephone transmission for many years; it is actually more efficient in terms of bandwidth than digital systems. The problem is that noise is amplified along with the voice signal. This fact, and the great decrease in the cost of digital electronics, has led to the widespread replacement of FDM systems with TDM systems in telephone networks.

Although the use of FDM for voice transmission is declining, it is still used widely for television distribution systems, including broadcast television and cable TV. The analog television signal discussed in Chapter 2 fits comfortably into a 6-MHz bandwidth. Figure 6.5 depicts the transmitted video signal and its bandwidth. The black-and-white video signal is amplitude-modulated on a carrier signal. The resulting signal has a bandwidth of about 5 MHz, most of which is above the carrier signal. A separate color subcarrier is used to transmit color information. This is spaced far enough from the main carrier that there is essentially no interference. Finally, the audio portion of the signal is modulated on a third carrier, outside the effective bandwidth of the other two signals. The composite signal fits into a 6-MHz bandwidth with the video, color, and audio signal carriers at 1.25 MHz, 4.799545 MHz, and 5.75 MHz above the lower edge of the band, respectively. Thus, multiple TV signals can be frequency-division multiplexed on a cable, each with a bandwidth of 6 MHz. Given the enormous bandwidth of coaxial cable (as much as 500 MHz), dozens of video signals can be simultaneously carried using FDM.

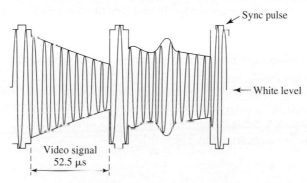

(a) Amplitude modulation with video signal

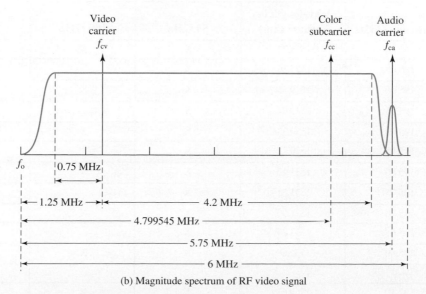

(b) Magnitude spectrum of RF video signal

Figure 6.5 Transmitted TV Signal

Wavelength–Division Multiplexing

The true potential of optical fiber is fully exploited when multiple beams of light at different frequencies are transmitted on the same fiber. This is a form of frequency-division multiplexing but is commonly called **wavelength-division multiplexing (WDM)**. With WDM, the light streaming through the fiber consists of many colors, or wavelengths, each carrying a separate channel of data. In 1997, a landmark was reached when Bell Laboratories was able to demonstrate a WDM system with 100 beams each operating at 10 Gbps, for a total data rate of 1 trillion bits per second (also referred to as 1 terabit per second or 1 Tbps). Commercial systems with 160 channels of 10 Gbps are now available. In a lab environment, Alcatel has carried 256 channels at 39.8 Gbps each, a total of 10.1 Tbps, over a 100-km span. Ongoing research and development suggests that channel speeds exceeding 100 Gbps are not untenable.

A typical WDM system has the same general architecture as other FDM systems. A number of sources generate a laser beam at different wavelengths. These are sent to a multiplexer that consolidates the sources for transmission over a single fiber line. Optical amplifiers, typically spaced tens of kilometers apart, amplify all of the wavelengths simultaneously. Finally, the composite signal arrives at a demultiplexer, where the component channels are separated and sent to receivers at the destination point.

Most WDM systems operate in the 1550-nm range. In early systems, 200 GHz was allocated to each channel, but today most WDM systems use 50-GHz spacing. The channel spacing defined in ITU-T G.692, which accommodates 80 50-GHz channels, is summarized in Table 6.1.

Table 6.1 ITU WDM Channel Spacing (G.692)

Frequency (THz)	Wavelength in Vacuum (nm)	50 GHz	100 GHz	200 GHz
196.10	1528.77	X	X	X
196.05	1529.16	X		
196.00	1529.55	X	X	
195.95	1529.94	X		
195.90	1530.33	X	X	X
195.85	1530.72	X		
195.80	1531.12	X	X	
195.75	1531.51	X		
195.70	1531.90	X	X	X
195.65	1532.29	X		
195.60	1532.68	X	X	
...	...			
192.10	1560.61	X	X	X

The term *dense wavelength-division multiplexing (DWDM)* is often seen in the literature. There is no official or standard definition of this term. The term connotes the use of more channels, more closely spaced, than ordinary WDM. In general, a channel spacing of 200 GHz or less could be considered dense.

WDM is also used in fiber-to-the-home (FTTH) systems. These were introduced in Chapter 5 and illustrated in Figure 5.5. Many providers deliver cable television services over their FTTH connections to subscribers. In FTTH cable television networks that provide interactive services such as pay-per-view, different wavelengths are used for downstream and upstream signals.

ADSL

The asymmetric digital subscriber line provides an interesting example of the use of FDM. ADSL was introduced in Chapter 5 and illustrated in Figure 5.4. In this section, we provide a brief overview of the method.

ADSL Design   The term *asymmetric* is used because ADSL provides more capacity downstream (from the carrier's central office to the customer's site) than upstream (from customer to carrier). ADSL was originally targeted at the expected need for video on demand (VOD) and related services. While VOD over ADSL has not taken off, since ADSL's introduction, the demand for high-speed Internet access. Typically, Internet users require far higher capacity for downstream than for upstream transmission. Most user transmissions are in the form of keyboard strokes or short e-mail messages, whereas incoming traffic, especially Web downloads, can involve large amounts of data that include images or even video. Thus, ADSL provides a perfect fit for consumer Internet access.

ADSL uses frequency-division modulation (FDM) in a novel way to exploit the 1-MHz capacity of twisted-pair telephone wire. There are three elements of the ADSL deployment strategy (Figure 6.6):

- Reserve the lowest 25 kHz for voice, known as POTS (plain old telephone service). The voice is carried only in the 0- to 4-kHz band; the additional bandwidth is to prevent crosstalk between the voice and data channels.

- Use either echo cancellation[1] or FDM to allocate two bands, a smaller upstream band and a larger downstream band.

- Use FDM within the upstream and downstream bands. In this case, a single bit stream is split into multiple parallel bit streams and each portion is carried in a separate frequency band. A commonly used technique is known as discrete multitone, explained subsequently.

When echo cancellation is used, the entire frequency band for the upstream channel overlaps the lower portion of the downstream channel. This has two advantages compared to the use of distinct frequency bands for upstream and downstream.

---

[1]Echo cancellation is a signal-processing technique that allows transmission of signals in both directions in the same frequency band on a single transmission line simultaneously. In essence, a transmitter must subtract the echo of its own transmission from the incoming signal to recover the signal sent by the other side.

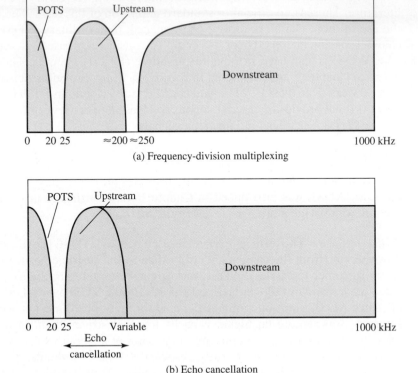

(a) Frequency-division multiplexing

(b) Echo cancellation

Figure 6.6   ADSL Channel Configuration

- The higher the frequency, the greater the attenuation. With the use of echo cancellation, more of the downstream bandwidth is in the "good" part of the spectrum.
- The echo cancellation design is more flexible for changing upstream capacity. The upstream channel can be extended upward (such as when large files must be uploaded) without running into the downstream; instead, the area of overlap is extended.

The disadvantage of the use of echo cancellation is the need for echo cancellation logic on both ends of the line.

The ADSL scheme provides a range of up to 5.5 km, depending on the diameter of the cable and its quality. This is sufficient to reach about 95% of all U.S. subscribers. Comparable coverage percentages can be provided in other nations.

DISCRETE MULTITONE   Discrete multitone (DMT) uses multiple carrier signals at different frequencies, sending some of the bits on each channel. The available transmission band (upstream or downstream) is divided into a number of 4-kHz subchannels. On initialization, the DMT modem sends out test signals on each subchannel to determine the signal-to-noise ratio. The modem then assigns more bits to channels with better signal transmission qualities and fewer bits to channels with poorer signal transmission qualities. Figure 6.7 illustrates this process.

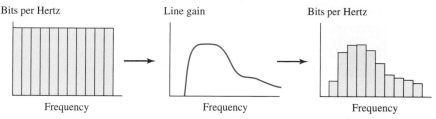

Figure 6.7 DMT Bits per Channel Allocation

Each subchannel can carry a data rate from 0 to 60 Kbps. The figure shows a typical situation in which there is increasing attenuation and hence decreasing signal-to-noise ratio at higher frequencies. As a result, the higher-frequency subchannels carry less of the load.

Present ADSL/DMT designs employ 256 downstream subchannels. In theory, with each 4-kHz subchannel carrying 60 Kbps, it would be possible to transmit at a rate of 15.36 Mbps. In practice, transmission impairments prevent attainment of this data rate. Current implementations operate at 1.5 to 9 Mbps, depending on line distance and quality.

6.4 SYNCHRONOUS TIME-DIVISION MULTIPLEXING

The TDM Mechanism

The other major form of multiplexing is **time-division multiplexing (TDM)**. In this section we examine **synchronous TDM**, which is often simply referred to as TDM.

Time-division multiplexing is possible when the data rate of the transmission medium exceeds the required data rate of signals to be transmitted. A number of digital signals, or analog signals carrying digital data, can be carried simultaneously by interleaving portions of each signal in time. A general case of TDM is shown in Figure 6.3b. In this figure, six signal sources are fed into a multiplexer, which interleaves the bits from each signal by taking turns transmitting bits from each of the signals in a round-robin fashion. For example, the multiplexer in Figure 6.3b has six inputs that might be, say, 9.6 Kbps each. A single line with a capacity of at least 57.6 Kbps accommodates all six sources.

A simple example of TDM is illustrated in Figure 6.8, which shows the transmission of three data signals simultaneously over a transmission medium. In this example, each source operates at 64 Kbps. The output from each source is briefly buffered. Each buffer is typically one bit or one character in length. The buffers are scanned in a round-robin fashion to form a composite digital data stream. The scan operations are sufficiently rapid so that each buffer is emptied before more data can arrive. The scanned data are combined by the multiplexer into a composite data stream. Thus, the data rate transmitted by the multiplexer must at least equal the sum of the data rates of the three inputs (3 × 64 = 192 Kbps). The digital signal produced by the multiplexer may be transmitted digitally or passed through a modem so that an analog signal is transmitted. In either case, transmission is

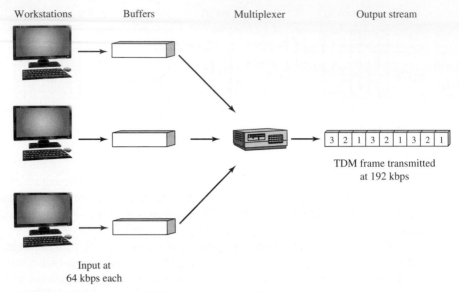

Figure 6.8 Synchronous TDM of Three Data Channels

typically synchronous (as opposed to asynchronous). At the receiving end, the demultiplexing process involves distributing the incoming data among three destination buffers.

The data transmitted by a synchronous TDM system have a format like that of Figure 6.9. The data are organized into *frames*, each of which contains a cycle of time slots. In each frame, one or more slots are dedicated to each data source. Transmission consists of the transmission of a sequence of frames. The set of time slots dedicated to one source, from frame to frame, is called a *channel*. Note that this is the same term used for FDM. The two uses of the term "channel" are logically equivalent. In both cases, a portion of the transmission capacity is dedicated to signals from a single source; that source sees a constant-data-rate or constant-bandwidth channel for transmission.

The slot length equals the transmitter buffer length, typically a bit or a byte (character). The byte-interleaving technique is used with both asynchronous and synchronous sources. Each time slot contains one byte of data. For asynchronous transmission, the start and stop bits of each character are typically eliminated before transmission and reinserted by the receiver, thus improving efficiency. The bit-interleaving technique is used with synchronous sources.

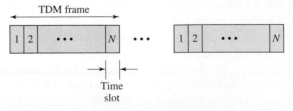

Figure 6.9 TDM Frame Structure

Synchronous TDM is called synchronous not because synchronous transmission is used but because the time slots are preassigned to sources and are fixed. The time slots for a given source are transmitted whether or not the source has data to send. This is, of course, also the case with FDM: A frequency band is dedicated to a particular source whether or not the source is transmitting at any given time. In both cases, capacity is wasted to achieve simplicity of implementation. Even when fixed assignment is used, however, it is possible for a synchronous TDM device to handle sources of different data rates. For example, the slowest input devices could be assigned one slot per frame, while faster devices are assigned multiple slots per frame.

Digital Carrier Systems

The long-distance carrier system provided in the United States and throughout the world was designed to transmit voice signals over high-capacity transmission links, such as optical fiber, coaxial cable, and microwave. Part of the evolution of these telecommunications networks to digital technology has been the adoption of synchronous TDM transmission structures. In the United States, AT&T developed a hierarchy of TDM structures of various capacities; this structure is used in Canada and Japan as well as the United States. A similar, but unfortunately not identical, hierarchy has been adopted internationally under the auspices of ITU-T; it is widely used in Europe and is often referred to as the E-carrier hierarchy, where E stands for European (Table 6.2).

The basis of the TDM hierarchy (in North America and Japan) is the DS-1 transmission format (Figure 6.10), which multiplexes 24 channels. Each frame contains 8 bits per channel, 24 channels, plus a framing bit. Hence, each frame is 193 bits (24 channels × 8 bits per channel + 1 framing bit = 193 bits). For voice transmission, the following rules apply. Each channel of each frame contains one byte (8 bits) of digitized voice data. The original analog voice signal is digitized using pulse code modulation (PCM) at a rate of 8000 samples per second. Therefore, each channel slot and hence each frame must repeat 8000 times per second. With a frame length of 193 bits, we have a data rate of 8000 frames per second × 193 bits per frame = 1.544 Mbps. For five of every six frames, 8-bit PCM samples are used. For every sixth frame, each channel contains a 7-bit PCM byte plus a signaling bit. The signaling bits form a

Table 6.2 North American and International TDM Carrier Standards

North American			International (ITU-T)		
Designation	**Number of Voice Channels**	**Data Rate (Mbps)**	**Level**	**Number of Voice Channels**	**Data Rate (Mbps)**
DS-1	24	1.544	1	30	2.048
DS-1C	48	3.152	2	120	8.448
DS-2	96	6.312	3	480	34.368
DS-3	672	44.736	4	1920	139.264
DS-4	4032	274.176	5	7680	565.148

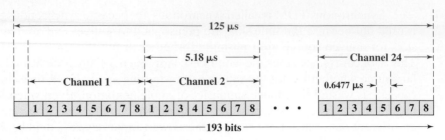

Figure 6.10 DS-1 Transmission Format

Notes:

1. The first bit is a framing bit, used for synchronization.
2. Voice channels:
   - 8-bit PCM used on five of six frames.
   - 7-bit PCM used on every sixth frame; bit 8 of each channel is a signaling bit.
3. Data channels:
   - Channel 24 is used for signaling only in some schemes.
   - Bits 1–7 used for 56 kbps service.
   - Bits 2–7 used for 9.6, 4.8, and 2.4 kbps service.

stream for each voice channel that contains network control and routing information. For example, control signals are used to establish a connection or terminate a call.

The same DS-1 format is used to provide digital data service. For compatibility with voice, the same 1.544-Mbps data rate is used. In this case, 23 channels of data are provided. The twenty-fourth channel position is reserved for a special sync byte, which allows faster and more reliable reframing following a framing error. Within each channel, 7 bits per frame are used for data, with the eighth bit used to indicate whether the channel, for that frame, contains user data or system control data. With 7 bits per channel, and because each frame is repeated 8000 times per second, a data rate of 56 Kbps can be provided per channel. Lower data rates are provided using a technique known as subrate multiplexing.[2]

Finally, the DS-1 format can be used to carry a mixture of voice and data channels. In this case, all 24 channels are utilized; no sync byte is provided.

Above this basic data rate of 1.544 Mbps, higher-level multiplexing is achieved by interleaving bits from DS-1 inputs. For example, the DS-2 transmission system combines four DS-1 inputs into a 6.312-Mbps stream. Data from the four sources are interleaved 12 bits at a time. Note that $1.544 \times 4 = 6.176$ Mbps. The remaining capacity is used for framing and control bits.

The designations DS-1, DS-1C, and so on refer to the multiplexing scheme used for carrying information. AT&T and other carriers supply transmission facilities that support these various multiplexed signals, referred to as carrier systems. These are designated with a "T" label. Thus, the T-1 carrier provides a data rate of 1.544 Mbps and is thus capable of supporting the DS-1 multiplex format and so on for higher data rates.

---

[2]For this technique, an additional bit is robbed from each channel to indicate which subrate multiplexing rate is being provided. This leaves a total capacity per channel of $6 \times 8000 = 48$ Kbps. This capacity is used to multiplex five 9.6-Kbps channels, ten 4.8-Kbps channels, or twenty 2.4-Kbps channels. For example, if channel 2 is used to provide 9.6-Kbps service, then up to five data subchannels share this channel. The data for each subchannel appear as six bits in channel 2 every fifth frame.

T-1 Facilities

The T-1 facility is widely used by companies as a way of supporting networking capability and controlling costs. The most common external use (not part of the public telephone network) of T-1 facilities is for leased dedicated transmission between customer premises. These facilities allow the customer to set up private networks to carry traffic throughout an organization. Examples of applications for such private networks include:

- **Private voice networks:** When there is a substantial amount of intersite voice traffic, a leased private network can provide significant savings over using dial-up facilities.

- **Private data network:** Similarly, high data volumes between two or more sites can be supported by T-1 lines.

- **Video teleconferencing:** Allows high-quality video to be transmitted. As the bandwidth requirement for video declines, private video conferencing links can share T-1 facilities with other applications.

- **High-speed digital facsimile:** Permits rapid transmission of facsimile images and, depending on the facsimile load, may be able to share the T-1 link with other applications.

- **Internet access:** If a high volume of traffic between the site and the Internet is anticipated, then a high-capacity access line to the local Internet service provider is needed.

For users with substantial data transmission needs, the use of private T-1 networking is attractive for two reasons. First, T-1 permits simpler configurations than the use of a mix of lower-speed offerings (such as multiple dedicated 56 Kbps links), and second, T-1 transmission services are less expensive.

Another popular use of T-1 is to provide high-speed access from the customer's premises to the telephone network. In this application, a local area network or PBX on the customer's premises supports a number of devices that generate sufficient off-site traffic to require the use of a T-1 access line to the public network.

Sonet/SDH

Synchronous Optical Network (SONET) is an optical transmission interface that was originally designed for the public telephone network. It began to be deployed in the 1980s and is still widely used. It has been standardized by ANSI for voice, long-haul data, and/or video traffic applications. A compatible version, referred to as Synchronous Digital Hierarchy (SDH), has been published by ITU-T in Recommendations G.707, G.708, and G.709.[3]

SONET is intended to provide a specification for taking advantage of the high-speed digital transmission capability of optical fiber. Similar to Ethernet, SONET provides a physical layer (layer 1 in the OSI model) interface technology that is

---

[3]In what follows, we will use the term *SONET* to refer to both specifications. Where differences exist, these will be addressed.

capable of carrying multiple higher level application protocols. For example, IP packets can be configured for transmission over SONET circuits.

SIGNAL HIERARCHY The SONET (Synchronous Optical Network) specification defines a hierarchy of standardized digital data rates (Table 6.3). The lowest level, referred to as STS-1 (Synchronous Transport Signal level 1) or OC-1 (Optical Carrier level 1),[4] is 51.84 Mbps. This rate can be used to carry a single DS-3 signal or a group of lower-rate signals, such as DS1, DS1C, DS2, plus ITU-T rates (e.g., 2.048 Mbps).

Multiple STS-1 signals can be combined to form an STS-N signal. The signal is created by interleaving bytes from *N* STS-1 signals that are mutually synchronized. For the ITU-T Synchronous Digital Hierarchy, the lowest rate is 155.52 Mbps, which is designated STM-1. This corresponds to SONET STS-3.

The most common data transmission speeds over SONET ranges between 155 Mbps and 2.5 Gbps. To build these data streams, SONET multiplexes lower-speed channels (with bandwidths as low as 64 Kbps) into STS frames.

FRAME FORMAT The basic SONET building block is the STS-1 frame, which consists of 810 octets and is transmitted once every 125 µs, for an overall data rate of 51.84 Mbps (Figure 6.11a). The frame can logically be viewed as a matrix of 9 rows of 90 octets each, with transmission being one row at a time, from left to right and top to bottom.

The first three columns (3 octets × 9 rows = 27 octets) of the frame are devoted to overhead octets, called section overhead and line overhead, which relate to different levels of detail in describing a SONET transmission. These octets convey not only synchronization information but network management information.

Table 6.3 SONET/SDH Signal Hierarchy

SONET Designation	ITU-T Designation	Data Rate	Payload Rate (Mbps)
STS-1/OC-1	STM-0	51.84 Mbps	50.112 Mbps
STS-3/OC-3	STM-1	155.52 Mbps	150.336 Mbps
STS-9/OC-9		466.56 Mbps	451.008 Mbps
STS-12/OC-12	STM-4	622.08 Mbps	601.344 Mbps
STS-18/OC-18		933.12 Mbps	902.016 Mbps
STS-24/OC-24		1.24416 Gbps	1.202688 Gbps
STS-36/OC-36		1.86624 Gbps	1.804032 Gbps
STS-48/OC-48	STM-16	2.48832 Gbps	2.405376 Gbps
STS-96/OC-96		4.87664 Gbps	4.810752 Gbps
STS-192/OC-192	STM-64	9.95328 Gbps	9.621504 Gbps
STS-768	STM-256	39.81312 Gbps	38.486016 Gbps
STS-3072		159.25248 Gbps	1.53944064 Gbps

---

[4]An OC-N rate is the optical equivalent of an STS-N electrical signal. End-user devices transmit and receive electrical signals; these must be converted to and from optical signals for transmission over optical fiber.

The remainder of the frame is payload, which is provided by the logical layer of SONET called the path layer. The payload includes a column of path overhead, which is not necessarily in the first available column position; the line overhead contains a pointer that indicates where the path overhead starts.

Figure 6.11b shows the general format for higher-rate frames, using the ITU-T designation.

Cellular and Cordless Telephone Systems

Frequency-division multiplexing has been used in analog cellular and cordless telephone systems. When *frequency-division multiple access (FDMA)* is used, the radio spectrum used to connect mobile devices and cell towers is divided into separate frequency channels; each channel is capable of carrying one call. *Frequency-division duplexing (FDD)* has also been used in analog cellular and cordless telephone systems. In FDD, two distinct frequency bands are used. One band carries uplink channels (e.g., from mobile device to cell tower) and the second carries downlink channels (from cell tower to mobile device).

As noted in Chapter 17, frequency-division approaches have been largely replaced by time-division multiple access (TDMA) and code-division multiple access (CDMA) in cellular networks. However, in some instances a combination of frequency-division and time-division multiplexing has been used. For example, in second generation GSM systems, the radio spectrum between cell towers and mobile devices is divided into frequency channels, but each frequency channel is further divided into time slots and each time slot carries the data of a voice call. Hence, second-generation GSM employs a combination of FDMA and TDMA.

Most cordless digital telephone systems used in homes employ TDMA or time-division duplexing (TDD) along with FDM. In TDD the uplink of the voice call is time multiplexed on the same frequency channel as the call's downlink.

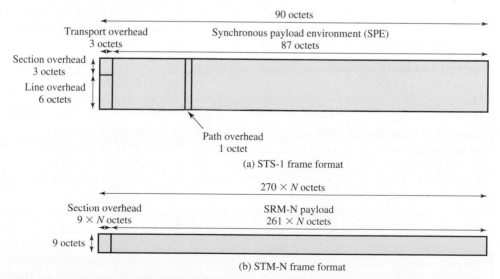

(a) STS-1 frame format

(b) STM-N frame format

Figure 6.11   SONET/SDH Frame Formats

APPLICATION NOTE

Changing Communications

It is interesting to follow data communications mechanisms as they change. Of special interest is how data gets from place to place compared to how it did ten or even five years ago. Like anything else, techniques put in place to ensure successful transmissions go out of date, only to be replaced by other fault eliminating tools. These changes are not always a result of advances in technology; many of them come about because of changes in *what* we communicate and with whom.

Technology certainly does advance and create new ways to get things done. When we examine wide area networks, and in particular the protocols used, we see many changes to the quality and speed of the connections. For example, X.25 was a popular protocol used to connect sites to the WAN. It has several functions built in to ensure error-free connectivity. All of the nodes that were part of the network performed these checks. With improvements in data transmission, both in the transmitting equipment and the media used, this amount of error checking is no longer necessary and is considered wasted overhead.

However, this overhead may not have been an issue had it not been for the huge demand for off-site connectivity. At one time, individual nodes did not require much in the way of external resources. With the advent of distributed processing, secure connections between business sites, Web sites, hotmail, search engines, and significant research resources available online, this rule has been almost completely reversed. Increasingly, we see people and organizations sending data to sites "beyond the horizon."

We make demands for increases in speed and accuracy to prevent clogging the outgoing lines with retransmissions. New applications can add to this need for external connectivity. The gaming industry is spending tremendous sums of money developing powerful virtual worlds that are engaging enough to secure their percentage of users moving online. Online games such as *World of Warcraft* and *Halo3* are perfect examples of this trend. We have seen migrations from X.25 to Frame Relay, T-carriers and ATM, which were followed by SONET. The next generation may accomplish all information transfer via 10 Gigabit Ethernet links or something even faster.

Universities are potentially the best illustration of organizations affected by this trend. Universities compete for a position on various "most wired" lists such as can be seen in *PC Magazine* and the older the Yahoo! Internet Life reports. Constant upgrades to improve desktop link speeds, router capability, protocol support, mobility, and off-site connectivity are all part of this drive to be super-wired. These goals also include a host of new policies for acceptable use and security for campus networks. Students can place very high demands on the infrastructure. Most network administrators and professors would probably agree that anytime there are new tools or techniques to communicate and share files over the network, students implement them.

But links to the external world are not the only changes to the way we swap information. Wireless communication is another area of demand for both educational and noneducational networks that certainly reflects change to our communication needs. It is difficult to imagine a world without wireless networking. Wireless has wide-ranging effects in terms of support, security, and management. People now want to be connected on the go and wherever they happen to be. So this means that the applications will require what is called persistence. Persistence refers to a connection's ability to weather changes to topology, protocol, and speed as a user moves. The most obvious technology is 802.11, but the list must also include MobileIP (to ensure roaming connectivity) and IPv6 to accommodate the larger number of users and the quality of service they will expect. Major changes to telephony will also be part of this migration as we move to a more IP-based existence.

Moving to wireless also means increased performance difficulties as users familiar with dedicated 10- or 100-Mbps connections must share slower, more error-prone links. This places demands on the providers to ensure some level of quality, increasing levels of access for individual nodes and radio interference control.

As we move from one architecture to the next and from one set of protocols to another, the methods of flow and error control may change, but the goals remain the same. Links must be managed to reduce errors and ensure connectivity. In addition to understanding the new protocols, it is important for providers to follow the flow of information as users take different pathways and change system requirements.

6.5   SUMMARY

Because of the possibility of transmission errors, and because the receiver of data may need to regulate the rate at which data arrive, it is necessary to impose a layer of control in each communicating device that provides functions such as flow control, error detection, and error control. This layer of control is known as a **data link control protocol**.

Transmission costs are the most substantial portion of the data communications budgets for most businesses. Companies that are faced with increasing needs to share business information among their operating locations must exploit techniques for increasing transmission efficiency across the communication lines that they use.

Multiplexing is commonly used to increase transmission efficiency. Multiplexing allows several transmission sources to share a single communication link. This enables businesses to realize the economies of scale of using fewer higher-capacity lines instead of many lower-capacity lines. With multiplexing, more sources can share the available capacity of a communications link thereby helping to ensure the efficient use of that link. Frequency-division multiplexing can be used with analog signals. A number of signals can be carried simultaneously on the same medium by allocating each signal a different frequency band. Modulation equipment is used to move each signal to the required frequency band, and multiplexing equipment is used to combine the modulated signals. This technique is used in both broadcast and cable TV video distribution systems. It has also been widely used in telephone networks to multiplex voice signals. However, this latter use is being displaced by synchronous time-division multiplexing techniques as telephone networks convert to digital operation. Wavelength division multiplexing and ADSL are forms of frequency-division multiplexing.

Synchronous time-division multiplexing can be used with digital signals or analog signals carrying digital data. In this form of multiplexing, data from various sources are carried in repetitive frames. Each frame consists of a set of time slots, and each source is assigned one or more time slots per frame. The effect is to interleave bits of data from the various sources. This technique is widely used in digital telephone networks and in data communications facilities within organizations. One of the most popular forms of synchronous TDM is known as T-1. This refers to a leased transmission facility of 1.544 Mbps available from various sources and the specific multiplex format used on this facility. T-1 is popular for constructing private networks within geographically dispersed organizations and is increasingly used to provide business-user access to public telephone networks.

Statistical time-division multiplexing provides a generally more efficient service than synchronous TDM for the support of terminals. With statistical TDM, time slots are not pre-assigned to particular data sources. Rather, user data are buffered and transmitted as rapidly as possible using available time slots. Statistical TDM has largely supplanted synchronous TDM for terminal networking applications.

TDM is also used on SONET (Synchronous Optical Network) to support long-haul voice, data, and video applications over fiber-optic circuits. SONET and the SDH (Synchronous Digital Hierarchy) use TDM to achieve multiple gigabit-per-second data rates. TDM and/or a mixture of TDM and FDM are used in cellular telephone networks.

Case Study IV: Broadband Access: Global and Local Issues

The major concepts addressed in this case study include Broadband Internet access options; "wired communities" and nations; digital divide. **This case study and more are available at www.pearsoninternationaleditions.com/stallings**

6.6 KEY TERMS, REVIEW QUESTIONS, AND PROBLEMS

Key Terms

automatic repeat request (ARQ)	flow control	synchronous TDM
data link control protocol	frame	time-division multiplexing (TDM)
discrete multitone (DMT)	frequency-division multiplexing (FDM)	wavelength-division multiplexing (WDM)
error control	multiplexing	

Review Questions

6.1 Why is transmission efficiency an issue for business computer network managers?

6.2 How do data link control protocols help in the transmission of data between senders and receivers?

6.3 What is the effect of an automatic repeat request (ARQ)?

6.4 What is *error control*?

6.5 What are the types of errors that occur in the transmission and reception process?

6.6 What is wavelength-division multiplexing?

6.7 Give an example where a combination of frequency-division and time-division multiplexing has been used.

6.8 How is a channel defined in FDM? How is a channel defined in TDM?

6.9 Why is multiplexing viewed as a cost-effective data transmission option by business computer network managers?

6.10 Identify several examples of FDM.

6.11 Briefly describe how FDM is used to multiplex analog voice signals? How is it used to multiplex analog cable television channels?

6.12 Define *upstream* and *downstream* with respect to subscriber lines.

6.13 What are the three elements in the ADSL deployment strategy?

6.14 Explain how synchronous time-division multiplexing (TDM) works.

6.15 Identify some of the major uses of T-1 lines.

6.16 Why is the use of private T-1 lines attractive to companies?

6.17 What is discrete multitone?

6.18 Briefly describe the role of the two distinct frequency bands used in frequency-division duplexing (FDD).

6.19 Briefly describe the DS-1 transmission format.

6.20 Identify the types of multiplexing used in cellular telephone networks.

Problems

6.1 Do some Internet research on the major functions performed by data link communication protocols. Identify examples of widely used data link control protocols. Summarize your findings in a 250–500 word paper.

6.2 Do some Internet research on flow control in data communications networks. Identify common examples of why flow control is needed and how it is used to ensure reliable data transfer between senders and receivers. Summarize your findings in a 250–500 word paper.

6.3 Find and view several YouTube on ARQ (automatic repeat request). Identify the URLs for three that you would recommend to fellow business data communication students who wanted/needed to learn more about ARQ and its role on error control. If you could only pick one to recommend to fellow students, which would you select? Why?

6.4 Do some Internet research on frequency-division multiplexing. Identify multiple everyday examples of FDM use. Summarize your findings in a brief paper (250–500 words) or five to eight slide PowerPoint presentation.

6.5 Do some Internet research on statistical time-division multiplexing. Summarize the major differences between STDM and synchronous TDM that business managers should know about in a 250–500 word paper or 8–12 slide PowerPoint presentation.

6.6 Do some Internet research on wavelength-division multiplexing. Find at least five images that you think do an especially good job illustrating how WDM works. Include these images in an 8–12 slide PowerPoint presentation that summarizes what WDM is, how it works, and why it is popular.

6.7 Do some Internet research on DSL access multiplexers (DSLAM) and their role in DSL services. Find several images/pictures of DSLAM technologies for inclusion in a 500–750 word paper or 8–12 slide PowerPoint presentation that focuses on DSL access multiplexers and their importance in DSL services.

6.8 Do some Internet research on T-1 multiplexers and the role of CSU/DSU (customer service unit/data service unit) technologies in T-1 services. Summarize your findings in a brief paper (250–500 words) or five to eight slide PowerPoint presentation.

6.9 To get some indication of the relative demands of voice and data traffic, consider the following:
    a. Calculate the number of bits used to send a three-minute telephone call using standard PCM.
    b. How many pages of IRA (ASCII—7 bit) text with an average of 65 characters a line and 55 lines a page corresponds to one three-minute telephone call?

6.10 Assume that you are the business network manager for a new company that is opening its door in your area. Also assume that it has already been determined that a T-1 connection to an ISP will be needed. Do some research on the ISPs that provide T-1 services in your local area and the costs of these services. Use this information to develop a PowerPoint presentation summarizing T-1 service options that are available.

6.11 Assume that you are to design a TDM carrier, which we call T-489, to support 30 voice channels using 6-bit samples and a structure similar to T-1. Determine the required bit rate.

6.12 What is the total bandwidth required to combine 25 voice signals using frequency-division multiplexing?

APPENDIX 6A   HIGH LEVEL DATA LINK CONTROL PROTOCOL

The most important data link control protocol is HDLC. HDLC is widely used and is the basis for many other important data link control protocols, which use the same or similar formats and the same mechanisms as employed in HDLC.

HDLC Frame Structure

Perhaps the best way to begin an explanation of HDLC is to look at the frame structure. The operation of HDLC involves the exchange of two sorts of information between the two connected stations. First, HDLC accepts user data from some higher layer of software and delivers that user data across the link to the other side. On the other side, HDLC accepts the user data and delivers it to a higher layer of software on that side. Second, the two HDLC modules exchange control information to provide for flow control, error control, and other control functions. The method by which this is done is to format the information that is exchanged into a **frame**. A frame is a predefined structure that provides a specific location for various kinds of control information and for user data.

Figure 6.12 depicts the format of the HDLC frame. The frame has the following fields:

- **Flag:** Used for synchronization. It appears at the beginning and end of the frame and always contains the pattern 01111110.

- **Address:** Indicates the secondary station for this transmission. It is needed in the case of a multidrop line, where a primary may send data to one of a number of secondaries, and one of a number of secondaries may send data to the primary. This field is usually 8 bits long but can be extended (Figure 6.12b).

- **Control:** Identifies the purpose and functions of the frame. It is described later in this subsection.

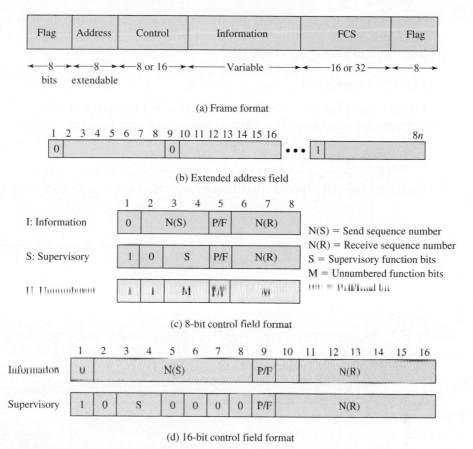

Figure 6.12 HDLC Frame Structure

- **Information:** Contains the user data to be transmitted.
- **Frame Check Sequence:** Contains a 16- or 32-bit cyclic redundancy check, used for error detection. CRC is discussed in Chapter 5.

HDLC defines three types of frames, each with a different control field format. Information frames (I frames) carry the user data to be transmitted for the station. Additionally, the information frames contain control information for flow control and error control. Supervisory frames (S frames) provide another means of exercising flow control and error control. Unnumbered frames (U frames) provide supplemental link control functions.

The first one or two bits of the control field serve to identify the frame type. The remaining bit positions are organized into subfields, as indicated in Figures 6.12c and 6.12d. Their use is explained in the discussion of HDLC operation, which follows. Note that the basic control field for S and I frames uses 3-bit sequence numbers. With the appropriate set-mode commands, an extended control field can be used that employs 7-bit sequence numbers.

All of the control field formats contain the poll/final (P/F) bit. Its use depends on context. Typically, in command frames, it is referred to as the P bit and is set to

1 to solicit (poll) a response frame from the peer HDLC entity. In response frames, it is referred to as the F bit and is set to 1 to indicate the response frame transmitted as a result of a soliciting command.

HDLC Operation

HDLC operation consists of the exchange of I frames, S frames, and U frames between two stations. The various commands and responses defined for these frame types are listed in Table 6.4. In describing HDLC operation, we discuss these three types of frames.

The operation of HDLC involves three phases. First, one side or another initializes the data link so that frames may be exchanged in an orderly fashion.

Table 6.4   HDLC Commands and Responses

Name	Command/Response	Description
Information (I)	C/R	Exchange user data
Supervisory (S)		
Receive ready (RR)	C/R	Positive acknowledgment; ready to receive I frame
Receive not ready (RNR)	C/R	Positive acknowledgment; not ready to receive
Reject (REJ)	C/R	Negative acknowledgment; go back N
Selective reject (SREJ)	C/R	Negative acknowledgment; selective reject
Unnumbered (U)		
Set normal response/extended mode (SNRM/SNRME)	C	Set mode; extended = 7-bit sequence numbers
Set asynchronous response/extended mode (SARM/SARME)	C	Set mode; extended = 7-bit sequence numbers
Set asynchronous balanced/extended mode (SABM, SABME)	C	Set mode; extended = 7-bit sequence numbers
Set initialization mode (SIM)	C	Initialize link control functions in addressed station
Disconnect (DISC)	C	Terminate logical link connection
Unnumbered acknowledgment (UA)	R	Acknowledge acceptance of one of the set-mode commands
Disconnected mode (DM)	R	Responder is in disconnected mode
Request disconnect (RD)	R	Request for DISC command
Request initialization mode (RIM)	R	Initialization needed; request for SIM command
Unnumbered information (UI)	C/R	Used to exchange control information
Unnumbered poll (UP)	C	Used to solicit control information
Reset (RSET)	C	Used for recovery; resets N(R), N(S)
Exchange identification (XID)	C/R	Used to request/report status
Test (TEST)	C/R	Exchange identical information fields for testing
Frame reject (FRMR)	R	Report receipt of unacceptable frame

During this phase, the options that are to be used are agreed upon. After initialization, the two sides exchange user data and the control information to exercise flow and error control. Finally, one of the two sides signals the termination of the operation.

INITIALIZATION   Either side may request initialization by issuing one of the six set-mode commands. This command serves three purposes:

1. It signals the other side that initialization is requested.
2. It specifies which of three modes is requested; these modes have to do with whether one side acts as a primary and controls the exchange or whether the two sides are peers and cooperate in the exchange.
3. It specifies whether 3- or 7-bit sequence numbers are to be used.

If the other side accepts this request, then the HDLC module on that end transmits an Unnumbered Acknowledgement (UA) frame back to the initiating side. If the request is rejected, then a Disconnected Mode (DM) frame is sent.

DATA TRANSFER   When initialization has been requested and accepted, a logical connection is established. Both sides may begin to send user data in I frames, starting with sequence number 0. The N(S) and N(R) fields of the I frame are sequence numbers that support flow control and error control. An HDLC module sending a sequence of I frames numbers them sequentially, modulo 8 or 128, depending on whether 3- or 7-bit sequence numbers are used, and place the sequence number in N(S). N(R) is the acknowledgment for I frames received; it enables the HDLC module to indicate which number I frame it expects to receive next.

S frames are also used for flow control and error control. The Receive Ready (RR) frame is used to acknowledge the last I frame received by indicating the next I frame expected. The RR is used when there is no reverse user data traffic (I frames) to carry an acknowledgment. Receive Not Ready (RNR) acknowledges an I frame, as with RR, but also asks the peer entity to suspend transmission of I frames. When the entity that issued RNR is again ready, it sends an RR. REJ initiates the go-back-N ARQ. It indicates that the last I frame received has been rejected and that retransmission of all I frames beginning with number N(R) is required. Selective reject (SREJ) is used to request retransmission of a single frame.

DISCONNECT   Either HDLC module can initiate a disconnect, either on its own initiative if there is some sort of fault or at the request of its higher-layer user. HDLC issues a disconnect by sending a Disconnect (DISC) frame. The other side must accept the disconnect by replying with a UA.

EXAMPLES OF OPERATION   To better understand HDLC operation, several examples are presented in Figure 6.13. In the example diagrams, each arrow includes a legend that specifies the frame type, the setting of the P/F bit, and, where appropriate, the values of N(R) and N(S). The setting of the P or F bit is 1 if the designation is present and 0 if absent.

Figure 6.13a shows the frames involved in link setup and disconnect. The HDLC entity for one side issues an SABM command[5] to the other side and starts a timer. The other side, upon receiving the SABM, returns a UA response and sets local variables and counters to their initial values. The initiating entity receives the UA response, sets its variables and counters, and stops the timer. The logical connection is now active, and both sides may begin transmitting frames. Should the

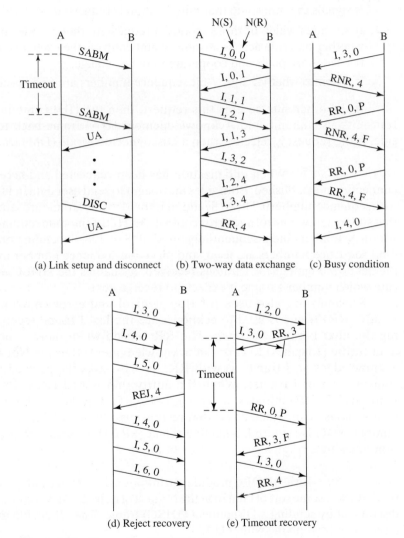

Figure 6.13   Examples of HDLC Operation

---

[5]This stands for Set Asynchronous Mode Balanced. The SABM command is a request to start an exchange. The ABM part of the acronym refers to the mode of transfer, a detail that need not concern us here.

timer expire without a response, the originator repeats the SABM, as illustrated. This would be repeated until a UA or DM is received or until, after a given number of tries, the entity attempting initiation gives up and reports failure to a management entity. In such a case, higher-layer intervention is necessary. The same figure (Figure 6.13a) shows the disconnect procedure. One side issues a DISC command, and the other responds with a UA response.

Figure 6.13b illustrates the full-duplex exchange of I frames. When an entity sends a number of I frames in a row with no incoming data, then the receive sequence number, N(R), is simply repeated (e.g., I,1,1; I,2,1 in the A-to-B direction). When an entity receives a number of I frames in a row with no outgoing frames, then the receive sequence number in the next outgoing frame must reflect the cumulative activity (e.g., I,1,3 in the B-to-A direction). Note that, in addition to I frames, data exchange may involve supervisory frames.

Figure 6.13c shows an operation involving a busy condition. Such a condition may arise because an HDLC entity is not able to process I frames as fast as they are arriving, or the intended user is not able to accept data as fast as they arrive in I frames. In either case, the entity's receive buffer fills up and it must halt the incoming flow of I frames, using an RNR command. In this example, station A issues an RNR, which requires the other side to halt transmission of I frames. The station receiving the RNR usually polls the busy station at some periodic interval by sending an RR with the P bit set. This requires the other side to respond with either an RR or an RNR. When the busy condition has cleared, A returns an RR, and I frame transmission from B can resume.

An example of error recovery using the REJ command is shown in Figure 6.13d. In this example, A transmits I frames numbered 3, 4, and 5. Frame 4 suffers an error. B detects the error and discards the frame. When B receives I frame 5, it discards this frame because it is out of order and sends an REJ with an N(R) of 4. This causes A to initiate retransmission of all I frames sent, beginning with frame 4. It may continue to send additional frames after the retransmitted frames.

An example of error recovery using a timeout is shown in Figure 6.13e. In this example, A transmits I frame number 3 as the last in a sequence of I frames. The frame suffers an error. B detects the error and discards it. However, B cannot send an REJ. This is because there is no way to know if this was an I frame. If an error is detected in a frame, all of the bits of that frame are suspect, and the receiver has no way to act upon it. A, however, started a timer as the frame was transmitted. This timer has a duration long enough to span the expected response time. When the timer expires, A initiates recovery action. This is usually done by polling the other side with an RR command with the P bit set, to determine the status of the other side. Because the poll demands a response, the entity will receive a frame containing an N(R) field and be able to proceed. In this case, the response indicates that frame 3 was lost, which A retransmits.

These examples are not exhaustive. However, they should give the reader a good feel for the behavior of HDLC.

THE INTERNET

Learning Objectives

After reading this chapter, you should be able to:

♦ Discuss the history of the Internet and explain its explosive growth.

♦ Describe the overall Internet architecture and its key components, including ISPs, POPs, and IXPs.

♦ Explain Internet domains and domain names.

♦ Discuss the operation of the Domain Name System.

7.1 THE STRUCTURE OF THE INTERNET

Business and the Internet

The Internet is a central component of most enterprise networks. Its publicly available infrastructure, applications, and protocols are leveraged by businesses in a wide variety of ways. Sophisticated inter-organizational supply chain management (SCM) systems are typically deployed via the Internet, and extranets are routinely used to link businesses with customers, suppliers, and other business partners. When combined with the Internet, enterprise resource planning (ERP) and other enterprise systems become global business software platforms. Businesses of all sizes use the Internet as an e-commerce platform to sell their products and deliver their services, and Internet marketing has become a standard component of advertising campaigns.

It is difficult to fathom how different business operations would be without the Internet. Most business strategies consider how to make greater use of the Internet to improve business processes, not how to unplug. Since living without the Internet is not a feasible alternative for most organizations, it is impossible to fully understand business data communications in enterprise networks without mastering fundamental Internet concepts.

Origins of the Internet

The Internet evolved from the ARPANET, which was developed in 1969 by the Advanced Research Projects Agency (ARPA) of the U.S. Department of Defense. It was the first operational packet-switching network. The ARPANET began operations in four locations. Today the number of hosts is in the hundreds of millions, the number of users is in the billions, and the number of countries participating is around 250. The number of connections to the Internet continues to grow exponentially (Figure 7.1).

The ARPANET made use of the new technology of packet switching, which offered advantages over circuit switching, both of which were briefly introduced in Section 1.8 and are discussed subsequently in this section.

The network was so successful that ARPA applied the same packet-switching technology to tactical radio communication (packet radio) and to satellite communication (SATNET). Because the three networks operated in very different communication environments, the appropriate values for certain parameters, such

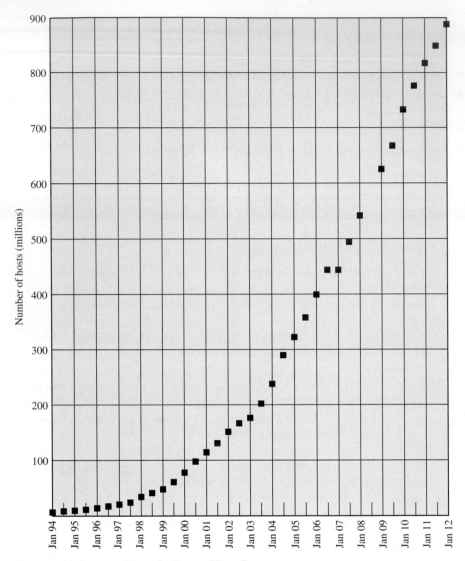

Figure 7.1 Internet Domain Survey Host Count
Source: Internet Software Consortium (http://www.isc.org)

as maximum packet size, were different in each case. Faced with the dilemma of integrating these networks, Vint Cerf and Bob Kahn of ARPA started to develop methods and protocols for *internetworking*—that is, communicating across arbitrary, multiple, packet-switched networks. They published a very influential paper in May 1974 [CERF74] outlining their approach to a Transmission Control Protocol (TCP). The proposal was refined and details filled in by the ARPANET community, with major contributions from participants from European networks eventually leading to TCP and IP (Internet Protocol), which, in turn, formed the basis for what eventually became the TCP/IP suite. This provided the foundation for the Internet.

The Federal Networking Council (subsequently merged into the Networking and Information Technology Research and Development [NITRD] Program of the U.S. government) adopted the following definition of the Internet:

The term *Internet* refers to the global information system that:

(i) is logically linked together by a globally unique address space based on the Internet Protocol (IP) or its subsequent extensions/follow-ons;

(ii) is able to support communications using the Transmission Control Protocol/Internet Protocol (TCP/IP) suite or its subsequent extensions/follow-ons, and/or other IP-compatible protocols; and

(iii) provides, uses or makes accessible, either publicly or privately, high level services layered on the communications and related infrastructure described herein.

The Use of Packet Switching

Traditionally, the two primary paradigms for electronic communications were circuit switching (essentially, voice communication; see Chapter 15) and message switching (telegraph and Telex). In **circuit switching** (Figure 7.2), when source S communicates with destination T through a network, a dedicated path of transmission facilities is established (e.g., S, A, C, E, T) connecting S to T. All of these facilities are held for the duration of the "call." In particular, if there were lulls in the conversation, the transmission path would remain unused during these periods. On the other hand, after the connection is established there is minimal delay through the network. Moreover, once the "call" was set up, the network could basically be passive. Because switching was often electromechanical, this was a big plus.

In **message switching** (Figure 7.2), a message is sent from S to T in stages. First the transmission facility from S to A might be seized and the message is transmitted from S to A, where it is temporarily stored. At this point the S to A channel is released. Then a channel from A to C is accessed and the message is sent to C, and so on. In this case the transmission channels are only used when they are needed, and not wasted when they are not needed. In exchange for this more efficient transmission, the delay can be substantial and quite variable. The messages were frequently stored at each intermediate location on slow peripheral processors such as disks, magnetic drums, or, in the early days, punched paper tapes. These peripherals are slow. Moreover, each time the message is transmitted, a transmission time equal to the length of the message divided by the channel's data rate was incurred. Very long messages would incur very long delays on each hop. There would be one such delay for each hop on the path connecting the source to the destination. So the delay due to transmissions would vary widely depending on the length of the message and the number of hops on the path connecting source to destination.

Packet switching is a special case of message switching, with substantially different properties. First the transmitted data unit, the packet, is limited in length. If a message is bigger than the maximum packet size, it is broken up into a number of packets. Second, when packets are passed from switch to switch they

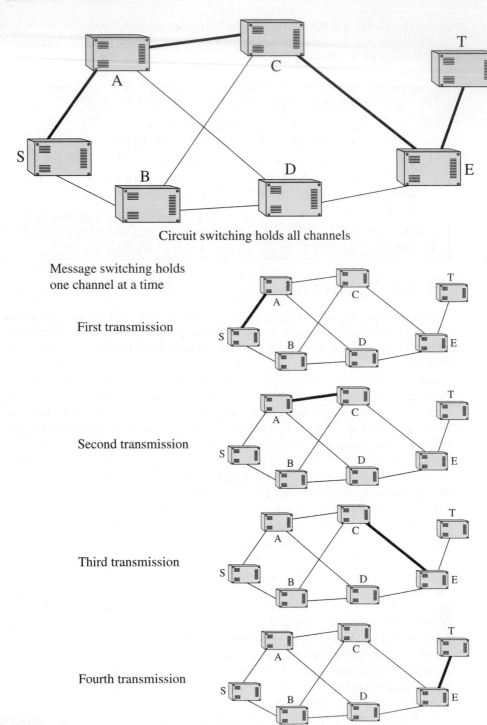

Figure 7.2 Circuit Switching versus Message Switching

are stored in high-speed random access memory (RAM) rather than in the slower peripherals ordinarily used in message-switching systems. Packet switching has several obvious advantages compared to message switching: The delay is much shorter. The delay of the first packet to arrive is only the transmission time of the first packet times the number of hops on the path used. Subsequent packets follow in sequence immediately behind. If high-speed channels are used, the delay, even across the United States, is a few hundred milliseconds. The ARPANET used 50-kbps links. Thus for a path with 5 or less hops and a packet length of less than 1000 bytes, the transmission time is less than $(1000 \times 8)/50,000 = 0.16$ second. At the same time, the channels are used as efficiently as for message switching.

When circuit switching is used for data transmission, the data rates of the transmitting device and the receiving device must be the same. With packet switching, this is not necessary. A packet can be sent at the data rate of the transmitting device into the network; travel through the network at a variety of different data rates, usually higher than the transmitter's rate; and then be metered out at the data rate that the receiver was expecting. The packet-switching network and its interfaces can buffer, look, drop data to make speed conversion from a higher rate to a lower one possible. It was not just differing data rates that made interconnections difficult at the time of the ARPANET's invention; the complete lack of open communication standards made it very difficult for a computer made by one manufacturer to communicate electronically with a computer made by another. Therefore, a key part of the ARPANET effort was the development of standardized communication and application protocols, as discussed subsequently. Of particular interest to its military sponsors, the ARPANET also offered adaptive routing. Each packet, individually, was routed to its destination by whatever route seemed fastest at the time of its transmission. Thus, if parts of the network got congested or failed, packets would automatically be routed around the obstacles.

Some of the early applications developed for the ARPANET also offered new functionality. The first two important applications were Telnet and the File Transfer Protocol (FTP). Telnet provided a universal language for remote computer terminals. When the ARPANET was introduced, each different computer system supported a different terminal. The Telnet application provided a common denominator terminal. If software was written for each type of computer to support the "Telnet terminal," then one terminal could interact with all computer types. FTP offered a similar open functionality. FTP allowed the transparent transfer of files from one computer to another over the network. This is not as trivial as it may sound because various computers had different word sizes, stored their bits in different orders, and used different word formats. However, the first "killer app" for the ARPANET was electronic mail. Before the ARPANET there were electronic mail systems, but they were all single-computer systems. In 1972, Ray Tomlinson of Bolt Beranek and Newman (BBN) wrote the first system to provide distributed mail service across a computer network using multiple computers. By 1973, an ARPA study had found that three-quarters of all ARPANET traffic was e-mail [HAFN96].

Key Elements

Figure 7.3 illustrates the key elements that comprise the Internet. The purpose of the Internet, of course, is to interconnect end systems, called **hosts**; these include PCs, workstations, servers, mainframes, and so on. Most hosts that use the Internet are connected to a **network**, such as a LAN or a wide area network (WAN). These networks are in turn connected by **routers**. Each router attaches to two or more networks. Some hosts, such as mainframes or servers, connect directly to a router rather than through a network.

In essence, the Internet operates as follows. A host may send data to another host anywhere on the Internet. The source host breaks the data to be sent into a sequence of packets, called **IP datagrams** or **IP packets**. Each packet includes a unique numeric address of the destination host. This address is referred to as an **IP address**, because the address is carried in an IP packet. Based on this destination address, each packet travels through a series of routers and networks from source to destination. Each router, as it receives a packet, makes a routing decision and forwards the packet along its way to the destination. We have more to say about this process in Chapter 8.

The World Wide Web

In the spring of 1989, at CERN (the European Laboratory for Particle Physics), Tim Berners-Lee proposed the idea of a distributed hypermedia technology to facilitate the international exchange of research findings using the Internet. Two years later, a prototype World Wide Web (WWW, or the Web for short) was developed at

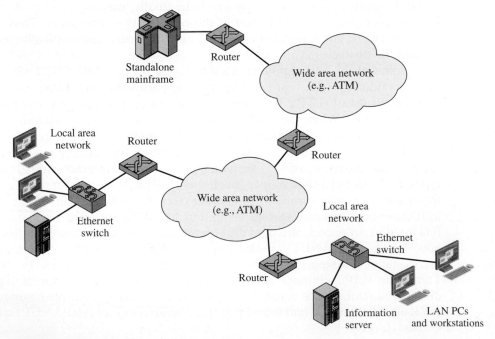

Figure 7.3 Key Elements of the Internet

CERN using the NeXT computer as a platform. By the end of 1991, CERN released a line-oriented *browser* or reader to a limited population. The explosive growth of the technology came with the development of the first graphically oriented browser, *Mosaic*, developed at the NCSA Center at the University of Illinois by Mark Andreessen and others in 1993. Two million copies of Mosaic were delivered over the Internet. Today, the characteristic Web addresses, the URLs (uniform resource locators), are ubiquitous. One cannot read a newspaper or watch TV without seeing the addresses everywhere.

The Web is a system consisting of an internationally distributed collection of *multimedia files* supported by clients (users) and servers (information providers). Each file is addressed in a consistent manner using its URL. The files from the providers are viewed by the clients using *browsers* such as Firefox or Microsoft's Internet Explorer. Most browsers have graphical display and support multimedia— text, audio, image, and video. The user can move from file to file by clicking with a mouse or other pointing device on specially highlighted text or image elements on the browser display; the transfer from one file to the next is called a *hyperlink*. The layout of the browser display is controlled by the *HyperText Markup Language* (HTML) standard, which defines embedded commands in text files that specify features of the browser display, such as the fonts, colors, images and their placement on the display, and the location of the locations where the user can invoke the hyperlinks and their targets. Another important feature of the Web is the Hypertext Transfer Protocol (HTTP), which is a communications protocol for use in TCP/IP networks for fetching the files from the appropriate servers as specified by the hyperlinks.

Internet Architecture

The Internet today is made up of thousands of overlapping hierarchical networks. Because of this, it is not practical to attempt a detailed description of the exact architecture or topology of the Internet. However, an overview of the common, general characteristics can be made. Figure 7.4 illustrates the discussion and Table 7.1 summarizes the terminology.

A key element of the Internet is the set of hosts attached to it. Simply put, a host is a computer. Today, computers come in many forms, including mobile phones and even cars. All of these forms can be hosts on the Internet. Hosts are sometimes grouped together in a LAN. This is the typical configuration in a corporate environment. Individual hosts and LANs are connected to an **Internet service provider (ISP)** through a **point of presence (POP)**. The connection is made in a series of steps starting with the **customer premises equipment (CPE)**. The CPE is the communications equipment located on-site with the host.

For many residential users, the CPE was traditionally a 56-kbps modem. This was adequate for e-mail and related services but marginal for graphics-intensive Web surfing. Today's CPE offerings provide greater capacity and guaranteed service in some cases. A sample of these access technologies includes DSL, cable modem, terrestrial wireless, and satellite. Users who connect to the Internet through their work often use workstations or PCs connected to their employer-owned LANs, which in turn connect through shared organizational trunks to an ISP. In these

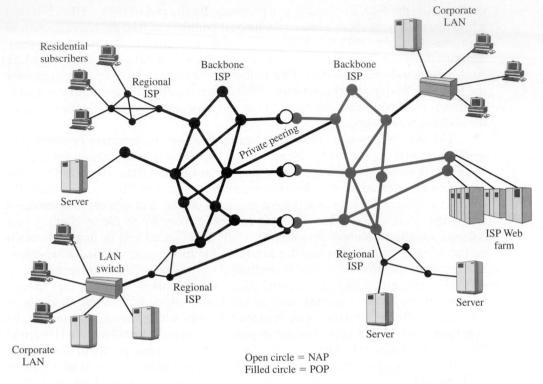

Figure 7.4   Simplified View of Portion of Internet

cases the shared circuit is often a T-1 connection (1.544 Mbps), while for very large organizations T-3 connections (44.736 Mbps) are sometimes found. Alternatively, an organization's LAN may be hooked to a WAN, such as a frame relay network, which in turn connects to an ISP.

The CPE is physically attached to the "local loop" or "last mile." This is the infrastructure between a provider's installation and the site where the host is located. For example, a home user with a 56-k modem attaches the modem to the telephone line. The telephone line is typically a pair of copper wires that runs from the house to a **central office (CO)** owned and operated by the telephone company. In this instance the local loop is the pair of copper wires running between the home and the CO. If the home user has a cable modem, the local loop is the coaxial cable that runs from the home to the cable company facilities. The preceding examples are a bit of an oversimplification but they suffice for this discussion. In many cases the wires that leave a home are aggregated with wires from other homes and then converted to a different media such as fiber. In these cases the term *local loop* still refers to the path from the home to the CO or cable facility. The local loop provider is not necessarily the ISP. In many cases the local loop provider is the telephone company and the ISP is a large, national service organization. Often, however, the local loop provider is also the ISP.

Other forms of CPE-ISP connection do not go through a telephone company CO. For example, a cable link would connect the local user to the cable company site, which would include or link to an ISP. Mobile users can take advantage of a

Table 7.1 Internet Terminology

Central Office (CO)

The place where telephone companies terminate customer lines and locate switching equipment to interconnect those lines with other networks.

Customer Premises Equipment (CPE)

Telecommunications equipment that is located on the customer's premises (physical location) rather than on the provider's premises or in between. Telephone handsets, modems, cable TV set-top boxes, and digital subscriber line routers are examples. Historically, this term referred to equipment placed at the customer's end of the telephone line and usually owned by the telephone company. Today, almost any end-user equipment can be called customer premises equipment, and it can be owned by the customer or by the provider.

Internet Service Provider (ISP)

A company that provides other companies or individuals with access to, or presence on, the Internet. An ISP has the equipment and the telecommunication line access required to have a POP on the Internet for the geographic area served. The larger ISPs have their own high-speed leased lines so that they are less dependent on the telecommunication providers and can provide better service to their customers.

Internet Exchange Point (IXP)

One of a number of major Internet interconnection points that serve to tie all the ISPs together. The IXPs provide major switching facilities that serve the public in general. Companies apply to use the IXP facilities. Much Internet traffic is handled without involving IXPs, using peering arrangements and interconnections within geographic regions.

Network Service Provider (NSP)

A company that provides backbone services to an ISP. Typically, an ISP connects Internet exchange point (IXP) to a regional ISP that in turn connects to an NSP backbone.

Point of Presence (POP)

A site that has a collection of telecommunications equipment, usually refers to ISP or telephone company sites. An ISP POP is the edge of the ISP's network; connections from users are accepted and authenticated here. An Internet access provider may operate several POPs distributed throughout its area of operation to increase the chance that their subscribers will be able to reach one with a local telephone call. The largest national ISPs have POPs all over the country.

wireless link to a Wi-Fi that provides access to the Internet. And corporate access to an ISP may be by dedicated high-speed links or through a WAN, such as an ATM (asynchronous transfer mode) or frame relay network.

The ISP provides access to its larger network through a POP. A POP is simply a facility where customers can connect to the ISP network. The facility is sometimes owned by the ISP, but often the ISP leases space from the local loop carrier. A POP can be as simple as a bank of modems and an access server installed in a rack at the CO. The POPs are usually spread out over the geographic area where the provider offers service. The ISP acts as a gateway to the Internet, providing many important services. For most home users, the ISP provides the unique numeric IP address needed to communicate with other Internet hosts. Most ISPs also provide name resolution and other essential network services. The most important service an ISP provides, though, is access to other ISP networks. Access is facilitated by formal peering agreements between providers. Physical access can be implemented by connecting POPs from different ISPs. This can be done directly with a local connection if the POPs are collocated or with leased lines when the POPs are not collocated. A more commonly used mechanism is the **Internet exchange point (IXP)**.

An IXP is a physical facility that provides the infrastructure to move data between connected networks. Most IXPs today have an ATM or Gigabit Ethernet core. The networks connected at an IXP are owned and operated by **network service providers (NSPs)**. A NSP can also be an ISP but this is not always the case. Peering agreements are between NSPs and do not include the network access point (NAP) operator. The NSPs install routers at the NAP and connect them to the NAP infrastructure. The NSP equipment is responsible for routing, and the IXP infrastructure provides the physical access paths between routers. At the time of this writing, there are 357 IXPs in operation in 91 countries, of which 85 are located in the United States. A current list is maintained at the Packet Clearing House (https://prefix.pch.net/applications/ixpdir).

Although there is no official, rigid organization to the Internet, it is commonly referred to as comprising thee tiers (Figure 7.5), defined as follows:

- **Tier 1:** A Tier 1 network is a top-level network on the Internet. There are about a dozen Tier 1 networks, most of which are in the United States, including AT&T, Global Crossing, Level 3, Qwest, Sprint, and Verizon (originally UUNET). Known as *settlement-free peering*, Tier 1 networks are private networks that

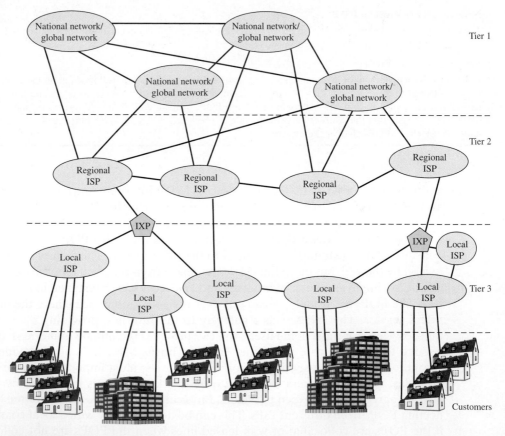

Figure 7.5   Internet Organization

allow traffic from other Tier 1 networks to transit their backbones without a fee. A Tier 1 network can reach every other network on the Internet without purchasing IP transit or paying settlements.

- **Tier 2:** Tier 2 networks peer with some networks without fees but pay to reach a large portion of the Internet. Typically, Tier 2 networks pay a fee to a Tier 1 network to access portions of the Internet that the Tier 2 network cannot reach directly or via peer networking arrangements.

- **Tier 3:** Tier 3 networks always pay fees to obtain access to the larger backbones via Tier 2 networks.

We can think of Tier 1 networks as forming an Internet backbone, with each Tier 1 network having access to an entire Internet routing table so that it knows how to direct traffic to any Internet network. There is a rough equivalence between the concepts of Tier 1 network and NSP, although there is no official definition of either term. Tier 2 networks are regional ISP networks, often provided by telecoms carriers. Tier 3 networks provide only a local presence and provide services to residential and business customers in a locality.

7.2 INTERNET DOMAINS

Internet Names and Addresses

Recall from Section 7.1 that data traverse the Internet in the form of packets, with each packet including a numeric destination address. These addresses are 32-bit binary numbers. The 32-bit IP address provides a way of uniquely identifying devices attached to the Internet. This address is interpreted as having two components: a network number, which identifies a network on the Internet, and a host address, which identifies a unique host on that network. The use of IP addresses presents two problems:

1. Routers devise a path through the Internet on the basis of the network number. If each router needed to keep a master table that listed every network and the preferred path to that network, the management of the tables would be cumbersome and time consuming. It would be better to group the networks in such a way as to simplify the routing function.

2. The 32-bit address is usually written as four decimal numbers, corresponding to the four octets of the address. This number scheme is effective for computer processing but is not convenient for users, who can more easily remember names than numeric addresses.

These problems are addressed by the concept of **domain** and the use of **domain names**. In general terms, a domain refers to a group of hosts that are under the administrative control of a single entity, such as a company or government agency. Domains are organized hierarchically, so that a given domain may consist of a number of subordinate domains. Names are assigned to domains and reflect this hierarchical organization.

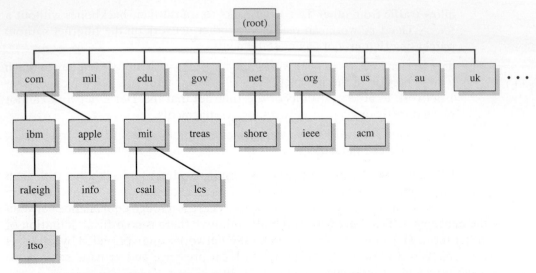

Figure 7.6 Portion of Internet Domain Tree

Figure 7.6 shows a portion of the domain naming tree. At the very top level are a small number of domains that encompass the entire Internet. Table 7.2 lists some of the currently defined top-level domains. These top-level domains are assigned by the Internet Assigned Numbers Authority (IANA). Each subordinate level is named by prefixing a subordinate name to the name at the next highest level. For example,

- edu is the domain of college-level educational institutions.
- mit.edu is the domain for the Massachusetts Institute of Technology (MIT).
- csail.mit.edu is the domain for the MIT Computer Science and Artificial Intelligence Laboratory.

As you move down the naming tree, you eventually get to leaf nodes that identify specific hosts on the Internet. These hosts are assigned Internet addresses. Domain names are assigned hierarchically in such a way that every domain name is unique. At a top level, the creation of new top-level names and the assignment of names and addresses are administered by the Internet Corporation for Assigned Names and Numbers (ICANN). The actual assignment of addresses is delegated down the hierarchy. Thus, the mil domain is assigned a large group of addresses. The U.S. Department of Defense (DoD) then allocates portions of this address space to various DoD organizations for eventual assignment to hosts.

For example, the main host at MIT, with a domain name of mit.edu, has the IP address 18.7.22.69. The subordinate domain csail.mit.edu has the IP address 128.30.2.121.[1]

---

[1]You should be able to demonstrate the name/address function by connecting your Web browser to your local ISP. The ISP should provide a ping or nslookup tool that allows you to enter a domain name and retrieve an IP address. Such a tool is typically available on user operating systems as well.

Table 7.2   Some Top-Level Internet Domains

Domain	Contents
com	Commercial organizations
edu	Educational institutions
gov	U.S. federal government agencies
mil	U.S. military
net	Network support centers, Internet service providers, and other network-related organizations
org	Nonprofit organizations
us	U.S. state and local government agencies, schools, libraries, and museums
country code	ISO standard 2-letter identifier for country-specific domains (e.g., au, ca, uk)
biz	Dedicated exclusively for private businesses
info	Unrestricted use
name	Individuals, for e-mail addresses and personalized domain names
museum	Restricted to museums, museum organizations, and individual members of the museum profession
coop	Member-owned cooperative organizations, such as credit unions
aero	Aviation community
pro	Medical, legal, and accounting professions
arpa	Temporary ARPA domain (still used)
int	International organizations
jobs	Human resource managers
mobi	Consumers and providers of mobile products and services
tel	For businesses and individuals to publish their contact data
travel	Entities whose primary area of activity is in the travel industry

Domain Name System

The Domain Name System (DNS) is a directory lookup service that provides a mapping between the name of a host on the Internet and its numeric address. DNS is essential to the functioning of the Internet.

Four elements comprise the DNS:

- **Domain name space:** DNS uses a tree-structured name space to identify resources on the Internet.
- **DNS database:** Conceptually, each node and leaf in the name space tree structure names a set of information (e.g., IP address, name server for this domain name) that is contained in resource record (RRs). The collection of all RRs is organized into a distributed database.
- **Name servers:** These are server programs that hold information about a portion of the domain name tree structure and the associated RRs.
- **Resolvers:** These are programs that extract information from name servers in response to client requests. A typical client request is for an IP address corresponding to a given domain name.

We have already looked at domain names. The remaining DNS elements are discussed in the remainder of this subsection.

THE DNS DATABASE   DNS is based on a hierarchical database containing **resource records (RRs)** that include the name, IP address, and other information about hosts. The key features of the database are as follows:

- **Variable-depth hierarchy for names:** DNS allows essentially unlimited levels and uses the period (.) as the level delimiter in printed names, as described earlier.
- **Distributed database:** The database resides in DNS servers scattered throughout the Internet.
- **Distribution controlled by the database:** The DNS database is divided into thousands of separately managed zones, which are managed by separate administrators. Distribution and update of records is controlled by the database software.

Using this database, DNS servers provide a name-to-address directory service for network applications that need to locate specific servers. For example, every time an e-mail message is sent or a Web page is accessed, there must be a DNS name lookup to determine the IP address of the e-mail server or Web server.

DNS OPERATION   DNS operation typically includes the following steps (Figure 7.7):

1. A user program requests an IP address for a domain name.
2. A resolver module in the local host or local ISP queries a local name server in the same domain as the resolver.

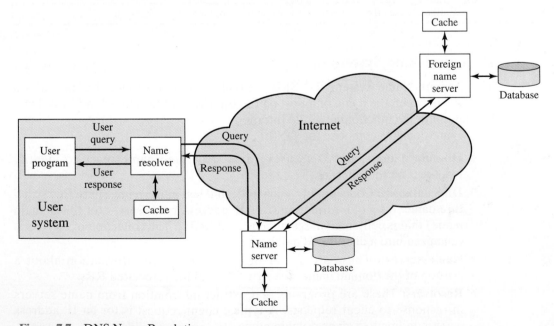

Figure 7.7   DNS Name Resolution

3. The local name server checks to see if the name is in its local database or cache, and, if so, returns the IP address to the requestor. Otherwise, the name server queries other available name servers, if necessary going to the root server, as explained subsequently.

4. When a response is received at the local name server, it stores the name/address mapping in its local cache and may maintain this entry for the amount of time specified in the Time to Live field of the retrieved RR.

5. The user program is given the IP address or an error message.

The distributed DNS database that supports the DNS functionality must be updated frequently because of the rapid and continued growth of the Internet. Further, the DNS must cope with dynamic assignment of IP addresses, such as is done for home DSL users by their ISP. Accordingly, dynamic updating functions for DNS have been defined. In essence, DNS name servers automatically send out updates to other relevant name servers as conditions warrant.

THE SERVER HIERARCHY   The DNS database is distributed hierarchically, residing in DNS name servers scattered throughout the Internet. Name servers can be operated by any organization that owns a domain; that is, any organization that has responsibility for a subtree of the hierarchical domain name space. Each name server is configured with a subset of the domain name space, known as a **zone**, which is a collection of one or more (or all) subdomains within a domain, along with the associated RRs. This set of data is called authoritative, because this name server is responsible for maintaining an accurate set of RRs for this portion of the domain name space. The hierarchical structure can extend to virtually any depth. Thus, a portion of the name space assigned to an authoritative name server can be delegated to a subordinate name server in a way that corresponds to the structure of the domain name tree. For example, a name server is authoritative for the domain ibm.com. A portion of that domain is defined by the name watson.ibm.com, which corresponds to the node watson.ibm.com and all of the branches and leaf nodes underneath the node watson.ibm.com.

At the top of the server hierarchy are 13 **root name servers** that share responsibility for the top-level zones (Table 7.3). This replication is to prevent the root server from becoming a bottleneck, and for reliability. Even so, each individual root server is quite busy. For example, the Internet Software Consortium reports that its server (F) answers almost 300 million DNS requests daily (www.isc.org/community/f-root). Note that some of the root servers exist as multiple servers that are geographically distributed. When there are multiple root servers with the same name, each has an identical copy of the database for that server and the same IP address. When a query is made to that root server, the IP routing protocol and algorithm direct the query to the most convenient server, which is generally the nearest server physically.

Consider a query by a program on a user host for watson.ibm.com. This query is sent to the local name server, and the following steps occur:

1. If the local server already has the IP address for watson.ibm.com in its local cache, it returns the IP address.

Table 7.3   Internet Root Servers

Server	Operator	Locations	IP Addr
A	VeriSign Global Registry Services	6 sites in the United States, Germany, Hong Kong	IPv4: 198.41.0.4 IPv6: 2001:503:BA3E::2:30
B	Information Sciences Institute	Marina Del Rey, CA, USA	IPv4: 192.228.79.201 IPv6: 2001:478:65::53
C	Cogent Communications	6 sites in the United States, Germany, Spain	192.33.4.12
D	University of Maryland	College Park, MD, USA	IPv4: 128.8.10.90 IPv6: 2001:500:2D::D
E	NASA Ames Research Center	Mountain View, CA, USA	192.203.230.10
F	Internet Software Consortium	49 sites in the United States and other countries	IPv4: 192.5.5.241 IPv6: 2001:500:2f::f
G	U.S. DOD Network Information Center	6 sites in United States, Japan, Germany, Italy	192.112.36.4
H	U.S. Army Research Lab	Aberdeen, MD, USA San Diego, CA, USA	IPv4: 128.63.2.53 IPv6: 2001:500:1::803f:235
I	Netnod	38 sites in the United States and other countries	IPv4: 192.36.148.17 IPv6: 2001:7fe::53
J	VeriSign Global Registry Services	70 sites in the United States and other countries	IPv4: 192.58.128.30 IPv6: 2001:503:C27::2:30
K	Reseaux IP Europeens—Network Coordination Centre	18 sites in the United States and other countries	IPv4: 193.0.14.129 IPv6: 2001:7fd::1
L	Internet Corporation for Assigned Names and Numbers	55 sites in the United States and other countries	IPv4: 199.7.83.42 IPv6: 2001:500:3::42
M	WIDE Project	6 sites in the United States, Japan, Korea, France	IPv4: 202.12.27.33 IPv6: 2001:dc3::35

2. If the name is not in the local name server's cache, it sends the query to a root server. The root server returns the names and addresses of the domain name servers that contain information for ibm.com.

3. If there is a delegated name server just for watson.ibm.com, then the ibm.com name server forwards the request to the watson.ibm.com name server, which returns the IP address.

NAME RESOLUTION   As Figure 7.7 indicates, each query begins at a name resolver located in the user host system (e.g., gethostbyname in UNIX). Each resolver is configured to know the IP address of a local DNS name server. If the resolver does not have the requested name in its cache, it sends a DNS query to the local DNS server, which either returns an address immediately or does so after querying one or more other servers.

There are two methods by which queries are forwarded and results returned. Suppose a resolver issues a request to local name server (A). If A has the name/address in its local cache or local database, it can return the IP address to the resolver. If not, then A can do either of the following:

1. Query another name server for the desired result and then send the result back to the resolver. This is known as a **recursive** technique.

2. Return to the resolver the address of the next server (B) to whom the request should be sent. The resolver then sends out a new DNS request to B. This is known as the **iterative** technique.

7.3 DYNAMIC HOST CONFIGURATION PROTOCOL

The Dynamic Host Configuration Protocol (DHCP) is an Internet protocol, defined in RFC 2131, that enables dynamic allocation of IP addresses to hosts.

DHCP was developed to deal with the shortage of IP addresses, a shortage that will remain an issue until the wholesale conversion to the longer IPv6 addresses. DHCP enables a local network, such as in a business enterprise, to assign IP addresses from a pool of available IP addresses to hosts currently in use. When a host is not in use, its IP address is returned to the pool managed by a DHCP server.

Even when there is not a shortage of IP addresses, DHCP is useful in environments with mobile systems, such as laptops and tablets, that travel among different networks or that are only used sporadically. DHCP also can assign permanent IP addresses to some systems, such as servers, so that the address remains the same when the system is rebooted.

DHCP operates on a client/server model, with any host acting as a client that needs an IP address upon booting up, and a DHCP server that provides the request IP address along with related configuration parameters (Figure 7.8). The configuration parameters may include the network address of a default router for communication outside the local network and the address of a local DNS server.

The following DHCP messages are used for protocol operation:

- **DHCPDISCOVER:** Client broadcast to locate available servers.

- **DHCPOFFER:** Server to client in response to DHCPDISCOVER with offer of configuration parameters.

- **DHCPREQUEST:** Client message to servers either (a) requesting offered parameters from one server and implicitly declining offers from all others, (b) confirming correctness of previously allocated address after, for example, system reboot, or (c) extending the lease on a particular network address.

- **DHCPACK:** Server to client with configuration parameters, including committed network address.

- **DHCPNACK:** Server to client indicating client's notion of network address is incorrect (e.g., client has moved to new subnet) or client's lease has expired.

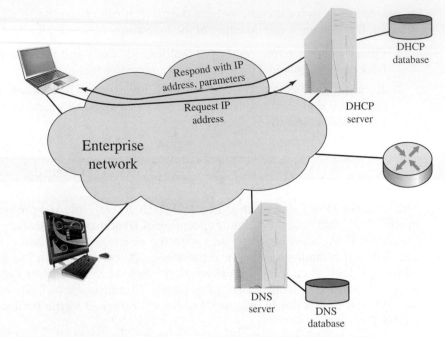

Figure 7.8 DHCP Role

- **DHCPDECLINE:** Client to server indicating network address is already in use. DHCP server should then notify sysadmin.
- **DHCPRELEASE:** Client to server relinquishing network address and canceling remaining lease.
- **DHCPINFORM:** Client to server, asking only for local configuration parameters; client already has externally configured network address.

Figure 7.9 illustrates a typical message exchange. The following steps are involved:

1. The client broadcasts a DHCPDISCOVER message on its local physical network. The message may include options that suggest values for the network address and lease duration. Relay agents may pass the message on to DHCP servers not on the same physical network.

2. Each server may respond with a DHCPOFFER message that includes an available network address.

3. The client receives one or more DHCPOFFER messages from one or more servers. The client may choose to wait for multiple responses. The client chooses one server from which to request configuration parameters, based on the configuration parameters offered in the DHCPOFFER messages. The client broadcasts a DHCPREQUEST message that includes the server identifier option to

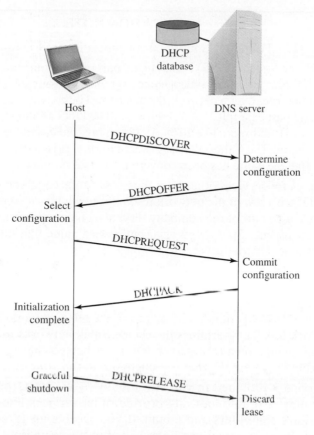

Figure 7.9 DHCP Message Exchange

indicate which server it has selected, and that may include other options specifying desired configuration values. This DHCPREQUEST message is broadcast and relayed through DHCP relay agents. The client times out and retransmits the DHCPDISCOVER message if the client receives no DHCPOFFER messages.

4. The servers receive the DHCPREQUEST broadcast from the client. Those servers not selected by the DHCPREQUEST message use the message as notification that the client has declined that server's offer. The server selected in the DHCPREQUEST message commits the binding for the client to persistent storage and responds with a DHCPACK message containing the configuration parameters for the requesting client.

5. The client receives the DHCPACK message with configuration parameters. At this point, the client is configured.

6. The client may choose to relinquish its lease on a network address by sending a DHCPRELEASE message to the server.

APPLICATION NOTE

Fitting DNS into Your Organizational Structure

The Domain Name System (DNS) is an integral part of communicating over your local area network and the Internet. Every time a name or uniform resource locator (URL) is entered into a program that runs over a network, the name must be converted to the Internet Protocol (IP) address. The best example is a Web browser. The DNS allows us to dispense with difficult to remember IP addresses like 207.42.16.185, in favor of easier "human readable" names like www.yahoo.com. The Yahoo Web site is actually comprised of servers accessed by their IP addresses after the name has been converted to these numbers.

DNS is also used for services other than those used to access Web sites. E-mail, network shares, and FTP are a few of the network resources to which we connect using names. End users typically contact all of the company servers by name rather than by IP address. For example, the command "ftp www.georgia.com" uses a name that must first be resolved to a numerical address for the server.

At the beginning of almost any network transaction, a computer (host) must contact the DNS in order to complete that transaction. So where is the DNS that is providing this service? An organization can either have this service provided by an outside entity or it can run its own DNS that connects to the rest of the DNS system. The size of your organizational network usually determines the choice. Small networks usually have no need or desire to maintain their own DNS server. It is only when you have large number of servers and services running internally that you might opt to run your own.

When the service is provided to you, it is usually by your Internet service provider or ISP. The ISP may also automatically provide other services like the IP addresses for the organization's computers and e-mail. If you receive an IP address automatically, the address of the DNS server can be provided at the same time. Another option is to manually configure the DNS server address on the individual computers. An institution may decide to do this if the network is configured with private IP addresses that do not come from the ISP.

Should the institution decide that it is time to run its own DNS server, there are several configurations possible. DNS is actually a huge collection of servers working together in a hierarchy. These servers will be both on site (your local DNS) and off site. The off-site systems are those servers used by everyone else connected to the Internet. This means that unless the server is designed to be isolated, it will have to communicate with DNS servers external to and upstream of the local network. Operationally, when the DNS system receives a request for name resolution, the closest server attempts to provide the answer (i.e., the IP address that goes with the name in the request). If that server does not know the answer, the request is passed upward and a server with the answer responds.

Just about any computer can be configured as a DNS server. While the technical details are beyond the scope of this text, running your own server adds an additional layer of complexity and management. The DNS server must be kept up to date and have a backup system. Should the local DNS server be off line, all the machines depending on it may have difficulty connecting. To mitigate this, companies running their own DNS server usually will run a secondary server for redundancy.

One consideration may be how much a company depends on Windows Active Directory. Active Directory is a repository or database of organization objects. These objects can describe people, groups, services, and many others. Previously, Windows networks were supported by domain controllers, NetBIOS, and DNS. Active Directory modifies this by increased reliance on DNS. Thus, the Windows system is even more dependent on the proper operation of DNS. In this case, it may be best to run a local DNS server because of all of the organization-specific information that must be stored there and on the Active Directory systems.

DNS is an integral and critical part of any data communications network. The decision to implement your own or rely on services provided from an external organization must be given a good deal of thought as it is a significant investment in time and management resources.

7.4   SUMMARY

The most important networking facility available to organizations is the Internet. The Internet can be used to link to customers and suppliers and can function as a portion of the wide area networking strategy for linking corporate facilities. The Internet is an unusual corporate tool in that it is not owned or managed by a single entity. Instead, each organization that uses the Internet must understand and deploy the standardized protocols necessary for communication across the Internet.

The Internet, and any private intranet, consists of multiple separate networks that are interconnected by routers. Data are transmitted in packets from a source system to a destination across a path involving multiple networks and routers. A router accepts packets and relays them on toward their destination and is responsible for determining the route, much the same way as packet-switching nodes operate.

An essential element of the Internet is its addressing scheme. It is necessary that each attached host have a unique address to make routing and delivery possible. Internet standards define a 32-bit addressing scheme for this purpose. The Domain Name System provides a means of translating host names to Internet addresses, making it easier for users to identify Internet resources.

Case Study V: Net Neutrality

The major concepts addressed in this case study include Internet traffic growth; business use of the Internet. **This case study and more are available at www.pearsoninternationaleditions.com/stallings**

7.5   KEY TERMS, REVIEW QUESTIONS, AND PROBLEMS

Key Terms

ARPANET	Internet exchange point (IXP)	point of presence (POP)
central office (CO)	Internet Protocol (IP)	root name server
customer premises	Internet service provider (ISP)	router
equipment (CPE)	IP address	Tier 1
domain	IP datagram	Tier 2
Domain Name System (DNS)	IP packet	Tier 3
Dynamic Host Configuration	message switching	Transmission Control
Protocol (DHCP)	network	Protocol (TCP)
host	network service provider (NSP)	World Wide Web (WWW)

Review Questions

7.1   What is the difference between the ARPANET and the Internet?

7.2   What two protocols form the foundation of and govern the way we communicate on the Internet?

7.3   What is the difference between message switching and packet switching?

7.4   What were two of the first applications developed for use over a network?

7.5   What are IP datagrams?

7.6   What is point of presence (POP)?

7.7   What are two applications programs that have taken the place of Mosaic?

7.8   What is the programming language used to display Web pages?

7.9   What is the difference between an ISP and a POP?

7.10   What is the difference between an NAP and an NSP?

7.11   What is an Internet exchange point (IXP)?

7.12   What is the use of root name servers in server hierarchy?

7.13   Name the four major components of the DNS.

7.14   What is the difference between a name server and a resolver in the DNS?

7.15   What is a DNS resource record?

7.16   Give a brief description of DNS operation.

7.17   What is a network service provider (NSP)?

7.18   What is DHCP?

7.19   Name three DHCP messages that are used for protocol operation.

Problems

7.1   Do some Internet research on how small businesses and entrepreneurs use the Internet. Look for information on why small businesses are attracted to the Internet and the benefits that they derive from using it. Also look for information on how small business use of the Internet is evolving. Summarize your findings in a short paper (500–750 words) or an 8–12 slide PowerPoint presentation that includes multiple case examples.

7.2   Do some Internet research on Internet marketing. Identify major types of Internet marketing strategies that are widely used and their relative effectiveness. Also identify the major trends that may be observed for Internet marketing. Summarize your findings in a short paper (500–750 words) or an 8–12 slide PowerPoint presentation that includes examples of effective Internet marketing approaches.

7.3 Find and view several YouTube videos that compare circuit switching and packet switching. Identify the URLs of three videos that you think do a good job communicating the essential differences between circuit switching and packet switching. If you could only recommend one to fellow business data communication students, which would you pick? Why? Summarize your recommendations and justification in a brief paper (250–500 words) or a three to five slide PowerPoint presentation.

7.4 Two seemingly unrelated events took place in late 1992 and early 1993 that together seeded the explosive growth of the Internet that is rooted in the early 1990s. One was a piece of legislation authored by Congressman Rick Boucher and the other was a piece of software authored by Marc Andreessen. Explain how and why these two events were major contributors to the state of the Internet as we know it today. References: http://www.neted.org/timeline/ http://www.nsf.gov/pubs/stis1993/oig9301/oig9301.txt http://www.webhistory.org/www.lists/www-talk.1993q1/0262.html

7.5 The dig tool provides easy interactive access to the DNS. The dig tool is available for UNIX and Windows operating systems. It can also be used from the Web. Here one site that, at the time of this writing, provided free access to dig: Reference: http://www.webmaster-toolkit.com/dig.shtml

Use the dig tool to get information about your university's domain.

7.6 Every machine connected to a network should have an IP address. This is true whether the address comes from a DHCP server or is manually configured. Use the following tools to determine your IP address. To use each one, you must first open up either a DOS shell (for Windows) or a Bourne shell (most often used Linux shell). These shells are sometimes called command windows. In Windows operating systems, the shell can be accessed by typing "command" in the Start/Run box. For Linux, the shell may be the default or can be accessed by the shell icon on the task bar.

Windows XP/7—type "ipconfig" in the shell window then press "Enter"

Linux—type "ifconfig eth0" in the shell window then press "Enter"

7.7 You can interact with the server providing the IP address for your computer. For Linux you can use the command ifdown eth0 followed by the command ifup eth0. This will send a series of requests to the server. On the Windows XP/7 machine, type the command ipconfig /? which will display a series of options. Type in ipconfig /all and get a screen capture of what is displayed. Paste the screen into a word processing document and then provide a brief explanation of each of element in the list.

7.8 Find and view several YouTube videos on the importance of DNS and DNS basic operations. Identify the URLs of three to five videos that you think do the best job of clearly describing the role of DNS in Internet operations and how DNS works. If you could only recommend one video to fellow business data communication students, which would you choose? Why? Summarize your recommendations and justification in a brief (250–500 word paper) or short (three to five slides) PowerPoint Presentation.

7.9 Windows XP/7 and Linux have a program built in that will allow you to interact with the DNS server. This program is called "nslookup." Type this name into the command windows and press "Enter." What is the automatic feedback you receive and what does it mean? Typing "exit" will close the program.

7.10 Do some Internet research on DHCP. Look for information that describes how it works and its advantages and disadvantages. Summarize your findings in a short paper (500–750 words) or an 8–12 slide PowerPoint presentation.

7.11 Do some Internet research on static versus dynamic IP addresses and how they can/ should be used in today's networks. Identify the pros and cons of each. Summarize your findings in a short paper (500–750 words) or an 8–12 slide PowerPoint presentation that includes general recommendations for using each in business networks.

TCP/IP

Learning Objectives

After reading this chapter, you should be able to:

♦ Define the term *protocol architecture* and explain the need for and benefits of a communications architecture.

♦ Describe the TCP/IP architecture and explain the functioning of each layer.

♦ Explain the motivation for the development of a standardized architecture and the reasons why a customer should use products based on a protocol architecture standard in preference to products based on a proprietary architecture.

♦ Explain the need for internetworking.

♦ Describe the operation of a router within the context of TCP/IP to provide internetworking.

This chapter examines the underlying communications software required to support distributed applications in businesses and other organizations. We will see that the required software is substantial. To make the task of implementing this communications software manageable, a modular structure known as a protocol architecture is used. The emergence of the Internet as a fundamental component in enterprise networks has meant that the TCP/IP suite has become the protocol architecture that is most important for business data communications students to know.

The transition to IP-based telecommunications has become so widespread that is beginning to spawn new buzzwords: everything over IP (EOIP) and IP over everything (IPOE). This transition has taken hold in both business enterprises and other organizations, including the U.S. Defense Department and its Defense Information Systems agency [JONE09]. EOIP has become the Holy Grail of enterprise networks and it fuels business interest in converged networks. EOIP encourages the development of IP applications for all major types of business data (voice, video, image, and data) as well as IP-based, or IP-compliant, telecommunications transport.

There is a lot to the multifaceted TCP/IP suite, so we begin this chapter by introducing a simple protocol architecture consisting of just three modules, or layers. This will allow us to present the key characteristics and design features of a protocol architecture without getting bogged down in details. With this background, we are then ready to examine the world's most important protocol architecture: TCP/IP (Transmission Control Protocol/Internet Protocol). TCP/IP is an Internet-based standard and is the framework for developing a complete range of computer communications standards. Virtually all computer vendors now provide support for this architecture. Open Systems Interconnection (OSI) is another standardized architecture that is often used to describe communications functions but that is now rarely implemented. For the interested reader, OSI is covered in Appendix L.

Following a discussion of TCP/IP, the important concept of internetworking is examined. Inevitably, a business will require the use of more than one communications network. Some means of interconnecting these networks is required, and this raises issues that relate to the protocol architecture.

8.1   A SIMPLE PROTOCOL ARCHITECTURE

The Need for a Protocol Architecture

When computers, terminals, and/or other data processing devices exchange data, the procedures involved can be quite complex. Consider, for example, the transfer of a file between two computers. There must be a data path between the two computers, either directly or via a communication network. But more is needed. Typical tasks to be performed include the following:

1. The source system must either activate the direct data communication path or inform the communication network of the identity of the desired destination system.

2. The source system must ascertain that the destination system is prepared to receive data.

3. The file transfer application on the source system must ascertain that the file management program on the destination system is prepared to accept and store the file for the user.

4. If the file formats or data representations used on the two systems are incompatible, one or the other system must perform a format translation function.

The exchange of information between computers for the purpose of cooperative action is generally referred to as *computer communications*. Similarly, when two or more computers are interconnected via a communication network, the set of computer stations is referred to as a *computer network*. Because a similar level of cooperation is required between a terminal and a computer, these terms are often used when some of the communicating entities are terminals.

In discussing computer communications and computer networks, two concepts are paramount:

- Protocols
- Computer communications architecture, or protocol architecture

A protocol is used for communication between entities in different systems. The terms *entity* and *system* are used in a very general sense. Examples of entities are user application programs, file transfer packages, database management systems, electronic mail facilities, and terminals. Examples of systems are computers, terminals, and remote sensors. Note that in some cases the entity and the system in which it resides are coextensive (e.g., terminals). In general, an entity is anything capable of sending or receiving information, and a system is a physically distinct object that contains one or more entities. For two entities to communicate successfully, they must "speak the same language." What is communicated, how it is communicated, and when it is communicated must conform to mutually agreed conventions among the entities involved. The conventions are referred to as a **protocol**, which may be defined as a set of rules governing the exchange of data between two entities. The key elements of a protocol are as follows:

- **Syntax:** Includes such things as data format and signal levels
- **Semantics:** Includes control information for coordination and error handling
- **Timing:** Includes speed matching and sequencing

Appendix 8B provides a specific example of a protocol, the Internet standard Trivial File Transfer Protocol (TFTP).

Having introduced the concept of a protocol, we can now introduce the concept of a **protocol architecture**. It is clear that there must be a high degree of cooperation between the two computer systems engaged in a cooperative application. Instead of implementing the logic for this as a single module, the task is broken up into sub-tasks, each of which is implemented separately. The result is a layered architecture, with **peer entities** at each layer performing subtasks appropriate to the layer. As an example, Figure 8.1 suggests the way in which a file transfer facility could be implemented between two computer systems connected by a network. Three modules are used. Tasks 3 and 4 in the preceding list could be performed by a *file transfer module*. The two modules on the two systems exchange files and commands. However, rather than requiring the file transfer module to deal with the details of actually transferring data and commands, the file transfer modules each rely on a *communications service module*. This module is responsible for making sure that the file transfer commands and data are reliably exchanged between systems. The manner in which a communications service module functions is explored subsequently. Among other things, this module would perform task 2. Finally, the nature of the exchange between the two communications service modules is independent of the nature of the network that interconnects them. Therefore, rather than building details of the network interface into the communications service module, it makes sense to have a third module, a *network access module*, that performs task 1 by interacting with the network.

To summarize, the file transfer module contains all the logic that is unique to the file transfer application, such as transmitting passwords, file commands, and file records. These files and commands must be transmitted reliably. However, the same sorts of reliability requirements are relevant to a variety of applications (e.g., electronic mail,

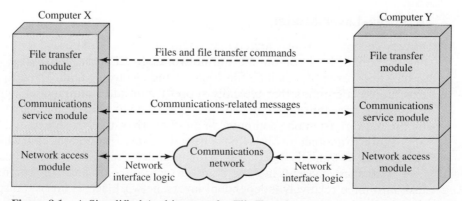

Figure 8.1   A Simplified Architecture for File Transfer

document transfer). Therefore, these requirements are met by a separate communications service module that can be used by a variety of applications. The communications service module is concerned with assuring that the two computer systems are active and ready for data transfer and for keeping track of the data that are being exchanged to assure delivery. However, these tasks are independent of the type of network that is being used. Therefore, the logic for actually dealing with the network is put into a separate network access module. If the network to be used is changed, only the network access module is affected.

Thus, instead of a single module for performing communications, there is a structured set of modules that implements the communications function. That structure is referred to as a **protocol architecture**. An analogy might be useful at this point. Suppose an executive in office X wishes to send a document to an executive in office Y. The executive in X prepares the document and perhaps attaches a note. This corresponds to the actions of the file transfer application in Figure 8.1. Then the executive in X hands the document to a secretary or administrative assistant (AA). The AA in X puts the document in an envelope and puts Y's address and X's return address on the outside. Perhaps the envelope is also marked "confidential." The AA's actions correspond to the communications service module in Figure 8.1. The AA in X then gives the package to the shipping department. Someone in the shipping department decides how to send the package: mail, UPS, or express courier. The shipping department attaches the appropriate postage or shipping documents to the package and ships it out. The shipping department corresponds to the network access module of Figure 8.1. When the package arrives at Y, a similar layered set of actions occurs. The shipping department at Y receives the package and delivers it to the appropriate AA or secretary based on the name on the package. The AA opens the package and hands the enclosed document to the executive to whom it is addressed.

Another important aspect of a protocol architecture is that modules in different systems communicate with peer modules on the same level. Thus, the file transfer module can focus on what it wants to communicate to a peer file transfer module on the other system (represented by the dotted line between the two modules in Figure 8.1).

In the remainder of this section, we generalize the example of Figure 8.1 to present a simplified protocol architecture. Following that, we look at the real-world example of TCP/IP.

A Three-Layer Model

In very general terms, distributed data communications can be said to involve three agents: applications, computers, and networks. In Chapter 10, we look at several applications; examples include file transfer and electronic mail. These applications execute on computers that typically support multiple simultaneous applications. Computers are connected to networks, and the data to be exchanged are transferred by the network from one computer to another. Thus, the transfer of data from one application to another involves first getting the data to the computer in which the application resides and then getting it to the intended application within the computer.

With these concepts in mind, it appears natural to organize the communication task into three relatively independent layers: network access layer, transport layer, and application layer.

The **network access layer** is concerned with the exchange of data between a computer and the network to which it is attached. The sending computer must provide the network with the address of the destination computer, so that the network may route the data to the appropriate destination. The sending computer may wish to invoke certain services, such as priority, that might be provided by the network. The specific software used at this layer depends on the type of network to be used; different standards have been developed for circuit switching, packet switching, local area networks (LANs), and others. For example, IEEE 802 is a standard that specifies the access to a LAN; this standard is described in Part Three. It makes sense to put those functions having to do with network access into a separate layer. By doing this, the remainder of the communications software, above the network access layer, need not be concerned about the specifics of the network to be used. The same higher-layer software should function properly regardless of the particular network to which the computer is attached.

Regardless of the nature of the applications that are exchanging data, there is usually a requirement that data be exchanged reliably. That is, we would like to be assured that all of the data arrive at the destination application and that the data arrive in the same order in which they were sent. As we shall see, the mechanisms for providing reliability are essentially independent of the nature of the applications. Thus, it makes sense to collect those mechanisms in a common layer shared by all applications; this is referred to as the **transport layer**.

Finally, the **application layer** contains the logic needed to support the various user applications. For each different type of application, such as file transfer, a separate module is needed that is peculiar to that application.

Figures 8.2 and 8.3 illustrate this simple architecture. Figure 8.2 shows three computers connected to a network. Each computer contains software at the

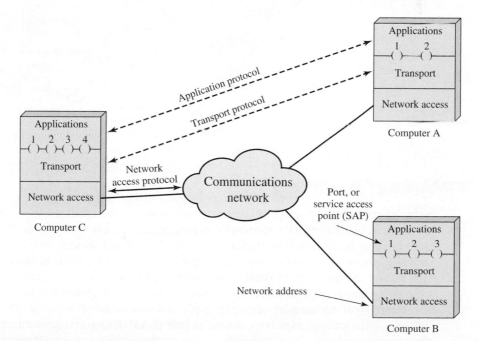

Figure 8.2 Protocol Architectures and Networks

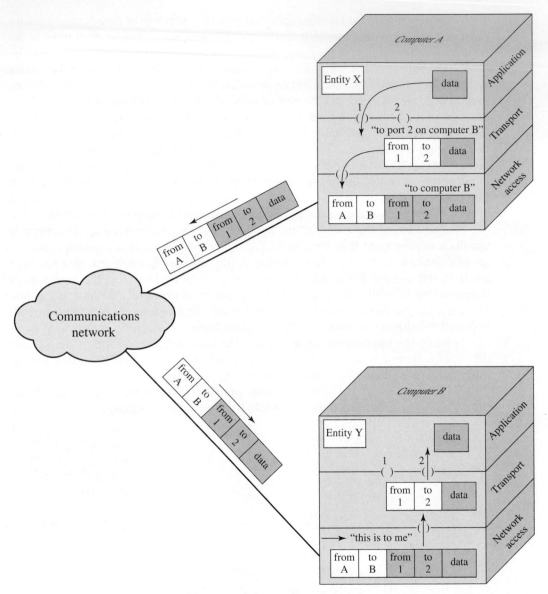

Figure 8.3 Protocols in a Simplified Architecture

network access and transport layers and software at the application layer for one or more applications. For successful communication, every entity in the overall system must have a unique address. In our three-layer model, two levels of addressing are needed. Each computer on the network has a unique network address; this allows the network to deliver data to the proper computer. Each application on a computer has an address that is unique within that computer; this allows the transport layer to support multiple applications at each computer. These latter addresses are known as **service access points (SAPs)**, or **ports**, connoting the fact that each application is individually accessing the services of the transport layer.

Figure 8.2 indicates that modules at the same level (peers) on different computers communicate with each other by means of a protocol. An application entity (e.g., a file transfer application) in one computer communicates with an application in another computer via an application-level protocol (e.g., the File Transfer Protocol). The interchange is not direct (indicated by the dashed line) but is mediated by a transport protocol that handles many of the details of transferring data between two computers. The transport protocol is also not direct, but relies on a network-level protocol to achieve network access and to route data through the network to the destination system. At each level, the cooperating peer entities focus on what they need to communicate to each other.

Let us trace a simple operation. Suppose that an application, associated with port 1 at computer A, wishes to send a message to another application, associated with port 2 at computer B. The application at A hands the message over to its transport layer with instructions to send it to port 2 on computer B. The transport layer hands the message over to the network access layer, which instructs the network to send the message to computer B. Note that the network need not be told the identity of the destination port. All that it needs to know is that the data are intended for computer B.

To control this operation, control information, as well as user data, must be transmitted, as suggested in Figure 8.3. Let us say that the sending application generates a block of data and passes this to the transport layer. The transport layer may break this block into two smaller pieces for convenience, as discussed subsequently. To each of these pieces the transport layer appends a transport **header**, containing protocol control information. The combination of data from the next higher layer and control information is known as a **protocol data unit (PDU)**; in this case, it is referred to as a transport PDU. Transport PDUs are typically called **segments**. The header in each segment contains control information to be used by the peer transport protocol at computer B. Examples of items that may be stored in this header include the following:

- **Source port:** This indicates that application that sent the data.
- **Destination port:** When the destination transport layer receives the segment, it must know to which application the data are to be delivered.
- **Sequence number:** Because the transport protocol is sending a sequence of segments, it numbers them sequentially so that if they arrive out of order, the destination transport entity may reorder them.
- **Error-detection code:** The sending transport entity may include a code that is a function of the contents of the segment. The receiving transport protocol performs the same calculation and compares the result with the incoming code. A discrepancy results if there has been some error in transmission. In that case, the receiver can discard the segment and take corrective action. This code is also referred to as a **checksum** or **frame check sequence**.

The next step is for the transport layer to hand each segment over to the network layer, with instructions to transmit it to the destination computer. To satisfy this request, the network access protocol must present the data to the network with a request for transmission. As before, this operation requires the use of control information. In this case, the network access protocol appends a network access header to the data it receives from the transport layer, creating a network access PDU, typically called a **packet**. Examples of the items that may be stored in the header include the following:

- **Source computer address:** Indicates the source of this packet.
- **Destination computer address:** The network must know to which computer on the network the data are to be delivered.
- **Facilities requests:** The network access protocol might want the network to make use of certain facilities, such as priority.

Note that the transport header is not "visible" at the network access layer; the network access layer is not concerned with the contents of the transport segment.

The network accepts the network packet from A and delivers it to B. The network access module in B receives the packet, strips off the packet header, and transfers the enclosed transport segment to B's transport layer module. The transport layer examines the segment header and, on the basis of the port field in the header, delivers the enclosed record to the appropriate application, in this case the file transfer module in B.

Standardized Protocol Architectures

When communication is desired among computers from different vendors, the software development effort can be a nightmare. Different vendors use different data formats and data exchange protocols. Even within one vendor's product line, different model computers may communicate in unique ways.

Now that computer communications and computer networking are ubiquitous, a one-at-a-time special-purpose approach to communications software development is too costly to be acceptable. The only alternative is for computer vendors to adopt and implement a common set of conventions. For this to happen, standards are needed. Such standards would have two benefits:

- Vendors feel encouraged to implement the standards because of an expectation that, because of wide usage of the standards, their products would be less marketable without them.

- Customers are in a position to require that the standards be implemented by any vendor wishing to propose equipment to them.

Two protocol architectures have served as the basis for the development of interoperable protocol standards: the TCP/IP suite and the OSI reference model. TCP/IP is by far the most widely used interoperable architecture. OSI, though well known, has never lived up to its early promise. There is also a widely used proprietary scheme: IBM's Systems Network Architecture (SNA). Although IBM provides support for TCP/IP, it continues to use SNA, and this latter architecture will remain important for some years to come. The remainder of the chapter looks in some detail at TCP/IP. OSI and SNA are summarized in Appendices I and F, respectively.

8.2   THE TCP/IP ARCHITECTURE

TCP/IP is a result of protocol research and development conducted on the experimental packet-switched network, ARPANET, funded by the Defense Advanced
Research Projects Agency (DARPA), and is generally referred to as the TCP/IP
suite. This protocol suite consists of a large collection of protocols that have been
issued as Internet standards by the Internet Activities Board (IAB). Appendix B
provides a discussion of Internet standards.

TCP/IP Layers

There is no official TCP/IP model as there is in the case of OSI. However, based on
the protocol standards that have been developed, we can organize the communication task for TCP/IP into five relatively independent layers:

- Application layer
- Host to host, or transport layer
- Internet layer
- Network access layer
- Physical layer

   The **application layer** and **transport layer** correspond to the top two layers
described in the three-layer model of Section 8.1. At the transport layer, TCP is the
most commonly used protocol.

   In those cases where two devices are attached to different networks, procedures are needed to allow data to traverse multiple interconnected networks. This is
the function of the internet layer. The **Internet Protocol (IP)** is used at this layer to
provide the routing function across multiple networks. This protocol is implemented
not only in the end systems but also in routers. A **router** is a device that connects two
networks and whose primary function is to relay data from one network to the other
on a route from the source to the destination end system.

   The **network access layer** was also discussed in our three-layer model. Let us
consider the case in which two computers that wish to communicate are both connected to the same network, such as the same LAN or the same wide area network
(WAN). The sending computer must provide the network with the address of the
destination computer, so that the network may route the data to the appropriate destination. In the case in which the two communicating computers are not connected to
the same network, the data transfer must occur as a sequence of hops across multiple
networks. In this latter case, the network access layer is concerned with access to one
network along the route. Thus, from the source computer, the network access layer
provides the attached network with the information needed to reach a router that
connects this network to the next network on the route to the destination.

   The **physical layer** covers the physical interface between a data transmission
device (e.g., workstation, computer) and a transmission medium or network. This
layer is concerned with specifying the characteristics of the transmission medium,
the nature of the signals, the data rate, and related matters.

Operation of TCP/IP

Figure 8.4 indicates how the TCP/IP architecture is configured for communications. Compare this with Figure 8.2. The architectural difference is the inclusion of the internet layer, which allows for multiple networks connected by routers. Some sort of network access protocol, such as the Ethernet or Wi-Fi logic, is used to connect a computer to a network. This protocol enables the host to send data across the network to another host or, in the case of a host on another network, to a router. IP is implemented in all end systems and routers. It acts as a relay to move a block of data from one host, through one or more routers, to another host. TCP is implemented only in the end systems; it keeps track of the blocks of data being transferred to assure that all are delivered reliably to the appropriate application.

The figure highlights the levels of addressing of the TCP/IP architecture. Each host on a network must have a unique network address that identifies the host on that network. In addition, each host has a unique global Internet address; this allows the data to be delivered to the proper host. This address is used by IP for routing and delivery. Each application within a host must have port number that is unique within the host; this allows the host-to-host protocol (TCP) to deliver data to the proper process.

As was shown in Figure 8.3 for a three-layer architecture, it is relatively easy to trace the operation of the four-layer TCP/IP model. For a transfer between applications in hosts A and B, control information as well as user data must be transmitted,

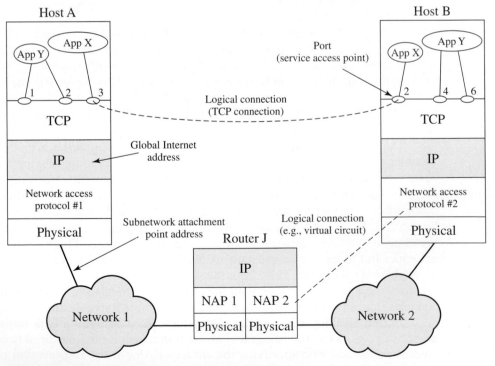

Figure 8.4   TCP/IP Concepts

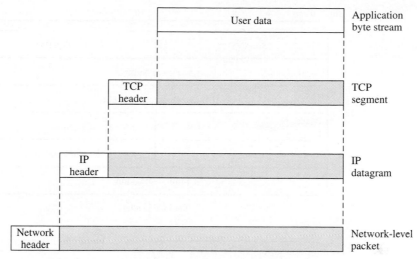

Figure 8.5   Protocol Data Units (PDUs) in the TCP/IP Architecture

as suggested in Figure 8.5. Let us say that the sending process generates a block of data and passes this to TCP. TCP appends control information known as the TCP header, forming a TCP segment. The control information is to be used by the peer TCP entity at host B.

Next, TCP hands each segment over to IP, with instructions to transmit it to B. These segments must be transmitted across one or more networks and relayed through one or more intermediate routers. This operation, too, requires the use of control information. Thus IP appends a header of control information to each segment to form an **IP datagram**. An example of an item stored in the IP header is the destination host address (in this example, B).

Finally, each IP datagram is presented to the network access layer for transmission across the first network in its journey to the destination. The network access layer appends its own header, creating a packet, or frame. The packet is transmitted across the network to router J. The packet header contains the information that the network needs in order to transfer the data across the network.

At router J, the packet header is stripped off and the IP header examined. On the basis of the destination address information in the IP header, the IP module in the router directs the datagram out across network 2 to B. To do this, the datagram is again augmented with a network access header.

When the data are received at B, the reverse process occurs. At each layer, the corresponding header is removed, and the remainder is passed on to the next higher layer, until the original user data are delivered to the destination process.

TCP and UDP

For most applications running as part of the TCP/IP architecture, the transport layer protocol is TCP. TCP provides a reliable connection for the transfer of data between applications. A connection is simply a temporary logical association between two processes in different systems. For the duration of the connection each process keeps

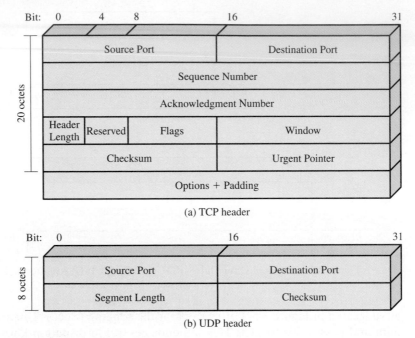

Bit: 0   4   8   16   31

(a) TCP header

Bit: 0   16   31

(b) UDP header

Figure 8.6   TCP and UDP Headers

track of segments coming from and going to the other process, in order to regulate the flow of segments and to recover from lost or damaged segments.

Figure 8.6a shows the header format for TCP, which is a minimum of 20 octets, or 160 bits. The Source Port and Destination Port fields identify the applications at the source and destination systems that are using this connection. The Sequence Number, Acknowledgment Number, and Window fields provide flow control and error control. The checksum is a 16-bit frame check sequence used to detect errors in the TCP segment. For the interested reader, Appendix 8A provides more detail.

In addition to TCP, there is one other transport-level protocol that is in common use as part of the TCP/IP suite: the User Datagram Protocol (UDP). UDP does not guarantee delivery, preservation of sequence, or protection against duplication. UDP enables a process to send messages to other processes with a minimum of protocol mechanism. Some transaction-oriented applications make use of UDP; one example is SNMP (Simple Network Management Protocol), the standard network management protocol for TCP/IP networks. Because it is connectionless, UDP has very little to do. Essentially, it adds a port addressing capability to IP. This is best seen by examining the UDP header, shown in Figure 8.6b.

IP and IPv6

For decades, the keystone of the TCP/IP architecture has been IP. Figure 8.7a shows the IP header format, which is a minimum of 20 octets, or 160 bits. The header, together with the segment from the transport layer, forms an IP-level PDU referred to as an IP datagram or an IP packet. The header includes 32-bit source

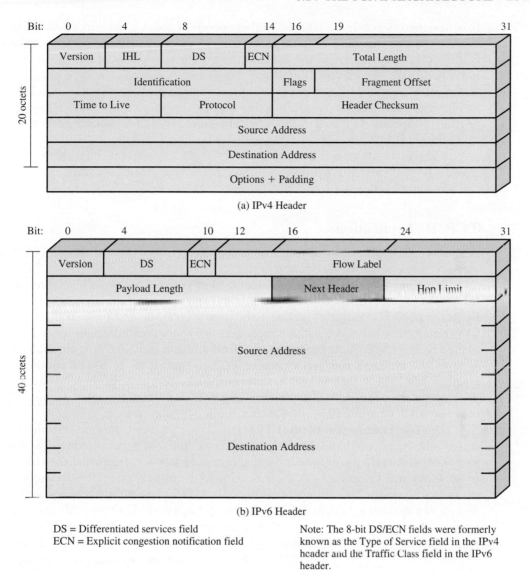

(a) IPv4 Header

(b) IPv6 Header

DS = Differentiated services field
ECN = Explicit congestion notification field

Note: The 8-bit DS/ECN fields were formerly known as the Type of Service field in the IPv4 header and the Traffic Class field in the IPv6 header.

Figure 8.7   IP Headers

and destination addresses. The Header Checksum field is used to detect errors in the header to avoid misdelivery. The Protocol field indicates which higher-layer protocol is using IP, such as TCP or UDP. The ID, Flags, and Fragment Offset fields are used in the fragmentation and reassembly process. For the interested reader, Section 8.4 provides more detail.

In 1995, the Internet Engineering Task Force (IETF), which develops protocol standards for the Internet, issued a specification for a next-generation IP, known then as IPng. This specification was turned into a standard in 1996 known as IPv6. IPv6 provides a number of functional enhancements over the existing IP.

It is designed to accommodate the higher speeds of today's networks and the mix of data streams, including graphic and video, which are becoming more prevalent. But the driving force behind the development of the new protocol was the need for more addresses. The current IP uses a 32-bit address to specify a source or destination. With the explosive growth of the Internet and of private networks attached to the Internet, this address length became insufficient to accommodate all systems needing addresses. As Figure 8.7b shows, IPv6 includes 128-bit source and destination address fields.

Ultimately, all installations using TCP/IP are expected to migrate from the current IP to IPv6, but this process will take many years, if not decades.

For more detail, see Appendix 8A.

TCP/IP Applications

A number of applications have been standardized to operate on top of TCP. We mention a few of the most common here.

The **Simple Mail Transfer Protocol (SMTP)** supports a basic electronic mail facility, by providing a mechanism for transferring messages among separate hosts. Features of SMTP include mailing lists, return receipts, and forwarding. SMTP does not specify the way in which messages are to be created; some local editing or native electronic mail facility is required. Once a message is created, SMTP accepts the message and makes use of TCP to send it to an SMTP module on another host. The target SMTP module will make use of a local electronic mail package to store the incoming message in a user's mailbox. SMTP is examined in more detail in Chapter 10.

The **File Transfer Protocol (FTP)** is used to send files from one system to another under user command. Both text and binary files are accommodated, and the protocol provides features for controlling user access. When a user wishes to engage in file transfer, FTP sets up a TCP connection to the target system for the exchange of control messages. This connection allows user ID and password to be transmitted and allows the user to specify the file and file actions desired. Once a file transfer is approved, a second TCP connection is set up for the data transfer. The file is transferred over the data connection, without the overhead of any headers or control information at the application level. When the transfer is complete, the control connection is used to signal the completion and to accept new file transfer commands.

SSH (Secure Shell) provides a secure remote logon capability, which enables a user at a terminal or personal computer to logon to a remote computer and function as if directly connected to that computer. SSH also supports file transfer between the local host and a remote server. SSH enables the user and the remote server to authenticate each other; it also encrypts all traffic in both directions. SSH traffic is carried on a TCP connection.

HTTP (HyperText Transfer Protocol) connects client systems to Web servers on the Internet or on an internet. Its primary function is to establish a connection with the server and send HTML pages back to the user's browser. It is also used to download files from the server either to the browser or to any other requesting application that uses HTTP.

SNMP (Simple Network Management Protocol) is a widely used network monitoring and control protocol. Data are passed from SNMP agents, which are hardware and/or software processes reporting activity in each network device (hub, router, bridge, etc.) to the workstation console used to oversee the network. The agents return information contained in an MIB (Management Information Base), which is a data structure that defines what is obtainable from the device and what can be controlled (turned off, on, etc.).

Protocol Interfaces

Each layer in the TCP/IP suite interacts with its immediate adjacent layers. At the source, the application layer makes use of the services of the transport layer and provides data down to that layer. A similar relationship exists at the interface between the transport and internet layers and at the interface of the internet and network access layers. At the destination, each layer delivers data up to the next higher layer.

This use of each individual layer is not required by the architecture. As Figure 8.8 suggests, it is possible to develop protocols that directly invoke the services of any one of the layers. Most applications require a reliable transport protocol and thus make use of TCP. Some special-purpose applications do not need the services of TCP. Some of these applications, such as SNMP, use another transport protocol known as the User Datagram Protocol (UDP); others may make use of IP directly. Applications or other protocols that do not involve internetworking and that do not need TCP have been developed to invoke the network access layer directly.

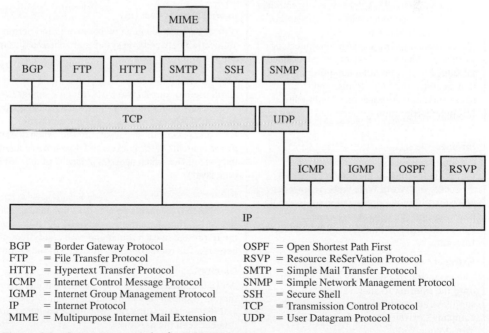

BGP	= Border Gateway Protocol	OSPF = Open Shortest Path First
FTP	= File Transfer Protocol	RSVP = Resource ReSerVation Protocol
HTTP	= Hypertext Transfer Protocol	SMTP = Simple Mail Transfer Protocol
ICMP	= Internet Control Message Protocol	SNMP = Simple Network Management Protocol
IGMP	= Internet Group Management Protocol	SSH = Secure Shell
IP	= Internet Protocol	TCP = Transmission Control Protocol
MIME	= Multipurpose Internet Mail Extension	UDP = User Datagram Protocol

Figure 8.8 Some Protocols in the TCP/IP Suite

8.3 INTERNETWORKING

In most cases, a LAN or WAN is not an isolated entity. An organization may have more than one type of LAN at a given site to satisfy a spectrum of needs. An organization may have multiple LANs of the same type at a given site to accommodate performance or security requirements. And an organization may have LANs at various sites and need them to be interconnected via WANs for central control of distributed information exchange.

Table 8.1 lists some commonly used terms relating to the interconnection of networks, or internetworking. An interconnected set of networks, from a user's point of view, may appear simply as a larger network. However, if each of the constituent networks retains its identity, and special mechanisms are needed for communicating across multiple networks, then the entire configuration is often referred to as an **internet**, and

Table 8.1 Internetworking Terms

Communication Network

A facility that provides a data transfer service among devices attached to the network.

Computer Network

A collection of host computers and other digital devices together with the communication network through which they can exchange data.

Internet

(1) (not capitalized): A collection of computer networks interconnected by switches and/or routers and/or gateways.
(2) (capitalized): The single, interconnected, worldwide system of commercial, governmental, educational, and other computer networks that share (a) the TCP/IP suite and (b) the name and address spaces managed by the Internet Corporation for Assigned Names and Numbers (ICANN).

Intranet

An internet used by a single organization that provides the key Internet applications, especially the World Wide Web. An intranet operates within the organization for internal purposes and can exist as an isolated, self-contained internet, or may have links to the Internet.

Extranet

The extension of a company's intranet out onto the Internet to allow selected customers, suppliers, and mobile workers to access the company's private data and applications via the World Wide Web.

Subnetwork

Refers to a constituent network of an internet. This avoids ambiguity because an entire internet, from a user's point of view, is a single network.

End System (ES)

A computer that is attached to a communication subnetwork or internetwork and can use services provided by the network to exchange data with other attached systems. Also: **Host**

Intermediate System (IS)

A device used to connect two networks and permit communication between end systems attached to different networks.

Layer 2 Switch

An IS used to connect two LANs that use similar LAN protocols. The switch acts as an address filter, picking up packets from one LAN that are intended for a destination on another LAN and passing those packets on. The switch does not modify the contents of the packets and does not add anything to the packet. The switch operates at layer 2 of the OSI model (link layer).

Router

An IS used to connect two networks that may or may not be similar but that share the use of the IP. The router employs the IP present in each router and each end system of the network. The router operates at layer 3 of the OSI model.

Gateway

An IS that attaches to two (or more) computer networks that have similar functions but dissimilar implementations and that enables either one-way or two-way communication between the networks.

each of the constituent networks as a **subnetwork**. The most important example of an internet is referred to simply as the Internet. As the Internet has evolved from its modest beginnings as a research-oriented packet-switching network, it has served as the basis for the development of internetworking technology and as the model for private internets within organizations. These latter are also referred to as **intranets**. If an organization extends access to its intranet, over the Internet, to selected customers and suppliers, then the resulting configuration is often referred to as an **extranet**.

Each constituent subnetwork in an internet supports communication among the devices attached to that subnetwork; these devices are referred to as **hosts**, or **end systems (ESs)**. In addition, subnetworks are connected by devices referred to in the ISO documents as **intermediate systems (ISs)**. ISs provide a communications path and perform the necessary relaying and routing functions so that data can be exchanged between devices attached to different subnetworks in the internet.

Two types of ISs of particular interest are **layer 2 switches** and **routers**. The differences between them have to do with the types of protocols used for the internetworking logic. We look at the role and functions of bridges in Chapter 12. The role and functions of routers were introduced in the context of IP earlier in this chapter. However, because of the importance of routers in the overall networking scheme, it is worth providing additional comment in this section.

Another type of IS is the **gateway**, which connects two or more subnetworks or internets that differ in some way. When two networks differ in the protocol by which they offer service to hosts, a gateway may translate one protocol into the other or otherwise facilitate interoperation of hosts. An example of an application-level gateway is one that translates between two different mail transfer protocols.

Routers

Internetworking is achieved by using intermediate systems, or routers, to interconnect a number of independent networks. Essential functions that the router must perform include the following:

1. Provide a link between networks.

2. Provide for the routing and delivery of data between end systems attached to different networks.

3. Provide these functions in such a way as to not require modifications of the networking architecture of any of the attached networks.

Point 3 means that the router must accommodate a number of differences among networks, such as the following:

- **Addressing schemes:** The networks may use different schemes for assigning addresses to devices. For example, an IEEE 802 LAN uses 48-bit binary addresses for each attached device; an ATM network typically uses 15-digit decimal addresses (encoded as 4 bits per digit for a 60-bit address). Some form of global network addressing must be provided, as well as a directory service.

- **Maximum packet sizes:** Packets from one network may have to be broken into smaller pieces to be transmitted on another network, a process known as **fragmentation**. For example, Ethernet imposes a maximum packet size of

1500 bytes; a maximum packet size of 1600 bytes is common on frame relay networks. A packet that is transmitted on a frame relay network and picked up by a router for forwarding on an Ethernet LAN may have to be fragmented into two smaller ones.

- **Interfaces:** The hardware and software interfaces to various networks differ. The concept of a router must be independent of these differences.
- **Reliability:** Various network services may provide anything from a reliable end-to-end virtual circuit to an unreliable service. The operation of the routers should not depend on an assumption of network reliability.

The preceding requirements are best satisfied by an internetworking protocol, such as IP, that is implemented in all end systems and routers.

Internetworking Example

Figure 8.9 depicts a configuration that we will use to illustrate the interactions among protocols for internetworking. In this case, we focus on a server attached to a frame relay WAN and a workstation attached to an IEEE 802 LAN such as Ethernet, with a router connecting the two networks. The router provides a link between the server and the workstation that enables these end systems to ignore the details of the intervening networks. For the frame relay network, what we have referred to as the network access layer consists of a single frame relay protocol. In the case of the IEEE 802 LAN, the network access layer consists of two sublayers: the logical link control (LLC) layer and the media access control (MAC) layer. For

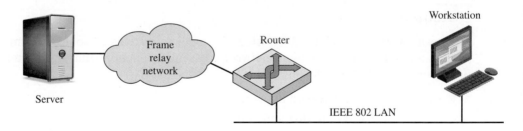

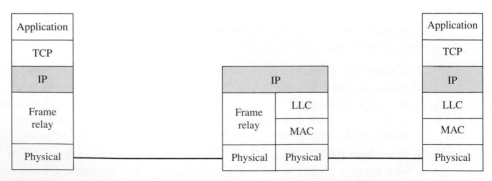

Figure 8.9   Configuration for TCP/IP Example

purposes of this discussion, we need not describe these layers in any detail, but they are explored in subsequent chapters.

Figures 8.10 through 8.12 outline typical steps in the transfer of a block of data, such as a file or a Web page, from the server, through an internet, and ultimately to an application in the workstation. In this example, the message passes through just one router. Before data can be transmitted, the application and transport layers in the server establish, with the corresponding layers in the workstation, the applicable ground rules for a communication session. These include character code to be used, error-checking method, and the like. The protocol at each layer is used for this purpose and then is used in the transmission of the message.

1. Preparing the data. The application protocol prepares a block of data for transmission. For example, an e-mail message (SMTP), a file (FTP), or a block of user input (TELNET).

2. Using a common syntax. If necessary, the data transmission is converted to a form expected by the destination. This may include a different character code, the use of encryption, and/or compression.

3. Segmenting the data. TCP may break the data block into a number of segments, keeping track of their sequence. Each TCP segment includes a header containing a sequence number and a frame check sequence to detect errors.

4. Duplicating segments. A copy is made of each TCP segment, in case the loss or damage of a segment necessitates retransmission. When an acknowledgment is received from the other TCP entity, a segment is erased.

5. Fragmenting the segments. IP may break a TCP segment into a number of datagrams to meet size requirements of the intervening networks. Each datagram includes a header containing a destination address, a frame check sequence, and other control information.

6. Framing. A frame relay header and trailer is added to each IP datagram. The header contains a connection identifier and the trailer contains a frame check sequence.

Peer-to-peer dialogue.
Before data are sent, the sending and receiving applications agree on format and encoding and agree to exchange data.

Peer-to-peer dialogue.
The two TCP entities agree to open a connection.

Peer-to-peer dialogue.
Each IP datagram is forwarded through networks and routers to the destination system.

Peer-to-peer dialogue.
Each frame is forwarded through the frame relay network.

7. Transmission. Each frame is transmitted over the medium as a sequence of bits.

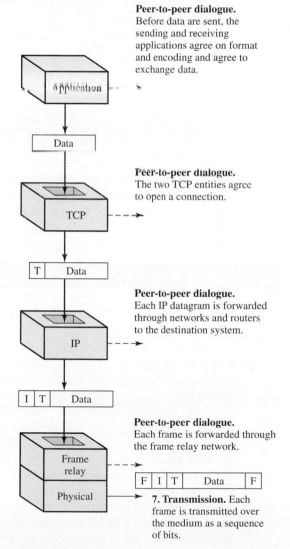

Figure 8.10   Operation of TCP/IP: Action at Sender

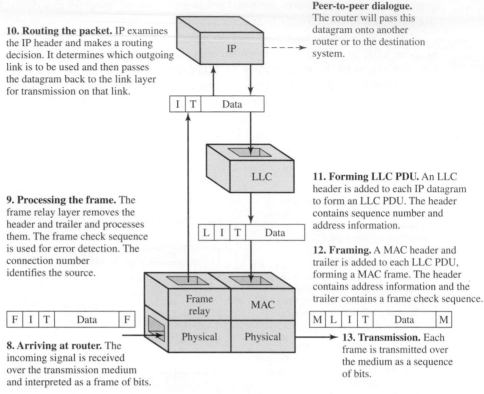

10. Routing the packet. IP examines the IP header and makes a routing decision. It determines which outgoing link is to be used and then passes the datagram back to the link layer for transmission on that link.

Peer-to-peer dialogue. The router will pass this datagram onto another router or to the destination system.

9. Processing the frame. The frame relay layer removes the header and trailer and processes them. The frame check sequence is used for error detection. The connection number identifies the source.

11. Forming LLC PDU. An LLC header is added to each IP datagram to form an LLC PDU. The header contains sequence number and address information.

12. Framing. A MAC header and trailer is added to each LLC PDU, forming a MAC frame. The header contains address information and the trailer contains a frame check sequence.

8. Arriving at router. The incoming signal is received over the transmission medium and interpreted as a frame of bits.

13. Transmission. Each frame is transmitted over the medium as a sequence of bits.

Figure 8.11 Operation of TCP/IP: Action at Router

8.4 VIRTUAL PRIVATE NETWORKS AND IP SECURITY

In today's distributed computing environment, the **virtual private network (VPN)** offers an attractive solution to network managers. In essence, a VPN consists of a set of computers that interconnect by means of a relatively unsecure network and that make use of encryption and special protocols to provide security. At each corporate site, workstations, servers, and databases are linked by one or more LANs. The LANs are under the control of the network manager and can be configured and tuned for cost-effective performance. The Internet or some other public network can be used to interconnect sites, providing a cost savings over the use of a private network and offloading the WAN management task to the public network provider. That same public network provides an access path for telecommuters and other mobile employees to log on to corporate systems from remote sites.

But the manager faces a fundamental requirement: security. Use of a public network exposes corporate traffic to eavesdropping and provides an entry point for unauthorized users. To counter this problem, the manager may choose from a variety of encryption and authentication packages and products. Proprietary solutions raise a number of problems. First, how secure is the solution? If proprietary

20. Delivering the data. The application performs any needed transformations, including decompression and decryption, and directs the data to the appropriate file or other destination.

19. Reassembling user data. If TCP has broken the user data into multiple segments, these are reassembled and the block is passed up to the application.

18. Processing the TCP segment. TCP removes the header. It checks the frame check sequence and acknowledges if there is a match and discards for mismatch. Flow control is also performed.

17. Processing the IP datagram. IP removes the header. The frame check sequence and other control information are processed.

16. Processing the LLC PDU. The LLC layer removes the header and processes it. The sequence number is used for flow and error control.

15. Processing the frame. The MAC layer removes the header and trailer and processes them. The frame check sequence is used for error detection.

14. Arriving at destination. The incoming signal is received over the transmission medium and interpreted as a frame of bits.

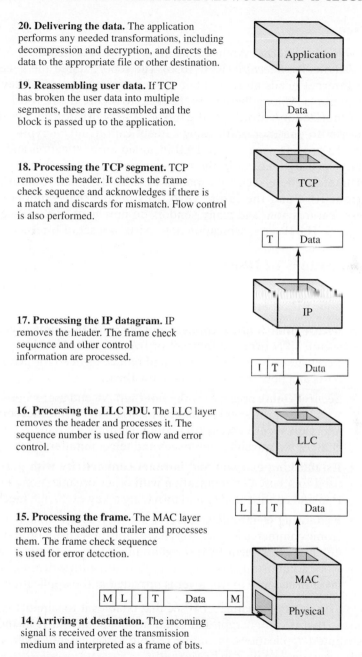

Figure 8.12   Operation of TCP/IP: Action at Receiver

encryption or authentication schemes are used, there may be little reassurance in the technical literature as to the level of security provided. Second is the question of compatibility. No manager wants to be limited in the choice of workstations, servers, routers, firewalls, and so on by a need for compatibility with the security facility. This is the motivation for the IP security (IPsec) set of Internet standards.

IPsec

In 1994, the Internet Architecture Board (IAB) issued a report titled *Security in the Internet Architecture* (RFC 1636). The report stated the general consensus that the Internet needs more and better security and identified key areas for security mechanisms. Among these were the need to secure the network infrastructure from unauthorized monitoring and control of network traffic and the need to secure end-user-to-end-user traffic using authentication and encryption mechanisms.

To provide security, the IAB included authentication and encryption as necessary security features in the next-generation IP, which has been issued as IPv6. Fortunately, these security capabilities were designed to be usable with both the current IPv4 and the future IPv6. This means that vendors can begin offering these features now, and many vendors do now have some IPsec capability in their products. The IPsec specification now exists as a set of Internet standards.

Applications of IPsec

IPsec provides the capability to secure communications across a LAN, across private and public WANs, and across the Internet. Examples of its use include the following:

- **Secure branch office connectivity over the Internet:** A company can build a secure VPN over the Internet or over a public WAN. This enables a business to rely heavily on the Internet and reduce its need for private networks, saving costs and network management overhead.

- **Secure remote access over the Internet:** An end user whose system is equipped with IPsec protocols can make a local call to an Internet service provider (ISP) and gain secure access to a company network. This reduces the cost of toll charges for traveling employees and telecommuters.

- **Establishing extranet and intranet connectivity with partners:** IPsec can be used to secure communication with other organizations, ensuring authentication and confidentiality and providing a key exchange mechanism.

- **Enhancing electronic commerce security:** Even though some Web and electronic commerce applications have built-in security protocols, the use of IPsec enhances that security. IPsec guarantees that all traffic designated by the network administrator is both encrypted and authenticated, adding an additional layer of security to whatever is provided at the application layer.

The principal feature of IPsec that enables it to support these varied applications is that it can encrypt and/or authenticate *all* traffic at the IP level. Thus, all distributed applications, including remote logon, client/server, e-mail, file transfer, Web access, and so on, can be secured.

Figure 8.13 is a typical scenario of IPsec usage. An organization maintains LANs at dispersed locations. Nonsecure IP traffic is conducted on each LAN. For traffic off-site, through some sort of private or public WAN, IPsec protocols are used. These protocols operate in networking devices, such as a router or firewall, that connect each LAN to the outside world. The IPsec networking device will typically encrypt and compress all traffic going into the WAN, and decrypt and decompress traffic coming from the WAN; these operations are transparent to workstations and

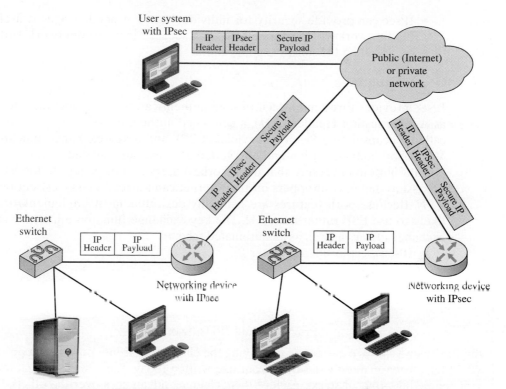

Figure 8.13 An IP Security Scenario

servers on the LAN. Secure transmission is also possible with individual users who dial into the WAN. Such user workstations must implement the IPsec protocols to provide security.

Benefits of IPsec

Some of the benefits of IPsec are as follows:

- When IPsec is implemented in a firewall or router, it provides strong security that can be applied to all traffic crossing the perimeter. Traffic within a company or workgroup does not incur the overhead of security-related processing.

- IPsec in a firewall is resistant to bypass if all traffic from the outside must use IP and the firewall is the only means of entrance from the Internet into the organization.

- IPsec is below the transport layer (TCP, UDP) and so is transparent to applications. There is no need to change software on a user or server system when IPsec is implemented in the firewall or router. Even if IPsec is implemented in end systems, upper-layer software, including applications, is not affected.

- IPsec can be transparent to end users. There is no need to train users on security mechanisms, issue keying material on a per-user basis, or revoke keying material when users leave the organization.

• IPsec can provide security for individual users if needed. This is useful for off-site workers and for setting up a secure virtual subnetwork within an organization for sensitive applications.

IPsec Functions

IPsec provides three main facilities: an authentication-only function referred to as Authentication Header (AH), a combined authentication/encryption function called Encapsulating Security Payload (ESP), and a key exchange function. For VPNs, both authentication and encryption are generally desired, because it is important both to (1) assure that unauthorized users do not penetrate the VPN and (2) assure that eavesdroppers on the Internet cannot read messages sent over the VPN. Because both features are generally desirable, most implementations are likely to use ESP rather than AH. The key exchange function allows for manual exchange of keys as well as an automated scheme.

IPsec is explored in Chapter 19.

APPLICATION NOTE

Practical Guide to Networking

Ten or fifteen years ago, an article describing the choices regarding networking protocols would have been markedly different from one written today. There were several models with competing protocol stacks, each of them claiming advantages over the others. While many of these protocols enjoyed some measure of popularity, TCP/IP as the language of the Internet finally won out. Currently networking architectures are very nearly standardized — at least in terms of the protocols used.

Gone are the days of choosing between various LAN transport mechanisms. Token Ring, FDDI, and LocalTalk have all been supplanted by the different forms of Ethernet. Gone too are the transport protocols that competed with TCP and UDP. Novell protocols (IPX and SPX), Appletalk, and the SNA architectures have all been replaced. At the center of it all we have the Internet Protocol (IP) as king of the hill with IPv6 on the remote horizon. While all of the core protocols may have been chosen for us, we still have plenty of decisions to make. New architectures and methodologies always seem to introduce their own rules and operations. Two of the most significant changes are 802.11 wireless networking and Voice over IP (VoIP).

Wireless networking brings with it the advantages of connectivity without being tethered, faster/lower cost deployment and the connection of geographically remote sites. On the downside, it also brings increased security risks, management headaches, and increased demands on the support staff. That said, before selecting a wireless technology, an organization must first decide whether or not it wants to support a wireless network. Even if the decision is against a WLAN, administrators still have to worry about wireless connections because they are built into so many devices. It turns out that wireless networks are often deployed with or without the aid of the network administrators.

Once the decision to adopt 802.11 is made, we must now decide on which version to use. 802.11b made WLANs popular but it doesn't really stand up to the rigors of a production network. As a result, two new standards, 802.11g and 802.11a, were developed. While they have similar top speeds, they are fundamentally different in their operational frequencies, range, coverage, and design parameters. On paper, 802.11a seems to have all of the advantages because it runs in the less populated 5-GHz portion of the spectrum. In fact, 802.11g has enjoyed much more popularity because it has a similar footprint when compared to 802.11b. Yet no matter how popular the WLAN standards get, they have not been designed to replace Ethernet, only supplement it. However, recent developments with the 802.11n version promise speeds that rival the wired infrastructure and, in fact, could supplant end node Ethernet connections.

Previously we mentioned that IP was "king" and nowhere is this more apparent than in VoIP. It turns out that while IP is the language of the Internet, it is also becoming the language of the telephone system. This technology is becoming so cost effective that almost any company can be presented with a viable business case for switching to VoIP. So, additional decisions now have to be made regarding the protocols to use when deploying voice on a data network. Once again we have several competing solutions including Session Initiation Protocol (SIP), H.323, and SKINNY. As VoIP gains more and more acceptance, we are beginning to see that SIP is enjoying an increasing amount of support from the communication industry. However, there is a tremendous install base of H.323 and Cisco SKINNY VoIP phones, with more still being deployed. However, each of these has its difficulties: H.323 is an older standard and SKINNY is a Cisco proprietary product.

Even though most vendors and manufacturers have standardized on the TCP/IP networking model, there are still many protocols and technologies to select from when building an entire communication system. Many times, the right choice emerges as more and more organizations adopt a particular set of standards, but we will have to decide for ourselves if it is the right time to jump and which way.

8.5   SUMMARY

The communication functionality required for distributed applications is quite complex. This functionality is generally implemented as a structured set of modules. The modules are arranged in a vertical, layered fashion, with each layer providing a particular portion of the needed functionality and relying on the next lower layer for more primitive functions. Such a structure is referred to as a protocol architecture.

One motivation for the use of this type of structure is that it eases the task of design and implementation. It is standard practice for any large software package to break the functions up into modules that can be designed and implemented separately. After each module is designed and implemented, it can be tested. Then the modules can be combined and tested together. This motivation has led computer vendors to develop proprietary layered protocol architectures. An example of this is the Systems Network Architecture (SNA) of IBM.

A layered architecture can also be used to construct a standardized set of communication protocols. In this case, the advantages of modular design remain. But, in addition, a layered architecture is particularly well suited to the development of standards. Standards can be developed simultaneously for protocols at each layer of the architecture. This breaks down the work to make it more manageable and speeds up the standards-development process. The TCP/IP architecture is the standard architecture used for this purpose. This architecture contains five layers. Each layer provides a portion of the total communications function required for distributed applications. Standards have been developed for each layer. Development work still continues, particularly at the top (application) layer, where new distributed applications are still being defined.

8.6　KEY TERMS, REVIEW QUESTIONS, AND PROBLEMS

Key Terms

application layer	IP datagram	protocol architecture
checksum	IPv4	protocol data unit (PDU)
end system	IPv6	router
extranet	network layer	service access point (SAP)
frame check sequence (FCS)	Open Systems	subnetwork
header	Interconnection (OSI)	Transmission Control Protocol
intermediate system	packet	(TCP)
Internet	peer entity	TCP segment
Internet Protocol (IP)	physical layer	transport layer
internetworking	port	User Datagram Protocol
intranet	protocol	(UDP)

Review Questions

8.1　What is an error-detection code?

8.2　Identify the key elements of a data communication protocol.

8.3　What is an extranet?

8.4　What are peer entities in a protocol architecture?

8.5　Identify and briefly describe the major communication functions performed at the network access layer.

8.6　Identify and briefly describe the major communication functions performed at the transport layer.

8.7　What is an intranet?

8.8　What is the difference between an internet (not capitalized) and the Internet (capitalized)?

8.9　What is a packet?

8.10　Identify and briefly describe each of TCP/IP's five layers.

8.11　Briefly describe each of the following TCP/IP application layer protocols: SMTP, FTP, HTTP.

8.12　Briefly describe the differences among the following subnetwork components: hosts, end systems, intermediate systems.

8.13　Briefly describe the differences among the following types of intermediate systems: layer 2 switches, routers, gateways.

8.14   What is SSH?

8.15   What is SNMP?

8.16   Identify several applications and advantages of IPsec.

8.17   Briefly describe the differences between TCP and UDP.

8.18   Briefly explain the differences between IPv4 and IPv6.

8.19   Identify and briefly describe the major functions performed by routers.

Problems

8.1   Do some Internet research on EOIP and IPOE. Look for sources that provide description of these, the business reasons behind their increasing popularity, and case examples that illustrate EOIP and IPOE best practices. Summarize your findings in a 750–1000 word paper or an 8–12 slide PowerPoint presentation.

8.2   Using the layer models in Figure 8.14, describe the ordering and delivery of a pizza, indicating the interactions at each level.

8.3   **a.**   The French and Chinese prime ministers need to come to an agreement by telephone, but neither speaks the other's language. Further, neither has on hand a translator that can translate to the language of the other. However, both prime ministers have English translators on their staffs. Draw a diagram similar to Figure 8.14 to depict the situation, and describe the interaction at each layer.

b.   Now suppose that the Chinese prime minister's translator can translate only into Japanese and that the French prime minister has a German translator available.

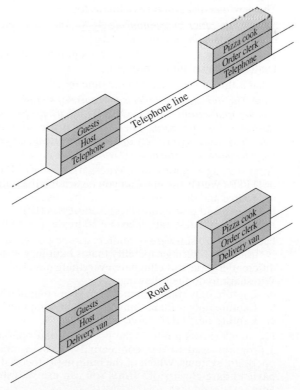

Figure 8.14   Architecture for Problem 8.2

A translator between German and Japanese is available in Germany. Draw a new diagram that reflects this arrangement and describe the hypothetical phone conversation.

8.4 Layering is common for communication protocols. Why? What are the advantages of layered communication protocols.

8.5 List the major disadvantages of the layered approach to protocols.

8.6 A TCP segment consisting of 1500 bits of data and 160 bits of header is sent to the IP layer, which appends another 160 bits of header. This is then transmitted through two networks, each of which uses a 24-bit packet header. The destination network has a maximum packet size of 800 bits. How many bits, including headers, are delivered to the network layer protocol at the destination?

8.7 Do some online research on protocols that use UDP instead of TCP (or that run on both UDP and TCP). Write a brief paper that identifies and briefly describes these protocols.

8.8 IP, TCP, and UDP all discard a packet that arrives with a checksum error and do not attempt to notify the source. Why?

8.9 Find and view several YouTube videos that illustrate how TCP/IP works. Identify the URLs for the three videos that you think best communicate how TCP/IP works. Identify the video that you think is the best overall and briefly explain the reasons behind your selection.

8.10 Why does the TCP header have a header length field while the UDP header does not?

8.11 The previous version of the TFTP specification, RFC 783, included the following statement:

All packets other than those used for termination are acknowledged individually unless a timeout occurs.

The new specification revises this as follows:

All packets other than duplicate ACKs and those used for termination are acknowledged unless a timeout occurs.

The change was made to fix a problem referred to as the "Sorcerer's Apprentice." Deduce and explain the problem.

8.12 What is the limiting factor in the time required to transfer a file using TFTP?

Note: The next three problems make use of Wireshark, a free packet sniffer that allows you to capture traffic on a LAN. A Wireshark projects package is part of the Instructor's Resource for this book. These exercises are additional mini-projects you can try. Wireshark runs on a variety of operating systems, and can be downloaded directly from the Wireshark Web site at www.wireshark.org.

8.13 After starting a capture from Wireshark, start a TCP-based application like SSH, FTP, or HTTP (Web browser). Can you determine the following from your capture?
   a. Source and destination layer 2 addresses (MAC)
   b. Source and destination layer 3 addresses (IP)
   c. Source and destination layer 4 addresses (port numbers)

8.14 Packet capture software or sniffers can be powerful management and security tools. By using the filtering capability that is built in, you can trace traffic based on several different criteria and eliminate everything else. Use the filtering capability built into Wireshark to do the following:
   a. Capture only traffic coming from your computer's MAC address.
   b. Capture only traffic coming from your computer's IP address.
   c. Capture only UDP-based transmissions.

8.15 Figure 8.8 shows a few of the protocols that operate directly on top of IP. Ping is a program used to test connectivity between machines and is available on all operating systems. Which of the built-in protocols does Ping use and what does the payload data consist of? *Hint:* You can use Wireshark to help you determine the answers.

8.16   What other programs are built into your operating system to help you troubleshoot or provide feedback about your connectivity?

8.17   Take a screen shot of the network connections detail window that includes your computer's IP and physical addresses.

8.18   Find and view several YouTube videos that illustrate how a router works. Identify the URLs for the three videos that you think best communicate how a router works. Identify the video that you think is the best overall and briefly explain the reasons behind your selection.

APPENDIX 8A   TCP, UDP, AND IP DETAILS

Having looked at the TCP/IP architecture and the basic functionality of internetworking, we can now return to TCP and IP and look at a few details.

TCP

TCP uses only a single type of segment. The header is shown in Figure 8.6a. Because one header must serve to perform all protocol mechanisms, it is rather large, with a minimum length of 20 octets. The fields are as follows:

- **Source Port (16 bits):** Source TCP user.

- **Destination Port (16 bits):** Destination TCP user.

- **Sequence Number (32 bits):** Sequence number of the first data octet in this segment except when the SYN flag is set. If SYN is set, this field contains the initial sequence number (ISN) and the first data octet in this segment has sequence number ISN + 1.

- **Acknowledgment Number (32 bits):** Contains the sequence number of the next data octet that the TCP entity expects to receive from the other TCP entity.

- **Header Length (4 bits):** Number of 32-bit words in the header.

- **Reserved (4 bits):** Reserved for future use.

- **Flags (8 bits):** For each flag, if set to 1, the meaning is as follows:
  CWR: congestion window reduced.
  ECE: ECN-Echo; the CWR and ECE bits, defined in RFC 3168, are used for the explicit congestion notification function.
  URG: urgent pointer field significant.
  ACK: acknowledgment field significant.
  PSH: push function.
  RST: reset the connection.
  SYN: synchronize the sequence numbers.
  FIN: no more data from sender.

- **Window (16 bits):** Flow control credit allocation, in octets. Contains the number of data octets, beginning with the sequence number indicated in the acknowledgment field that the sender is willing to accept.

Table 8.2 Some Assigned Port Numbers

5	Remote Job Entry	79	Finger
7	Echo	80	World Wide Web (HTTP)
20	FTP (Default Data)	88	Kerberos
21	FTP (Control)	119	Network News Transfer Protocol
23	TELNET	161	SNMP Agent Port
25	SMTP	162	SNMP Manager Port
43	WhoIs	179	Border Gateway Protocol
53	Domain Name Server	194	Internet Relay Chat Protocol
69	TFTP	389	Lightweight Directory Access Protocol

- **Checksum (16 bits):** The ones complement of the ones complement sum modulo of all the 16-bit words in the segment plus a pseudoheader, described subsequently. (Appendix E describes this checksum.)

- **Urgent Pointer (16 bits):** This value, when added to the segment sequence number, contains the sequence number of the last octet in a sequence of urgent data. This allows the receiver to know how much urgent data are coming.

- **Options (Variable):** Zero or more options may be included.

The Source Port and Destination Port specify the sending and receiving users of TCP. There are a number of common users of TCP that have been assigned fixed numbers; some examples are shown in Table 8.2. These numbers should be reserved for that purpose in any implementation. Other port numbers must be arranged by agreement between the two communicating parties.

The Sequence Number and Acknowledgment Number are bound to octets rather than to entire segments. For example, if a segment contains Sequence Number 1001 and includes 600 octets of data, the Sequence Number refers to the first octet in the data field; the next segment in logical order will have Sequence Number 1601. Thus, TCP is logically stream oriented: It accepts a stream of octets from the user, groups them into segments as it sees fit, and numbers each octet in the stream. These numbers are used for flow control, together with the Window field. The scheme works as follows, for a TCP segment traveling from X to Y: The Acknowledgment Number is the number of the next octet expected by X; that is, X has already received data octets up to this number. The Window indicates how many additional octets X is prepared to receive from Y. By limiting the value of Window, X can limit the rate at which data arrive from Y.

The Checksum field is used to detect errors. This field is calculated based on the bits in the entire segment plus a pseudoheader prefixed to the header at the time of calculation (at both transmission and reception). The sender calculates this Checksum and adds it to the segment. The receiver performs the same calculation on the incoming segment and compares that calculation to the Checksum field in that incoming segment. If the two values don't match, then one or more bits have been accidentally altered in transit. The pseudoheader includes the following fields from the IP header: Source and Destination Address and Protocol, plus a segment length field. By including the pseudoheader, TCP protects itself from misdelivery by IP. That is, if IP delivers a segment to the wrong host, even if the segment contains no bit errors, the receiving TCP entity will detect the delivery error.

UDP

UDP uses only a single type of segment, shown in Figure 8.6b. The header includes a source port and destination port. The Length field contains the length of the entire UDP segment, including header and data. The checksum is the same algorithm used for TCP and IP. For UDP, the checksum applies to the entire UDP segment plus a pseudoheader prefixed to the UDP header at the time of calculation and which is the same pseudoheader used for TCP. If an error is detected, the segment is discarded and no further action is taken.

The Checksum field in UDP is optional. If it is not used, it is set to zero. However, it should be pointed out that the IP checksum applies only to the IP header and not to the data field, which in this case consists of the UDP header and the user data. Thus, if no checksum calculation is performed by UDP, then no check is made on the user data at either the transport or IP layers.

IPv4

Figure 8.7a shows the IP header format, which is a minimum of 20 octets, or 160 bits. The fields are as follows:

- **Version (4 bits):** Indicates version number, to allow evolution of the protocol; the value is 4.
- **Internet Header Length (IHL) (4 bits):** Length of header in 32-bit words. The minimum value is 5, for a minimum header length of 20 octets.
- **DS/ECN (8 bits):** Prior to the introduction of differentiated services, this field was referred to as the **Type of Service (ToS)** field and specified reliability, precedence, delay, and throughput parameters. This interpretation has now been superseded. The first 6 bits of the TOS field are now referred to as the DS (differentiated services) field, discussed in Chapter 11. The remaining 2 bits are reserved for an ECN (explicit congestion notification) field, which is beyond our scope.
- **Total Length (16 bits):** Total datagram length, including header plus data, in octets.
- **Identification (16 bits):** A sequence number that, together with the source address, destination address, and user protocol, is intended to identify a datagram uniquely. Thus, this number should be unique for the datagram's source address, destination address, and user protocol for the time during which the datagram will remain in the internet.
- **Flags (3 bits):** Only two of the bits are currently defined. The More bit is used for fragmentation and reassembly, as previously explained. The Don't Fragment bit prohibits fragmentation when set. This bit may be useful if it is known that the destination does not have the capability to reassemble fragments. However, if this bit is set, the datagram will be discarded if it exceeds the maximum size of an en route network. Therefore, if the bit is set, it may be advisable to use source routing to avoid networks with small maximum packet size.
- **Fragment Offset (13 bits):** Indicates where in the original datagram this fragment belongs, measured in 64-bit units. This implies that fragments other

Table 8.3 Some Assigned Protocol Numbers

1	Internet Control Message Protocol	17	User Datagram Protocol
2	Internet Group Management Protocol	46	Reservation Protocol (RSVP)
6	Transmission Control Protocol	89	Open Shortest Path First (OSPF)
8	Exterior Gateway Protocol		

than the last fragment must contain a data field that is a multiple of 64 bits in length.

- **Time to Live (8 bits):** Specifies how long, in seconds, a datagram is allowed to remain in the internet. Every router that processes a datagram must decrease the TTL by at least one, so the TTL is somewhat similar to a hop count.
- **Protocol (8 bits):** Indicates the next-higher-level protocol that is to receive the data field at the destination; thus, this field identifies the type of the next header in the packet after the IP header.
- **Header Checksum (16 bits):** An error-detecting code applied to the header only. Because some header fields may change during transit (e.g., time to live, fragmentation-related fields), this is reverified and recomputed at each router. The checksum is formed by taking the ones complement of the 16-bit ones complement addition of all 16-bit words in the header. For purposes of computation, the checksum field is itself initialized to a value of zero. (Appendix E describes this checksum.)
- **Source Address (32 bits):** Coded to allow a variable allocation of bits to specify the network and the end system attached to the specified network, as discussed subsequently.
- **Destination Address (32 bits):** Same characteristics as source address.
- **Options (variable):** Encodes the options requested by the sending user.
- **Padding (variable):** Used to ensure that the datagram header is a multiple of 32 bits in length.
- **Data (variable):** The data field must be an integer multiple of 8 bits in length. The maximum length of the datagram (data field plus header) is 65,535 octets.

The protocol field indicates to which IP user the data in this IP datagram are to be delivered. Although TCP is the most common user of IP, other protocols can access IP. For common protocols that use IP, specific protocol numbers have been assigned and should be used. Table 8.3 lists some of these assignments.

IPv6

The IPv6 header has a fixed length of 40 octets, consisting of the following fields (Figure 8.7b):

- **Version (4 bits):** IP version number; the value is 6.
- **DS/ECN (8 bits):** Available for use by originating nodes and/or forwarding routers for differentiated services and congestion functions, as described for the IPv4 DS/ECN field.

- **Flow Label (20 bits):** May be used by a host to label those packets for which it is requesting special handling by routers within a network, as discussed subsequently.

- **Payload Length (16 bits):** Length of the remainder of the IPv6 packet following the header, in octets. In other words, this is the total length of all of the extension headers plus the transport-level PDU.

- **Next Header (8 bits):** Identifies the type of header immediately following the IPv6 header; this will either be an IPv6 extension header or a higher-layer header, such as TCP or UDP.

- **Hop Limit (8 bits):** The remaining number of allowable hops for this packet. The hop limit is set to some desired maximum value by the source and decremented by 1 by each node that forwards the packet. The packet is discarded if Hop Limit is decremented to zero. This is a simplification over the processing required for the Time to Live field of IPv4. The consensus was that the extra effort in accounting for time intervals in IPv4 added no significant value to the protocol. In fact, IPv4 routers, as a general rule, treat the Time to Live field as a hop limit field.

- **Source Address (128 bits):** The address of the originator of the packet.

- **Destination Address (128 bits):** The address of the intended recipient of the packet. This may not in fact be the intended ultimate destination if a Routing header is present, as explained subsequently.

Although the IPv6 header is longer than the mandatory portion of the IPv4 header (40 octets versus 20 octets), it contains fewer fields (8 versus 12). Thus, routers have less processing to do per header, which should speed up routing.

APPENDIX 8B   THE TRIVIAL FILE TRANSFER PROTOCOL

This appendix provides an overview of the Internet standard Trivial File Transfer Protocol (TFTP). Our purpose is to give the reader some flavor for the elements of a protocol.

Introduction to TFTP

TFTP is far simpler than the Internet standard File Transfer Protocol (FTP). There are no provisions for access control or user identification, so TFTP is only suitable for public access file directories. Because of its simplicity, TFTP is easily and compactly implemented. For example, some diskless devices use TFTP to download their firmware at boot time.

TFTP runs on top of UDP. The TFTP entity that initiates the transfer does so by sending a read or write request in a UDP segment with a destination port of 69 to the target system. This port is recognized by the target UDP module as the identifier of the TFTP module. For the duration of the transfer, each side uses a transfer identifier (TID) as its port number.

TFTP Packets

TFTP entities exchange commands, responses, and file data in the form of packets, each of which is carried in the body of a UDP segment. TFTP supports five types of packets (Figure 8.15); the first two bytes contain an opcode that identifies the packet type:

- **RRQ:** The read request packet requests permission to transfer a file from the other system. The packet includes a file name, which is a sequence of ASCII[1] bytes terminated by a zero byte. The zero byte is the means by which the receiving TFTP entity knows when the file name is terminated. The packet also includes a mode field, which indicates whether the data file is to be interpreted as a string of ASCII bytes or as raw 8-bit bytes of data.

- **WRQ:** The write request packet requests permission to transfer a file to the other system.

- **Data:** The block numbers on data packets begin with one and increase by one for each new block of data. This convention enables the program to use a single number to discriminate between new packets and duplicates. The data field is

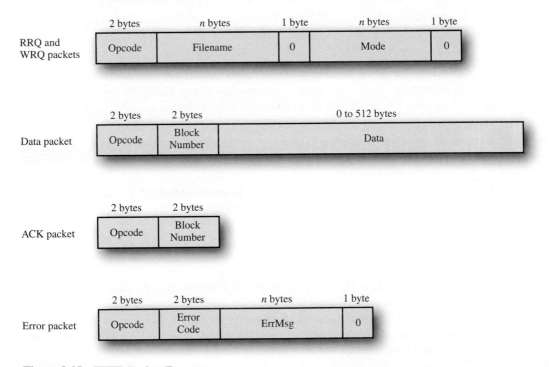

Figure 8.15   TFTP Packet Formats

---

[1]ASCII is the American Standard Code for Information Interchange, a standard of the American National Standards Institute. It designates a unique 7-bit pattern for each letter, with an eighth bit used for parity. ASCII is equivalent to the International Reference Alphabet (IRA), defined in ITU-T Recommendation T.50. Appendix D provides a description and table of the IRA code.

Table 8.4   TFTP Error Codes

Value	Meaning
0	Not defined, see error message (if any)
1	File not found
2	Access violation
3	Disc full or allocation exceeded
4	Illegal TFTP operation
5	Unknown transfer ID
6	File already exists
7	No such user

from zero to 512 bytes long. If it is 512 bytes long, the block is not the last block of data; if it is from zero to 511 bytes long, it signals the end of the transfer.

- **ACK:** This packet is used to acknowledge receipt of a data packet or a WRQ packet. An ACK of a data packet contains the block number of the data packet being acknowledged. An ACK of a WRQ contains a block number of zero.

- **Error:** An error packet can be the acknowledgment of any other type of packet. The error code is an integer indicating the nature of the error (Table 8.4). The error message is intended for human consumption, and should be in ASCII. Like all other strings, it is terminated with a zero byte.

All packets other than duplicate ACKs (explained subsequently) and those used for termination are to be acknowledged. Any packet can be acknowledged by an error packet. If there are no errors, then the following conventions apply: A WRQ or a data packet is acknowledged by an ACK packet. When a RRQ is sent, the other side responds (in the absence of error) by beginning to transfer the file; thus, the first data block serves as an acknowledgment of the RRQ packet. Unless a file transfer is complete, each ACK packet from one side is followed by a data packet from the other, so that the data packet functions as an acknowledgment. An error packet can be acknowledged by any other kind of packet, depending on the circumstance.

Figure 8.16 shows a TFTP data packet in context. When such a packet is handed down to UDP, UDP adds a header to form a UDP segment. This is then passed to IP, which adds an IP header to form an IP datagram.

Overview of a Transfer

The example illustrated in Figure 8.17 is of a simple file transfer operation from A to B. No errors occur and the details of the option specification are not explored.

The operation begins when the TFTP module in system A sends a write request (WRQ) to the TFTP module in system B. The WRQ packet is carried as the body of a UDP segment. The write request includes the name of the file (in this case, XXX) and a mode of octet, or raw data. In the UDP header, the destination port number is 69, which alerts the receiving UDP entity that this message is intended for the TFTP application. The source port number is a TID selected by A, in this case

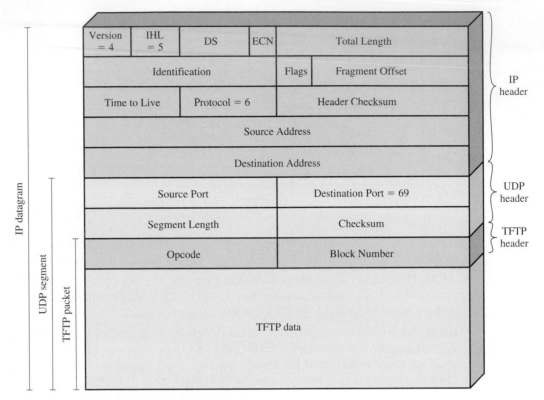

Figure 8.16 A TFTP Packet in Context

1511. System B is prepared to accept the file and so responds with an ACK with a block number of 0. In the UDP header, the destination port is 1511, which enables the UDP entity at A to route the incoming packet to the TFTP module, which can match this TID with the TID in the WRQ. The source port is a TID selected by B for this file transfer, in this case 1660.

Following this initial exchange, the file transfer proceeds. The transfer consists of one or more data packets from A, each of which is acknowledged by B. The final data packet contains less than 512 bytes of data, which signals the end of the transfer.

Errors and Delays

If TFTP operates over a network or internet (as opposed to a direct data link), it is possible for packets to be lost. Because TFTP operates over UDP, which does not provide a reliable delivery service, there needs to be some mechanism in TFTP to deal with lost packets. TFTP uses the common technique of a timeout mechanism. Suppose that A sends a packet to B that requires an acknowledgment (i.e., any packet other than duplicate ACKs and those used for termination). When A has transmitted the packet, it starts a timer. If the timer expires before the acknowledgment is received from B, A retransmits the same packet. If in fact the original

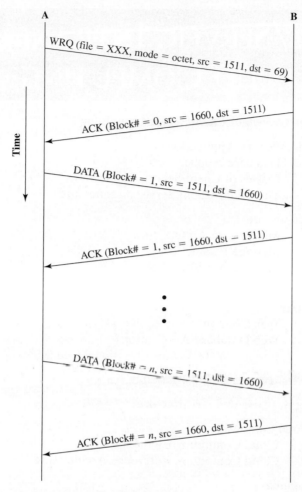

Figure 8.17   Example TFTP Operation

packet was lost, then the retransmission will be the first copy of this packet received by B. If the original packet was not lost but the acknowledgment from B was lost, then B will receive two copies of the same packet from A and simply acknowledges both copies. Because of the use of block numbers, this causes no confusion. The only exception to this rule is for duplicate ACK packets. The second ACK is ignored.

Syntax, Semantics, and Timing

In Section 8.1, it was mentioned that the key features of a protocol can be classified as syntax, semantics, and timing. These categories are easily seen in TFTP. The formats of the various TFTP packets form the **syntax** of the protocol. The **semantics** of the protocol are shown in the definitions of each of the packet types and the error codes. Finally, the sequence in which packets are exchanged, the use of block numbers, and the use of timers are all aspects of the **timing** of TFTP.

CLIENT/SERVER, INTRANET, AND CLOUD COMPUTING

Learning Objectives

After reading this chapter, you should be able to:

♦ Discuss the reasons for the growing interest in and availability of client/server computing systems.

♦ Describe the features and characteristics of client/server computing.

♦ Describe the architecture of client/server applications.

♦ Explain the role of middleware in client/server systems.

♦ Assess the networking requirements and implications of client/server computing.

♦ Define *intranet* and contrast it with *Internet*.

♦ Compare client/server and intranet approaches to distributed computing.

♦ List the benefits of and communications options for extranets.

Most distributed applications in a business environment involve a style of distributed computing known as client/server computing. We begin this chapter with a general description of the client/server philosophy and the implications for businesses. Next, we examine the nature of the application support provided by the client/server architecture. Then we look at the rather fuzzy but very important concept of middleware.

Following this survey of client/server computing, we examine a more recent approach referred to as an intranet. An intranet uses Internet technology and applications (especially Web-based applications) to provide in-house support for distributed applications. Next, this chapter covers the concept of the extranet. Finally, we examine the increasingly important service-oriented architecture (SOA).

9.1 THE GROWTH OF CLIENT/SERVER COMPUTING

The concept of client/server computing, and related concepts, has become increasingly important in information technology systems. As with other new waves in the computer field, client/server computing comes with its own set of jargon words. Table 9.1 lists some of the terms that are commonly found in descriptions of client/server products and applications.

Figure 9.1 attempts to capture the essence of these themes. **Client** machines are typically single-user PCs or workstations that provide a highly user-friendly interface to the end user. The client-based station generally presents the type of graphical interface that is most comfortable to users, including the use of windows and a mouse. Common examples of such interfaces are provided by Microsoft Windows and Macintosh OS X. Client-based applications are tailored for ease of use and include such familiar tools as the spreadsheet.

Each **server** in the client/server environment provides a set of shared user services to the clients. The most common type of server is the database server, usually controlling a relational database. The server enables many clients to share access to

Table 9.1 Client/Server Terminology

Application Programming Interface (API)

A set of function and call programs that allow clients and servers to intercommunicate.

Client

A networked information requester, usually a PC or workstation, that can query database and/or other information from a server.

Middleware

A set of drivers, APIs, or other software that improves connectivity between a client application and a server.

Relational Database

A database in which information access is limited to the selection of rows that satisfy all search criteria.

Server

A computer, usually a high-powered workstation or a mainframe, that houses information for manipulation by networked clients.

Structured Query Language (SQL)

A language developed by IBM and standardized by ANSI for addressing, creating, updating, or querying relational databases.

---

the same database and enables the use of a high-performance computer system to manage the database.

In addition to clients and servers, the third essential ingredient of the client/server environment is the **network**. Client/server computing is distributed computing. Users, applications, and resources are distributed in response to business requirements and linked by a single LAN or WAN or by an internet.

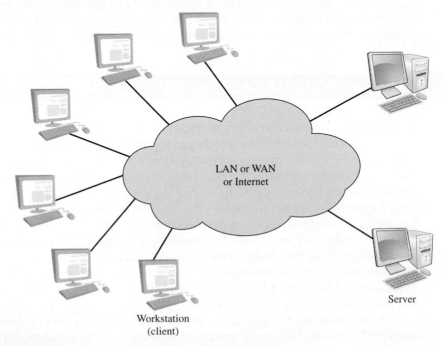

Workstation
(client)

Server

LAN or WAN
or Internet

Figure 9.1 Generic Client/Server Environment

There are a number of characteristics that together make client/server distinct from ordinary distributed processing:

- There is a heavy reliance on bringing user-friendly applications to the user on his or her system. This gives the user a great deal of control over the timing and style of computer usage and gives department-level managers the ability to be responsive to their local needs.

- Although the applications are dispersed, there is an emphasis on centralizing corporate databases and many network management and utility functions. This enables corporate management to maintain overall control of the total capital investment in computing and information systems and enables corporate management to provide interoperability so that systems are tied together. At the same time, it relieves individual departments and divisions of much of the overhead of maintaining sophisticated computer-based facilities but enables them to choose just about any type of machine and interface they need to access data and information.

- There is an emphasis on open and modular systems. This means that the user has greater choice in selecting products and in mixing equipment from a number of vendors.

- Networking is fundamental to the operation. Thus, network management and network security have a high priority in organizing and operating information systems.

Client/server computing is, on the one hand, a natural solution from the product point of view, because it exploits the declining cost of microcomputers and networks. On the other hand, client/server computing may be the ideal choice to support the direction that business is taking in the organization of work.

This latter point deserves elaboration. The success of client/server computing in the marketplace is not just a matter of new jargon on top of old solutions. Client/server computing is indeed a relatively new technical approach to distributed computing. But beyond that, client/server computing is responsive to, and indeed creates the conditions for, new ways of organizing business. Let us consider two significant trends in industry that illustrate the point.

The first of these is the permanent shedding of jobs by companies in an effort to downsize and streamline for success in a fiercely competitive market. Why have companies needed to shed jobs to remain competitive and how have they managed to increase productivity so fast as to have sales growth without payroll growth? The cost per employee is rising rapidly, with wage increases coupled to mandated benefits increases. At the same time, business equipment, especially computer and network equipment and services, has suffered only modest cost increases. This has led, as one might expect, to substantial increases in investment in computers and other information technology in an effort to compensate for a smaller employee base.

This trend occurs in small as well as large businesses and is affecting middle managers as well as clerical staff. What client/server computing provides is a way of automating tasks and eliminating barriers to information, which allows companies to eliminate layers of management and to add work without adding workers.

Another trend that illustrates the effectiveness of client/server computing is the so-called internal market. This is a business strategy that affects primarily large businesses, which seek to combine entrepreneurial zeal with corporate might to have the best of both worlds: the economies of scale of a large business with the agility of a small business. In an era of rapid technological and market changes, many large companies are tearing down traditional functional hierarchies and replacing them with collections of relatively independent business units. These units must then compete with external companies for business from other units. In an internal market, every business unit operates as an independent company. Each one decides to buy its inputs from internal sources (other units of the corporation) or from outside suppliers. Even traditional "overhead" departments, such as information systems, accounting, and legal, must sell their services to other units and compete with outside providers.

This dose of internal competition is designed to correct the flaws of the traditional way of doing business. As Jay Forrester of MIT observes [ROTH93], "American corporations are some of the largest socialist bureaucracies in the world. They have central planning, central ownership of capital, central allocation of resources, subjective evaluation of people, lack of internal competition, and decisions made at the top in response to political pressures."

Internal markets have already transformed some companies and promise to have a major impact on others. But, until recently, there has been a formidable obstacle to implementing such a scheme. In a large company, the use of an internal market can result in thousands of teams making agreements among themselves and with outsiders. Somehow, the ledgers for all the resulting transactions have to be reconciled. Analyses of this situation have suggested that the cost and complexity of bookkeeping would overwhelm the benefits of an internal market. The evolution of computing technology has overcome this obstacle. Today, a number of multinationals are using the latest database software running on client/server networks to set up internal markets.

9.2 CLIENT/SERVER APPLICATIONS

The central feature of a client/server architecture is the allocation of application-level tasks between clients and servers. Figure 9.2 illustrates the general case. In both client and server, the basic software is an operating system running on the hardware platform. The platforms and the operating systems of client and server may differ. Indeed, there may be a number of different types of client platforms and operating systems and a number of different types of server platforms and operating systems in a single environment. As long as a particular client and server share the same communications protocols and support the same applications, these lower-level differences are irrelevant.

It is the communications software that enables client and server to interoperate. The principal example of such software is TCP/IP. Of course, the point of all this support software (communications and operating system) is to provide a base for distributed applications. Ideally, the actual functions performed by the application can be split up between client and server in a way that optimizes platform

Client workstation

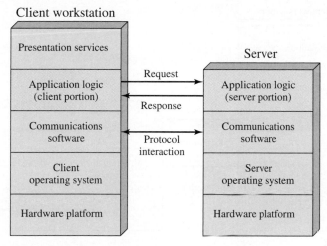

Figure 9.2   Generic Client/Server Architecture

and network resources and that optimizes the ability of users to perform various tasks and to cooperate with one another in using shared resources. In some cases, these requirements dictate that the bulk of the applications software executes at the server, while in other cases, most of the application logic is located at the client.

An essential factor in the success of a client/server environment is the way in which the user interacts with the system as a whole. Thus, the design of the user interface to the client machine is critical. In most client/server systems, there is heavy emphasis on providing a **graphical user interface (GUI)** that is easy to use, easy to learn, yet powerful and flexible. Thus, we can think of a presentation services module[1] in the client workstation that is responsible for providing a user-friendly interface to the distributed applications available in the environment.

Database Applications

As an example that illustrates the concept of splitting application logic between client and server, we consider the most common family of client/server applications: those that make use of relational databases. In this environment, the server is essentially a database server. Interaction between client and server is in the form of transactions in which the client makes a database request and receives a database response.

Figure 9.3 illustrates, in general terms, the architecture of such a system. The server is responsible for maintaining the database, for which purpose a complex database management system software module is required. A variety of applications that make use of the database can be housed on client machines. The "glue" that ties client and server together is software that enables the client to make requests for access to the server's database. A popular example of such logic is the Structured Query Language (SQL).

---

[1]Not to be confused with the presentation layer of the OSI model. The presentation layer is concerned with the formatting of data so that they can be properly interpreted by the two communicating machines. A presentation services module is concerned with the way in which the user interacts with an application and with the layout and functionality of what is presented to the user on the screen.

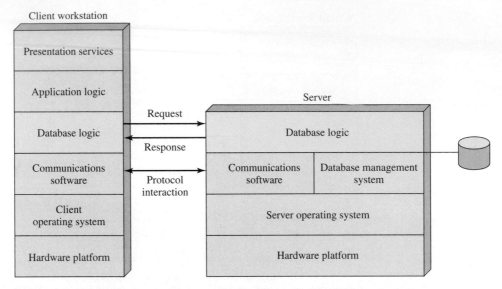

Figure 9.3 Client/Server Architecture for Database Applications

Figure 9.3 suggests that all of the application logic—the software for "number crunching" or other types of data analysis—is on the client side, while the server is only concerned with managing the database. Whether such a configuration is appropriate depends on the style and intent of the application. For example, suppose that the primary purpose is to provide online access for record lookup. Figure 9.4a suggests how this might work. Suppose that the server is maintaining a database of one million records (called rows in relational database jargon), and the user wants to perform a lookup that should result in zero, one, or at most a few records. The user could search for these records using a number of search criteria (e.g., records older than 1992; records referring to individuals in Ohio; records referring to a specific event or characteristic). An initial client query may yield a server response that there are 100,000 records that satisfy the search criteria. The user then adds additional qualifiers and issues a new query. This time, a response indicating that there are 1000 possible records is returned. Finally, the client issues a third request with additional qualifiers. The resulting search criteria yield a single match, and the record is returned to the client.

The preceding application is well suited to a client/server architecture for two reasons:

1. There is a massive job of sorting and searching the database. This requires a large disc or bank of discs, a high-speed processor, and a high-speed I/O architecture. Such capacity and power are not needed and are too expensive for a single-user workstation or PC.

2. It would place too great a traffic burden on the network to move the entire one-million-record file to the client for searching. Therefore, it is not enough for the server to just be able to retrieve records on behalf of a client; the server needs to have database logic that enables it to perform searches on behalf of a client.

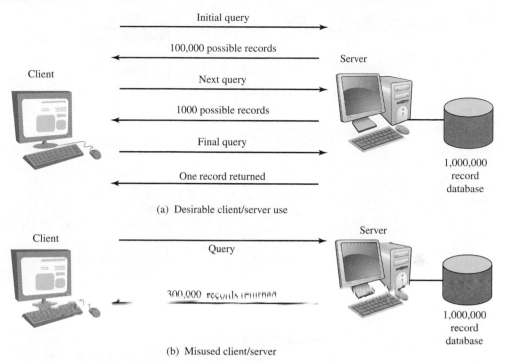

Figure 9.4   Client/Server Database Usage

Now consider the scenario of Figure 9.4b, which has the same one-million-record database. In this case, a single query results in the transmission of 300,000 records over the network. This might happen if, for example, the user wishes to find the grand total or mean value of some field across many records or even the entire database.

Clearly, this latter scenario is unacceptable. One solution to this problem, which maintains the client/server architecture with all its benefits, is to move part of the application logic over to the server. That is, the server can be equipped with application logic for performing data analysis as well as data retrieval and data searching.

Classes of Client/Server Applications

Within the general framework of client/server, there is a spectrum of implementations that divide the work between client and server differently. The exact distribution of data and application processing depends on the nature of the database information, the types of applications supported, the availability of interoperable vendor equipment, and the usage patterns within an organization.

Figure 9.5 illustrates some of the major options for database applications. Other splits are possible, and the options may have a different characterization for other types of applications. In any case, it is useful to examine this figure to get a feel for the kind of trade-offs possible.

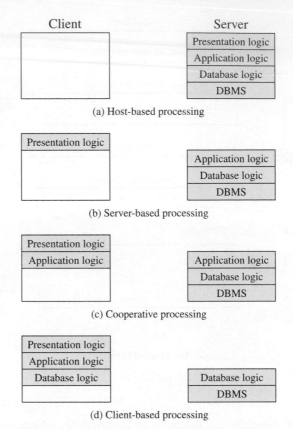

Figure 9.5   Classes of Client/Server Applications

The figure depicts four classes:

- **Host-based processing:** Host-based processing is not true client/server computing as the term is generally used. Rather, host-based processing refers to the traditional mainframe environment in which all or virtually all of the processing is done on a central host. Often the user interface is via a dumb terminal. Even if the user is employing a microcomputer, the user's station is generally limited to the role of a terminal emulator.

- **Server-based processing:** The simplest class of client/server configuration is one in which the client is principally responsible for providing a graphical user interface, while virtually all of the processing is done on the server.

- **Client-based processing:** At the other extreme, virtually all application processing may be done at the client, with the exception of data validation routines and other database logic functions that are best performed at the server. Generally, some of the more sophisticated database logic functions are housed on the client side. This architecture is perhaps the most common client/server approach in current use. It enables the user to employ applications tailored to local needs.

- **Cooperative processing:** In a cooperative processing configuration, the application processing is performed in an optimized fashion, taking advantage of the strengths of both client and server machines and of the distribution of data. Such a configuration is more complex to set up and maintain but, in the long run, this type of configuration may offer greater user productivity gains and greater network efficiency than other client/server approaches.

Figure 9.5c and 9.5d corresponds to configurations in which a considerable fraction of the load is on the client. This so-called **thick client** model has been popularized by application development tools such as Powersoft Corp.'s PowerBuilder. Applications developed with these tools are typically departmental in scope, supporting between 25 and 150 users. The main benefit of the thick client model is that it takes advantage of desktop power, off-loading application processing from servers and making them more efficient and less likely to be bottlenecks.

There are, however, several disadvantages to the thick client strategy. The addition of more functions rapidly overloads the capacity of desktop machines, forcing companies to upgrade. If the model extends beyond the department to incorporate many users, the company must install high-capacity LANs to support the large volumes of transmission between the thin servers and the thick clients. Finally, it is difficult to maintain, upgrade, or replace applications distributed across tens or hundreds of desktops.

Figure 9.5b is representative of a **thin client**, or fat server, approach. This approach more nearly mimics the traditional host-centered approach and is often the migration path for evolving corporate-wide applications from the mainframe to a distributed environment.

Figure 9.6 illustrates five client/server categories based on the distribution of computational services between the client process and the server process. Each category is defined by the client-side functionality.

Three–Tier Client/Server Architecture

The traditional client/server architecture involves two levels, or tiers: a client tier and a server tier. In recent years, a three-tier architecture has become increasingly common (Figure 9.7). In this architecture, the application software is distributed among three types of machines: a user machine, a middle-tier server, and a backend server. The user machine is the client machine we have been discussing and, in the three-tier model, is typically a thin client. The middle-tier machines are essentially gateways between the thin user clients and a variety of backend database servers.

	Thin client				Thick client
Computational services	Distributed presentation	Local presentation	Distributed application logic	Local application logic	
Presentation services	Shared	Client	Client	Client	Client
Application services	Server	Server	Shared	Client	Client
Data services	Server	Server	Server	Server	Shared

Figure 9.6   Three-Level Architectural Client/Server Framework

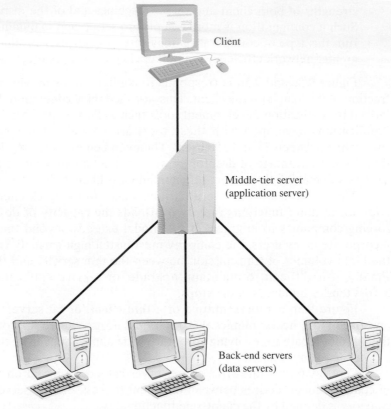

Figure 9.7 Three-Tier Client/Server Architecture

The middle-tier machines can convert protocols and map from one type of database query to another. In addition, the middle-tier machine can merge/integrate results from different data sources. Finally, the middle-tier machine can serve as a gateway between the desktop applications and the backend legacy applications by mediating between the two worlds.

The interaction between the middle-tier server and the backend server also follows the client/server model. Thus, the middle-tier system acts as both a client and a server.

9.3 MIDDLEWARE

The development and deployment of client/server products has far outstripped efforts to standardize all aspects of distributed computing, from the physical layer up to the application layer. This lack of standards makes it difficult to implement an integrated, multivendor, enterprise-wide client/server configuration. Because much of the benefit of the client/server approach is tied up with its modularity and the ability to mix and match platforms and applications to provide a business solution, this interoperability problem must be solved.

To achieve the true benefits of the client/server approach, developers need tools that provide a uniform means and style of access to system resources across all platforms. This will enable programmers to build applications that not only look and feel the same on various PCs and workstations but that use the same method to access data regardless of the location of that data.

The most common way to meet this requirement is by the use of standard programming interfaces and protocols that sit between the application above and communications software and operating system below. Such standardized interfaces and protocols have come to be referred to as **middleware**. With standard programming interfaces, it is easy to implement the same application on a variety of server types and workstation types. This obviously benefits the customer, but vendors are also motivated to provide such interfaces. The reason is that customers buy applications, not servers; customers will only choose among those server products that run the applications they want. The standardized protocols are needed to link these various server interfaces back to the clients that need access to them.

There is a variety of middleware packages ranging from the very simple to the very complex. What they all have in common is the capability to hide the complexities and disparities of different network protocols and operating systems. Client and server vendors generally provide a number of the more popular middleware packages as options. Thus, a user can settle on a particular middleware strategy and then assemble equipment from various vendors that support that strategy.

Middleware Architecture

Figure 9.8 suggests the role of middleware in a client/server architecture. The exact role of the middleware component will depend on the style of client/server computing being used. Referring back to Figure 9.5, recall that there are a number

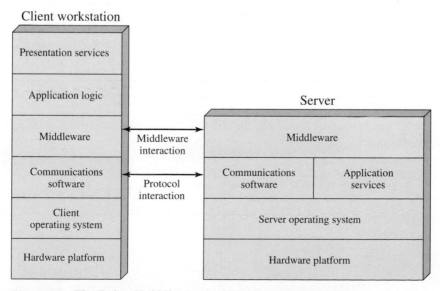

Figure 9.8 The Role of Middleware in Client/Server Architecture

of different client/server approaches, depending on the way in which application functions are split up. In any case, Figure 9.8 gives a good general idea of the architecture involved.

Note that there is both a client and server component of middleware. The basic purpose of middleware is to enable an application or user at a client to access a variety of services on servers without being concerned about differences among servers. To look at one specific application area, the Structured Query Language (SQL) is supposed to provide a standardized means for access to a relational database by either a local or remote user or application. However, many relational database vendors, although they support SQL, have added their own proprietary extensions to SQL. This enables vendors to differentiate their products but also creates potential incompatibilities.

As an example, consider a distributed system used to support, among other things, the personnel department. The basic employee data, such as employee name and address, might be stored on a Gupta database, whereas salary information might be contained on an Oracle database. When a user in the personnel department requires access to particular records, that user does not want to be concerned with which vendor's database contains the records needed. Middleware provides a layer of software that enables uniform access to these differing systems.

It is instructive to look at the role of middleware from a logical, rather than an implementation, point of view. This viewpoint is illustrated in Figure 9.9. Middleware enables the realization of the promise of distributed client/server computing. The entire distributed system can be viewed as a set of applications and resources available to users. Users need not be concerned with the location of data or indeed the location of applications. All applications operate over a uniform **application programming interface (API)**. The middleware, which cuts across all client and server platforms, is responsible for routing client requests to the appropriate server.

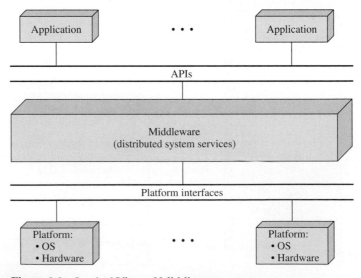

Figure 9.9 Logical View of Middleware

Although there are a wide variety of middleware products, these products are typically based on one of three underlying mechanisms: message passing, remote procedure calls, and object-oriented mechanisms. The remainder of this section provides an overview of these mechanisms.

Message Passing

Figure 9.10a shows the use of distributed message passing to implement client/ server functionality. A client process requires some service (e.g., read a file, print) and sends a message containing a request for service to a server process. The server process honors the request and sends a message containing a reply. In its simplest form, only two functions are needed: Send and Receive. The Send function specifies a destination and includes the message content. The Receive function tells from whom a message is desired (including "all") and provides a buffer where the incoming message is to be stored.

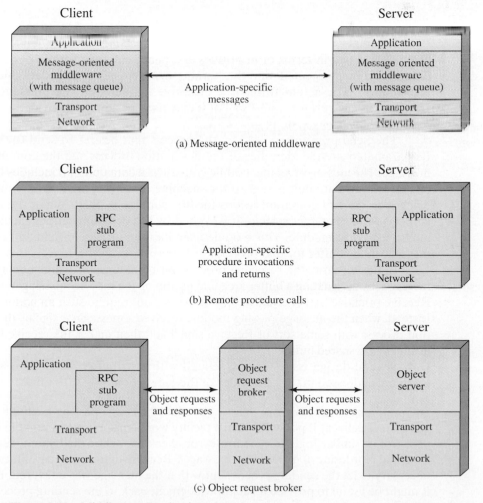

(a) Message-oriented middleware

(b) Remote procedure calls

(c) Object request broker

Figure 9.10 Middleware Mechanisms

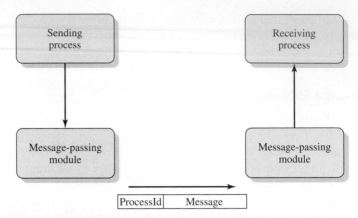

Figure 9.11 Basic Message-Passing Primitives

Figure 9.11 suggests an implementation approach for message passing. Processes make use of the services of a message-passing module. Service requests can be expressed in terms of primitives and parameters. A primitive specifies the function to be performed, and the parameters are used to pass data and control information. The actual form of a primitive depends on the message-passing software. It may be a procedure call or it may itself be a message to a process that is part of the operating system.

The Send primitive is used by the process that desires to send the message. Its parameters are the identifier of the destination process and the contents of the message. The message-passing module constructs a data unit that includes these two elements. This data unit is sent to the machine that hosts the destination process, using some sort of communications facility, such as TCP/IP. When the data unit is received in the target system, it is routed by the communications facility to the message-passing module. This module examines the processId field and stores the message in the buffer for that process.

In this scenario, the receiving process must announce its willingness to receive messages by designating a buffer area and informing the message-passing module by a Receive primitive. An alternative approach does not require such an announcement. Instead, when the message-passing module receives a message, it signals the destination process with some sort of Receive signal and then makes the received message available in a shared buffer.

Several design issues are associated with distributed message passing, and these are addressed in the remainder of this subsection.

RELIABILITY VERSUS UNRELIABILITY   A reliable message-passing facility is one that guarantees delivery if possible. Such a facility would make use of a reliable transport protocol or similar logic to perform error checking, acknowledgment, retransmission, and reordering of misordered messages. Because delivery is guaranteed, it is not necessary to let the sending process know that the message was delivered. However, it might be useful to provide an acknowledgment back to the sending process so that it knows that delivery has already taken place. In either case, if the facility fails to achieve delivery (e.g., persistent network failure, crash of destination system), the sending process is notified of the failure.

At the other extreme, the message-passing facility may simply send the message out into the communications network but will report neither success nor failure. This alternative greatly reduces the processing and communications overhead of the message-passing facility. For those applications that require confirmation that a message has been delivered, the applications themselves may use request and reply messages to satisfy the requirement.

BLOCKING VERSUS NONBLOCKING   With nonblocking, or asynchronous, primitives, a process is not suspended as a result of issuing a Send or Receive. Thus, when a process issues a Send primitive, the operating system returns control to the process as soon as the message has been queued for transmission or a copy has been made. If no copy is made, any changes made to the message by the sending process before or even while it is being transmitted are made at the risk of the process. When the message has been transmitted, or copied to a safe place for subsequent transmission, the sending process is interrupted to be informed that the message buffer may be reused. Similarly, a non-blocking Receive is issued by a process that then proceeds to run. When a message arrives, the process is informed by interrupt, or it can poll for status periodically.

Nonblocking primitives provide for efficient, flexible use of the message-passing facility by processes. The disadvantage of this approach is that it is difficult to test and debug programs that use these primitives. Irreproducible, timing-dependent sequences can create subtle and difficult problems.

The alternative is to use blocking, or synchronous, primitives. A blocking Send does not return control to the sending process until the message has been transmitted (unreliable service) or until the message has been sent and an acknowledgment received (reliable service). A blocking Receive does not return control until a message has been placed in the allocated buffer.

Remote Procedure Calls

A variation on the basic message-passing model is the remote procedure call (RPC), which is a common method for encapsulating communication in a distributed system. The essence of the technique is to allow programs on different machines to interact using simple procedure call/return semantics, just as if the two programs were on the same machine. That is, the procedure call is used for access to remote services. The popularity of this approach is due to the following advantages:

1. The procedure call is a widely accepted, used, and understood abstraction.

2. The use of RPCs enables remote interfaces to be specified as a set of named operations with designated types. Thus, the interface can be clearly documented and distributed programs can be statically checked for type errors.

3. Because a standardized and precisely defined interface is specified, the communication code for an application can be generated automatically.

4. Because a standardized and precisely defined interface is specified, developers can write client and server modules that can be moved among computers and operating systems with little modification and recoding.

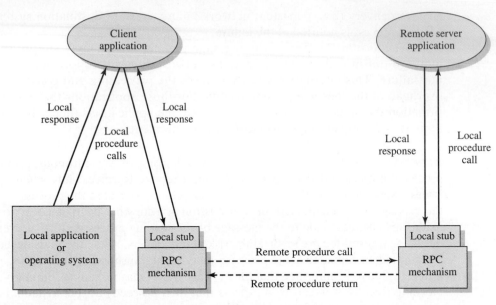

Figure 9.12   Remote Procedure Call Mechanism

The RPC mechanism can be viewed as a refinement of reliable, blocking message passing. Figure 9.10b illustrates the general architecture, and Figure 9.12 provides a more detailed look. The calling program makes a normal procedure call with parameters on its machine. For example,

$$CALL\ P\ (X, Y)$$

where

    P = procedure name
    X = passed arguments
    Y = returned values

It may or may not be transparent to the user that the intention is to invoke a remote procedure on some other machine. A dummy or stub procedure P must be included in the caller's address space or be dynamically linked to it at call time. This procedure creates a message that identifies the procedure being called and includes the parameters. It then sends this message to a remote system and waits for a reply. When a reply is received, the stub procedure returns to the calling program, providing the returned values.

At the remote machine, another stub program is associated with the called procedure. When a message comes in, it is examined and a local CALL P (X, Y) is generated. This remote procedure is thus called locally, so its normal assumptions about where to find parameters, the state of the stack, and so on, are identical to the case of a purely local procedure call.

Figure 9.13 illustrates the flow of control for an RPC operation.

CLIENT/SERVER BINDING   Binding specifies how the relationship between a remote procedure and the calling program will be established. A binding is formed when

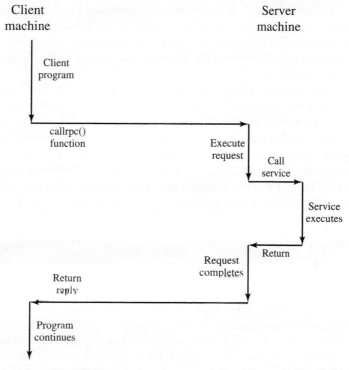

Figure 9.13 RPC Flow

two applications have made a logical connection and are prepared to exchange commands and data.

Nonpersistent binding means that a logical connection is established between the two processes at the time of the RPC and that as soon as the values are returned, the connection is dismantled. Because a connection requires the maintenance of state information on both ends, it consumes resources. The nonpersistent style is used to conserve those resources. On the other hand, the overhead involved in establishing connections makes nonpersistent binding inappropriate for remote procedures that are called frequently by the same caller.

With **persistent binding**, a connection that is set up for an RPC is sustained after the procedure return. The connection can then be used for future RPCs. If a specified period of time passes with no activity on the connection, the connection is terminated. For applications that make many repeated calls to remote procedures, persistent binding maintains the logical connection and allows a sequence of calls and returns to use the same connection.

Object-Oriented Mechanisms

As object-oriented technology becomes more prevalent in operating system design, client/server designers have begun to embrace this approach. In this approach, clients and servers ship messages back and forth between objects. Object communications may rely on an underlying message or RPC structure or be developed directly on top of object-oriented capabilities in the operating system.

A client that needs a service sends a request to an object request broker, which acts as a directory of all the remote services available on the network (Figure 9.10c). The broker calls the appropriate object and passes along any relevant data. Then the remote object services the request and replies to the broker, which returns the response to the client.

The success of the object-oriented approach depends on standardization of the object mechanism. Unfortunately, there are several competing designs in this area. One is Microsoft's Component Object Model (COM), the basis for Object Linking and Embedding (OLE). COM is used on Windows and has also been implemented by a number of vendors for UNIX. A competing approach, developed by the Object Management Group, is the Common Object Request Broker Architecture (CORBA), which has wide industry backing. IBM, Apple, Sun, and many other vendors support the CORBA approach.

9.4   INTRANETS

Intranet is a term used to refer to the implementation of Internet technologies within a corporate organization rather than for external connection to the global Internet. This concept has resulted in the most rapid change of direction in the history of business data communications. By any measure, including product announcements by vendors, statements of intent by customers, actual deployment of products, and even books on the shelves of bookstores, intranets have enjoyed a more rapid penetration of the corporate consciousness than personal computers, client/server computing, or even the Internet and the World Wide Web.

What accounts for this growth is a long list of attractive features and advantages of an intranet-based approach to corporate computing, including the following:

- Rapid prototyping and deployment of new services (can be measured in hours or days)
- Scales effectively (start small, build as needed)
- Virtually no training required on the part of users and little training required of developers, because the services and user interfaces are familiar from the Internet
- Can be implemented on virtually all platforms with complete interoperability
- Open architecture means a large and growing number of add-on applications is available across many platforms
- Supports a range of distributed computing architectures (few central servers or many distributed servers)
- Structured to support integration of "legacy" information sources (databases, existing word processing documents, groupware databases)
- Supports a range of media types (audio, video, interactive applications)
- Inexpensive to start, requires little investment either in new software or infrastructure

The enabling technologies for the intranet are the high processing speed and storage capacity of personal computers together with the high data rates of LANs.

Although the term *intranet* refers to the whole range of Internet-based applications, including network news, e-mail, and FTP, Web technology is responsible for the almost instant acceptance of intranets. Thus, this section is devoted to a discussion of Web systems.

The Web browser has become the universal information interface. An increasing number of employees have had experience using the Internet Web and are comfortable with the access model it provides. The intranet Web takes advantage of this experience base.

Web Content

An organization can use the intranet Web to enhance management–employee communication and to provide job-related information easily and quickly. Figure 9.14 suggests, at a top level, the kinds of information that can be provided by a corporate Web. Typically, there is an internal corporate home page that serves as an entry point for employees into the corporate intranet. From this home page, there are links to areas of interest company-wide or to large groups of employees, including human resources, finance, and information system service. Other links are to areas of interest to groups of employees, such as sales and manufacturing.

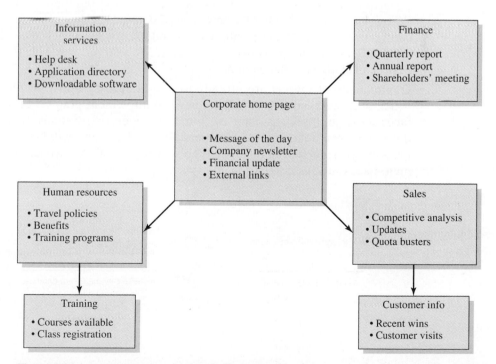

Figure 9.14 Example Corporate Web Page Structure

Beyond these broad-based Web services, an intranet Web is ideal for providing department- and project-level information and services. A group can set up its own Web pages to disseminate information and to maintain project data. With the widespread availability of easy-to-use WYSIWYG Web authoring tools, such as Adobe Dreamweaver, it is relatively easy for employees outside the information services group to develop their own Web pages for specific needs.

Web/Database Applications

Although the Web is a powerful and flexible tool for supporting corporate requirements, the HTML used to construct Web pages provides a limited capability for maintaining a large, changing base of data. For an intranet to be truly effective, many organizations will want to connect the Web service to a database with its own database management system.

Figure 9.15 illustrates a general strategy for Web/database integration in simple terms. To begin, a client machine (running a Web browser) issues a request for information in the form of a URL reference. This reference triggers a program at the Web server that issues the correct database command to a database server. The output returned to the Web server is converted into HTML format and returned to the Web browser.

[WHET96] lists the following advantages of a Web/database system compared to a more traditional database approach:

- **Ease of administration:** The only connection to the database server is the Web server. The addition of a new type of database server does not require configuration of all the requisite drivers and interfaces at each type of client machine. Instead, it is only necessary for the Web server to be able to convert between HTML and the database interface.

- **Deployment:** Browsers are already available across almost all platforms, which relieves the developer of the need to implement graphical user interfaces across multiple customer machines and operating systems. In addition, developers can assume that customers already have and will be able to use browsers as soon as the intranet Web server is available, avoiding deployment issues such as installation and synchronized activation.

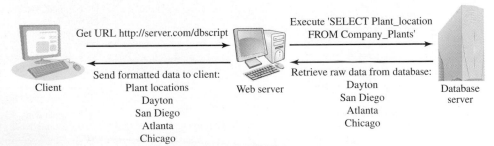

Figure 9.15 Web/Database Connectivity

- **Development speed:** Large portions of the normal development cycle, such as deployment and client design, do not apply to Web-based projects. In addition, the text-based tags of HTML allow for rapid modification, making it easy to continually improve the look and feel of the application based on user feedback. By contrast, changing form or content of a typical graphical-based application can be a substantial task.

- **Flexible information presentation:** The hypermedia base of the Web enables the application developer to employ whatever information structure is best for a given application, including the use of hierarchical formats in which progressive levels of detail are available to the user.

These advantages are compelling in the decision to deploy a Web-based database interface. However, managers need to be aware of potential disadvantages, also listed in [WHET96]:

- **Functionality:** Compared to the functionality available with a sophisticated graphical user interface (GUI), a typical Web browser interface may be more limited.

- **Stateless operation.** The nature of HTTP is such that each interaction between a browser and a server is a separate transaction, independent of prior or future exchanges. Typically, the Web server keeps no information between transactions to track the state of the user. Such history information can be important. For example, consider an application that allows the user to query a database of parts for cars and trucks. Once the user has indicated that he or she is looking for a specific truck part, subsequent menus should show only parts that pertain to trucks. It is possible to work around this difficulty, but it is awkward.

Intranet Webs Versus Traditional Client/Server

Although traditional client/server systems have become increasingly widespread and popular, displacing older corporate computing models, their use is not without problems, including the following:

- Long development cycles
- Difficulty of partitioning applications into client and server modules and the even greater difficulty of modifying the partition in response to user feedback
- Effort involved in distributing upgrades to clients
- Difficulty of scaling the servers to respond to increased load in a distributed environment
- Continuous requirement for increasingly powerful desktop machines

Much of this difficulty can be traced to the typical client/server design, which puts much of the load on the client; this thick client strategy corresponds to Figure 9.5c and 9.5d. As was mentioned earlier, this strategy may not scale well to corporate-wide applications. Thus, many companies opt for a fat server approach. An intranet Web can be viewed as one realization of the fat server.

Viewed as an alternative to other fat server schemes, the intranet Web has the advantages of ease of deployment, use of a small number of widely accepted standards, and integration with other TCP/IP-based applications. However, it is unlikely that the intranet Web will kill or even slow down traditional client/server deployment, at least in the near term. Longer term, the intranet Web may come to dominate corporate computing or it may simply be a widely used alternative to other client/server strategies that also flourish.

9.5 EXTRANETS

A concept similar to that of the intranet is the **extranet**. Like the intranet, the extranet makes use of TCP/IP and their applications, especially the Web. The distinguishing feature of the extranet is that it provides access to corporate resources by outside clients, typically suppliers and customers of the organization. This outside access can be through the Internet or through other data communications networks. An extranet provides more than the simple Web access for the public that virtually all companies now provide. Instead, the extranet provides more extensive access to corporate resources, usually in a fashion that enforces a security policy. As with the intranet, the typical model of operation for the extranet is client/server.

The essential feature of an extranet is that it enables the sharing of information among companies. [BIDG08b] lists the following benefits of extranets:

- **Reduced costs:** Information sharing is done in a highly automated fashion, with minimized paperwork and human involvement.
- **Coordination:** Critical information from one partner can be made available so that another partner can quickly make decisions. For example, a manufacturer can coordinate its production by checking the inventory status of a customer.
- **Customer satisfaction:** By linking the customer to an organization, an extranet provides more information about the current status of products and services of the vendor.
- **Expedited communications:** Extranets increase the efficiency and effectiveness of communication among business partners by linking intranets for immediate access to critical information.

An important consideration with extranets is security. Because corporate Web resources and database resources are made available to outside parties and transactions against these resources are allowed, privacy and authentication concerns must be addressed. This is typically done with the use of a virtual private network (VPN), which is discussed in Chapter 19. Here, we can simply list some of the communications options available for opening up the corporate intranet to outsiders to create an extranet:

- **Long-distance dial-up access:** This enables outsiders to access the intranet directly, using a logon procedure to authenticate the user. This approach may provide the weakest security because of the risk of impersonation, with few tools to counteract such risks.

- **Internet access to intranet with security:** Authentication of users and encryption of communications between user and intranet provide enhanced security. The encryption prevents eavesdropping, and authentication is intended to prevent unauthorized access. However, as with dial-up access, if a hacker is able to defeat the authentication mechanism, then the entire resources of the intranet become vulnerable.

- **Internet access to an external server that duplicates some of a company's intranet data:** This approach reduces the risk of hacker penetration but may also reduce the value of the extranet to external partners.

- **Internet access to an external server that originates database queries to internal servers:** The external server acts as a firewall to enforce the company's security policy. The firewall may employ encryption in communicating to external users, will authenticate external users, and filters the information flow to restrict access on the basis of user. If the firewall is itself secure from hacker attacks, this is a powerful approach.

- **Virtual private network:** The VPN in effect is a generalization of the firewall approach and takes advantage of IP security capabilities to allow secure communications between external users and the company's intranet. VPNs are discussed in Chapter 19.

9.6 SERVICE-ORIENTED ARCHITECTURE

The service-oriented architecture (SOA) is a form of client/server architecture that now enjoys widespread use in enterprise systems. A recent Forrester survey found that over 70% of enterprises were using SOA by 2011 [KANA11].

[WELK11] lists three ways in which SOA differs from previous client/server approaches:

1. A service's functional scope can range from very low-level or fine-grained up to functionality that maps directly in scope, terminology, and interest to business users. To permit this range of possibilities, an SOA organizes business functions into a modular structure rather than as monolithic applications for each department. As a result, common functions can be used by different departments internally and by external business partners as well. The more fine-grained the modules, the more they can be reused. In general, an SOA consists of a set of services and a set of client applications that use these services. A client request may involve a single service or may involve two or more services to coordinating some activity, requiring communication of services with each other. The services are available through published and discoverable interfaces.

2. A well-evolved—and still evolving—set of open standards define everything from service description, to communication with the service, to discovering and connecting to the service, to details on combining services to create composite service, transaction completion, and security. Standardized interfaces are used to enable service modules to communicate with one another and to enable client applications to communicate with service modules. The most

popular interface is the use of XML (Extensible Markup Language) over HTTP (Hypertext Transfer Protocol), known as *Web services*. SOAs are also implemented using other standards, such as CORBA (Common Object Request Broker Architecture).

3. The means for communicating with services, regardless of scope, is an Internet protocol. This means that the service can be local or remote, and can be provided within an enterprise or by an outside service provider. Further, the details of the service processing can change without affecting the user, because communication is via standardized interfaces and protocols.

At a top level, an SOA contains three types of architectural elements [BIH06], illustrated in Figure 9.16:

- **Service provider:** A network node that provides a service interface for a software asset that manages a specific set of tasks. A service provider node can represent the services of a business entity or it can simply represent the service interface for a reusable subsystem.

- **Service requestor:** A network node that discovers and invokes other software services to provide a business solution. Service requestor nodes will often represent a business application component that performs RPCs to a distributed object, the service provider. In some cases, the provider node may reside locally within an intranet or in other cases it could reside remotely over the Internet. The conceptual nature of SOA leaves the networking, transport protocol, and security details to the specific implementation.

- **Service broker:** A specific kind of service provider that acts as a registry and allows for the lookup of service provider interfaces and service locations. The service broker can pass on service requests to one or more additional service providers.

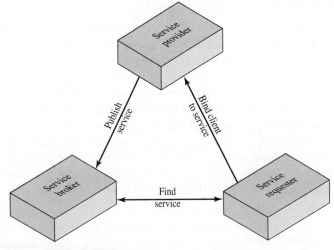

Figure 9.16   SOA Model

The following are key characteristics for effective use of services:

- **Coarse-grained:** Operations on services are frequently implemented to encompass more functionality and operate on larger data sets, compared with component-interface design.

- **Interface-based design:** Services implement separately defined interfaces. The benefit of this is that multiple services can implement a common interface and a service can implement multiple interfaces.

- **Discoverable:** Services need to be found at both design time and run time, not only by unique identity but also by interface identity and by service kind.

- **Single instance:** Unlike component-based development, which instantiates components as needed, each service is a single, always running instance that a number of clients communicate with.

- **Loosely coupled:** Services are connected to other services and clients using standard, dependency-reducing, decoupled message-based methods such as XML document exchanges.

- **Asynchronous:** In general, services use an asynchronous message-passing approach; however, this is not required. In fact, many services will use synchronous message passing at times.

To give the reader some feel for the use of SOA, we look at an example. Figure 9.17a shows a common approach to building applications targeted at specific user categories. For each specific application, a single self-contained application module is built. What ties together the various applications in the enterprise is an application-independent database management system that supports a number of databases. Multiple applications may have access to a single database. For example, in this configuration all three applications require access to a customer information database. The advantages of this arrangement are clear. By separating the data from the applications and providing a uniform database interface, multiple applications can be developed and revised independently from one another.

This typical approach, of a variety of applications using a common set of databases, has some drawbacks. The addition of a new feature or user service, such as ATM (automatic teller machine), generally requires building a new application independent of existing applications—despite the fact that much of the necessary logic has already been implemented in related applications.

We can achieve greater efficiency and flexibility by migrating to an SOA, as shown in Figure 9.17b. Here, the strategy is to isolate services that may be of common use to multiple applications and implement these as separate service modules. In this particular example of the SOA, there are some core applications that deal with the functionality of individual databases. These applications are accessible by application programming interfaces (APIs) by service modules that implement common services. Finally, the specific applications visible to users deal primarily with presentation issues and with specific business logic.

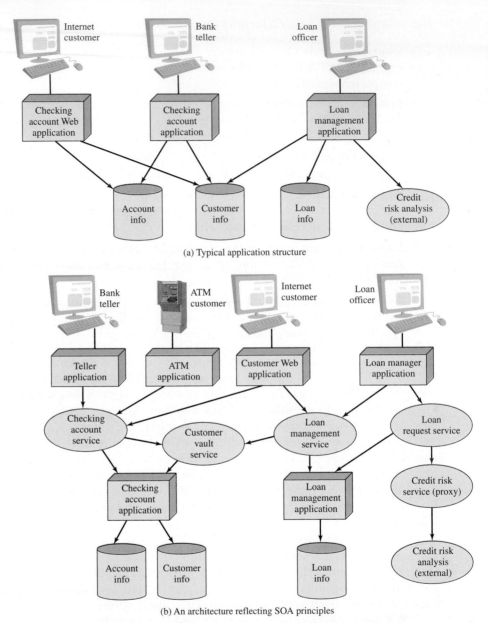

(a) Typical application structure

(b) An architecture reflecting SOA principles

Figure 9.17   Example Use of SOA

9.7 CLOUD COMPUTING

There is an increasingly prominent trend in many organizations to move a substantial portion or even all information technology (IT) operations to an Internet-connected infrastructure known as enterprise cloud computing. This section provides an overview of cloud computing.

Cloud Computing Elements

NIST defines cloud computing, in NIST SP-800-145 (*The NIST Definition of Cloud Computing*) as follows:

> **Cloud computing:** A model for enabling ubiquitous, convenient, on-demand network access to a shared pool of configurable computing resources (e.g., networks, servers, storage, applications, and services) that can be rapidly provisioned and released with minimal management effort or service provider interaction. This cloud model promotes availability and is composed of five essential characteristics, three service models, and four deployment models.

The definition refers to various models and characteristics, whose relationship is illustrated in Figure 9.18. The **essential characteristics** of cloud computing include the following:

- **Broad network access:** Capabilities are available over the network and accessed through standard mechanisms that promote use by heterogeneous thin or thick client platforms (e.g., mobile phones, laptops, and PDAs) as well as other traditional or cloud-based software services.

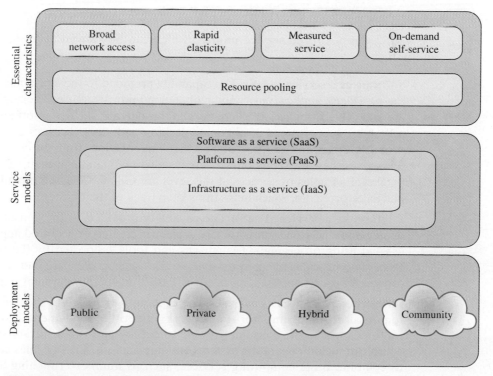

Figure 9.18   Cloud Computing Elements

- **Rapid elasticity:** Cloud computing gives you the ability to expand and reduce resources according to your specific service requirement. For example, you may need a large number of server resources for the duration of a specific task. You can then release these resources upon completion of the task.

- **Measured service:** Cloud systems automatically control and optimize resource use by leveraging a metering capability at some level of abstraction appropriate to the type of service (e.g., storage, processing, bandwidth, and active user accounts). Resource usage can be monitored, controlled, and reported, providing transparency for both the provider and consumer of the utilized service.

- **On-demand self-service:** A consumer can unilaterally provision computing capabilities, such as server time and network storage, as needed automatically without requiring human interaction with each service provider. Because the service is on demand, the resources are not permanent parts of your IT infrastructure.

- **Resource pooling:** The provider's computing resources are pooled to serve multiple consumers using a multi-tenant model, with different physical and virtual resources dynamically assigned and reassigned according to consumer demand. There is a degree of location independence in that the customer generally has no control or knowledge of the exact location of the provided resources, but may be able to specify location at a higher level of abstraction (e.g., country, state, or data center). Examples of resources include storage, processing, memory, network bandwidth, and virtual machines. Even private clouds tend to pool resources between different parts of the same organization.

NIST defines three **service models**, which can be viewed as nested service alternatives:

- **Software as a service (SaaS):** The capability provided to the consumer is to use the provider's applications running on a cloud infrastructure. The applications are accessible from various client devices through a thin client interface such as a Web browser. Instead of obtaining desktop and server licenses for software products it uses, an enterprise obtains the same functions from the cloud service. SaaS saves the complexity of software installation, maintenance, upgrades, and patches. Examples of services at this level are Gmail, Google's e-mail service, and Salesforce.com, which helps firms keep track of their customers.

- **Platform as a service (PaaS):** The capability provided to the consumer is to deploy onto the cloud infrastructure consumer-created or acquired applications created using programming languages and tools supported by the provider. PaaS often provides middleware-style services such as database and component services for use by applications. In effect, PaaS is an operating system in the cloud.

- **Infrastructure as a service (IaaS):** The capability provided to the consumer is to provision processing, storage, networks, and other fundamental computing resources where the consumer is able to deploy and run arbitrary software, which can include operating systems and applications. IaaS enables customers to combine basic computing services, such as number crunching and data storage, to build highly adaptable computer systems.

NIST defines four **deployment models**:

- **Public cloud:** The cloud infrastructure is made available to the general public or a large industry group and is owned by an organization selling cloud services. Both the infrastructure and control of the cloud is with the service provider.

- **Private cloud:** The cloud infrastructure is operated solely for an organization. It may be managed by the organization or a third party and may exist on premise or off premise. The cloud provider is responsible only for the infrastructure and not for the control.

- **Community cloud:** The cloud infrastructure is shared by several organizations and supports a specific community that has shared concerns (e.g., mission, security requirements, policy, and compliance considerations). It may be managed by the organizations or a third party and may exist on premise or off premise.

- **Hybrid cloud:** The cloud infrastructure is a composition of two or more clouds (private, community, or public) that remain unique entities but are bound together by standardized or proprietary technology that enables data and application portability (e.g., cloud bursting for load balancing between clouds).

Figure 9.19 illustrates the typical cloud service context. An enterprise maintains workstations within an enterprise LAN or set of LANs, which are connected by a router through a network or the Internet to the cloud service provider. The cloud service provider maintains a massive collection of servers, which it manages with a variety of network management, redundancy, and security tools. In the figure, the cloud infrastructure is shown as a collection of blade servers, which is a common architecture.

Cloud Computing Reference Architecture

NIST SP 500-292 (*NIST Cloud Computing Reference Architecture*) establishes a reference architecture, described as follows:

> The NIST cloud computing reference architecture focuses on the requirements of "what" cloud services provide, not a "how to" design solution and implementation. The reference architecture is intended to facilitate the understanding of the operational intricacies in cloud computing. It does not represent the system architecture of a specific cloud computing system; instead it is a tool for describing, discussing, and developing a system-specific architecture using a common framework of reference.

NIST developed the reference architecture with the following objectives in mind:

- to illustrate and understand the various cloud services in the context of an overall cloud computing conceptual model

- to provide a technical reference for consumers to understand, discuss, categorize, and compare cloud services

- to facilitate the analysis of candidate standards for security, interoperability, and portability and reference implementations

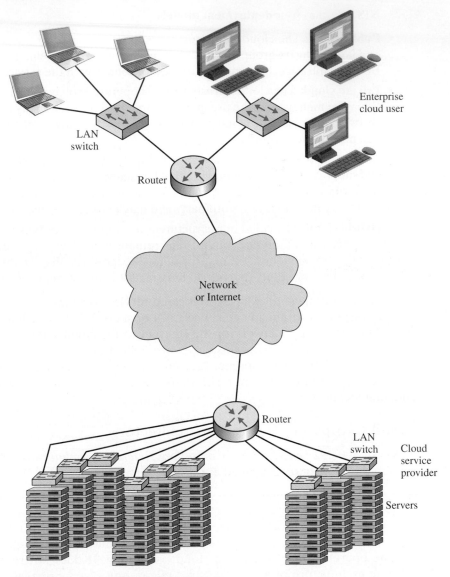

Figure 9.19 Cloud Computing Context

The reference architecture, depicted in Figure 9.20, defines five major actors in terms of the roles and responsibilities:

- **Cloud consumer:** A person or organization that maintains a business relationship with, and uses service from, cloud providers.
- **Cloud provider:** A person, organization, or entity responsible for making a service available to interested parties.
- **Cloud auditor:** A party that can conduct independent assessment of cloud services, information system operations, performance, and security of the cloud implementation.

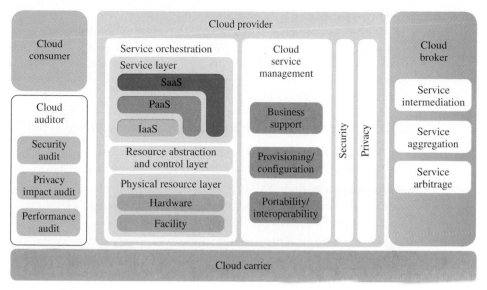

Figure 9.20   NIST Cloud Computing Reference Architecture

- **Cloud broker:** An entity that manages the use, performance, and delivery of cloud services, and negotiates relationships between cloud providers and cloud consumers,

- **Cloud carrier:** An intermediary that provides connectivity and transport of cloud services from cloud providers to cloud consumers.

The roles of the cloud consumer and provider have already been discussed. To summarize, a **cloud provider** can provide one or more of the cloud services to meet IT and business requirements of **cloud consumers**. For each of the three service models (SaaS, PaaS, IaaS), the cloud provider provides the storage and processing facilities needed to support that service model, together with a cloud interface for cloud service consumers. For SaaS, the cloud provider deploys, configures, maintains, and updates the operation of the software applications on a cloud infrastructure so that the services are provisioned at the expected service levels to cloud consumers. The consumers of SaaS can be organizations that provide their members with access to software applications, end users who directly use software applications, or software application administrators who configure applications for end users.

For PaaS, the cloud provider manages the computing infrastructure for the platform and runs the cloud software that provides the components of the platform, such as runtime software execution stack, databases, and other middleware components. Cloud consumers of PaaS can employ the tools and execution resources provided by cloud providers to develop, test, deploy, and manage the applications hosted in a cloud environment.

For IaaS, the cloud provider acquires the physical computing resources underlying the service, including the servers, networks, storage, and hosting infrastructure. The IaaS cloud consumer in turn uses these computing resources, such as a virtual computer, for their fundamental computing needs.

The **cloud carrier** is a networking facility that provides connectivity and transport of cloud services between cloud consumers and cloud providers. Typically, a cloud provider will set up service level agreements (SLAs) with a cloud carrier to provide services consistent with the level of SLAs offered to cloud consumers, and may require the cloud carrier to provide dedicated and secure connections between cloud consumers and cloud providers.

A **cloud broker** is useful when cloud services are too complex for a cloud consumer to easily manage. Three areas of support can be offered by a cloud broker:

- **Service intermediation:** These are value-added services, such as identity management, performance reporting, and enhanced security.
- **Service aggregation:** The broker combines multiple cloud services to meet consumer needs not specifically addressed by a single cloud provider, or to optimize performance or minimize cost.
- **Service arbitrage:** This is similar to service aggregation except that the services being aggregated are not fixed. Service arbitrage means a broker has the flexibility to choose services from multiple agencies. The cloud broker, for example, can use a credit-scoring service to measure and select an agency with the best score.

A **cloud auditor** can evaluate the services provided by a cloud provider in terms of security controls, privacy impact, performance, and so on. The auditor is an independent entity that can assure that the cloud provider conforms to a set of standards.

APPLICATION NOTE

To Be Fat or Thin—That Is the Question

One of the most popular communications architectures is the client/server model. Figure 9.2 illustrates this relationship. In a nutshell, the client computer has a small program that makes specific requests of the server. For example, when you access a Web page on a Web server, you are making the requests through a Web browser. The browser is your client application. The usual configuration for a computer is to have its own hard drive, processing power, memory, a collection of programs for doing work (e.g., Microsoft Office), and a collection of programs that are used to connect to other machines or resources. The latter are called client applications or simply "clients." This configuration is also true of network components. With the exception of the hard drive, routers, switches, and access points all have processors, memory, and software. In most cases the hard drive has simply been replaced by flash memory. Computers and devices built in this fashion are considered "fat" because they have everything that they need built in.

However, this is not the only way to configure computers or the other machines in a network. There are many products that sacrifice one or more of these parts in order to reduce cost or to fit a particular use. The following examples show how the configuration of the network and systems can be modified.

When you set up a printer for your home, it is dedicated to the computer directly attached. Even for a small company, individual printers for everyone may be appropriate. This is certainly something that becomes less feasible as the number of users increases. In this case, it is far more likely that the printers will be shared and that one of the servers will be operating as a print server, handling all of the printing requests from the clients.

Inventory software is an application that will run on the server or mainframe. Clients may work via serial or network connections, but very little processing or storage will occur on the clients. This is to ensure that the database information is accurate and up to date. The user keystrokes are passed to the mainframe or server and the information is sent back to the user after the "number crunching" has been completed. With respect to this application, the clients may be considered "thin." The user cannot work with these applications unless they are connected and possibly authenticated. This type of installation allows controlled use of the program and the software licenses.

Software licenses can cost a great deal of money, and there is always the possibility of fines if licenses are improperly administered. The server can act to control the number of users using the applications at any one time. This can also create problems if the number of licenses is not updated when new users are added. More than one user has been locked out of a network application because there were too many people already logged in.

Applications such as word processors and spreadsheets typically reside in full on computers. Again, clients configured in this way are considered fat. In a fully distributed environment with fat clients, the users will have a complete set of applications whose operation does not require any network connectivity.

It is also possible that the word processor exists entirely or in part on the server. In fact, the computer itself may be configured to be thin, in which case there are very few resources on the computer itself. The hard drive is only large enough to store essential operating system components, and all of the applications are stored on, and run from, the server out in the network. In this case, the installation potentially saves space on the client machines. Thin clients also have the advantage of being less expensive and easier to use. They are also less at risk for data corruption and theft. The downside is that the devices are now heavily dependent on the network. One can expect an increase of network traffic and, in the case of a loss of network access, a decrease in productivity.

Network devices can also be configured as fat or thin depending on their use. In the case of a wireless network for a large company, there can be dozens of deployed access points. The usual way of managing all of these is to configure each one individually and allow it to handle security and forwarding for that area, in other words, "fat" access points. This approach can be very time consuming, especially with the threats leveled against wireless networks today. An alternative would be to connect all of the access points back to a network controller and have all of the decisions made at this central location. The access points only have enough processing capability to provide feedback to the controller. All of the operational decisions are made in the central location. While this does make management easier, the controller is a single point of failure. Even if the failure is short in duration, the entire wireless network may be down completely.

There are some significant choices to be made when deciding on fat versus thin servers and clients. The choices made can have a significant effect on cost, security, performance, and impact on end users. Both fat and thin clients have particular areas to which they are well suited, and every installation is different from the next. It is important to understand the capabilities of the installed system, the services required, and the use of the client machines.

9.8 SUMMARY

Client/server computing is the key to realizing the potential of information systems and networks to significantly improve productivity in organizations. With client/server computing, applications are distributed to users on single-user workstations and personal computers. At the same time, resources that can and should be shared are maintained on server systems that are available to all clients. Thus, the client/server architecture is a blend of decentralized and centralized computing.

Typically, the client system provides a graphical user interface (GUI) that enables a user to exploit a variety of applications with minimal training and relative ease. Servers support shared utilities, such as database management systems. The actual application is divided between client and server in a way intended to optimize ease of use and performance.

Because there are no generally accepted standards for client/server networking, a number of products have been developed to bridge the gap between client and server and to enable users to develop multivendor configurations. Such products generally are referred to as middleware. Middleware products are based on either a message-passing or a remote-procedure-call mechanism.

A more recent organizational model that competes with the client/server model is the intranet. An intranet leverages existing Internet applications, especially the Web, to provide an internal suite of applications suited to the needs of an organization. Intranets are easy to set up, involve standardized software, can be deployed on multiple platforms, and require virtually no user training.

The service-oriented architecture (SOA) is a form of client/server computing. SOA systems are built from loosely-coupled software modules deployed as services, typically communicating via a network. This allows different modules to be implemented and deployed in different ways, for example, owned by different organizations, developed by different teams, written in different programming languages, running on different hardware and operating systems. The key to making it work is interoperability and standards so that modules can exchange data.

Cloud computing is a term that refers to any system providing access via the Internet to processing power, storage, software, or other computing services, often via a Web browser. Typically these services will be rented from an external company that hosts and manages them.

Case Study VI: Shifting Sands: Chevron's Migration to the Cloud

The major concepts addressed in this case study include Cloud computing and web services. **This case study and more are available at www.pearsoninternationaleditions.com/stallings**

9.9 KEY TERMS, REVIEW QUESTIONS, AND PROBLEMS

Key Terms

application programming interface (API)	community cloud	private cloud
	extranet	public cloud
client	graphical user interface (GUI)	remote procedure call (RPC)
client/server	infrastructure as	server
cloud auditor	a service (IaaS)	service aggregation
cloud broker	intranet	service arbitrage
cloud carrier	message	service intermediation
cloud computing	middleware	service-oriented
cloud consumer	object-oriented middleware	architecture (SOA)
cloud provider	platform as a service (PaaS)	software as a service (SaaS)

Review Questions

9.1 What is client/server computing?

9.2 What distinguishes client/server computing from any other form of distributed data processing?

9.3 Discuss the rationale for locating applications on the client, the server, or split between client and server.

9.4 What are four different ways processing can be divided between machines communicating with each other?

9.5 How are machines interacting in client/server-based systems different from a typical laptop or desktop computer?

9.6 What is the role of the middleware component in client/server architecture?

9.7 What is thin client, or fat server, approach?

9.8 What is client/server binding?

9.9 Middleware is often required for clients accessing data in different locations. Are Telnet and FTP examples of applications requiring middleware?

9.10 What are the three types of SOA architectural elements?

9.11 What are remote procedure calls?

9.12 What is reliable message-passing?

9.13 Define cloud computing.

9.14 What is a cloud carrier?

9.15 What are the communications options available for converting an intranet into an extranet?

Problems

9.1 You have just been hired as the CIO of an organization that has been in business for a while and has recently acquired another smaller organization in order to increase market share. The original organization operated a fleet of buses that conducted tours and travel packages along the northern portion of the U.S. eastern coast. All of its computer applications existed on a central mainframe at company headquarters in

Baltimore, Maryland. The acquired organization conducted helicopter tours around New York City and Washington, DC. All of its systems were C/S based (primarily thick clients accessing thin DB servers) and they were based outside Baltimore, near the BWI airport. Due to the mergers, the organization's IT architecture is now a disparate combination of computer systems and manual procedures. Given the general description of the stakeholder groups below and using the general C/S classes defined in Figure 9.5, prepare a cohesive IT architectural plan for the new organization and present it to the CEO for approval. Address all potential advantages and disadvantages of the plan from the perspectives of the various groups of stakeholders.

- bus/helicopter maintenance workers and mechanics (10 employees)
  - —system for ordering parts/supplies
- drivers/pilots (20 employees)
  - —logs and route/schedule information
- administration/HR (5 employees)
  - —employee records
  - —financial records
- marketing (8 employees)
  - —marketing activities
  - —customer interactions (CRM)
- management (9 employees)
  - —reports

9.2 The Java programming language is referred to by some as the language of the Web, due to its platform independent nature. Java uses a hybrid form of RPC and CORBA called RMI (Remote Method Invocation). How does RMI differ from these two technologies and for what type of environment might RMI be an acceptable (or even optimal) solution? Reference: http://www.kuro5hin.org/story/2001/2/9/213758/1156. A copy of this paper is in the Document section of the Premium Content for this book.

9.3 A relatively new term that has been introduced to the Web environment is *Web service*. What is a Web service and how does it differ from the concept of a Web application? Reference: http://www.w3.org/TR/2003/WD-ws-gloss-20030514/

9.4 What are the client/server-based applications that are part of your operating system?

9.5 What are some of the servers on your local network operating within the client/server paradigm? Where are these servers located? What are the IP addresses of the servers? What are the names of the servers?

9.6 This chapter discusses thick clients. There has been a good deal of work, past and present, in the area of thin clients. How would you characterize a thin client?

9.7 This chapter introduced the term *intranet*. Previously the term *Internet* was introduced. Based on your understanding of these terms, draw a diagram depicting your local intranet (school network) and your organization's (school's) connection to the Internet.

- How big is your network?
- Who is your Internet service provider?
- How many networks comprise your school network?
- How many users does the network serve?
- What kind of network performance have you received?

INTERNET-BASED APPLICATIONS

Learning Objectives

After reading this chapter, you should be able to:

♦ Discuss the applications for electronic mail.
♦ Explain that basic functionality of SMTP.
♦ Explain the need for MIME as an enhancement to ordinary e-mail.
♦ Describe the key elements of MIME.
♦ Explain the role of HTTP in the operation of the Web.
♦ Describe the functions of proxies, gateways, and tunnels in HTTP.
♦ Explain Web caching.
♦ Discuss the need for and use of acceptable use policies.

As we discussed in Chapters 2 and 3, distributed information processing is essential in virtually all businesses. Much of the distributed processing is tailored to specific types of data and is supported by proprietary vendor software. However, there is a growing use of distributed applications for both intracompany and intercompany exchanges that are general purpose in nature and that are defined by international standards or by industry de facto standards. These applications can have a direct impact on the efficiency and competitiveness of a business. In this chapter, we look at three of the most important and widespread of these distributed applications: electronic mail (e-mail), Web access, and multimedia support. In each case, international standards have been developed. As these standards become more widely implemented by computer vendors and software houses, these applications become increasingly important and useful in the business environment. This chapter also examines acceptable use policies for Internet- and network-based applications.

10.1 ELECTRONIC MAIL

Electronic mail is a facility that allows users at workstations and terminals to compose and exchange messages. The messages need never exist on paper unless the user (sender or recipient) desires a paper copy of the message. Some e-mail systems only serve users on a single computer; others provide service across a network of computers. Table 10.1 lists some of the common features provided by an e-mail facility.

In this section, we look at the standard Internet mail architecture and then examine the key protocols to support e-mail applications.

Internet Mail Architecture

To understand the operation of an electronic mail system and its supporting protocols, it is useful to have a basic grasp of the Internet mail architecture, which is currently defined in RFC 5598 (*Internet Mail Architecture*). At its most fundamental level, the Internet mail architecture consists of a user world, in the form of message user agents (MUA), and the transfer world, in the form of the **message handling service (MHS)**,

Table 10.1 Typical Electronic Mail Facilities

Message Preparation

Word Processing

Facilities for the creation and editing of messages. Usually these need not be as powerful as a full word processor, since electronic mail documents tend to be simple. However, most electronic mail packages allow "off-line" access to word processors: The user creates a message using the computer's word processor, stores the message as a file, and then uses the file as input to the message preparation function of the e-mail facility.

Annotation

Messages often require some sort of short reply. A simple technique is to allow the recipient to attach annotation to an incoming message and send it back to the originator or on to a third party.

Message Sending

User Directory

Used by the system. May also be accessible to users to be able to look up addresses.

Timed Delivery

Allows the sender to specify that a message be delivered before, at, or after a specified date/time. A message is considered delivered when it is placed in the recipient's mailbox.

Multiple Addressing

Copies of a message are sent to multiple addressees. The recipients are designated by listing each in the header of the message or by the use of a distribution list. The latter is a file containing a list of users. Distribution lists can be created by the user and by central administrative functions.

Message Priority

A message may be labeled at a given priority level. Higher-priority messages will be delivered more rapidly, if that is possible. Also, the recipient will be notified or receive some indication of the arrival of high-priority messages.

Status Information

A user may request notification of delivery or of actual retrieval by the recipient. A user may also be able to query the current status of a message (e.g., queued for transmission, transmitted but receipt confirmation not yet received).

Interface to Other Facilities

These would include other electronic systems, such as telex, and physical distribution facilities, such as couriers and the public mail service (e.g., U.S. postal service).

Message Receiving

Mailbox Scanning

Allows the user to scan the current contents of mailbox. Each message may be indicated by subject, author, date, priority, and so on.

Message Selection

The user may select individual messages from the mailbox for display, printing, storing in a separate file, or deletion.

Message Notification

Many systems notify an online user of the arrival of a new message and indicate to a user during log on that there are messages in his or her mailbox.

Message Reply

A user may reply immediately to a selected message, avoiding the necessity of keying in the recipient's name and address.

Message Rerouting

A user who has moved, either temporarily or permanently, may reroute incoming messages. An enhancement is to allow the user to specify different forwarding addresses for different categories of messages.

which is composed of message transfer agents (MTA). The MHS accepts a message from one user and delivers it to one or more other users, creating a virtual MUA-to-MUA exchange environment. This architecture involves three types of interoperability. One is directly between users: Messages must be formatted by the MUA on behalf of the message author so that the message can be displayed to the message recipient by the destination MUA. There are also interoperability requirements between the MUA and the MHS—first when a message is posted from an MUA to the MHS and later when it is delivered from the MHS to the destination MUA. Interoperability is required among the MTA components along the transfer path through the MHS.

Figure 10.1 illustrates the key components of the Internet mail architecture, which include the following.

- **Message user agent (MUA):** Works on behalf of user actors and user applications. It is their representative within the e-mail service. Typically, this function is housed in the user's computer and is referred to as a client e-mail program or a local network e-mail server. The author MUA formats a message and performs initial submission into the MHS via an MSA. The recipient MUA processes received mail for storage and/or display to the recipient user.
- **Mail submission agent (MSA):** Accepts the message submitted by an MUA and enforces the policies of the hosting domain and the requirements of

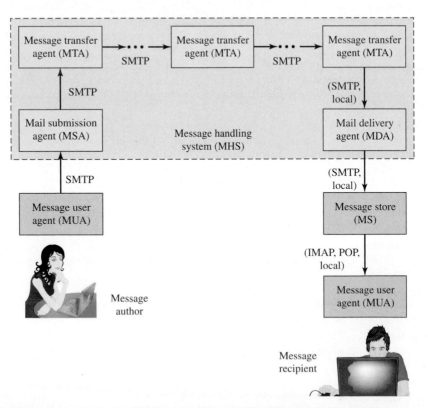

Figure 10.1 Function Modules and Standardized Protocols Used Between Them in the Internet Mail Architecture

Internet standards. This function may be located together with the MUA or as a separate functional model. In the latter case, the Simple Mail Transfer Protocol (SMTP) is used between the MUA and the MSA.

- **Message transfer agent (MTA):** Relays mail for one application-level hop. It is like a packet switch or IP router in that its job is to make routing assessments and to move the message closer to the recipients. Relaying is performed by a sequence of MTAs until the message reaches a destination MDA. An MTA also adds trace information to the message header. SMTP is used between MTAs and between an MTA and an MSA or MDA.

- **Mail delivery agent (MDA):** Responsible for transferring the message from the MHS to the message store (MS).

- **Message store (MS):** An MUA can employ a long-term MS. An MS can be located on a remote server or on the same machine as the MUA. Typically, an MUA retrieves messages from a remote server using POP (Post Office Protocol) or IMAP (Internet Message Access Protocol).

Two other concepts need to be defined. An **administrative management domain (ADMD)** is an Internet e mail provider. Examples include a department that operates a local mail relay (MTA), an IT department that operates an enterprise mail relay, and an ISP that operates a public shared e-mail service. Each ADMD can have different operating policies and trust-based decision making. One obvious example is the distinction between mail that is exchanged within an organization and mail that is exchanged between independent organizations. The rules for handling the two types of traffic tend to be quite different.

The **Domain Name System (DNS)** is a directory lookup service that provides a mapping between the name of a host on the Internet and its numerical address. DNS is discussed in Chapter 7.

The user agent functions are visible to the e-mail user. These include facilities for preparing and submitting messages for routing to the destination(s), as well as utility functions to assist the user in filing, retrieving, replying, and forwarding. The MHS accepts messages from the user agent for transmission across a network or internetwork. The MHS is concerned with the protocol operation needed to transmit and deliver messages.

The user does not directly interact with the MHS. If the user designates a local recipient for a message, the MUA stores the message in the local recipient's mailbox. If a remote recipient is designated, the MUA passes the message to the MHS for transmission to a remote MTA and ultimately to a remote mailbox.

To implement the Internet mail architecture, a set of standards is needed. Four standards are noteworthy:

- **Post Office Protocol (POP3):** POP3 allows an e-mail client (user agent) to download an e-mail from an e-mail server (MTA). POP3 user agents connect via TCP/IP to the server (typically port 110). The user agent enters a username and password (either stored internally for convenience or entered each time by the user for stronger security). After authorization, the user agent can issue POP3 commands to retrieve and delete mail.

- **Internet Mail Access Protocol (IMAP):** As with POP3, IMAP also enables an e-mail client to access mail on an e-mail server. IMAP also uses TCP/IP, with server TCP port 143. IMAP is more complex than POP3. IMAP provides stronger authentication than POP3 and provides other functions not supported by POP3.

- **Simple Mail Transfer Protocol (SMTP):** This protocol is used for transfer of mail from a user agent to an MTA and from one MTA to another.

- **Multipurpose Internet Mail Extensions (MIME):** MIME supplements SMTP and allows the encapsulation of multimedia (nontext) messages inside of a standard SMTP message.

In the remainder of this section, we elaborate on these standards.

Simple Mail Transfer Protocol

SMTP is the standard protocol for transferring mail between hosts in the TCP/IP suite; it is defined in RFC 821.

Although messages transferred by SMTP usually follow the format defined in RFC 822, described subsequently, SMTP is not concerned with the format or content of messages themselves, with two exceptions. This concept is often expressed by saying that SMTP uses information written on the envelope of the mail (message header) but does not look at the contents (message body) of the envelope. The two exceptions are as follows:

1. SMTP standardizes the message character set as 7-bit ASCII. (The American Standard Code for Information Interchange is described in Appendix D.)

2. SMTP adds log information to the start of the delivered message that indicates the path the message took.

BASIC E-MAIL OPERATION   Figure 10.2 illustrates the overall flow of mail in a typical distributed system. Although much of this activity is outside the scope of SMTP, the figure illustrates the context within which SMTP typically operates.

To begin, mail is created by a user agent program in response to user input. Each created message consists of a header that includes the recipient's e-mail address and other information, and a body containing the message to be sent. These messages are then queued in some fashion and provided as input to an SMTP sender program, which is typically an always-present server program on the host.

Although the structure of the outgoing mail queue will differ depending on the host's operating system, each queued message conceptually has two parts:

1. The message text, consisting of
   - The 822 header: This constitutes the message envelope and includes an indication of the intended recipient or recipients.
   - The body of the message, composed by the user.
2. A list of mail destinations.

The list of mail destinations for the message is derived by the user agent from the message header. In some cases, the destination or destinations are literally

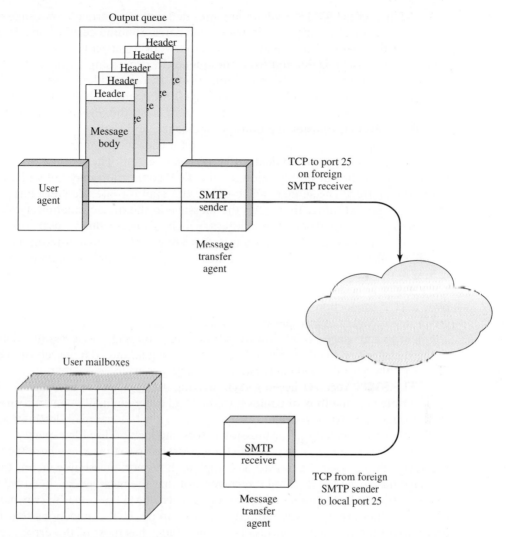

Figure 10.2   SMTP Mail Flow

specified in the message header. In other cases, the user agent may need to expand mailing list names, remove duplicates, and replace mnemonic names with actual mailbox names. If any blind carbon copies (BCCs) are indicated, the user agent needs to prepare messages that conform to this requirement. The basic idea is that the multiple formats and styles preferred by humans in the user interface are replaced by a standardized list suitable for the SMTP sender program.

The **SMTP sender** takes messages from the outgoing mail queue and transmits them to the proper destination host via SMTP transactions over one or more TCP connections to port 25 on the target hosts. A host may have multiple SMTP senders active simultaneously if it has a large volume of outgoing mail and should also have the capability of creating SMTP receivers on demand so that mail from one host cannot delay mail from another.

Whenever the SMTP sender completes delivery of a particular message to one or more users on a specific host, it deletes the corresponding destinations from that message's destination list. When all destinations for a particular message are processed, the message is deleted from the queue. In processing a queue, the SMTP sender can perform a variety of optimizations. If a particular message is sent to multiple users on a single host, the message text needs to be sent only once. If multiple messages are ready to send to the same host, the SMTP sender can open a TCP connection, transfer the multiple messages, and then close the connection, rather than opening and closing a connection for each message.

The SMTP sender must deal with a variety of errors. The destination host may be unreachable or out of operation, or the TCP connection may fail while mail is being transferred. The sender can re-queue the mail for later delivery but give up after some period rather than keep the message in the queue indefinitely. A common error is a faulty destination address, which can occur due to user input error or because the intended destination user has a new address on a different host. The SMTP sender must either redirect the message if possible or return an error notification to the message's originator.

SMTP is used to transfer a message from the SMTP sender to the SMTP receiver over a TCP connection. SMTP attempts to provide reliable operation but does not guarantee recovery of lost messages. SMTP does not return an end-to-end acknowledgment to a message's originator to indicate that a message is successfully delivered to the message's recipient. Error indications are not guaranteed to be returned either. However, the SMTP-based mail system is generally considered reliable.

The **SMTP receiver** accepts each arriving message and either places it in the appropriate user mailbox or copies it to the local outgoing mail queue if forwarding is required. The SMTP receiver must be able to verify local mail destinations and deal with errors, including transmission errors and lack of disc file capacity.

The SMTP sender is responsible for a message up to the point where the SMTP receiver indicates that the transfer is complete; however, this simply means that the message has arrived at the SMTP receiver, not that the message has been delivered to and retrieved by the intended final recipient. The SMTP receiver's error-handling responsibilities are generally limited to giving up on TCP connections that fail or are inactive for very long periods. Thus, the sender has most of the error recovery responsibility. Errors during completion indication may cause duplicate, but not lost, messages.

In most cases, messages go directly from the mail originator's machine to the destination machine over a single TCP connection. However, mail will occasionally go through intermediate machines via an SMTP forwarding capability, in which case the message must traverse a series of TCP connections between source and destination. One way for this to happen is for the sender to specify a route to the destination in the form of a sequence of servers. A more common event is forwarding required because a user has moved.

It is important to note that SMTP is limited to the conversation that takes place between the SMTP sender and the SMTP receiver. SMTP's main function is the transfer of messages, although there are some ancillary functions dealing with mail destination verification and handling. The rest of the mail-handling functionality depicted in Figure 10.2 is beyond the scope of SMTP and may differ from one system to another.

RFC 822   RFC 822 defines a format for text messages that are sent using e-mail. The SMTP standard adopts RFC 822 as the format for use in constructing messages for transmission via SMTP. In the RFC 822 context, messages are viewed as having an envelope and contents. The envelope contains whatever information is needed to accomplish transmission and delivery. The contents compose the object to be delivered to the recipient. The RFC 822 standard applies only to the contents. However, the content standard includes a set of header fields that may be used by the mail system to create the envelope, and the standard is intended to facilitate the acquisition of such information by programs.

An RFC 822 message consists of a sequence of lines of text and uses a general "memo" framework. That is, a message consists of some number of header lines, which follow a rigid format, followed by a body portion consisting of arbitrary text.

A header line usually consists of a keyword, followed by a colon, followed by the keyword's arguments; the format allows a long line to be broken up into several lines. The most frequently used keywords are From, To, Subject, and Date. Here is an example message:

```
Date. Mon, 10 Mar 2008 10:37:17 (EDT)
From: "William Stallings" <ws@host.com>
Subject: The Syntax in RFC 822
To: Smith@Other-host.com
Cc: Jones@Yet-Another-Host.com

Hello. This section begins the actual message body, which
is delimited from the message heading by a blank line.
```

Another field that is commonly found in RFC 822 headers is Message-ID. This field contains a unique identifier associated with this message.

Multipurpose Internet Mail Extensions (MIME)

MIME is an extension to the RFC 822 framework that is intended to address some of the problems and limitations of the use of SMTP and RFC 822 for e-mail. [PARZ06] lists the following limitations of the SMTP/822 scheme:

1. SMTP cannot transmit executable files or other binary objects. A number of schemes are in use for converting binary files into a text form that can be used by SMTP mail systems, including the popular UNIX uuencode/uudecode scheme. However, none of these is a standard or even a de facto standard.

2. SMTP cannot transmit text data that include national language characters because these are represented by 8-bit codes with values of 128 decimal or higher, and SMTP is limited to 7-bit ASCII.

3. SMTP servers may reject mail message over a certain size.

4. SMTP gateways that translate between ASCII and the character code EBCDIC do not use a consistent set of mappings, resulting in translation problems.

5. SMTP gateways to X.400 e-mail networks cannot handle nontextual data included in X.400 messages.

6. Some SMTP implementations do not adhere completely to the SMTP standards defined in RFC 821. Common problems include the following:

- Deletion, addition, or reordering of carriage return and linefeed
- Truncating or wrapping lines longer than 76 characters
- Removal of trailing white space (tab and space characters)
- Padding of lines in a message to the same length
- Conversion of tab characters into multiple space characters

These limitations make it difficult to use encryption with electron mail and to use SMTP to carry multimedia objects and electronic data interchange (EDI) messages. MIME is intended to resolve these problems in a manner that is compatible with existing RFC 822 implementations.

OVERVIEW   The MIME specification includes the following elements:

1. Five new message header fields are defined, which may be included in an RFC 822 header. These fields provide information about the body of the message.
2. A number of content formats are defined, thus standardizing representations that support multimedia e-mail.
3. Transfer encodings are defined that enable the conversion of any content format into a form that is protected from alteration by the mail system.

The five header fields defined in MIME are as follows:

- **MIME-Version:** Must have the parameter value 1.0. This field indicates that the message conforms to the RFCs.
- **Content-Type:** Describes the data contained in the body with sufficient detail that the receiving user agent can pick an appropriate agent or mechanism to represent the data to the user or otherwise deal with the data in an appropriate manner.
- **Content-Transfer-Encoding:** Indicates the type of transformation that has been used to represent the body of the message in a way that is acceptable for mail transport.
- **Content-ID:** Used to uniquely identify MIME entities in multiple contexts.
- **Content-Description:** A plain text description of the object with the body; this is useful when the object is not readable (e.g., audio data).

Any or all of these fields may appear in a normal RFC 822 header. A compliant implementation must support the MIME-Version, Content-Type, and Content-Transfer-Encoding fields; the Content-ID and Content-Description fields are optional and may be ignored by the recipient implementation.

MIME CONTENT TYPES   The bulk of the MIME specification is concerned with the definition of a variety of content types. This reflects the need to provide standardized ways of dealing with a wide variety of information representations in a multimedia environment.

Table 10.2 MIME Content Types

Type	Subtype	Description
Text	Plain	Unformatted text; may be ASCII or ISO 8859.
Multipart	Mixed	The different parts are independent but are to be transmitted together. They should be presented to the receiver in the order that they appear in the mail message.
	Parallel	Differs from Mixed only in that no order is defined for delivering the parts to the receiver.
	Alternative	The different parts are alternative versions of the same information. They are ordered in increasing faithfulness to the original and the recipient's mail system should display the "best" version to the user.
	Digest	Similar to Mixed, but the default type/subtype of each part is message/rfc822.
Message	rfc822	The body is itself an encapsulated message that conforms to RFC 822.
	Partial	Used to allow fragmentation of large mail items, in a way that is transparent to the recipient.
	External-body	Contains a pointer to an object that exists elsewhere.
Image	jpeg	The image is in JPEG format, JFIF encoding.
	gif	The image is in GIF format.
Video	mpeg	MPEG format.
Audio	Basic	Single-channel 8-bit ISDN mu-law encoding at a sample rate of 8 kHz.
Application	PostScript	Adobe Postscript.
	octet-stream	General binary data consisting of 8 bit bytes.

Table 10.2 lists the MIME content types. There are seven different major types of content and a total of 14 subtypes. In general, a content type declares the general type of data, and the subtype specifies a particular format for that type of data.

POP and IMAP

The Post Office Protocol and the Internet Message Access Protocol support retrieval of mail between a client system (message user agent) and a server that holds the mail for the client (message store).

POST OFFICE PROTOCOL   Version 3 of POP, identified as POP3, is an Internet standard defined in RFC 1939. POP3 supports the basic functions of download and delete for e-mail retrieval. To perform a function from the client (MUA) to the server (MS), the MUA establishes a TCP connection to the MS, using port 110. Then, the interaction passes through three distinct states:

- **Authentication state:** During this state, the client must authenticate itself to the user. This is often done with a simple user ID/password combination, although more sophisticated options are available.
- **Transaction state:** Once the server successfully authenticates the client, the client can access the mailbox to retrieve and delete messages.
- **Update state:** During this state, the server enacts all of the changes requested by the client's commands and then closes the connection.

INTERNET MESSAGE ACCESS PROTOCOL IMAP version 4 is defined by RFC 3501. Similar to POP, IMAP4 servers store messages for multiple users to be retrieved upon client requests, but the IMAP4 model provides more functionality to users than does the POP model, including the following features:

- Clients can have multiple remote mailboxes from which messages can be retrieved.
- Clients can also specify criteria for downloading messages, such as not transferring large messages over slow links.
- IMAP always keeps messages on the server and replicates copies to the clients.
- IMAP4 allows clients to make changes both when connected and when disconnected. When disconnected (referred to as a disconnected client), changes made on the client take effect on the server by periodic re-synchronization of the client and server.

10.2 WEB ACCESS AND HTTP

The Hypertext Transfer Protocol (HTTP) is the foundation protocol of the World Wide Web (WWW) and can be used in any client/server application involving hypertext. The name is somewhat misleading in that HTTP is not a protocol for transferring hypertext; rather it is a protocol for transmitting information with the efficiency necessary for making hypertext jumps. The data transferred by the protocol can be plaintext, hypertext, audio, images, or any Internet-accessible information.

We begin with an overview of HTTP concepts and operation and then look at some of the details, basing our discussion on the most recent version to be put on the Internet standards track, HTTP 1.1. A number of important terms defined in the HTTP specification are summarized in Table 10.3; these will be introduced as the discussion proceeds.

HTTP Overview

HTTP is a transaction-oriented client/server protocol. The most typical use of HTTP is between a Web browser and a Web server. To provide reliability, HTTP makes use of TCP. Nevertheless, HTTP is a **stateless protocol**: Each transaction is treated independently. Accordingly, a typical implementation will create a new TCP connection between client and server for each transaction and then terminate the connection as soon as the transaction completes, although the specification does not dictate this one-to-one relationship between transaction and connection lifetimes.

The stateless nature of HTTP is well suited to its typical application. A normal session of a user with a Web browser involves retrieving a sequence of Web pages and documents. The sequence is, ideally, performed rapidly, and the locations of the various pages and documents may be a number of widely distributed servers.

Table 10.3   Key Terms Related to HTTP

Cache

A program's local store of response messages and the subsystem that controls its message storage, retrieval, and deletion. A cache stores cacheable responses in order to reduce the response time and network bandwidth consumption on future, equivalent requests. Any client or server may include a cache, though a cache cannot be used by a server while it is acting as a tunnel.

Client

An application program that establishes connections for the purpose of sending requests.

Connection

A transport layer virtual circuit established between two application programs for the purposes of communication.

Entity

A particular representation or rendition of a data resource, or reply from a service resource, that may be enclosed within a request or response message. An entity consists of entity headers and an entity body.

Gateway

A server that acts as an intermediary for some other server. Unlike a proxy, a gateway receives requests as if it were the original server for the requested resource; the requesting client may not be aware that it is communicating with a gateway. Gateways are often used as server-side portals through network firewalls and as protocol translators for access to resources stored on non-HTTP systems.

Message

The basic unit of HTTP communication, consisting of a structured sequence of octets transmitted via the connection.

Origin Server

The server on which a given resource resides or is to be created.

Proxy

An intermediary program that acts as both a server and a client for the purpose of making requests on behalf of other clients. Requests are serviced internally or by passing them, with possible translation, on to other servers. A proxy must interpret and, if necessary, rewrite a request message before forwarding it. Proxies are often used as client-side portals through network firewalls and as helper applications for handling requests via protocols not implemented by the user agent.

Resource

A network data object or service that can be identified by a URI.

Server

An application program that accepts connections in order to service requests by sending back responses.

Tunnel

An intermediary program that is acting as a blind relay between two connections. Once active, a tunnel is not considered a party to the HTTP communication, though the tunnel may have been initiated by an HTTP request. A tunnel ceases to exist when both ends of the relayed connections are closed. Tunnels are used when a portal is necessary and the intermediary cannot, or should not, interpret the relayed communication.

User Agent

The client that initiates a request. These are often browsers, editors, spiders, or other end-user tools.

Another important feature of HTTP is that it is flexible in the formats that it can handle. When a client issues a request to a server, it may include a prioritized list of formats that it can handle, and the server replies with the appropriate format. For example, a Lynx browser cannot handle images, so a Web server need not transmit any images on Web pages. This arrangement prevents the transmission of unnecessary information and provides the basis for extending the set of formats with new standardized and proprietary specifications.

Figure 10.3 illustrates three examples of HTTP operation. The simplest case is one in which a user agent establishes a direct connection with an origin server. The **user agent** is the client that initiates the request, such as a Web browser being run on behalf of an end user. The **origin server** is the server on which a resource of interest resides; an example is a Web server at which a desired

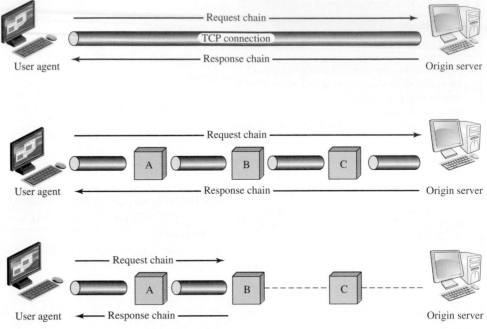

Figure 10.3 Examples of HTTP Operation

Web home page resides. For this case, the client opens a TCP connection that is end-to-end between the client and the server. The client then issues an HTTP request. The request consists of a specific command, referred to as a method, an address [referred to as a Uniform Resource Locator (URL—Appendix C provides a discussion of URLs)], and a MIME-like message containing request parameters, information about the client, and perhaps some additional content information.

When the server receives the request, it attempts to perform the requested action and then returns an HTTP response. The response includes status information, a success/error code, and a MIME-like message containing information about the server, information about the response itself, and possible body content. The TCP connection is then closed.

The middle part of Figure 10.3 shows a case in which there is not an end-to-end TCP connection between the user agent and the origin server. Instead, there are one or more intermediate systems with TCP connections between logically adjacent systems. Each intermediate system acts as a relay, so that a request initiated by the client is relayed through the intermediate systems to the server, and the response from the server is relayed back to the client.

Three forms of intermediate system are defined in the HTTP specification: proxy, gateway, and tunnel, all of which are illustrated in Figure 10.4.

PROXY   A proxy acts on behalf of other clients and presents requests from other clients to a server. The proxy acts as a server in interacting with a client and as a client in interacting with a server. There are two scenarios that call for the use of a proxy:

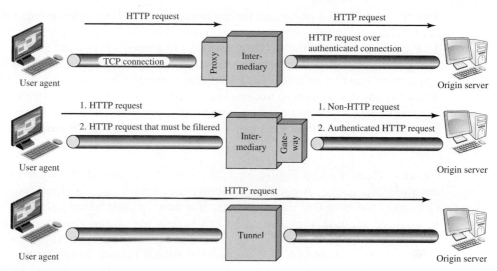

Figure 10.4 Intermediate HTTP Systems

- **Security intermediary:** The client and server may be separated by a security intermediary such as a firewall, with the proxy on the client side of the firewall. Typically, the client is part of a network secured by a firewall and the server is external to the secured network. In this case, the server must authenticate itself to the firewall to set up a connection with the proxy. The proxy accepts responses after they have passed through the firewall.

- **Different versions of HTTP:** If the client and server are running different versions of HTTP, then the proxy can implement both versions and perform the required mapping.

In summary, a proxy is a forwarding agent, receiving a request for a URL object, modifying the request, and forwarding the request toward the server identified in the URL.

GATEWAY   A gateway is a server that appears to the client as if it were an origin server. It acts on behalf of other servers that may not be able to communicate directly with a client. There are two scenarios in which gateways can be used.

- **Security intermediary:** The client and server may be separated by a security intermediary such as a firewall, with the gateway on the server side of the firewall. Typically, the server is connected to a network protected by a firewall, with the client external to the network. In this case the client must authenticate itself to the gateway, which can then pass the request on to the server.

- **Non-HTTP server:** Web browsers have built into them the capability to contact servers for protocols other than HTTP, such as FTP and Gopher servers. This capability can also be provided by a gateway. The client makes an HTTP request to a gateway server. The gateway server then contacts the relevant FTP or Gopher server to obtain the desired result. This result is then converted into a form suitable for HTTP and transmitted back to the client.

TUNNEL   Unlike the proxy and the gateway, the tunnel performs no operations on HTTP requests and responses. Instead, a tunnel is simply a relay point between two TCP connections, and the HTTP messages are passed unchanged as if there were a single HTTP connection between user agent and origin server. Tunnels are used when there must be an intermediary system between client and server but it is not necessary for that system to understand the contents of messages. An example is a firewall in which a client or server external to a protected network can establish an authenticated connection and then maintain that connection for purposes of HTTP transactions.

CACHE   Returning to Figure 10.3, the lowest portion of the figure shows an example of a cache. A cache is a facility that may store previous requests and responses for handling new requests. If a new request arrives that is the same as a stored request, then the cache can supply the stored response rather than accessing the resource indicated in the URL. The cache can operate on a client or server or on an intermediate system other than a tunnel. In the figure, intermediary B has cached a request/response transaction, so that a corresponding new request from the client need not travel the entire chain to the origin server but is handled by B.

   Not all transactions can be cached, and a client or server can dictate that a certain transaction may be cached only for a given time limit.

Messages

The best way to describe the functionality of HTTP is to describe the individual elements of the HTTP message. HTTP consists of two types of messages: **requests** from clients to servers, and **responses** from servers to clients. Figure 10.5 provides an example.

   The Simple-Request and Simple-Response messages were defined in HTTP/0.9. The request is a simple GET command with the requested URL; the response is simply a block containing the information identified in the URL. In HTTP/1.1, the use of these simple forms is discouraged because it prevents the client from using content negotiation and the server from identifying the media type of the returned entity.

   All of the HTTP headers consist of a sequence of fields, following the same generic format as RFC 822 (described in Section 10.1). Each field begins on a new line and consists of the field name followed by a colon and the field value.

   A full request uses the following fields:

- **Request-Line:** Indicates the requested action, the resource on which the action is to be performed, and the version of HTTP used in this message.
- **General-Headers:** Contains fields that are applicable to the request message but that do not apply to the entity being transferred.
- **Request-Headers:** Contains information about the request and the client. For example, a request may be conditional, specifying under what conditions the requested action is to be determined. A field in this header may also indicate which formats and encodings the client is able to handle.

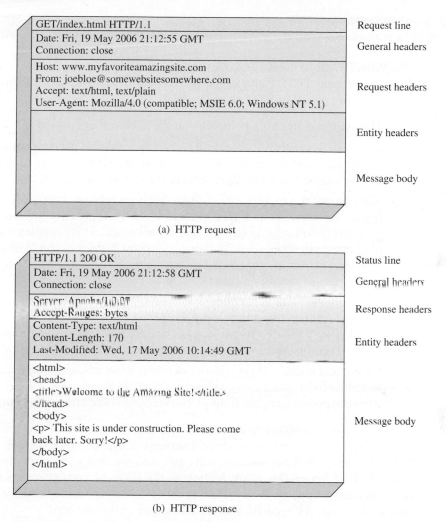

(a) HTTP request

(b) HTTP response

Figure 10.5   Examples of HTTP Message Format

- **Entity-Header:** Contains information about the resource identified by the request and information about the entity body, if any.
- **Entity-Body:** The body of the message.

A response message has the same structure as a request message, but substitutes the following headers for the request line and the request headers:

- **Status-Line:** Indicates the version of HTTP used in this message and provides status information about this response. For example, "OK" means that the request was successfully completed.
- **Response-Headers:** Provides additional data that expand on the status information in the status line.

10.3 WEB SECURITY

The World Wide Web is fundamentally a client/server application running over the Internet and TCP/IP intranets. [GARF02] points out the following security challenges presented by the use of the Web:

- The Web is vulnerable to attacks on the Web servers over the Internet.

- The Web is a highly visible outlet for corporate and product information and as the platform for business transactions. Reputations can be damaged and money can be lost if the Web servers are subverted.

- Web browsers are very easy to use, Web servers are relatively easy to configure and manage, and Web content is increasingly easy to develop, but the underlying software is extraordinarily complex. This complex software may hide many potential security flaws. The short history of the Web is filled with examples of new and upgraded systems, properly installed, that are vulnerable to a variety of security attacks.

- A Web server can be exploited as a launching pad into the corporation's or agency's entire computer complex. Once the Web server is subverted, an attacker may be able to gain access to data and systems not part of the Web itself but connected to the server at the local site.

- Casual and untrained (in security matters) users are common clients for Web-based services. Such users are not necessarily aware of the security risks that exist and do not have the tools or knowledge to take effective countermeasures.

One way to classify Web security threats is in terms of the location of the threat: Web server, Web browser, and network traffic between browser and server. Issues of server and browser security fall into the category of computer system security; Part Six of this book addresses the issue of system security in general but is also applicable to Web system security. Issues of traffic security fall into the category of network security and are addressed in this section.

Web Traffic Security Approaches

A number of approaches to providing Web security are possible. The various approaches that have been considered are similar in the services they provide and, to some extent, in the mechanisms that they use, but they differ with respect to their scope of applicability and their relative location within the TCP/IP stack.

One way to provide Web security is to use IP security (IPsec), described in Chapter 8. The advantage of using IPsec is that it is transparent to end users and applications and provides a general-purpose solution. Further, IPsec includes a filtering capability so that only selected traffic need incur the overhead of IPsec processing. The disadvantage of IPsec is the need to configure a relatively complex security architecture on all of the systems supporting both Web browsers and Web servers. An enterprise network that allows access from both enterprise systems and partner (vendor, customer) systems may not be a good candidate for such a configuration.

Another relatively general-purpose solution is to implement security just above TCP. This is the approach defined by the Secure Sockets Layer (SSL) and the follow-on Internet standard known as Transport Layer Security (TLS). At this level, there are two implementation choices. For full generality, SSL (or TLS) could be provided as part of the underlying protocol suite and therefore be transparent to applications. Alternatively, SSL can be embedded in specific packages. In the case of the Web, virtually all browsers and Web servers incorporate SSL.

The remainder of this chapter is devoted to a discussion of SSL/TLS and the related concept of HTTPS.

Secure Sockets Layer

Figure 10.6 illustrates the position of SSL in the TCP/IP architecture. Before discussing this architecture, we need to define the term *socket*. In essence, a socket is a method of directing data to the appropriate application in a TCP/IP network. The combination of the IP address of the host and a TCP port number make up a socket address. From the application point of view, a socket interface is an application-programming interface (API). The socket interface is a generic communication programming interface implemented on UNIX and many other systems. Two applications communicate through TCP sockets. An application connects to TCP through a socket address and tells TCP what remote application is requested by means of the remote application's socket address.

With SSL in place, an application has an SSL socket address and communicates to the SSL socket of the remote application. The security functions provided by SSL are transparent to the application and also to TCP. Thus, neither TCP nor the application needs to be modified to invoke the security features of SSL. As shown in Figure 10.6, SSL supports not only HTTP, but also any other application that uses TCP.

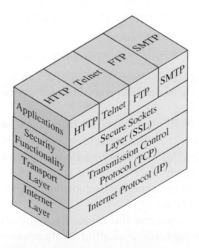

Figure 10.6   The Role of SSL
in the TCP/IP Architecture

SSL provides three categories of security:

- **Confidentiality:** All data that pass between the two applications (e.g., the two HTTP modules) are encrypted so that they cannot be eavesdropped on the Internet.

- **Message integrity:** SSL assures that the message is not altered or substituted for en route.

- **Authentication:** SSL can validate the identity of one or both partners to the exchange.

SSL consists of two phases: handshake and data transfer. During handshake, the two sides perform an authentication function and establish an encryption key to be used for data transfer. During data transfer, the two sides use the encryption key to encrypt all transmitted data.

HTTPS

HTTPS (HTTP over SSL) refers to the combination of HTTP and SSL to implement secure communication between a Web browser and a Web server. The HTTPS capability is built into all modern Web browsers. Its use depends on the Web server supporting HTTPS communication. For example, search engines do not support HTTPS.

The principal difference seen by a user of a Web browser is that URL addresses begin with http:// rather than http://. A normal HTTP connection uses port 80. If HTTPS is specified, port 443 is specified, which invokes SSL.

When HTTPS is used, the following elements of the communication are encrypted:

- URL of the requested document
- Contents of the document
- Contents of browser forms (filled in by browser user)
- Cookies sent from browser to server and from server to browser
- Contents of HTTP header

10.4 MULTIMEDIA APPLICATIONS

With the increasing availability of broadband access to the Internet has come an increased interest in Web-based and Internet-based multimedia applications. The terms *multimedia* and *multimedia applications* are used rather loosely in the literature and in commercial publications, and no single definition of the term *multimedia* has been agreed. For our purposes, the definitions in Table 10.4 provide a starting point.

One way to organize the concepts associated with multimedia is to look at a taxonomy that captures a number of dimensions of this field. Figure 10.7 looks at multimedia from the perspective of three different dimensions: type of media, applications, and the technology required to support the applications.

Table 10.4   Multimedia Terminology

Media
Refers to the form of information and includes text, still images, audio, and video.
Multimedia
Human–computer interaction involving text, graphics, voice, and video. Multimedia also refers to storage devices that are used to store multimedia content.
Streaming Media
Refers to multimedia files, such as video clips and audio, that begin playing immediately or within seconds after it is received by a computer from the Internet or Web. Thus, the media content is consumed as it is delivered from the server rather than waiting until an entire file is downloaded.

Media Types

Typically, the term *multimedia* refers to four distinct types of media: text, audio, graphics, and video.

From a communications perspective, the term **text** is self-explanatory, referring to information that can be entered via a keyboard and is directly readable and printable. Text messaging, instant messaging, and text (non-html) e-mail are common examples, as are chat rooms and message boards. However, the term often is used in the broader sense of data that can be stored in files and databases and that do not fit into the other three categories. For example, an organization's database may contain files of numerical data, in which the data are stored in a more compact form than printable characters.

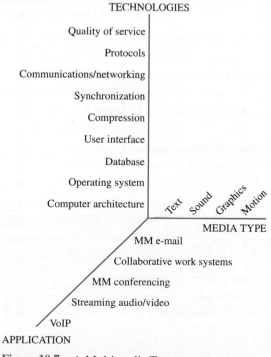

Figure 10.7   A Multimedia Taxonomy

The term **audio** generally encompasses two different ranges of sound. Voice, or speech, refers to sounds that are produced by the human speech mechanism. Generally, a modest bandwidth (under 4 kHz) is required to transmit voice. Telephony and related applications (e.g., voice mail, audio teleconferencing, telemarketing) are the most common traditional applications of voice communications technology. A broader frequency spectrum is needed to support music applications, including the download of music files.

The **image** service supports the communication of individual pictures, charts, or drawings. Image-based applications include facsimile, computer-aided design (CAD), publishing, and medical imaging. Images can be represented in a vector graphics format, such as is used in drawing programs and PDF files. In a raster graphics format, an image is represented as a two-dimensional array of spots, called pixels.[1] The compressed JPG format is derived from a raster graphics format.

The **video** service carries sequences of pictures in time. In essence, video makes use of a sequence of raster-scan images.

Multimedia Applications

The Internet, until recently, has been dominated by information retrieval applications, e-mail, and file transfer, plus Web interfaces that emphasized text and images. Increasingly, the Internet is being used for multimedia applications that involve massive amounts of data for visualization and support of real-time interactivity. Streaming audio and video are perhaps the best known of such applications. An example of an interactive application is a virtual training environment involving distributed simulations and real-time user interaction. Some other examples are shown in Table 10.5.

Multimedia application domains include the following:

- **Multimedia information systems:** Databases, information kiosks, hypertexts, electronic books, and multimedia expert systems
- **Multimedia communication systems:** Computer-supported collaborative work, videoconferencing, streaming media, and multimedia teleservices
- **Multimedia entertainment systems:** 3D computer games, multiplayer network games, infotainment, and interactive audiovisual productions
- **Multimedia business systems:** Immersive electronic commerce, marketing, multimedia presentations, video brochures, virtual shopping, and so on

Table 10.5 Domains of Multimedia Systems and Example Applications

Domain	Example Application
Information management	Hypermedia, multimedia-capable databases, content-based retrieval
Entertainment	Computer games, digital video, audio (MP3)
Telecommunication	Videoconferencing, shared workspaces, virtual communities
Information publishing/delivery	Online training, electronic books, streaming media

---

[1]A pixel, or picture element, is the smallest element of a digital image that can be assigned a gray level. Equivalently, a pixel is an individual dot in a dot-matrix representation of a picture.

- **Multimedia educational systems:** Electronic books, flexible teaching materials, simulation systems, automatic testing, distance learning, and so on

One point worth noting is highlighted in Figure 10.7. Although traditionally the term *multimedia* has connoted the simultaneous use of multiple media types (e.g., video annotation of a text document), the term has also come to refer to applications that require real-time processing or communication of video or audio alone. Thus, voice over IP (VoIP), streaming audio, and streaming video are considered multimedia applications even though each involves a single media type.

Multimedia Technologies

Figure 10.7 lists some of the technologies that are relevant to the support of multimedia applications. As can be seen, a wide range of technologies is involved. The lowest four items on the list are beyond the scope of this book. The other items represent only a partial list of communications and networking technologies for multimedia. These technologies and others are explored throughout the book. Here, we give a brief comment on each area.

- **Compression:** Digitized video, and to a much lesser extent audio, can generate an enormous amount of traffic on a network. A streaming application, which is delivered to many users, magnifies the traffic. Accordingly, standards have been developed for producing significant savings through compression. The most notable standards are JPG for still images and MPG for video.
- **Communications/networking:** This broad category refers to the transmission and networking technologies (e.g., SONET, ATM) that can support high-volume multimedia traffic.
- **Protocols:** A number of protocols are instrumental in supporting multimedia traffic. One example is the Real-time Transport Protocol (RTP), which is designed to support inelastic traffic. RTP uses buffering and discarding strategies to assure that real-time traffic is received by the end user in a smooth continuous stream. Another example is the Session Initiation Protocol (SIP), an application-level control protocol for setting up, modifying, and terminating real-time sessions between participants over an IP data network.
- **Quality of service (QoS):** The Internet and its underlying local area and wide area networks must include a QoS capability to provide differing levels of service to different types of application traffic. A QoS capability can deal with priority, delay constraints, delay variability constraints, and other similar requirements.

10.5 ACCEPTABLE USE POLICIES

E-mail and Internet access for most or all employees are common in office environments and is typically provided for at least some employees in other environments, such as a factory. A growing number of companies incorporate specific e-mail and Internet use policies into the organization's security policy document. This section examines some important considerations for these policies.

Motivation

Widespread use of e-mail and the Internet by employees raises a number of concerns for employers, including the following:

1. Significant employee work time may be consumed in non-work-related activities, such as surfing the Web, playing games on the Web, shopping on the Web, chatting on the Web, and sending and reading personal e-mail.

2. Significant computer and communications resources may be consumed by such non-work-related activity, compromising the mission that the IS resources are designed to support.

3. Excessive and casual use of the Internet and e-mail unnecessarily increases the risk of introduction of malicious software into the organization's IS environment.

4. The non-work-related employee activity could result in harm to other organizations or individuals outside the organization, thus creating a liability for the organization.

5. E-mail and the Internet may be used as tools of harassment by one employee against another.

6. Inappropriate online conduct by an employee may damage the reputation of the organization.

Policy Issues

The development of a comprehensive e-mail and Internet use policy raises a number of policy issues. The following is a suggested set of policies, based on [KING06].

- **Business use only:** Company-provided e-mail and Internet access are to be used by employees only for the purpose of conducting company business.

- **Policy scope:** Policy covers e-mail access; contents of e-mail messages; Internet and intranet communications; and records of e-mail, Internet, and intranet communications.

- **Content ownership:** Electronic communications, files, and data remain company property even when transferred to equipment not owned by the company.

- **Privacy:** Employees have no expectation of privacy in their use of company-provided e-mail or Internet access, even if the communication is personal in nature.

- **Standard of conduct:** Employees are expected to use good judgment and act courteously and professionally when using company-provided e-mail and Internet access.

- **Reasonable personal use:** Employees may make reasonable personal use of company-provided e-mail and Internet access provided that such use does not interfere with the employee's duties, violate company policy, or unduly burden company facilities.

- **Unlawful activity prohibited:** Employees may not use company-provided e-mail and Internet access for any illegal purpose.

- **Security policy:** Employees must follow the company's security policy when using e-mail and Internet access.

- **Company policy:** Employees must follow all other company policies when using e-mail and Internet access. Company policy prohibits viewing, storing, or distributing pornography; making or distributing harassing or discriminatory communications; and unauthorized disclosure of confidential or proprietary information.

- **Company rights:** The company may access, monitor, intercept, block access, inspect, copy, disclose, use, destroy, recover using computer forensics, and/or retain any communications, files, or other data covered by this policy. Employees are required to provide passwords upon request.

- **Disciplinary action:** Violation of this policy may result in immediate termination of employment or other discipline deemed appropriate by the company.

Table 10.6 suggests how the roles and responsibilities for acceptable use might be defined in an organization.

Guidelines for Developing a Policy

A useful document to consult when developing an e-mail and Internet use policy is *Guidelines to Assist Agencies in Developing Email and Internet Use Policies*, from the Office of e-Government, the Government of Western Australia, July 2004. Another useful document is the example *Acceptable Use Policy Document* put out by the SANS Institute in 2003. There are several related documents available at this book's Premium Content site.

Table 10.6 Acceptable Use Responsibilities

Activity	Executive Sponsors	All Managers	System Admins	CISO	All Personnel	Auditors
Inform users	X	X		X		A
Implement user sanctions	X	X		C		A
Acquire hardware and software properly	X	X		C		X/A
Comply with copyright and licensing	X	X	X	X	X	X/A
Comply with personally-owned software policy	X	X	X	X	X	X/A
Protect intellectual property	X	X	X	X	X	X/A
Comply with e-mail policy	X	X	X	X	X	X/A
Comply with e-mail encryption policy	X	X	X	X	X	X/A
Comply with Internet policy	X	X	X	X	X	X/A
Comply with information resources policy	X	X	X	X	X	X/A

Note: CISO = chief information security officer; X = responsible for accomplishment; C = consulting support as required; A = independent compliance auditing.

APPLICATION NOTE

To Serve or Not to Serve

Web servers and mail servers are possibly the most difficult kinds of systems to manage. They are constantly barraged with requests from valid users and assailed by attacks from not so valid users. Before deciding to deploy either of these, there are some questions that an organization should ask itself. Very often, there is no need to manage these types of services internally.

Perhaps the best place to start is determining what the system will be required to do. In other words, what do you need and want? For mail servers, questions such as the number of accounts needed, security required, and internal versus external mail should be answered. Small companies or individuals running their own companies may be able to take advantage of free mail services such as Gmail. This does not provide a real identity for the organization but does facilitate communication.

Groups falling into the small office home office (SOHO) category often have their Web pages hosted by their Internet service provider (ISP) or a specialized hosting firm. This allows them to have a Web presence without the need to run a Web server. In addition, Web hosting services or ISPs will often register a domain name with the DNS for you. At a small cost (typically less than $100/year) this provides an identity to the group and often includes several e-mail accounts, some security/logging tools, and management services.

Using Web hosting and mail services from an ISP or hosting company can serve companies with several employees. For a few extra dollars the number of accounts can be increased and the space or scripting required by the Web site can be expanded. However, there is a point at which the outside services become less attractive. For large organizations with dozens or hundreds of people, complex human resources or internal communication demands, and a fully staffed IT department, it may be much more attractive to run your own services.

Setting up e-mail or Web servers internally can be a daunting task for the unprepared. Like most installations, it is not difficult to put the software on a machine or set up a few accounts. It is the maintenance and security of the systems that can be a struggle. In addition, installing services internally can affect other systems. For example, if you are running your own Web site that generates sales or provides support, what is the response if it goes down? How many hits does the site get? What is the network utilization? It is important to understand the operation and requirements of such a system before it is installed.

When running a Web or mail server that is to be accessed from outside the company network, any firewalls that have been configured need to be updated to allow this sort of traffic. This is directly related to the ports used by these applications. The firewall rules may also be written based on other criterion such as IP address. In addition, the type of client software must be considered as not all external systems will have what is required. Are the users carrying their laptops around with them? If so, they may need additional support and a full suite of applications. Do they access the corporate resources from outside? Do they need virtual private network (VPN) access? What about the additional security necessary when accessing information from a restaurant wireless hotspot?

Allowing access from outside can be tricky if the organization regularly handles sensitive data or has to contend with compliance issues. If this is the case, security will be a top priority with encryption and firewalls as main focal points. A security policy should be established and careful consideration given to the personnel allowed external access to internal systems. Often companies will have two sets of servers running. These will be for internal or external use exclusively. For example, employee information and benefits may be run on an internal server while the company Web site and contact information may be on the external one. Often, authentication servers are deployed in conjunction with certain Web site features.

For the staff running the servers, the never-ending tasks of security patching and virus protection take up a good deal of time. Exploits for security installations pop up as fast as older holes can be closed and new viruses arrive as we are filtering out the existing ones. Viruses are a particularly tricky problem and this has led many administrators to do a good amount of mail filtering on the server itself. This means that many messages will arrive to the end user with a note describing how a potentially dangerous file was automatically removed from the original message. This is especially true of executable files. End users should also be running virus protection software that examines incoming mail and the local computer. In the end, the real problem with viruses is that the end users often download them to a computer either by going around the installed security or because the security measures didn't catch it. The answer here is training for everyone.

There are Advantages and disadvantages to running your own services. On one hand, local configuration permits tailored security changes, rapid account creation, and content modification. On the other hand, server management headaches, costs, and man hours can make external provisioning attractive.

10.6 SUMMARY

Standardized distributed applications are becoming increasingly important to businesses, for three main reasons:

- Standardized applications are more readily acquired and used than special-purpose software, which may have inadequate support and is accompanied by inadequate training.
- Standardized software allows the user to procure computers from a variety of vendors and yet have those computers work together.
- Standards promote the ability for different companies to exchange data.

This chapter examines three important distributed applications. Standards have been developed for these applications, and their use continues to grow.

A general-purpose e-mail facility provides a means of exchanging unstructured messages, usually text messages. E-mail is a rapid and convenient method for communication, supplementing, and, in many instances, replacing telephone and paper communications. Because e-mail is so general purpose in nature, it is perhaps the most popular distributed application and can have the most widespread benefits.

The most widely used protocol for the transmission of e-mail is SMTP. SMTP assumes that the content of the message is a simple text block. The recent MIME standard expands SMTP to support transmission of multimedia information.

The rapid growth in the use of the Web is due to the standardization of all the elements that support Web applications. A key element is HTTP, which is the protocol for the exchange of Web-based information between Web browsers and Web servers. Three types of intermediate devices can be used in an HTTP networks: proxies, gateways, and tunnels. HTTP uses a request/response style of communication.

Case Study VII: E-Business at Guardian Life

The major concepts addressed in this case study include E-business/digital commerce; web portals. **This case study and more are available at www.pearsoninternationaleditions .com/stallings**

10.7 KEY TERMS, REVIEW QUESTIONS, AND PROBLEMS

Key Terms

acceptable use policies	Hypertext Transfer Protocol	message user agent (MUA)
administrative management	(HTTP)	multimedia
domain (ADMD)	Internet Message Access	Multipurpose Internet Mail
Domain Name System	Protocol (IMAP)	Extensions (MIME)
(DNS)	mail delivery agent (MDA)	Post Office Protocol (POP)
electronic mail	message handling service	RFC 822
HTTP gateway	(MHS)	Simple Mail Transfer Protocol
HTTP method	message store (MS)	(SMTP)
HTTP proxy	mail submission agent (MSA)	Uniform Resource Locator
HTTP tunnel	message transfer agent (MTA)	(URL)

Review Questions

10.1   What is a tunnel?
10.2   What is the difference between an MUA and an MSA?
10.3   What are the SMTP and MIME standards?
10.4   What advantage does IMAP have over POP3?
10.5   What is meant by saying that HTTP is a stateless protocol?
10.6   Explain the differences among HTTP proxy, gateway, and tunnel.
10.7   What is the function of a mail delivery agent (MDA)?
10.8   What is a proxy?

Problems

10.1   E-mail systems differ in the manner in which multiple recipients are handled. In some systems, the originating user agent or mail sender makes all the necessary copies and these are sent out independently. An alternative approach is to determine the route for each destination first. Then a single message is sent out on a common portion of the route and copies are only made when the routes diverge; this process is referred to as mail bagging. Discuss the relative advantages and disadvantages of the two methods.

10.2 Excluding the connection establishment and termination, what is the minimum number of network round trips to send a small e-mail message using SMTP?

10.3 Suppose you need to send one message to three different users: user1@example.com, user2@example.com, and user3@example.com. Is there any difference between sending one separate message per user and sending only one message with multiple (three) recipients? Explain.

10.4 Users are free to define and use additional header fields other than the ones defined in RFC 87. Such header fields must begin with the string "X-". Why?

10.5 Suppose you find some technical problems with the mail account user@example.com. Who should you try to contact in order to solve them?

10.6 HTTP caching is an operation that can be controlled at the originating server, at an intermediate node, or at the client browser application. What are the potential benefits and detriments associated with this mechanism (from the perspective of both the originator and client) as it is implemented?

10.7 RFC 3298 describes the Spirits protocol requirements. What is Sprits and how might it be relative to a discussion of SIP and PINT?

10.8 Many mail clients allow you to view the mail header that will display the path that the message traveled. Does your mail client or program have this option? If so, can you trace the message from source to destination?

10.9 What TCP port does your mail system use?

10.10 In discovering the port your mail system uses, what port is your machine using?

10.11 Why is it important for the local systems administrator to understand what ports are being used by applications?

10.12 What are POP3 and IMAP?

10.13 What is HTTPS?

10.14 Netmeeting is a video conferencing program built into the Windows family of operating systems. It allows video, audio, or video/audio combined communications. Using Netmeeting and some basic communications gear (microphone, speakers, camera), establish communication between two stations. What protocols and codecs are being used?

CHAPTER 11

INTERNET OPERATION

Learning Objectives

After reading this chapter, you should be able to:

♦ Describe Internet addressing and appreciate the key issues involved in address assignment.

♦ Understand the difference between an interior routing protocol and an exterior routing protocol.

♦ Explain the basic mechanisms in a routing protocol.

♦ Understand the concept of quality of service.

♦ Explain the difference between elastic traffic and inelastic traffic.

♦ Discuss the services provided by a differentiated services facility.

This chapter looks at some of the details "under the hood" of the Internet. We begin by examining the rather complicated issue of addressing in such a far-flung, massive, and dynamic configuration. Next, we provide an overview of routing protocols, by which routers cooperate to design routes, or paths, through the Internet from source to destination. Then, we introduce the issue of quality of service. Next, we look at the most important approach to providing quality of service on the Internet, known as differentiated services. Finally, we introduce the topics of service level agreements and IP performance metrics.

11.1 INTERNET ADDRESSING

To identify a host on the Internet, each host is assigned a unique IP address, which consists of two logical components: a *network* component, which identifies a network on the Internet, and a *host* component, which identifies a host connected to a particular network. The *host* portion of the address need only be unique within its designated network. Thus, the IP address is of the form

IP address = <network number><host number>

The *network number* portion of the IP address is administered by one of five Regional Internet Registries. The *host* portion is assigned by the authority that manages the network, which is typically the organization that owns the network.

The IP address is assigned to a network interface on a host (there may be multiple network interfaces) when the OS boots up. As discussed in Chapter 7, the IP address is obtained either by looking it up in a configuration file or dynamically, via the Dynamic Host Configuration Protocol (DHCP).

In this section, we examine the form of IP addressing used in IPv4 and IPv6.

IPv4 Addressing

IPv4 uses 32-bit address field. IP addresses are usually written in what is called **dotted decimal notation**, with a decimal number representing each of the octets of the 32-bit address. For example, the IP address 11000000 11100100 00010001 00111001 is written as 192.228.17.57.

CLASS-BASED IP ADDRESSES   In general terms, the rightmost, or least significant, bits of the 32-bit IP address designate a host, and the leftmost, or most significant, bits designate a network. A fixed allocation of bits, such as 16 bits for network number and 16 bits for host, was deemed inadequate to handle the global Internet, where some organizations might have a few networks, each with many hosts and some organizations might have many networks, each with a few hosts. Therefore, a scheme known as **class-based**, or **classful**, IP addressing was adopted.

Class-based IP addresses allow for a variable allocation of bits to specify network and host. For this scheme, the first few leftmost bits specify how the rest of the address should be separated into network and host fields. This encoding provides flexibility in assigning addresses to hosts and allows a mix of network sizes on an internet. Class A addresses are best suited to a configuration with few networks, each with many hosts. The Class A address has the following format:

0	network (7 bits)	host (24 bits)

Class B addresses are best suited to a configuration with a medium number of networks, each with a medium number of hosts, and have the following format:

1	0	network (14 bits)	host (16 bits)

Class C addresses are best suited to a configuration with many networks, each with a few hosts, and have the following format:

1	1	1	network (21 bits)	host (8 bits)

An organization would be assigned one or more blocks from these classes.

SUBNETS AND SUBNET MASKS   The concept of subnet was introduced to address the following requirement. Consider an internet that includes one or more WANs and a number of sites, each of which has a number of LANs. We would like to allow arbitrary complexity of interconnected LAN structures within an organization while insulating the overall internet against explosive growth in network numbers and routing complexity. One approach to this problem is to assign a single network number to all of the LANs at a site. From the point of view of the rest of the internet, there is a single network at that site, which simplifies addressing and routing. To allow the routers within the site to function properly, each LAN is assigned a subnet number. The *host* portion of the internet address is partitioned into a subnet number and a host number to accommodate this new level of addressing.

Within the subnetted network, the local routers must route on the basis of an extended network number consisting of the *network* portion of the IP address and the subnet number. The address mask indicates the bit positions containing this extended network number. The use of the address mask allows the host to determine whether an outgoing datagram is destined for a host on the same LAN (send directly) or another LAN (send datagram to router). It is assumed that some other means (e.g., manual configuration) are used to create address masks and make them known to the local routers.

Table 11.1 IP Addresses and Subnet Masks

(a) Dotted decimal and binary representations of IP address and subnet masks

	Binary Representation	Dotted Decimal
IP address	11000000.11100100.00010001.00111001	192.228.17.57
Subnet mask	11111111.11111111.11111111.11100000	255.255.255.224
Bitwise AND of address and mask (resultant network/subnet number)	11000000.11100100.00010001.00100000	192.228.17.32
Subnet number	11000000.11100100.00010001.001	1
Host number	00000000.00000000.00000000.00011001	25

(b) Default subnet masks

	Binary Representation	Dotted Decimal
Class A default mask	11111111.00000000.00000000.00000000	255.0.0.0
Example Class A mask	11111111.11000000.00000000.00000000	255.192.0.0
Class B default mask	11111111.11111111.00000000.00000000	255.255.0.0
Example Class B mask	11111111.11111111.11111000.00000000	255.255.248.0
Class C default mask	11111111.11111111.11111111.00000000	255. 255. 255.0
Example Class C mask	11111111.11111111.11111111.11111100	255. 255. 255.252

Table 11.1a shows the calculations involved in the use of a subnet mask. Note that the effect of the subnet mask is to erase the portion of the host field that refers to an actual host on a subnet. What remain are the network number and the subnet number.

> **Example** Figure 11.1 shows an example of the use of subnetting. The figure shows a local complex consisting of three LANs and two routers. To the rest of the internet, this complex is a single network with a Class C address of the form 192.228.17.x, where the leftmost three octets are the network number and the rightmost octet contains a host number x. Both routers R1 and R2 are configured with a subnet mask with the value 255.255.255.224 (see Table 11.1a). For example, if a datagram with the destination address 192.228.17.57 arrives at R1 either from the rest of the internet or from LAN Y, R1 applies the subnet mask to determine that this address refers to subnet 1, which is LAN X, and so forwards the datagram to LAN X. Similarly, if a datagram with that destination address arrives at R2 from LAN Z, R2 applies the mask and then determines from its forwarding database that datagrams destined for subnet 1 should be forwarded to R1. Hosts must also employ a subnet mask to make routing decisions.

The default subnet mask for a given class of addresses is a null mask (Table 11.1b), which yields the same network and host number as the non-subnetted address.

CLASSLESS INTER-DOMAIN ROUTING (CIDR)   By the mid-1990s, it became evident to Internet designers and administrators that the 32-bit class-based addressing scheme was woefully inadequate for the growing demand for IP addresses. The long-term

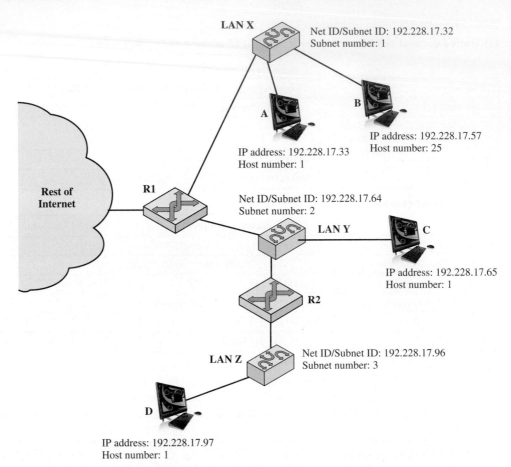

LAN X

Net ID/Subnet ID: 192.228.17.32
Subnet number: 1

B

A

IP address: 192.228.17.57
Host number: 25

IP address: 192.228.17.33
Host number: 1

Rest of Internet

R1

Net ID/Subnet ID: 192.228.17.64
Subnet number: 2

LAN Y   C

IP address: 192.228.17.65
Host number: 1

R2

Net ID/Subnet ID: 192.228.17.96
Subnet number: 3

LAN Z

D

IP address: 192.228.17.97
Host number: 1

Figure 11.1   Example of Subnetworking

solution to this problem, as described in Chapter 8, was the development of IPv6, which includes 128-bit address fields. The use of 128-bit addresses increases the number of possible unique addresses by a factor of almost 10^{29} compared to the use of 32-bit addresses.

However, the deployment of IPv6 would take many years so, as an interim measure, CIDR was adopted. CIDR makes more efficient use of the 32-bit IP address than the class-based method primarily because it makes more efficient use of the address space. With class-based addressing, an organization can request a block of addresses that provides 8, 16, or 24 bits for host addresses. Because Internet addresses were typically only assigned as blocks of a certain class, there were a lot of wasted addresses.

CIDR does away with the class designation and with the use of leading bits to identify a class. Instead, each 32-bit address consists of a leftmost *network* part and a *rightmost* host part, with all 32 bits used for addressing. Associated with each IP address is a *prefix* value that indicates the length of the network portion of the address. A CIDR IP address is written as *a.b.c.d/p*, where *a* is the value of the first byte of the address, *b* the value of the second byte, *c* the value of the third byte, and *d* the value of the fourth byte. Each of these values is in the range of 0 to 255. The prefix value *p* is in the range of 1 through 32 and indicates the length of the network portion of the address.

In CIDR notation, a prefix is shown as a 4-octet quantity, just like a traditional IPv4 address or network number, followed by the "/" (slash) character, followed by a decimal value from 0 through 32. For example, the legacy "Class B" network 172.16.0.0, with an implied network mask of 255.255.0.0, is defined as the prefix 172.16.0.0/16, the "/16" indicating that the mask to extract the network portion of the prefix is a 32-bit value where the most significant 16 bits are ones and the least significant 16 bits are zeros. Similarly, the legacy "Class C" network number 192.168.99.0 is defined as the prefix 192.168.99.0/24; the most significant 24 bits are ones and the least significant 8 bits are zeros.

Note that each 32-bit address still has (and must have) a unique interpretation. That is, each IP address must have associated with it a prefix value *p* for proper routing to the correct network and delivery to the correct host. However, the IP address field only provides space for the 32-bit IP address and not for the prefix value. Accordingly, each CIDR routing table entry in each Internet router contains a 32-bit IP address and a 32-bit network mask, which together give the length of the IP prefix. Clearly, it would be impractical to have an entry for each of the 2^{32} possible IP addresses together with a mask at each router. Instead, multiple IP addresses referring to a block of CIDR addresses can be identified with a single mask, a process known as **supernetting**. A discussion of this technique is beyond our scope.

IPv6 Addressing

IPv6 addresses are 128 bits in length. Addresses are assigned to individual interfaces on nodes, not to the nodes themselves.[1] A single interface may have multiple unique unicast addresses. Any of the unicast addresses associated with a node's interface may be used to uniquely identify that node. As with IPv4, IPv6 addresses use CIDR rather than address classes.

The combination of long addresses and multiple addresses per interface enables improved routing efficiency over IPv4. Longer internet addresses allow for aggregating addresses by hierarchies of network, access provider, geography, corporation, and so on. Such aggregation should make for smaller routing tables and faster table lookups. The allowance for multiple addresses per interface would allow a subscriber that uses multiple access providers across the same interface to have separate addresses aggregated under each provider's address space.

IPv6 allows three types of addresses (Figure 11.2):

- **Unicast:** An identifier for a single interface. A packet sent to a unicast address is delivered to the interface identified by that address.

- **Anycast:** An identifier for a set of interfaces (typically belonging to different nodes). A packet sent to an anycast address is delivered to one of the interfaces identified by that address (the "nearest" one, according to the routing protocols' measure of distance).

---

[1] In IPv6, a *node* is any device that implements IPv6; this includes hosts and routers.

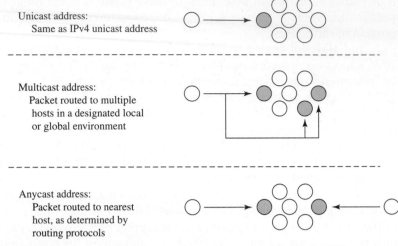

Unicast address:
    Same as IPv4 unicast address

Multicast address:
    Packet routed to multiple
    hosts in a designated local
    or global environment

Anycast address:
    Packet routed to nearest
    host, as determined by
    routing protocols

Figure 11.2   IPv6 Addresses

- **Multicast:** An identifier for a set of interfaces (typically belonging to different nodes). A packet sent to a multicast address is delivered to all interfaces identified by that address.

The notation for an IPv6 address uses eight hexadecimal number to represent the eight 16-bit blocks in the 128-bit address, with the numbers divided by colons. For example:

FE80:0000:0000:0000:0001:0800:23E7:F5DB

To make the notation more compact, leading zeroes in any hexadecimal number are omitted. For the preceding example, the result is:

FE80:0:0:0:1:800:23E7:F5DB

To further compress the representation, a zero or any contiguous sequence of zeroes is replaced by a double colon. For our example, the result is:

FE80::1:800:23E7:F5DB

11.2 INTERNET ROUTING PROTOCOLS

The routers in an internet are responsible for receiving and forwarding packets through the interconnected set of networks. Each router makes routing decisions based on knowledge of the topology and traffic/delay conditions of the internet. In a simple internet, a fixed routing scheme is possible, in which a single, permanent route is configured for each source–destination pair of nodes in the network. The routes are fixed, or at most only change when there is a change in the topology of the network. Thus, the link costs used in designing routes cannot be based any dynamic variable such as traffic. They could, however, be based on estimated traffic volumes between various source–destination pairs or the capacity of each link.

In more complex internets, a degree of dynamic cooperation is needed among routers. In particular, routers **must** avoid portions of the network that have failed and **should** avoid portions of the network that are congested. To make such dynamic routing decisions, routers exchange routing information using a special routing protocol for that purpose. Information is needed about which networks can be reached by which routes, and the delay characteristics of various routes.

In considering the routing function, it is important to distinguish two concepts:

- **Routing information:** Information about the topology and delays of the internet
- **Routing algorithm:** The algorithm used to make a routing decision for a particular datagram, based on current routing information

Autonomous Systems

To proceed with our discussion of routing protocols, we need to introduce the concept of an **autonomous system (AS)**. An AS exhibits the following characteristics:

1. An AS is a set of routers and networks managed by a single organization.
2. An AS consists of a group of routers exchanging information via a common routing protocol.
3. Except in times of failure, an AS is connected (in a graph-theoretic sense); that is, there is a path between any pair of nodes.

A shared routing protocol, which we shall refer to as an **interior router protocol (IRP)**, passes routing information between routers within an AS. The protocol used within the AS does not need to be implemented outside of the system. This flexibility allows IRPs to be custom tailored to specific applications and requirements.

It may happen, however, that an internet will be constructed of more than one AS. For example, all of the LANs at a site, such as an office complex or campus, could be linked by routers to form an AS. This system might be linked through a wide area network to other ASs. The situation is illustrated in Figure 11.3. In this case, the routing algorithms and information in routing tables used by routers in different ASs may differ. Nevertheless, the routers in one AS need at least a minimal level of information concerning networks outside the system that can be reached. We refer to the protocol used to pass routing information between routers in different ASs as an **exterior router protocol (ERP)**.[2]

In general terms, IRPs and ERPs have a somewhat different flavor. An IRP needs to build up a rather detailed model of the interconnection of routers within an AS in order to calculate the least-cost path from a given router to any network within the AS. An ERP supports the exchange of summary reachability information between separately administered ASs. Typically, this use of summary information means that an ERP is simpler and uses less detailed information than an IRP.

---

[2]In the literature, the terms *interior gateway protocol* (IGP) and *exterior gateway protocol* (EGP) are often used for what are referred to here as IRP and ERP. However, because the terms *IGP* and *EGP* also refer to specific protocols, we avoid their use to define the general concepts.

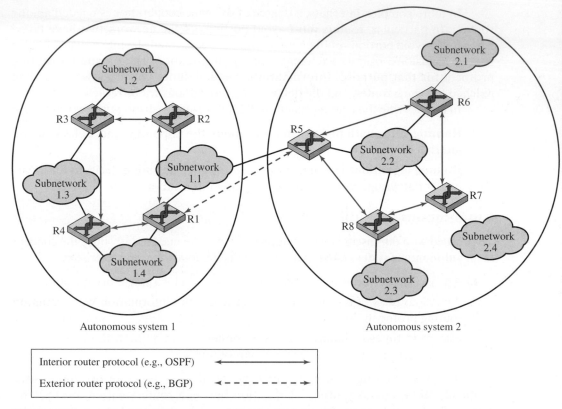

Figure 11.3   Application of Exterior and Interior Routing Protocols

In the remainder of this section, we look at what are perhaps the most important examples of these two types of routing protocols: BGP and OSPF.

Border Gateway Protocol

The Border Gateway Protocol (BGP) was developed for use in conjunction with internets that employ the TCP/IP suite, although the concepts are applicable to any internet. BGP has become the preferred exterior router protocol for the Internet.

BGP was designed to allow routers, called gateways in the standard, in different ASs to cooperate in the exchange of routing information. The protocol operates in terms of messages, which are sent over TCP connections. The current version of BGP is known as BGP-4.

Three functional procedures are involved in BGP:

- Neighbor acquisition
- Neighbor reachability
- Network reachability

Two routers are considered to be neighbors if they are attached to the same network. If the two routers are in different autonomous systems, they may wish to exchange routing information. For this purpose, it is necessary first to perform **neighbor acquisition**. The term *neighbor* refers to two routers that share the same network. In essence, neighbor acquisition occurs when two neighboring routers in different autonomous systems agree to exchange routing information regularly. A formal acquisition procedure is needed because one of the routers may not wish to participate. For example, the router may be overburdened and may not want to be responsible for traffic coming in from outside the AS. In the neighbor acquisition process, one router sends a request message to the other, which may either accept or refuse the offer. The protocol does not address the issue of how one router knows the address or even the existence of another router, nor how it decides that it needs to exchange routing information with that particular router. These issues must be dealt with at configuration time or by active intervention of a network manager.

To perform neighbor acquisition, one router sends an Open message to another. If the target router accepts the request, it returns a Keepalive message in response.

Once a neighbor relationship is established, the **neighbor reachability** procedure is used to maintain the relationship. Each partner needs to be assured that the other partner still exists and is still engaged in the neighbor relationship. For this purpose, the two routers periodically issue Keepalive messages to each other.

The final procedure specified by BGP is **network reachability**. Each router maintains a database of the networks that it can reach and the preferred route for reaching each network. Whenever a change is made to this database, the router issues an Update message that is broadcast to all other routers for which it has a neighbor relationship. Because the Update message is broadcast, all BGP routers can build up and maintain their routing information.

Open Shortest Path First (OSPF) Protocol

The OSPF protocol is widely used as an interior router protocol in TCP/IP networks. OSPF uses what is known as a link state routing algorithm. Each router maintains descriptions of the state of its local links to networks, and from time to time transmits updated state information to all of the routers of which it is aware. Every router receiving an update packet must acknowledge it to the sender. Such updates produce a minimum of routing traffic because the link descriptions are small and rarely need to be sent.

OSPF computes a route through the internet that incurs the least cost based on a user-configurable metric of cost. The user can configure the cost to express a function of delay, data rate, dollar cost, or other factors. OSPF is able to equalize loads over multiple equal-cost paths.

Each router maintains a database that reflects the known topology of the autonomous system of which it is a part. The topology is expressed as a directed graph. The graph consists of the following:

- Vertices, or nodes, of two types:
  - Router

—Network, which is in turn of two types:
  - Transit, if it can carry data that neither originates nor terminates on an end system attached to this network
  - Stub, if it is not a transit network
- Edges, of two types:
  —A graph edge that connects two router vertices when the corresponding routers are connected to each other by a direct point-to-point link
  —A graph edge that connects a router vertex to a network vertex when the router is directly connected to the network

Figure 11.4 shows an example of an autonomous system (only one host is shown). A link cost is associated with a transmission from each router along each of its interfaces to a network or directly to a host. If a router is connected to other autonomous systems, then the path cost to each network in the other system must be obtained by some exterior routing protocol (ERP).

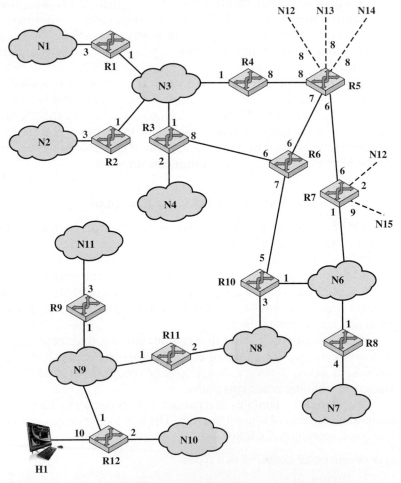

Figure 11.4 A Sample Autonomous System

11.3 MULTICASTING

Typically, an IP address refers to an individual host on a particular network. IP also accommodates addresses that refer to a group of hosts on one or more networks. Such addresses are referred to as **multicast addresses**, and the act of sending a packet from a source to the members of a multicast group is referred to as **multicasting**.

Multicasting has a number of practical applications. For example,

- **Multimedia:** A number of users "tune in" to a video or audio transmission from a multimedia source station.

- **Teleconferencing:** A group of workstations form a multicast group such that a transmission from any member is received by all other group members.

- **Database:** All copies of a replicated file or database are updated at the same time.

- **Distributed computation:** Intermediate results are sent to all participants.

- **Real-time workgroup:** Files, graphics, and messages are exchanged among active group members in real time.

Multicasting done within the scope of a single LAN segment is straightforward. IEEE 802 and other LAN protocols include provision for MAC-level multicast addresses. A packet with a multicast address is transmitted on a LAN segment. Those stations that are members of the corresponding multicast group recognize the multicast address and accept the packet. In this case, only a single copy of the packet is ever transmitted. This technique works because of the broadcast nature of a LAN: a transmission from any one station is received by all other stations on the LAN.

Multicast Transmission

In an internet environment, multicasting is a far more difficult undertaking. To see this, consider the configuration of Figure 11.5, in which a number of LANs are interconnected by routers. Routers connect to each other either over high-speed links or across a wide area network (network N4). A cost is associated with each link or network in each direction, indicated by the value shown leaving the router for that link or network. Suppose that the multicast server on network N1 is transmitting packets to a multicast address that represents the workstations indicated on networks N3, N5, and N6. Suppose that the server does not know the location of the members of the multicast group. Then one way to assure that the packet is received by all members of the group is to **broadcast** a copy of each packet to each network in the configuration, over the least-cost route for each network. For example, one packet would be addressed to N3 and would traverse N1, link L3, and N3. Router B is responsible for translating the IP-level multicast address to a MAC-level multicast address before transmitting the MAC frame onto N3. Table 11.2 summarizes the number of packets generated on the various links and networks in order to transmit one packet to a multicast group by this method. In this table, the source is the multicast server on network N1 in Figure 11.5; the multicast address includes the group members on N3, N5, and N6. Each column in the table refers to

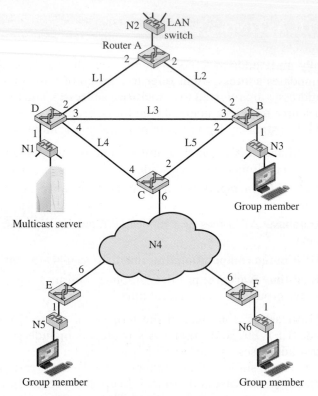

Figure 11.5 Example Configuration to Illustrate Multicasting

Table 11.2 Traffic Generated by Various Multicasting Strategies

	Broadcast					Multiple Unicast				Multicast
	S → N2	S → N3	S → N5	S → N6	Total	S → N3	S → N5	S → N6	Total	
N1	1	1	1	1	4	1	1	1	3	1
N2										
N3		1			1	1			1	1
N4			1	1	2		1	1	2	2
N5			1		1		1		1	1
N6				1	1			1	1	1
L1	1				1					
L2										
L3		1			1	1			1	1
L4			1	1	2		1	1	2	1
L5										
Total	2	3	4	4	13	3	4	4	11	8

the path taken from the source host to a destination router attached to a particular destination network. Each row of the table refers to a network or link in the configuration of Figure 11.5. Each entry in the table gives the number of packets that traverse a given network or link for a given path. A total of 13 copies of the packet are required for the broadcast technique.

Now suppose the source system knows the location of each member of the multicast group. That is, the source has a table that maps a multicast address into a list of networks that contain members of that multicast group. In that case, the source need only send packets to those networks that contain members of the group. We could refer to this as the **multiple unicast** strategy. Table 11.2 shows that in this case, 11 packets are required.

Both the broadcast and multiple unicast strategies are inefficient because they generate unnecessary copies of the source packet. In a true **multicast** strategy, the following method is used:

1. The least-cost path from the source to each network that includes members of the multicast group is determined. This results in a *spanning tree* of the configuration. The spanning tree is a set of all the networks that include multicast members, plus sufficient links between networks to establish a route from a source to all multicast members.
2. The source transmits a single packet along the spanning tree.
3. The packet is replicated by routers only at branch points of the spanning tree.

Multicast Routing Protocols

For multicasting to work, the source of a multicast packet, together with Internet routers, must identify networks that include hosts with the given multicast address and determine a route that will reach all hosts in the group. For this purpose, a number of address discovery and routing protocols are used at different levels of the Internet architecture.

LOCAL NETWORKS   At the local level, individual hosts need a method of joining or leaving a multicast group. The host needs to be able to alert a router on its local network of its membership status in a multicast group. On a broadcast network, such as Ethernet or a wireless LAN, the **Internet Group Management Protocol (IGMP)** is used between hosts and routers to exchange multicast group membership information. IGMP takes advantage of the broadcast nature of a LAN to provide an efficient technique for the exchange of information among multiple hosts and routers. In general, IGMP supports two principal operations:

1. Hosts send messages to routers to subscribe to and unsubscribe from a multicast group defined by a given multicast address.
2. Routers periodically check which multicast groups are of interest to which hosts.

INTERIOR ROUTING PROTOCOLS   IGMP enables a router to know of hosts on an attached network that are using a particular multicast IP address. Next, routers must cooperate across an organization's internet or across the Internet to route and deliver multicast IP packets. Routers must exchange two sorts of information. First, routers need to know which networks include members of a given multicast group. Second, routers need sufficient information to calculate the shortest path to each network containing group members. These requirements imply the need for a multicast routing protocol.

Within an AS, a number of alternative multicast routing protocols have been developed. We mention two here. **Multicast Extensions to OSPF (MOSPF)** is an enhancement to OSPF for the exchange of multicast routing information. Periodically, each router floods information about local group membership to all other routers in its AS. The result is that all routers in an AS are able to build up a complete picture of the location of all group members for each multicast group. Each router constructs the shortest-path spanning tree from a source network to all networks containing members of a multicast group.

Protocol Independent Multicast (PIM) provides a more general solution to multicast routing than MOSPF. As the name suggests, PIM is a separate routing protocol, independent of any existing unicast routing protocol. PIM is designed to extract needed routing information from any unicast routing protocol and may support routing protocols that operate across multiple ASs with a number of different unicast routing protocols.

EXTERIOR ROUTING PROTOCOLS Much of the early work on multicasting focused on multicasting within a single domain. For inter-domain routing, several new classes of protocols have been developed, but all of these are experimental. However, the problems associated with both interior and exterior routing protocols for multicasting have not been successfully solved. A general solution to multicast routing and delivery across the Internet has yet to emerge.

11.4 QUALITY OF SERVICE

The traffic that the Internet and other internetworks must carry continues to grow and change. The demand generated by traditional data-based applications, such as electronic mail, Usenet news, file transfer, and remote logon, is sufficient to challenge these systems. But the driving factors are the heavy use of the World Wide Web, which demands real-time response, and the increasing use of audio, image, and video over internetwork architectures.

These internetwork schemes are essentially datagram packet-switching technology with routers functioning as the switches. This technology was not designed to handle voice and video and is straining to meet the demands placed on it.

To cope with these demands, it is not enough to increase Internet capacity. Sensible and effective methods for managing the traffic and controlling congestion are needed. Historically, IP-based internets have been able to provide a simple best-effort delivery service to all applications using an internet. But the needs of users have changed. A company may have spent millions of dollars installing an IP-based internet designed to transport data among LANs but now finds that new real-time, multimedia, and multicasting applications are not well supported by such a configuration.

Thus, there is a strong need to be able to support a variety of traffic with a variety of QoS (quality of service) requirements, within the TCP/IP architecture.

In this section, we survey some of the end-user factors relating to QoS. We begin with the need for high-speed LANs in the business environment, because this need has appeared first and has forced the pace of networking development. Then we look at business WAN requirements. Finally, we relate the requirements for QoS to the Internet.

The Emergence of High-Speed LANs

Traditionally, office LANs provided basic connectivity services—connecting personal computers and terminals to mainframes and midrange systems that ran corporate applications and providing workgroup connectivity at the departmental or divisional level. In both cases, traffic patterns were relatively light, with an emphasis on file transfer and electronic mail. The LANs that were available for this type of workload, primarily Ethernet and token ring, were well suited to this environment.

In recent years, two significant trends altered the role of the personal computer and therefore the requirements on the LAN:

1. The speed and computing power of personal computers continued to enjoy explosive growth. These more powerful platforms support graphics intensive applications and ever more elaborate graphical user interfaces to the operating system.

2. IT (information technology) organizations have recognized the LAN as a viable and essential computing platform, resulting in the focus on network computing. This trend began with client/server computing, which has become a dominant architecture in the business environment and the more recent Web-focused intranet trend. Both of these approaches involve the frequent transfer of potentially large volumes of data in a transaction-oriented environment.

The effect of these trends has been to increase the volume of data to be handled over LANs and, because applications are more interactive, to reduce the acceptable delay on data transfers. The earlier generation of 10-Mbps Ethernets and 16-Mbps token rings is simply not up to the job of supporting these requirements.

Corporate Wide Area Networking Needs

As recently as the early 1990s, there was an emphasis in many organizations on a centralized data processing model. In a typical environment, there might be significant computing facilities at a few regional offices, consisting of mainframes or well-equipped midrange systems. These centralized facilities could handle most corporate applications, including basic finance, accounting, and personnel programs, as well as many of the business-specific applications. Smaller, outlying offices (e.g., a bank branch) could be equipped with terminals or basic personal computers linked to one of the regional centers in a transaction-oriented environment.

This model began to change in the early 1990s, and the change accelerated through the mid-1990s. Many organizations have dispersed their employees into multiple smaller offices. There is a growing use of telecommuting. Most significant, the nature of the application structure has changed. First client/server computing and, more recently, intranet computing have fundamentally restructured the organizational data processing environment. There is now much more reliance on personal computers, workstations, and servers and much less use of centralized mainframe and midrange systems. Furthermore, the virtually universal deployment of graphical user interfaces to the desktop enables the end user to exploit graphic applications, multimedia, and other data-intensive applications. In addition, most organizations require access to the Internet. Because a few clicks of the mouse can trigger huge volumes of data, traffic patterns have become more unpredictable while the average load has risen.

All of these trends mean that more data must be transported off premises and onto WANs. It has long been accepted that in the typical business environment, about 80% of the traffic remains local and about 20% traverses wide area links. But this rule no longer applies to most companies, with a greater percentage of the traffic going into the WAN environment. This traffic flow shift places a greater burden on LAN backbones and, of course, on the WAN facilities used by a corporation. Thus, just as for LANs, changes in corporate data traffic patterns are driving the creation of high-speed WANs.

Internet Traffic

Traffic on a network or internet can be divided into two broad categories: elastic and inelastic. A consideration of their differing requirements clarifies the need for an enhanced internet architecture.

Elastic traffic can adjust, over wide ranges, to changes in delay and throughput across an internet and still meet the needs of its applications. This is the traditional type of traffic supported on TCP/IP-based internets and is the type of traffic for which internets were designed. With TCP, traffic on individual connections adjusts to congestion by reducing the rate at which data are presented to the network.

Elastic applications include common Internet-based applications, such as file transfer, electronic mail, remote logon, network management, and Web access. But there are differences among the requirements of these applications. For example,

- E-mail is generally insensitive to changes in delay.

- When file transfer is done interactively, as it frequently is, the user expects the delay to be proportional to the file size and so is sensitive to changes in throughput.

- With network management, delay is generally not a serious concern. However, if failures in an internet are the cause of congestion, then the need for network management messages to get through with minimum delay increases with increased congestion.

- Interactive applications, such as remote logon and Web access, are sensitive to delay.

So, even if we confine our attention to elastic traffic, a QoS-based internet service could be of benefit. Without such a service, routers are dealing evenhandedly with arriving IP packets, with no concern for the type of application and whether this packet is part of a large transfer or a small one. Under such circumstances, and if congestion develops, it is unlikely that resources will be allocated in such a way as to meet the needs of all applications fairly. When inelastic traffic is added to the mix, matters are even more unsatisfactory.

Inelastic traffic does not easily adapt, if at all, to changes in delay and throughput across an internet. The prime example is real-time traffic, such as voice and video. The requirements for inelastic traffic may include the following:

- **Throughput:** A minimum throughput value may be required. Unlike most elastic traffic, which can continue to deliver data with perhaps degraded service, many inelastic applications require a firm minimum throughput.

- **Delay:** An example of a delay-sensitive application is stock trading; someone who consistently receives later service will consistently act later, and with greater disadvantage.

- **Jitter:** The magnitude of delay variation, called **jitter**, is a critical factor in real-time applications. Because of the variable delay imposed by the Internet, the interarrival times between packets are not maintained at a fixed interval at the destination. To compensate for this, the incoming packets are buffered, delayed sufficiently to compensate for the jitter, and then released at a constant rate to the software that is expecting a steady real-time stream. The larger the allowable delay variation, the longer the real delay in delivering the data and the greater the size of the delay buffer required at receivers. Real-time interactive applications, such as teleconferencing, may require a reasonable upper bound on jitter.

- **Packet loss:** Real-time applications vary in the amount of packet loss, if any, that they can sustain.

These requirements are difficult to meet in an environment with variable queuing delays and congestion losses. Accordingly, inelastic traffic introduces two new requirements into the internet architecture. First, some means is needed to give preferential treatment to applications with more demanding requirements. Applications need to be able to state their requirements, either ahead of time in some sort of service request function, or on the fly, by means of fields in the IP packet header.

A second requirement in supporting inelastic traffic in an internet architecture is that elastic traffic must still be supported. Inelastic applications typically do not back off and reduce demand in the face of congestion, in contrast to TCP-based applications. Therefore, unless some control is imposed, in times of congestion inelastic traffic will continue to supply a high load and elastic traffic will be crowded off the internet.

Several mechanisms for providing QoS services on the Internet have been proposed. The one that has received the broadest acceptance is known as differentiated services. We turn to this topic next.

11.5 DIFFERENTIATED SERVICES

As the burden on the Internet grows, and as the variety of applications grows, there is an immediate need to provide differing levels of QoS to different users. The differentiated services (DS) architecture is designed to provide a simple, easy-to-implement, low-overhead tool to support a range of network services that are differentiated on the basis of performance. In essence, **differentiated services** do not provide QoS on the basis of flows but rather on the basis of the needs of different groups of users. This means that all the traffic on the Internet is split into groups with different QoS requirements and that routers recognize different groups on the basis of a label in the IP header.

Several key characteristics of DS contribute to its efficiency and ease of deployment:

- IP packets are labeled for differing QoS treatment using the 6-bit DS field in the IPv4 and IPv6 headers (Figure 8.7). No change is required to IP.
- A service level agreement (SLA) is established between the service provider (internet domain) and the customer prior to the use of DS. This avoids the need to incorporate DS mechanisms in applications. Thus, existing applications need not be modified to use DS.
- DS provides a built-in aggregation mechanism. All traffic with the same DS octet is treated the same by the network service. For example, multiple voice connections are not handled individually but in the aggregate. This provides for good scaling to larger networks and traffic loads.
- DS is implemented in individual routers by queuing and forwarding packets based on the DS octet. Routers deal with each packet individually and do not have to save state information on packet flows.

Today, DS is the most widely accepted QoS mechanism in enterprise networks.

Services

The DS type of service is provided within a DS domain, which is defined as a contiguous portion of the Internet over which a consistent set of DS policies are administered. Typically, a DS domain would be under the control of one administrative entity. The services provided across a DS domain are defined in a service level agreement, which is a service contract between a customer and the service provider that specifies the forwarding service that the customer should receive for various classes of packets. A customer may be a user organization or another DS domain. Once the SLA is established, the customer submits packets with the DS octet marked to indicate the packet class. The service provider must assure that the customer gets at least the agreed QoS for each packet class. To provide that QoS, the service provider must configure the appropriate forwarding policies at each router (based on DS octet value) and must measure the performance being provided to each class on an ongoing basis.

If a customer submits packets intended for destinations within the DS domain, then the DS domain is expected to provide the agreed service. If the destination is beyond the customer's DS domain, then the DS domain will attempt to forward the packets through other domains, requesting the most appropriate service to match the requested service.

A DS framework document lists the following detailed performance parameters that might be included in an SLA:

- Service performance parameters, such as expected throughput, drop probability, and latency
- Constraints on the ingress and egress points at which the service is provided, indicating the scope of the service
- Traffic profiles that must be adhered to for the requested service to be provided
- Disposition of traffic submitted in excess of the specified profile

The framework document also gives some examples of services that might be provided:

1. Traffic offered at service level A will be delivered with low latency.
2. Traffic offered at service level B will be delivered with low loss.
3. Ninety percent of in-profile traffic delivered at service level C will experience no more than 50 ms latency.
4. Ninety-five percent of in-profile traffic delivered at service level D will be delivered.
5. Traffic offered at service level E will be allotted twice the bandwidth of traffic delivered at service level F.
6. Traffic with drop precedence X has a higher probability of delivery than traffic with drop precedence Y.

The first two examples are qualitative and are valid only in comparison to other traffic, such as default traffic that gets a best-effort service. The next two examples are quantitative and provide a specific guarantee that can be verified by measurement on the actual service without comparison to any other services offered at the same time. The final two examples are a mixture of quantitative and qualitative.

DS Field

Packets are labeled for service handling by means of the 6-bit DS field in the IPv4 header or the IPv6 header (Figure 8.7). The value of the DS field, referred to as the **DS codepoint**, is the label used to classify packets for differentiated services.

With a 6-bit codepoint, there are, in principle, 64 different classes of traffic that could be defined. These 64 codepoints are allocated across three pools of codepoints, as follows:

- Codepoints of the form xxxxx0, where x is either 0 or 1, are reserved for assignment as standards.
- Codepoints of the form xxxx11 are reserved for experimental or local use.
- Codepoints of the form xxxx01 are also reserved for experimental or local use but may be allocated for future standards action as needed.

Within the first pool, the codepoint 000000 is the default packet class. The default class is the best-effort forwarding behavior in existing routers. Such packets are forwarded in the order that they are received as soon as link capacity becomes available. If other higher-priority packets in other DS classes are available for transmission, these are given preference over default best-effort packets.

The codepoint is set to indicate the degree of urgency or priority to be associated with a datagram. If a router supports DS, there are three approaches to responding:

- **Route selection:** A particular route may be selected if the router has a smaller queue for that route or if the next hop on that route supports network precedence or priority (e.g., a token ring network supports priority).

- **Network service:** If the network on the next hop supports precedence, then that service is invoked.

- **Queuing discipline:** A router may use precedence to affect how queues are handled. For example, a router may give preferential treatment in queues to datagrams with higher precedence.

DS Configuration and Operation

Figure 11.6 illustrates the type of configuration envisioned in the DS documents. A DS domain consists of a set of contiguous routers; that is, it is possible to get from any router in the domain to any other router in the domain by a path that does not include routers outside the domain. Within a domain, the interpretation of DS codepoints is uniform, so that a uniform, consistent service is provided.

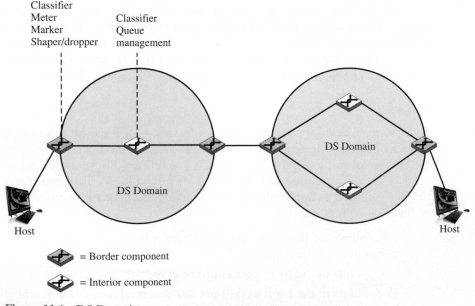

Figure 11.6 DS Domains

Routers in a DS domain are either boundary nodes or interior nodes. Typically, the interior nodes implement simple mechanisms for handling packets based on their DS codepoint values. This includes a queuing discipline to give preferential treatment depending on codepoint value, and packet-dropping rules to dictate which packets should be dropped first in the event of buffer saturation. The DS specifications refer to the forwarding treatment provided at a router as per-hop behavior (PHB). This PHB must be available at all routers, and typically PHB is the only part of DS implemented in interior routers.

The boundary nodes not only include PHB mechanisms but also more sophisticated traffic conditioning mechanisms required to provide the desired service. Thus, interior routers have minimal functionality and minimal overhead in providing the DS service, while most of the complexity is in the boundary nodes. The boundary node function can also be provided by a host system attached to the domain, on behalf of the applications at that host system.

The traffic conditioning function consists of five elements:

- **Classifier:** Separates submitted packets into different classes. This is the foundation of providing differentiated services. A classifier may separate traffic only on the basis of the DS codepoint (behavior aggregate classifier) or based on multiple fields within the packet header or even the packet payload (multifield classifier).

- **Meter:** Measures submitted traffic for conformance to a profile. The meter determines whether a given packet stream class is within or exceeds the service level guaranteed for that class.

- **Marker:** Re-marks packets with a different codepoint as needed. This may be done for packets that exceed the profile; for example, if a given throughput is guaranteed for a particular service class, any packets in that class that exceed the throughput in some defined time interval may be re-marked for best-effort handling. Also, re-marking may be required at the boundary between two DS domains. For example, if a given traffic class is to receive the highest supported priority, and this is a value of 3 in one domain and 7 in the next domain, then packets with a priority 3 value traversing the first domain are re-marked as priority 7 when entering the second domain.

- **Shaper:** Delays packets as necessary so that the packet stream in a given class does not exceed the traffic rate specified in the profile for that class.

- **Dropper:** Drops packets when the rate of packets of a given class exceeds that specified in the profile for that class.

Figure 11.7 illustrates the relationship between the elements of traffic conditioning. After a flow is classified, its resource consumption must be measured. The metering function measures the volume of packets over a particular time interval to determine a flow's compliance with the traffic agreement.

If a traffic flow exceeds some profile, several approaches can be taken. Individual packets in excess of the profile may be re-marked for lower-quality handling and allowed to pass into the DS domain. A traffic shaper may absorb a burst of packets in a buffer and pace the packets over a longer period of time. A dropper may drop packets if the buffer used for pacing becomes saturated.

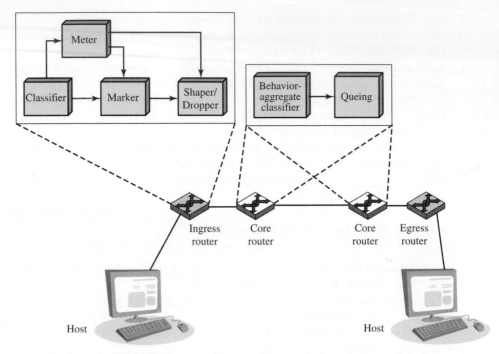

Figure 11.7   DS Functions

11.6 SERVICE LEVEL AGREEMENTS

A service level agreement (SLA) is a contract between a network provider and a customer that defines specific aspects of the service that is to be provided. The definition is formal and typically defines quantitative thresholds that must be met. An SLA typically includes the following information:

- **A description of the nature of service to be provided:** A basic service would be IP-based network connectivity of enterprise locations plus access to the Internet. The service may include additional functions such as Web hosting, maintenance of domain name servers, and operation and maintenance tasks.

- **The expected performance level of the service:** The SLA defines a number of metrics, such as delay, reliability, and availability, with numerical thresholds.

- **The process for monitoring and reporting the service level:** This describes how performance levels are measured and reported.

Figure 11.8 shows a typical configuration that lends itself to an SLA. In this case, a network service provider maintains an IP-based network. A customer has a number of private networks (e.g., LANs) at various sites. Customer networks are connected to the provider via access routers at the access points. The SLA dictates service and performance levels for traffic between access routers across the provider network. In addition, the provider network links to the Internet and thus provides

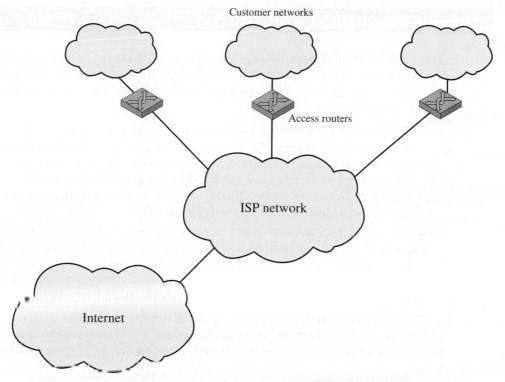

Figure 11.8 Typical Framework for Service Level Agreement

Internet access for the enterprise. For example, for the Internet Dedicated Service provided by one major carrier, the SLA includes the following items:

- **Availability:** 100% availability.
- **Latency (delay):** Average round-trip transmissions of ≤45 ms between access routers in the contiguous United States. Average round-trip transmissions of ≤90 ms between an access router in the New York metropolitan area and an access router in the London metropolitan area. Latency is calculated by averaging sample measurements taken during a calendar month between routers.
- **Network packet delivery (reliability):** Successful packet delivery rate of ≥99.5%.
- **Denial of service (DoS):** Responds to DoS attacks reported by customer within 15 minutes of customer opening a complete trouble ticket. MCI defines a DoS attack as more than 95% bandwidth utilization.
- **Network jitter:** Jitter is defined as the variation or difference in the end-to-end delay between received packets of an IP or packet stream. Jitter performance will not exceed 1 ms between access routers.

An SLA can be defined for the overall network service. In addition, SLAs can be defined for specific end-to-end services available across the carrier's network, such as a virtual private network, or differentiated services.

11.7 IP PERFORMANCE METRICS

The IP Performance Metrics Working Group (IPPM) is chartered by IETF to develop standard metrics that relate to the quality, performance, and reliability of Internet data delivery. Two trends dictate the need for such a standardized measurement scheme:

1. The Internet has grown and continues to grow at a dramatic rate. Its topology is increasingly complex. As its capacity has grown, the load on the Internet has grown at an even faster rate. Similarly, private internets, such as corporate intranets and extranets, have exhibited similar growth in complexity, capacity, and load. The sheer scale of these networks makes it difficult to determine quality, performance, and reliability characteristics.

2. The Internet serves a large and growing number of commercial and personal users across an expanding spectrum of applications. Similarly, private networks are growing in terms of user base and range of applications. Some of these applications are sensitive to particular QoS parameters, leading users to require accurate and understandable performance metrics.

A standardized and effective set of metrics enables users and service providers to have an accurate common understanding of the performance of the Internet and private internets. Measurement data is useful for a variety of purposes, including

- Supporting capacity planning and troubleshooting of large complex internets
- Encouraging competition by providing uniform comparison metrics across service providers
- Supporting Internet research in such areas as protocol design, congestion control, and quality of service
- Verification of service level agreements

Table 11.3 lists the metrics that have been defined in RFCs at the time of this writing. Table 11.3a lists those metrics which result in a value estimated based on a sampling technique. The metrics are defined in three stages:

- **Singleton metric:** The most elementary, or atomic, quantity that can be measured for a given performance metric. For example, for a delay metric, a singleton metric is the delay experienced by a single packet.
- **Sample metric:** A collection of singleton measurements taken during a given time period. For example, for a delay metric, a sample metric is the set of delay values for all of the measurements taken during a one-hour period.
- **Statistical metric:** A value derived from a given sample metric by computing some statistic of the values defined by the singleton metric on the sample. For example, the mean of all the one-way delay values on a sample might be defined as a statistical metric.

The measurement technique can be either active or passive. **Active techniques** require injecting packets into the network for the sole purpose of measurement. There are several drawbacks to this approach. The load on the network is increased.

Table 11.3   IP Performance Metrics

(a) Sampled metrics

Metric Name	Singleton Definition	Statistical Definitions
One-Way Delay	Delay = dT, where Src transmits first bit of packet at T and Dst received last bit of packet at T + dT	Percentile, median, minimum, inverse percentile
Round-Trip Delay	Delay = dT, where Src transmits first bit of packet at T and Src received last bit of packet immediately returned by Dst at T + dT	Percentile, median, minimum, inverse percentile
One-Way Loss	Packet loss = 0 (signifying successful transmission and reception of packet); = 1 (signifying packet loss)	Average
One-Way Loss Pattern	Loss distance: Pattern showing the distance between successive packet losses in terms of the sequence of packets Loss period: Pattern showing the number of bursty losses (losses involving consecutive packets)	Number or rate of loss distances below a defined threshold, number of loss periods, pattern of period lengths, pattern of inter-loss period lengths
Packet Delay Variation	Packet delay variation (pdv) for a pair of packets with a stream of packets = difference between the one-way delay of the selected packets	Percentile, inverse percentile, jitter, peak-to-peak pdv

Note: Src — IP address of a host; Dst = IP address of a host

(b) Other metrics

Metric Name	General Definition	Metrics
Connectivity	Ability to deliver a packet over a transport connection	One-way instantaneous connectivity, two-way instantaneous connectivity, one-way interval connectivity, two-way interval connectivity, two-way temporal connectivity
Bulk Transfer Capacity	Long-term average data rate (bps) over a single congestion-aware transport connection	BTC = (data sent)/(elapsed time)

This in turn can affect the desired result. For example, on a heavily loaded network, the injection of measurement packets can increase network delay, so that the measured delay is greater than it would be without the measurement traffic. In addition, an active measurement policy can be abused for denial-of-service attacks disguised as legitimate measurement activity. **Passive techniques** observe and extract metrics from existing traffic. This approach can expose the contents of Internet traffic to unintended recipients, creating security and privacy concerns. So far, the metrics defined by the IPPM working group are all active.

Figure 11.9 illustrates the packet delay variation metric. This metric is used to measure jitter, or variability, in the delay of packets traversing the network. The singleton metric is defined by selecting two packet measurements and measuring the difference in the two delays. The statistical measures make use of the absolute values of the delays.

Table 11.3b lists two metrics that are not defined statistically. Connectivity deals with the issue of whether a transport-level connection is maintained by the network. The current specification (RFC 2678) does not detail specific sample and statistical metrics but provides a framework within which such metrics could

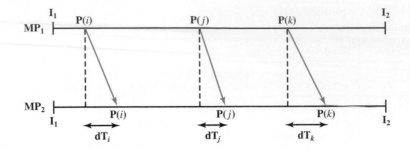

I_1, I_2 = times that mark that beginning and ending of the interval
 in which the packet stream from which the singleton
 measurement is taken occurs
MP_1, MP_2 = source and destination measurement points
$P(i)$ = ith measured packet in a stream of packets
dT_i = one-way delay for $P(i)$

Figure 11.9   Model for Defining Packet Delay Variation

be defined. Connectivity is determined by the ability to deliver a packet across a connection within a specified time limit. The other metric, bulk transfer capacity, is similarly specified (RFC 3148) without sample and statistical metrics but begins to address the issue of measuring the transfer capacity of a network service with the implementation of various congestion control mechanisms.

APPLICATION NOTE

Where Does My Network Address Come From?

All computers connecting to a network must get a network address. This address is an IP (Internet Protocol) address. If your network connects to the Internet, then at least one node must have an address that is valid for use on the public net. This address usually is assigned by an Internet service provider or ISP. The approach used to assign the addresses for the internal network and the network nodes is usually based on the number of computers that will have globally unique Internet addresses.

Globally unique addresses are those that can only be used by one computer in the public Internet space. All communication interfaces connected to the Internet have globally unique addresses. These computers or interfaces are sometimes referred to as the "visible" machines. Visible means that these computers are directly attached to the public Internet. Being visible also implies that the machines are more exposed to attack from hackers; this is true.

An organization may decide to have all of their machines use these globally unique addresses and be visible. In this case, the ISP must assign many addresses to the organization by assigning a full or partial class address. The Internet address space is organized by classes A, B, and C, with class A networks being very large and class C's being much smaller. ISPs often control large chunks of address space that they can parcel out to their customers. For example, a company having 200 nodes may request that a class C network address be assigned to them.

Large ISPs can control millions of IP addresses and, using the subnet mask, can assign a slice of this address space to their clients. The subnet mask is used to determine what network a host is on and the size of that network. For example, an ISP like Time Warner may control a portion of the address space within a class A network. A small percentage of these addresses can be provided to an individual company. When this is done, it is also common to see the ISP handling a good number of services for the company like DNS, domain name registration, security, and mail.

Another option is to have a small number of globally unique addresses assigned by the ISP and use these addresses as the outside connection to the company firewalls. It is possible to "hide" some or all of the computers behind a router running network address translation or NAT. The computers using the NAT box will all use the same global Internet address, effectively making them invisible. This does not mean that "invisible" machines are barred from communicating over the Internet or that they are immune from attack.

However, this presents the problem of addressing for the inside nodes. These addresses are not coming from the ISP and so must be assigned by the local network administrator, either by static configuration or by DHCP. Care must be taken to avoid using standard Internet addressing internally. If internal machines are assigned the same addresses as external visible machines, the routers on the Internet will not be able to route traffic back to the internal company machines.

For this reason, private IP addressing has been established. The following Internet addresses have been reserved for organizations wishing to deploy networks in this manner:

10.0.0.0–10.255.255.255
172.16.0.0–172.31.255.255
192.168.0.0–192.168.255.255

Private addressing is described in detail in RFC 1918. Aside from the benefit of security for the internal machines, this scheme was introduced to alleviate the problem of increasing numbers of users on the Internet. With this tremendous growth, the number of globally unique addresses in IPv4 is insufficient for everyone to have their own unique public address.

There are benefits and drawbacks to each of the methods outlined above. Private addressing usually requires more management, but it does provide increased security and a reduction in the public address space used. Using public addressing throughout does ease the management and has the potential for easing connectivity concerns. However, it can make the organization dependent on the ISP for a large number of its concerns, including security.

11.8 SUMMARY

An essential element of the Internet is its addressing scheme. It is necessary that each attached host have a unique address to make routing and delivery possible. Internet standards define a 32-bit addressing scheme for this purpose.

An Internet routing protocol is used to exchange information about reachability and traffic delays, allowing each router to construct a next-hop routing table for paths through the internet. Typically, relatively simple routing protocols are used between autonomous systems within a larger internet and more complex routing protocols are used within each autonomous system.

The increasing data rate (capacity) requirements of applications have spurred the development of higher speeds in data networks and the Internet. The higher available capacity has in turn encouraged ever more data-intensive applications. To cope with the varying demands on the Internet, the concept of quality of service has been introduced. A QoS facility allows the Internet to treat diffcrent classes of traffic differently in order to optimize the service to all customers.

The differentiated services architecture is designed to provide a simple, easy-to-implement, low-overhead tool to support a range of network services that are differentiated on the basis of performance. Differentiated services are provided on the basis of a 6-bit label in the IP header, which classifies traffic in terms of the type of service to be given by routers for that traffic.

11.9 KEY TERMS, REVIEW QUESTIONS, AND PROBLEMS

Key Terms

anycast	inelastic traffic	packet loss
autonomous system (AS)	interior routing protocol	Protocol Independent
availability	Internet Group Management	Multicast (PIM)
best effort	Protocol (IGMP)	quality of service (QoS)
Border Gateway Protocol	jitter	routing
(BGP)	latency	routing algorithm
broadcast	multicast	routing protocol
Classless Inter-Domain	Multicast Extensions to	service level agreement
Routing (CIDR)	OSPF (MOSPF)	(SLA)
delay	neighbor	subnet
denial of service	neighbor acquisition	subnet mask
differentiated services	neighbor reachability	supernetting
dotted decimal notation	network reachability	throughput
elastic traffic	Open Shortest Path First	unicast
exterior routing protocol	(OSPF)	

Review Questions

11.1   Briefly describe IPv4 addressing.

11.2   What is a subnet?

11.3   What is the purpose of the subnet mask?

11.4   What is the use of classless inter-domain routing (CIDR)?

11.5   What is the difference between an interior router protocol and an exterior router protocol?

11.6   List and briefly explain the three main functions of BGP.

11.7   What is a service level agreement (SLA)?

11.8   OSPF is designed as what type of routing protocol?

11.9 What are the types of addresses that IPv6 allows?

11.10 Explain the difference between elastic and inelastic traffic.

11.11 What is the use of a protocol independent multicast (PIM)?

11.12 What is the use of border gateway protocols?

11.13 List and briefly explain the five main functions of DS traffic conditioning.

Problems

11.1 Provide the following parameter values for each of the network classes A, B, and C. Be sure to consider any special or reserved addresses in your calculations.
   a. Number of bits in network portion of address
   b. Number of bits in host portion of address
   c. Number of distinct networks allowed
   d. Number of distinct hosts per network allowed
   e. Integer range of first octet

11.2 What percentage of the total IP address space does each of the network classes represent?

11.3 What is the difference between the subnet mask for a Class A address with 16 bits for the subnet ID and a Class B address with 8 bits for the subnet ID?

11.4 Is the subnet mask 255.255.0.255 valid for a Class A address?

11.5 Given a network address of 192.168.100.0 and a subnet mask of 255.255.255.192,
   a. How many subnets are created?
   b. How many hosts are there per subnet?

11.6 Given a company with six individual departments and each department having ten computers or networked devices, what mask could be applied to the company network to provide the subnetting necessary to divide up the network equally?

11.7 In contemporary routing and addressing, the notation commonly used is called classless interdomain routing or CIDR. With CIDR, the number of bits in the mask is indicated in the following fashion: 192.168.100.0/24. This corresponds to a mask of 255.255.255.0. If this example would provide for 256 host addresses on the network, how many addresses are provided with the following?
   a. 192.168.100.0/23
   b. 192.168.100.0/25

11.8 If an IPv4 address is given out every tenth of a second, how many years until all the IPv4 addresses are exhausted? If an IPv6 address is given out every second, how many years until all the IPv6 addresses are exhausted? Assume that, for practical purposes, 2^{125} IPv6 addresses are available.

11.9 Find out about your network. Using the command "ipconfig," "ifconfig," or "winipcfg," we can learn not only our IP address but other network parameters as well. Can you determine your mask, gateway, and the number of addresses available on your network?

11.10 Using your IP address and your mask, what is your network address? This is determined by converting the IP address and the mask to binary and then proceeding with a bitwise logical AND operation. For example, given the address 172.16.45.0 and the mask 255.255.224.0, we would discover that the network address would be 172.16.32.0.

11.11 Provide three examples (each) of elastic and inelastic Internet traffic. Justify each example's inclusion in their respective category.

11.12 Why does a differentiated services (DS) domain consist of a set of contiguous routers? How are the boundary node routers different from the interior node routers in a DS domain?

LAN ARCHITECTURE AND INFRASTRUCTURE

Learning Objectives

After reading this chapter, you should be able to:

♦ Define the various types of local area networks (LANs) and list the requirements that each is intended to satisfy.

♦ Identify the major characteristics of office networks, backbone LANs, factory LANs, and tiered LANs.

♦ Discuss the transmission media commonly used for LANs.

♦ Discuss the characteristics of structured cabling systems and LAN protocol architectures.

Local area networks (LANs) are pervasive in businesses of all sizes. Today, they are standard building blocks for creating enterprise networks and many business users access the Internet on a daily basis through LAN-connected devices. Being knowledgeable about LANs and how they work is essential for making informed decisions about business computing infrastructures.

Recent years have seen rapid changes in the technology, design, and commercial applications of LANs. A major feature of this evolution is the introduction of a variety of new schemes for high-speed local networking. These changes have benefitted businesses in a number of ways, especially in terms of being able to use LANs to share all types of business data (voice, data, image, and video) among decision makers. Enhanced data and information sharing has, in turn, contributed to increased business agility, responsiveness, and innovation.

In this chapter we look at the underlying technology of LANs. Chapters 13 and 14 are devoted to a discussion of specific LAN systems. This chapter begins with a discussion of various types of LANs and various LAN configuration options. Next we look at alternatives for wired transmission media, putting off a discussion of wireless transmission until Chapter 14. This is followed by a discussion of LAN protocol architecture.

12.1 BACKGROUND

The variety of applications of LANs is wide. To provide some insight into the types of requirements that LANs are intended to meet, this section discusses some of the most important general application areas of these networks. In the next section, we look at the implications for LAN configuration.

Personal Computer LANs

A common LAN configuration is one that supports personal computers. With the relatively low cost of personal computers, managers within organizations often independently procure personal computers for departmental applications, such as collaboration and project management tools, and Internet access. Desktop systems have traditionally been the most common type of personal computers acquired to support users in work units, but in recent years, laptop computers, with or without docking stations, have become increasing common in business LANs. In some organizations, desktop systems are being phased out in favor of laptops and/or tablets.

In larger businesses, a collection of department-level processors is rarely capable of meeting all of the organization's computing needs and centralized computer processing facilities continue to be important parts of the computing landscape. This is particularly true in organizations that use enterprise resource planning (ERP) systems and other enterprise systems to support integrated business processes across their operating locations. Some applications, such as econometric forecasting models, may be too big or complex to run efficiently on a personal computer in someone's office; in such instances, it makes more sense to run the applications on powerful servers located in a centralized data center. As noted in Chapter 3, "big data" applications are most likely to be hosted in centralized facilities, so are in-memory computing applications and real-time analytics supported by high-performance analytic appliance (HANA) boxes. In-house collaboration software applications that support project teams and other business teams, such as SharePoint or SAP's StreamWork, are also likely to be housed in centralized facilities. When employees need to share work and information, by far the most efficient way to do so is digitally.

Certain expensive resources, such as copiers, high-speed black and white or color laser printers, and high-capacity network-attached storage (NAS) systems, can be shared by all users of a departmental LAN. In addition, LANs that support individual work units can tie into larger corporate-wide network facilities. For example, the corporation may have a building-wide LAN at each of its operating locations as well as a wide area private network. A communications server can provide each location with controlled access to enterprise-wide resources.

LANs for the support of personal computers and workstations have become nearly universal in organizations of all sizes. Even those sites that still depend heavily on mainframes and centralized data centers have transferred much of the processing load to personal computer networks. Perhaps the prime example of the way in which personal computers are being used is to implement client/server business applications.

Backend Networks and Storage Area Networks

Backend networks are used to interconnect large systems such as mainframes, supercomputers, and mass storage devices that typically need to transfer large volumes of data between one another. Backend networks are sometimes called *computer room networks* because the large devices that they interconnect are often located physically in centralized climate-controlled computer rooms. This means that backend networks are physically small in size because the machines that they interconnect are located close to one another. By putting such large devices on the same network segment, the data traffic that they interchange is less likely to overwhelm the LAN and degrade the overall performance of the network. The key requirement for creating a backend network is for bulk data transfer among a limited number of devices in a small area. High reliability is generally also a requirement. Typical characteristics also include the following:

- **High data rate:** To satisfy the high-volume demand, data rates of 1000 Mbps or more are required.

- **High-speed interface:** Data transfer operations between a large host system and a mass storage device are typically performed through high-speed parallel I/O interfaces, such as Fibre Channel, rather than slower communications interfaces. The high-speed interface is needed because the mainframes and supercomputers may need to exchange high volumes of data over the network.

- **Distributed access:** Some sort of distributed media access control (MAC) technique is needed to ensure that all devices get fair, efficient, and reliable access to the network.

- **Limited distance:** Typically, a backend network is employed in a computer room or a small number of contiguous rooms.

- **Limited number of devices:** The number of mainframes, supercomputers, and mass storage devices included in a backend network is usually small because they are expensive. Also, limiting the number of machines contributes to network efficiency.

Typically, backend networks are found in centralized facilities in large companies or in research installations that have large data processing budgets. Because of the scale involved, even a small increase in backend network–enabled productivity can be worth millions of dollars.

Consider a business computing site that uses a dedicated mainframe computer to run an enterprise-wide ERP system or another set of applications that are used organization-wide. Powerful applications such as medical imaging, e-commerce, social media, and data warehousing require servers that can process larger files and move data faster than ever before. As the data processing load at the site grows, the existing mainframe may be replaced by a more powerful one or a multiprocessor system (e.g., a server cluster or server farm). At some sites, a single-system replacement may not be sufficient to keep up, especially if equipment performance growth rates are exceeded by user demand growth rates. In such instances, the facility may require multiple independent mainframes (or server clusters/farms) to satisfy user needs. And, there are compelling reasons for interconnecting these systems. For example, if the cost of network interruption is very high, interconnecting the high-performance machines makes it possible to shift applications easily and quickly to backup systems. Using one system to back up another also makes it possible to test new procedures and applications on the backup without degrading the production system.

As computing capabilities and equipment increase within backend networks, it becomes more desirable to move large bulk storage files to storage systems that can be accessed from more than one computer. Load leveling technologies also become more attractive because of their ability to maximize utilization and performance.

As it can be seen in this brief introduction, key requirements for backend networks often differ from those for personal computer LANs. High data rates are required to keep up with the work, which typically involves the transfer of large blocks of data. The equipment for achieving high speeds is expensive. Fortunately, investments for increased computing capabilities and ability to better serve business users enterprise-wide can be justified.

A concept related to that of the backend network is the **storage area network** (SAN). A SAN can be described as a separate network of storage devices that are physically removed from, but still connected to, the network. SANs evolved from the concept of taking storage devices and storage traffic off the LAN and creating a separate backend network specifically designed for data.

In essence, a SAN is a separate network to handle storage needs. The SAN decouples storage tasks from specific servers and creates a shared storage facility across a high-speed network. The collection of networked storage devices can include hard disks, tape libraries, and CD arrays. Most SANs use Fibre Channel, which is described in online Appendix G.

In early client/server LANs, data were stored on devices (typically disk drives) inside or directly attached to the server. *Network-attached storage (NAS)* systems were the next step in the evolution of LAN storage systems. NAS separated storage devices from the server and connected them directly to the network. SANs go one step further by allowing storage devices to exist on their own separate network and communicate directly with each other over very fast interfaces. Business users access these storage devices via server systems that are connected to both the LAN and the SAN. The SAN arrangement improves client-to-storage access efficiency, as well as direct storage-to-storage communications for backup and replication functions.

Figure 12.1 suggests a typical SAN configuration. Users attached to the Internet send file requests (store, retrieve) to a bank of servers. These servers do not maintain the files locally but are connected to a SAN, which supports a number of mass storage devices. The SAN includes network devices optimized to handle storage tasks.

Solid-state storage technologies are increasingly being deployed in enterprise networks as alternatives to SANs or NAS. Unlike traditional storage technologies, solid-state storage devices do not have moving mechanical components such as spinning magnetic disks or movable read-write heads. In addition, most use flash memory and are able to retain data without power. Relative to magnetic disk storage, solid-state storage technologies have lower latency and data access times;

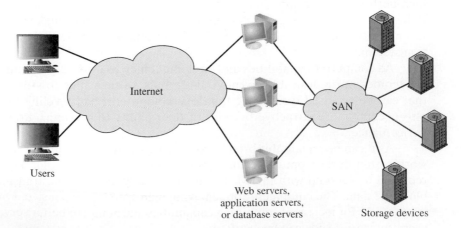

Figure 12.1   Storage Area Network Configuration

they also make less noise (almost none) and are more durable (less susceptible to physical shock). Faster data access contributes to the popularity of solid-state storage solutions among cloud computing service providers.

High-Speed Office Networks

Traditionally, the office environment has included a variety of devices with low- to medium-speed data transfer requirements. However, the evolution of office applications has required businesses to move to higher-speed LANs. Bandwidth hungry applications such as video, audio, or data conferencing, computer-based training, and e-learning systems have increased network data flow by unprecedented amounts. Other LAN applications that are bandwidth hogs include fax machines, document scanners, interactive graphics, and collaboration software programs. Even when compression techniques are used, such applications can still generate tremendous data traffic loads. These new demands require high-speed LANs that can support larger numbers of machines over a greater geographic extent when compared to backend networks.

Backbone LANs

The increasing use of distributed processing applications and personal computing devices, including mobile devices, has led to a need for a flexible strategy for local networking. Support of premises-wide data communications requires a networking service that is capable of spanning the distances involved and that interconnects equipment in a single (perhaps large) building or a cluster of buildings. Although it is possible to develop a single LAN to interconnect all on premises data processing equipment, this is probably not a practical alternative in most cases. There are several drawbacks to a single-LAN strategy:

- **Reliability:** With a single LAN, a service interruption, even of short duration, could result in a major disruption for users.
- **Capacity:** A single LAN could be saturated as the number of devices attached to the network grows over time, especially if the use of bandwidth hungry applications also grows.
- **Cost:** A single LAN technology is not typically optimized for the diverse requirements of interconnection and communication. The presence of large numbers of low-cost microcomputers dictates that network support for these devices be provided at low cost. LANs that support very low cost attachments are not likely to be suitable for meeting the overall communication requirements of enterprise networks.

A more attractive alternative is to employ lower-cost, lower-capacity LANs within buildings or departments and to interconnect these networks with a higher-capacity LAN. This latter network is referred to as a backbone LAN. If confined to a single building or cluster of buildings, a high-capacity LAN can perform the backbone function. The backbone network provides the infrastructure for the exchange of data and information among the LANs that it interconnects. Typically, the backbone's capacity is greater than that of any the networks that connect to it.

Factory LANs

Factory environments are increasingly dominated by automated equipment: programmable controllers, automated materials handling devices, machine vision inspection devices, and various forms of robots. To manage the production or manufacturing process, it is essential to tie this equipment together.

The most dynamic and data-intensive part of a manufacturing organization is the factory floor. Microprocessor devices used in manufacturing have the potential to collect information from the shop floor and accept commands. A variety of specialized machines from multiple vendors may populate the production line. Each of these is likely to include *programmable logic controllers (PLCs)* and when these are found in each step of the manufacturing process, data processing and information transmission within the manufacturing environment can be improved.

In general, the more that a factory is automated, the greater is its need for integrated communications. Only by interconnecting devices and by providing mechanisms for their cooperation can the automated factory achieve its full potential. In general, a factory LAN should be:

- Of high capacity
- Able to handle a variety of data traffic
- Capable of a having a large geographic footprint
- Highly reliable
- Able to specify and control transmission delays

Factory LANs are a niche market requiring, in general, more flexible and reliable LANs than are found in typical business office environments.

12.2 LAN CONFIGURATION

Tiered LANs

Consider the kinds of data processing equipment to be supported in a typical business organization. In rough terms, we can group this equipment into three categories:

- **Personal computers and workstations:** The workhorse in most office environments is the microcomputer, including personal computers and workstations. Laptops and mobile tablets have joined the list of business user devices in many organizations. Most of this equipment is found at the departmental level, used by individual professionals and secretarial personnel. When used for network applications, the load generated ranges from modest to heavy depending on the nature of the applications needed by employees to perform their jobs.
- **Servers:** Servers, used within a department or shared by users in a number of departments, can perform a variety of functions. Generic examples include supporting expensive peripherals such as mass storage devices, providing applications that require large amounts of processor resources, and

maintaining databases accessible by many users. Because of this shared use, these machines may generate substantial traffic.

- **Mainframes:** For large database and scientific applications, the mainframe is often the machine of choice. When the machines are networked to exchange information with one another, bulk data transfers dictate that a high-capacity network, such as a backend network, be used.

The requirements indicated by this spectrum suggest that combining all of these technologies in a single LAN is not, in many cases, the most cost-effective solution. A single network would have to have very high speed to support the aggregate demand. However, the cost of attachment to a LAN tends to increase as a function of the network data rate. For example, a 10-Gbps Ethernet adapter card can cost several hundred dollars, while a 100-/1000-Mbps Ethernet adapter may cost $15 or less. Accordingly, attaching low-cost personal computers to a very high speed LAN can be very expensive.

An alternative approach, which is becoming increasingly common, is to employ two or three tiers of LANs (Figure 12.2). Within a department, a low-cost, moderate-speed LAN supports a cluster of personal computers and workstations. These departmental LANs are lashed together with a backbone LAN of higher capacity. In addition, shared systems are also supported off of this backbone. If mainframes are also part of the office equipment suite, then a separate high-speed, backend network that supports these devices may be linked, as a whole, to the backbone LAN to support the traffic between the mainframes and the departmental LANs. We shall see that LAN standards and products address the need for all three types of LANs.

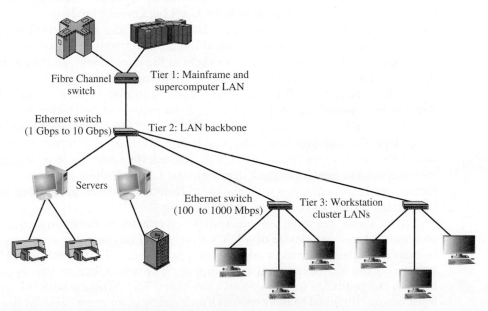

Figure 12.2 Tiered Local Area Networks

Evolution Scenario

One final aspect of the tiered architecture should be mentioned: the way in which such a networking implementation comes about in an organization. This varies widely from one business organization to the next, but two general scenarios can be defined. It is useful to be aware of both scenarios because of their implications for the selection and management of LANs.

In the first scenario, the LAN decisions are made from the bottom up, with each department making decisions more or less in isolation. In this scenario, the particular application requirements of a department are typically well known. For example, an engineering department has very high data rate requirements to support its CAD environment, whereas the sales department has much more modest data rate requirements for its order entry and order inquiry needs. Because the applications are well known, decisions about the infrastructure needed for each department LAN can be made quickly. Departmental budgets are often sufficient to cover all or most of the costs of these networks, so approval by upper level management may not be required. When a bottom-up scenario is followed, the potential exists for each department to develop its own cluster network (tier 3). In the meantime, if this is a large organization, the information services department may acquire a high-speed (tier 1) LAN or backend network to interconnect its mainframes.

Over time, departments with their own cluster tier LAN realize the need to connect to other networks in the enterprise in order to access other computing resources. For example, the marketing department may have to access cost information from the finance department as well as last month's order volumes from sales. When cluster-to-cluster communication requirements become important, the company make a conscious decision to provide interconnect capability. This interconnection may be realized through the LAN backbone (tier 2).

The advantage of this scenario is that, since the department manager is closest to the department's needs, local interconnect strategies can be responsive to the specific applications used by workers in the department, and acquisition can be timely. There are several disadvantages to this approach. First, there is the problem of suboptimization. If procurement is not centralized within the organization, department-by-department purchase requests may wind up costing the company more, especially when similar types of equipment are being purchased. In addition, larger-volume purchases may result in more favorable terms from quantity discounts, site licenses for software, etc. Second, the company is eventually faced with the need to interconnect all departmental LANs. If there are a wide variety of cluster tier LANs equipped with hardware from many different vendors, the interconnection problem becomes more challenging.

For these reasons, an alternative scenario is becoming increasingly common: a top-down design of a LAN strategy. In this case, the company decides to map out a total local networking strategy. The decision is centralized because it impacts the entire location or company. The advantage of this approach is built-in compatibility to interconnect the users. The difficulty with this approach is, of course, the need to be responsive and timely in meeting needs at the departmental level.

12.3 GUIDED TRANSMISSION MEDIA

In a data transmission system, the **transmission medium** is the physical path between transmitter and receiver. Transmission media can be classified as guided or unguided. In both cases, communication is in the form of electromagnetic waves. With **guided media**, the waves are guided along a solid medium, such as copper twisted pair, copper coaxial cable, or optical fiber. The atmosphere and outer space are examples of **unguided media**, which provide a means of transmitting electromagnetic signals but do not guide them; this form of transmission is usually referred to as **wireless transmission**.

The characteristics and quality of a data transmission system are determined both by the characteristics of the medium and the characteristics of the signal. In the case of guided media, the medium itself is more important in determining the limitations of transmission. For unguided media, the bandwidth of the signal produced by the transmitting antenna is more important than the medium in determining transmission characteristics. One key property of signals transmitted by antenna is directionality. In general, signals at lower frequencies are omnidirectional; that is, the signal propagates in all directions from the antenna. At higher frequencies, it is possible to focus the signal into a directional beam.

In considering the design of data transmission systems, key concerns include data rate and distance: The greater the data rate and distance capability, the greater the importance of having a well-designed network. A number of design factors relating to the transmission medium and the signal determine the data rate and distance:

- **Bandwidth:** All other factors remaining constant, the wider the bandwidth of a signal, the higher the data rate that can be achieved.

- **Transmission impairments:** Impairments, such as attenuation, limit effective distance. For guided media, twisted pair generally suffers more impairment than does coaxial cable, which in turn suffers more than optical fiber.

- **Interference:** Interference from competing signals in overlapping frequency bands can distort or wipe out a signal. Interference is of particular concern for unguided media but is also a problem with guided media. For guided media, interference can be caused by emanations from nearby cables. For example, twisted pairs are often bundled together and conduits often carry multiple cable bundles. Interference can also be experienced from unguided transmissions. Proper shielding of a guided medium can minimize this problem.

- **Number of receivers:** A guided medium can be used to construct a point-to-point link or a shared link with multiple attachments. In the latter case, each attachment introduces some attenuation and distortion on the line, limiting distance and/or data rate.

Figure 12.3 depicts the electromagnetic spectrum and indicates the frequencies at which various guided media and unguided transmission techniques operate. In this section, we look at the guided media alternatives for LANs; a discussion of wireless media alternatives for LANs is deferred to Chapter 14.

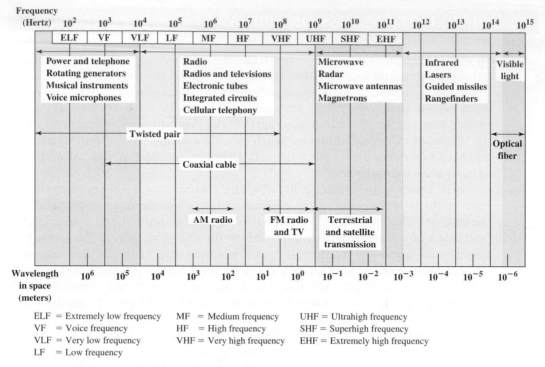

Figure 12.3 Electromagnetic Spectrum for Telecommunications

Twisted Pair

A twisted pair consists of two insulated copper wires arranged in a regular spiral pattern (Figure 12.4a). A wire pair acts as a single communication link. Typically, a number of these pairs are bundled together into a cable by wrapping them in a tough protective sheath. Over longer distances, cables may contain hundreds of pairs.

Twisted pair is much less expensive than the other commonly used guided transmission media (coaxial cable, optical fiber) and is easier to work with. Compared to other transmission media, twisted pair is limited in distance, bandwidth, and data rate. The medium is quite susceptible to interference and noise because of its potential for coupling with electromagnetic fields. For example, a wire run parallel to an AC power line will pick up 60-Hz energy. Impulse noise also easily intrudes into twisted pair.

Several measures are taken to reduce impairments. Shielding the wire with metallic braid or sheathing reduces interference. The twisting of the wire reduces low-frequency interference, and the use of different twist lengths in adjacent pairs reduces crosstalk.

Unshielded and Shielded Twisted Pair   Twisted pair comes in two varieties: unshielded and shielded. One of the best known examples of **unshielded twisted pair** (UTP) is ordinary telephone wire. Office buildings, by universal practice, are prewired with excess UTP, more than is needed for simple telephone support. Business buildings are also wired with one or more of the several categories of

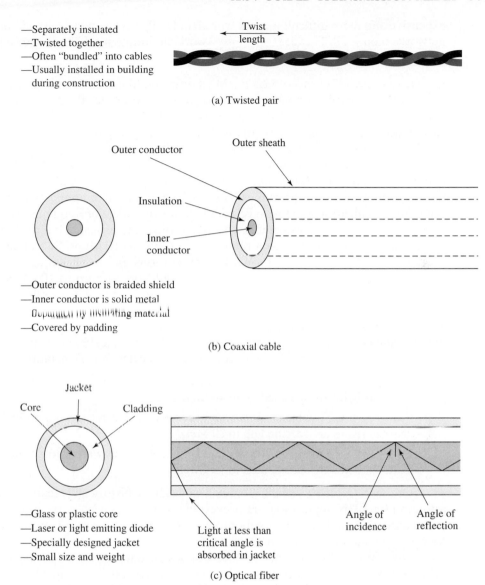

—Separately insulated
—Twisted together
—Often "bundled" into cables
—Usually installed in building
 during construction

Twist
length

(a) Twisted pair

Outer conductor

Outer sheath

Insulation

Inner
conductor

—Outer conductor is braided shield
—Inner conductor is solid metal
 Separated by insulating material
—Covered by padding

(b) Coaxial cable

Jacket

Core

Cladding

—Glass or plastic core
—Laser or light emitting diode
—Specially designed jacket
—Small size and weight

Light at less than
critical angle is
absorbed in jacket

Angle of
incidence

Angle of
reflection

(c) Optical fiber

Figure 12.4   Guided Transmission Media

UTP that have been developed for data communications. Because UTP is the least expensive of all the transmission media commonly used for LANs and is easy to work with and install, it is the most widely deployed communications medium in enterprise networks.

UTP is subject to external electromagnetic interference, including interference from nearby twisted pair and from noise generated in the environment. A way to improve the characteristics of this medium is to shield the twisted pair with a metallic braid or sheathing that reduces interference. This **shielded twisted pair** (STP) provides better performance at lower data rates. However, because it is more expensive and more difficult to work with than UTP, it is less widely used in business networks than UTP. However, in "noisy" work environments, STP or optical fiber is preferred over UTP.

CATEGORY 3 AND CATEGORY 5 UTP   Most office buildings are prewired with a type of twisted-pair cable commonly referred to as voice grade. Because voice-grade twisted pair is already installed, it may appear to be an attractive alternative for use as a medium in LAN implementations. Unfortunately, the data rates and distances achievable with voice-grade twisted pair are limited.

In 1991, the Electronic Industries Association published standard EIA-568, *Commercial Building Telecommunications Cabling Standard*, which specifies the use of voice-grade UTP as well as STP for in-building data applications. At that time, the specification was felt to be adequate for the range of frequencies and data rates found in office environments. Up to that time, the principal interest for LAN designs was in the range of data rates from 1 Mbps to 16 Mbps. Subsequently, as users migrated to higher-performance workstations and applications, there was increasing interest in providing LANs that could operate up to 100 Mbps over inexpensive cable. In response to this need, TIA/EIA-568-A was issued in 1995; TIA/EIA 568-B was published in 2001. Both of these have been superseded by TIA/EIA 568-C, which was published in 2009. The new standard reflects advances in cable and connector design and test methods. It covers STP and UTP.

TIA/EIA-568-A and B recognized three categories of UTP cabling:

- **Category 3:** UTP cables and associated connecting hardware whose transmission characteristics are specified up to 16 MHz
- **Category 4:** UTP cables and associated connecting hardware whose transmission characteristics are specified up to 20 MHz
- **Category 5:** UTP cables and associated connecting hardware whose transmission characteristics are specified up to 100 MHz

Of these, Category 3 and Category 5 cables have historically received the most attention for LAN applications. However, in recent years, Category 5e (enhanced) and Category 6 cables have largely replaced Category 5 for new LAN implementations. These are addressed in TIA/EIA 568-C.

Over limited distances, and with proper design, data rates of up to 100 Mbps are achievable with Category 5. Category 5 and Category 5e cabling is capable of supporting faster Ethernet LANs such as 100BASE-TX and 1000BASE-T. Category 6 UTP provides performance up to 250 MHz and is capable of supporting 100BASE-TX (Fast Ethernet), 1000BASE-T/1000BASE-TX (Gigabit Ethernet), or 10BASE-TX (10-Gigabit Ethernet). The "T" or "TX" in each of these Ethernet varieties stands for "twisted pair." As you might guess, the ability to support fast LANs has made Category 5e and Category 6 cables increasingly common for preinstallation in new office buildings.

A key difference between the categories of twisted-pair cable is the number of twists in the cable per unit distance. For example, Category 5 is much more tightly twisted, with a typical twist length of 0.6–0.85 cm (3–4 twists per inch), compared to 7.5–10 cm (or 3–4 twists per foot) for Category 3. Category 5e has more twists per inch than Category 5. The tighter twisting of Category 5e and Category 5 is one of the

Table 12.1 Comparison of Shielded and Unshielded Twisted Pair

Frequency	Attenuation (dB per 100 m)				Near-end Crosstalk (dB)			
	Category 5	Category 5e	Category 6	STP	Category 5	Category 5e	Category 6	STP
1	2.0	2.0	2.0	1.1	62	65.3	74.3	58
4	4.1	4.1	3.8	2.2	53	56.3	65.3	58
16	8.2	8.2	7.6	4.4	44	47.2	56.2	50.4
25	10.4	10.4	9.5	6.2	41	44.3	53.3	47.7
100	22.0	22.0	19.8	12.3	32.2	35.3	44.3	38.5
250	—	—	32.8	21.4	—	—	38.3	31.3

factors that make these more expensive than Category 3, but this is also one of the reasons why they provide much better performance than does Category 3.

Table 12.1 summarizes the performance of Category 5, Category 5e, and Category 6 UTP, as well as the STP specified in EIA-568. The first parameter used for comparison, attenuation, is fairly straightforward. The strength of a signal falls off with distance over any transmission medium. For guided media, attenuation is generally exponential and therefore is typically expressed as a constant number of decibels per unit distance (see Appendix 12A).

Attenuation introduces three considerations for the network designer. First, a received signal must have sufficient magnitude so that the electronic circuitry in the receiver can detect and interpret the signal. Second, the signal must maintain a level sufficiently higher than noise to be received without error. Third, attenuation is an increasing function of frequency.

Near-end crosstalk (NEXT), as it applies to twisted-pair wiring systems, is the coupling of the signal from one pair of conductors to another pair. These conductors may be the metal pins in a connector or wire pairs in a cable. The near end refers to coupling that takes place when the transmit signal entering the link couples back to the receive conductor pair at that same end of the link (i.e., the near transmitted signal is picked up by the near receive pair).

Since the publication of TIA/EIA-568-C, there has been ongoing work on the development of standards for premises cabling. These are being driven by two issues. First, the Gigabit Ethernet specification requires the definition of parameters that are not specified completely in any published cabling standard. Second, there is a desire to specify cabling performance to higher levels, namely Enhanced Category 5 (Cat 5e), Category 6, Category 6e, Category 6a (augmented), and Category 7. Table 12.2 compares these schemes to the existing standards.

Coaxial Cable

Coaxial cable, like twisted pair, consists of two conductors but is constructed differently to permit it to operate over a wider range of frequencies. It consists of a hollow outer cylindrical conductor that surrounds a single inner wire conductor (Figure 12.4b). The inner conductor is held in place by either regularly spaced

Table 12.2 Twisted Pair Categories and Classes

	Category 5 Class D	Category 5e	Category 6 Class E	Category 6e	Category 6a	Category 7 Class F
Bandwidth	100 MHz	100 MHz	250 MHz	500 MHz	500 MHz	600 MHz
Cable Type	UTP; STP	UTP; STP	UTP; S/UTP	S/UTP; S/STP	S/UTP; S/STP	S/STP
Link Cost (Category 5 = 1)	1	1.2	1.5	1.6	3.0	10.0
Differences from Preceding Standard	Replaced Category 3 using only two pairs	More twists per inch than 5; four pairs required in each cable	Thicker wire gauge than and more twists per inch than 5e	More twists per inch than Category 6. Grounded foil shielding	New 6a connectors that are 3 dB better than 6e connectors	Stricter requirements for crosstalk and noise than Class E
Speed	100 Mbps/ 100 m	350 Mbps/ 100 m 1 Gbps/50 m	1 Gbps/100 m 10 Gbps/50 m	10 Gbps/ 100 m	10 Gbps/ 100 m	10 Gbps/ 100 m 40 Gbps/50 m

Note: UTP = unshielded twisted pair; S/UTP = screened unshielded twisted pair; S/STP = screened shielded twisted pair.

insulating rings or a solid dielectric material. The outer conductor is covered with a jacket or shield. A single coaxial cable has a diameter of 1–2.5 cm. Because of its shielded, concentric construction, coaxial cable is much less susceptible to interference and crosstalk than is twisted pair. Coaxial cable can be used over longer distances and can support more stations on a shared line than twisted pair.

Coaxial cable, like STP, provides good immunity from electromagnetic interference. Coaxial cable is more expensive than STP but provides greater capacity.

Traditionally, coaxial cable was an important transmission medium for LANs, beginning with the early popularity of Ethernet. However, in recent years, the emphasis has been on low-cost, limited distance LANs using twisted pair, and high-performance LANs using optical fiber. The effect is the gradual but steady decline in the use of coaxial cable for LAN implementation, to the point that it is rarely used today except in legacy LANs.

Optical Fiber

An optical fiber is a thin (2–125 μm), flexible medium capable of conducting an optical ray. Various glasses and plastics can be used to make optical fibers. The lowest losses have been obtained using fibers of ultrapure fused silica. Ultrapure fiber is difficult to manufacture; higher-loss multicomponent glass fibers are more economical and still provide good performance. Plastic fiber is even less costly and can be used for short-haul links, for which moderately high losses are acceptable.

An optical fiber has a cylindrical shape and consists of three concentric sections (Figure 12.4c). The two innermost are two types of glass with different indexes of refraction. The center one is called the core, and the next layer the cladding. These two sections of glass are covered by a protective, light-absorbing jacket. Optical fibers are grouped together into optical cables.

One of the most significant technological breakthroughs in information transmission has been the development of practical fiber optic communications systems. Optical fiber already enjoys considerable use in long-distance telecommunications, and its use in military applications is growing. The continuing improvements in performance and decline in prices, together with the inherent advantages of optical fiber, have made it increasingly attractive for local area networking. The following characteristics distinguish optical fiber from twisted pair or coaxial cable:

- **Greater capacity:** The potential bandwidth, and hence data rate, of optical fiber is immense; data rates of hundreds of Gbps over tens of kilometers have been demonstrated. Compare this to the practical maximum of hundreds of Mbps over about 1 km for coaxial cable and just a few Mbps over 1 km or up to 100 Mbps to 10 Gbps over a few tens of meters for twisted pair.

- **Smaller size and lighter weight:** Optical fibers are considerably thinner than coaxial cable or bundled twisted-pair cable—at least an order of magnitude thinner for comparable information transmission capacity. For cramped conduits in buildings and underground along public rights-of-way, the advantage of small size is considerable. The corresponding reduction in weight reduces structural support requirements.

- **Lower attenuation:** Attenuation is significantly lower for optical fiber than for coaxial cable or twisted pair and is constant over a wide frequency range.

- **Electromagnetic isolation:** Optical fiber systems are not affected by external electromagnetic fields. Thus the system is not vulnerable to interference, impulse noise, or crosstalk. By the same token, fibers do not radiate energy, causing little interference with other equipment and providing a high degree of security from eavesdropping. In addition, fiber is inherently difficult to tap.

Optical fiber systems operate in the range of about 10^{14}–10^{15} Hz; this covers portions of the infrared and visible spectrums. The principle of optical fiber transmission is as follows. Light from a source enters the cylindrical glass or plastic core. Rays at shallow angles are reflected and propagated along the fiber; other rays are absorbed by the surrounding material. This form of propagation is called **step-index multimode**, referring to the variety of angles of reflection. With multimode transmission, multiple propagation paths exist, each with a different path length and hence time to traverse the fiber. This causes signal elements (light pulses) to spread out in time, which limits the rate at which data can be accurately received. Put another way, the need to leave spacing between the pulses limits data rate. This type of fiber is best suited for transmission over very short distances. When the fiber core radius is reduced, fewer angles will reflect. By reducing the radius of the core to the order of a wavelength, only a single angle or mode can pass: the axial ray. This **single-mode** propagation provides superior performance for the following reason. Because there is a single transmission path with single-mode transmission, the distortion found in multimode cannot occur. Single mode is typically used for long-distance applications, including telephone and cable television. Finally, by varying the index of refraction of the core, a third type of transmission, known as **graded-index multimode**, is possible. This type is intermediate between the other two in characteristics. The higher refractive index at the center makes the light rays moving down the axis advance more slowly than those near the cladding. Rather than zigzagging off the cladding, light in the core curves helically because of the graded index, reducing its travel distance. The shortened path and higher speed allow light at the periphery to arrive at a receiver at about the same time as the straight rays in the core axis. Graded-index fibers are often used in LANs.

Two different types of light source are used in fiber optic systems: the light-emitting diode (LED) and the injection laser diode (ILD). Both are semiconductor devices that emit a beam of light when a voltage is applied. The LED is less costly, operates over a greater temperature range, and has a longer operational life. The ILD, which operates on the laser principle, is more efficient and can sustain higher data rates.

There is a relationship among the wavelength employed, the type of transmission, and the achievable data rate. Both single mode and multimode can support several different wavelengths of light and can employ laser or LED light source. In optical fiber, light propagates best in three distinct wavelength "windows," centered on 850, 1300, and 1550 nm. These are all in the infrared portion of the frequency spectrum, below the visible-light portion, which is 400–700 nm. The loss is lower at higher wavelengths, allowing greater data rates over longer distances. Most local applications today use 850-nm LED light sources. Although this combination is relatively inexpensive, it is generally limited to data rates under 100 Mbps and distances of a few kilometers. To achieve higher data rates and longer distances, a 1300-nm LED or laser source is needed. The highest data rates and longest distances require 1500-nm laser sources.

Structured Cabling

As a practical matter, network managers need a cabling plan that deals with the selection of cable and the layout of the cable in a building. The cabling plan should be easy to implement and accommodate future growth. In campus environments, the cabling plan also includes cable connections among buildings within a campus area network (CAN).

To aid in the development of cabling plans, standards have been issued that specify the cabling types and layout for office, data center, and apartment buildings. These standards are referred to as *structured cabling systems*. A structured cabling system is a generic wiring scheme with the following characteristics:

- The scheme refers to the telecommunications infrastructure wiring within a building or campus.
- The scope of the system includes cabling to support all types of information transfer, including voice, LANs, video and image transmission, and other forms of data transmission.
- The cabling layout and cable selection are independent of vendor and end-user equipment.
- The cable layout is designed to encompass distribution to all work or living areas within the building, so that relocation of equipment does not require rewiring but simply requires plugging the equipment into a preexisting outlet in the new location.

One advantage of such standards is that they provide guidance for preinstallation of cable in new buildings so that future voice and data networking needs

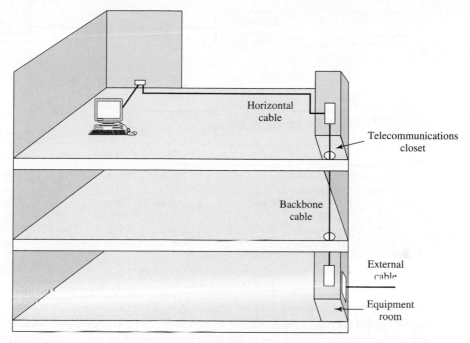

Figure 12.5   Elements of a Structured Cabling Layout

can be met without the need to rewire the building. The standards also simplify cable layout design for network managers. Two standards for structured cabling systems have been issued: TIA/EIA-568, issued jointly by the Electronic Industries Association and the Telecommunications Industry Association, and ISO 11801, issued by the International Organization for Standardization. The two standards are quite similar; the details in this section are from the TIA/EIA-568 document.

A structured cabling strategy is based on the use of a hierarchical, star-wired cable layout. Figure 12.5 illustrates the key elements for a typical commercial building. External cables, from the local telephone company and from wide area networks (WANs), terminate in an equipment room that is generally on the ground floor or a basement level. Patch panel and cross-connect equipment in the equipment room connect the external cables to internal distribution cable. Typically, the first level of distribution consists of backbone cables. In the simplest implementation, a single backbone cable or set of cables run from the equipment room to telecommunications closets (called *wiring closets*) on each floor. A telecommunications closet differs from the equipment room only in that it is less complex; the telecommunications closet generally contains cross-connect equipment for interconnecting cable on a single floor to the backbone. The cables distributed on a single floor are referred to as *horizontal cabling*. This cabling connects the backbone to wall outlets that service individual telephone and data equipment.

The use of a structured cabling plan enables an enterprise to use the transmission media appropriate for its requirements in a systematic and standardized fashion. Figure 12.6 indicates the recommended media for each portion of the structured cabling hierarchy. For horizontal cabling, a maximum distance of 90 m

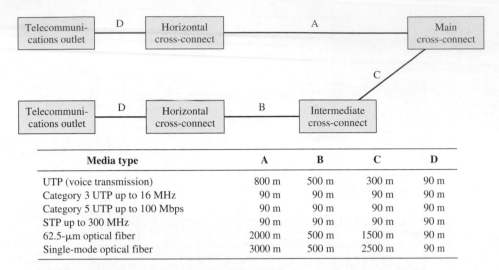

Media type	A	B	C	D
UTP (voice transmission)	800 m	500 m	300 m	90 m
Category 3 UTP up to 16 MHz	90 m	90 m	90 m	90 m
Category 5 UTP up to 100 Mbps	90 m	90 m	90 m	90 m
STP up to 300 MHz	90 m	90 m	90 m	90 m
62.5-μm optical fiber	2000 m	500 m	1500 m	90 m
Single-mode optical fiber	3000 m	500 m	2500 m	90 m

Figure 12.6   Cable Distances Specified in EIA-568-A

is recommended independent of media type. This distance is adequate to provide coverage for an entire floor for many commercial buildings. For buildings with very large floor space, backbone cable may be required to interconnect multiple telecommunications closets on a single floor. For backbone cabling, distances range from 90 to 3000 m, depending on cable type and position in the hierarchy.

12.4 LAN PROTOCOL ARCHITECTURE

LAN infrastructure focuses primarily on the hardware and media that provide the network platform needed to transmit data and information among attached devices. As we have seen in the preceding sections, cabling is a key aspect of LAN infrastructure, especially in environments where tiered LANs make sense. LAN architecture is less closely related to connections among physical equipment. Instead, it primarily focuses on the protocols used by LAN devices to share transmission media.

The architecture of a LAN is best described in terms of a layering of protocols that organize the basic functions of a LAN. This section opens with a description of the standardized protocol architecture for LANs, which encompasses physical, media access control (MAC), and logical link control (LLC) layers. This section then provides an overview of the MAC and LLC layers.

IEEE 802 Reference Model

Protocols defined specifically for LAN and MAN transmission address issues relating to the transmission of blocks of data over the network. In Open Systems Interconnection (OSI) terms, higher-layer protocols (layer 3 or 4 and above) are independent of network architecture and are applicable to LANs, MANs, and WANs. Thus, a discussion of LAN protocols is concerned principally with lower layers of the OSI model, especially layers 1 and 2.

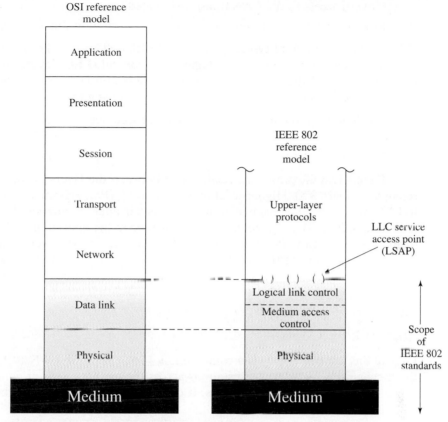

Figure 12.7 IEEE 802 Protocol Layers Compared to OSI Model

Figure 12.7 relates the LAN protocols to the OSI architecture (Figure L.1). This architecture was developed by the IEEE 802 committee and has been adopted by all organizations working on the specification of LAN standards. It is generally referred to as the IEEE 802 reference model.

Working from the bottom up, the lowest layer of the IEEE 802 reference model corresponds to the **physical layer** of the OSI model and includes such functions as encoding/decoding of signals and bit transmission/reception. In addition, the physical layer includes a specification of the transmission medium. Generally, the transmission medium is considered "below" the lowest layer of the OSI model. However, the choice of transmission medium is critical in LAN design, and so a specification of the medium is included.

Above the physical layer are the functions associated with providing service to LAN users. These include the following:

- On transmission, assemble data into a frame with address and error-detection fields.

- On reception, disassemble frame, and perform address recognition and error detection.

- Govern access to the LAN transmission medium.
- Provide an interface to higher layers and perform flow and error control.

These are functions typically associated with OSI layer 2. The functions in the last bullet item are grouped into a **logical link control (LLC)** layer. The functions in the first three bullet items are treated as a separate layer, called **media access control (MAC)**. The separation is done for the following reasons:

- The logic required to manage access to a shared-access medium is not found in traditional layer 2 data link control.
- For the same LLC, several MAC options may be provided.

Figure 12.8 illustrates the relationship between the layers of the architecture (compare Figure 8.5). Higher-level data, such as an IP datagram, are passed down to LLC, which appends control information as a header, creating an **LLC protocol data unit (PDU)**. This control information is used in the operation of the LLC protocol. The entire LLC PDU is then passed down to the MAC layer, which appends control information at the front and back of the packet, forming a **MAC frame**. Again, control information in the frame is needed for the operation of the MAC protocol. For context, the figure also shows the use of TCP/IP and an application layer above the LAN protocols.

Logical Link Control

Logical link control (LLC) is a common link protocol for all LANs. LLC specifies the mechanisms for addressing stations across the medium and for controlling the exchange of data between two users. It can be thought of as residing between the

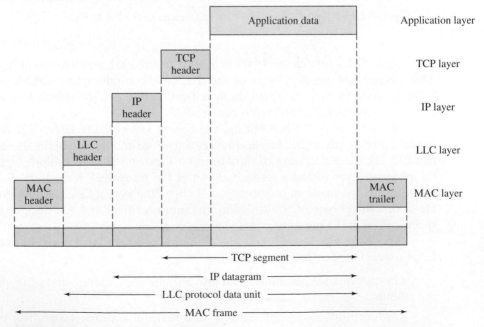

Figure 12.8 LAN Protocols in Context

network layer and the media access control sublayer of the data link layer. LLC enables LANs with different MAC protocols (such as Ethernet and Token Ring) to interface with a common network layer protocol, such as IP. Three services are provided as alternatives for attached devices using LLC:

- **Unacknowledged connectionless service:** This service is a datagram-style service. It is a very simple service that does not involve any of the flow control and error control mechanisms. Thus, the delivery of data is not guaranteed. However, in most devices there is some higher layer of software that deals with reliability issues.

- **Connection-mode service:** This service is similar to that offered by typical data link control protocols, such as HDLC (see Chapter 6). A logical connection is set up between two users exchanging data, and flow control and error control are provided.

- **Acknowledged connectionless service:** This is a cross between the previous two services. It provides that datagrams are to be acknowledged, but no prior logical connection is set up.

The **unacknowledged connectionless service** requires minimum logic and is useful in two contexts. First, it is often the case that higher layers of software provide the necessary reliability and flow-control mechanism, and it is efficient to avoid duplicating them. For example, TCP provides the mechanisms needed to ensure that data are delivered reliably. Second, there are instances in which the overhead of connection establishment and maintenance is unjustified or even counterproductive. One example is data collection activity that involves the periodic sampling of data sources, such as sensors and automatic self-test reports from security equipment or network components. In a monitoring application, the loss of an occasional data unit would not cause distress, as the next report should arrive shortly. Thus, in most cases, the unacknowledged connectionless service is the preferred option.

The **connection-mode service** could be used in very simple devices, such as terminal controllers, that have little software operating above this level. In these cases, it would provide the flow control and reliability mechanisms normally implemented at higher layers of the communications software.

The **acknowledged connectionless service** is useful in several contexts. With connection-mode service, the logical link control software must maintain some sort of table for each active connection, to keep track of the status of that connection. If the user needs guaranteed delivery, but there are a large number of destinations for data, connection-mode service may be impractical because of the large number of tables required. An example is a process control or automated factory environment where a central site may need to communicate with a large number of processors and programmable controllers. Another use of this is the handling of important and time-critical alarm or emergency control signals in a factory. Because of their importance, an acknowledgment is needed so that the sender can be assured that the signal got through. Because of the urgency of the signal, the user might not want to take the time to first establish a logical connection and then send the data.

The LLC PDU includes destination and source service access point (DSAP, SSAP) addresses. These refer to the next higher-layer protocol that uses LLC (typically IP). The LLC PDU also includes a control field that provides a sequencing and flow control mechanism. Such a control field is typical for data link control protocols and is described in Chapter 6.

Media Access Control

All LANs and MANs (metropolitan area networks) consist of collections of devices that must share the network's transmission capacity. Some means of controlling access to the transmission medium is needed to provide an orderly and efficient use of that capacity. This is the function of a **media access control** (MAC) protocol.

The relationship between LLC and the MAC protocols can be seen by considering the transmission formats involved. User data are passed down to the LLC layer, which prepares a link-level frame, known as an LLC protocol data unit (PDU). This PDU is then passed down to the MAC layer, where it is enclosed in a MAC frame.

The exact format of the MAC frame differs somewhat for the various MAC protocols in use. In general, all of the MAC frames have a format similar to that of Figure 12.9. The fields of this frame are as follows:

- **MAC:** This field contains any protocol control information needed for the functioning of the MAC protocol. For example, a priority level could be indicated here.
- **Destination MAC address:** The destination physical attachment point on the LAN for this frame. This is the physical (MAC) address of the device within the LAN that is the intended recipient of the frame.
- **Source MAC address:** The source physical attachment point on the LAN for this frame. This is the physical (MAC) address of the sender of the frame.

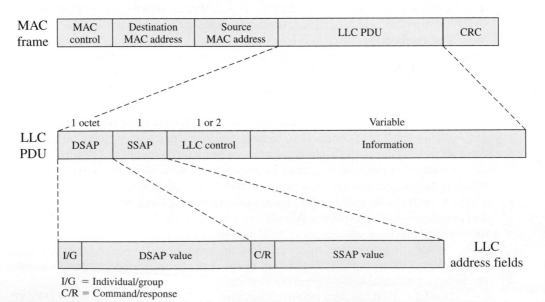

I/G = Individual/group
C/R = Command/response

Figure 12.9 LLC PDU in a Generic MAC Frame Format

- **LLC PDU:** The LLC data from the next higher layer. This includes the user data plus the source and destination service access point (SSAP and DSAP), which indicate the user of LLC.
- **CRC:** The cyclic redundancy check field (also known as the Frame Check Sequence, FCS, field). This is an error-detecting code, such as is used in other data link control protocols (Chapter 6). CRC's role in the error control process is described in Chapter 5. The CRC is calculated based on the bits in the entire frame. The sender calculates the CRC and adds it to the frame. The receiver performs the same calculation on the incoming frame and compares that calculation to the CRC field in that incoming frame. If the two values don't match, then one or more bits have been accidentally altered in transit; this typically triggers retransmission of the frame by the sender.

In most data link control protocols, the data link protocol entity is responsible not only for detecting errors using the CRC, but for recovering from those errors by retransmitting damaged frames. In the LAN protocol architecture, these two functions are split between the MAC and LLC layers. The MAC layer is responsible for detecting errors and discarding any frames that contain errors. The LLC layer optionally keeps track of which frames have been successfully received and retransmits unsuccessful frames.

APPLICATION NOTE

Cabling Infrastructure

A solid cabling infrastructure is the basis for all reliable communications. For new buildings, proper procedures must be followed to ensure that the network will perform as expected and that the job will adhere to the budget. In building with existing cabling infrastructure, a good understanding of the cable plant can help us understand the limitations of the system and to troubleshoot bottlenecks. Even with tremendous growth in the use of wireless communications, the cable plant is extremely important because wireless equipment is eventually connected to the wired backbone.

There are several important components to the cabling infrastructure, of which cabling is only a part. The network will be an integral part of the building systems and so space must be allocated for the wiring closets and consideration given for the location of the data cables. This is similar in scope to the attention given to electrical and plumbing systems. Wiring closets are the termination points for all of the cabling and where the networking equipment will be located. Wiring closets also include connections to the data center or the backbone, and eventually lead to the Internet. Adequate space, cooling, drainage, and cleanliness should be provided to ensure long life of the equipment and dependable connectivity. Often wiring closets are seen as a painful necessity and are relegated to the most inhospitable locations within the building. This can result in poor network performance as corrosion, heat, dirt, and interference all serve to degrade communications capability.

The wiring closet should also be located where distance limitations will not be violated. Every communication standard has its own maximum range. For example Ethernet

(*Continued*)

requires that each segment be no more than 100 m in length for 10-Mbps and 100-Mbps transmissions. The 100 m includes the installed cabling and patch cables at either end. While many buildings are not 100 m in length or width, going through floors, through ceilings, and around obstacles can add distance quickly.

The quality of the cabling can make a big difference as well. There is saying that goes, "Communication can be done over barbed wire; it's just not high quality." While there can be a cost savings between Cat 5, Cat 5e, and Cat 6 cable, investment should be in the best available wiring. This provides some longevity to the network and the best possible transmission rates. It will usually save money in the long run as upgrades are less frequent.

Other cable installation issues include, but are not limited to, the following: proximity to power wiring, equipment installed near cable runs (motors, vent ducts, etc.), management of the cable in the run (cable trays, tie wraps, cable rings), proper cable used, spares, damage during and after installation, enough cable pulled to allow modification of termination locations (office occupant desires a jack to be moved), and labels. All cabling should be labeled on both ends, at the jack and in the wiring closet, to facilitate troubleshooting and modification. The growing popularity of power over Ethernet (PoE) is also forcing network designers to rethink how cable is run within buildings. This is especially true for PoE systems with higher voltage levels where gathering cables into bundles within conduits is no longer an option.

Termination quality is also very important. Increasingly, modular equipment is being used on new networks. This means that connections can be easily moved and terminations completed quickly but care must be taken to ensure that the correct components are purchased. Every type of cable and every type of application has a separate type of terminator. For example, a Category 6 solid cable will use a different jack than a Category 5 stranded cable. All terminations should be checked with the proper network test equipment such as a Fluke cable meter. This device will test the cable for crosstalk, return, attenuation, and wire mapping to ensure that all runs are within specification.

Inside the wiring closet a suitable amount of wire management should be used. Wire management is used to organize and "tidy up" installations. Without it, a wiring closet can be an absolute mess that can make troubleshooting, maintenance, or additions all but impossible. Wire management includes items such as vertical and horizontal management, front/back pieces, covers, guides, and cable rings for bundling.

Finally, the entire cable installation should be clean and neat. No one wants cables hanging out of the wall or a crooked wall plate in their office. No network technician wants to work in a closet that looks like a bad day at the spaghetti factory. A clean, professional installation allows for faster troubleshooting and easier maintenance, facilitates future modifications, and does not take up unnecessary room in the floor, ceiling, or closet.

Most companies will use contractors for the installation because they do not have the manpower or expertise. In this case, having a local supervisor that understands the issues can mean the difference between a well-built installation and a poor one. Organizations should develop their own standards for the installation and ensure that these standards are met before payment is made.

12.5 SUMMARY

The requirement for networking capability within the individual building is just as strong as the requirement for wide area networking. Every business environment is populated with a large and growing collection of data processing equipment. Local area networks (LANs) are needed to tie this equipment together to ensure intraoffice communications and to provide cost-effective links to wide area networks (WANs).

A LAN consists of a shared transmission medium and a set of hardware and software for interfacing devices to the medium and regulating the orderly access to the medium.

The transmission media that are used to convey information can be classified as guided or unguided. Guided media provide a physical path along which the signals are propagated; these include twisted pair, coaxial cable, and optical fiber. Unguided media employ an antenna for transmitting through air, vacuum, or water. Traditionally, twisted pair has been the workhorse for communications of all sorts. More recently, optical fiber has come to play a dominant role and has displaced other media in many applications. Of these two, optical fiber has the most promising future for the widest range of applications.

A set of standards has been defined for LANs that specifies a range of data rates and a variety of transmission media. These standards are widely accepted, and most of the products on the market conform to one of these standards.

Structured cabling systems provide guidance for wiring buildings to support LANs. Guidelines exist to assist network and building designers to locate telecommunications closets, connect to WAN services, and to run network cabling both horizontally and vertically within buildings.

LAN protocol architectures are less concerned with cabling infrastructure than with providing services needed by network attached devices to share the LAN transmission medium. These map most directly to the data link layer of the OSI reference model and address both media access and logical link control.

Case Study VIII: Carlson Companies

The major concepts addressed in this case study include Mass storage systems; storage area networks; backend networks. **This case study and more are available at www.pearsoninternationaleditions.com/stallings**

12.6 KEY TERMS, REVIEW QUESTIONS, AND PROBLEMS

Key Terms

backend network	decibel (dB)	logical link control (LLC)
backbone LAN	guided media	media access control
coaxial cable	IEEE 802	(MAC)

optical fiber	structured cabling	unguided media
server farm	tiered LAN	unshielded twisted pair
shielded twisted pair (STP)	transmission medium	(UTP)
storage area network (SAN)	twisted pair	wireless transmission

Review Questions

12.1   How do the key requirements for computer room networks differ from those for personal computer local networks?

12.2   What are the different categories of data processing equipment that are supported in a typical business organization?

12.3   Other than large storage capacity, what other advantage does a SAN provide?

12.4   What is the protocol typically used in storage area networks?

12.5   Differentiate between guided media and unguided media.

12.6   Why are the wires twisted in twisted-pair copper wire?

12.7   What are some major limitations of twisted-pair wire?

12.8   What is the difference between unshielded twisted pair and shielded twisted pair?

12.9   Describe the components of optical fiber cable.

12.10   How is optical fiber different from twisted-pair or coaxial cable?

12.11   What are the differences between multimode and single-mode propagation?

12.12   What are the characteristics of structured cabling systems?

12.13   Arrange the following in order from highest to lowest regarding bandwidth: UTP, fiber, and coaxial cable.

12.14   Arrange the following in order from highest to lowest regarding cost: UTP, fiber, and coaxial cable.

12.15   What is the purpose of the IEEE 802 committee?

12.16   List the different characteristics of backend networks.

12.17   List and briefly define the types of operation provided by the LLC protocol.

12.18   List some basic functions performed at the MAC layer.

Problems

12.1   The semiconductor industry requires a large degree of automation in the processing of microelectronics devices. This is primarily due to the fact that extremely small tolerances are required in the manufacturing process of most semiconductor devices and therefore semiconductor fabrication plants must be many times "cleaner" than the average hospital surgical facility. For example, the conducting channel of a MOSFET (Metal Oxide Semiconductor Field Effect Transistor) is typically <1 micron in length. Conversely, a human hair is approximately 50 microns in diameter. Thus, seemingly minute biological contaminants (e.g., a single skin flake) can potentially render numerous transistors inoperable. Since the human process operator can be detrimental to the semiconductor fabrication process, robotics and automation must be instituted wherever possible. To facilitate this automation, the SEMI organization developed the SECS/GEM (Semiconductor Equipment Communication Standard/Generic Equipment Model) Protocol. Do some Internet research on SEMI/GEM. Provide a basic overview of this standard and discuss the associated benefits relative to the design and operation of a factory LAN and its impact on general fabrication communications. Summarize your findings in a 500–750 word paper or a 5–8 slide PowerPoint presentation.

12.2   In campus environments, cabling plans include those for the outside service plant (OSP). Do some Internet research on OSP standards and guidelines that are used to guide cable infrastructures for interconnecting buildings in campus environments. Gather several images from online sources that illustrate OSP recommendations. Include these images in a 6–10 slide PowerPoint presentation.

12.3 Develop, in general terms, a cost-effective structured cabling plan for a tiered LAN within a scientific R&D organization that is building a new five-story research facility. The first floor will contain the lobby and administrative offices. The second and third floors will contain labs that utilize fairly large pieces of heavy-power-consumption equipment (e.g., small linear accelerators and reactive ion chambers). Numerous technicians and scientists will be working on this floor and data requirements include high-speed transmission of high bandwidth data (e.g., color video). The fourth floor will contain offices for the lab personnel and the fifth floor will contain executive offices. Your plan should describe and illustrate the horizontal cabling for each floor as well as the vertical cabling runs.

12.4 Some organizations are implementing wide area networks as a high-speed backbone in order to increase communication efficiency and effectiveness of services throughout a particular region. One such example of this is NetworkVirginia, which delivers Internet and intranet services to organizations throughout the state of Virginia. NetworkVirginia also provides a regional interconnection point for Internet 2 members. Do some Internet research on NetworkVirginia and discuss the importance of this concept in the evolution of networking strategy, with particular reference to LAN support in enterprise networks. Summarize your findings in a 750–1000 word paper or an 8–12 slide PowerPoint presentation.

12.5 Do some Internet research on structured cabling systems and gather several images illustrating the range of meanings that structured cabling has in enterprise networks. Include the images in an 8–12 slide PowerPoint presentation that summarizes the many facets of structured cabling in business networks.

12.6 Do some Internet research on power over Ethernet (PoE) cabling and how it differs from cabling used in traditional Ethernet networks. Identify the wiring (or rewiring) requirements needed to move from traditional to PoE. Also describe trends in the voltage levels for PoE cables. Summarize your findings in a 500–750 word paper or an 8–12 slide PowerPoint presentation.

12.7 Gather multiple images that illustrate the differences among Category 5e, Category 6, and Category 7 cables. Include these in a 5–8 slide PowerPoint presentation that summarizes how these cables physically differ from one another.

12.8 Do some Internet research on transcontinental fiber optic cable runs and the ships used to deploy undersea fiber optic cable. Collect several images illustrating the major fiber optic connections among continents. Summarize your findings in an 8–12 slide PowerPoint presentation.

12.9 Use Wireshark to capture packets on your network. Do some screen captures that illustrate the contents of Ethernet LLC PDUs and MAC frames.

APPENDIX 12A   DECIBELS AND SIGNAL STRENGTH

An important parameter in any transmission system is the signal strength. As a signal propagates along a transmission medium, there is a loss, or *attenuation*, of signal strength. To compensate, amplifiers may be inserted at various points to impart a gain in signal strength.

It is customary to express gains, losses, and relative levels in decibels because

- Signal strength often falls off exponentially, so loss is easily expressed in terms of the decibel, which is a logarithmic unit.

- The net gain or loss in a cascaded transmission path can be calculated with simple addition and subtraction.

The decibel is a measure of the ratio between two signal levels. The decibel gain is given by

$$G_{dB} = 10 \log_{10} \frac{P_{out}}{P_{in}}$$

where

G_{dB} = gain, in decibels

P_{in} = input power level

P_{out} = output power level

$\log_{10}$ = logarithm to the base 10

Table 12.3 shows the relationship between decibel values and powers of 10.

There is some inconsistency in the literature over the use of the terms *gain* and *loss*. If the value of G_{dB} is positive, it represents an actual gain in power. For example, a gain of 3 dB means that the power has doubled. If the value of G_{dB} is negative, it represents an actual loss in power. For example a gain of –3 dB means that the power has halved, and this is a loss of power. Normally, this is expressed by saying there is a loss of 3 dB. However, some of the literature would say that this is a loss of –3 dB. It makes more sense to say that a negative gain corresponds to a positive loss. Therefore, we define a decibel loss as

$$L_{dB} = -10 \log_{10} \frac{P_{out}}{P_{in}} = 10 \log_{10} \frac{P_{in}}{P_{out}}$$

Example If a signal with a power level of 10 mW is inserted onto a transmission line and the measured power some distance away is 5 mW, the loss can be expressed as $L_{dB} = 10\log(10/5) = 10(0.3) = 3$ dB.

Note that the decibel is a measure of relative, not absolute, difference. A loss from 1000 mW to 500 mW is also a loss of 3 dB. Thus, a loss of 3 dB halves the power level; a gain of 3 dB doubles the power.

Table 12.3 Decibel Values

Power Ratio	dB	Power Ratio	dB
10^1	10	10^{-1}	–10
10^2	20	10^{-2}	–20
10^3	30	10^{-3}	–30
10^4	40	10^{-4}	–40
10^5	50	10^{-5}	–50
10^6	60	10^{-6}	–60

The decibel is also used to measure the difference in voltage, taking into account that power is proportional to the square of the voltage:

$$P = \frac{V^2}{R}$$

where

      P = power dissipated across resistance R
      V = voltage across resistance R

Thus

$$L_{dB} = 10\log\frac{P_{in}}{P_{out}} = 10\log\frac{V_{in}^2/R}{V_{out}^2/R} = 20\log\frac{V_{in}}{V_{out}}$$

Example Decibels are useful in determining the gain or loss over a series of transmission elements. Consider a series in which the input is at a power level of 4 mW, the first element is a transmission line with a 12-dB loss (−12-dB gain), the second element is an amplifier with a 35-dB gain, and the third element is a transmission line with a 10-dB loss. The net gain is (−12 + 35 − 10) = 13 dB. To calculate the output power P_{out},

$$G_{dB} = 13 = 10\log(P_{out}/4\,mW)$$
$$P_{out} = 4 \times 10^{1.3}\,mW = 712.8\,mW$$

ETHERNET, SWITCHES, AND VIRTUAL LANs

CHAPTER

13

Learning Objectives

After reading this chapter, you should be able to:

♦ Explain the continued interest in Ethernet-type systems at higher and higher data rates.

♦ Describe the various Ethernet alternatives.

♦ Explain the differences among bridges, hubs, layer 2 switches, and layer 3 switches.

♦ Describe the characteristics of Power over Ethernet (PoE).

Recent years have seen rapid changes in the technology, design, and business applications of local area networks (LANs). A major feature of this evolution is new schemes for high-speed local area networking. To keep pace with the changing local networking needs of business, several approaches to high-speed LAN design have become pervasive in enterprise networks. The most important of these include the following:

- **Fast Ethernet and Gigabit Ethernet:** The migration from 10-Mbps CSMA/CD (carrier sense multiple access with collision detection) to higher speeds is a logical strategy, because it helps preserve the investment in existing systems.
- **High-speed wireless LANs:** Wireless LAN technology and standards have come of age, and high-speed standards and products have been introduced.
- **Fibre Channel:** As noted in Chapter 12, this standard provides a low-cost, easily scalable approach to achieving very high data rates and is used in storage area networks (SANs) and for other types of storage networking.

Table 13.1 lists characteristics of these approaches. The remainder of this chapter is devoted to Ethernet. Chapter 14 covers wireless LANs. Appendix G covers Fibre Channel.

13.1 TRADITIONAL ETHERNET

The most widely used high-speed LANs in today's enterprise networks are referred to as Ethernet and were developed by the IEEE 802.3 standards committee. Collectively, Ethernet and Ethernet-like LANs are the dominant force in the wired LAN market. As with other LAN standards, much of the content of the Ethernet

Table 13.1   Characteristics of Some High-Speed LANs

	Fast Ethernet	Gigabit Ethernet	Fibre Channel	Wireless LAN
Data Rate	100 Mbps	1 Gbps, 10 Gbps, 100 Gbps	100 Mbps to 3.2 Gbps	1 Mbps to 600 Mbps
Transmission Media	UTP, STP, optical fiber	UTP, shielded cable, optical fiber	Optical fiber, coaxial cable, STP	2.4-GHz, 5-GHz microwave
Access Method	CSMA/CD	Switched	Switched	CSMA/Polling
Supporting Standard	IEEE 802.3	IEEE 802.3	Fibre Channel Association	IEEE 802.11

standard is focused on the medium access control sublayer and physical layer, which are found, respectively, on layers 2 and 1 of the Open Systems Interconnection (OSI) reference model.

Early Ethernet networks that complied with the original IEEE 802.3 standard operated at 10 Mbps. Subsequently, standards were developed for Ethernet networks operating at 100 Mbps, 1 Gbps, and 10 Gbps. Today, standards for 40-Gbps and 100-Gbps versions of Ethernet are being formulated by IEEE 802.3 committees. Power over Ethernet (PoE) is another important development in the evolution of 802.3 networks.

Before looking at PoE and high-speed Ethernet LANs, we provide a brief overview of the original 10-Mbps Ethernet because it is a good vehicle for understanding Ethernet's traditional media access control (MAC) protocol. We also introduce the concept of switched LANs to help you better understand why fully-switched Ethernet networks dominate today's business networks.

Classical Ethernet operates at 10 Mbps over a bus topology LAN using the CSMA/CD (carrier sense multiple access with collision detection) medium access control protocol. In this section, we introduce the concepts of bus LANs and CSMA/CD operation, and then briefly discuss transmission medium options.

Bus Topology LAN

Early Ethernet LANs had a bus topology and the original IEEE 802.3 standard assumed that a bus topology was in place. In a bus topology LAN, all stations attach, through appropriate hardware interfacing known as a tap, directly to a linear transmission medium, or bus. Full-duplex operation between the station and the tap allows data to be transmitted onto the bus and received from the bus. A transmission from any station's tap propagates the length of the medium in both directions and can be received by all other stations. At each end of the bus is a terminator, which absorbs any signal, removing it from the bus, and keeping the signal from echoing back across the medium.

Two communication challenges are present in bus LANs. First, because a transmission from any one station can be received by all other stations, there needs to be some way of indicating for whom the transmission is intended. Second, a mechanism is needed to regulate station transmissions. To see the reason for this, consider that if two stations on the bus attempt to transmit at the same time, their signals overlap and become garbled. Or consider that one station decides to transmit continuously for a long period of time, blocking other users from accessing the transmission medium.

To address these challenges, stations are required to transmit data in small blocks, known as **frames**. Each frame consists of a portion of the data that a station wishes to transmit, plus a frame header that contains control information. Each station on the bus is assigned a unique address, or identifier, and the destination address for the intended recipient of a frame is included in its header.

Figure 13.1 illustrates the scheme. In this example, station C wishes to transmit a frame of data to A. The frame header includes A's address. As the frame propagates along the bus, it passes B. B observes that A is the intended recipient and ignores the frame. A, on the other hand, sees that the frame is addressed to itself and therefore copies the data from the frame as it goes by.

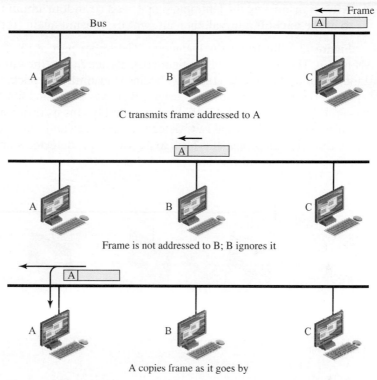

Figure 13.1 Frame Transmission on a Bus LAN

So the frame structure solves the first challenge mentioned previously: It provides a mechanism for indicating the intended recipient of the data. It also provides the basic tool for solving the second challenge, the regulation of access. In particular, the stations take turns sending frames in some cooperative fashion, as explained in the next subsection.

Medium Access Control

For CSMA/CD, a station wishing to transmit first listens to the medium (the bus) to determine if another transmission is in progress (carrier sense). If the medium is idle, the station may transmit. It may happen that two or more stations attempt to transmit at about the same time. If this happens, there will be a **collision**; the signals from both transmissions will be garbled and not received successfully by their intended recipients. The following procedure is the essence of CSMA/CD; it specifies what a station with data to transmit should do if the medium is found busy and what it should do if a collision occurs:

1. If the medium is idle, transmit; otherwise, go to step 2.
2. If the medium is busy, continue to listen until it is idle, then transmit immediately.
3. If a collision is detected during transmission, transmit a brief jamming signal to assure that all stations know that there has been a collision and then cease transmission.

4. After transmitting the jamming signal, wait a random amount of time, referred to as the **backoff** interval, then attempt to transmit again (repeat from step 1).

Figure 13.2 illustrates the technique. The upper part of the figure shows a bus LAN layout. The remainder of the figure depicts activity on the bus at four successive instants in time. At time t_0, station A begins transmitting a packet addressed to D. At t_1, both B and C are ready to transmit. B senses a transmission and so defers. C, however, is still unaware of A's transmission and begins its own transmission. When A's transmission reaches C, at t_2, C detects the collision and ceases transmission. The effect of the collision propagates back to A, where it is detected some time later, t_3, at which time A ceases transmission.

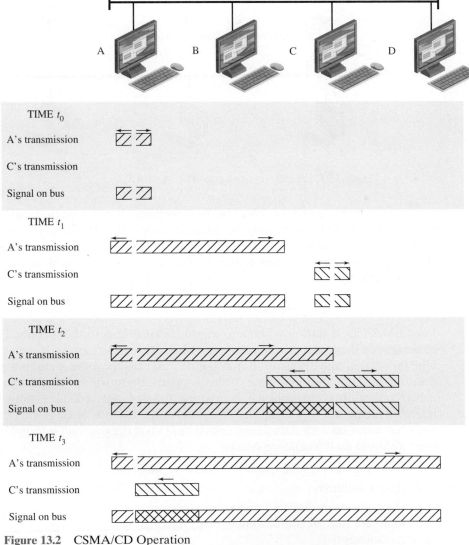

Figure 13.2 CSMA/CD Operation

The advantage of CSMA/CD is its simplicity. It is easy to implement the logic required for this protocol. Furthermore, there is little to go wrong in the execution of the protocol. For example, if for some reason a station fails to detect a collision, the worst that can happen is that it continues to transmit its frame, wasting some time on the medium. Once the transmission is over, the algorithm continues to function as before.

MAC Frame

Figure 13.3 depicts the frame format for the 802.3 protocol. It consists of the following fields:

- **Preamble:** A seven-octet pattern of alternating 0s and 1s used by the receiver to establish bit synchronization.
- **Start Frame Delimiter (SFD):** The sequence 10101011, which indicates the actual start of the frame and enables the receiver to locate the first bit of the rest of the frame.
- **Destination Address (DA):** Specifies the station(s) for which the frame is intended. It may be a unique physical address, a group address, or a broadcast address.
- **Source Address (SA):** Specifies the station that sent the frame.

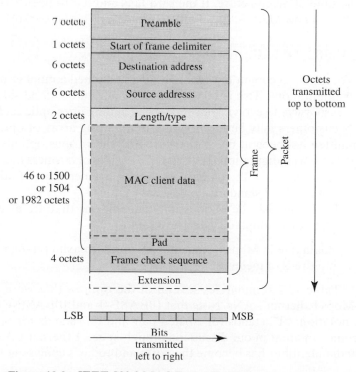

Figure 13.3　IEEE 802.3 MAC Frame Format

- **Length/Type:** Takes on one of two meanings, depending on its numeric value. If the value of this field is less than or equal to 1500 decimal, then the Length/Type field indicates the number of MAC Client Data octets contained in the subsequent MAC Client Data field of the basic frame (length interpretation). If the value of this field is greater than or equal to 1536 decimal, then the Length/Type field indicates the nature of the MAC client protocol (Type interpretation). The Length and Type interpretations of this field are mutually exclusive.

- **MAC Client Data:** Data unit supplied by LLC. The maximum size of this field is 1500 octets for a basic frame, 1504 octets for a Q-tagged frame, and 1982 octets for an envelope frame.

- **Pad:** Octets added to ensure that the frame is long enough for proper CD operation.

- **Frame Check Sequence (FCS):** A 32-bit cyclic redundancy check (CRC), based on all fields except preamble, SFD, and FCS.

- **Extension:** This field is added, if required for 1-Gbps half-duplex operation. The extension field is necessary to enforce the minimum carrier event duration on the medium in half-duplex mode at an operating speed of 1 Gbps.

A station's source address is also called its MAC address. If the station is a personal computer (PC), the MAC address is hardwired into its network adapter card, when the card is manufactured. A card's backoff interval may also be randomly assigned at the time of manufacture. If the card fails and has to been replaced, the machine will have a new MAC address and may have a different backoff interval.

IEEE 802.3 Medium Options at 10 Mbps

The IEEE 802.3 committee has traditionally defined a number of alternative physical configurations. This is both good and bad. On the good side, the standard has been responsive to evolving technology, including fiber optic cable. On the bad side, LAN customers may be faced with a bewildering array of options. However, the committee has been at pains to ensure that the various options can be easily integrated into a configuration that satisfies a variety of business needs. Thus, enterprise network designers with complex sets of requirements may find the flexibility and variety of the 802.3 standards to be an asset.

To distinguish the various implementations that are available, the original 802.3 committee adopted a concise notation:

> <data rate in Mbps> <signaling method><maximum segment length in hundreds of meters>

Table 13.2 summarizes several of the options that were available for early 10-Mbps Ethernet LANs. Note that 10BASE-T and 10BASE-F do not quite follow the notation: "T" stands for twisted pair and "F" stands for optical fiber. As will become apparent in our discussion of high-speed Ethernet LANs, the inclusion of a media identifier has become the norm and today's concise notation is as follows:

> <data rate in Mbps or Gbps> <signaling method><media identifier>

Table 13.2   IEEE 802.3 10-Mbps Physical Layer Medium Alternatives

	10BASE5	**10BASE2**	**10BASE-T**	**10BASE-F**
Transmission Medium	Coaxial cable	Coaxial cable	Unshielded twisted pair	850-nm optical fiber pair
Topology	Bus	Bus	Star	Star
Maximum Segment Length (m)	500	185	100	500
Nodes per Segment	100	30	—	33
Cable Diameter	10 mm	5 mm	0.4–0.6 mm	62.5/125 μm

13.2 BRIDGES, HUBS, AND SWITCHES

Before continuing our discussion of Ethernet, we need to take a detour and introduce the concepts of bridges, hubs, and switches.

Bridges

In virtually all cases, there is a need to expand beyond the confines of a single LAN, to provide interconnection to other LANs and to wide area networks (WANs). Two general approaches are used for this purpose: bridges and routers. The **bridge** is the simpler of the two devices and provides a means of interconnecting similar LANs. The router is a more general-purpose device, capable of interconnecting a variety of LANs and WANs.

Both bridging and routing are forms of data control, but work through different methods. Bridging takes place at the data link layer of the OSI reference model while routing takes place at the network layer. This difference means that a bridge uses MAC addresses to direct frames while a router bases its forwarding decisions on network layer (e.g., IP) addresses.

Basic bridges are designed for use between LANs or LAN segments that use identical protocols for the physical and link layers (e.g., all conforming to IEEE 802.3). Because the devices all use the same protocols, the amount of processing required at the bridge is minimal. More sophisticated bridges are capable of mapping from one MAC format to another (e.g., to interconnect an Ethernet and a Fibre Channel LAN).

Because the bridge is used in a situation in which all the LANs have the same characteristics, the reader may ask, why not simply have one large LAN? Depending on circumstance, there are several reasons for the use of multiple LANs or LAN segments connected by bridges in place of one large LAN:

- **Reliability:** The danger in connecting all data processing devices in an organization to one network is that a fault on the network may disable communication for all devices. By using bridges, the network can be partitioned into self-contained units. Each self-contained unit is called a *collision domain* because it is a group of computers amongst which data collisions can occur. Segmenting a larger network into collision domains can help to prevent a fault in one network segment from affecting the entire network.

- **Performance:** In general, performance on a LAN declines with an increase in the number of devices or the length of the wire. Adding devices to an Ethernet LAN increases the probability of collisions and an increase in collisions can degrade network performance. Dividing a large LAN into smaller segments can give improved performance, especially when devices can be clustered so that intranetwork traffic significantly exceeds internetwork traffic.

- **Security:** The establishment of multiple LANs may improve security of communications. It is desirable to keep different types of traffic (e.g., accounting, personnel, strategic planning) that have different security needs on physically separate media. At the same time, the different types of users with different levels of security need to communicate through controlled and monitored mechanisms.

- **Geography:** Clearly, two separate LANs are needed to support devices clustered in two geographically distant locations. Even in the case of two buildings separated by a highway, it may be far easier to use a microwave bridge link than to attempt to string cable between the two buildings.

Figure 13.4 shows the action of a bridge connecting two LANs, A and B, using the same MAC protocol. In this example, a single bridge attaches to both LANs; frequently, the bridge function is performed by two "half-bridges," one on each LAN. The functions of the bridge are few and simple:

- Read all frames transmitted on A and accept those addressed to any station on B.

- Using the medium access control protocol for B, retransmit each frame on B.

- Do the same for B-to-A traffic.

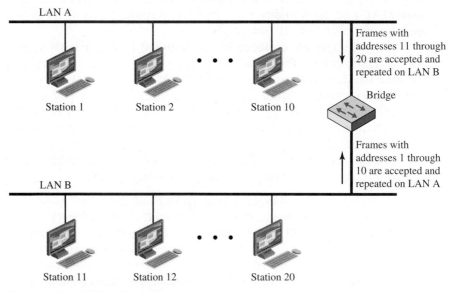

Figure 13.4 Bridge Operation

Several design aspects of a bridge are worth highlighting:

- The bridge makes no modification to the content or format of the frames it receives, nor does it encapsulate them with an additional header. Each frame to be transferred is simply copied from one LAN and repeated with exactly the same bit pattern on the other LAN. Because the two LANs use the same LAN protocols, it is permissible to do this.
- The bridge should contain enough buffer space to meet peak demands. Over a short period of time, frames may arrive faster than they can be retransmitted.
- The bridge must contain addressing and routing intelligence. At a minimum, the bridge must know which addresses are on each network to know which frames to pass. Further, there may be more than two LANs interconnected by a number of bridges. In that case, a frame may have to be routed through several bridges in its journey from source to destination.
- A bridge may connect more than two LANs.

In summary, the bridge provides an extension to the LAN that requires no modification to the communications software in the stations attached to the LANs. It appears to all stations on the two (or more) LANs that there is a single LAN on which each station has a unique address. The station uses that unique address and need not explicitly discriminate between stations on the same LAN and stations on other LANs; the bridge takes care of that.

Hubs

In recent years, there has been a proliferation of types of devices for interconnecting LANs that go beyond bridges and the routers. These devices can conveniently be grouped into the categories of layer 2 switches and layer 3 switches. We begin with a discussion of hubs and then explore these two concepts.

A hub is an alternative to the bus topology. Each station is connected to the hub by two lines (transmit and receive). The hub acts as a repeater: When a single station transmits, the hub repeats the signal on the outgoing line to every station. Like other repeaters, hubs are relatively simple network devices that operate at the physical layer (layer 1) of the OSI reference model. Hubs do not manage the traffic that comes through them. Any frame entering one of its ports broadcasts out or is "repeated" on every other port, except for the port of entry. Since every packet is repeated on every other port, collisions can occur and these can affect the performance of the entire network.

Ordinarily, the line between a station and a hub consists of two unshielded twisted pairs. Because of the high data rate and transmission qualities of UTP, the length of a line is limited to about 100 m. As an alternative, an optical fiber link may be used. In this case, the maximum length is about 500 m.

Multiple levels of hubs can be cascaded in a hierarchical configuration. Figure 13.5 depicts a two-level configuration. There is one **header hub** (HHUB) and one or more **intermediate hubs** (IHUBs). Each hub may have a mixture of stations and other hubs attached to it from below. This layout fits well with building wiring practices. Typically, there is a wiring closet on each floor of an office building, and a hub can be placed in each one. Each hub could service the stations on its floor.

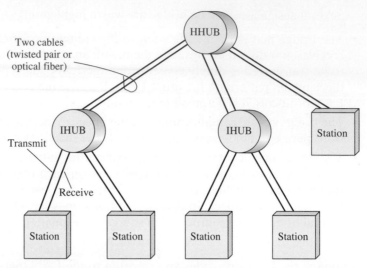

Figure 13.5 Two-Level Star Topology

A hub uses a star wiring arrangement to attach stations to the hub. Note that although this topology is physically a star, it is logically a bus. In this arrangement, a transmission from any one station is received by the hub and retransmitted on all of the outgoing lines to every station. If two stations transmit at the same time, there will be a collision. Therefore, to avoid collisions, only one station should transmit at a time. All attached devices share the LANs total transmission (e.g., 10 Mbps) just as they do in a shared medium bus LAN such as that depicted in Figure 13.6a.

The hub has several advantages over the simple bus arrangement. It exploits standard building wiring practices in the layout of cable. In addition, the hub can be configured to recognize a malfunctioning station that is jamming the network and to cut that station out of the network. Figure 13.6b illustrates the operation of a hub. Here again, station B is transmitting. This transmission goes from B, across the transmit line from B to the hub, and from the hub along the receive lines of each of the other attached stations.

Layer 2 Switches

In recent years, the layer 2 switch has replaced the hub in popularity, particularly for high-speed LANs. The layer 2 switch is also sometimes referred to as a switching hub or a multiport network bridge that processes and routes data at the data link layer (layer 2) of the OSI model.

To clarify the distinction between hubs and switches, Figure 13.6a shows a typical bus layout of a traditional 10-Mbps LAN. A bus is installed that is laid out so that all the devices to be attached are in reasonable proximity to a point on the bus. In the figure, station B is transmitting. This transmission goes from B, across the link from B to the bus, along the bus in both directions, and along the access lines of each of the other attached stations. In this configuration, all the stations must share the total capacity of the bus, which is 10 Mbps.

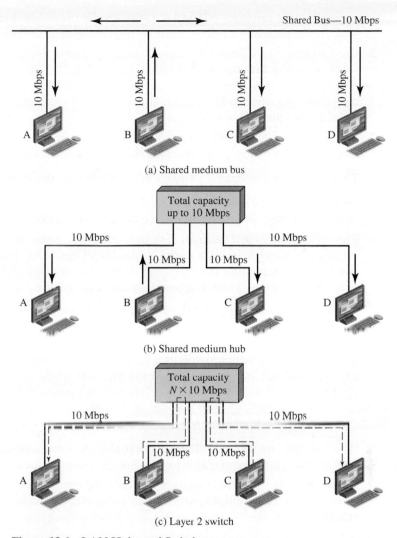

Figure 13.6   LAN Hubs and Switches

We can achieve greater performance with a layer 2 switch. In this case, the central hub acts as a switch, similar to a packet switch. An incoming frame from a particular station is switched to the appropriate output line to be delivered to the intended destination. At the same time, other unused lines can also be used for switching other traffic. Figure 13.6c shows an example in which B is transmitting a frame to A and at the same time C is transmitting a frame to D. So, in this example, the current throughput on the LAN is 20 Mbps, although each individual device is limited to 10 Mbps. The layer 2 switch has several attractive features:

1. No change is required to the software or hardware of the attached devices to convert a bus LAN or a hub LAN to a switched LAN. In the case of an Ethernet LAN, each attached device continues to use the Ethernet medium

access control protocol (CSMA/CD) to access the LAN. From the point of view of the attached devices, nothing has changed in the access logic.

2. Each attached device has a dedicated capacity equal to that of the entire original LAN, assuming that the layer 2 switch has sufficient capacity to keep up with all attached devices. For example, in Figure 13.6c, if the layer 2 switch can sustain a throughput of 20 Mbps, each attached device appears to have a dedicated capacity for either input or output of 10 Mbps.

3. The layer 2 switch scales easily. Additional switches can be attached to the layer 2 switch by increasing the capacity of the layer 2 switch correspondingly.

Two major types of layer 2 switches are available for use in business networks:

- **Store-and-forward switch:** The layer 2 switch accepts a frame on an input line, buffers it briefly, and then routes it to the appropriate output line.

- **Cut-through switch:** The layer 2 switch takes advantage of the fact that the destination address appears at the beginning of the MAC frame. The layer 2 switch begins repeating the incoming frame onto the appropriate output line as soon as the layer 2 switch recognizes the destination address.

The cut-through switch yields the highest possible throughput but at some risk of propagating bad frames, because the switch is not able to perform the cyclical redundancy check (CRC, described in Chapter 5) prior to retransmission. The store-and-forward switch involves a delay between sender and receiver while the CRC is performed, but boosts the overall integrity of the network.

A layer 2 switch can be viewed as a full-duplex version of the hub. It can also incorporate logic that allows it to function as a multiport bridge. The following are differences between layer 2 switches and bridges:

- Bridge frame handling is done in software. A layer 2 switch performs the address recognition and frame forwarding functions in hardware.

- A bridge can typically only analyze and forward one frame at a time, whereas a layer 2 switch has multiple parallel data paths and can handle multiple frames at a time.

- A bridge uses store-and-forward operation. With a layer 2 switch, it is possible to have cut-through instead of store-and-forward operation.

Because a layer 2 switch has higher performance and can incorporate the functions of a bridge, bridges are much less common in today's LANs than they were in the past. New installations typically include layer 2 switches with bridge functionality rather than bridges.

Layer 3 Switches

When compared to shared media hubs, layer 2 switches provide increased performance to meet the needs of high-volume traffic generated by PCs, workstations, and servers. However, as the number of devices in a building or complex of buildings grows, layer 2 switches reveal some inadequacies.

Generally speaking, layer 2 switches have the same limitations as bridged networks. Similar to bridges, layer 2 switches are good if a network is designed by the 80/20 rule and where users spend 80% of their time communicating with devices on their local segment. In addition, while bridges and layer 2 switches enable a network to be broken up into collision domains, the whole network is still a large broadcast domain. Large broadcast domains are problematic and can cause performance issues as the network grows. Because of these problems, layer 2 switches cannot completely replace routers.

A set of devices and LANs connected by layer 2 switches is considered to have a flat address space. The term *flat* means that all users share a common MAC broadcast address. Thus, if any device issues a MAC frame with a broadcast address, that frame is to be delivered to all devices attached to the overall network connected by layer 2 switches and/or bridges. In a large network, frequent transmission of broadcast frames can create tremendous overhead. Worse, a malfunctioning device can create a *broadcast storm*, in which numerous broadcast frames clog the network and crowd out legitimate traffic.

A second performance-related problem with the use of bridges and/or layer 2 switches is that the current standards for bridge protocols dictate that there be no closed loops in the network. That is, there can only be one path between any two devices. Thus, it is impossible, in a standards-based implementation, to provide multiple paths through multiple switches between devices. This restriction limits both performance and network resiliency.

To overcome these problems, it seems logical to break up a large local network into a number of **subnetworks** connected by routers. A MAC broadcast frame is then limited to only the devices and switches contained in a single subnetwork. Furthermore, IP-based routers employ sophisticated routing algorithms that allow the use of multiple paths between subnetworks going through different routers.

However, the problem with using routers to overcome some of the inadequacies of bridges and layer 2 switches is that routers typically do all of the IP-level processing involved in the forwarding of IP traffic in software rather than hardware. High-speed LANs and high-performance layer 2 switches may pump millions of packets per second whereas a software-based router may only be able to handle less than a million packets per second. To accommodate the higher traffic loads associated with today's high-speed LANs, a number of vendors have developed layer 3 switches, which implement the packet-forwarding logic of the router in hardware. Hence, a layer 3 switch can be described as a hardware-based router.

There are various layer 3 schemes on the market, but fundamentally they fall into two categories: packet-by-packet and flow based. The packet-by-packet layer 3 switch operates in the identical fashion as a traditional router. However, because the forwarding logic is in hardware, the packet-by-packet switch can achieve an order of magnitude increase in performance compared to the software-based router.

A flow-based layer 3 switch tries to enhance performance by identifying flows of IP packets that have the same source and destination. This can be done by observing ongoing traffic or by using a special flow label in the packet header (allowed in IPv6 but not in IPv4; see Figure 8.7). Once a flow is identified, a predefined route can be established through the network to speed up the forwarding process. Again, huge performance increases over a pure software-based router are achieved.

Figure 13.7 is a typical example of the approach taken to local networking in an organization with a large number of PCs and workstations (thousands to tens

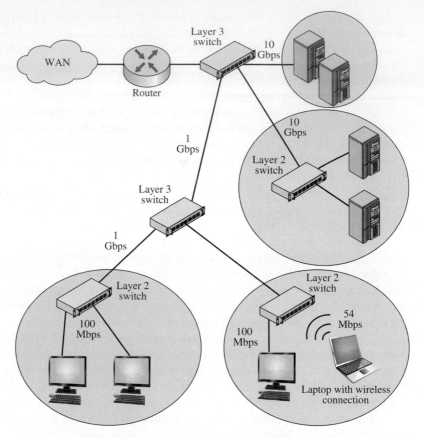

Figure 13.7 Typical Premises Network Configuration

of thousands). Desktop systems have links of 100 Mbps to 1000 Mbps (1 Gbps) into a LAN controlled by a layer 2 switch. Wireless LAN connectivity is also likely to be available for mobile users. Layer 3 switches are at the local network's core, forming a local backbone. Typically, these switches are interconnected at 1 Gbps or 10 Gbps and connect to layer 2 switches at 1 Gbps to 10 Gbps. Servers connect directly to layer 2 or layer 3 switches at 1 Gbps or possibly 10 Gbps. A lower-cost software-based router provides WAN connection. The circles in the figure identify separate LAN subnetworks; a MAC broadcast frame is limited to its own subnetwork.

13.3 HIGH-SPEED ETHERNET

Fast Ethernet

If one were to design a high-speed (100 Mbps or more) LAN from scratch, one would not choose CSMA/CD as the basis for the design. CSMA/CD is simple to implement and robust in the face of faults. However, it does not scale well. As the load on a bus increases, the number of collisions increases, degrading performance. Furthermore, as the data rate for a given system increases, performance also decreases. The reason for this is that at a higher data rate, a station can transmit more bits before it recognizes a collision, and therefore more wasted bits are transmitted when collisions occur.

These problems can be overcome. To accommodate higher loads, a system can be designed to have a number of different segments, interconnected with switching hubs. As mentioned previously, the switches can act as barriers, separating the LAN into collision domains, so that a collision in one domain does not spread to other domains. The use of switched Ethernet hubs in effect eliminates collisions, further increasing efficiency.

Despite some drawbacks to the use of CSMA/CD as a MAC protocol, Ethernet-style LANs have been developed that operate at 100 Mbps, 1 Gbps, and 10 Gbps. The reasons for this are instructive. From the vendor's point of view, the CSMA/CD protocol is well understood and vendors have experience building the hardware, firmware, and software for such systems. Scaling the system up to 100 Mbps or more may be easier than implementing an alternative protocol and topology. From the customer's point of view, it is relatively easy to integrate older Ethernet systems running at 10 Mbps with newer systems running at higher speeds if all the systems use the same frame format and the same access protocol. In other words, the continued use of Ethernet-style LANs is attractive because Ethernet is already there. This same situation is encountered in other areas of data communications. Vendors and customers do not always, or even in the majority of cases, choose the technically superior solution. Cost, ease of management, and other factors relating to the already-existing base of equipment are often more important factors in the selection of new LAN equipment than technically superior alternatives. This is the reason that Ethernet-style systems continue to dominate the LAN market and show every sign of continuing to do so in the foreseeable future.

Fast Ethernet refers to a set of specifications developed by the IEEE 802.3 committee to provide a low-cost, Ethernet-compatible LAN operating at 100 Mbps. The blanket designation for these standards is 100BASE-T. The committee defined a number of alternatives to be used with different transmission media.

Table 13.3 summarizes key characteristics of the 100BASE-T options. All of the 100BASE-T options use the IEEE 802.3 MAC protocol and frame format. 100BASE-X refers to a set of options that use the physical medium

Table 13.3   IEEE 802.3 100-Mbps Physical Layer Medium Alternatives

	100BASE-TX		100BASE-FX	100BASE-T4
Transmission Medium	2 pair, STP	2 pair, Category 5 UTP	2 optical fibers	4 pair, Category 3, 4, or 5 UTP
Maximum Segment Length	100 m	100 m	100 m	100 m
Network Span	200 m	200 m	400 m	200 m

specifications. All of the 100BASE-X schemes use two physical links between nodes: one for transmission and one for reception. 100BASE-TX makes use of shielded twisted pair (STP) or high-quality (Category 5e or higher) UTP. (See Chapter 12 for a discussion of Category 3 and Category 5 cables.) 100BASE-FX uses optical fiber.

For all of the 100BASE-T options, the topology is similar to that of 10BASE-T, namely a star-wire topology.

A traditional Ethernet 10 Mbps bus LAN is half duplex: A station can either transmit or receive a frame, but it cannot do both simultaneously. With full-duplex operation, a station can transmit and receive simultaneously. In a 100-Mbps Ethernet running in full-duplex mode, the theoretical transfer rate becomes 200 Mbps. To operate in full-duplex mode, the attached stations must have full-duplex adapter cards; these are now standard equipment in switched Ethernet environments.

The central points in a fully-switched Ethernet network are the switches. Each station attaches to a switch and the link between the switch and the station is essentially a separate collision domain. In full-duplex Ethernet LANs, traffic can be simultaneously flowing in both directions between the station and the switch, which essentially means that there are no collisions and the CSMA/CD algorithm is no longer needed. However, the same 802.3 MAC frame format is used and the attached stations can continue to execute the CSMA/CD algorithm, even though there are no collisions to be detected.

Gigabit Ethernet

The strategy for Gigabit Ethernet is the same as that for Fast Ethernet. While defining a new medium and transmission specification, Gigabit Ethernet retains the CSMA/CD protocol and frame format of its 10-Mbps and 100-Mbps predecessors. It is compatible with both 100BASE-T and 10BASE-T, preserving a smooth migration path. Most business organizations have moved to 100BASE-T and many have jumped to Gigabit Ethernet for at least some of their LANs. These LANs are putting huge traffic loads on backbone networks, which further increases demand for Gigabit Ethernet and 10 Gigabit Ethernet.

Figure 13.8 shows a typical application of Gigabit Ethernet. A 1-/10-Gbps LAN switch provides backbone connectivity for central servers and high-speed workgroup switches. Each workgroup LAN switch supports both 1-Gbps links, to connect to the backbone LAN switch and to support high-performance workgroup servers, and 100-Mbps links, to support high-performance workstations, servers, and 100-/1000-Mbps LAN switches.

The current 1-Gbps specification for IEEE 802.3 includes the following physical layer alternatives (Figure 13.9):

- **1000BASE-LX:** This long-wavelength option supports duplex links of up to 550 m of 62.5-μm or 50-μm multimode fiber or up to 5 km of 10-μm single-mode fiber. Wavelengths are in the range of 1270–1355 nm.
- **1000BASE-SX:** This short-wavelength option supports duplex links of up to 275 m using 62.5-μm multimode or up to 550 m using 50-μm multimode fiber. Wavelengths are in the range of 770–860 nm.

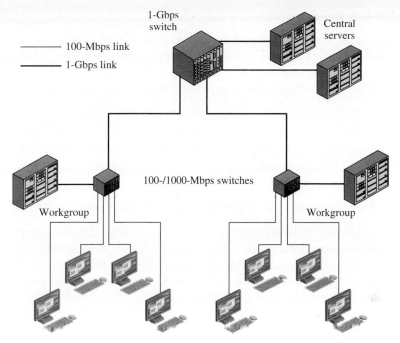

Figure 13.8   Example Gigabit Ethernet Configuration

- **1000BASE-CX:** This option supports 1-Gbps links among devices located within a single room or equipment rack, using copper jumpers (specialized STP cable that spans no more than 25 m). Each link is composed of a separate STP running in each direction.

- **1000BASE-T:** This option makes use of four pairs of Category 5 UTP to support devices over a range of up to 100 m.

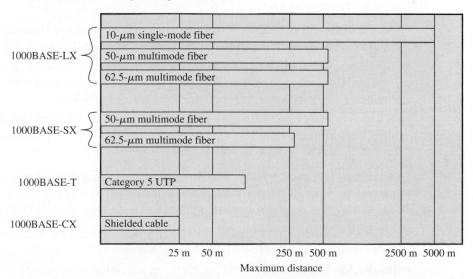

Figure 13.9   Gigabit Ethernet Medium Options (log scale)

10–Gbps Ethernet

In recent years, 10-Gbps Ethernet switches have made considerable inroads in the LAN market. The principal driving requirement for 10 Gigabit Ethernet is the increase in Internet and intranet traffic. A number of factors contribute to the explosive growth in both Internet and intranet traffic:

- An increase in the number of network connections
- An increase in the connection speed of each end-station (e.g., 10-Mbps users moving to 100 Mbps, analog 56-kbps users moving to DSL and cable modems)
- An increase in the deployment of bandwidth-intensive applications such as high-quality video
- An increase in Web hosting and application hosting traffic

Initially, network managers are using 10-Gbps Ethernet to provide high-speed, local backbone interconnection between large-capacity switches. As the demand for bandwidth increases, 10-Gbps Ethernet will be deployed throughout the entire network and will include data center, backbone, and campus-wide connectivity. This technology enables Internet service providers (ISPs) and network service providers (NSPs) to create very high-speed links at a low cost, between co-located, carrier-class switches and routers.

The technology also allows the construction of metropolitan area networks (MANs) and WANs that connect geographically dispersed LANs between campuses or points of presence (PoPs). Thus, Ethernet now competes with ATM and other wide area transmission/networking technologies. Carrier Ethernet, Metro Ethernet, and Wide Area Ethernet services are increasingly common components of enterprise networks. In most cases where the primary form of business communications traffic is data and TCP/IP is the preferred mode of transport, 10-Gbps Ethernet provides substantial value over ATM transport for both network end users and service providers:

- No expensive, bandwidth-consuming conversion between Ethernet packets and ATM cells is required; the network is Ethernet, end to end.
- The combination of IP and Ethernet offers quality of service and traffic policing capabilities that approach those provided by ATM, so that advanced traffic engineering technologies are available to users and providers.
- A wide variety of standard optical interfaces (wavelengths and link distances) have been specified for 10-Gbps Ethernet, optimizing its operation and cost for LAN, MAN, or WAN applications.

Maximum link distances for 10-Gbps Ethernet ranges from 300 m to 40 km. The links operate in full-duplex mode only, using a variety of optical fiber physical media. Four physical layer options are defined for 10-Gbps Ethernet (Figure 13.10):

- **10GBASE-S (short):** Designed for 850-nm transmission on multimode fiber. This medium can achieve distances up to 300 m.
- **10GBASE-L (long):** Designed for 1310-nm transmission on single-mode fiber. This medium can achieve distances up to 10 km.

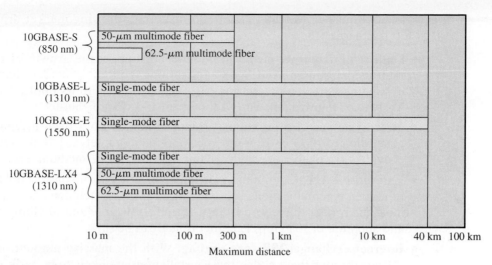

Figure 13.10   10-Gbps Ethernet Distance Options (log scale)

- **10GBASE-E (extended):** Designed for 1550-nm transmission on single mode fiber. This medium can achieve distances up to 40 km.
- **10GBASE-LX4:** Designed for 1310-nm transmission on single-mode or multi-mode fiber. This medium can achieve distances up to 10 km. This medium uses wavelength-division multiplexing (WDM) to multiplex the bit stream across four light waves.

100–Gbps Ethernet

Ethernet is widely deployed and is the preferred technology for wired local area networking. Ethernet dominates enterprise LANs, broadband access, and data center networking, and has also become popular for communication across MANs and even WANs. Further, it is now the preferred carrier wire line vehicle for bridging wireless technologies, such as Wi-Fi and WiMAX, into local Ethernet networks.

This popularity of Ethernet technology is due to the availability of cost-effective, reliable, and interoperable networking products from a variety of vendors. Over the years, a number of industry consortiums have participated in the development of ever-faster versions of Ethernet, including the Fast Ethernet Alliance (100 Mbps), the Gigabit Ethernet Alliance, the 10 Gigabit Ethernet Alliance, the Ethernet Alliance, and the Road to 100G Alliance. As a testament to the continuing evolution of Ethernet, the first three of the alliances just mentioned no longer exist. The Ethernet Alliance is devoted to promoting the development of Ethernet, whatever the speed. The Road to 100G Alliance is focused on the development of standards and technologies for 100-Gbps Ethernet.

As this alliance evolution reflects, the development of converged and unified communications, the evolution of data centers, and the continuing expansion of VoIP, TVoIP, and Web 2.0 applications have driven the need for ever-faster Ethernet switches. [HUFF06] lists the following market drivers for 100-Gbps Ethernet:

- **Data center/Internet media providers:** To support the growth of Internet multimedia content and Web applications, content providers have been expanding data centers, pushing 10-Gbps Ethernet to its limits. These are likely to be high-volume early adopters of 100-Gbps Ethernet.

- **Metro-video/service providers:** Video on demand has been driving a new generation of 10-Gbps Ethernet metropolitan/core network buildouts. These providers are likely to be high-volume adopters in the medium term.

- **Enterprise LANs:** Continuing growth in convergence of voice/video/data and in unified communications is driving up network switch demands. However, most enterprises still rely on 1-Gbps or a mix of 1-Gbps and 10-Gbps Ethernet, and adoption of 100-Gbps Ethernet is likely to be slow.

- **Internet exchanges/ISP core routing:** With the massive amount of traffic flowing through these nodes, these installations are likely to be early adopters of 100-Gbps Ethernet.

In 2007, the IEEE 802.3 working group authorized the *IEEE P802.3ba 40Gb/s and 100Gb/s Ethernet Task Force.* Table 13.4 indicates the physical layer objectives for this task force. As can be seen, these high-speed switches will be standardized to operate at distances from 1 m to 40 km over a variety of physical media.

An example of the application of 100-Gbps Ethernet is shown in Figure 13.11, taken from [NOWE07]. The trend at large data centers, with substantial banks of blade servers,[1] is the deployment of 10-Gbps ports on individual servers to handle the massive multimedia traffic provided by these servers. Such arrangements are stressing the on-site switches needed to interconnect large numbers of servers.

Table 13.4 Media Options for 40-Gbps and 100-Gbps Ethernet

	40 Gbps	100 Gbps
1-m backplane	40GBASE-KR4	
10-m copper	40GBASE-CR4	1000GBASE-CR10
100-m multimode fiber	40GBASE-SR4	1000GBASE-SR10
10-km single-mode fiber	40GBASE-LR4	1000GBASE-LR4
40-km single-mode fiber		1000GBASE-ER4

Naming nomenclature:
  Copper: K = backplane; C = cable assembly
  Optical: S = short reach (100m); L = long reach (10 km); E = extended long reach (40 km)
  Coding scheme: R = 64B/66B block coding
  Final number: number of lanes (copper wires or fiber wavelengths)

---

[1]A blade server is a server architecture that houses multiple server modules ("blades") in a single chassis. It is widely used in data centers to save space and improve system management. Either self-standing or rack mounted, the chassis provides the power supply, and each blade has its own processor, memory, and hard disk.

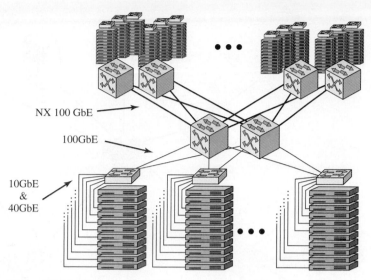

Figure 13.11   Example 100-Gbps Ethernet Configuration for Massive Blade Server Sites

A 100-Gigabit Ethernet rate was proposed to provide the bandwidth required to handle the increased traffic load. It is expected that 100 Gigabit Ethernet will be deployed in switch uplinks inside the data center as well as providing interbuilding, intercampus, MAN, and WAN connections for enterprise networks.

The success of Fast Ethernet, Gigabit Ethernet, and 10-Gbps Ethernet highlights the importance of network management concerns in choosing a network technology. Both ATM and Fibre Channel, explored subsequently, may be technically superior choices for a high-speed backbone, because of their flexibility and scalability. However, the Ethernet alternatives offer compatibility with existing installed LANs, network management software, and applications. This compatibility has accounted for the survival of 30-year-old technology in today's fast-evolving network environment.

13.4 VIRTUAL LANs

Figure 13.12 shows a relatively common type of hierarchical LAN configuration. In this example, the devices on the LAN are organized into four groups, each served by a LAN switch. The three lower groups might correspond to different departments, which are physically separated, and the upper group could correspond to a centralized server farm or data center that is used by all the departments.

Let us consider the transmission of a single MAC frame from workstation X. Suppose the destination MAC address in the frame (see Figure 12.9) is workstation Y. This frame is transmitted from X to the local switch, which then directs the frame along the link to Y. If X transmits a frame addressed to Z or W, then its local switch routes the MAC frame through the appropriate switches to the intended destination. All these are examples of *unicast addressing*, in which

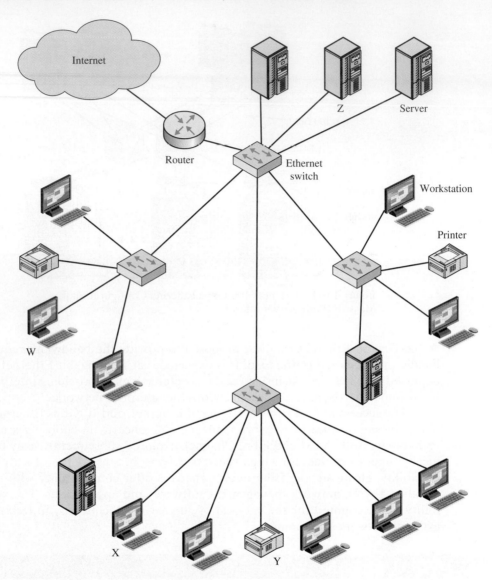

Figure 13.12 A LAN Configuration

the destination address in the MAC frame designates a unique destination. A MAC frame may also contain a *broadcast address*, in which case the destination MAC address indicates that all devices on the LAN should receive a copy of the frame. Thus, if X transmits a frame with a broadcast destination address, all of the devices on all of the switches in Figure 13.12 receive a copy of the frame. The total collection of devices that receive broadcast frames from each other is referred to as a *broadcast domain*.

In many situations, a broadcast frame is used for a purpose, such as network management or the transmission of some type of alert, that has a relatively local significance. Thus, in Figure 13.12, if a broadcast frame has information that is only useful to a particular department, then transmission capacity is wasted on the other portions of the LAN and on the other switches.

One simple approach to improving efficiency is to physically partition the LAN into separate broadcast domains, as shown in Figure 13.13. We now have four separate LANs connected by a router. In this case, an IP packet from X intended for Z is handled as follows. The IP layer at X determines that the next hop to the destination is via router V. This information is handed down to X's MAC layer which prepares a MAC frame with a destination MAC address of router V. When V receives the

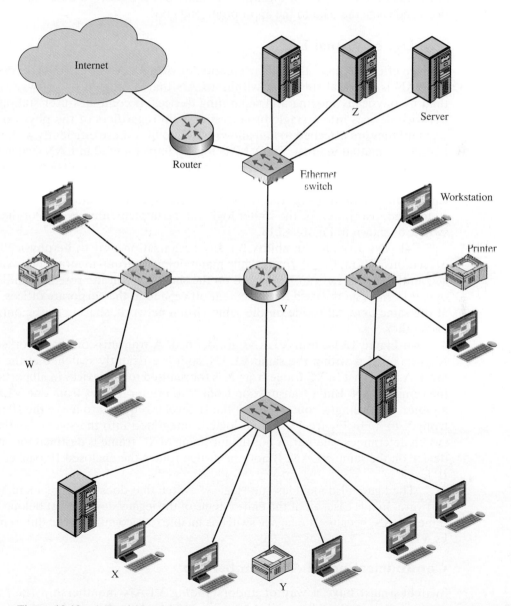

Figure 13.13 A Partitioned LAN

frame, it strips off the MAC header, determines the destination, and encapsulates the IP packet in a MAC frame with a destination MAC address of Z. This frame is then sent to the appropriate Ethernet switch for delivery.

The drawback to this approach is that the traffic pattern may not correspond to the physical distribution of devices. For example, some departmental workstations may generate a lot of traffic with one of the central servers. Further, as the networks expand, more routers are needed to separate users into broadcast domains and provide connectivity among broadcast domains. Routers introduce more latency than switches because the router must process more of the packet to determine destinations and route the data to the appropriate end node.

The Use of Virtual LANs

A more effective alternative is the creation of virtual LANs (VLANs). In essence, a VLAN is a logical subgroup within a LAN that is created by software rather than by physically moving and separating devices. It combines user stations and network devices into a single broadcast domain regardless of the physical LAN segment they are attached to and allows traffic to flow more efficiently within populations of mutual interest. The VLAN logic is implemented in LAN switches and functions at the MAC layer. Because the objective is to isolate traffic within the VLAN, in order to link from one VLAN to another, a router is required. Routers can be implemented as separate devices, so that traffic from one VLAN to another is directed to a router, or the router logic can be implemented as part of the LAN switch, as shown in Figure 13.14.

VLANs provide the ability for any organization unit to be physically dispersed throughout the company while maintaining its group identity. For example, accounting personnel can be located on the shop floor, in the research and development center, in the cash disbursement office, and in the corporate offices, while at the same time, all reside on the same virtual network, sharing traffic only with each other.

In Figure 13.14, four VLANs are defined. A transmission from workstation X to server Z is within the same VLAN, so it is efficiently switched at the MAC level. A broadcast MAC frame from X is transmitted to all devices in all portions of the same VLAN. But a transmission from X to printer Y goes from one VLAN to another. Accordingly, router logic at the IP level is required to move the IP packet from X to Y. In Figure 13.14, that logic is integrated into the switch, so that the switch determines whether or not the incoming MAC frame is destined for another device on the same VLAN. If not, the switch routes the enclosed IP packet at the IP level.

The figure also includes one "legacy" switch that does not implement VLAN software. In this case, all of the end systems of the legacy device must belong to the same VLAN, because the legacy switch is unable to recognize traffic differentiated by VLAN.

Communicating VLAN Membership

Switches must have a way of understanding VLAN membership (i.e., which stations belong to which VLAN) when network traffic arrives from other

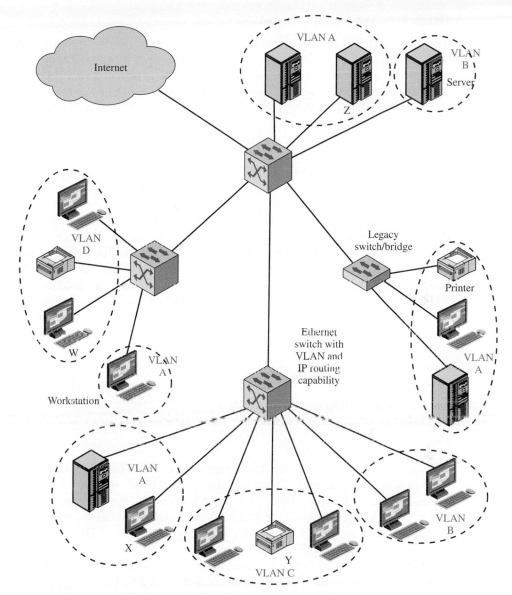

Figure 13.14   A VLAN Configuration

switches; otherwise, VLANs would be limited to a single switch. One possibility is to configure the information manually or with some type of network management signaling protocol, so that switches can associate incoming frames with the appropriate VLAN.

A more common approach is frame tagging, in which a header is typically inserted into each frame on interswitch trunks to uniquely identify to which VLAN a particular MAC-layer frame belongs. The IEEE 802 committee has developed a standard for frame tagging, IEEE 802.1Q, which we examine in the next section.

IEEE 802.1Q VLAN Standard

The IEEE 802.1Q standard, last updated in 2005, defines the operation of VLAN bridges and switches that permits the definition, operation, and administration of VLAN topologies within a bridged/switched LAN infrastructure. In this section, we will concentrate on the application of this standard to 802.3 LANs.

Recall that a VLAN is an administratively configured broadcast domain, consisting of a subset of end stations attached to a LAN. A VLAN is not limited to one switch but can span multiple interconnected switches. In that case, traffic between switches must indicate VLAN membership. This is accomplished in 802.1Q by inserting a tag with a VLAN identifier (VID) with a value in the range from 1 to 4094. Each VLAN in a LAN configuration is assigned a globally unique VID. By assigning the same VID to end systems on many switches, one or more VLAN broadcast domains can be extended across a large network. The tag also contains a priority level.

Figure 13.14 illustrates a LAN configuration that includes three switches that implement 802.1Q and one "legacy" switch or bridge that does not. The MAC frames that traverse trunks between VLAN-aware switches include the 802.1Q tag. This tag is stripped off before a frame is routed to a legacy switch. For end systems connected to a VLAN-aware switch, the MAC frame may or may not include the tag, depending on the implementation. The important point is that the tag is used between VLAN-aware switches so that appropriate routing and frame handling can be performed.

13.5 POWER OVER ETHERNET

Power over Ethernet (PoE) is another form of Ethernet that is increasingly found in enterprise networks. As the name suggests, PoE makes it possible to distribute both power and data using Ethernet cabling. The IEEE standard for PoE requires Category 3 cable for low power levels and Category 5 cable or higher for high power levels. PoE uses two or more twisted pairs in the Ethernet cable to distribute power; the other pairs are used to transmit data. PoE switches and DC battery arrays are the primary power supplies in PoE networks.

PoE provides network designers with more flexibility for deploying LAN devices. In many instances, PoE eliminates the need to locate equipment close to AC power sources. As is illustrated in Figure 13.15, PoE can be used to power VoIP phones, Wi-Fi access points, and LCD monitors. PoE can also be used to distribute power to IP surveillance cameras, Web cams, industrial devices (such as sensors, controllers, and meters), lighting controllers, remote network switches, access control devices (such as keyless entry and intercom systems), and remote POS (point of sale) kiosks. Industry pundits predict that PoE will increasingly be used to power the motherboards of network-attached workstations.

There are numerous advantages of PoE. For example, PoE can be used in situations where AC power would be expensive, infeasible, or inconvenient to use to power network devices. While USB could also be an option in such situations, PoE is often a superior choice to either USB or AC wire because:

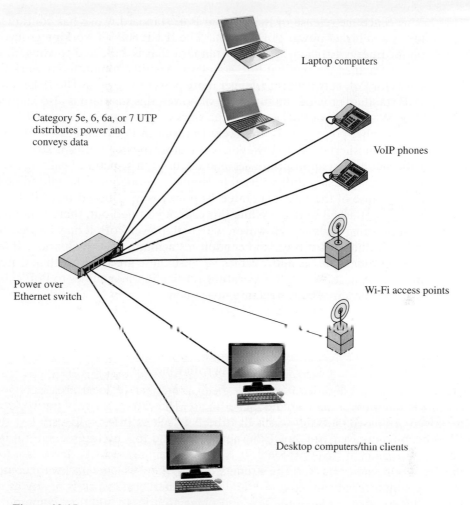

Laptop computers

Category 5e, 6, 6a, or 7 UTP
distributes power and
conveys data

VoIP phones

Power over
Ethernet switch

Wi-Fi access points

Desktop computers/thin clients

Figure 13.15   Power over Ethernet (PoE)

- It can be deployed over Category 5 UTP, which is less expensive than using USB repeaters or AC wire.

- Gigabit connections are possible; this is faster than USB 2.0 and AC power line networking capabilities. Furthermore, a 10-Gbps PoE standard is being developed.

- Companies with multiple international locations can deploy PoE everywhere without regard to local differences in AC power levels, plugs, outlets, or reliability. It can be deployed in buildings without having to worry about AC cabling building codes.

Like other versions of Ethernet, PoE standards continue to evolve. The original IEEE 802.3af-2003 PoE standard provides up to 15.4 W of direct current (DC) power (or a minimum of 44 V DC and 350 mA) to each device. This standard only assures 12.95 W to each powered device because some power is dissipated in the cable.

Since the release of the original PoE standard, work has continued on both lower and higher power PoE systems. The IEEE 802.3af working group is working on an Energy Efficient Ethernet standard that is expected to consume 60% less electricity than the original PoE standard. Another committee is working on standards for PoE networks that deliver more power to devices. The IEEE 802.3at-2009 PoE standard provides up to 25.5 W of power; this standard is also known as PoE+. A 60 W standard of PoE is also in the works.

Higher power levels are likely to result in PoE being used to power workstation motherboards. However, with more power being distributed through Ethernet cables, appropriate accommodations in structured cabling schemes may be necessary. Using PoE with cable bundles is sometimes thought to be a fire hazard because of the heat generated as power is distributed from PoE switches to network attached devices. While this cannot be ruled out, there is not a great deal of supporting evidence. However, with high-power PoE, it may be wise to separate cables within cables trays and conduit to facilitate heat dissipation. It is also wise to use Category 6, 6a, and 7 cables because these are superior than Category 5e in dissipating heat. Adding temperature-sensing thermocouples to PoE cable bundles may also be a wise infrastructure investment.

APPLICATION NOTE

Networking with Ethernet

Over the past two decades there have been a number of local area network (LAN) protocols, but most of them are no longer in use. The vast majority of networks currently deployed are based on faster forms of Ethernet such as 100/1000BASE-TX, 100BASE-FX, Gigabit, and even 10-Gbps Ethernet. Today, and for the foreseeable future, Ethernet is the dominant LAN protocol. It is even beginning to make inroads into the last mile common carrier market. The strength of Ethernet lies in its backward compatibility, industry support, and simplicity. Setting up an Ethernet network is nearly as simple as taking the equipment out of the box and plugging it in. In addition, common Ethernet components are becoming very inexpensive. In contrast, maintaining or installing any of the less popular, legacy systems can be very costly.

While the "under the hood" operation of Ethernet makes for good engineering reading, there are some very practical aspects of Ethernet that are good to know in order to get the most out of the network. An organization must analyze its communication requirements and decide how much bandwidth is required for present and future use, what applications will be running over the network architecture, and how much money will be spent.

For several years, most networking equipment sold have 10/100/1000 Ethernet ports. This means that the equipment port and the network interface card (NIC) in the computer will "auto-sense" the network conditions and determine what speed is available. However, computer bus speeds and operating system delays represent barriers to actually making use of a network running at gigabit speeds. In addition, there are not very many computers that need to send that much data. For standard machines, the 100-Mbps or 100/1000 cards are usually sufficient, and this is not likely to change in the near future. Even without gigabit capability, network cards and devices can be set for full-duplex operation, which increases the two-way throughput to 200 Mbps.

For new installations or planned network upgrades, the purchase of gigabit equipment may certainly be justified. This is especially true with the growth of "big data" that many business networks can expect. However, the cost per port for enterprise level equipment can still be expensive, and for many applications, the cost of this high-speed equipment may not justify itself outside of specific situations. Gigabit, 10-Gbps, and even 40-Gbps Ethernet networks are well suited to fiber backbone connections such as those between wiring closets, connections going off-site, and hard working servers. Of course fiber adds to the cost of any implementation.

While virtually no new networks will be installed at less than 100 Mbps, older networks may run at slower speeds and have a mix of technologies. Any new equipment that is purchased in such environments should be of the 10/100/1000 models to ensure compatibility with both the old system and any newer equipment purchased. However, new equipment will only transmit as fast as is permitted by the wiring. Older Category 5 wiring will not facilitate gigabit speeds. Even Category 5e wiring may not support the higher speeds depending on distance. The problem is that while replacing equipment represents a certain fixed cost, when the cable plant itself must be replaced the cost can increase dramatically.

Hubs are another item that seems destined for extinction. In early Ethernet networks, the cost per port for bridges and switches made the transition to them painfully expensive. However, in the last few years the cost for these components has been reduced to points that more than justify their purchase. The advanced features offered by switches make it easier to manage and secure networks. For example, many switches come with built-in statistics and support virtual LANs (VLANs). In addition, switches offer firewall filtering and fault isolation as part of their standard operation.

For any new installation the shopping list should include the best quality UTP cabling, network cards capable of 10/100/1000 full-duplex operation, and switches with ports capable of 10/100/1000 full-duplex operation. When upgrading the old system, network administrators should follow these guidelines with the understanding that for best performance the equipment should be matched with the appropriate cabling infrastructure.

13.6 SUMMARY

High-speed LANs have emerged as a critical element of corporate information systems. Such LANs are needed not only to provide an on-premises backbone for linking departmental LANs, but also to support the high-performance requirements of graphics-based client/server and intranet applications.

For most applications, Fast Ethernet and Gigabit Ethernet technologies dominate corporate high-speed LAN choices. These systems involve the least risk and cost for managers for a number of reasons, including compatibility with the existing large Ethernet installed base, maturity of the basic technology, and compatibility with existing network management and configuration software.

In most cases, an organization will have multiple LANs that need to be inter-connected. The simplest approach to meeting this requirement is the bridge or layer 2 switch; however, in enterprise networks, layer 3 switches may also be needed to ensure performance.

Power over Ethernet (PoE) is increasing in popularity. With PoE, the same Ethernet cable can be used to transmit data and distribute power to attached devices.

13.7 KEY TERMS, REVIEW QUESTIONS, AND PROBLEMS

Key Terms

bridge	Fibre Channel	power over Ethernet
cut-through switch	frame	(PoE)
Ethernet	frame check sequence (FCS)	store-and-forward switch
Fast Ethernet	hub	switch

Review Questions

13.1 Why is it important for business data communication students to have a fundamental understanding of Ethernet?

13.2 Explain why data rates of 100 Mbps, 1 Gbps, and 10 Gbps are increasingly common in business networks.

13.3 What is CSMA/CD? How does it operate?

13.4 What functions are performed by a bridge?

13.5 What is the difference between a hub and a layer 2 switch?

13.6 What are the factors responsible for the explosive growth in both Internet and intranet traffic?

13.7 What are the differences between a bridge and a switch?

13.8 What is the difference between a layer 2 switch and a layer 3 switch?

13.9 What is the use of Fast Ethernet?

13.10 What are the transmission medium options for Gigabit Ethernet?

13.11 Name four physical layer options that are defined for 10-Gbps Ethernet.

13.12 What are the characteristics of virtual local area networks (VLANs)?

13.13 What is power over Ethernet (PoE)?

13.14 Why is PoE increasingly popular in business networks?

Problems

13.1 Determine the type of network interface card installed in your computer? Describe this card's major properties including its speed(s), layer 2 protocol, and the type of medium used to connect to the communication medium.

13.2 Using capture programs such as Wireshark and built-in programs like ping, nslookup, and ipconfig, find and capture screen shots showing the following information:
   a. Your computer's MAC address (using ipconfig or ifconfig).
   b. The code value for IP in the frames you have captured. This can be found in the control field of the Ethernet frame.

13.3 Use Wireshark to capture frames transmitted by your computer. (Hint: After starting the capture, launch a browser and visit several Web sites.) Explore one or more of the captured frames to a level that illustrates destination and source MAC addresses. Does your MAC address match the one found in Problem 13.2a?

13.4 An argument that has been ongoing for some time now involves the question as to whether ATM or Gigabit Ethernet is the best choice for a high-speed networking solution. Do some Internet research that compares these two technologies and formulate a 500–1000 word position paper outlining a potential scenario for each technology where it might constitute the optimal solution for a business.

13.5 Explain the advantages of having the FCS field of IEEE 802.3 frames in the trailer of the frame rather than in the header of the frame.

13.6 Token-Ring is an alternative (but largely considered obsolete) technology to Ethernet. Do some Internet research on Token-Ring to identify the major reasons why it is relatively rare in today's networks. Summarize your findings in a 500–750 word paper or a 5–8 slide PowerPoint presentation.

13.7 Find and view multiple YouTube videos that illustrate how CSMA/CD works. Identify the URLs of three videos that you think do an especially good job of illustrating CSMA/CD. If you only could choose one to recommend to other business data communications students, which would you select? Why?

13.8 Find and view multiple YouTube videos that compare hubs and switches. Identify the URLs of three videos that you think do an especially good job of illustrating the differences between hubs and switches. If you only could choose one to recommend to other business data communications students, which would you select? Why?

13.9 Do some Internet research comparing the advantages and uses of store-and-forward and cut-through switches. Identify several situations in which store-and-forward switches are a better choice than a cut-through switch. Identify situations in which a cut-through switch is an appropriate choice. Summarize your finding in a 500–750 word paper or a 5–8 slide PowerPoint presentation.

13.10 Do some Internet research on how businesses use VLANs. Identify the business advantages of VLANs and cite several specific examples of how businesses benefit from VLAN creation and use. Summarize your findings in a 500–750 word paper or a 5–8 slide PowerPoint presentation.

13.11 Do some Internet research to find at least five images of power over Ethernet (PoE) that do an especially good job illustrating PoE capabilities and deployment essentials. Compose an 8–12 slide PowerPoint presentation on PoE that provides a clear explanation of what it is, why it is being deployed, how it is being used, and includes the illustrative images that you found while doing your PoE research.

13.12 Do some Internet research on the structured cabling implications of power over Ethernet (PoE) in business networks. Summarize your findings in a 500–1000 word paper or an 8–12 slide PowerPoint presentation.

13.13 Do some Internet research on power line networking alternatives to PoE in homes or small business networks. Identify the major characteristics of power line networks. Summarize your findings in a 500–1000 word paper or an 8–12 slide PowerPoint presentation.

CHAPTER 14

WIRELESS LANs

Wireless LANs have become a significant segment of the LAN market. Organizations are using wireless LANs as an indispensable adjunct to traditional wired LANs, to satisfy requirements for mobility, relocation, ad hoc networking, and coverage of locations difficult to wire.

This chapter provides a survey of wireless LANs. We begin with an overview that looks at the motivations for using wireless LANs and summarizes the various approaches in current use. Then, the most widely used wireless LAN schemes, IEEE 802.11, also known as Wi-Fi, is examined. Appendix H examines another popular scheme known as Bluetooth.

14.1 OVERVIEW

As the name suggests, a wireless LAN is one that makes use of a wireless transmission medium.

Wireless LAN Applications

Like wired LANs, such as Ethernet, wireless LANs (WLANs) provide connectivity within a limited geographic area. One key feature of WLANs, not readily provided by a wired LAN, is mobility: the ability to move around while remaining connected. WLANs are a necessity in a working environment in which staff need to be mobile but remain constantly connected to the local network. A good example of this is the need for doctors and nurses to access patient information, hospital records, and other medical information as they move about the hospital.

WLANs also provide outdoor connectivity. This is now found in many locations in the form of Wi-Fi "hot spots," which can be secured to allow employees to remain connected in the vicinity of the building, or unsecured, such as public access hot spots found in many municipalities.

WLANs are also useful as an adjunct to wired LANs, such as for connecting wired LANs in adjacent building where wired connection is difficult, expensive, or even impossible because of an intervening public area.

Figure 14.1 indicates a simple WLAN configuration that is typical of many environments. There is a backbone wired LAN, such as Ethernet, that supports servers, workstations, and one or more bridges or routers to link with other networks. In addition, there is a control module (CM) that acts as an interface to

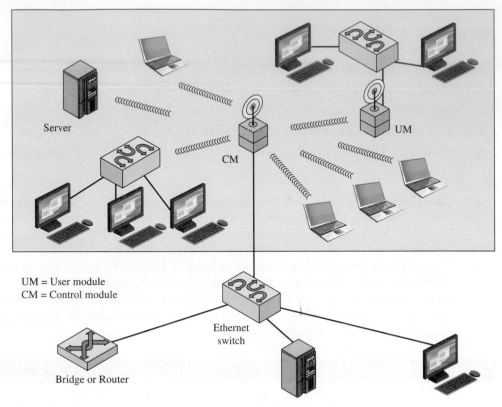

Figure 14.1   Example Single-Cell Wireless LAN Configuration

a WLAN. The control module includes either bridge or router functionality to link the WLAN to the backbone. It includes some sort of access control logic, such as a polling or token-passing scheme, to regulate the access from the end systems. Note that some of the end systems are standalone devices, such as a workstation or a server. Hubs or other user modules (UMs) that control a number of stations off a wired LAN may also be part of the WLAN configuration.

The configuration of Figure 14.1 can be referred to as a single-cell WLAN; all of the wireless end systems are within range of a single control module. Another common configuration, suggested by Figure 14.2, is a multiple-cell WLAN. In this case, there are multiple control modules interconnected by a wired LAN. Each control module supports a number of wireless end systems within its transmission range. For example, with an infrared LAN, transmission is limited to a single room; therefore, one cell is needed for each room in an office building that requires wireless support.

Wireless LAN Requirements

A WLAN must meet the same sort of requirements typical of any LAN, including high capacity, ability to cover short distances, full connectivity among attached stations, and broadcast capability. In addition, there are a number of requirements

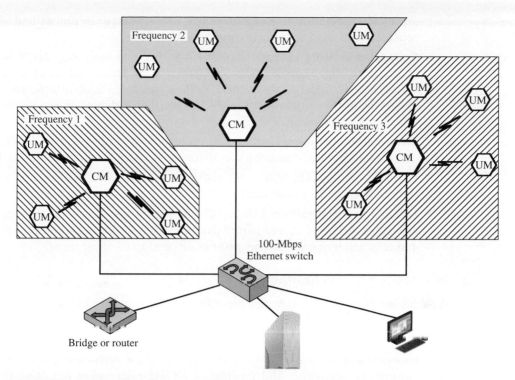

Figure 14.2   Example Multiple-Cell Wireless LAN Configuration

specific to the WLAN environment. The following are among the most important requirements for WLANs:

- **Throughput:** The medium access control (MAC) protocol should make as efficient use as possible of the wireless medium to maximize capacity.
- **Number of nodes:** WLANs may need to support hundreds of nodes across multiple cells.
- **Connection to backbone LAN:** In most cases, interconnection with stations on a wired backbone LAN is required. For infrastructure WLANs, this is easily accomplished through the use of control modules that connect to both types of LANs. There may also need to be accommodation for mobile users and ad hoc wireless networks.
- **Service area:** A typical coverage area for a WLAN has a diameter of 100–300 m.
- **Battery power consumption:** Mobile workers use battery-powered worksta- tions that need to have a long battery life when used with wireless adapters. This suggests that a MAC protocol that requires mobile nodes to monitor access points constantly or engage in frequent handshakes with a base station is inappropriate. Typical WLAN implementations have features to reduce power consumption while not using the network, such as a sleep mode.
- **Transmission robustness and security:** Unless properly designed, a WLAN may be interference prone and easily eavesdropped. The design of a WLAN

must permit reliable transmission even in a noisy environment and should provide some level of security from eavesdropping.

- **Collocated network operation:** As WLANs become more popular, it is quite likely for two or more WLANs to operate in the same area or in some area where interference between the LANs is possible. Such interference may thwart the normal operation of a MAC algorithm and may allow unauthorized access to a particular LAN.

- **License-free operation:** Users would prefer to buy and operate WLAN products without having to secure a license for the frequency band used by the LAN.

- **Handoff/roaming:** The MAC protocol used in the WLAN should enable mobile stations to move from one cell to another.

- **Dynamic configuration:** The MAC addressing and network management aspects of the LAN should permit dynamic and automated addition, deletion, and relocation of end systems without disruption to other users.

Wireless LAN Technology

WLANs are generally categorized according to the transmission technique that is used. All current WLAN products fall into one of the following categories:

- **Spread spectrum LANs:** This type of LAN makes use of spread spectrum transmission technology. In most cases, these LANs operate in the ISM (industrial, scientific, and medical) 2.4-GHz microwave bands so that no Federal Communications Commission (FCC) licensing is required for their use in the United States.

- **OFDM LANs:** For higher speeds, a technology known as orthogonal frequency division multiplexing is superior to spread spectrum, and products with this technology are now common. These LANs typically operate in either the 2.4-GHz band or the 5-GHz band.

- **Infrared (IR) LANs:** An individual cell of an IR LAN is limited to a single room, because infrared light does not penetrate opaque walls.

14.2 WI-FI ARCHITECTURE AND SERVICES

In 1990, the IEEE 802 Committee formed a new working group, IEEE 802.11, specifically devoted to WLANs, with a charter to develop a MAC protocol and physical medium specification. Since that time, the demand for WLANs, at different frequencies and data rates, has exploded. Keeping pace with this demand, the IEEE 802.11 working group has issued an ever-expanding list of standards (Table 14.1). Table 14.2 briefly defines key terms used in the IEEE 802.11 standard.

With any networking standard, there is a concern whether products from different vendors will successfully interoperate. To meet this concern, the Wireless Ethernet Compatibility Alliance (WECA), an industry consortium, was formed in 1999. This organization, subsequently renamed the **Wi-Fi (Wireless Fidelity) Alliance**, creates a test suite to certify interoperability for 802.11 products. The term

Table 14.1   Key IEEE 802.11 Task Groups

Standard	Scope
IEEE 802.11a	Physical layer: 5-GHz OFDM at rates from 6 to 54 Mbps
IEEE 802.11b	Physical layer: 2.4-GHz DSSS at 5.5 and 11 Mbps
IEEE 802.11c	Bridge operation at 802.11 MAC layer
IEEE 802.11d	Physical layer: Extend operation of 802.11 WLANs to new regulatory domains (countries)
IEEE 802.11e	MAC: Enhance to improve quality of service and enhance security mechanisms
IEEE 802.11g	Physical layer: Extend 802.11b to data rates >20 Mbps
IEEE 802.11i	MAC: Enhance security and authentication mechanisms
IEEE 802.11n	Physical/MAC: Enhancements to enable higher throughput
IEEE 802.11T	Recommended practice for the evaluation of 802.11 wireless performance
IEEE 802.11ac	Physical/MAC: Enhancements to support 0.5–1 Gbps in 5-GHz band
IEEE 802.11ad	Physical/MAC: Enhancements to support ≥1 Gbps in the 60-GHz band

Table 14.2   IEEE 802.11 Terminology

Access point (AP)	Any entity that has station functionality and provides access to the distribution system via the wireless medium for associated stations
Basic service set (BSS)	A set of stations controlled by a single coordination function
Coordination function	The logical function that determines when a station operating within a BSS is permitted to transmit and may be able to receive PDUs
Distribution system (DS)	A system used to interconnect a set of BSSs and integrated LANs to create an ESS
Extended service set (ESS)	A set of one or more interconnected BSSs and integrated LANs that appear as a single BSS to the LLC layer at any station associated with one of these BSSs
MAC protocol data unit (MPDU)	The unit of data exchanged between two peer MAC entities using the services of the physical layer
MAC service data unit (MSDU)	Information that is delivered as a unit between MAC users
Station	Any device that contains an IEEE 802.11 conformant MAC and physical layer

used for certified products is *Wi-Fi*. The Wi-Fi Alliance is concerned with a range of market areas for WLANs, including enterprise, home, and hot spots.

IEEE 802.11 Architecture

Figure 14.3 illustrates the model developed by the 802.11 working group. The smallest building block of a WLAN is a **basic service set (BSS)**, which consists of some number of stations executing the same MAC protocol and competing for access to the same shared wireless medium. A BSS may be isolated or it may connect to a backbone **distribution system (DS)** through an **access point (AP)**. The AP functions as a bridge and a relay point. In a BSS, client stations do not communicate directly with one another. Rather, if one station in the BSS wants to communicate with

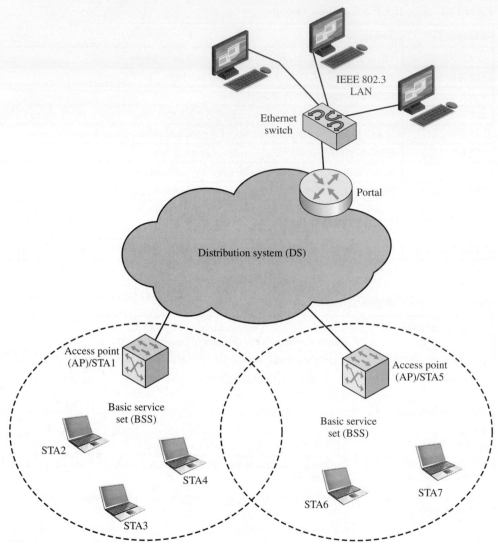

IEEE 802.3 LAN

Ethernet switch

Portal

Distribution system (DS)

Access point (AP)/STA1

Basic service set (BSS)

STA2

STA4

STA3

Access point (AP)/STA5

Basic service set (BSS)

STA6

STA7

Figure 14.3   Example WLAN Extended Service Set

another station in the same BSS, the MAC frame is first sent from the originating station to the AP, and then from the AP to the destination station. Similarly, a MAC frame from a station in the BSS to a remote station is sent from the local station to the AP and then relayed by the AP over the DS on its way to the destination station. The BSS generally corresponds to what is referred to as a cell in the literature. The DS can be a switch, a wired network, or a wireless network.

When all the stations in the BSS are mobile stations, with no connection to other BSSs, the BSS is called an **independent BSS (IBSS)**. An IBSS is typically an ad hoc network. In an IBSS, the stations all communicate directly, and no AP is involved.

A simple configuration is shown in Figure 14.3, in which each station belongs to a single BSS; that is, each station is within wireless range only of other stations within the same BSS. It is also possible for two BSSs to overlap geographically, so that a single station could participate in more than one BSS. Further, the association between a station and a BSS is dynamic. Stations may turn off, come within range, and go out of range.

An **extended service set (ESS)** consists of two or more BSSs interconnected by a distribution system. Typically, the distribution system is a wired backbone LAN but can be any communications network. The extended service set appears as a single logical LAN to the logical link control (LLC) level.

Figure 14.3 indicates that an AP is implemented as part of a station; the AP is the logic within a station that provides access to the DS by providing DS services in addition to acting as a station. To integrate the IEEE 802.11 architecture with a traditional wired LAN, a **portal** is used. The portal logic is implemented in a device, such as a bridge or router, that is part of the wired LAN and that is attached to the DS.

IEEE 802.11 Services

IEEE 802.11 defines nine services that need to be provided by the WLAN to achieve functionality equivalent to that which is inherent to wired LANs. The following are two ways of categorizing the services.

1. The service provider can be either the station or the DS. Station services are implemented in every 802.11 station, including AP stations. Distribution services are provided between BSSs; these services may be implemented in an AP or in another special-purpose device attached to the distribution system.

2. Three of the services are used to control IEEE 802.11 LAN access and confidentiality. Six of the services are used to support delivery of MAC service data units (MSDUs) between stations. The MSDU is a block of data passed down from the MAC user to the MAC layer; typically this is a LLC PDU. If the MSDU is too large to be transmitted in a single MAC frame, it may be fragmented and transmitted in a series of MAC frames.

Following the IEEE 802.11 document, we next discuss the services in an order designed to clarify the operation of an IEEE 802.11 ESS network. **MSDU delivery**, which is the basic service, has already been mentioned. Services related to security are introduced in Section 14.3 and discussed in Chapter 19.

DISTRIBUTION OF MESSAGES WITHIN A DS The two services involved with the distribution of messages within a DS are distribution and integration. **Distribution** is the primary service used by stations to exchange MAC frames when the frame must traverse the DS to get from a station in one BSS to a station in another BSS. For example, suppose a frame is to be sent from station 2 (STA 2) to STA 7 in Figure 14.3. The frame is sent from STA 2 to STA 1, which is the AP for this BSS. The AP gives the frame to the DS, which has the job of directing the frame to the AP associated with STA 5 in the target BSS. STA 5 receives the frame and forwards it to STA 7. How the message is transported through the DS is beyond the scope of the IEEE 802.11 standard.

If the two stations that are communicating are within the same BSS, then the distribution service logically goes through the single AP of that BSS.

The **integration** service enables transfer of data between a station on an IEEE 802.11 LAN and a station on an integrated IEEE 802.x LAN. The term *integrated* refers to a wired LAN that is physically connected to the DS and whose stations may be logically connected to an IEEE 802.11 LAN via the integration service. The integration service takes care of any address translation and media conversion logic required for the exchange of data.

ASSOCIATION-RELATED SERVICES The primary purpose of the MAC layer is to transfer MSDUs between MAC entities; this purpose is fulfilled by the distribution service. For that service to function, it requires information about stations within the ESS that is provided by the association-related services. Before the distribution service can deliver data to or accept data from a station, that station must be *associated*. Before looking at the concept of association, we need to describe the concept of mobility. The standard defines three transition types, based on mobility:

- **No transition:** A station of this type either is stationary or moves only within the direct communication range of the communicating stations of a single BSS.

- **BSS transition:** This is defined as a station movement from one BSS to another within the same ESS. In this case, delivery of data to the station requires that the addressing capability be able to recognize the new location of the station.

- **ESS transition:** This is defined as a station movement from a BSS in one ESS to a BSS within another ESS. This case is supported only in the sense that the station can move. Maintenance of upper-layer connections supported by 802.11 cannot be guaranteed. In fact, disruption of service is likely to occur.

To deliver a message within a DS, the distribution service needs to know where the destination station is located. Specifically, the DS needs to know the identity of the AP to which the message should be delivered in order for that message to reach the destination station. To meet this requirement, a station must maintain an association with the AP within its current BSS. Three services relate to this requirement:

- **Association:** Establishes an initial association between a station and an AP. Before a station can transmit or receive frames on a WLAN, its identity and address must be known. For this purpose, a station must establish an association with an AP within a particular BSS. The AP can then communicate this information to other APs within the ESS to facilitate routing and delivery of addressed frames.

- **Reassociation:** Enables an established association to be transferred from one AP to another, allowing a mobile station to move from one BSS to another.

- **Disassociation:** A notification from either a station or an AP that an existing association is terminated. A station should give this notification before leaving an ESS or shutting down. However, the MAC management facility protects itself against stations that disappear without notification.

14.3 IEEE 802.11 MAC AND PHYSICAL LAYER STANDARDS

IEEE 802.11 Medium Access Control

The IEEE 802.11 MAC layer covers three functional areas: reliable data delivery, access control, and security. In this section we examine reliable data delivery and access control. Security is covered in the Section 14.4.

RELIABLE DATA DELIVERY As with any wireless network, a WLAN using the IEEE 802.11 physical and MAC layers is subject to considerable unreliability. Noise, interference, and other propagation effects may result in the loss of a significant number of frames. Even with error-correction codes, a number of MAC frames may not successfully be received. This situation can be dealt with by reliability mechanisms at a higher layer, such as TCP. However, timers used for retransmission at higher layers are typically on the order of seconds. It is therefore more efficient to deal with errors at the MAC level. For this purpose, IEEE 802.11 includes a frame exchange protocol. When a station receives a data frame from another station, it returns an acknowledgment (ACK) frame to the source station. This exchange is treated as an atomic unit, not to be interrupted by a transmission from any other station. If the source does not receive an ACK within a short period of time, either because its data frame was damaged or because the returning ACK was damaged, the source retransmits the frame.

Thus, the basic data transfer mechanism in IEEE 802.11 involves an exchange of two frames. To further enhance reliability, a four-frame exchange may be used. In this scheme, a source first issues a Request to Send (RTS) frame to the destination. The destination then responds with a Clear to Send (CTS). After receiving the CTS, the source transmits the data frame, and the destination responds with an ACK. The RTS alerts all stations that are within reception range of the source that an exchange is under way; these stations refrain from transmission in order to avoid a collision between two frames transmitted at the same time. Similarly, the CTS alerts all stations that are within reception range of the destination that an exchange is under way. The RTS/CTS portion of the exchange is a required function of the MAC but may be disabled.

ACCESS CONTROL The 802.11 working group considered two types of proposals for a MAC algorithm: distributed access protocols, which, like Ethernet, distribute the decision to transmit among all the nodes using a carrier-sense mechanism; and centralized access protocols, which involve regulation of transmission by a centralized decision maker. A distributed access protocol makes sense for an ad hoc network of peer workstations and may also be attractive in other WLAN configurations that consist primarily of bursty traffic. A centralized access protocol is natural for configurations in which a number of wireless stations are interconnected with each other and some sort of base station that attaches to a backbone wired LAN; it is especially useful if some of the data are time sensitive or high priority.

The end result for 802.11 is a MAC algorithm called DFWMAC (distributed foundation wireless MAC) that provides a distributed access control mechanism with an optional centralized control built on top of that. Figure 14.4 illustrates the architecture. The lower sublayer of the MAC layer is the distributed coordination

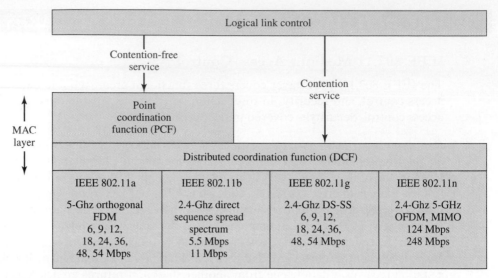

Figure 14.4   IEEE 802.11 Protocol Architecture

function (DCF). DCF uses an Ethernet-style contention algorithm to provide access to all traffic. Ordinary asynchronous traffic directly uses DCF. The point coordination function (PCF) is a centralized MAC algorithm used to provide contention-free service; this is done by polling stations in turn. Higher-priority traffic, or traffic with greater timing requirements, makes use of the PCF. PCF is built on top of DCF and exploits features of DCF to assure access for its users. Finally, the logical link control (LLC) layer provides an interface to higher layers and performs basic link layer functions such as error control.

IEEE 802.11 Physical Layer

The physical layer for IEEE 802.11 has been issued in five stages. The first part, simply called **IEEE 802.11**, includes the MAC layer and three physical layer specifications, two in the 2.4-GHz band (ISM) and one in the infrared, all operating at 1 and 2 Mbps. **IEEE 802.11a** operates in the 5-GHz band at data rates up to 54 Mbps. **IEEE 802.11b** operates in the 2.4-GHz band at 5.5 and 11 Mbps. **IEEE 802.11g** also operates in the 2.4-GHz band, at data rates up to 54 Mbps. Finally, **IEEE 802.11n** operates in either the 2.4-GHz band or the 5-GHz band with data rates in the hundreds of Gbps. Table 14.3 provides some details. We look at each of these in turn.

ORIGINAL IEEE 802.11   Three physical media are defined in the original 802.11 standard:

- Direct-sequence spread spectrum (DSSS) operating in the 2.4-GHz ISM band, at data rates of 1 and 2 Mbps
- Frequency-hopping spread spectrum (FHSS) operating in the 2.4-GHz ISM band, at data rates of 1 and 2 Mbps
- Infrared at 1 and 2 Mbps, operating at a wavelength between 850 and 950 nm

Table 14.3   IEEE 802.11 Physical Layer Standards

	802.11a	802.11b	802.11g	802.11n
Peak data throughput*	23 Mbps	6 Mbps	23 Mbps	60 Mbps (20-MHz channel)
				90 Mbps (40-MHz channel)
Peak signaling rate	54 Mbps	11 Mbps	54 Mbps	124 Mbps (20-MHz channel)
				248 Mbps (40-MHz channel)
RF band	5 GHz	2.4 GHz	2.4 GHz	2.4 GHz or 5 GHz
Channel width	20 MHz	20 MHz	20 Mhz	20 MHz or 40 MHz
Number of spatial streams	1	1	1	1, 2, 3, or 4

*This is the actual data throughput you get with real equipment under ideal conditions. Real-world performance is lower than this due to noise. Capacity is also shared among wireless clients. When two devices use the same access point, the capacity is typically divided in two, though it's possible some clients will use more of the capacity than others. *Source*: [OU07].

The infrared option never gained market support. The other two schemes use spread spectrum approaches. In essence, spread spectrum involves the use of a much wider bandwidth than is actually necessary to support a given data rate. The purpose of using a wider bandwidth is to minimize interference and drastically reduce the error rate. In the case of FHSS, spread spectrum is achieved by frequently jumping from one carrier frequency to another; thus, if there is interference or performance degradation at a given frequency, it only affects a small fraction of the transmission. DSSS effectively increases the data rate of a signal by mapping each data bit into a string of bits, with one string used for binary 1 and another used for binary 0. The higher data rate uses a greater bandwidth. The effect is to spread each bit out over time, which minimizes the effects of interference and degradation. FHSS, which is simpler, was employed in most early 802.11 networks. Products using DSSS, which is more effective in the 802.11 scheme, followed. However, all of the original 802.11 products were of limited utility because of the low data rates.

IEEE 802.11B   IEEE 802.11b is an extension of the IEEE 802.11 DSSS scheme, providing data rates of 5.5 and 11 Mbps within the 2.4-GHz band. A higher data rate is achieved by using a more complex modulation technique. The 802.11b specification quickly led to product offerings, including chipsets, PC cards, access points, and systems. Apple Computer was the first company to offer 802.11b products, with its iBook portable computer using the AirPort wireless network option. Other companies, including Cisco, 3Com, and Dell, have followed. Although these new products are all based on the same standard, there is always a concern whether products from different vendors will successfully interoperate. To meet this concern, the Wireless Ethernet Compatibility Alliance (now called the Wi-Fi Alliance) created a test suite to certify interoperability for 802.11b products. Interoperability tests have been conducted, and a number of products have achieved certification.

One other concern for both the original 802.11 and the 802.11b products is interference with other systems that operate in the 2.4-GHz band, such as Bluetooth,

HomeRF, and many other devices that use the same portion of the spectrum (including baby monitors and garage door openers). A coexistence study group (IEEE 802.15) is examining this issue and so far the prospects are encouraging.

IEEE 802.11a Although 802.11b achieved a certain level of success, its limited data rate results in limited appeal. To meet the needs for a truly high-speed LAN, **IEEE 802.11a** was developed. IEEE 802.11a makes use of the frequency band called the Universal Networking Information Infrastructure (UNII), which is divided into three parts. The UNNI-1 band (5.15–5.25 GHz) is intended for indoor use; the UNNI-2 band (5.25–5.35 GHz) can be used either indoor or outdoor; and the UNNI-3 band (5.725–5.825 GHz) is for outdoor use.

Unlike the 2.4-GHz specifications, IEEE 802.11a does not use a spread spectrum scheme but rather uses **orthogonal frequency division multiplexing (OFDM)**. OFDM, also called *multicarrier modulation*, uses multiple carrier signals (up to 52) at different frequencies, sending some of the bits on each channel. The possible data rates for IEEE 802.11a are 6, 9, 12, 18, 24, 36, 48, and 54 Mbps.

At high data rates, OFDM is particularly effective in dealing with a major problem with wireless networks known as **multipath interference**. The essence of the problem is that in a transmission from one antenna to another, multiple copies of the signal may be received, one by a direct line of sight and other copies of the signal by reflection off objects in the vicinity. Because these signals travel different paths of different lengths, they arrive at slightly different times, causing interference. The higher the data rate, the more damaging the interference. With OFDM, instead of sending a single data stream at a high data rate over a given channel, the channel is broken up into many subchannels and a portion or the data stream is sent on each subchannel. Thus, roughly speaking, if there are 10 subchannels, each carries a portion of the data stream at a data rate of only 1/10 of the original data rate. For a more detailed discussion of multipath interference and OFDM, see Appendix I.

IEEE 802.11g Although 802.11a offered higher data rates than those by 802.11b, acceptance of this new scheme was limited. This is because the equipment was relatively expensive and the scheme is not compatible with either the original 802.11 or 802.11b. Instead manufacturers and customers turned to a more recent standard, IEEE 802.11g.

IEEE 802.11g is a higher-speed extension to IEEE 802.11b, providing data rates up to 54 Mbps, matching IEEE 802.11a. Like 802.11b, 802.11g operates in the 2.4-GHz range and thus the two are compatible. The standard is designed so that 802.11b devices will work when connected to an 802.11g AP, and 802.11g devices will work when connected to an 802.11b AP, in both cases using the lower 802.11b data rate.

IEEE 802.11g offers a wider array of data rate and modulation scheme options. At higher data rates, 802.11g adopts the 802.11a OFDM scheme, adapted for the 2.4-GHz rate; this is referred to as ERP-OFDM, with ERP standing for extended rate physical layer.

The IEEE 802.11 standards do not include a specification of speed versus distance objectives. Different vendors will give different values, depending on environment. Table 14.4, based on [LAYL04], gives estimated values for a typical office environment.

Table 14.4 Estimated Distance (m) Versus Data Rate

Data Rate (Mbps)	802.11b	802.11a	802.11g
1	90+	—	90+
2	75	—	75
5.5(b)/6(a/g)	60	60+	65
9	—	50	55
11(b)/12(a/g)	50	45	50
18	—	40	50
24	—	30	45
36	—	25	35
48	—	15	25
54	—	10	20

IEEE 802.11n   With increasing demands being placed on WLANs, the 802.11 committee looked for ways to increase the data throughput and overall capacity of 802.11 networks. The goal of this effort is not only to increase the bit rate of the transmitting antennas but also to increase the effective throughput of the network. Increasing effective throughput involves improvements to the antenna architecture and the MAC frame structure, not simply improvements to the signal encoding scheme. The result of these efforts is a package of improvements and enhancements embodied in IEEE 802.11n. This standard is defined to operate in both the 2.4-GHz and the 5-GHz bands and can therefore be made upwardly compatible with either 802.11a or 802.11b/g.

IEEE 802.11n embodies changes in three general areas: use of MIMO, enhancements in radio transmission, and MAC enhancements. We briefly examine each of these.

Multiple-input-multiple-output (MIMO) antenna architecture is the most important of the enhancements provided by 802.11n. A discussion of MIMO is beyond our scope, so we content ourselves with a brief overview (see Figure 14.5). In a MIMO scheme, the transmitter employs multiple antennas. The source data stream is divided into n substreams, one for each of the n transmitting antennas. The individual substreams are the input to the transmitting antennas (multiple input). At the receiving end, m antennas receive the transmissions from the n source antennas via a combination of line-of-sight transmission and multipath. The outputs from the m receiving antennas (multiple output) are combined with the signals from the other receive radios. With a lot of complex math, the result is a much better receive signal than can be achieved with either a single antenna or multiple frequency channels. The 802.11n standard defines a number of different combinations for the number of transmitters and the number of receivers, from 2×1 to 4×4. Each additional transmitter or receiver in the system increases the SNR (signal-to-noise ratio). However, the incremental gains from each additional transmitter or receiver diminish rapidly. The gain in SNR is large for each step from 2×1 to 2×2 and to 3×2, but the improvement with 3×3 and beyond is relatively small [CISC07].

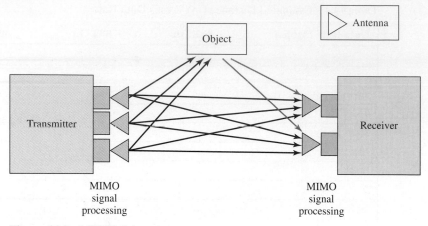

Figure 14.5 MIMO Scheme

In addition to MIMO, 802.11n makes a number of changes in the **radio transmission scheme** to increase capacity. The most significant of these techniques, known as channel bonding, combines two 20-MHz channels to create a 40-MHz channel. Using OFDM, this allows for twice as many subchannels, doubling the transmission rate.

Finally, 802.11 provides some **MAC enhancements**. The most significant change is to aggregate multiple MAC frames into a single block for transmission. Once a station acquires the medium for transmission, it can transmit long packets without significant delays between transmissions. The receiver sends a single block acknowledgment. Frame aggregation can result in significantly improved efficiency in the use of the transmission capacity.

Figure 14.6 gives an indication of the effectiveness of 802.11n compared to 802.11g [DEBE07]. The chart shows the average throughput per user on a shared system. As expected, the more active users competing for the wireless capacity,

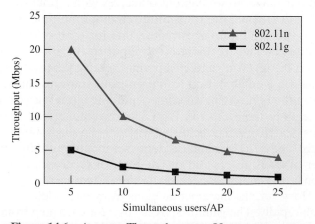

Figure 14.6 Average Throughput per User

the smaller the average throughput per user. IEEE 802.11n provides a significant improvement, especially for networks in which a small number of users are actively competing for transmission time.

14.4 GIGABIT WLANs

Just as wired LANs have evolved into the gigabit range to meet the relentless demand for increasing transmission capacity, wireless LANs are headed into the same range. We look at the two areas of development in this field.

Gigabit Wi-Fi

Several approaches to gigabit wireless LANs are in the works. IEEE 802.11, whose standards will determine the products that become available, is developing two standards.

The **IEEE 802.11ac** standard is the next step up for the old 802.11a Wi-Fi standard. Recall that 802.11a is a 5-GHz standard with a data rate up to 54 Mbps. Vendors were slow to get 802.11a equipment out the door. When 802.11g came along, which works in the 2.4-GHz range, could produce the same speed, and was compatible with the older and slower 802.11b, 802.11a became something of an orphaned technology. Now with 802.11ac, 802.11a is seeing renewed interest. The new standard is in the 5-Ghz band, but provides wider channels for higher data throughput. IEEE 802.11a uses channels with a width of 20 MHz; 802.11ac uses a channel width of either 40 MHz or 80 MHz or perhaps even 160 MHz to deliver data. 802.11ac may also make use of MU-MIMO (multiuser multiple-input multiple-output). In MU MIMOs simultaneous streams will be transmitted to different users on the same channels. As of this writing, not all of these details have been worked out, but already products have been announced that support data rates up to 1 Gbps.

The **IEEE 802.11ad** standard operates in the 60-GHz band and is expected to deliver data rates of up to 6 Gbps. The downside of this millimeter band Wi-Fi is that its range will be in feet rather than yards. 802.11ad will be able to cover a room, but not much more. As with 802.11ac, products have been announced and will soon appear, as of the time of this writing.

Li-Fi

In October of 2011, a number of companies and industry groups formed the Li-Fi Consortium, whose objective is to promote high-speed optical wireless systems. The motivation for optical WLANs is that optical systems can help to deal with a looming capacity problem. As radio-based wireless becomes ever more prevalent, more and more devices are using the WLAN frequencies to transmit large volumes of data. But there is only a limited amount of radio spectrum available. Using light waves offers the potential of overcoming this problem by exploiting an entirely separate part of the electromagnetic spectrum, one that is already ubiquitous because it is used for illumination.

The basic technical approach is to vary the intensity of the light from a light source to encode binary data. The flickering is so slight that it is imperceptible to the human eye. Incandescent light bulbs and fluorescent tubes are not suitable for the rapid modulation required. However, LEDs, which are replacing these older technologies at a rapid rate, are well-suited to high-speed modulation. Some are already equipped with photosensors (to be able to turn on at night) and adding photosensors to existing products is not a big technical challenge. Speeds of 10 Gbps have been achieved and speeds of up to 100 Gbps are contemplated.

One limitation of Li-Fi is that it requires line-of-sight between transmitter and receiver, either direct or by reflection from walls and ceilings. Yet for secure applications, this could be an asset. Further, with the use of strategically placed switches and routers, the line-of-sight limitation is manageable.

14.5 IEEE 802.11 SECURITY CONSIDERATIONS

There are two characteristics of a wired LAN that are not inherent in a WLAN.

1. In order to transmit over a wired LAN, a station must be physically connected to the LAN. On the other hand, with a WLAN, any station within radio range of the other devices on the LAN can transmit. In a sense, there is a form of authentication with a wired LAN, in that it requires some positive and presumably observable action to connect a station to a wired LAN.

2. Similarly, in order to receive a transmission from a station that is part of a wired LAN, the receiving station must also be attached to the wired LAN. On the other hand, with a WLAN, any station within radio range can receive. Thus, a wired LAN provides a degree of privacy, limiting reception of data to stations connected to the LAN.

Access and Privacy Services

IEEE 802.11 defines three services that provide a WLAN with the two features just mentioned:

- **Authentication:** Used to establish the identity of stations to each other. In a wired LAN, it is generally assumed that access to a physical connection conveys authority to connect to the LAN. This is not a valid assumption for a WLAN, in which connectivity is achieved simply by having an attached antenna that is properly tuned. The authentication service is used by stations to establish their identity with stations they wish to communicate with. IEEE 802.11 supports several authentication schemes and allows for expansion of the functionality of these schemes. The standard does not mandate any particular authentication scheme, which could range from relatively unsecure handshaking to public-key encryption schemes. However, IEEE 802.11 requires mutually acceptable, successful authentication before a station can establish an association with an AP.

- **Deauthentication:** This service is invoked whenever an existing authentication is to be terminated.

- **Privacy:** Used to prevent the contents of messages from being read by other than the intended recipient. The standard provides for the optional use of encryption to assure privacy.

Wireless LAN Security Standards

The original 802.11 specification included a set of security features for privacy and authentication that, unfortunately, were quite weak. For **privacy**, 802.11 defined the Wired Equivalent Privacy (WEP) algorithm. The privacy portion of the 802.11 standard contained major weaknesses. Subsequent to the development of WEP, the 802.11i task group has developed a set of capabilities to address the WLAN security issues. In order to accelerate the introduction of strong security into WLANs, the Wi-Fi Alliance promulgated **Wi-Fi Protected Access (WPA)** as a Wi-Fi standard. WPA is a set of security mechanisms that eliminates most 802.11 security issues and was based on the current state of the 802.11i standard. As 802.11i evolves, WPA will evolve to maintain compatibility. WPA is examined in Chapter 19.

APPLICATION NOTE

Deploying WLANs

Many organizations are faced with the problem of deciding whether or not to deploy a wireless local area network, or WLAN. This problem is exacerbated by several issues regarding WLANs, such as security, management of deployed devices, and a confusing array of standards. Finally, deployment of a WLAN increases the responsibility of the support staff without necessarily providing them with the training or expertise to manage it.

That said, there are a few reasons for deploying a WLAN: mobility, reduction in the cost of an installation, speed of deployment, ad hoc networking, and the ability to connect geographically remote nodes. The first thing that an organization should probably ask itself is if a WLAN is a requirement or simply something that would be nice to have. Many companies decide not to deploy a WLAN because of the security hole that the wireless network represents. It is understandable that it may simply be too much of a risk or a management nightmare to deploy. This approach comes with some danger, especially if the company also decides not to bother with wireless training. Most end-user equipment has built-in wireless capability. In addition, employees, students, and visitors will deploy wireless equipment without company approval. This is not usually done to attack the company network; it is simply because more and more devices come equipped with wireless capability. Laptops are a very good example of this.

Wireless devices also have the annoying ability to find connections automatically. This is made worse with operating systems like Windows XP, which handles many wireless issues transparently and has the functionality of connection sharing. Connection sharing will allow multiple users to access the network through a single computer's network connection. Further, the Windows wireless networking client does not provide very many control features. If you decide not to deploy a wireless network, you still should prepare for someone else deploying one within your organization.

Choosing the right standard can be very difficult. The 802.11 family has had several generations, with 802.11b being the most successful. However, there have been significant

(*Continued*)

problems with the 802.11b standard, including relatively low bandwidth, a small number of access points able to operate in an area, and interference from other devices sharing the 2.4-GHz portion of the spectrum.

The next-generation standards, 802.11a and 802.11g, both attempt to address these problems, with 802.11a being the more successful at avoiding interference because it has moved up to 5 GHz. This introduces the problem of smaller coverage areas; the higher frequencies do not propagate as far. If you already have a wireless network, then your decision may be slightly different than if you are deploying one from scratch. In order to be compatible with an existing 802.11b network, you may opt for 802.11g, which has higher data capacity but still can communicate directly with 802.11b nodes. 802.11g has been the choice for most businesses.

Depending on the intended use, new installations may decide on one of the new standards exclusively. Remember that there is a tremendous amount of pre-existing 802.11b equipment so a decision must be made about its support. For many, 802.11a will be the best choice because of its high data rates, low interference, and the number of available channels. The strength of 802.11a is also its weakness. A basic rule of thumb for radio-based communication is that the higher the frequency, the shorter the transmission distance. Thus, because it uses higher frequencies, 802.11a has a shorter range than does 802.11b. Another rule of thumb is that as the frequency increases, the easier it is to disrupt the signal. This last problem is highly dependent on your operating environment. For these reasons, 802.11g may be the best choice as it closely matches the model of 802.11b.

Our last discussion point will be about security. While there is never a silver bullet regarding security measures, there are some basic practices that will help reduce exposure and vulnerability. These include the following:

- Place access points outside the company firewall to ensure that company data are not broadcast.
- Turn on WEP or WPA-PSK. They do have their problems, but they will stop most casual eavesdroppers and bandwidth hogs.
- Run access points back to switches instead of hubs, to provide increased traffic filtering.
- Complete a wireless site survey to determine your level of exposure.
- Use a VPN for wireless nodes.
- Deploy some basic layer 2 or 3 filters for securing access.
- When in doubt, use encryption on your data.
- Understand that most problems (both malicious and accidental) do not come from external hackers, but from internal users.

The real problem with wireless communication is that very few network administrators have spent much time with it. As a result, there is a tremendous lack of understanding and experience with the issues. While this short discussion is not meant to be the ultimate guide to wireless networking, it should help you understand some of the larger problems and thought processes associated with WLANs.

14.6 SUMMARY

In recent years, a whole new class of local area networks (LANs) has arrived to provide an alternative to LANs based on twisted pair, coaxial cable, and optical fiber: WLANs. The key advantages of the WLAN are that it eliminates the wiring cost, which is often the most costly component of a LAN, and that it accommodates mobile workstations.

WLANs use one of three transmission techniques: spread spectrum, narrow-band microwave, and infrared. The most significant set of standards defining WLANs are those defined by the IEEE 802.11 committee.

**Case Study IX St. Luke's Health Care System: Using Mobility
to Advance Health Care Delivery**

The major concepts addressed in this case study include Wireless LANs; mobile applications. **This case study and more are available at www.pearsoninternationaleditions .com/stallings**

14.7 KEY TERMS, REVIEW QUESTIONS, AND PROBLEMS

Key Terms

access point (AP)	IEEE 802.11	OFDM
ad hoc networking	independent BSS	portal
basic service set (BSS)	(IBSS)	service area
distribution system (DS)	infrared LAN	spread spectrum LAN
extended service set	Li-Fi MIMO	Wi-Fi
(ESS)	narrowband microwave LAN	wireless LAN (WLAN)

Review Questions

14.1 List and briefly define four application areas of WLANs.
14.2 List and briefly define key requirements for WLANs.
14.3 What is the difference between a single-cell and a multiple-cell WLAN?
14.4 What is the basic building block of an 802.11 WLAN?
14.5 Define an extended service set.
14.6 List and briefly define IEEE 802.11 services.
14.7 What is the difference between an access point and a portal?
14.8 Is a distribution system a wireless network?
14.9 How is the concept of an association related to that of mobility?
14.10 In general terms, what application areas are supported by Bluetooth?
14.11 What is the difference between a core specification and a profile specification?
14.12 What is a usage model?

Problems

14.1   Answer the following questions about your wireless network:
  a. What is the SSID?
  b. Who is the equipment vendor?
  c. What standard are you using?
  d. What is the size of the network?

14.2   Using what you know about wired and wireless networks, draw the topology of your network.

14.3   There are many free tools and applications available for helping decipher wireless networks. One of the most popular is Netstumbler. Obtain the software at www.netstumbler.com and follow the links for downloads. The site has a list of supported wireless cards. Using the Netstumbler software, determine the answers for the following:
  a. How many access points in your network have the same SSID?
  b. What is your signal strength to your access point?
  c. How many other wireless networks and access points can you find?

14.4   Most wireless cards come with a small set of applications that can perform tasks similar to Netstumbler. Using your own client software, determine the same items you did with Netstumbler. Do they agree?

14.5   Try this experiment: How far can you go and still be connected to your network? This will depend to a large extent on your physical environment.

14.6   Compare and contrast wired and wireless LANs. What unique concerns must be addressed by the designer of a WLAN network?

14.7   Two documents related to safety concerns associated with wireless media are the FCC OET-65 Bulletin and the ANSI/IEEE C95.1-1999. Briefly describe the purpose of these documents and briefly outline the safety concerns associated with WLAN technology.

WAN TECHNOLOGY AND PROTOCOLS

CHAPTER 15

Learning Objectives

After reading this chapter, you should be able to:

♦ Explain the need for a communications network for wide area voice and data communications.

♦ Define circuit switching and describe the key elements of circuit-switching networks.

♦ Discuss the important applications of circuit switching, including public networks, private networks, and software-defined networks.

♦ Define packet switching and describe the key elements of packet-switching technology.

♦ Discuss the important applications of packet switching, including public and private networks.

♦ Discuss the relative merits of circuit switching and packet switching and analyze the circumstances for which each is most appropriate.

♦ Present an overview of VoIP networks.

♦ Explain the concept of presence and how it is implemented.

Switching technologies are pervasive in enterprise networks. Fully switched Ethernet networks are the norm in business local area networks (LANs). Switches are also the dominant internetworking devices that underlie the wide area network (WAN) services that businesses use to interconnect geographically dispersed operating locations. Developing an understanding of fundamental switching techniques is essential for understanding data and voice transmission in today's enterprise networks.

This chapter begins with a general discussion of switched communications networks. The chapter next focuses on WANs and, in particular, on traditional approaches to WAN design: circuit switching and packet switching. Next we examine voice over IP as the most important example of providing traditional WAN services over the Internet. Finally, the chapter discusses the concept of presence, which is a service that can be built on WAN and LAN infrastructures.

15.1 SWITCHING TECHNIQUES

For transmission of data[1] beyond a local area, communication is typically achieved by transmitting data from source to destination through a network of intermediate switching nodes; this switched network design is typically used to implement LANs as well. The switching nodes are not concerned with the content of the data; rather, their purpose is to provide a switching facility that will move the data from node to node until they reach their destination. Figure 15.1 illustrates a simple network. The end devices that wish to communicate may be referred to as *stations*. The

---

[1]We use this term here in a very general sense, to include audio, image, and video, as well as ordinary data (e.g., numerical, text).

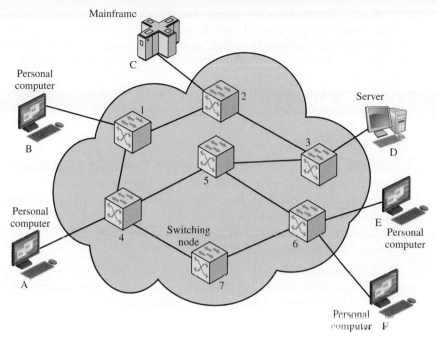

Figure 15.1 Simple Switching Network

stations may be computers, terminals, telephones, or other communicating devices. We shall refer to the switching devices whose purpose is to provide communication as *nodes*. The nodes are connected to one another in some topology by transmission links. Each station attaches to a node, and the collection of nodes is referred to as a *communications network*.

In a *switched communication network*, data entering the network from a station are routed to the destination by being switched from node to node.

Example   In Figure 15.1, data from station A intended for station F are sent to node 4. They may then be routed via nodes 5 and 6 or nodes 7 and 6 to the destination. Several observations are in order:

1. Some nodes connect only to other nodes (e.g., 5 and 7). Their sole task is the internal (to the network) switching of data. Other nodes have one or more stations attached as well; in addition to their switching functions, such nodes accept data from and deliver data to the attached stations.

2. Node–station links are generally dedicated point-to-point links. Node–node links are usually multiplexed, using either frequency division multiplexing (FDM) or time division multiplexing (TDM).

3. Usually, the network is not fully connected; that is, there is not a direct link between every possible pair of nodes. However, it is always desirable to have more than one possible path through the network for each pair of stations. This enhances the reliability of the network. Partial mesh topologies are often used to ensure multiple paths.

Two different technologies are used in wide area switched networks: circuit switching and packet switching. These two technologies differ in the way the nodes switch information from one link to another on the way from source to destination. We next look at the details of these two technologies.

15.2 CIRCUIT-SWITCHING NETWORKS

Basic Operation

Communication via circuit switching implies that there is a dedicated communication path between two stations. That path is a connected sequence of links between network nodes. On each physical link, a channel is dedicated to the connection. The most common example of circuit switching is the telephone network.

Communication via circuit switching involves three phases, which can be explained with reference to Figure 15.1.

1. **Circuit establishment.** Before any signals can be transmitted, an end-to-end (station-to-station) circuit must be established. For example, station A sends a request to node 4 requesting a connection to station E. Typically, the link from A to 4 is a dedicated line, so that part of the connection already exists. Node 4 must find the next leg in a route leading to E. Based on routing information and measures of availability and perhaps cost, node 4 selects the link to node 5, allocates a free channel (using FDM or TDM) on that link, and sends a message requesting connection to E. So far, a dedicated path has been established from A through 4 to 5. Because a number of stations may attach to node 4, it must be able to establish internal paths from multiple stations to multiple nodes. How this is done is discussed later in this section. The remainder of the process proceeds similarly. Node 5 allocates a channel to node 6 and internally ties that channel to the channel from node 4. Node 6 completes the connection to E. In completing the connection, a test is made to determine if E is busy or is prepared to accept the connection.

2. **Data transfer.** Data can now be transmitted from A through the network to E. The data may be analog voice, digitized voice, or binary data, depending on the nature of the network. As the carriers evolve to fully integrated digital networks, the use of digital (binary) transmission for both voice and data is becoming the dominant method. The path is as follows: A–4 link, internal switching through 4, 4–5 channel, internal switching through 5, 5–6 channel, internal switching through 6, 6–E link. Generally, the connection is full duplex, and signals may be transmitted in both directions simultaneously.

3. **Circuit disconnect.** After some period of data transfer, the connection is terminated, usually by the action of one of the two stations. Signals must be propagated to nodes 4, 5, and 6 to deallocate the dedicated resources.

Note that the connection path is established before data transmission begins. Thus, channel capacity must be reserved between each pair of nodes in the path, and each node must have available internal switching capacity to handle the requested connection. The switches must have the intelligence to make these allocations and to devise a route through the network.

Circuit switching can be rather inefficient. Channel capacity is dedicated for the duration of a connection, even if no data are being transferred. For a voice connection, utilization may be rather high, but it still does not approach 100%. For a client/server connection, the capacity may be idle during most of the time of the connection. There is a delay prior to signal transfer for call establishment. However, once the circuit is established, the network is effectively transparent to the users. Data are transmitted at a fixed data rate with no delay other than the propagation delay through the transmission links. The delay at each node is negligible.

Circuit switching was developed to handle voice traffic but is now also used for data traffic. The best-known example of a circuit-switching network is the public telephone network (Figure 15.2). This is actually a collection of national networks interconnected to form the international service. Although originally designed and implemented to service analog telephone subscribers, it handles substantial data traffic via modem and is now primarily a digital network. Another well-known application of circuit switching is the private branch exchange (PBX), used to interconnect telephones within a building or office. Circuit switching is also used in private networks. Typically, such a network is set up by a corporation or other large organization to interconnect its various sites. Such a network usually consists of PBX systems at each site interconnected by dedicated, leased lines obtained from a carrier, such as AT&T.

A public telecommunications network can be described using four generic architectural components:

- **Subscribers:** The devices that attach to the network. It is still the case that most subscriber devices to public telecommunications networks are telephones, but the percentage of data traffic increases year by year.

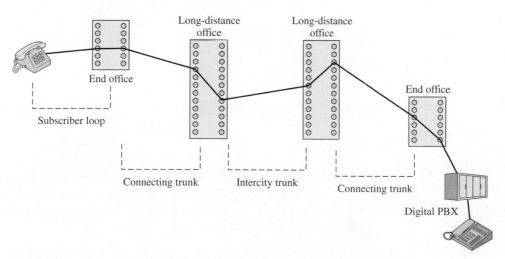

Figure 15.2 Example Connection over a Public Circuit-Switching Network

- **Subscriber line:** The link between the subscriber and the network, also referred to as the *subscriber loop* or *local loop*. Almost all local loop connections use twisted-pair wire. The length of a local loop is typically in a range from a few kilometers to a few tens of kilometers.

- **Exchanges:** The switching centers in the network. A switching center that directly supports subscribers is known as an end office. Typically, an end office will support many thousands of subscribers in a localized area. There are over 19,000 end offices in the United States, so it is clearly impractical for each end office to have a direct link to each of the other end offices; this would require on the order of 2×10^8 links. Rather, intermediate switching nodes are used.

- **Trunks:** The branches between exchanges. Trunks carry multiple voice-frequency circuits using either FDM or synchronous TDM. These are also referred to as *carrier systems*.

Subscribers connect directly to an end office, which switches traffic between subscribers and between a subscriber and other exchanges. The other exchanges are responsible for routing and switching traffic between end offices. This distinction is shown in Figure 15.3. To connect two subscribers attached to the same end office, a circuit is set up between them in the same fashion as described before. If two subscribers connect to different end offices, a circuit between them consists of a chain of circuits through one or more intermediate offices. In the figure, a connection is established between lines a and b by simply setting up the connection through the end office. The connection between c and d is more complex. In c's end office, a connection is established between line c and one channel on a TDM trunk to the intermediate switch. In the intermediate switch, that channel is connected to a channel on a TDM trunk to d's end office. In that end office, the channel is connected to line d.

Circuit-switching technology has been driven by its use to carry voice traffic. One of the key requirements for voice traffic is that there must be virtually no transmission delay and certainly no variation in delay. A constant signal transmission rate must be

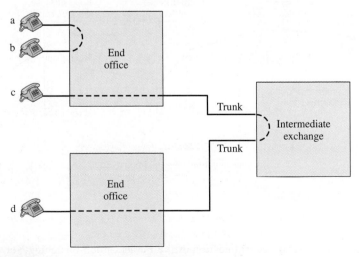

Figure 15.3 Circuit Establishment

maintained, because transmission and reception occur at the same signal rate. These requirements are necessary to allow normal human conversation. Further, the quality of the received signal must be sufficiently high to provide, at a minimum, intelligibility.

Circuit switching achieved its widespread, dominant position because it is well suited to the analog transmission of voice signals. In today's digital world, its inefficiencies are more apparent. However, despite the inefficiency, circuit switching is and will remain an attractive choice for both local area and wide area networking. One of its key strengths is that it is transparent. Once a circuit is established, it appears like a direct connection to the two attached stations; no special networking logic is needed at the station.

Control Signaling

Control signals are the means by which the network is managed and by which calls are established, maintained, and terminated. Both call management and overall network management require that information be exchanged between subscriber and switch, among switches, and between switch and network management center. For a large public telecommunications network, a relatively complex control-signaling scheme is required.

Control signals affect many aspects of network behavior, including both network services visible to the subscriber and internal mechanisms. As networks become more complex, the number of functions performed by control signaling necessarily grows. The following functions are among the most important:

1. Audible communication with the subscriber, including dial tone, ringing tone, busy signal, and so on.
2. Transmission of the number dialed to switching offices that will attempt to complete a connection.
3. Transmission of information between switches indicating that a call cannot be completed.
4. Transmission of information between switches indicating that a call has ended and that the path can be disconnected.
5. A signal to make a telephone ring.
6. Transmission of information used for billing purposes.
7. Transmission of information giving the status of equipment or trunks in the network. This information may be used for routing and maintenance purposes.
8. Transmission of information used in diagnosing and isolating system failures.
9. Control of special equipment such as satellite channel equipment.

As an example of the use of control signaling, consider a typical telephone connection sequence from one line to another in the same central office:

1. Prior to the call, both telephones are not in use (on-hook). The call begins when one subscriber lifts the receiver (off-hook); this action is automatically signaled to the end office switch.
2. The switch responds with an audible dial tone, signaling the subscriber that a number may be dialed.

3. The caller dials a number, which is communicated as a called address to the switch.

4. If the called subscriber is not busy, the switch alerts that subscriber to an incoming call by sending a ringing signal, which causes the telephone to ring.

5. Feedback is provided to the calling subscriber by the switch:

   a. If the called subscriber is not busy, the switch returns an audible ringing tone to the caller while the ringing signal is being sent to the called subscriber.

   b. If the called subscriber is busy, the switch sends an audible busy signal to the caller.

   c. If the call cannot be completed through the switch, the switch sends an audible "reorder" message to the caller.

6. The called party accepts the call by lifting the receiver (off-hook), which is automatically signaled to the switch.

7. The switch terminates the ringing signal and the audible ringing tone, and it establishes a connection between the two subscribers.

8. The connection is released when either subscriber hangs up.

When the called subscriber is attached to a different switch than the calling subscriber, the following switch-to-switch trunk signaling functions are required:

1. The originating switch seizes an idle interswitch trunk and sends an off-hook indication on the trunk so that the address may be communicated.

2. The terminating switch sends an off-hook followed by an on-hook signal, known as a "wink." This indicates a register-ready status.

3. The originating switch sends the address digits to the terminating switch.

This example illustrates some of the functions performed using control signals. Signaling can also be classified functionally as supervisory, address, call information, and network management.

The term **supervisory** is generally used to refer to control functions that have a binary character (true/false; on/off), such as request for service, answer, alerting, and return to idle. They deal with the availability of the called subscriber and of the needed network resources. Supervisory control signals are used to determine if a needed resource is available and, if so, to seize it. They are also used to communicate the status of requested resources.

Address signals identify a subscriber. Initially, an address signal is generated by a calling subscriber when dialing a telephone number. The resulting address may be propagated through the network to support the routing function and to locate and ring the called subscriber's phone.

The term **call information** refers to those signals that provide information to the subscriber about the status of a call. This is in contrast to internal control signals between switches used in call establishment and termination. Such internal signals are analog or digital electrical messages. By contrast, call information signals are audible tones that can be heard by the caller or an operator with the proper phone set.

Supervisory, address, and call information control signals are directly involved in the establishment and termination of a call. **Network management** signals are used for the maintenance, troubleshooting, and overall operation of the network. Such signals may be in the form of messages, such as a list of preplanned routes being sent to a station to update its routing tables. These signals cover a broad scope, and it is this category that will expand most with the increasing complexity of switched networks.

15.3 PACKET-SWITCHING NETWORKS

Around 1970, research began on a new form of architecture for long-distance digital data communications: **packet switching**. Although the technology of packet switching has evolved substantially since that time, it is remarkable that (1) the basic technology of packet switching is fundamentally the same today as it was in the early-1970s networks, and (2) packet switching remains one of the few effective technologies for long-distance data communications. The two newest WAN technologies, frame relay and ATM, are essentially variations on the basic packet-switching approach. In this chapter, we provide an overview of traditional packet switching, which is still in use; frame relay and ATM are discussed in Chapter 16.

Basic Operation

The long-haul circuit-switching telecommunications network was originally designed to handle voice traffic, and the majority of traffic on these networks continues to be voice. A key characteristic of circuit-switching networks is that resources within the network are dedicated to particular calls. For voice connections, the resulting circuit will enjoy a high percentage of utilization because, most of the time, one party or the other is talking. However, as the circuit-switching network began to be used increasingly for data connections, two shortcomings became apparent:

- In a typical user/host data connection (e.g., PC user logged on to a database server), much of the time the line is idle. Thus, with data connections, a circuit-switching approach is inefficient.

- In a circuit-switching network, the connection provides for transmission at a constant data rate. Thus, each of the two devices that are connected must transmit and receive at the same data rate as the other. This limits the utility of the network in interconnecting a variety of host computers and workstations.

To understand how packet switching addresses these problems, let us briefly summarize packet-switching operation. Data are transmitted in short packets. A typical upper bound on packet length is approximately 1500 octets (bytes). If a source has a longer message to send, the message is broken up into a series of packets (Figure 15.4). Each packet contains a portion (or all for a short message) of the user's data plus some control information. The control information, at a minimum, includes the information that the network requires to be able to route the packet through the network and deliver it to the intended destination. At each node en route, the packet is received, stored briefly, and passed on to the next node.

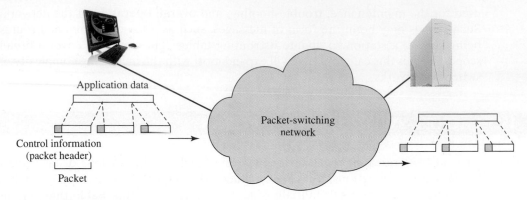

Figure 15.4 The Use of Packets

Figure 15.5 illustrates the basic operation. A transmitting computer or other device sends a message as a sequence of packets (Figure 15.5a). Each packet includes control information indicating the destination station (computer, terminal, etc.). The packets are initially sent to the node to which the sending station attaches. As each packet arrives at this node, it stores the packet briefly, determines the next leg of the route, and queues the packet to go out on that link. When the link is available, each packet is transmitted to the next node (Figure 15.5b). All of the packets eventually work their way through the network and are delivered to the intended destination.

The packet-switching approach has a number of advantages over circuit switching:

- Line efficiency is greater, because a single node-to-node link can be dynamically shared by many packets over time. The packets are queued up and transmitted as rapidly as possible over the link. By contrast, with circuit switching, time on a node-to-node link is preallocated using synchronous TDM. Much of the time, such a link may be idle because a portion of its time is dedicated to a connection that is idle.

- A packet-switching network can carry out data-rate conversion. Two stations of different data rates can exchange packets, because each connects to its node at its proper data rate.

- When traffic becomes heavy on a circuit-switching network, some calls are blocked; that is, the network refuses to accept additional connection requests until the load on the network decreases. On a packet-switching network, packets are still accepted, but delivery delay increases.

- Priorities can be used. If a node has a number of packets queued for transmission, it can transmit the higher-priority packets first. These packets will therefore experience less delay than lower-priority packets.

Packet switching also has disadvantages relative to circuit switching:

- When a packet passes through a packet-switching node, it incurs a delay not experienced in circuit switching. At a minimum, it incurs a transmission delay equal to the length of the packet in bits divided by the incoming channel rate

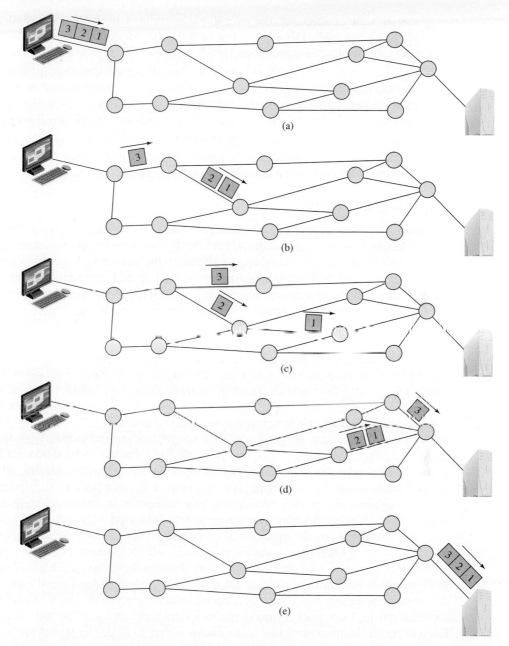

Figure 15.5   Packet Switching: Datagram Approach

in bits per second; this is the time it takes to absorb the packet into an internal buffer. In addition, there may be a variable delay due to processing and queuing in the node.

- Because the packets between a given source and destination may vary in length, may take different routes, and may be subject to varying delay in the switches they encounter, the overall packet delay can vary substantially. This phenomenon, called **jitter**, may not be desirable for some applications (e.g., in real-time applications including telephone voice and real-time video).

- To route packets through the network, overhead information including the address of the destination and often sequencing information must be added to each packet, which reduces the communication capacity available for carrying user data. This is not needed in circuit switching once the circuit is set up.

- More processing is involved in the transfer of information using packet switching than in circuit switching at each node. In the case of circuit switching, there is virtually no processing at each switch once the circuit is set up.

Switching Technique

A station has a message to send through a packet-switching network that is of greater length than the maximum packet size. It therefore breaks the message into packets and sends these packets, one at a time, to the network. A question arises as to how the network will handle this stream of packets as it attempts to route them through the network and deliver them to the intended destination. Two approaches are used in contemporary networks: datagram and virtual circuit.

In the **datagram** approach, each packet is treated independently, with no reference to packets that have gone before. This approach is illustrated in Figure 15.5. Each node chooses the next node on a packet's path, taking into account information received from neighboring nodes on traffic, line failures, and so on. So the packets, each with the same destination address, do not all follow the same route, and they may arrive out of sequence at the exit point. In this example, the exit node restores the packets to their original order before delivering them to the destination. In some datagram networks, it is up to the destination rather than the exit node to do the reordering. Also, it is possible for a packet to be damaged in the network. For example, if a packet-switching node crashes momentarily, all of its queued packets may be lost. Again, it is up to either the exit node or the destination to detect the loss of a packet and decide how to recover it. In this technique, each packet, treated independently, is referred to as a datagram.

In the **virtual circuit** approach, a preplanned route is established before any packets are sent. Once the route is established, all the packets between a pair of communicating parties follow this same route through the network. This is illustrated in Figure 15.6. Because the route is fixed for the duration of the logical connection, it is somewhat similar to a circuit in a circuit-switching network and is referred to as a virtual circuit. Each packet now contains a virtual circuit identifier as well as data. Each node on the preestablished route knows where to direct such packets; no routing decisions are required. At any time, each station can have more than one virtual circuit to any other station and can have virtual circuits to more than one station.

So the main characteristic of the virtual circuit technique is that a route between stations is set up prior to data transfer. Note that this does not mean that this is a dedicated path, as in circuit switching. A packet is still buffered at each node and queued for output over a line. The difference from the datagram approach is that, with virtual circuits, the node need not make a routing decision for each packet. It is made only once for all packets using that virtual circuit.

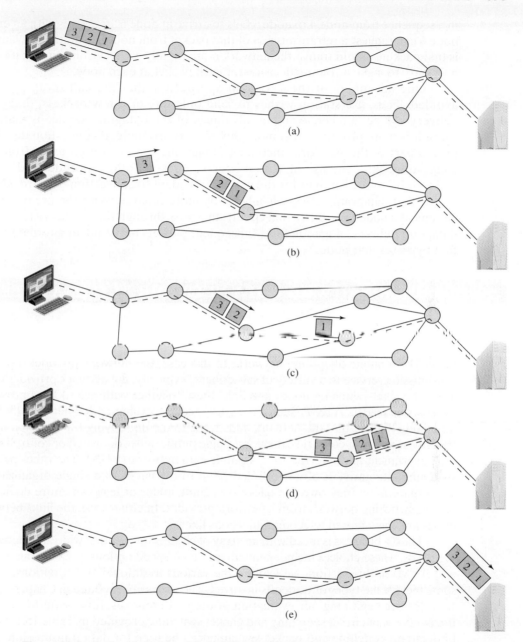

Figure 15.6   Packet Switching: Virtual Circuit Approach

If two stations wish to exchange data over an extended period of time, there are certain advantages to virtual circuits. First, the network may provide services related to the virtual circuit, including sequencing and error control. Sequencing refers to the fact that, because all packets follow the same route, they arrive in the original order. Error control is a service that assures not only that packets arrive in proper sequence but also that all packets arrive correctly. For example, if a packet in a sequence from node 4 to node 6 fails to arrive at node 6, or arrives with an error, node 6 can request a retransmission of that packet from node 4. Another advantage is that packets should transit the network more rapidly with a virtual circuit; it is not necessary to make a routing decision for each packet at each node.

One advantage of the datagram approach is that the call setup phase is avoided. Thus, if a station wishes to send only one or a few packets, datagram delivery will be quicker. Another advantage of the datagram service is that, because it is more primitive, it is more flexible. For example, if congestion develops in one part of the network, incoming datagrams can be routed away from the congestion. With the use of virtual circuits, packets follow a predefined route, and thus it is more difficult for the network to adapt to congestion. A third advantage is that datagram delivery is inherently more reliable. With the use of virtual circuits, if a node fails, all virtual circuits that pass through that node are lost. With datagram delivery, if a node fails, subsequent packets may find an alternate route that bypasses that node.

15.4 TRADITIONAL WIDE AREA NETWORK ALTERNATIVES

Just as there are public and private circuit-switching networks, there are also public and private packet-switching networks. A public packet-switching network works much like a public telephone network. In this case, the network provides a packet transmission service to a variety of subscribers. Typically, the network provider owns a set of packet-switching nodes and links these together with leased lines provided by a carrier such as AT&T. Such a network is called a **value-added network (VAN)**, reflecting the fact that the network adds value to the underlying transmission facilities. In a number of countries, there is a single public network owned or controlled by the government and referred to as a **public data network (PDN)**. The other packet-switching alternative is a network dedicated to the needs of a single organization. The organization may own the packet-switching nodes or lease an entire dedicated packet-switching network from a network provider. In either case, the links between nodes are again leased telecommunications lines.

Thus, a business is faced with an array of choices for meeting wide area networking needs. These choices include a number of high-speed options, such as frame relay and ATM. In this section, we explore the various traditional WAN options, to get some feel for the types of tradeoffs involved. The issues are revisited in Chapter 16.

Before beginning our evaluation of these alternatives, it is useful to consider the overview of circuit switching and packet switching provided in Table 15.1. While both circuit switching and packet switching can be used for data transmission, each has its particular strengths and weaknesses for a given application.

Wide Area Networks for Voice

Traditionally, the preferred business alternatives for wide area voice communications all employed circuit switching. With the increasing competition and advancing technology of recent years, the manager has a number of circuit-switching network alternatives, including private networks, software-defined networks, ordinary telephone service, and a variety of special services such as toll-free numbers.

Table 15.1   Relative Merits of Circuit Switching and Packet Switching of Data

Circuit Switching	
Advantages	**Disadvantages**
Compatible with voice. Economies of scale can be realized by using the same network for voice and data.	Subject to blocking. This makes it difficult to size the network properly. The problem is less severe with the use of dynamic nonhierarchical routing techniques.
Commonality of calling procedures for voice and data. No special user training or communication protocols are needed to handle data traffic.	Requires subscriber compatibility. The devices at each end of a circuit must be compatible in terms of protocol and data rate, since the circuit is a transparent connection.
Predictable, constant rate for data traffic.	Large processing and signal burden. For transaction-type applications, data calls are of short duration and need to be set up rapidly. This proportionally increases the overhead burden on the network.
Packet Switching	
Advantages	**Disadvantages**
Provides speed conversion. Two attached devices with different data rates may exchange data; the network buffers the data and delivers them at the appropriate data rate.	Complex routing and control. To achieve efficiency and resilience, a packet-switched network must employ a complex set of routing and control algorithms.
Appears nonblocking. As the network load increases, the delay increases, but new exchanges are usually permitted.	Delay. Delay is a function of load. It can be long and it is variable.
Efficient utilization. Switches and trunks are used on demand rather than dedicating capacity for a particular call.	
Logical multiplexing. A host system can have simultaneous conversations with a number of terminals over a single line.	

With all of these choices, and with the constantly changing prices attached to the various choices, it is difficult to generalize. What can be said is that business relies heavily on the public telephone networks and related services. Private networks are appropriate for an organization with a number of sites and with a substantial amount of voice traffic between them.

A new entry in the competition is voice over IP (VoIP). VoIP uses a packet transmission approach over Internets and intranets. VoIP is enjoying gradually growing acceptance as an alternative. We discuss VoIP in Section 15.5.

Wide Area Networks for Data

For data traffic, the number of wide area networking choices is even broader. Roughly, we can list the following categories as alternatives:

- **Public packet-switching networks:** There are a number of such networks in the United States and at least one in most industrialized countries. Typically, the user must lease a line from the user's computing equipment to the nearest packet-switching node.

- **Private packet-switching networks:** In this case, the user owns or leases the packet-switching nodes, which are generally collocated with the user's data processing equipment. Leased lines, typically 56- or 64-kbps digital lines, interconnect the nodes.

- **Private leased lines:** Dedicated lines can be used between sites. No switching is involved, so a leased line is needed between any pair of sites that wish to exchange data.

- **Public circuit-switching networks:** With the use of modems or switched digital service, the user can employ dial-up telephone lines for data communications.

- **Private circuit-switching networks:** If the user has an interconnected set of digital PBXs, either by leased 56-kbps lines or by T-1 lines, then this network can carry data as well as voice.

- **ISDN:** ISDN offers both packet switching and traditional circuit switching in an integrated service.

The last two alternatives are likely to be justified on the basis of the voice traffic, with data traffic being a sort of bonus that comes with the network. Because this approach is therefore not directly comparable to the others, we do not consider it further in this chapter.

As with voice, the choice of approach for data networking is complex and depends on current prices. In comparing the alternatives for wide area data networks, we look first at the cost and performance considerations, which are more easily quantified and analyzed. Then we consider some other issues that are also important in selecting a network.

COST/PERFORMANCE CONSIDERATIONS   Data communications traffic can be roughly classified into two categories: stream and bursty. Stream traffic is characterized by lengthy and fairly continuous transmission. Examples are file transfer, telemetry, other sorts of batch data processing applications, and digitized voice communication. Bursty traffic is characterized by short, sporadic transmissions. Interactive client/server traffic, such as transaction processing, data entry, and time sharing, fits this description. Facsimile transmission is also bursty.

The public circuit-switching network approach makes use of dial-up lines. The cost is based on data rate, connection time, and distance. As we have said, this is quite inefficient for bursty traffic. However, for occasional stream-oriented requirements, this may be the most appropriate choice. For example, a corporation may have distributed offices. At the close of the day, each office transfers a file to headquarters summarizing the activities for that day. A dial-up line used for the single transfer from each office appears to be the most cost-effective solution. When there is a high volume of stream traffic among a few sites, the most economical solution is to obtain dedicated circuits among sites. These circuits, also known as leased lines or semipermanent circuits, may be leased from a telecommunications provider, such as a telephone company, or from a satellite provider. The dedicated circuit carries a constant fixed cost based on data rate and, in some cases, distance. If the traffic volume is high enough, then the utilization will be high enough to make this approach the most attractive.

On the other hand, if the traffic is primarily bursty, then packet switching has the advantage. Furthermore, packet switching permits terminals and computer ports of various data rates to be interconnected. If the traffic is primarily bursty but is of relatively modest volume for an organization, a public packet-switching network provides the best solution. In this case, the network provides a packet transmission service to a variety of subscribers, each of which has moderate traffic requirements. If there are a number of different subscribers, the total traffic should be great enough to result in high utilization. Hence, the public network is cost effective from the provider's point of view. The subscriber gets the advantages of packet switching without the fixed cost of implementing and maintaining the network. The cost to the subscriber is based on both connection time and traffic volume but not distance.

If the volume of an organization's bursty traffic is high and is concentrated among a small number of sites, a private packet-switching network is the best solution. With a lot of bursty traffic among sites, the private packet-switching network provides much better utilization and hence lower cost than using circuit switching or simple dedicated lines. The cost of a private network (other than the initial fixed cost of the packet-switching nodes and the dedicated lines) is based solely on distance. Thus, it combines the efficiencies of public packet switching with the time and volume independence of dedicated circuits.

OTHER CONSIDERATIONS   In addition to the issues of cost and performance, the choice of network should also take into account control, reliability, and security.

An organization large enough to need a wide area data network will come to rely heavily on that network. Accordingly, it is vital that management be able to maintain proper control of the network to provide an efficient and effective service to users. We will explore this topic at some length in Part Six. For our purposes here, we can say that three aspects of control are significant in comparing various network approaches: strategic control, growth control, and day-to-day operation of the network.

Strategic control involves the process of designing and implementing the network to meet the organization's unique requirements. With public packet switching, the subscriber has virtually no strategic control over service levels, reliability, or maintenance. The network is intended as a public utility to serve the average customer. With either dedicated lines or a private packet-switching network, the user organization can decide on the capacity and level of redundancy that it is willing to pay for. **Growth control** allows users to plan for network expansion and modifications arising as their needs change. A private packet-switching network provides the most flexibility in accommodating needs for growth. Additional packet-switching nodes, more trunks, and higher-capacity trunks can be added as needed. These raise the overall capacity and reliability of the network. Although the user has control over the number and capacity of lines in a dedicated-line design, there is less flexibility for incrementally expanding the network. Again, with a public packet-switching network, the user has no control over growth. The user's needs are satisfied only if they happen to be within the capabilities of the public network. With respect to **day-to-day operation**, the user is concerned with accommodating peaks of traffic and with quickly diagnosing and repairing faults. Packet-switching networks can be designed with effective centralized network control that allows the network to be adjusted to changing conditions. Of course, in the case of the public network, the user is dependent on

Table 15.2 Features of Wide Area Networks

Feature	Dedicated (leased lines)	Public Packet	Private Packet
Strategic control	Network design, service, and maintenance can be given priority and controlled by user.	Service limited to that which suits average customer.	Network design, service, and maintenance can be given priority and controlled by user.
Growth control and operation control	Not integrated; decentralized fault detection may be expensive.	Provided by service supplier to satisfy average requirements.	Integrated into all equipment; centralized fault isolation and detection.
Reliability	Manual and user-visible recovery from failure.	Transparent and automatic recovery from failure.	Transparent and automatic recovery from failure.
Security	Private users only.	Public users, network access control.	Private users only, network access control.

the network provider. As in any public utility, such as a transportation system, there tend to be "rush hours" in public networks when service levels decline. Day-to-day control is more difficult to automate in the case of dedicated lines; available tools are comparatively few and crude because we are not dealing with a unified network.

The inherent reliability of a packet-switching network is higher than that of a collection of dedicated lines. The network consists of a set of shared facilities and is equipped with centralized, automated network control facilities. Faults can be easily located and isolated and the traffic shifted to the healthy part of the network. A public network may be able to afford a greater investment in redundancy and control tools, because the cost is spread over many users. Further, the user is relieved of the burden of developing the expertise required to keep a large data communications network operational.

Finally, data security is vital to most corporations. We explore this topic in detail in Part Six. For purposes of the present discussion, we can say that use of a private network or dedicated lines will clearly afford greater security than a public packet-switching network. Public networks can use various access control mechanisms to limit the ways in which users can obtain data across the network. Those same control mechanisms are useful in private networks, because an organization may wish to segregate various communities of users.

Table 15.2 summarizes the difference among the various communications approaches.

15.5 VOICE OVER IP

We have referred a number of times in this text to the trend toward the convergence of data, voice, and video transmission using IP-based networks. This convergence enables the delivering of advanced services at lower cost for residential users, business customers of varying sizes, and service providers. One of the key technologies underlying this convergence is VoIP (voice over IP), which has become increasingly prevalent in organizations of all sizes.

In essence VoIP is the transmission of speech across IP-based network. VoIP works by encoding voice information into a digital format, which can be carried across IP networks in discrete packets. VoIP has two main advantages over traditional telephony.

1. A VoIP system is usually cheaper to operate than an equivalent telephone system with a PBX and conventional telephone network service. There are several reasons for this. Whereas traditional telephone networks allocate dedicated circuits for voice communications using circuit switching, VoIP uses packet switching, allowing the sharing of transmission capacity. Further, packetized voice transmission fits well in the framework of the TCP/IP suite, enabling the use of application- and transport-level protocols to support communications.

2. VoIP readily integrates with other services, such as combining Web access with telephone features through a single PC or terminal.

VoIP Signaling

Before voice can be transferred using VoIP, a call must be placed. In a traditional phone network, the caller enters the digits of the called number. The telephone number is processed by the provider's signaling system to ring the called number. With VoIP, the calling user (program or individual) supplies the phone number of a URI (Universal Resource Indicator, a form of URL), which then triggers a set of protocol interactions resulting in the placement of the call.

The heart of the call placement process for VoIP is the Session Initiation Protocol (SIP), defined in RFC 3261, which is an application-level control protocol for setting up, modifying, and terminating real-time sessions between participants over an IP data network. SIP supports not only VoIP but also many multimedia applications.

Figure 15.7 shows how some of the SIP components relate to one another and the protocols that are employed. A user agent (alice) uses SIP to set up a session with a user agent that will act as a server (bob). The session initiation dialogue uses SIP and involves one or more proxy servers to forward requests and responses between the two user agents. A proxy server primarily plays the role of routing, which means its job is to ensure that a request is sent to another entity closer to the targeted user. Proxies are also useful for enforcing policy (e.g., making sure a user is allowed to make a call). The user agents also make use of the Session Description Protocol (SDP), which is used to describe the media session.

The proxy servers may need to determine the address of the called device. If so, a proxy server consults a location service database. DNS is also an important part of SIP operation. Typically, a caller will make a request using the domain name of the called agent, rather than an IP address. A proxy server will need to consult a DNS server to find a proxy server for the target domain.

Associated with SIP is SDP, defined in RFC 4566. SIP is used to invite one or more participants to a session, while the SDP-encoded body of the SIP message contains information about what media encodings (e.g., voice, video) the parties can and will use. Once this information is exchanged and acknowledged, all participants are aware of the participants' IP addresses, available transmission capacity, and media type. Then data transmission begins, using an appropriate transport protocol. Typically, the Real-Time Transport Protocol (RTP), described subsequently,

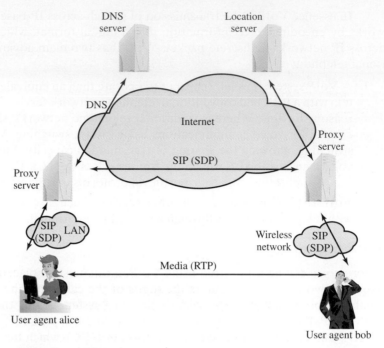

Figure 15.7 SIP Components and Protocols

is used. Throughout the session, participants can make changes to session param-eters, such as new media types or new parties to the session, using SIP messages.

VoIP Processing

Once a called party responds, a logical connection is established between the two parties (or more for a conference call), and voice data may be exchanged in both directions. Figure 15.8 illustrates the basic flow of voice data in one direction in a VoIP system. On the sending side, the analog voice signal is first converted into a digital bit stream and then segmented into packets. The packetization is performed, typically, by RTP. This protocol includes mechanisms for labeling the packets so that they can be reassembled in the proper order at the receiving end, plus a buff-ering function to smooth out reception and deliver the voice data in a continuous flow. The RTP packets are then transmitted over the Internet or a private internet using the User Datagram Protocol (UDP) and IP.

At the receiving end, the process is reversed. The packet payloads are reas-sembled by RTP and put into the proper order. The data are then decompressed and the digitized voice is processed by a digital-to-analog converter to produce analog signals for the receiver's telephone or headset speaker.

VoIP Context

Ultimately, VoIP using IP-based networks may replace the public circuit-switched networks in use today. But for the foreseeable future, VoIP must coexist with the existing telephony infrastructure. Figure 15.9 suggests some of the key elements involved in the coexistence of the older and newer technologies.

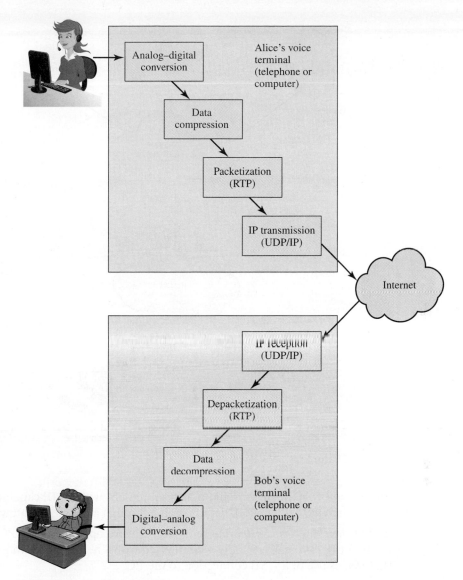

Figure 15.8   VoIP Processing

The deployment of the VoIP infrastructure has been accompanied by a variety of end-user products including the following:

- **Traditional telephone handset:** These corded or cordless units function much like a traditional telephone but are VoIP capable. They typically have many additional features, making use of a screen and providing capabilities found in smart mobile phones.

- **Conferencing units:** These provide the same basic service of conventional conference calling phone systems. These units also allow users to coordinate other data communications services, such as text, graphics, video, and whiteboarding.

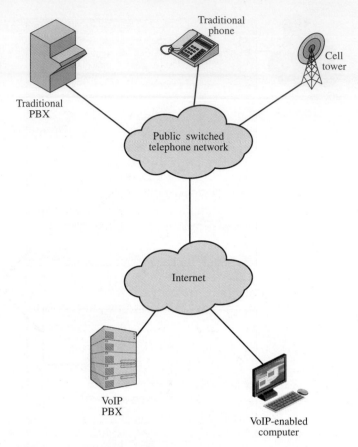

Figure 15.9 VoIP Context

- **Mobile units:** Smart phones and other cell phones with VoIP capability can tie directly into a VoIP network without going through any kind of gateway system.

- **Softphone:** The term *softphone* refers to software operating on a PC to implements VoIP. Typically, the PC is configured with a headset or with a telephone that makes use of a USB connection to the PC.

There is a wide variety of infrastructure equipment developed for to support VoIP. Here we mention two noteworthy types:

- **IP PBX:** The IP PBX is designed to support digital and analog phones and connect to IP-based networks using VoIP, as well as provide if needed a connection to the public switched telephone network using traditional technology.

- **Media gateway:** The media gateway connects different physical networks in order to provide end-to-end connectivity. An important type of media gateway connects a VoIP network to a circuit-switched telephone network, providing the necessary conversion and signaling.

The VoIP environment continues to evolve with a large number of products being developed for providers, businesses, and residential/personal users.

15.6 PRESENCE

The presence service is familiar to any instant message (IM) user who sees evidence of it in his or her buddy list as a little icon that indicates someone is online. But the presence service has evolved from a supporting feature of IM and similar applications to an underlying network service tapped by applications and corporate communication services, including telephony. Presence is becoming essential to the way employees collaborate and communicate.

A fully realized presence service is a real-time communications, messaging, and routing infrastructure that not only supports collaborative applications for user-to-user interaction, but also supports communication between applications and users. It also supports application-to-application integration, whereby presence infrastructure is used to announce which applications are up, what their functions are, and what types of protocols they accept.

The discussion in this section is based on the specification of a presence service defined by the Internet Engineering Task Force (IETF) in several RFC documents. RFC 2778 defines a model and terminology for describing systems that provide presence information, and RFC 2779 defines the requirements that a presence protocol must fulfill.

Presence Service Structure

A presence system allows users to subscribe to each other and be notified of changes in state. A presence service has two categories of clients: presentities and watchers. Any entity may take on the status of either or both types of clients.

A **presentity** (presence entity) provides presence information to a presence service. The presentity is not (usually) located within the presence service; the presence service only has a recent version of the presentity's presence information. The presentity initiates changes in the presence information, which is then distributed by the presence service.

A **watcher** requests presence information about a presentity, or watcher information about a watcher, from the presence service. Watcher information consists of information about watchers that have received presence information about a particular presentity within a particular recent span of time. Watcher information is maintained by the presence service, which can choose to present it in the same form as presence information; that is, the service can make watchers look like a special form of presentity. Three types of watcher are defined in RFC 2778:

- **Fetcher:** A fetcher plays an active role. It requests the current value of some presentity's presence information from the presence service. This role corresponds to a user who wishes at a particular time to know if another user, application, or service is available and/or wishes to know related presence information about the user, application, or service.
- **Poller:** A poller is a specific type of fetcher that fetches information on a regular basis.

- **Subscriber:** A subscriber uses the presence service to notify it immediately of changes in the presence information of one or more presentities. A user might use this role to ask to be notified when another user, application, or service becomes available.

Figure 15.10 shows the general model of a presence service. In addition to watchers and presentities, the model includes the following key components:

- **Principal:** A principal is a human, program, or a collection of humans, programs, or both that chooses to appear to the presence service as a single actor, distinct from all other principals. Principals use the presence system as a means of coordination and communication.

- **User agent:** A user agent is the means by which a principal interacts with the presence system. The user agent is software that implements a presence protocol, enabling the agent, on behalf of a principal, to invoke the presence service.

- **Presence service:** The presence service accepts, stores, and distributes presence information concerning presentities in the system that are known to the presence service.

Here is an example of the use of the presence service. A department manager wishes to teleconference with task leaders at the beginning of the day, to coordinate any cooperative actions that need to be taken. The conference is not urgent and has not been scheduled, so the department manager asks to be informed when all of the task leaders are available.

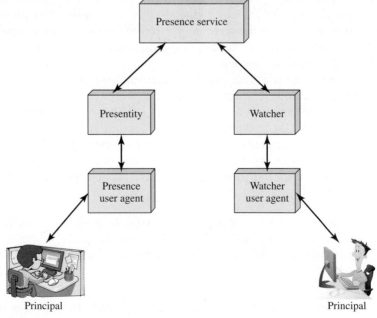

Figure 15.10 Presence Service Elements

Presence Information

Presence information is associated with every presentity in the system and is maintained by the presence service. Any change in the status of a presentity is transmitted by the presence user agent to the presence service using a presence protocol.

Presence information consists of two elements components:

- **URL:** The Uniform Resource Locator (URL) of the presentity.
- **Presence tuples:** One or more tuples of information that characterize the presentity.

The number of presence tuples is variable, and allows a number of presence properties to be associated with a particular user. Each tuple includes a STATUS marker, which conveys information such as online/offline, busy, away, do not disturb, and so on. The tuple may also include a COMMUNICATION ADDRESS, which specifies a means of contact, such as a telephone number, an e-mail address, a URL for a shared cloud element, such as a file or folder, or other means of contact and communication. Finally, a tuple may contain an OTHER PRESENCE MARKUP element, which contains other relevant information. Examples include priority, time-stamp for the last time this tuple was changed, the activity the presentity is engaged in, physical location, whether the communication is likely to be private or observed by others, and various other parameters.

Thus, the presence information structure allows an organization to create a presence system that provides basic information for simple collaboration and communication tasks, or much more elaborate schemes for support of sophisticated collaboration and communications applications.

15.7 SUMMARY

The use of a direct point-to-point link for information communications is impractical for all but the most limited requirements. For cost-effective, practical information communications, some sort of communications network is needed. For communications outside the range of a single building or a cluster of buildings, a wide area network (WAN) is employed. Two basic technologies are employed: circuit switching and packet switching.

Circuit switching is used in public telephone networks and is the basis for private networks built on leased lines and using on-site circuit switches. Circuit switching was developed to handle voice traffic but can also handle digital data, although this latter use is often inefficient. With circuit switching, a dedicated path is established between two stations for communication. Switching and transmission resources within the network are reserved for the exclusive use of the circuit for the duration of the connection. The connection is transparent: Once it is established, it appears to attached devices as if there were a direct connection.

Packet switching is employed to provide an efficient means of using the shared facilities in a data communications network. With packet switching, a station transmits data in small blocks called packets. Each packet contains some portion of the user data plus control information needed for proper functioning of the network.

Public packet-switching networks are available to be shared by a number of separate subscriber communities. The technology may also be employed to build a private packet-switching network.

The choice between circuit and packet switching depends on a host of considerations, including cost, performance, reliability, and flexibility. Both technologies will continue to be important in wide area networking.

15.8 KEY TERMS, REVIEW QUESTIONS, AND PROBLEMS

Key Terms

circuit switching	packet switching	subscriber loop
control signaling	presence	trunk
datagram	public data network	value-added network
exchange	(PDN)	(VAN)
local loop	subscriber	virtual circuit
packet	subscriber line	voice over IP (VoIP)

Review Questions

15.1 Why is it useful to have more than one possible path through a network for each pair of stations?

15.2 Concerning a switched communications network, answer the following as either true or false:
  a. All switching nodes are connected to every other node.
  b. Links between switching nodes utilize some sort of multiplexing technique.
  c. Switching nodes provide connectivity for a single end station.

15.3 What are the four generic architectural components of a public communications network? Define each term.

15.4 Answer the following as either true or false regarding circuit switching.
  a. A complete connection from end to end must be completed before data transmission can occur:
  b. There are three basic stages: connection setup, data transfer, and connection termination.
  c. Circuit switching is very efficient.

15.5 What is the principal application that has driven the design of circuit-switching networks?

15.6 Explain the difference between datagram and virtual circuit operation.

15.7 What are some advantages of private networks?

15.8 What are some of the limitations of using a circuit-switching network for data transmission?

15.9 What is a value-added network (VAN)?

15.10 What are the advantages of VoIP?

15.11 Briefly describe the role of SIP and SDP in VoIP applications.

15.12 Identify and briefly describe the major characteristics and components of presence services.

Problems

15.1   How far away from your local switching center is your business or home?

15.2   In the public switched telephone network, your call is set up and switched based on the numbers that you dial. These numbers actually provide different frequency sounds or tones to the switching center. What is this signaling called?

15.3   Find and view several YouTube videos comparing circuit switching to packet switching. Identify the URLs for at least three videos that you think do an especially good job explaining and illustrating the differences between circuit switching and packet switching. If you had to select only one video to recommend to fellow business data communications students, which would you choose? Why?

15.4   Consider a simple telephone network consisting of two end offices and one intermediate switch with a 1-MHz full-duplex trunk between each end office and the intermediate switch. The average telephone is used to make four calls per eight-hour workday, with a mean call duration of six minutes. Ten percent of the calls are long distance. What is the maximum number of telephones an end office can support?

15.5   Do some Internet research to compare datagram approach to the virtual circuit approach in packet-switching networks. Identify several business data communication applications that perform acceptably using the datagram approach. Also identify several business applications that are better suited to the virtual circuit approach.

15.6   Both temporary and permanent virtual circuits can be supported in packet-switching networks. Temporary virtual circuits are also called switched virtual circuits. Do some Internet research on the differences between switched and permanent virtual circuits and identify examples of the types of applications for which each is used in business data communication networks.

15.7   Consider a packet-switching network of N nodes, connected by the following topologies:
   a. Star: One central node with no attached station; all other nodes attach to the central node.
   b. Loop: Each node connects to two other nodes to form a closed loop.
   c. Fully connected: Each node is directly connected to all other nodes.
   For each case, give the average number of hops between stations.

15.8   Do some Internet research on switching techniques used in cellular telephone networks. Are cell phone networks examples of circuit-switched networks? Why or why not? Justify your decision in a 500–750 word paper.

15.9   VoIP has increased in popularity alongside the increased deployment of power over Ethernet (PoE) in business networks. Do some Internet research focusing how and why these systems have evolved in parallel. Summarize your findings in a 500–750 word paper or a 5–8 slide PowerPoint presentation.

15.10   Do some Internet research on SIP and SDP that focuses on the range of services that each can support. Explain how these protocols are used in unified communications to blend VoIP and presence services. Summarize your findings in a 500–1000 word paper or an 8–12 slide PowerPoint presentation.

WAN SERVICES

Learning Objectives

After reading this chapter, you should be able to:

◆ Discuss the reasons for the growing interest in and availability of high-speed alternatives for wide area networking.

◆ Describe the features and characteristics of frame relay networks.

◆ Describe the features and characteristics of asynchronous transfer mode (ATM) networks.

◆ Describe the features and characteristics of multiprotocol label switching (MPLS) and wide area Ethernet (WAE) services.

As the speed and number of local area networks (LANs) continue their relentless growth, increasing demand is placed on wide area packet-switching networks to support the tremendous throughput generated by these LANs. In the early days of wide area networking, X.25 emerged to support direct connection of terminals and computers over long distances. At speeds of up to 64 kbps, X.25 copes well with these demands. With the proliferation of high-speed LANs in business networks, the need to find more robust alternatives for interconnecting geographically dispersed business LANs was soon realized. Several generations of high-speed switched services for wide area networking have built on the X.25 technical base, and today, there are a number of high-speed WAN services available for inclusion in enterprise networks.

Indeed, business network managers are often faced with so many choices for solving capacity problems that it can be time consuming to due diligence for each. In this chapter, we begin with an overview of various wide area networking alternatives, and their relative strengths and weaknesses. We then focus on perhaps the four of the most important WAN services being consumed by businesses: frame relay, asynchronous transfer mode (ATM), multiprotocol label switching (MPLS), and wide area Ethernet (WAE).

In most business networks, the public Internet is often used as the primary or secondary WAN infrastructure for connecting computers at dispersed sites. It is increasingly rare for a business to not have a presence on the public Internet and as we have observed in previous chapters, many organizations have taken advantage of Internet technologies to develop intranets, extranets, and virtual private networks (VPNs). However, many businesses supplement the Internet's public communication infrastructure with the types of WAN services discussed in this chapter because they can exert more direct control over transmission speeds, the quality and consistency of application performance, and the security of transmitted data. Hence, the rationale for investing in the WAN services described in this chapter is similar to reasons why businesses invest in T-1 facilities or SONET services, which were discussed in Chapter 6.

16.1 WIDE AREA NETWORKING ALTERNATIVES

When considering wide area networking strategies for businesses and other organizations, two distinct but related trends need to be analyzed. The first is the need for a distributed processing architecture to support business applications and communications requirements, and the second is the wide area networking technologies and services available to meet those needs.

WAN Offerings

To meet the demands of the new corporate computing paradigm, service and equipment providers have developed a variety of high-speed services. These include faster multiplexed line schemes, such as T-3 and SONET/SDH, as well as faster switched networks schemes, including frame relay, ATM, MPLS, and WAE.

Figure 16.1 lays out the primary alternatives available from public U.S. carriers; a similar mix is available in other countries. A non-switched, or dedicated, line is a transmission link leased for a fixed price. Such lines can be leased from a carrier and used to link offices of an organization. Common offerings include the following:

- **Analog:** The least expensive option is to lease a twisted-pair analog link. With dedicated private line modems, data rates of 4.8–56 kbps are common.

- **Digital data service:** High-quality digital lines that require digital signaling units rather than modems are more expensive but can be leased at higher data rates.

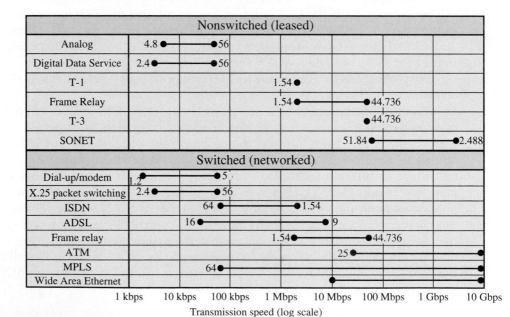

Figure 16.1   U.S. Carriers' Communications Services

- **T-1, T-3:** For many years, the most common leased line for high-traffic voice and data needs was the T-1 line, which is still quite popular. For greater needs, the T-3 is widely available.

- **Frame relay:** Although frame relay is a switched network technology, the frame relay protocol can be used over a dedicated line to provide a convenient and flexible multiplexing technique. Frame relay devices are required at the customer's premises for this approach.

- **SONET:** Some of the highest-speed leased lines that are available use SONET/SDH, discussed in Chapter 6.

Public switched services include the following:

- **Dial-up/modem:** Modems connected to the public telephone network provide a relatively inexpensive way to obtain low-speed data services. The modems themselves are inexpensive, and the telephone rates are reasonable for modest connect times. This is the near-universal access technique for residential users. In organizations, many LANs and private branch exchanges (PBXs) are equipped with modem banks to provide low-cost, supplemental data transmission service.

- **X.25 packet switching:** Although largely replaced by frame relay services in North America, this elderly standby is still used in networks worldwide. Typically, X.25 network charges are based on the volume of data transferred.

- **Integrated Services Digital Network (ISDN):** ISDN provides both circuit switching and X.25 packet switching over 64-kbps B channels. Higher data rates are also achievable. Typically, network charges are based on the duration of the call regardless of the amount of data transferred.

- **Frame relay:** Frame relay provides switched capability at speeds equivalent to the leased T-1 rate and, in some offerings, higher rates up to T-3. Its low overhead makes it suitable for interconnecting LANs and high-speed standalone systems.

- **ATM:** From the 1990s to 2005, ATM was widely viewed as a universal networking technology, destined to replace other WAN services offerings.

- **MPLS:** MPLS is a highly scalable data-carrying mechanism. Data packets are assigned labels in an MPLS network and packet-forwarding decisions are based solely on the contents of the labels. This eliminates the need to examine the entire packet and enables the creation of end-to-end circuits across any type of transport medium. MPLS can encapsulate packets from most other data communication protocols including T-1, ATM, frame relay, Ethernet, and digital subscriber line (DSL).

- **Wide area Ethernet:** WAE uses Ethernet connectivity to deliver high-speed WAN service. WAE is basically a VPN that simplifies linking Ethernet LANs at remote locations. WAE is marketed as an alternative to traditional WAN services such as T-1, leased lines, and frame relay.

Choosing among the various WAN alternatives is no easy task, and the proliferation of alternatives has increased the difficulty. Table 16.1 indicates

Table 16.1 WAN Alternatives (U.S. pricing)

Service	Usage Rate	Distance Rate
Leased line	Fixed price per month for a specific capacity (e.g., T-1 or T-3) and no additional fee for usage.	More for greater distance.
ISDN	Fixed price per month for service plus a usage charge based on amount of connect time.	Long-distance charges apply.
Frame relay	Fixed price per month for a port connection and a flat rate for a permanent virtual circuit (PVC) based on the capacity of the link.	Not distance sensitive.
ATM	Pricing policies vary.	Not distance sensitive.
MPLS	Pricing policies vary.	Not distance sensitive.
Carrier Ethernet	Pricing policies vary.	Not distance sensitive.

common pricing practices in the United States; comparable practices are used in other countries. As can be seen, the pricing structures of the various services are not directly comparable. This is one complication. Other issues that complicate the selection process include the difficulty of forecasting future traffic volumes by WAN services users, and the difficulty in forecasting traffic distributions given the flexibility of applications and the increasing mobility of users.

Evolution of WAN Architectures

Figure 16.2a shows the type of WAN architecture that was dominant in business networks until recently and continues to be a popular model. In a typical configuration, all the devices at a customer's premises are fed through a synchronous time division multiplexer onto a high-speed subscriber line to a telecommunications carrier. This includes a PBX that controls phone and fax machines for voice and fax traffic as well as an interface to a LAN. Typically, the LAN is interfaced by means of a router or layer 3 switch, as discussed in Chapter 13. There may also be a number of dumb terminals or thin clients connected to a controller that interfaces with the multiplexer. The line itself can be either T-1 or T-3; as demand has risen, SONET links, such as OC-1, have become more common.

At the carrier end, the multiplexed traffic can be split up into a number of leased circuits. These enable the creation of a private network linking to PBXs, LANs, and mainframe hosts at other locations for this customer. In addition, for data traffic, the carrier can provide an interface to one or more public high-speed switched networks, such as frame relay, ATM, MPLS, or WAE. Finally, a link to the Internet is also typically provided.

The configuration of Figure 16.2a can be very attractive to a business. It integrates all of the organization's voice and data traffic onto a single external line, which simplifies network management and configuration. One drawback is its relative lack of flexibility. The capacity on the synchronous time division multiplexing (TDM) line is divided into fixed partitions allocated to the various elements at the customer site, such as PBX, LANs, and terminal controllers. This makes it difficult if not impossible to allocate capacity dynamically as needed without the use of more expensive statistical time division multiplexers.

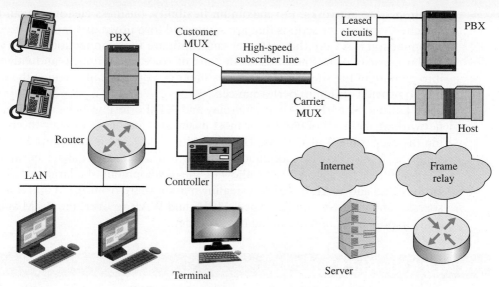

(a) Integrated network access using dedicated channels

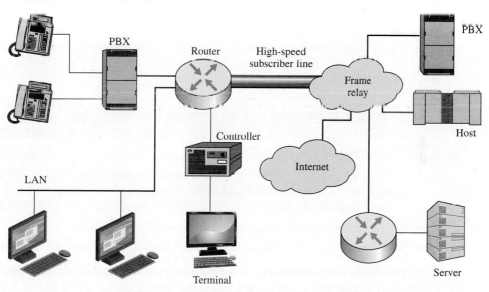

(b) Integrated network access using public switched WAN

Figure 16.2   Integrated Network Strategies

   With the advent of faster and faster switched networks, a more flexible solution is now possible, an example of which is shown in Figure 16.2b. In this arrangement, the high-speed external line connects directly to a public switched network, such as frame relay or ATM. Virtual connections can be used to set up temporary "pipes" or to various destinations. In addition, most frame relay, ATM, MPLS, and WAE suppliers offer what are called permanent virtual connections; these provide the equivalent of dedicated synchronous TDM channels and can be used to set up private networks. For maximum flexibility, business customers can rely on switched virtual connections that are set up and torn down dynamically. Each time a connection is set up, the customer can configure that connection to carry a particular capacity of traffic. Thus, as the mix of voice, data, image, and video traffic into and out of the site changes, the customer can dynamically change the capacity mix to provide optimum performance.

During the early 1990s, frame relay and ATM offerings became the wide area networking methods of choice for most businesses and large organizations, including the Department of Defense (DOD). Although ATM is considered technically superior, frame relay has continued to enjoy a sizable market share because it has been available for a longer time, allowing the development of a large installed base. Both MPLS and WAE have been stealing market share from ATM and frame relay services and industry pundits expect MPLS and WAE to overtake ATM and frame relay in popularity and use in the next decade.

16.2 FRAME RELAY

Frame relay was designed to provide a more efficient transmission scheme than traditional packet switching. The standards for frame relay matured earlier than those for ATM, and frame relay services from carriers and other providers also arrived earlier. Accordingly, there is a large installed base of frame relay products.

Background

The traditional approach to packet switching makes use of a protocol between the user and the network known as X.25. X.25 not only determines the user–network interface but also influences the internal design of the network. Several key features of the X.25 approach are the following:

- Call control packets, used for setting up and terminating virtual circuits, are carried on the same channel and same virtual circuit as data packets. In effect, in-band signaling is used.
- Multiplexing of virtual circuits takes place at layer 3.
- Both layer 2 and layer 3 include flow control and error control mechanisms.

The X.25 approach results in considerable overhead. At each hop through the network, the data link control protocol involves the exchange of a data frame and an acknowledgment frame. Furthermore, at each intermediate node, state tables must be maintained for each virtual circuit to deal with the call management and flow control/error control aspects of the X.25 protocol. All of this overhead may be justified when there is a significant probability of error on any of the links in the network. This approach is not suitable for modern digital communication facilities with very low link error rates. Today's networks employ reliable digital transmission technology over high-quality, reliable transmission links, many of which are optical fiber. In addition, with the use of optical fiber and digital transmission, high data rates can be achieved. In this environment, X.25's overhead is not only unnecessary but degrades the effective utilization of the available high-capacity links.

Frame relay was designed to eliminate much of the overhead that X.25 imposes on end-user systems and on the packet-switching network. The key differences between frame relaying and a conventional X.25 packet-switching service are as follows:

- Call control signaling, which is information needed to set up and manage a connection, is carried on a separate logical connection from user data. Thus, intermediate nodes need not maintain state tables or process messages relating to call control on an individual per-connection basis.

- Multiplexing and switching of logical connections take place at layer 2 instead of layer 3, eliminating one entire layer of processing.

- There is no hop-by-hop flow control and error control. End-to-end flow control and error control are the responsibility of a higher layer, if they are employed at all.

Thus, with frame relay, a sender's data frame is sent from source to destination, and an acknowledgment, generated at a higher layer, may be carried back in a response frame. There are no hop-by-hop exchanges of data frames and acknowledgments.

Let us consider the advantages and disadvantages of this approach. The principal potential disadvantage of frame relay, compared to X.25, is that we have lost the ability to do link-by-link flow and error control. (Although frame relay does not provide end-to-end flow and error control, this is easily provided at a higher layer.) In X.25, multiple virtual circuits are carried on a single physical link, and the link-layer protocol provides reliable transmission from the source to the packet-switching network and from the packet-switching network to the destination. In addition, at each hop through the network, the link control protocol can be used for reliability. With the use of frame relay, this hop-by-hop link control is lost. However, with the increasing reliability of transmission and switching facilities, this is not a major disadvantage.

The advantage of frame relay is that we have streamlined the communications process. The protocol functionality required at the user–network interface is reduced, as is the internal network processing. As a result, lower delay and higher throughput can be expected. Studies indicate an improvement in throughput using frame relay, compared to X.25, of an order of magnitude or more [HARB92]. The ITU-T Recommendation I.233 indicates that frame relay is to be used at access speeds up to 2 Mbps. However, frame relay service at much higher data rates is now available. Ultimately, frame relay may be replaced by MPLS and WAE networks. A recent market study projects a growth rate of frame relay connections over the 2011–2016 period of only 2% per year, after which these legacy systems will begin to decline as these networks are replaced by MPLS [INSI12].

Frame Relay Protocol Architecture

Figure 16.3 depicts the protocol architecture to support the frame relay. We need to consider two separate planes of operation: a control (C) plane, which is involved in the establishment and termination of logical connections, and a user (U) plane, which is responsible for the transfer of user data between subscribers. Thus, C-plane protocols are between a subscriber and the network, while U-plane protocols provide end-to-end functionality.

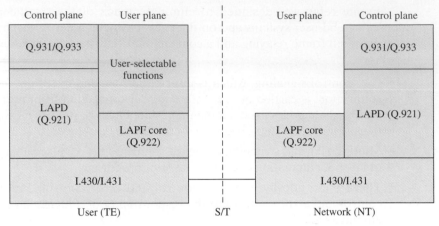

Figure 16.3 Frame Relay User–Network Interface Protocol Architecture

CONTROL PLANE The control plane for frame relay is similar to that for common channel signaling for circuit-switching services, in that a separate logical channel is used for control information. At the data link layer, LAPD (Q.921) provides a reliable data link control service, with error control and flow control, between user (TE) and network (NT). This data link service is used for the exchange of Q.933 control signaling messages.

USER PLANE For the actual transfer of information between end users, the user-plane protocol is LAPF (Link Access Procedure for Frame Mode Bearer Services), which is defined in Q.922. Only the core functions of LAPF are used for frame relay:

- Frame delimiting, alignment, and transparency
- Frame multiplexing/demultiplexing using the address field
- Inspection of the frame to ensure that it is neither too long nor too short
- Detection of transmission errors
- Congestion control functions

The core functions of LAPF in the user plane constitute a sublayer of the data link layer. This provides the base service of transferring data link frames from one subscriber to another, with no flow control or error control. Above this, the user may choose to select additional data link or network-layer end-to-end functions. These are not part of the frame relay service. Based on the core functions, a network offers frame relaying as a connection-oriented link layer service with the following properties:

- Preservation of the order of frame transfer from one edge of the network to the other
- A small probability of frame loss

As with X.25, frame relay involves the use of logical connections, in this case called data link connections rather than virtual circuits. Figure 16.4b emphasizes that the frames transmitted over these data link connections are not protected by a data link control pipe with flow and error control.

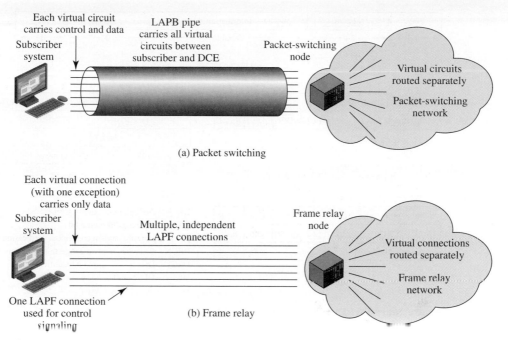

Figure 16.4   Virtual Circuits and Frame Relay Virtual Connections

Another difference between X.25 and frame relay is that the latter devotes a separate data link connection to call control. The setting up and tearing down of data link connections are done over this permanent control-oriented data link connection.

The frame relay architecture significantly reduces the amount of work required of the network. User data are transmitted in frames with virtually no processing by the intermediate network nodes, other than to check for errors and to route based on connection number. A frame in error is simply discarded, leaving error recovery to higher layers.

User Data Transfer

The operation of frame relay for user data transfer is best explained by beginning with the frame format, illustrated in Figure 16.5. The format is similar to that of other data link control protocols, such as HDLC (described in Chapter 6), with one omission: There is no Control field.

The lack of a Control field in the frame relay format means that the process of setting up and tearing down connections must be carried out on a separate channel at a higher layer of software. It also means that it is not possible to perform flow control and error control at the data link layer.

The Flag and Frame Check Sequence (FCS) fields function as in HDLC. The Flag field is a unique pattern that delimits the start and end of the frame. The FCS field is used for error detection. On transmission, the FCS checksum is calculated and stored in the FCS field. On reception, the checksum is again calculated and compared to the value stored in the incoming FCS field. If there is a mismatch, then the frame is assumed to be in error and is discarded.

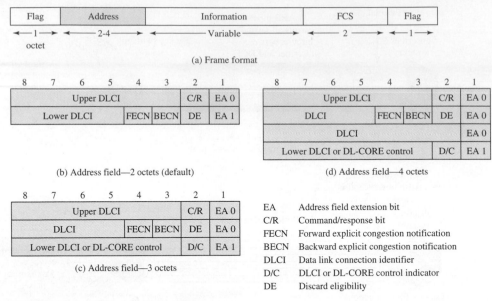

Figure 16.5   LAPE-core Formats

The information field carries higher-layer data. The higher-layer data may be either user data or call control messages.

The address field has a default length of two octets and may be extended to three or four octets. It carries a data link connection identifier (DLCI) of 10, 16, or 23 bits. The DLCI allows multiple logical frame relay connections to be multiplexed over a single channel.

The length of the address field, and hence of the DLCI, is determined by the address field extension (EA) bits. The C/R bit is application specific and is not used by the standard frame relay protocol. The remaining bits in the address field have to do with congestion control and are explained later.

Frame Relay Call Control

The actual details of the call control procedure for frame relay depend on the context of its use. Here, we summarize the essential elements of frame relay call control.

Frame relay supports multiple connections over a single link, and each has a locally unique DLCI. Data transfer involves the following stages:

1. Establish a logical connection between two endpoints, and assign a unique DLCI to the connection.

2. Exchange information in data frames. Each frame includes a DLCI field to identify the connection.

3. Release the logical connection.

The establishment and release of a logical connection is accomplished by the exchange of messages over a connection dedicated to call control, with DLCI = 0. A frame with DLCI = 0 contains a call control message in the information field.

At a minimum, four message types are needed: SETUP, CONNECT, RELEASE, and RELEASE COMPLETE.

Either side may request the establishment of a logical connection by sending a SETUP message. The other side, upon receiving the SETUP message, must reply with a CONNECT message if it accepts the connection; otherwise it responds with a RELEASE COMPLETE message. The side sending the SETUP message may assign the DLCI by choosing an unused value and including this value in the SETUP message. Otherwise, the DLCI value is assigned by the accepting side in the CONNECT message.

Either side may request to clear a logical connection by sending a RELEASE message. The other side, upon receipt of this message, must respond with a RELEASE COMPLETE message.

Congestion Control

Congestion control for a frame relay network is challenging because only a limited set of tools is available. The frame relay protocol has been streamlined to maximize throughput and efficiency. A consequence of this is that frame relay switches cannot control the flow of frames coming from business subscribers or adjacent frame relay switches using the typical flow control mechanisms included in other data link control protocols.

Congestion control is the joint responsibility of the network and its end users. The network (i.e., the collection of frame relay switches) is in the best position to monitor the degree of congestion, while the end users are in the best position to control congestion by limiting the flow of traffic. With this in mind, two general congestion control strategies are supported in frame relay: congestion avoidance and congestion recovery.

Congestion avoidance procedures are used at the onset of congestion to minimize the effect on the network. At a point at which the network detects a build-up of queue lengths and the danger of congestion, there would be little evidence available to end users that congestion is increasing. Thus, there must be some explicit signaling mechanism from the network that will trigger the congestion avoidance.

Congestion recovery procedures are used to prevent network collapse in the face of severe congestion. These procedures are typically initiated when the network has begun to drop frames due to congestion. Such dropped frames will be reported by some higher layer of software, and serve as an implicit signaling mechanism.

For explicit signaling, 2 bits in the address field of each frame are provided. Either bit may be set by the frame relay switch that detects congestion. If a switch forwards a frame in which one or both of these bits are set, it must not clear the bits. Thus, the bits constitute signals from the network to the end user. The 2 bits are as follows:

- **Backward explicit congestion notification (BECN):** Notifies the user that congestion avoidance procedures should be initiated where applicable for traffic in the opposite direction of the received frame. It indicates that the frames that the user transmits on this logical connection may encounter congested resources.

- **Forward explicit congestion notification (FECN):** Notifies the user that congestion avoidance procedures should be initiated where applicable for traffic in the same direction as the received frame. It indicates that this frame, on this logical connection, has encountered congested resources.

Implicit signaling occurs when the network discards a frame, and this fact is detected by the end user at a higher layer. The network role, of course, is to discard frames as necessary. One bit in the address field of each frame can be used to provide guidance:

- **Discard eligibility (DE):** Indicates a request that a frame should be discarded instead of other frames in which this bit is not set, when it is necessary to discard frames

The DE capability makes it possible for the frame relay subscriber to temporarily send more frames than it is allowed to on average. In this case, the user sets the DE bit on the excess frames. The network will forward these frames if it has the capacity to do so.

The DE bit also can be set by a frame relay switch that handles the frame. The network can monitor the influx of frames from subscribers and use the DE bit to protect the network. That is, if the switch to which the subscriber is directly connected decides that the input is potentially excessive, it sets the DE bit on each frame and then forwards it further into the network.

The DE bit can be used in such a way as to provide guidance for the discard decision and at the same time as a tool for providing a guaranteed level of service. This tool can be used on a per data link connection basis to ensure that heavy users can get the throughput they need without penalizing lighter users. The mechanism works as follows: Each user can negotiate a *committed information rate* (CIR) (in bits per second) at connection setup time. The requested CIR represents the user's estimate of its "normal" traffic during a busy period; the granted CIR, which is less than or equal to the requested CIR, is the network's commitment to deliver data at that rate in the absence of errors. The frame relay switch to which the subscriber's station attaches then performs a metering function (Figure 16.6). If the user is

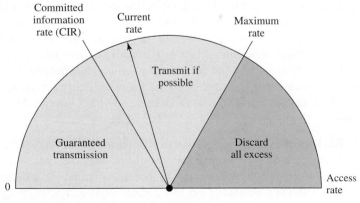

Figure 16.6 Operation of the CIR

sending data at less than the CIR, the incoming switch does not alter the DE bit. If the rate exceeds the CIR, the incoming switch will set the DE bit on the excess frames and then forward them; such frames may get through or may be discarded if congestion is encountered. Finally, a maximum rate is defined, such that any frames above the maximum are discarded at the entry frame relay switch.

16.3 ASYNCHRONOUS TRANSFER MODE (ATM)

Frame relay was designed to support access speeds up to 2 Mbps. Although it has evolved to provide services up to 45 Mbps, frame relay is not able to meet the needs of businesses that require wide area access speeds in the hundreds or thousands of megabits per second. One of the first technologies developed to accommodate such gargantuan requirements was **asynchronous transfer mode (ATM)**, also known as *cell relay*.

Cell relay is similar in concept to frame relay. Both frame relay and cell relay take advantage of the reliability and dependability of modern digital facilities to provide faster packet switching than X.25. Cell relay is even more streamlined than frame relay in its functionality and can support data rates several orders of magnitude greater than frame relay.

Virtual Channels and Virtual Paths

ATM is a packet-oriented transfer mode. Like frame relay and X.25, it allows multiple logical connections to be multiplexed over a single physical interface. The information flow on each logical connection is organized into fixed-size packets, called **cells**. As with frame relay, there is no link-by-link error control or flow control.

Logical connections in ATM are referred to as **virtual channels**. A virtual channel is analogous to a virtual circuit in X.25 or a frame relay data link connection. It is the basic unit of switching in an ATM network. A virtual channel is set up between two end users through the network, and a variable-rate, full-duplex flow of fixed-size cells is exchanged over the connection. Virtual channels are also used for user–network exchange (control signaling) and network–network exchange (network management and routing).

For ATM, a second sublayer of processing has been introduced that creates and manages virtual paths (Figure 16.7). A **virtual path** is a bundle of virtual channels that have the same endpoints. Thus, all of the cells flowing over all of the virtual channels in a single virtual path are switched together.

Figure 16.7   ATM Connection Relationships

Several advantages can be listed for the use of virtual paths:

- **Simplified network architecture:** Network transport functions can be separated into those related to an individual logical connection (virtual channel) and those related to a group of logical connections (virtual path).
- **Increased network performance and reliability:** The network deals with fewer, aggregated entities.
- **Reduced processing and short connection setup time:** Much of the work is done when the virtual path is set up. The addition of new virtual channels to an existing virtual path involves minimal processing.
- **Enhanced network services:** The virtual path is used internal to the network but is also visible to the end user. Thus, the user may define closed user groups or closed networks of virtual channel bundles.

VIRTUAL PATH/VIRTUAL CHANNEL CHARACTERISTICS ITU-T Recommendation I.150 lists the following as characteristics of virtual channel connections:

- **Quality of service:** A user of a virtual channel is provided with a quality of service specified by parameters such as cell loss ratio (ratio of cells lost to cells transmitted) and cell delay variation.
- **Switched and semipermanent virtual channel connections:** Both switched connections, which require call control signaling, and dedicated channels, called semipermanent, can be provided.
- **Cell sequence integrity:** The sequence of transmitted cells within a virtual channel is preserved.
- **Traffic parameter negotiation and usage monitoring:** Traffic parameters can be negotiated between a user and the network for each virtual channel. The input of cells to the virtual channel is monitored by the network to ensure that the negotiated parameters are not violated.

The types of traffic parameters that can be negotiated include average rate, peak rate, burstiness, and peak duration. The network may need a number of strategies to deal with congestion and to manage existing and requested virtual channels. At the crudest level, the network may simply deny new requests for virtual channels to prevent congestion. Additionally, cells may be discarded if negotiated parameters are violated or if congestion becomes severe. In an extreme situation, existing connections might be terminated.

I.150 also lists characteristics of virtual paths. The first four characteristics listed are identical to those of virtual channels. That is, quality of service, switched and semipermanent virtual paths, cell sequence integrity, and traffic parameter negotiation and usage monitoring are all characteristics of a virtual path. There are a number of reasons for this duplication. First, this provides some flexibility in how the network manages the requirements placed upon it. Second, the network must be concerned with the overall requirements for a virtual path and, within a virtual path, may negotiate the establishment of virtual circuits with given characteristics. Finally, once a virtual path is set up, it is possible for the end users to negotiate the creation of new virtual channels. The virtual path characteristics impose a discipline on the choices that the end users may make.

In addition, a fifth characteristic is listed for virtual paths:

- **Virtual channel identifier restriction within a virtual path:** One or more virtual channel identifiers, or numbers, may not be available to the user of the virtual path but may be reserved for network use. Examples would be virtual channels used for network management.

CONTROL SIGNALING   In ATM, a mechanism is needed for the establishment and release of virtual paths and virtual channels. The exchange of information involved in this process is referred to as control signaling and takes place on connections separate from those that are being managed.

For virtual channels, I.150 specifies four methods for providing an establishment/release facility. One or a combination of these methods will be used in any particular network:

1. *Semipermanent virtual channels* may be used for user-to-user exchange. In this case, no control signaling is required.

2. If there is no preestablished call control signaling channel, one must be set up. Such a channel is called a *meta-signaling channel*, because the channel is used to set up signaling channels.

3. The meta-signaling channel can be used to set up a virtual channel between the user and the network for call control signaling.

4. The meta-signaling channel can also be used to set up a user-to-user signaling virtual channel. It can then be used to allow the two end users, without network intervention, to establish and release user-to-user virtual channels to carry user data.

For virtual paths, three methods are defined in I.150:

1. A virtual path can be established on a *semipermanent* basis by prior agreement. In this case, no control signaling is required.

2. Virtual path establishment/release may be *customer controlled*. In this case, the customer uses a signaling virtual channel to request the virtual path from the network.

3. Virtual path establishment/release may be *network controlled*. In this case, the network establishes a virtual path for its own convenience. The path may be network to network, user to network, or user to user.

ATM Cells

ATM makes use of fixed-size cells, consisting of a 5-octet header and a 48-octet information field. There are several advantages to the use of small, fixed-size cells. First, the use of small cells may reduce queuing delay for a high-priority cell, because it waits less if it arrives slightly behind a lower-priority cell that has gained access to a resource (e.g., the transmitter). Second, fixed-size cells can be switched more efficiently, which is important for the very high data rates of ATM. With fixed-size cells, it is easier to implement the switching mechanism in hardware.

Figure 16.8a shows the header format at the user–network interface. Figure 16.8b shows the cell header format internal to the network.

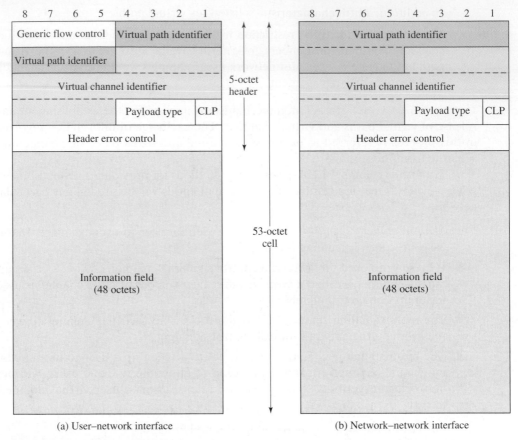

Figure 16.8 ATM Cell Format

The *Generic Flow Control* (GFC) field does not appear in the cell header internal to the network, but only at the user–network interface. Hence, it can be used for control of cell flow only at the local user–network interface. The GFC mechanism is used to alleviate short-term overload conditions in the network.

The *Virtual Path Identifier* (VPI) field constitutes a routing field for the network. It is 8 bits at the user–network interface and 12 bits at the network–network interface, allowing for more virtual paths to be supported within the network. The *Virtual Channel Identifier* (VCI) field is used for routing to and from the end user. Thus, it functions much as a service access point.

The *Payload Type* (PT) field indicates the type of information in the information field. Table 16.2 shows the interpretation of the PT bits. A value of 0 in the first bit indicates user information (i.e., information from the next higher layer). In this case, the second bit indicates whether congestion has been experienced; the third bit, known as the service data unit (SDU)[1] type bit, is a 1-bit field that can be used

---

[1]This is the term used in ATM Forum documents. In ITU-T documents, this bit is referred to as the ATM-user-to-ATM-user (AAU) indication bit. The meaning is the same.

Table 16.2   Payload Type (PT) Field Coding

PT Coding	Interpretation	
0 0 0	User data cell, congestion not experienced	SDU type = 0
0 0 1	User data cell, congestion not experienced	SDU type = 1
0 1 0	User data cell, congestion experienced	SDU type = 0
0 1 1	User data cell, congestion experienced	SDU type = 1
1 0 0	OAM segment associated cell	
1 0 1	OAM end-to-end associated cell	
1 1 0	Resource management cell	
1 1 1	Reserved for future function	

SDU = Service data unit
OAM = Operations, administration, and maintenance

to discriminate two types of ATM SDUs associated with a connection. The term *SDU* refers to the 48-octet payload of the cell. A value of 1 in the first bit of the payload type field indicates that this cell carries network management or maintenance information. This indication allows the insertion of network management cells onto a user's virtual channel without impacting the user's data. Thus, the PT field can provide inband control information.

The *cell loss priority* (CLP) bit is used to provide guidance to the network in the event of congestion. A value of 0 indicates a cell of relatively higher priority, which should not be discarded unless no other alternative is available. A value of 1 indicates that this cell is subject to discard within the network. The user might employ this field so that extra cells (beyond the negotiated rate) may be inserted into the network, with a CLP of 1, and delivered to the destination if the network is not congested. The network may set this field to 1 for any data cell that is in violation of the agreement concerning traffic parameters between the user and the network. In this case, the switch that does the setting realizes that the cell exceeds the agreed traffic parameters but that the switch is capable of handling the cell. At a later point in the network, if congestion is encountered, this cell has been marked for discard in preference to cells that fall within agreed traffic limits.

The *Header Error Control* (HEC) field is an 8-bit error code that can be used to correct single-bit errors in the header and to detect double-bit errors. In the case of most existing data link layer protocols, such as LAPD and HDLC, the data field that serves as input to the error code calculation is in general much longer than the size of the resulting error code. This allows for error detection. In the case of ATM, there is also sufficient redundancy in the code to recover from certain error patterns.

ATM Service Categories

An ATM network is designed to be able to transfer many different types of traffic simultaneously, including real-time flows such as voice, video, and bursty TCP flows. Although each such traffic flow is handled as a stream of 53-octet cells traveling through a virtual channel, the way in which each data flow is handled within the network depends on the characteristics of the traffic flow and the QoS requirements of the application. For example, real-time video traffic must be delivered within minimum variation in delay.

In this subsection, we summarize ATM service categories, which are used by an end system to identify the type of service required. The following service categories have been defined by the ATM Forum:

- **Real-Time Service**
  - —Constant bit rate (CBR)
  - —Real-time variable bit rate (rt-VBR)
- **Non-Real-Time Service**
  - —Non-real-time variable bit rate (nrt-VBR)
  - —Available bit rate (ABR)
  - —Unspecified bit rate (UBR)
  - —Guaranteed frame rate (GFR)

REAL-TIME SERVICES The most important distinction among applications concerns the amount of delay and the variability of delay, referred to as jitter, that the application can tolerate. Real-time applications typically involve a flow of information to a user that is intended to reproduce that flow at a source. For example, a user expects a flow of audio or video information to be presented in a continuous, smooth fashion. A lack of continuity or excessive loss results in significant loss of quality. Applications that involve interaction between people have tight constraints on delay. Typically, any delay above a few hundred milliseconds becomes noticeable and annoying. Accordingly, the demands in the ATM network for switching and delivery of real-time data are high.

The **constant bit rate (CBR)** service is perhaps the simplest service to define. It is used by applications that require a fixed data rate that is continuously available during the connection lifetime and a relatively tight upper bound on transfer delay. CBR is commonly used for uncompressed audio and video information. Examples of CBR applications include the following:

- Videoconferencing
- Interactive audio (e.g., telephony)
- Audio/video distribution (e.g., television, distance learning, pay per view)
- Audio/video retrieval (e.g., video on demand, audio library)

The **real-time variable bit rate (rt-VBR)** category is intended for time-sensitive applications; that is, those requiring tightly constrained delay and delay variation. The principal difference between applications appropriate for rt-VBR and those appropriate for CBR is that rt-VBR applications transmit at a rate that varies with time. Equivalently, an rt-VBR source can be characterized as somewhat bursty. For example, the standard approach to video compression results in a sequence of image frames of varying sizes. Because real-time video requires a uniform frame transmission rate, the actual data rate varies.

The rt-VBR service allows the network more flexibility than CBR. The network is able to statistically multiplex a number of connections over the same dedicated capacity and still provide the required service to each connection.

NON-REAL-TIME SERVICES   Non-real-time services are intended for applications that have bursty traffic characteristics and do not have tight constraints on delay and delay variation. Accordingly, the network has greater flexibility in handling such traffic flows and can make greater use of statistical multiplexing to increase network efficiency.

For some non-real-time applications, it is possible to characterize the expected traffic flow so that the network can provide substantially improved quality of service (QoS) in the areas of loss and delay. Such applications can use the **non-real-time variable bit rate (nrt-VBR)** service. With this service, the end system specifies a peak cell rate (PCR), a sustainable or average cell rate, and a measure of how bursty or clumped the cells may be. With this information, the network can allocate resources to provide relatively low delay and minimal cell loss.

The nrt-VBR service can be used for data transfers that have critical response-time requirements. Examples include airline reservations, banking transactions, and process monitoring.

At any given time, a certain amount of the capacity of an ATM network is consumed in carrying CBR and the two types of VBR traffic. Additional capacity is available for one or both of the following reasons: (1) Not all of the total resources have been committed to CBR and VBR traffic, and (2) the bursty nature of VBR traffic means that at some times less than the committed capacity is being used. All of this unused capacity could be made available for the **unspecified bit rate (UBR)** service. This service is suitable for applications that can tolerate variable delays and some cell losses, which is typically true of TCP-based traffic. With UBR, cells are forwarded on a first-in, first-out (FIFO) basis using the capacity not consumed by other services; both delays and variable losses are possible. No initial commitment is made to a UBR source and no feedback concerning congestion is provided; this is referred to as a *best-effort service*. Examples of UBR applications include the following:

- Text/data/image transfer, messaging, distribution, retrieval
- Remote terminal (e.g., telecommuting)

Bursty applications that use a reliable end-to-end protocol such as TCP can detect congestion in a network by means of increased round-trip delays and packet discarding. However, TCP has no mechanism for causing the resources within the network to be shared fairly among many TCP connections. Further, TCP does not minimize congestion as efficiently as is possible using explicit information from congested nodes within the network.

To improve the service provided to bursty sources that would otherwise use UBR, the **available bit rate (ABR)** service has been defined. An application using ABR specifies a PCR that it will use and a minimum cell rate (MCR) that it requires. The network allocates resources so that all ABR applications receive at least their MCR capacity. Any unused capacity is then shared in a fair and controlled fashion among all ABR sources. The ABR mechanism uses explicit feedback to sources to assure that capacity is fairly allocated. Any capacity not used by ABR sources remains available for UBR traffic.

An example of an application using ABR is LAN interconnection. In this case, the end systems attached to the ATM network are routers.

The most recent addition to the set of ATM service categories is **guaranteed frame rate (GFR)**, which is designed specifically to support IP backbone subnetworks. GFR provides better service than UBR for frame-based traffic, including IP and Ethernet. A major goal of GFR is to optimize the handling of frame-based traffic that passes from a LAN through a router onto an ATM backbone network. Such ATM networks are increasingly being used in large enterprise, carrier, and Internet service provider networks to consolidate and extend IP services over the wide area. While ABR is also an ATM service meant to provide a greater measure of guaranteed packet performance over ATM backbones, ABR is relatively difficult to implement between routers over an ATM network. With the increased emphasis on using ATM to support IP-based traffic, especially traffic that originates on Ethernet LANs, GFR may offer the most attractive alternative for providing ATM service.

16.4 MULTIPROTOCOL LABEL SWITCHING (MPLS)

Multiprotocol label switching (MPLS) services are IP-based networking services that are available from a number of carriers. MPLS services are designed to speed up the IP packet-forwarding process while retaining the types of traffic management and connection-oriented QoS mechanisms found in ATM networks.

MPLS is often described as being "protocol agnostic" because it can carry many different kinds of traffic, including ATM cells, IP packets, and Ethernet or SONET frames. Carriers have been able to cost effectively implement MPLS infrastructure because it is possible for MPLS-enabled routers to coexist with ordinary IP routers. MPLS has also been designed to work with ATM and frame relay networks via MPLS-enabled ATM switches and MPLS-enabled frame relay switches.

Because of its ability to provide higher-performance network capabilities, MPLS has the potential to completely replace frame relay and ATM. MPLS recognizes that small ATM cells are not needed in the core of modern optical networks with speeds of 40 Gbps or more. In these environments, neither 53-byte cells nor full-length 1500 byte packets experience real-time queuing delays. In addition, MPLS preserves many of the same traffic engineering and out-of-band network control mechanisms that have made frame relay and ATM attractive WAN services for business subscribers.

MPLS Operation

An MPLS network consists of a set of nodes, called *label switched routers* (LSRs), that are capable of switching and routing packets on the basis of a label which has been appended to each packet. Labels define a flow of packets between two endpoints. For each distinct flow, a specific path through the network of LSRs is defined. This path is called a *forwarding equivalence class* (FEC) and each FEC has an associated traffic characterization that defines the QoS requirements for that flow. LSRs forward each packet based on its label value; they do not need to examine or process the packet's IP header. This means that an LSR's forwarding process is simpler and faster than that for an IP router.

Figure 16.9 illustrates the operation of MPLS within a domain of MPLS-enabled routers. The first step in the process involves establishing a *label switched path* (LSP) for the packets that are to be routed and delivered and the QoS parameters that must be established for the LSP. QoS parameters include the queuing and discarding policy for each LSR along the path and the resources that need to be committed to the path. The process of establishing the LSP and its QoS parameters results in the creation of the FEC; this is illustrated in (1) in Figure 16.9. Once the FEC is created, labels can be assigned to the packets for the FEC.

Packets enter an MPLS switching domain through an ingress LSR at the edge of the MPLS network. The ingress LSR processes the packet, determines the QoS services that it requires, and assigns the packet to a FEC and LSP. It then appends the appropriate label and forwards the packet to the next LSR along the LSP. This is illustrated in Figure 16.9 (2). Within the MPLS network, each LSR along the LSP receives the labeled packet and forwards it to the next LSR along the LSP; see Figure 16.9 (3). When the packet arrives at the egress LSR at the edge of the network closest to the packet's destination, the edge LSR strips the label from the packet, reads its IP packet header, and forwards to packet to its final destination. In the example illustrated in Figure 16.9 (4), the final destination is a server.

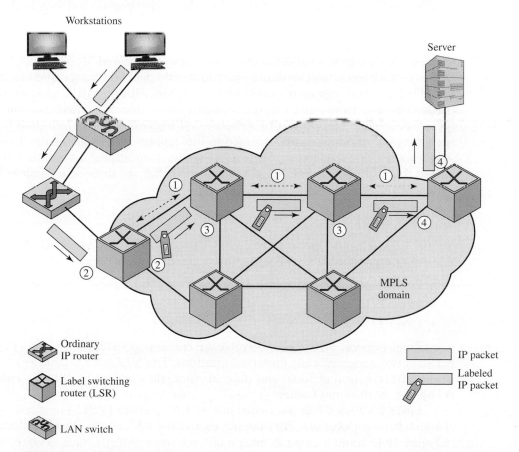

Figure 16.9   MPLS Operation

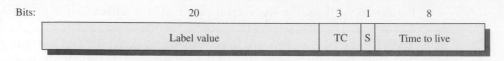

TC = traffic class
S = bottom of stack bit

Figure 16.10 MPLS Label Format

As may be observed in Figure 16.10, an MPLS label is a 32-bit field that includes the following elements:

- Local value: a 20-bit label that has local significance
- Traffic class: a 3-bit label that signifies QoS priority and explicit congestion notification (ECN)
- Bottom of stack bit: If this is set to 1, it indicates that the current label is the last in the stack.
- Time to live: 8 bits are used to encode a hop count, or time-to-live value. This is included to avoid looping or having the packet remain too long in the network because of faulty routing.

In short, with MPLS, the first time the packet enters the network, it is assigned to a specific FEC that is indicated in the label that is allocated. Because each router in the network has a table indicating how to handle packets of a specific FEC type, the MPLS network can consistently handle packets with particular characteristics (such as coming from particular ports or carrying traffic of particular application types). Assigning packets to FECs means that packets carrying real-time traffic, such as voice or video, can be mapped to low-latency routes across the network. A key point is that the labels provide a way to attach additional information to each packet that facilitates traffic engineering in ways that are difficult to achieve in IP networks and other WAN services.

MPLS VPN

MPLS VPN refers to methods to create VPNs over MPLS networks. There are three major types of MPLS VPNs deployed in today's networks:

- Point-to-point (Pseudowire)
- Layer 2 (VPLS)
- Layer 3 (VPRN)

Point-to-point MPLS VPNs involve the creation of virtual leased lines (VLLs) between two geographically dispersed locations. The VLLs are established similar to the FEC creation process, and once in place, they can be used to encapsulate ATM, T-1, or Ethernet frames.

Layer 2 MPLS VPNs use virtual private LAN service (VPLS) to create virtual channels between locations. For example, each of the MPLS VPN channels illustrated in Figure 16.11 could be used to route a different type of traffic such as voice, video, and data.

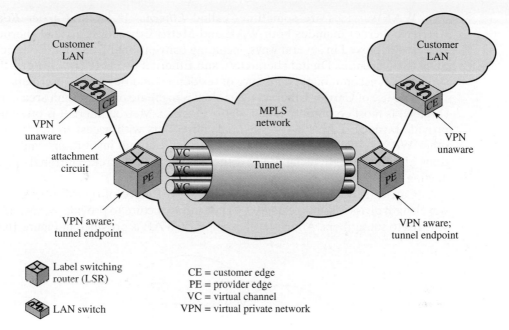

Figure 16.11 Layer 2 MPLS VPN Concepts

Layer 3 MPLS VPNs employ the use of VPRN (virtual private routed network) to segment the network traffic for each customer utilizing the service. A specific routing table for each customer is created and is used to route network traffic among that customer's locations. For example, a business might use a MPLS layer 3 VPN to route traffic between its corporate offices and data centers.

VPNs are popular with businesses because they make it possible to create private networks across shared WAN circuits. Because they combine privacy and high-performance networking capabilities, MPLS VPNs are becoming increasingly common in enterprise networks.

16.5 WIDE AREA ETHERNET

Wide area Ethernet (WAE) is the delivery of WAN services using Ethernet connectivity. It is a high-speed alternative to traditional WAN services such as frame relay, leased lines, ATM, or T-1 services. WAE maintains the simplicity, high bandwidth, and flat network design of layer 2 Ethernet. To WAE subscribers, connected sites look like one single logical network. WAE is essentially a VPN service for linking remote locations.

Most WAE implementations use virtual private LAN services (VPLS) to interconnect network endpoints. VPLS allows carriers to define QoS levels for wide area connections and commit resources, such as sufficient bandwidth, for applications such as video or audio. VPLS also enables carries to create logical Ethernet networks from a variety of WAN services including IP or MPLS networks.

WAE services are sometimes called *Ethernet WAN* or *Carrier Ethernet*. Carrier Ethernet includes both WAE and Metro Ethernet. Carrier Ethernet services are deployed in several ways, including conventional Ethernet, Ethernet over SDH (Synchronous Digital Hierarchy), and Ethernet over MPLS. Carrier Ethernet services can accommodate a mixture of residential and business subscribers.

The use of Carrier Ethernet technologies to create metropolitan area networks (MANs) is most commonly called *Metro Ethernet*. Metro Ethernet is often used to provide business LANs and residential subscribers with access to the Internet or other WAN services. Government agencies, educational institutions, and corporations are increasingly using Metro Ethernet services to create intranets interconnecting branch offices or campuses.

Carrier Ethernet often capitalizes on the existence of optical fiber and dense wavelength division multiplexing (DWDM) infrastructure to provide WAN and MAN services to subscribers. A high-level example of WAE is provided in Figure 16.12.

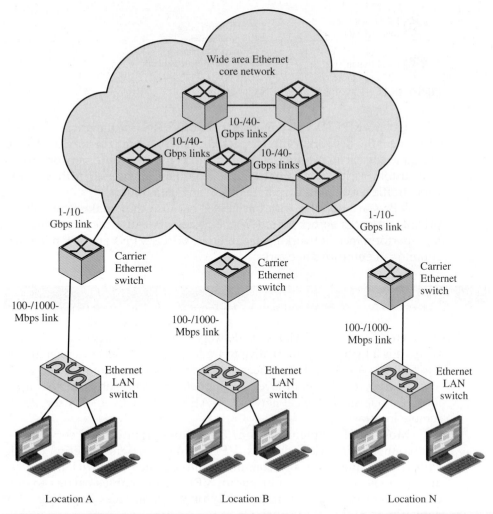

Figure 16.12 Wide Area Ethernet

APPLICATION NOTE

Off-Site Connectivity Solutions

There was a rule of thumb called the 80/20 rule which described where data were headed. There are actually several of these rules but this one stated that about 80% of your network data would be local and 20% was going to head off-site. This is referred to as your "locality of reference." Increasingly, we see organizations turning this rule on its head and sending/receiving 80% of their data to off-site locations as part of their normal business routine. As a result, traditional solutions will not be sufficient to handle the load. In addition to the protocols and services already mentioned in this chapter, there are other transport systems that have emerged as robust connectivity alternatives. Originally viewed as solutions for the home, cable and digital subscriber line (DSL) systems have proven themselves to be appropriate for businesses and so should be part of any site evaluation.

Like ATM and frame relay, cable and DSL can be "throttled." This means that the data transmission rate can be modified to suit a particular need. As you have seen in Chapters 5 and 6, DSL also has several different types of service available. Cable providers also have different service plans for businesses.

As with most services, there is the question of regional availability. Geographic offerings vary quite a bit. The pricing from area to area can also be significantly different. For example, in the Northeast, frame relay has been very popular while ISDN and ATM remain available but expensive solutions. In the same region, cable and DSL services are both available and in fact directly compete with each other in advertising campaigns.

Cable simply means that the data are being sent down the same cabling infrastructure that provides cable television. Another channel (like the television channels) is allocated for this transmission. All of the channels are allocated 6 MHz, and the data channel is no different. The upstream and downstream data transmissions are provided with different carriers, and the modems simply modulate or demodulate the signal. Cable is capable of long-range transmission because of the coaxial cable. This medium serves to protect the signal from outside interference.

The problem that most people complain about with cable is the number of users that may be on a particular segment. Cable distribution is a shared medium, and because of this, all of the users in a neighborhood or building are often on the same line, fighting for bandwidth. Because of this, cable often starts to behave like shared Ethernet: The higher the number of users, the lower the bandwidth allocated to each individual. Even with this drawback, cable offers a high-speed alternative worth considering.

DSL runs over the same line that your telephone uses. Like cable, DSL providers advertise that you can use your telephone while transmitting data. While cable transmissions use a completely different system, DSL requires a mechanism for "stepping around" a telephone conversation. DSL data transmissions use different frequencies than that of voice. Voice output is low frequency, and DSL modems transmit at frequencies above this to prevent interference. It is interesting to note that cable and DSL use the same modulation technique—quadrature amplitude modulation (QAM).

Unlike cable, DSL users do not share a line with others. However, DSL has other restrictions. The most prominent problem is distance. This, coupled with the quality of the

(*Continued*)

copper connecting a site to the central office, can eliminate DSL as a viable solution for some areas. DSL does not perform well beyond a few miles, and the farther the distance, the greater the noise and therefore the lower the data rate. Even with the best unshielded twisted pair (UTP), the maximum distance is limited to about 18,000 feet.

While neither cable nor DSL is currently capable of very high speed connections (100 Mbps), they represent successful alternatives to traditional services. Companies providing these solutions are constantly adding bandwidth to make themselves more competitive. In addition, services are often bundled, which may make them very attractive. Depending on the organization's needs and service availability, cable and DSL are definitely worth considering.

This discussion wouldn't be complete without noting another last-mile connectivity solution—Ethernet, both Gigabit and 10 Gigabit. Targeted specifically for this particular market, it leverages a well-known technology (Ethernet) and runs over fiber. The result is an extremely high speed alternative to other services that is able to transmit over long distances. To compare, a high data transfer site like a university that might purchase an expensive OC-3 at 155 Mbps could get a 10-gigabit connection that is up to 60 times faster. However, the equipment is still quite expensive and the service may not be available. The list of off-site connectivity solutions is already quite long, and we keep adding different technologies. Yet it won't be too long before several of the older technologies simply will not be able to keep up with bandwidth demands as companies push more and more data over their external links.

16.6 SUMMARY

A major change has occurred in the provision of wide area telecommunications services. The increasing capacity requirements of distributed computing systems, coupled with the introduction of transmission facilities of high speed and high reliability, have led to the introduction of a variety of WAN services that far outstrip the capabilities of traditional packet-switching networks.

Historically, frame relay has been one of the most popular WAN services for business subscribers. Frame relay is used globally and is offered by a wide variety of providers for both public and private network configurations. Frame relay makes use of variable-sized packets, called frames, and a processing scheme that is considerably simpler than traditional packet-switching networks. Data rates of up to 44.736 Mbps are readily achievable.

Asynchronous transfer mode (ATM) is even more streamlined than frame relay and provides capacity in the Gbps range. ATM technology is widely found in today's enterprise networks, especially for wide area networking.

Multiprotocol label switching (MPLS) directs data from one network node to the next based on short path labels rather than longer IP network addresses. This speeds up the packet forwarding process. MPLS can encapsulate packets of various protocols and supports a wide range of access technologies including Ethernet, T-1, ATM, frame relay, and DSL.

Wide area Ethernet (WAE) has emerged as another high-speed WAN service alternative to frame relay and ATM. Because Ethernet is pervasive in business LANs, WAE has become an attractive WAN service option to enterprise network managers.

16.7 KEY TERMS, REVIEW QUESTIONS, AND PROBLEMS

Key Terms

asynchronous transfer mode (ATM)	multiprotocol label switching (MPLS)	T-3
available bit rate (ABR)	non-real-time variable bit rate (nrt-VBR)	unspecified bit rate (UBR)
cell		variable bit rate (VBR)
constant bit rate (CBR)	real-time variable bit rate (rt-VBR)	virtual channel
frame relay		virtual path
guaranteed frame rate (GFR)	T-1	wide area Ethernet (WAE)
		wide area network (WAN)

Review Questions

16.1 What are the key high-speed networking services available for wide area networking?

16.2 How does frame relay differ from packet switching?

16.3 What are the relative advantages and disadvantages of frame relay compared to packet switching?

16.4 Why is all of the error checking used by an X.25 system not required on modern communication facilities?

16.5 How is congestion control handled in a frame relay network?

16.6 How does ATM differ from frame relay?

16.7 What are the relative advantages and disadvantages of ATM compared to frame relay?

16.8 What is the difference between a virtual channel and a virtual path?

16.9 List and briefly define ATM real-time services.

16.10 List and briefly define ATM non-real-time services.

16.11 What are the characteristics of MPLS networks?

16.12 Briefly describe the role of a forwarding equivalence class (FEC) in MPLS.

16.13 What are the characteristics of MPLS VPNs?

16.14 What are the characteristics of wide area Ethernet networks?

Problems

16.1 Do some Internet research on growth rates for frame relay, ATM, MPLS, and Carrier Ethernet services. What conclusions can be reached about the future of each of these WAN services? Summarize your findings in a 750–1000 word paper or an 8–10 slide PowerPoint presentation.

16.2 Do some Internet research on virtual private networks (VPNs) and their use by business organizations. Describe the major types of VPNs and technologies, protocols, and services used to deploy VPNs. Also describe the business benefits of VPNs.

Summarize your findings in a 750–1000 word paper or an 8–10 slide PowerPoint presentation.

16.3 The proliferation of support for mobility and mobile applications in enterprise networks has increased the importance of mobile VPNs to support mobile business users. Do some Internet research on mobile VPNs, how they differ from conventional VPNs, and the types of business applications they support. Summarize your findings in a 500–750 word paper or a 5–8 slide PowerPoint presentation.

16.4 Do some Internet research to identify some of the major vendors of Carrier Ethernet services. The following Web site may assist in your search for information: www. carrierethernetservices.com. Focus on at least three vendors that provide national and/or international Carrier Ethernet services and summarize the access speeds, transmission speeds, and VPN services that they provide to their subscribers. Summarize your findings in a 500–750 word paper or a 5–8 slide PowerPoint presentation.

16.5 Consider the following situations. In each case indicate whether you would use frame relay, ATM, MPLS, or Carrier Ethernet services. Assume that the facilities are available and "competitively" priced. For each situation, determine which services could be used to satisfy the functional requirements of the application. For each situation, select the service(s) you would recommend and explain the reasons for your choice.

   a. You have a large number of locations in a metropolitan area. At each location there is a large number of real-time data transactions processed. Information about the transactions must be sent independently and more or less randomly among the locations. That is, the transaction are not batched or do not occur in bunches. Performance requirements are such that the delay must be short. Volumes at each location are modest but in the range of up to a few Mbps in total.

   b. You have a national WAN with about a half dozen locations in relatively remote areas. The transmission facilities are varied and include radio links, satellite links, and phone links using modems. The data rates are relatively modest.

   c. In this case, you have multimedia applications. These include image communication and significant real-time video and audio services. These are interspersed with a multitude of other data services. The number of locations is small, but with the image and video applications, the volume is quite large, nearing Gbps ranges. There is also a large number of users and applications involved so that a large number of virtual circuits are needed even though the number of locations is small.

16.6 Do some Internet research to identify some of the major vendors of MPLS service providers. The Web site www.mplsprovider.com/mpls-service-provider.asp may be helpful in your search for information. Focus on three or four vendors that you think do a particularly good job describing the business benefits of MPLS to potential subscribers and explain why you are particularly impressed by these providers. If you were in charge and had to select the MPLS service vendor for your business, which would you choose? Why?

16.7 When doing Internet research on MPLS and Ethernet, you are likely to encounter discussions of virtual local area networks (VLANs). Do some Internet research on VLANs and how they are used in business organizations. Summarize the characteristics, typical uses, and business advantages of VLANs in a 5–8 slide PowerPoint presentation or a 500–750 word paper. Identify the WAN services (ATM, frame relay, MPLS, Carrier Ethernet) that are most conducive to supporting VLANs.

WIRELESS WANs

Learning Objectives

After reading this chapter, you should be able to:

♦ Identify the advantages and disadvantages of unguided (wireless communication) relative to guided communication.

♦ Distinguish among four generations of mobile telephony.

♦ Understand the relative merits of time division multiple access (TDMA) and code division multiple access (CDMA) approaches to mobile telephony.

♦ Describe the characteristics of third-generation (3G) and fourth-generation (4G) cellular networks.

♦ Understand the properties and applications of low-earth-orbiting satellites (LEOSs), medium-earth-orbiting satellites (MEOSs), and geostationary earth orbit satellites (GEOSs).

We have entered the post-PC era. In 2011, more smartphones were sold than personal computers, and Web services/applications made up the vast majority of the new software that was developed. The proliferation of mobile devices and Web applications underscores the fact that electronic information systems affect every aspect of our lives, and that it is increasingly bothersome to be tethered to these systems by wires. Wireless communications offers us mobility and much more. Wireless communications is likely to be viewed as an essential part of an enterprise network infrastructure when

- Mobile communication is needed.
- Communication must take place in a hostile or difficult terrain that makes wired communication difficult or impossible.
- A communication system must be deployed quickly.
- Communication facilities must be installed at low initial cost.
- The same information must be broadcast to many locations.

However, business network designers cannot overlook the disadvantages of wireless communications relative to guided media such as twisted pair, coaxial cable, or optical fiber:

- Wireless communication operates in a less controlled environment and is therefore more susceptible to interference, signal loss, noise, and eavesdropping.
- Generally, wireless facilities have lower data rates than guided facilities.
- Frequencies can be more easily reused with guided media than with wireless media.

In this chapter we consider wide area wireless systems, including mobile telephony, third- and fourth-generation wireless systems, and satellite communications. Wireless LANs are discussed in Chapter 14.

17.1 CELLULAR WIRELESS NETWORK

Of all the significant advances in data communications and telecommunications, one of the most revolutionary has been the development and evolution of cellular networks. Cellular technology is the foundation of mobile wireless communications and supports users in locations that are not easily served by wired networks. It is the underlying technology for mobile telephones, personal communications systems, wireless Internet and mobile Web applications, and much more.

Cellular radio is a technique that was developed to increase the capacity available for mobile radio telephone service. Prior to the introduction of cellular radio, mobile radio telephone service was only provided by a high-power transmitter/receiver. A typical system would support about 25 channels with an effective radius of about 80 km. The way to increase the capacity of the system is to use lower-power transmitters with shorter radius and to use numerous transmitters/receivers.

Cellular Network Organization

The essence of a cellular network is the use of multiple low-power transmitters, on the order of 100 W or less. Because the range of such a transmitter is small, an area can be divided into cells, each one served by its own antenna. Each cell is allocated a band of frequencies and is served by a **base station** (BS), consisting of transmitter, receiver, and control unit. Adjacent cells are assigned different frequencies to avoid interference or crosstalk. However, cells sufficiently distant from each other can use the same frequency band.

The first design decision to make is the shape of cells to cover an area. A matrix of square cells would be the simplest layout to define (Figure 17.1a). However, this geometry is not ideal.[1] As a mobile user within a cell moves toward the cell's boundaries, it is best if all of the adjacent antennas are equidistant. This simplifies the task of determining when to switch the user to an adjacent antenna and which antenna to choose. A hexagonal pattern provides for equidistant antennas (Figure 17.1b).[2] In practice, a precise hexagonal pattern is not used. Variations from the ideal are due to topographical limitations, local signal propagation conditions, and practical limitations on siting antennas.

A wireless cellular system limits the opportunity to use the same frequency for different communications because the signals, not being constrained, can interfere with one another even if geographically separated. Systems supporting a large number of communications simultaneously need mechanisms to conserve spectrum.

FREQUENCY REUSE   In a cellular system, each cell has a base transceiver. The transmission power is carefully controlled (to the extent that it is possible in the highly variable mobile communication environment) to allow communication within the

---

[1]If the width of a square cell is d, then a cell has four neighbors at a distance d and four neighbors at a distance $\sqrt{2}d$.

[2]The radius of a hexagon is defined to be the radius of the circle that circumscribes it (equivalently, the distance from the center to each vertex; also equal to the length of a side of a hexagon). For a cell radius R, the distance between the cell center and each adjacent cell center is $d = \sqrt{3}R$.

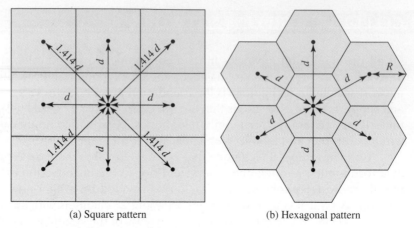

(a) Square pattern   (b) Hexagonal pattern

Figure 17.1 Cellular Geometries

cell using a given frequency while limiting the power at that frequency that escapes the cell into adjacent ones. The objective is to use the same frequency in other nearby (but not adjacent) cells, thus allowing the frequency to be used for multiple simultaneous conversations. Generally, 10–50 frequencies are assigned to each cell, depending on the traffic expected.

The essential issue is to determine how many cells must intervene between two cells using the same frequency so that the two cells do not interfere with each other. Various patterns of frequency reuse are possible. Figure 17.2 shows some examples. If the pattern consists of N cells and each cell is assigned the same number of frequencies, each cell can have K/N frequencies, where K is the total number of frequencies allotted to the system.[3]

Several parameters are typically considered when determining frequency reuse. These include the radius of a cell (R), the distance between the centers of adjacent cells ($d = \sqrt{3}R$), the minimum distance between centers of cells that use the same band of frequencies (D), and additional parameters associated with frequency reuse.[4]

---

[3]For AMPS (Advanced Mobile Phone Service, a widely used first-generation cellular scheme), $K = 395$, and $N = 7$ is the smallest pattern that can provide sufficient isolation between two uses of the same frequency. This implies that there can be at most 57 frequencies per cell on average.

[4]Commonly used parameters in frequency reuse calculations include:

D = minimum distance between centers of cells that use the same band of frequencies (called cochannels)

R = radius of a cell

d = distance between centers of adjacent cells ($d = \sqrt{3}R$)

N = number of cells in a repetitious pattern (each cell in the pattern uses a unique band of frequencies), termed the *reuse factor*

In a hexagonal cell pattern, only the following values of N are possible:

$$N = I^2 + J^2 + (I \times J), \ldots I, J = 0, 1, 2, 3, \ldots$$

Hence, possible values of N are 1, 3, 4, 7, 9, 12, 13, 16, 19, 21, and so on. The following relationship holds:

$$\frac{D}{R} = \sqrt{3N}$$

This can also be expressed as $D/d = \sqrt{N}$.

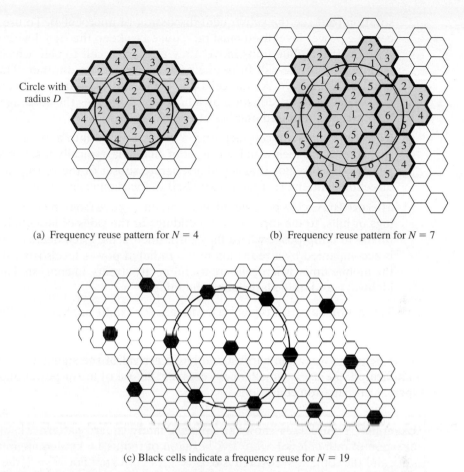

(a) Frequency reuse pattern for $N = 4$

(b) Frequency reuse pattern for $N = 7$

(c) Black cells indicate a frequency reuse for $N = 19$

Figure 17.2   Frequency Reuse Patterns

INCREASING CAPACITY   In time, as more customers use the system, traffic may build up so that there are not enough frequencies assigned to a cell to handle its calls. A number of approaches have been used to cope with this situation, including the following:

- **Adding new channels:** Typically, when a system is set up in a region, not all of the channels are used, and growth and expansion can be managed in an orderly fashion by adding new channels.

- **Frequency borrowing:** In the simplest case, frequencies are taken from adjacent cells by congested cells. The frequencies can also be assigned to cells dynamically.

- **Cell splitting:** In practice, the distribution of traffic and topographic features is not uniform, and this presents opportunities for capacity increase. Cells in areas of high usage can be split into smaller cells. Generally, the original cells are about 6.5–13 km in size. The smaller cells can themselves be split; however, 1.5-km cells are close to the practical minimum size as a general solution (but see the subsequent discussion of microcells). To use a smaller cell, the power level used must be reduced to keep the signal within the cell. Also, as the mobile units move, they pass from cell to cell, which requires transferring of the call from one base transceiver to another. This process is called a *handoff*. As the cells get smaller, these handoffs become more frequent. A radius reduction by a factor of F reduces the coverage area and increases the required number of BSs by a factor of F^2.

- **Cell sectoring:** With cell sectoring, a cell is divided into a number of wedge-shaped sectors, each with its own set of channels, typically three or six sectors per cell. Each sector is assigned a separate subset of the cell's channels, and directional antennas at the BS are used to focus on each sector.

- **Microcells:** As cells become smaller, antennas move from the tops of tall buildings or hills, to the tops of small buildings or the sides of large buildings, and finally to lamp posts, where they form microcells. Each decrease in cell size is accompanied by a reduction in the radiated power levels from the BS and the mobile units. Microcells are useful in city streets, in congested areas along highways, and inside large public buildings.

Table 17.1 suggests typical parameters for traditional cells, called macrocells, and microcells with current technology. The average delay spread refers to multipath delay spread (i.e., the same signal follows different paths and there is a time delay between the earliest and latest arrival of the signal at the receiver). As indicated, the use of smaller cells enables the use of lower power and provides superior propagation conditions.

Example. Figure 17.3a shows an approximately square pattern. The area of a hexagon of radius R is $1.5R^2\sqrt{3}$. A hexagon of radius 1.6 km has an area of 6.65 km^2, and the total area covered is $6.65 \times 32 = 213$ km^2. For $N = 7$, the number of channels per cell is $336/7 = 48$, for a total channel capacity of $48 \times 32 = 1536$ channels. For the layout of Figure 17.3b, the area covered is $1.66 \times 128 = 213$ km^2. The number of channels per cell is $336/7 = 48$, for a total channel capacity of $48 \times 128 = 6144$ channels.

Operation of Cellular Systems

Figure 17.4 shows the principal elements of a cellular system. In the approximate center of each cell is a BS. The BS includes an antenna, a controller, and a number of transceivers, all of which are used for communicating on the channels assigned

Table 17.1 Typical Parameters for Macrocells and Microcells

	Macrocell	**Microcell**
Cell radius	1–20 km	0.1–1 km
Transmission power	1–10 W	0.1–1 W
Average delay spread	0.1–10 µs	10–100 ns
Maximum bit rate	0.3 Mbps	1 Mbps

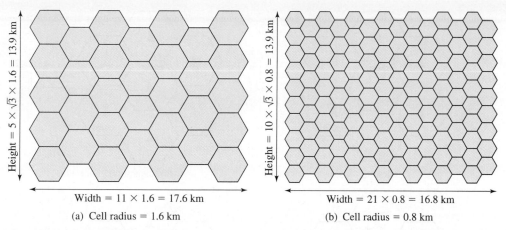

Figure 17.3   Frequency Reuse Example

to that cell. The controller is used to handle the call process between the mobile unit and the rest of the network. At any time, a number of mobile user units may be active and moving about within a cell, communicating with the BS. Each BS is connected to a mobile telecommunications switching office (MTSO), with one MTSO serving multiple BSs. Typically, the link between an MTSO and a BS is by a wire line, although a wireless link is also possible. The MTSO connects calls between mobile units. The MTSO is also connected to the public telephone or telecommunications network and can make a connection between a fixed subscriber to the public network and a mobile subscriber to the cellular network. The MTSO assigns the voice channel to each call, performs handoffs, and monitors the call for billing information.

The use of a cellular system is fully automated and requires no action on the part of the user other than placing or answering a call. Two types of channels are available between the mobile unit and the BS: control channels and traffic channels. **Control channels** are used to exchange information having to do with setting up

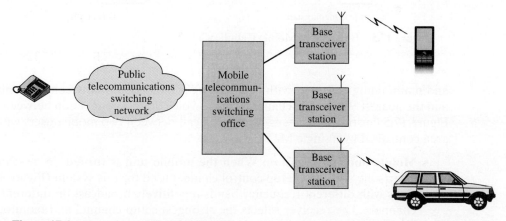

Figure 17.4   Overview of Cellular System

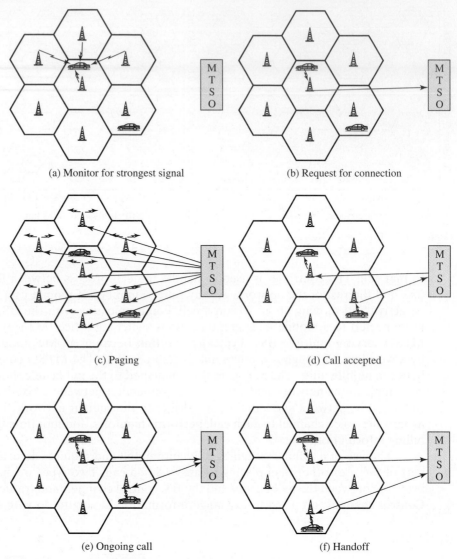

(a) Monitor for strongest signal

(b) Request for connection

(c) Paging

(d) Call accepted

(e) Ongoing call

(f) Handoff

Figure 17.5 Example of Mobile Cellular Call

and maintaining calls and with establishing a relationship between a mobile unit and the nearest BS. **Traffic channels** carry a voice or data connection between users. Figure 17.5 illustrates the steps in a typical call between two mobile users within an area controlled by a single MTSO:

- **Mobile unit initialization:** When the mobile unit is turned on, it scans and selects the strongest setup control channel used for this system (Figure 17.5a). Cells with different frequency bands repetitively broadcast on different setup channels. The receiver selects the strongest setup channel and monitors that channel. The effect of this procedure is that the mobile unit has automatically selected the BS antenna of the cell within which it will operate.[5] Then a handshake takes place between the mobile unit and the MTSO controlling this cell, through the BS in this cell. The handshake is used to identify the user and register its location. As long as the mobile unit is on, this scanning procedure is repeated periodically to account for the motion of the unit. If the unit enters a new cell, then a new BS is selected. In addition, the mobile unit is monitoring for pages, discussed subsequently.

- **Mobile-originated call:** A mobile unit originates a call by sending the number of the called unit on the preselected setup channel (Figure 17.5b). The receiver at the mobile unit first checks that the setup channel is idle by examining information in the forward (from the BS) channel. When an idle is detected, the mobile may transmit on the corresponding reverse (to BS) channel. The BS sends the request to the MTSO.

- **Paging:** The MTSO then attempts to complete the connection to the called unit. The MTSO sends a paging message to certain BSs depending on the called mobile number (Figure 17.5c). Each BS transmits the paging signal on its own assigned setup channel.

- **Call accepted:** The called mobile unit recognizes its number on the setup channel being monitored and responds to that BS, which sends the response to the MTSO. The MTSO sets up a circuit between the calling and called BSs. At the same time, the MTSO selects an available traffic channel within each BS's cell and notifies each BS, which in turn notifies its mobile unit (Figure 17.5d). The two mobile units tune to their respective assigned channels.

- **Ongoing call:** While the connection is maintained, the two mobile units exchange voice or data signals, going through their respective BSs and the MTSO (Figure 17.5e).

- **Handoff:** If a mobile unit moves out of range of one cell and into the range of another during a connection, the traffic channel has to change to one assigned to the BS in the new cell (Figure 17.5f). The system makes this change without either interrupting the call or alerting the user.

Other functions performed by the system but not illustrated in Figure 17.5 include the following:

- **Call blocking:** During the mobile-initiated call stage, if all the traffic channels assigned to the nearest BS are busy, then the mobile unit makes a preconfigured number of repeated attempts. After a certain number of failed tries, a busy tone is returned to the user.

- **Call termination:** When one of the two users hangs up, the MTSO is informed and the traffic channels at the two BSs are released.

- **Call drop:** During a connection, because of interference or weak signal spots in certain areas, if the BS cannot maintain the minimum required signal strength for a certain period of time, the traffic channel to the user is dropped and the MTSO is informed.

---

[5]Usually, but not always, the antenna and therefore the base station selected is the closest one to the mobile unit. However, because of propagation anomalies, this is not always the case.

- **Calls to/from fixed and remote mobile subscriber:** The MTSO connects to the public switched telephone network (PSTN). Thus, the MTSO can set up a connection between a mobile user in its area and a fixed subscriber via the telephone network. Further, the MTSO can connect to a remote MTSO via the telephone network or via dedicated lines and set up a connection between a mobile user in its area and a remote mobile user.

17.2 MULTIPLE ACCESS

One can categorize mobile telephone systems into generations. The first-generation systems are based on analog voice communication using frequency modulation. A widely used first-generation system was the Advanced Mobile Phone System (AMPS), which was widely used in North and South America, Australia, and China through the 1980s and into the 2000s. Due to rapid adoption of first generation mobile telephones by consumers and businesses, systems that use the spectrum more efficiently became necessary to reduce congestion. This requirement was addressed by the second generation, which uses digital techniques and time division multiple access (TDMA) or code division multiple access (CDMA) for channel access. Advanced call processing features are present as well. The third generation evolved from several second-generation wireless systems and fourth-generation systems are currently being rolled out.

In this section, we describe the basic concept of multiple access, which is a key design element of any cellular system.

The primary motivation for the transition from the first-generation cellular telephones to the second was the need to conserve spectrum. The first-generation systems were extremely successful and the number of subscribers had been growing exponentially for years. However, use (and provider profit) is constrained by spectrum capacity. Hence there is a premium on the efficient use of spectrum. In the United States this interest has not been dampened by the recent policy of the Federal Communications Commission (FCC) to auction spectrum (for very large sums of money) rather than give it away. For these reasons, it is important to understand how the spectrum is divided among users in current and planned systems. There are basically four ways to divide the spectrum among active users: frequency division multiple access (FDMA), time division multiple access (TDMA), code division multiple access (CDMA), and space division multiple access (SDMA).[6] The first two types are discussed in Chapter 6; the remaining two we treat here.

Space division multiplexing is simply the idea of using the same spectral band in two physically separate places. A simple example is frequency reuse in cells, which is discussed in this chapter. The same frequency can be used in two different cells as long as the cells are sufficiently far apart so that their signals do not interfere. Another form of space division that has been proposed for cellular telephony is to use highly directional antennas so that the same frequency may be used for two

---

[6]The terms *FDMA, TDMA, CDMA,* and *SDMA* are essentially equivalent to the terms *FDM, TDM, CDM,* and *SDM,* respectively. The phrase *multiple access* emphasizes that a single channel is being shared (accessed) by multiple users.

communications. This idea can be carried further by using steered beam antennas; these antennas can actually be aimed electronically and dynamically at a specific user. The ideas behind code division multiplexing are a little more complex, but because of their importance, we discuss them next.

Code Division Multiple Access (CDMA)

CDMA is based on direct sequence spread spectrum (DSSS). DSSS, which was briefly introduced in Chapter 14, is grounded in the following rather counterintuitive notion. We take a signal that we wish to communicate that has a data rate of, say, D bits per second and we convert it for transmission into a longer message and transmit it at a higher rate say, kD, where k is called the *spreading factor*. It might be about 100. Several things can be gained from this apparent waste of spectrum. For example, we can gain immunity from various kinds of noise and multipath distortion.

The earliest applications of spread spectrum were military, where it was used for its immunity to jamming. It can also be used for hiding and encrypting signals. However, of interest to us is that several users can independently use the same (higher) bandwidth with very little interference. Figure 17.6 shows the codes for three users, A, B, and C, each of which is communicating with the same BS receiver, R.

In practice, the CDMA receiver can filter out the contribution from unwanted users or they appear as low-level noise. However, if there are many users competing for the channel with the user the receiver is trying to listen to, or if the signal power of one or more competing signals is too high, perhaps because it is very near the receiver (the "near/far" problem), the system breaks down. The coding gain may be greater than 100 so that the ability of our decoder to filter out unwanted codes can be quite effective. A more detailed description of CDMA is provided in Appendix M.

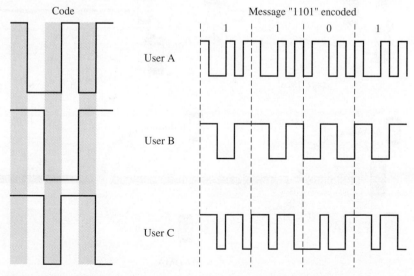

Figure 17.6 CDMA Example

Which Access Method to Use

Figure 17.7 illustrates the differences among FDMA, TDMA, and CDMA. In summary, with FDMA, each user communicates with the BS on its own narrow frequency band. For TDMA, the users share a wider frequency band and take turns communicating with the BS. For CDMA, many users can simultaneously use the same wide frequency band. Each user's signal is scrambled using a unique code so that it resembles random background noise to other users. The BS uses the same codes to unscramble the different user signals. CDMA allows more users to share a given bandwidth than does FDMA or TDMA.

Besides the pure forms of splitting the channel (FDMA, TDMA, CDMA, SDMA), hybrids are also possible. For example, the second-generation system known as Global System for Mobile communications (GSM) uses FDM to divide the allotted spectrum into 124 carriers. Each carrier is then split in up to eight parts using TDMA. The number of potential users in any one cell is potentially enormous. Any subscriber in the area could enter the cell; in addition, a whole world of roamers could show up. Fortunately, the number of customers who are in a given cell at one time and are using their units for calls is usually quite modest. The problem is how to determine which users are active in a cell and how to assign them to vacant subchannels. Mobiles/subscribers entering a cell by a handoff can be allocated a channel directly through the mobile switching office. The question remains what to do about mobiles/subscribers that are just becoming active. A common answer is to use a random access channel, in which any user can transmit at any time. If two users transmit at approximately the same time, their signals interfere and each must retransmit. Since the message from

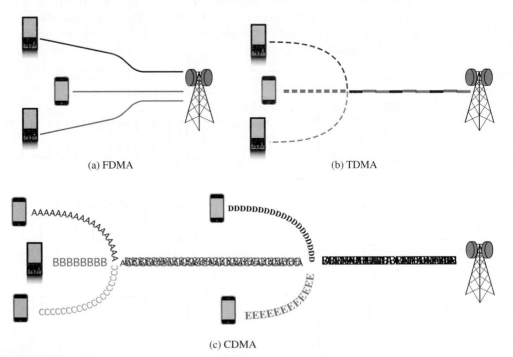

(a) FDMA   (b) TDMA

(c) CDMA

Figure 17.7   Cellular Multiple Access Schemes

a mobile/subscriber announcing its presence is quite short and infrequent, the poor utilization that is characteristic of random access channels is not a problem. Similarly, control information originating from a mobile/subscriber can be carried in the same random access mode. One control message is to assign the mobile/subscriber a dedicated channel when a conversation or data transfer is necessary.

So the assignment of channels and other control functions that are relatively short and rare can be initiated using a random access method, while the higher-traffic activities can be carried out in dedicated conversation subchannels derived by a multiple access scheme.

The primary multiple access schemes used in cellular telephony (and satellite communications as well) are FDMA (e.g., the first-generation system AMPS), TDMA (e.g., Digital AMPS, the digital successor to AMPS, and GSM, which also uses FDM), and CDMA, pioneered by Qualcomm. This listing is in order of increasing complexity of implementation and also of increasing spectral efficiency. In Digital AMPS the 30-kHz channels of AMPS are divided into subchannels using TDM, giving about a 3:1 improvement in spectrum utilization. Qualcomm claims a tenfold improvement for CDMA systems over AMPS. CDMA uses *soft handoff*, wherein the power from the codes in the old and new cells is summed by the mobile. In the other direction, the two signals received by the two base transceivers can be compared to make better communication.

In the United States there has been debate over the access method to use. FDMA is clearly too wasteful of spectrum for contemporary systems. Moreover, with the development of inexpensive, high-performance digital signal processing chips, FDMA is no longer necessarily easier to implement than TDMA. But the choice between TDMA and CDMA is a matter debated. Adherents of TDMA argue that the theoretical advantages of the CDMA scheme are hard to realize in practice and that there is a lot more successful experience with TDMA. CDMA proponents argue that the theoretical advantages can be realized and that CDMA offers additional features as well, such as increased range. The TDMA systems achieved an early lead in actual implementations worldwide. But large wireless providers soon began to sign up with CDMA vendors, making CDMA the access method of choice for third-generation systems.

17.3 THIRD-GENERATION WIRELESS COMMUNICATION

The objective of the third generation of wireless communication is to provide fairly high speed wireless communications to support multimedia, data, and video in addition to voice. The ITU's International Mobile Telecommunications for the year 2000 (IMT-2000) initiative defined the ITU's view of third-generation capabilities as follows:

- Voice quality comparable to the PSTN
- 144-kbps data rate available to users in high-speed motor vehicles over large areas
- 384-kbps data rate available to pedestrians standing or moving slowly over small areas

- Support (to be phased in) for 2.048 Mbps for office use
- Support for both packet-switched and circuit-switched data services
- An adaptive interface to the Internet to reflect efficiently the common asymmetry between inbound and outbound traffic
- More efficient use of the available spectrum in general
- Support for a wide variety of mobile equipment
- Flexibility to allow the introduction of new services and technologies

Competition among service providers has spawned a wide variety of 3G networks and services that meet or exceed the minimum capabilities outlined by the ITU in 2000. Many vendors have focused their mobile product offerings around the concepts of universal personal telecommunications and universal communications access. The first concept refers to the ability of a person to identify himself or herself easily in terms of a single account, and use conveniently any communication system in an entire country, over a continent, or even globally. The second refers to the capability of using one's computing device in a wide variety of environments to connect to information services (e.g., to have a portable device that will work in the office, on the street, and on airplanes equally well). This ongoing revolution in personal computing has shaped the evolution of wireless communications in several fundamental ways.

Personal communications services (PCSs) and personal communication networks (PCNs) are names attached to these concepts of global wireless communications, and they also form objectives for third-generation wireless. Generally speaking, PCSs and PCNs have relied on TDMA or CDMA to provide efficient use of the spectrum and high capacity.

PCS handsets are designed to be low power and relatively small and light. Several efforts have been made internationally to provide universal PCS. For example, worldwide frequency allocations have been made for second-generation cordless telephones (CT-2) in the 800-MHz region and for more advanced personal communications in the 1.7–2.2-GHz band of the spectrum.

The 1992 World Administrative Radio Conference (WARC 92) identified worldwide allocations for future public land mobile telecommunications systems (FPLMTS). This concept includes both terrestrial and satellite-based services. In addition, allocations were made for low-earth-orbiting satellite (LEOS) services that can be used to support personal communications.

Some proposed technologies that fall under the umbrella of PCS are American Digital Cellular System, Japanese Digital Cellular System, second-generation cordless telephones (CT-2), the European Community's GSM for digital cellular service, and Digital European Cordless Telephone (DECT). These involve advanced wireless telephony, which may also be supported by LEOSs and geostationary earth orbit satellites (GEOSs), as well as by terrestrial antennas. Among the technologies that have become the hallmark of third-generation services are mobile telephones ("smartphones") and other mobile devices that can access Web services.

Third-generation mobile networks were first launched in the United States in 2003. They were arguably the first "mobile broadband" networks in North America. Providers have deployed many varieties of 3G with Internet speeds ranging anywhere from 400 kbps to 4 Mbps or more.

The popularity of 3G technologies and services can be observed in consumer buying patterns. In 2011, more smartphones were purchased than personal computers. This has caused some industry experts to proclaim that we have entered the "post-PC" era of business data communications.

The ability to access the Internet, check e-mail, send text messages, and run mobile applications has helped to fuel consumer demand for smartphones. The ability to also use them for voice communications (phone calls) seems almost an afterthought for some mobile users. These capabilities also underlie the proliferation of mobile devices in business communication networks. In addition to the mobile applications popular among consumers, businesses are moving rapidly to ensure that their business software applications are supported on mobile platforms.

By 2012, four major mobile device platforms emerged to dominate the business mobility market: the iPhone, the Blackberry (from RIM), the Droid, and the iPad. Most large corporations have adopted a "device agnostic" or BYOD (bring your own device) attitude toward their mobility initiative. Rather than telling users what they will or will not support, companies are leaving the decision up to the preferences of their mobile workers. Support for the iPad is consistent with the spirit of the ITU's original vision for universal telecommunications services. Although the iPad is not used for cellular voice services, it is capable of using cellular networks to access the Internet.

The ability for smartphones and mobile tablet devices to access the Internet is one of the primary reasons why they are popular among business users. These capabilities are based on the evolution of Wireless Application Protocol.

Wireless Application Protocol (WAP)

The Wireless Application Protocol (WAP) is a universal, open standard developed by the WAP Forum to provide mobile users to access telephony and information services including the Internet and the Web. WAP is designed to work with all wireless network technologies (e.g., GSM, CDMA, and TDMA). It is also based on existing Internet standards, such as IP, XML, HTML, and HTTP, as much as possible, and it includes security facilities. Ericsson, Motorola, Nokia, and Phone.com established the WAP Forum in 1997; it subsequently consolidated into the Open Mobile Alliance in 2002, and it is this group which oversees the evolution of WAP. The WAP Forum released v1.1 of WAP in June 1999; as of 2012, WAP 2.0 was the most current version of WAP.

WAP was developed to address the limitations of cellular and other wireless networks for providing data services to mobile devices. Relative to personal computers, mobile devices have traditionally had limited processors, memory, and battery life. On some devices, the user interface is also limited, and the displays are small. In comparison to wire-based WAN services, wireless networks are characterized by relatively low bandwidth, high latency, and less predictable availability and stability. Moreover, all these features vary widely from mobile device to mobile device and from wireless network to wireless network. Finally, mobile, wireless users have different expectations and needs from other information systems users. For instance, mobile devices must be extremely easy to use, often much easier than desktop workstations, laptops, and personal computers. WAP was initially developed to deal with these challenges and its evolution has paralleled the evolution of the mobile devices on which it runs.

The WAP specification includes the following:

- A programming model based on the WWW Programming Model
- A markup language, the Wireless Markup Language (WML), adhering to XML
- A specification of a small browser suitable for a mobile, wireless device
- A lightweight communications protocol stack
- A framework for wireless telephony applications (WTAs)

The WAP Programming Model

The WAP Programming Model is based on three elements: the *client*, the *gateway*, and the *original server* (Figure 17.8). HTTP is used between the gateway and the original server to transfer content. The gateway acts as a proxy server for the wireless domain. Its processor(s) provide services that offload the limited capabilities of the hand-held, mobile, wireless terminals. For example, the gateway provides Domain Name System (DNS) services, converts between WAP protocol stack and the WWW stack (HTTP and TCP/IP), encodes information from the Web into a more compact form that minimizes wireless communication, and, in the other direction, decodes the compacted form into standard Web communication conventions. The gateway also caches frequently requested information.

The Wireless Markup Language (WML)

WML does not assume a standard keyboard or a mouse as an input device. It is designed to work with telephone keypads, styluses, and other input devices common to mobile, wireless communication. WML documents are subdivided into small, well-defined units of user interaction called *cards*. Users navigate by moving back and forth between cards. WML uses a small set of markup tags appropriate to telephony-based systems.

The Microbrowser

The microbrowser specified in the WAP1.1 release was designed to provide users with Internet access using a traditional 12-key phone keypad to enter alphanumeric characters. Users navigate among the WML cards using up and down scroll keys rather than a mouse. Navigation features familiar from the Web (e.g., Back, Home, and Bookmark) are provided as well.

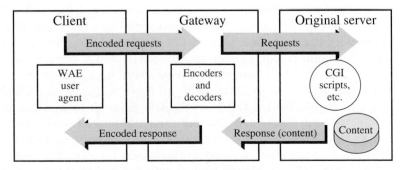

Figure 17.8 The WAP Programming Model

Today's microbrowsers are more robust. These have a variety of names including mobile browser, minibrowser, or wireless Internet browser (WIB). All are browsers designed for use on a mobile device such as mobile phones, tablets, or personal digital assistants (PDAs).

Microbrowsers are optimized to effectively display Web content on the small screens of portable devices. The browser software is typically small and efficient in order to accommodate the limited memory capacity of wireless devices and the low-bandwidth connections of the networks that they use to access the Internet. In essence, mobile browsers have traditionally been stripped-down Web browsers. However, since the mid-2000s, some mobile browsers have evolved to handle more recent technologies such as Ajax, CSS 2.1, and JavaScript.

The *Mobile Web* is another name for the collection of Web sites and wireless portals that have been designed for access from mobile browsers. Some automatically create "mobile" versions of their Web pages for users who use mobile devices to access the Web site. A mobile browser usually connects via cellular network and/ or via a wireless LAN, using standard HTTP. Most display Web pages written in HTML, WML, or XHTML Mobile Profile (WAP 2.0).

Wireless Telephony Applications (WTAs)

WTA provides an interface to the local and wide area telephone systems. Thus, using WTA, application developers can use the microbrowser to originate telephone calls and to respond to events from the telephone network.

A Sample Configuration

Figure 17.9 represents schematically a possible WAP configuration. There are three networks: the Internet (excluding the wireless net), the PSTN, and a wireless network

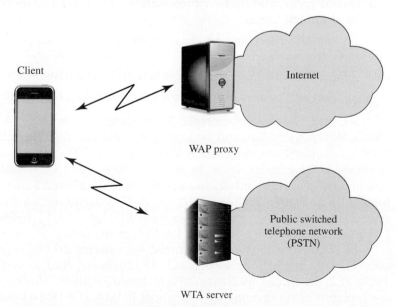

Figure 17.9 WAP Network Schematic

(e.g., cellular or Wi-Fi). The client could be a hand-held, smartphone in the wireless network. It communicates, in this example, with two gateways; one is the WAP Proxy to the Internet. The WAP Proxy communicates on the device's behalf with servers on the Internet. The Proxy translates HTML information to WML, HTML, or WAP 2.0 and sends it to the device. Materials on the Mobile Web are passed directly to the mobile device without translation. The other gateway, the WTA Server, is a gateway to the PSTN so that the mobile device can access telephony-based functionality such as call control, phone book access, and messaging through the microbrowser.

17.4 FOURTH-GENERATION WIRELESS COMMUNICATION

The evolution of smartphones and cellular networks has ushered in a new generation of capabilities and standards which is collectively called 4G. 4G systems are designed to provide ultra-broadband Internet access for a variety of mobile devices including laptops, smartphones, and tablet PCs. 4G networks are designed to support Mobile Web access and high-bandwidth applications such as high-definition mobile TV, mobile video conferencing, and gaming services.

Fourth-Generation (4G) Network Requirements

The ITU has issued directives for 4G networks. According to the ITU, an IMT-Advanced (or 4G) cellular system must fulfill a number of minimum requirements, including the following:

- Be based on an all-IP packet-switched network.
- Support peak data rates of up to approximately 100 Mbps for high-mobility mobile access and up to approximately 1 Gbps for low-mobility access such local wireless access.
- Dynamically share and use the network resources to support more simultaneous users per cell.
- Support smooth handovers across heterogeneous networks.
- Support high quality of service for next-generation multimedia applications.

By 2012, two systems emerged as the standard bearers for 4G networks: the Mobile WiMAX standard and the long-term evolution (LTE) standard. The Mobile WiMAX standard was launched in South Korea in 2006 and was first adopted for use in the U.S. by Sprint Nextel beginning in 2008. The LTE standard was released in Scandinavia in 2009 and has been available in the United States since 2010 from MetroPCS and other cellular providers. LTE smartphones have been available since 2011 and WiMAX smartphones since 2010. As of 2012, neither WiMAX nor LTE smartphones were available in the European market.

In contrast to earlier generations, 4G systems do not support traditional circuit-switched telephony service, only IP telephony. And, as may be observed in Table 17.2, the spread spectrum radio technologies that characterized 3G systems are replaced in 4G systems by orthogonal FDMA (OFDMA) multicarrier transmission and frequency domain equalization schemes.

Table 17.2 Third-Generation (3G) vs. Fourth-Generation (4G) Networks

Factor	3G	4G
Frequency Band	1.8–2.5 GHz	2–8 GHz
Network	Wide Area Cell Based	Wireless LAN + Wide Area
Services	CDMA 2000, EDGE, UMTS	WiMAX 2, LTE-Advance
Peak Upload Rate	50 Mbps	500 Mbps
Peak Download Rate	100 Mbps	1 Gbps
Stationary Bandwidth	2 Mbps	1 Gbps
Moving Bandwidth	384 kbps	100 Mbps
Data Rate	3 MB per second	1 GB per second
Switching Technique(s)	Packet switching; circuit switching	Packet switching (IP)
Radio Technology	Spread spectrum; TDMA; CDMA	OFDMA; MIMO; OFDM

Figure 17.10 illustrates several major differences between 3G and 4G cellular networks. As may be observed in Figure 17.10a, the connections between BSs and switching offices in 3G networks are typically cable-based, either copper or fiber wires. Circuit switching is supported to enable voice connections between mobile users and phones connected to the PSTN. Internet access in 3G networks may also be routed through switching offices. By contrast, in 4G networks, IP telephony is the norm as are IP packet-switched connections for Internet access. These are enabled by wireless connections, such as WiMAX, between BSs and switching offices (see Figure 17.10b). Connections among mobile users with 4G-capable smartphones may never be routed over cable-based, circuit-switched connections—all communications between them can be IP-based and handled by wireless links. This setup facilitates deployment of mobile-to-mobile video call/video conferencing services

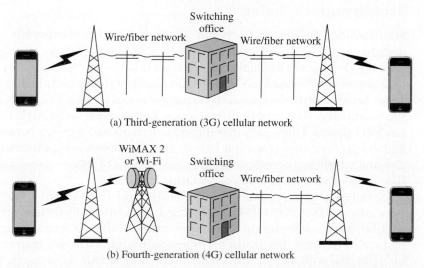

(a) Third-generation (3G) cellular network

(b) Fourth-generation (4G) cellular network

Figure 17.10 Third-Generation vs. Fourth-Generation Cellular Networks

and the simultaneous delivery of voice and data services (such as Web browsing while engaged in a phone call). 4G mobile users can still connect with 3G network users and PSTN subscribers over cable/fiber circuit-switched connections between the switching offices.

Orthogonal Frequency Division Multiple Access (OFDMA)

New spectrum sharing schemes are important in 4G systems and these are bringing FDMA, once viewed as a bandwidth waster, back to the table. The new multiple access schemes include single-carrier FDMA (SC-FDMA), orthogonal FDMA (OFDMA), interleaved FDMA, and multicarrier CDMA (MC-CDMA). These are based on Fast Fourier Transform (FFT) algorithms and frequency domain equalization mechanisms. Collectively, these enable 4G service providers to control bandwidth and spectrum in flexible ways. However, they also require advanced capabilities such as dynamic channel allocation and traffic adaptive scheduling.

OFDMA resembles CDMA spread spectrum in that users can achieve different data rates via the assignment of different spreading factors. It also enables the assignment of a different number of spreading codes to each user. OFDMA can also be described as a combination of frequency domain and time domain multiple access. With OFDMA, transmission resources are partitioned by time slots within an assigned frequency range.

OFDMA is considered to be highly suitable for broadband wireless networks. It is used in WiMAX, the IEEE 802.16 Wireless MAN standard, and IEEE 802.20 Mobile Wireless MAN networks. It is also used in LTE-Advance downlink channels. Some of OFDMA's major advantages include scalability, MIMO friendliness, and ability to leverage channel frequency selectivity. A key advantage of the new 4G techniques is that they require less complexity for equalization at the receiver. This can be especially advantageous in MIMO environments where spatial multiplexing transmission inherently requires high complexity equalization at the receiver.

4G Network Evolution

4G networks, devices, and services are expected to evolve rapidly over the next decade. As of 2012, 4G services were limited geographically and, in the United States, were typically available only in larger urban areas. Because they use new multiple access schemes such as OFDMA, and support significantly higher upstream and downstream speeds, the rollout of 4G networks and services will also be tempered by the evolution of 4G-capable smartphones. For example, as of 2012, the iPhone was not a 4G device. This meant that iPhone adherents had a choice between the device and 4G services; they could not have both. 4G iPhones will undoubtedly be in high demand when they become available, but millions of iPhone users will have to buy the new phones to be able to connect to 4G networks.

Industry experts expect that CDMA and OFDM will coexist in cellular networks into the 2020s. 3G CDMA-based solutions are likely to remain as the core cellular service offering for mobile operators while 4G technologies evolve and mature. Over time, the world's wireless subscriber base will migrate to 4G technologies, but with an ever-increasing number of mobile device uses, the migration period is likely to be lengthy.

17.5 SATELLITE COMMUNICATIONS

Satellite communications is comparable in importance to optical fiber in the evolution of telecommunications and data communications.

The heart of a satellite communications system is a satellite-based antenna in a stable orbit above the earth. In a satellite communications system, two or more stations on or near the earth communicate via one or more satellites that serve as relay stations in space. The antenna systems on or near the earth are referred to as **earth stations**. A transmission from an earth station to the satellite is referred to as **uplink**, whereas transmissions from the satellite to the earth station are **downlink**. The electronics in the satellite that takes an uplink signal and converts it to a downlink signal is called a **transponder**.

Satellite Orbits

Geostationary Earth Orbit Satellites   The most common type of communications satellite today is the geostationary earth orbit (GEO) satellite (GEOS), first proposed by the science-fiction author Arthur C. Clarke in 1945. If the satellite is in a circular orbit 35,863 km above the earth's surface and rotates in the equatorial plane of the earth, it will rotate at exactly the same angular speed as the earth and will remain above the same spot on the equator as the earth rotates.[7] Figure 17.11 depicts the GEO in scale with the size of the earth; the satellite symbols are intended to suggest that there are many satellites in GEO, some of which are quite close to each other.

The GEO has several advantages to recommend it:

- Because the satellite is stationary relative to the earth, there is no problem with frequency changes due to the relative motion of the satellite and antennas on earth (Doppler effect).

- Tracking of the satellite by its earth stations is simplified.

- At 35,863 km above the earth, the satellite can communicate with roughly a fourth of the earth's surface; three satellites in GEO separated by 120° can cover most of the inhabited portions of the entire earth excluding only the areas near the north and south poles.

On the other hand, there are problems:

- The signal can get quite weak after traveling over 35,000 km.

- The polar regions and the far northern and southern hemispheres are poorly served by GEOSs.

- Even at the speed of light, about 300,000 km/s, the delay in sending a signal from a point on the equator beneath the satellite to the satellite and back is substantial.

---

[7]The term *geosynchronous* is often used in place of *geostationary*. For purists, the difference is that a geosynchronous orbit is any circular orbit at an altitude of 35,863 km, and a geostationary orbit is a geosynchronous orbit with zero inclination, so the satellite hovers over one spot on the earth's equator.

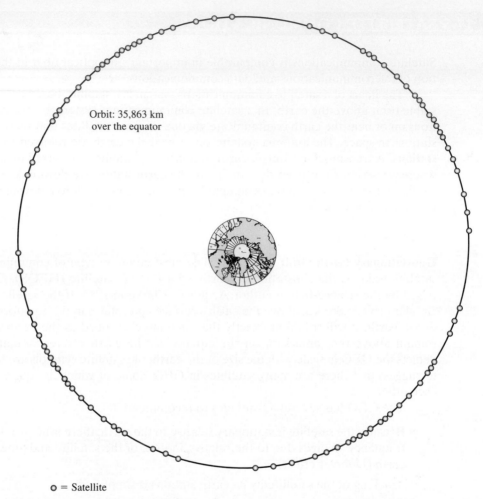

Orbit: 35,863 km
over the equator

○ = Satellite

Figure 17.11 Geostationary Earth Orbit (GEO)

The delay of communication between two locations on earth directly under the satellite is in fact $(2 \times 35,863)/300,000 \approx 0.24$ s. For other locations not directly under the satellite, the delay is even longer. If the satellite link is used for telephone communication, the added delay between when one person speaks and the other responds is increased twofold, to almost 0.5 s. This is definitely noticeable. Another feature of GEOSs is that they use their assigned frequencies over a very large area. For point-to-multipoint applications such as broadcasting TV programs, this can be desirable, but for point-to-point communications it is very wasteful of spectrum. Special spot and steered beam antennas, which restrict the area covered by the satellite's signal, can be used to control the "footprint" or signaling area. To solve some of these problems, orbits other than GEOs have been designed for satellites. *Low-earth-orbiting satellites (LEOSs)* and *medium-earth-orbiting satellites (MEOSs)* are important for third-generation personal communications.

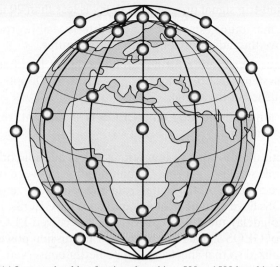

(a) Low-earth orbit: often in polar orbit at 500 to 1500 km altitude

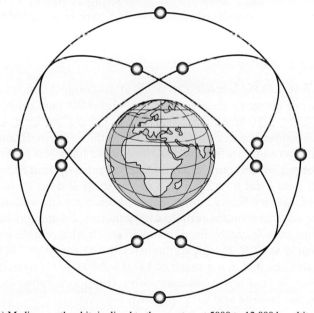

(b) Medium-earth orbit: inclined to the equator, at 5000 to 12,000 km altitude

Figure 17.12   Low-Earth and Medium-Earth Orbits

LEOSs   LEOSs (Figure 17.12a) have the following characteristics:

- Circular or slightly elliptical orbit at less than 2000 km. Proposed and actual systems are in the range of 500–1500 km.
- The orbit period is in the range of 1.5–2 hours.
- The diameter of coverage is about 8000 km.

- Round-trip signal propagation delay is less than 20 ms.
- The maximum time that the satellite is visible from a fixed point on earth (above the radio horizon) is up to 20 minutes.
- Because the motion of the satellite relative to a fixed point on earth is high, the system must be able to cope with large Doppler shifts, which change the frequency of the signal.
- The atmospheric drag on a LEOS is significant, resulting in gradual orbital deterioration.

Practical use of this system requires that multiple orbital planes be used, each with multiple satellites in orbit. Communication between two earth stations typically will involve handing off the signal from one satellite to another.

LEOSs have a number of advantages over GEOSs. In addition to the reduced propagation delay mentioned previously, a received LEOS signal is much stronger than that of GEOS signals for the same transmission power. LEOS coverage can be better localized so that spectrum can be better conserved. For this reason, this technology is currently being proposed for communicating with mobile devices and with personal computing devices that need stronger signals to function. On the other hand, to provide broad coverage over 24 hours, many satellites are needed.

A number of commercial proposals have been made to use clusters of LEOSs to provide communications services. These proposals can be divided into two categories:

- **Little LEOS:** Intended to work at communication frequencies below 1 GHz using no more than 5 MHz of bandwidth and supporting data rates up to 10 kbps. These systems are aimed at paging, tracking, and low-rate messaging. Orbcomm is an example of such a satellite system. It was the first (little) LEOS in operation; its first two satellites were launched in April 1995. It is designed for paging and burst communication and is optimized for handling small bursts of data from 6 to 250 bytes in length. It is used by businesses to track trailers, railcars, heavy equipment, and other remote and mobile assets. It can also be used to monitor remote utility meters, oil and gas storage tanks, wells, and pipelines. It can be used to stay in touch with remote workers anywhere in the world as well. It uses frequencies in the range of 148.00–150.05 MHz to the satellites, and in the range of 137.00–138.00 MHz from the satellites. It has well over 30 satellites in low earth orbit. It supports subscriber data rates of 2.4 kbps to the satellite and 4.8 kbps down.
- **Big LEOS:** Work at frequencies above 1 GHz and support data rates up to a few Mbps. These systems tend to offer the same services as those of the small LEOS, with the addition of voice and positioning services. Globalstar is one example of a Big LEOS system. Its satellites are fairly rudimentary. Unlike some of the little LEOS systems, it has no onboard processing or communications between satellites. Most processing is done by the system's earth stations. It uses CDMA as in the CDMA cellular standard. It uses the S-Band (about 2 GHz) for the downlink to mobile users. Globalstar is tightly integrated with traditional voice carriers. All calls must be processed through earth stations. The satellite constellation consists of 48 operating satellites and 8 spares. They are in 1413-km-high orbits.

MEOSs   MEOSs (Figure 17.12b) have the following characteristics:

- Circular orbit at an altitude in the range of 5000–12,000 km.
- The orbit period is about 6 hours.
- The diameter of coverage is from 10,000 to 15,000 km.
- Round-trip signal propagation delay is less than 50 ms.
- The maximum time that the satellite is visible from a fixed point on earth (above the radio horizon) is a few hours.

MEOSs require much fewer handoffs than LEOSs. While propagation delay to earth from such satellites and the power required are greater than for LEOSs, they are still substantially less than for GEOSs. New ICO, established in January 1995, proposed a MEOS system. Launches began in 2000. Twelve satellites, including two spares, are planned in 10,400-km-high orbits. The satellites will be divided equally between two planes tilted 45° to the equator. Proposed applications are digital voice, data, facsimile, high-penetration notification, and messaging services.

Satellite Network Configurations

Figure 17.14 depicts in a general way two common configurations for satellite communication. In the first, the satellite is being used to provide a point-to-point link between two distant ground-based antennas. In the second, the satellite provides communications between one ground-based transmitter and a number of ground-based receivers.

Applications

The communications satellite is a technological revolution as important as fiber optics. Among the most important applications for satellites are the following:

- Television distribution
- Satellite radio services
- Long-distance telephone transmission
- Private business networks

Because of their broadcast nature, satellites are well suited to television distribution and are being used extensively for this purpose in the United States and throughout the world. In its traditional use, a network provides programming from a central location. Programs are transmitted to the satellite and then broadcast down to a number of stations, which then distribute the programs to individual viewers. Another application of satellite technology to television distribution is direct broadcast satellite (DBS), in which satellite video signals are transmitted directly to the home user.

Satellite radio services such as Sirius XM and Worldspace allow mobile subscribers to listen to the same audio programming anywhere they go; some have continent-wide footprints. Other audio services, such as Music Choice or Muzak's satellite-delivered content, require a dish antenna and a fixed-location

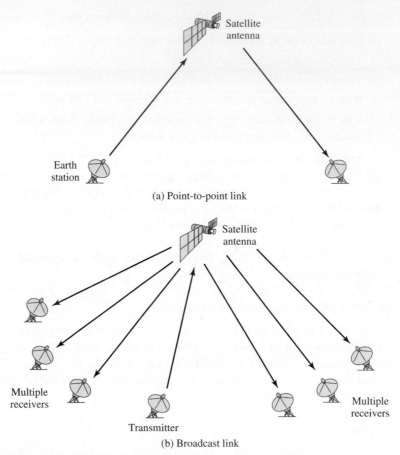

Figure 17.13 Satellite Communication Configurations

receiver. In both fixed-location and mobile radio services, the antenna must have a clear view to the satellites. In areas where tall buildings, bridges, or parking garages obscure the signal, repeaters can be used to make the signal available to listeners. Radio services are usually subscription-based that use proprietary signals and require specialized receiving hardware for decoding and playback. Providers such as Sirius XM enable subscribers to access a large range of news, weather, sports, talk, comedy, and music channels; most music channels are broadcast commercial-free.

Satellite transmission is also used for point-to-point trunks between telephone exchange offices in public telephone networks. It is a useful medium for high-usage international trunks and is competitive with terrestrial systems for many long-distance intranational links, particularly in remote and undeveloped areas.

Finally, there are a number of business data applications for satellite. The satellite provider can divide the total capacity into a number of channels and lease these channels to individual business users. A user equipped with antennas at a number of sites can use a satellite channel for a private network. Traditionally, such applications have been quite expensive and limited to larger organizations

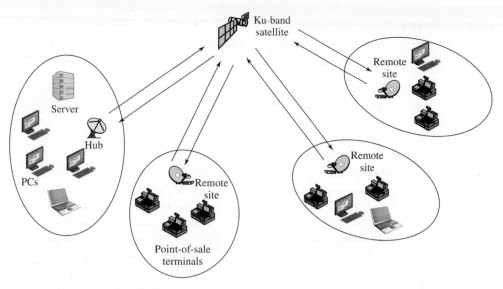

Figure 17.14 Typical VSAT Configuration

with high-volume requirements. Today, the very small aperture terminal (VSAT) system provides a low-cost alternative. Figure 17.14 depicts a typical VSAT configuration. A number of subscriber stations are equipped with low-cost VSAT antennas. Using some discipline, these stations share a satellite transmission capacity for transmission to a hub station. The hub station can exchange messages with each of the subscribers and can relay messages between subscribers.

APPLICATION NOTE

Laptops, Netbooks, PDAs, and Cell Phones

Businesses are faced with several questions regarding computing resources. While it is common for an organization to purchase dozens or even hundreds of desktop computers, increasingly organizations must also make mobile computing device decisions. The choices really depend on the application or use for which the device is intended. More than one company has stretched its budget by buying devices that are overpowered for the application or the devices may be left to gather dust because they are unsatisfactory for the tasks they are purchased to support. In order to make the right decision, some analysis for matching business tools to tasks must be undertaken.

Laptops have traditionally been among the first options that come to mind when businesses think of mobile devices. Laptops have a great deal of processing power, memory, and hard drive capacity. They typically come equipped with built-in Wi-Fi connectivity that makes them very attractive because there is no need to purchase the wireless network cards, unless there is a need to gain Internet access via cellular networks. Combined with a docking station, a laptop can double as a desktop station.

(Continued)

As attractive as they are, laptops do have a darker side. Laptops are sometimes more difficult to use because of the keyboard style and built-in touchpad instead of a mouse. Many users opt to have larger monitors, extended keyboards, and an extra mouse when working in desktop mode. Another downside to laptop purchases, if the laptop is actually used as a mobile station, is that batteries rarely behave as advertised. Every activity drains the battery further, and the true mobile user must become familiar with power-saving settings or have a second battery on hand. Yet for a user that requires the processing power, large storage capacity, and easy access to all of his/her files when moving from home to the office, the laptop may represent the best solution.

Netbooks and mini-laptops have experienced a wave of popularity among mobile workers. These are smaller and lighter in weight, and often have a better battery life than standard sized laptops. Many users think that they are easier and more comfortable to travel with. However, netbook processors are typically less powerful than those installed in laptops and this makes it more difficult for them to handle large file downloads or uploads.

A personal digital assistant (PDA) is a mobile device that mobile workers can use as a personal information manager. PDAs are also known as palmtop computers or a personal data assistant. Most PDAs have the ability to connect to the Internet. Because it has a visual display, PDAs typically support a microbrowser. Most access the Internet, intranets, or extranets via Wi-Fi or cellular connections. Current models also have audio capabilities enabling them to be used as portable media players.

A PDA is not a replacement for a laptop as it does not have the processing capability or the storage capacity. This has limited the popularity of PDAs as computing devices. In addition, today, almost all PDAs are smartphones. The evolution of smartphones and their ability to substitute for PDAs have significantly diminished PDA sales.

Smartphones have become standard business computing platforms. Although 3G and 4G Mobile Web services have evolved quickly in the United States, mobile broadband services offered in the United States are not at the level of those offered in several other developed countries. The real strength of the smartphone lies in its anywhere, anytime voice and Internet connectivity. While a PDA can often connect over the same networks, they typically provide less versatility than smartphones for business users. The same is true for laptop users who require both Internet access and voice (soft phone) support.

Tablet computers have also emerged as important mobile computing devices. The iPad has helped Apple make significant inroads into business computing. Although tablet computers typically lack voice capabilities, they do provide Wi-Fi and/or cellular network connectivity. This and user-friendly touch screen interfaces provided by tablet PC operating systems have made them extremely popular among business users and consumers.

As is often the case, we must first ask ourselves, "What are we trying to do?" or "What do we need to do?" Once these questions are answered, it is usually easier to find a solution that fits the needs of the organization. Netbooks, smartphones, and tablets, while often considered necessary tools, are not usually a replacement for a more powerful laptop or desktop computer. For sheer portability, it is often much more feasible to carry around a wallet-sized or tablet-sized device rather than full-size laptop. On the other hand, there is a big difference between wanting and needing, especially where the bottom line is concerned. Companies would be well advised to look at usage patterns before and after smartphone purchases to determine if they are indeed necessary. Even if the power of a laptop is currently the best solution, improvements in smartphones and tablets can have us struggling to decide which device is best for the next generation of connectivity as the lines between them are no longer well defined.

17.6 SUMMARY

Cellular wireless networks have traditionally supported mobile telephony but now also support wireless Internet access and other wireless data networking applications. Cellular networks are pervasive worldwide and carry an increasing portion of long-distance voice and data traffic. A cellular system is based on the principle of using a large number of relatively small geographic areas, called cells, to cover a large area. Each cell is allocated a band of frequencies and is served by a BS, consisting of transmitter, receiver, and control unit. Adjacent cells are assigned different frequencies to avoid interference or crosstalk. However, cells sufficiently distant from each other can use the same frequency band.

The capacity available within each cell is shared among a number of users by means of some sort of multiple-access scheme. For a given system, multiple access is based on TDMA, FDMA, CDMA, or some combination of these.

The evolution of cellular networks is ongoing. Both third-generation (3G) and fourth-generation (4G) technologies and solutions have been developed. 4G technologies and services are currently being rolled out by mobile operators and have the potential to provide significant performance increases for subscribers. However, both 3G and 4G systems are likely to coexist for another decade.

Another important form of wireless communications is satellite communications. The bulk of satellite traffic has traditionally been carried by GEOSs. Recently, networks using LEOSs and MEOSs have been introduced.

> **Case Study X: Choice Hotels**
>
> The major concepts addressed in this case study include Satellite-based communications and wireless WANs. **This case study and more are available at www.pearsoninternationaleditions.com/stallings**

17.7 KEY TERMS, REVIEW QUESTIONS, AND PROBLEMS

Key Terms

base station	earth station	orthogonal frequency division
cell sectoring	fourth generation (4G)	multiple access (OFMDA)
cell splitting	geostationary earth orbit	transponder
cellular wireless	satellite (GEOS)	uplink
network	microcells	Wireless Markup
downlink	multiple access	Language (WML)

Review Questions

17.1 What geometric shape of cells is used in cellular networks?

17.2 What is the principle of frequency reuse in the context of a cellular network? Why is frequency reuse important?

17.3 What are the differences between control channels and traffic channels in cellular networks?

17.4 What is a cellular handoff?

17.5 Describe what is meant by the term *multiple access* as it applies to cellular communication.

17.6 Identify the most prevalent multiple access methods deployed in today's cellular networks.

17.7 Briefly explain the principle behind CDMA.

17.8 What is the Wireless Application Protocol (WAP)?

17.9 What are the major characteristics of third-generation (3G) networks?

17.10 What are the major characteristics of fourth-generation (4G) networks?

17.11 Identify and briefly describe the key components of satellite communication systems.

17.12 Explain what GEOSs, LEOSs, and MEOSs are (including what the acronyms stand for). Compare the three types with respect to factors such as size and shape of orbits, signal power, frequency reuse, propagation delay, number of satellites for global coverage, and handoff frequency.

17.13 Identify how organizations use GEOS, LEOS, and MEOS, respectively.

17.14 Identify and briefly describe the characteristics and uses of VSAT systems.

Problems

17.1 There are many cellular providers serving each geographic area and each one may use a different technology.
   a. Who are the providers in your area and what are the multiple access technologies used?
   b. What are the technologies behind the cellular phones you or your family and friends use?

17.2 Do some Internet research on microcells in urban areas with high population densities. Locate information relevant to microcell sizes and the deployment of base stations and switching offices. Summarize your findings in a 500–750 word paper or a 5–8 slide PowerPoint presentation.

17.3 Describe a sequence of events similar to that of Figure 17.5 for
   a. a call from a mobile unit to a fixed subscriber
   b. a call from a fixed subscriber to a mobile unit

17.4 Do some Internet research on the Mobile Web. Locate information that compares the Mobile Web to traditional Internet resources. Identify examples of Mobile Web applications that are especially popular among consumers and compare these to applications that are popular among business users. Summarize your findings in a 500–750 word paper or a 5–8 slide PowerPoint presentation.

17.5 Do some Internet research to locate information comparing cellular network systems and services in the United States to those in other highly developed nations around the world. How does the United States stack up and what are some of the reasons why cellular systems in some highly developed nations are superior to those in others? Summarize your findings in a 500–750 word paper or a 5–8 slide PowerPoint presentation.

17.6 Do some Internet research on business use of VSAT systems. Locate information relevant to the types of applications that businesses are likely to support via VSAT systems and the costs of VSAT systems in comparison to other business data communication facilities. Summarize your findings in a 500–750 word paper or a 5–8 slide PowerPoint presentation.

17.7 Global System for Mobile communications (GSM) is an international standard for digital cellular communication. Provide a basic overview of GSM, focusing on the three primary functional entities of a GSM network. Is the GSM strategy a superior or inferior alternative to CDMA? Support your answer.

17.8 Some concern has been expressed regarding potential health hazards related to cellular phone use. Discuss potential health risks related to cellular phone technology. What precautions can be taken to minimize potential dangers involved in cell phone use?

COMPUTER AND NETWORK SECURITY THREATS

CHAPTER

18

Learning Objectives

After reading this chapter, you should be able to:

♦ Describe the key security requirements of confidentiality, integrity, and availability.

♦ Describe the major categories of threats to computers and networks.

♦ Discuss the types of intruders and the techniques used by intruders to access computer systems.

♦ Discuss the types of malicious software.

This chapter provides an overview of security threats. We begin with a discussion of what we mean by computer security. In essence, computer security deals with computer-related assets that are subject to a variety of threats and for which various measures are taken to protect those assets. The remainder of the chapter looks at the two broad categories of computer and network security threats: intruders and malicious software.

Cryptographic algorithms, such as encryption and hash functions, play a role both in computer security threats and computer security techniques. Appendix J provides an overview of these algorithms.

18.1 COMPUTER SECURITY CONCEPTS

The NIST *Computer Security Handbook* [NIST95] defines the term *computer security* as follows:

Computer Security: The protection afforded to an automated information system in order to attain the applicable objectives of preserving the integrity, availability, and confidentiality of information system resources (includes hardware, software, firmware, information/data, and telecommunications).

This definition introduces three key objectives that are at the heart of computer security:

- **Confidentiality:** This term covers two related concepts:
  - **Data[1] confidentiality:** Assures that private or confidential information is not made available or disclosed to unauthorized individuals

---

[1]RFC 2828 (*Internet Security Glossary*) defines *information* as "facts and ideas, which can be represented (encoded) as various forms of data," and *data* as "information in a specific physical representation, usually a sequence of symbols that have meaning; especially a representation of information that can be processed or produced by a computer." Security literature typically does not make much of a distinction; nor does this chapter.

—**Privacy:** Assures that individuals control or influence what information related to them may be collected and stored and by whom and to whom that information may be disclosed

- **Integrity:** This term covers two related concepts:

  —**Data integrity:** Assures that information and programs are changed only in a specified and authorized manner

  —**System integrity:** Assures that a system performs its intended function in an unimpaired manner, free from deliberate or inadvertent unauthorized manipulation of the system

- **Availability:** Assures that systems work promptly and service is not denied to authorized users

These three concepts form what is often referred to as the **CIA triad** (Figure 18.1). The three concepts embody the fundamental security objectives both for data and for information and computing services. For example, the NIST standard FIPS 199 (*Standards for Security Categorization of Federal Information and Information Systems*) lists confidentiality, integrity, and availability as the three security objectives for information and for information systems. FIPS PUB 199 provides a useful characterization of these three objectives in terms of requirements and the definition of a loss of security in each category:

- **Confidentiality:** Preserving authorized restrictions on information access and disclosure, including means for protecting personal privacy and proprietary information. A loss of confidentiality is the unauthorized disclosure of information.

- **Integrity:** Guarding against improper information modification or destruction, including ensuring information nonrepudiation and authenticity. A loss of integrity is the unauthorized modification or destruction of information.

- **Availability:** Ensuring timely and reliable access to and use of information. A loss of availability is the disruption of access to or use of information or an information system.

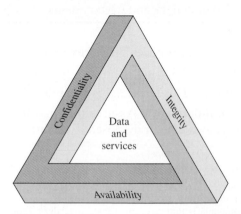

Figure 18.1   The Security Requirements Triad

Although the use of the CIA triad to define security objectives is well established, some in the security field feel that additional concepts are needed to present a complete picture. Two of the most commonly mentioned are as follows:

- **Authenticity:** The property of being genuine and being able to be verified and trusted; confidence in the validity of a transmission, a message, or message originator. This means verifying that users are who they say they are and that each input arriving at the system came from a trusted source.

- **Accountability:** The security goal that generates the requirement for actions of an entity to be traced uniquely to that entity. This supports nonrepudiation, deterrence, fault isolation, intrusion detection and prevention, and after-action recovery and legal action. Because truly secure systems aren't yet an achievable goal, we must be able to trace a security breach to a responsible party. Systems must keep records of their activities to permit later forensic analysis to trace security breaches or to aid in transaction disputes.

Note that FIPS PUB 199 includes authenticity under integrity.

18.2 THREATS, ATTACKS, AND ASSETS

We turn now to a look at threats, attacks, and assets as related to computer security.

Threats and Attacks

Table 18.1, based on RFC 2828, describes four kinds of threat consequences and lists the kinds of attacks that result in each consequence.

Unauthorized disclosure is a threat to confidentiality. The following types of attacks can result in this threat consequence:

- **Exposure:** This can be deliberate, as when an insider intentionally releases sensitive information, such as credit card numbers, to an outsider. It can also be the result of a human, hardware, or software error, which results in an entity gaining unauthorized knowledge of sensitive data. There have been numerous instances of this, such as universities accidentally posting student confidential information on the Web.

- **Interception:** Interception is a common attack in the context of communications. On a shared local area network (LAN), such as a wireless LAN or a broadcast Ethernet, any device attached to the LAN can receive a copy of packets intended for another device. On the Internet, a determined hacker can gain access to e-mail traffic and other data transfers. All of these situations create the potential for unauthorized access to data.

- **Inference:** An example of inference is traffic analysis, in which an adversary is able to gain information from observing the pattern of traffic on a network, such as the amount of traffic between particular pairs of hosts on the network. Another example is the inference of detailed information from a database by a user who has only limited access; this is accomplished by repeated queries whose combined results enable inference.

Table 18.1 Threat Consequences, and the Types of Threat Actions That Cause Each Consequence (Based on RFC 2828)

Threat Consequence	Threat Action (attack)
Unauthorized Disclosure A circumstance or event whereby an entity gains access to data for which the entity is not authorized.	**Exposure:** Sensitive data are directly released to an unauthorized entity. **Interception:** An unauthorized entity directly accesses sensitive data traveling between authorized sources and destinations. **Inference:** A threat action whereby an unauthorized entity indirectly accesses sensitive data (but not necessarily the data contained in the communication) by reasoning from characteristics or byproducts of communications. **Intrusion:** An unauthorized entity gains access to sensitive data by circumventing a system's security protections.
Deception A circumstance or event that may result in an authorized entity receiving false data and believing it to be true.	**Masquerade:** An unauthorized entity gains access to a system or performs a malicious act by posing as an authorized entity. **Falsification:** False data deceive an authorized entity. **Repudiation:** An entity deceives another by falsely denying responsibility for an act.
Disruption A circumstance or event that interrupts or prevents the correct operation of system services and functions.	**Incapacitation:** Prevents or interrupts system operation by disabling a system component. **Corruption:** Undesirably alters system operation by adversely modifying system functions or data. **Obstruction:** A threat action that interrupts delivery of system services by hindering system operation.
Usurpation A circumstance or event that results in control of system services or functions by an unauthorized entity.	**Misappropriation:** An entity assumes unauthorized logical or physical control of a system resource. **Misuse:** Causes a system component to perform a function or service that is detrimental to system security.

- **Intrusion:** An example of intrusion is an adversary gaining unauthorized access to sensitive data by overcoming the system's access control protections.

Deception is a threat to either system integrity or data integrity. The following types of attacks can result in this threat consequence:

- **Masquerade:** One example of masquerade is an attempt by an unauthorized user to gain access to a system by posing as an authorized user; this could happen if the unauthorized user has learned another user's logon ID and password. Another example is malicious logic, such as a Trojan horse, that appears to perform a useful or desirable function but actually gains unauthorized access to system resources or tricks a user into executing other malicious logic.
- **Falsification:** This refers to the altering or replacing of valid data or the introduction of false data into a file or database. For example, a student may alter his or her grades on a school database.
- **Repudiation:** In this case, a user either denies sending data or a user denies receiving or possessing the data.

Disruption is a threat to availability or system integrity. The following types of attacks can result in this threat consequence:

- **Incapacitation:** This is an attack on system availability. This could occur as a result of physical destruction of or damage to system hardware. More typically, malicious software, such as Trojan horses, viruses, or worms, could operate in such a way as to disable a system or some of its services.

- **Corruption:** This is an attack on system integrity. Malicious software in this context could operate in such a way that system resources or services function in an unintended manner. Or a user could gain unauthorized access to a system and modify some of its functions. An example of the latter is a user placing back door logic in the system to provide subsequent access to a system and its resources by other than the usual procedure.

- **Obstruction:** One way to obstruct system operation is to interfere with communications by disabling communication links or altering communication control information. Another way is to overload the system by placing excess burden on communication traffic or processing resources.

Usurpation is a threat to system integrity. The following types of attacks can result in this threat consequence:

- **Misappropriation:** This can include theft of service. An example is a distributed denial of service attack, when malicious software is installed on a number of hosts to be used as platforms to launch traffic at a target host. In this case, the malicious software makes unauthorized use of processor and operating system resources.

- **Misuse:** Misuse can occur either by means of malicious logic or by a hacker that has gained unauthorized access to a system. In either case, security functions can be disabled or thwarted.

Threats and Assets

The assets of a computer system can be categorized as hardware, software, data, and communication lines and networks. In this subsection, we briefly describe these four categories and relate these to the concepts of integrity, confidentiality, and availability introduced in Section 18.1 (see Figure 18.2 and Table 18.2).

HARDWARE A major threat to computer system hardware is the threat to availability. Hardware is the most vulnerable to attack and the least susceptible to automated controls. Threats include accidental and deliberate damage to equipment, as well as theft. The proliferation of personal computers and workstations and the widespread use of LANs increase the potential for losses in this area. Theft of CD-ROMs and DVDs can lead to loss of confidentiality. Physical and administrative security measures are needed to deal with these threats.

SOFTWARE Software includes the operating system, utilities, and application programs. A key threat to software is an attack on availability. Software, especially application software, is often easy to delete. Software can also be altered or damaged to render it useless. Careful software configuration management, which

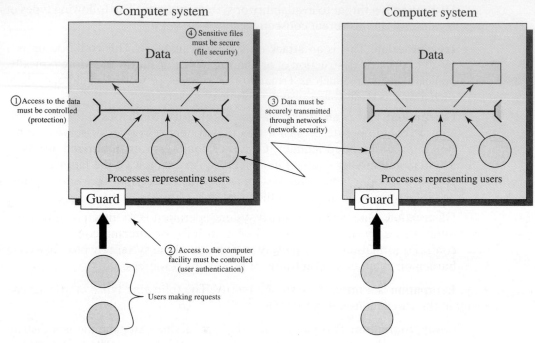

Figure 18.2   Scope of System Security

includes making backups of the most recent version of software, can maintain high availability. A more difficult problem to deal with is software modification that results in a program that still functions but that behaves differently than before, which is a threat to integrity/authenticity. Computer viruses and related attacks fall into this category. A final problem is protection against software

Table 18.2   Computer and Network Assets, with Examples of Threats

	Availability	**Confidentiality**	**Integrity**
Hardware	Equipment is stolen or disabled, thus denying service.		
Software	Programs are deleted, denying access to users.	An unauthorized copy of software is made.	A working program is modified, either to cause it to fail during execution or to cause it to do some unintended task.
Data	Files are deleted, denying access to users.	An unauthorized read of data is performed. An analysis of statistical data reveals underlying data.	Existing files are modified or new files are fabricated.
Communication Lines	Messages are destroyed or deleted. Communication lines or networks are rendered unavailable.	Messages are read. The traffic pattern of messages is observed.	Messages are modified, delayed, reordered, or duplicated. False messages are fabricated.

piracy. Although certain countermeasures are available, by and large the problem of unauthorized copying of software has not been solved.

DATA Hardware and software security are typically concerns of computing center professionals or individual concerns of personal computer users. A much more widespread problem is data security, which involves files and other forms of data controlled by individuals, groups, and business organizations.

Security concerns with respect to data are broad, encompassing availability, secrecy, and integrity. In the case of availability, the concern is with the destruction of data files, which can occur either accidentally or maliciously.

The obvious concern with secrecy is the unauthorized reading of data files or databases, and this area has been the subject of perhaps more research and effort than any other area of computer security. A less obvious threat to secrecy involves the analysis of data and manifests itself in the use of so-called statistical databases, which provide summary or aggregate information. Presumably, the existence of aggregate information does not threaten the privacy of the individuals involved. However, as the use of statistical databases grows, there is an increasing potential for disclosure of personal information. In essence, characteristics of constituent individuals may be identified through careful analysis. For example, if one table records the aggregate of the incomes of respondents A, B, C, and D and another records the aggregate of the incomes of A, B, C, D, and E, the difference between the two aggregates would be the income of E. This problem is exacerbated by the increasing desire to combine data sets. In many cases, matching several sets of data for consistency at different levels of aggregation requires access to individual units. Thus, the individual units, which are the subject of privacy concerns, are available at various stages in the processing of data sets.

Finally, data integrity is a major concern in most installations. Modifications to data files can have consequences ranging from minor to disastrous.

COMMUNICATION LINES AND NETWORKS Network security attacks can be classified as *passive attacks* and *active attacks*. A passive attack attempts to learn or make use of information from the system but does not affect system resources. An active attack attempts to alter system resources or affect their operation.

Passive attacks are in the nature of eavesdropping on, or monitoring of, transmissions. The goal of the attacker is to obtain information that is being transmitted. Two types of passive attacks are release of message contents and traffic analysis.

The **release of message contents** is easily understood. A telephone conversation, an electronic mail message, and a transferred file may contain sensitive or confidential information. We would like to prevent an opponent from learning the contents of these transmissions.

A second type of passive attack, **traffic analysis**, is subtler. Suppose that we had a way of masking the contents of messages or other information traffic so that opponents, even if they captured the message, could not extract the information from the message. The common technique for masking contents is encryption. If we had encryption protection in place, an opponent might still be able to observe the pattern of these messages. The opponent could determine the location and identity of communicating hosts and could observe the frequency and length of messages being exchanged. This information might be useful in guessing the nature of the communication that was taking place.

Passive attacks are very difficult to detect because they do not involve any alteration of the data. Typically, the message traffic is sent and received in an apparently normal fashion, and neither the sender nor receiver is aware that a third party has read the messages or observed the traffic pattern. However, it is feasible to prevent the success of these attacks, usually by means of encryption. Thus, the emphasis in dealing with passive attacks is on prevention rather than detection.

Active attacks involve some modification of the data stream or the creation of a false stream and can be subdivided into four categories: replay, masquerade, modification of messages, and denial of service.

Replay involves the passive capture of a data unit and its subsequent retransmission to produce an unauthorized effect.

A **masquerade** takes place when one entity pretends to be a different entity. A masquerade attack usually includes one of the other forms of active attack. For example, authentication sequences can be captured and replayed after a valid authentication sequence has taken place, thus enabling an authorized entity with few privileges to obtain extra privileges by impersonating an entity that has those privileges.

Modification of messages simply means that some portion of a legitimate message is altered, or that messages are delayed or reordered, to produce an unauthorized effect. For example, a message stating "Allow John Smith to read confidential file `accounts`" is modified to say "Allow Fred Brown to read confidential file `accounts`."

The **denial of service** prevents or inhibits the normal use or management of communications facilities. This attack may have a specific target; for example, an entity may suppress all messages directed to a particular destination (e.g., the security audit service). Another form of service denial is the disruption of an entire network, either by disabling the network or by overloading it with messages so as to degrade performance.

Active attacks present the opposite characteristics of passive attacks. Whereas passive attacks are difficult to detect, measures are available to prevent their success. On the other hand, it is quite difficult to prevent active attacks absolutely, because to do so would require physical protection of all communications facilities and paths at all times. Instead, the goal is to detect them and to recover from any disruption or delays caused by them. Because the detection has a deterrent effect, it may also contribute to prevention.

18.3 INTRUDERS

One of the two most publicized threats to security is the intruder (the other is viruses), often referred to as a hacker or cracker. In an important early study of intrusion, Anderson [ANDE80] identified three classes of intruders:

- **Masquerader:** An individual who is not authorized to use the computer and who penetrates a system's access controls to exploit a legitimate user's account

- **Misfeasor:** A legitimate user who accesses data, programs, or resources for which such access is not authorized, or who is authorized for such access but misuses his or her privileges
- **Clandestine user:** An individual who seizes supervisory control of the system and uses this control to evade auditing and access controls or to suppress audit collection

The masquerader is likely to be an outsider; the misfeasor generally is an insider; and the clandestine user can be either an outsider or an insider.

Intruder attacks range from the benign to the serious. At the benign end of the scale, there are many people who simply wish to explore internets and see what is out there. At the serious end are individuals who are attempting to read privileged data, perform unauthorized modifications to data, or disrupt the system.

The following are examples of intrusion:

- Performing a remote root compromise of an e-mail server
- Defacing a Web server
- Guessing and cracking passwords
- Copying a database containing credit card numbers
- Viewing sensitive data, including payroll records and medical information, without authorization
- Running a packet sniffer on a workstation to capture usernames and passwords
- Using a permission error on an anonymous FTP server to distribute pirated software and music files
- Dialing into an unsecured modem and gaining internal network access
- Posing as an executive, calling the help desk, resetting the executive's e-mail password, and learning the new password
- Using an unattended, logged-in workstation without permission

Intruder Behavior Patterns

The techniques and behavior patterns of intruders are constantly shifting, to exploit newly discovered weaknesses and to evade detection and countermeasures. Even so, intruders typically follow one of a number of recognizable behavior patterns, and these patterns typically differ from those of ordinary users. In the following, we look at three broad examples of intruder behavior patterns to give the reader some feel for the challenge facing the security administrator. Table 18.3 summarizes the behavior.

HACKERS Traditionally, those who hack into computers do so for the thrill of it or for status. The hacking community is a strong meritocracy in which status is determined by level of competence. Thus, attackers often look for targets of opportunity and then share the information with others. A typical example is a break-in at a large financial institution reported in [RADC04]. The intruder took advantage of the fact that the corporate network was running unprotected services, some of which were not even needed. In this case, the key to the break-in was the pcAnywhere application.

Table 18.3   Some Examples of Intruder Patterns of Behavior

(a) Hacker

1. Select the target using IP lookup tools such as NSLookup, Dig, and others.
2. Map network for accessible services using tools such as NMAP.
3. Identify potentially vulnerable services (in this case, pcAnywhere).
4. Brute force (guess) pcAnywhere password.
5. Install remote administration tool called DameWare.
6. Wait for administrator to log on and capture his password.
7. Use that password to access remainder of network.

(b) Criminal Enterprise

1. Act quickly and precisely to make their activities harder to detect.
2. Exploit perimeter through vulnerable ports.
3. Use Trojan horses (hidden software) to leave back doors for reentry.
4. Use sniffers to capture passwords.
5. Do not stick around until noticed.
6. Make few or no mistakes.

(c) Internal Threat

1. Create network accounts for themselves and their friends.
2. Access accounts and applications they wouldn't normally use for their daily jobs.
3. E-mail former and prospective employers.
4. Conduct furtive instant-messaging chats.
5. Visit Web sites that cater to disgruntled employees, such as f'dcompany.com.
6. Perform large downloads and file copying.
7. Access the network during off hours.

The manufacturer, Symantec, advertises this program as a remote control solution that enables secure connection to remote devices. But the attacker had an easy time gaining access to pcAnywhere; the administrator used the same three-letter username and password for the program. In this case, there was no intrusion detection system on the 700-node corporate network. The intruder was only discovered when a vice president walked into her office and saw the cursor moving files around on her Windows workstation.

Benign intruders might be tolerable, although they do consume resources and may slow performance for legitimate users. However, there is no way in advance to know whether an intruder will be benign or malign. Consequently, even for systems with no particularly sensitive resources, there is a motivation to control this problem.

Intrusion detection systems (IDSs) and intrusion prevention systems (IPSs), of the type described in Chapter 19, are designed to counter this type of hacker threat. In addition to using such systems, organizations can consider restricting remote logons to specific IP addresses and/or use virtual private network technology.

One of the results of the growing awareness of the intruder problem has been the establishment of a number of computer emergency response teams (CERTs). These cooperative ventures collect information about system vulnerabilities and disseminate it to systems managers. Hackers also routinely read CERT reports. Thus, it is important for system administrators to quickly insert all software patches to discovered vulnerabilities. Unfortunately, given the complexity of many IT systems and the rate at which patches are released, this is increasingly difficult to achieve without automated updating. Even then, there are problems caused by incompatibilities resulting from the updated software (hence the need for multiple layers of defense in managing security threats to IT systems).

CRIMINALS   Organized groups of hackers have become a widespread and common threat to Internet-based systems. These groups can be in the employ of a corporation or government but often are loosely affiliated gangs of hackers. Typically, these gangs are young, often Eastern European, Russian, or Southeast Asian hackers who do business on the Web [ANTE06]. They meet in underground forums with names like DarkMarket.org and theftservices.com to trade tips and data and coordinate attacks. A common target is a credit card file at an e-commerce server. Attackers attempt to gain root access. The card numbers are used by organized crime gangs to purchase expensive items and are then posted to carder sites, where others can access and use the account numbers; this obscures usage patterns and complicates investigation.

Whereas traditional hackers look for targets of opportunity, criminal hackers usually have specific targets, or at least classes of targets in mind. Once a site is penetrated, the attacker acts quickly, scooping up as much valuable information as possible and exiting.

IDSs and IPSs can also be used for these types of attackers but may be less effective because of the quick in-and-out nature of the attack. For e-commerce sites, database encryption should be used for sensitive customer information, especially credit cards. For hosted e-commerce sites (provided by an outsider service), the e-commerce organization should make use of a dedicated server (not used to support multiple customers) and closely monitor the provider's security services.

INSIDER ATTACKS   Insider attacks are among the most difficult to detect and prevent. Employees already have access to and knowledge of the structure and content of corporate databases. Insider attacks can be motivated by revenge or simply a feeling of entitlement. An example of the former is the case of Kenneth Patterson, fired from his position as data communications manager for American Eagle Outfitters. Patterson disabled the company's ability to process credit card purchases during five days of the holiday season of 2002. As for a sense of entitlement, there have always been many employees who felt entitled to take extra office supplies for home use, but this now extends to corporate data. An example is that of a vice president of sales for a stock analysis firm who resigned to go to a competitor. Before she left, she copied the customer database to take with her. The offender reported feeling no animus toward her former employee; she simply wanted the data because it would be useful to her.

Although IDS and IPS facilities can be useful in countering insider attacks, other more direct approaches are of higher priority. Examples include the following:

- Enforce least privilege, only allowing access to the resources employees need to do their job.
- Set logs to see what users access and what commands they are entering.
- Protect sensitive resources with strong authentication.
- Upon termination, delete employee's computer and network access.
- Upon termination, make a mirror image of employee's hard drive before reissuing it. That evidence might be needed if your company information turns up at a competitor.

Intrusion Techniques

The objective of the intruder is to gain access to a system or to increase the range of privileges accessible on a system. Most initial attacks use system or software vulnerabilities that allow a user to execute code that opens a back door into the system. Intruders can get access to a system by exploiting attacks such as buffer overflows on a program that runs with certain privileges.

Alternatively, the intruder attempts to acquire information that should have been protected. In some cases, this information is in the form of a user password. With knowledge of some other user's password, an intruder can log in to a system and exercise all the privileges accorded to the legitimate user.

18.4 MALICIOUS SOFTWARE OVERVIEW

Perhaps the most sophisticated types of threats to computer systems are presented by programs that exploit vulnerabilities in computing systems. Such threats are referred to as **malicious software**, or **malware**. In this context, we are concerned with application programs as well as utility programs, such as editors and compilers. Malware is software designed to cause damage to or use up the resources of a target computer. It is frequently concealed within or masquerades as legitimate software. In some cases, it spreads itself to other computers via e-mail or infected discs.

The terminology in this area presents problems because of a lack of universal agreement on all of the terms and because some of the categories overlap. Table 18.4 is a useful guide.

Malicious software can be divided into two categories: those that need a host program, and those that are independent. The former, referred to as **parasitic**, are essentially fragments of programs that cannot exist independently of some actual application program, utility, or system program. Viruses, logic bombs, and back doors are examples. The latter are self-contained programs that can be scheduled and run by the operating system. Worms and bot programs are examples.

We can also differentiate between those software threats that do not replicate and those that do. The former are programs or fragments of programs that are activated by a trigger. Examples are logic bombs, back doors, and bot programs. The latter consist of either a program fragment or an independent program that,

Table 18.4   Terminology of Malicious Programs

Name	Description
Virus	Malware that, when executed, tries to replicate itself into other executable code; when it succeeds, the code is said to be infected. When the infected code is executed, the virus also executes.
Worm	A computer program that can run independently and can propagate a complete working version of itself onto other hosts on a network.
Logic bomb	A program inserted into software by an intruder. A logic bomb lies dormant until a predefined condition is met; the program then triggers an unauthorized act.
Trojan horse	A computer program that appears to have a useful function, but also has a hidden and potentially malicious function that evades security mechanisms, sometimes by exploiting legitimate authorizations of a system entity that invokes the Trojan horse program.
Back door (trap door)	Any mechanisms that bypasses a normal security check; it may allow unauthorized access to functionality.
Mobile code	Software (e.g., script, macro, or other portable instruction) that can be shipped unchanged to a heterogeneous collection of platforms and execute with identical semantics.
Exploits	Code specific to a single vulnerability or set of vulnerabilities.
Downloaders	Program that installs other items on a machine that is under attack. Usually, a downloader is sent in an e-mail.
Auto-rooter	Malicious hacker tools used to break into new machines remotely.
Kit (virus generator)	Set of tools for generating new viruses automatically.
Spammer programs	Used to send large volumes of unwanted e-mail.
Flooders	Used to attack networked computer systems with a large volume of traffic to carry out a denial of service (DoS) attack.
Keyloggers	Captures keystrokes on a compromised system.
Rootkit	Set of hacker tools used after attacker has broken into a computer system and gained root-level access.
Zombie, bot	Program activated on an infected machine that is activated to launch attacks on other machines.
Spyware	Software that collects information from a computer and transmits it to another system.
Adware	Advertising that is integrated into software. It can result in pop-up ads or redirection of a browser to a commercial site.

when executed, may produce one or more copies of itself to be activated later on the same system or some other system. Viruses and worms are examples.

In the remainder of this section, we briefly survey some of the key categories of malicious software, deferring discussion on the key topics of viruses, worms, and bots until the following section.

Back Door

A **back door**, also known as a **trap door**, is a secret entry point into a program that allows someone who is aware of the back door to gain access without going through the usual security access procedures. Programmers have used back doors legitimately for many years to debug and test programs; such a back door is called a **maintenance hook**. This usually is done when the programmer is developing an application that has an authentication procedure, or a long setup, requiring the user to enter many different values to run the application. To debug the program, the developer may wish to gain special privileges or to avoid all the necessary setup and authentication. The programmer may also want to ensure that there is a method of activating the program should something be wrong with the authentication procedure that is being built into the application. The back door is code that recognizes some special sequence of input or is triggered by being run from a certain user ID or by an unlikely sequence of events.

Back doors become threats when unscrupulous programmers use them to gain unauthorized access. The back door was the basic idea for the vulnerability portrayed in the movie *War Games*. Another example is that during the development of Multics, penetration tests were conducted by an Air Force "tiger team" (simulating adversaries). One tactic employed was to send a bogus operating system update to a site running Multics. The update contained a Trojan horse (described later) that could be activated by a back door and that allowed the tiger team to gain access. The threat was so well implemented that the Multics developers could not find it, even after they were informed of its presence [ENGE80].

It is difficult to implement operating system controls for back doors. Security measures must focus on the program development and software update activities.

Logic Bomb

One of the oldest types of program threat, predating viruses and worms, is the logic bomb. The logic bomb is code embedded in some legitimate program that is set to "explode" when certain conditions are met. Examples of conditions that can be used as triggers for a logic bomb are the presence or absence of certain files, a particular day of the week or date, or a particular user running the application. Once triggered, a bomb may alter or delete data or entire files, cause a machine halt, or do some other damage. A striking example of how logic bombs can be employed was the case of Tim Lloyd, who was convicted of setting a logic bomb that cost his employer, Omega Engineering, more than $10 million, derailed its corporate growth strategy, and eventually led to the layoff of 80 workers [GAUD00]. Ultimately, Lloyd was sentenced to 41 months in prison and ordered to pay $2 million in restitution.

Trojan Horse

A Trojan horse is a useful, or apparently useful, program or command procedure containing hidden code that, when invoked, performs some unwanted or harmful function.

Trojan horse programs can be used to accomplish functions indirectly that an unauthorized user could not accomplish directly. For example, to gain access to the files of another user on a shared system, a user could create a Trojan horse program that, when executed, changes the invoking user's file permissions so that the files are readable by any user. The author could then induce users to run the program by placing it in a common directory and naming it such that it appears to be a useful utility program or application. An example is a program that ostensibly produces a listing of the user's files in a desirable format. After another user has run the program, the author of the program can then access the information in the user's files. An example of a Trojan horse program that would be difficult to detect is a compiler that has been modified to insert additional code into certain programs as they are compiled, such as a system login program. The code creates a back door in the login program that permits the author to log on to the system using a special password. This Trojan horse can never be discovered by reading the source code of the login program.

Another common motivation for the Trojan horse is data destruction. The program appears to be performing a useful function (e.g., a calculator program), but it may also be quietly deleting the user's files. For example, a CBS executive was victimized by a Trojan horse that destroyed all information contained in his computer's memory [TIME90]. The Trojan horse was implanted in a graphics routine offered on an electronic bulletin board system.

Trojan horses fit into one of three models:

- Continuing to perform the function of the original program and additionally performing a separate malicious activity
- Continuing to perform the function of the original program but modifying the function to perform malicious activity (e.g., a Trojan horse version of a login program that collects passwords) or to disguise other malicious activity (e.g., a Trojan horse version of a process listing program that does not display certain processes that are malicious)
- Performing a malicious function that completely replaces the function of the original program

Mobile Code

Mobile code refers to programs (e.g., script, macro, or other portable instruction) that can be shipped unchanged to a heterogeneous collection of platforms and execute with identical semantics. The term also applies to situations involving a large homogeneous collection of platforms (e.g., Microsoft Windows).

Mobile code is transmitted from a remote system to a local system and then executed on the local system without the user's explicit instruction. Mobile code often acts as a mechanism for a virus, worm, or Trojan horse to be transmitted to the user's workstation. In other cases, mobile code takes advantage of vulnerabilities to perform its own exploits, such as unauthorized data access or root compromise. Popular vehicles for mobile code include Java applets, ActiveX, JavaScript, and VBScript. The most common ways of using mobile code for malicious operations on local system are cross-site scripting, interactive and dynamic Web sites, e-mail attachments, and downloads from untrusted sites or of untrusted software.

Multiple-Threat Malware

Viruses and other malware may operate in multiple ways. The terminology is far from uniform; this subsection gives a brief introduction to several related concepts that could be considered multiple-threat malware.

A **multipartite** virus infects in multiple ways. Typically, the multipartite virus is capable of infecting multiple types of files, so that virus eradication must deal with all of the possible sites of infection.

A **blended attack** uses multiple methods of infection or transmission, to maximize the speed of contagion and the severity of the attack. Some writers characterize a blended attack as a package that includes multiple types of malware. An example of a blended attack is the Nimda attack, erroneously referred to as simply a worm. Nimda uses four distribution methods:

- **E-mail:** A user on a vulnerable host opens an infected e-mail attachment; Nimda looks for e-mail addresses on the host and then sends copies of itself to those addresses.

- **Windows shares:** Nimda scans hosts for unsecured Windows file shares; it can then use NetBIOS86 as a transport mechanism to infect files on that host in the hopes that a user will run an infected file, which will activate Nimda on that host.

- **Web servers:** Nimda scans Web servers, looking for known vulnerabilities in Microsoft IIS. If it finds a vulnerable server, it attempts to transfer a copy of itself to the server and infect it and its files.

- **Web clients:** If a vulnerable Web client visits a Web server that has been infected by Nimda, the client's workstation will become infected.

Thus, Nimda has worm, virus, and mobile code characteristics. Blended attacks may also spread through other services, such as instant messaging and peer-to-peer file sharing.

18.5 VIRUSES, WORMS, BOTS, AND SPAM

Viruses

A computer virus is a piece of software that can "infect" other programs by modifying them; the modification includes injecting the original program with a routine to make copies of the virus program, which can then go on to infect other programs.

Biological viruses are tiny scraps of genetic code—DNA or RNA—that can take over the machinery of a living cell and trick it into making thousands of flawless replicas of the original virus. Like its biological counterpart, a computer virus carries in its instructional code the recipe for making perfect copies of itself. The typical virus becomes embedded in a program on a computer. Then, whenever the infected computer comes into contact with an uninfected piece of software, a fresh copy of the virus passes into the new program. Thus, the infection can be spread from computer to computer by unsuspecting users who either swap disks or send programs to one another over a network. In a network environment, the ability to access applications and system services on other computers provides a perfect culture for the spread of a virus.

THE NATURE OF VIRUSES   A virus can do anything that other programs do. The only difference is that it attaches itself to another program and executes secretly when the host program is run. Once a virus is executing, it can perform any function that is allowed by the privileges of the current user, such as erasing files and programs.

A computer virus has three parts:

- **Infection mechanism:** The means by which a virus spreads, enabling it to replicate. The mechanism is also referred to as the **infection vector**.
- **Trigger:** The event or condition that determines when the payload is activated or delivered.
- **Payload:** What the virus does, besides spreading. The payload may involve damage or may involve benign but noticeable activity.

During its lifetime, a typical virus goes through the following four phases:

- **Dormant phase:** The virus is idle. The virus will eventually be activated by some event, such as a date, the presence of another program or file, or the capacity of the disk exceeding some limit. Not all viruses have this stage.
- **Propagation phase:** The virus places an identical copy of itself into other programs or into certain system areas on the disk. Each infected program will now contain a clone of the virus, which will itself enter a propagation phase.
- **Triggering phase:** The virus is activated to perform the function for which it was intended. As with the dormant phase, the triggering phase can be caused by a variety of system events, including a count of the number of times that this copy of the virus has made copies of itself.
- **Execution phase:** The function is performed. The function may be harmless, such as a message on the screen, or damaging, such as the destruction of programs and data files.

Most viruses carry out their work in a manner that is specific to a particular operating system and, in some cases, specific to a particular hardware platform. Thus, they are designed to take advantage of the details and weaknesses of particular systems.

VIRUS STRUCTURE   A virus can be prepended or postpended to an executable program, or it can be embedded in some other fashion. The key to its operation is that the infected program, when invoked, will first execute the virus code and then execute the original code of the program.

A very general depiction of virus structure is shown in Figure 18.3 (based on [COHE94]). In this case, the virus code, V, is prepended to infected programs, and it is assumed that the entry point to the program, when invoked, is the first line of the program.

The infected program begins with the virus code and works as follows. The first line of code is a jump to the main virus program. The second line is a special marker that is used by the virus to determine whether or not a potential victim program has already been infected with this virus. When the program is invoked, control is immediately transferred to the main virus program. The virus program may first seek out uninfected executable files and infect them. Next, the virus may perform some action, usually detrimental to the system. This action could be performed

```
      program V :=
{goto main;
    1234567;

    subroutine infect-executable :=
      {loop:
      file := get-random-executable-file;
      if (first-line-of-file = 1234567)
          then goto loop
          else prepend V to file; }

    subroutine do-damage :=
      {whatever damage is to be done}

    subroutine trigger-pulled :=
      {return true if some condition holds}

main: main-program :=
      {infect-executable;
      if trigger-pulled then do-damage;
      goto next;}

next:

}
```

Figure 18.3   A Simple Virus

every time the program is invoked, or it could be a logic bomb that triggers only under certain conditions. Finally, the virus transfers control to the original program. If the infection phase of the program is reasonably rapid, a user is unlikely to notice any difference between the execution of an infected and an uninfected program.

A virus such as the one just described is easily detected because an infected version of a program is longer than the corresponding uninfected one. A way to thwart such a simple means of detecting a virus is to compress the executable file so that both the infected and uninfected versions are of identical length. Figure 18.4 shows in general terms the logic required. The important lines in this virus are numbered. We assume that program P_1 is infected with the virus CV. When this program is invoked, control passes to its virus, which performs the following steps:

1. For each uninfected file P_2 that is found, the virus first compresses that file to produce P_2', which is shorter than the original program by the size of the virus.

2. A copy of the virus is prepended to the compressed program.

3. The compressed version of the original infected program, P_1', is uncompressed.

4. The uncompressed original program is executed.

```
    program CV :=

{goto main;
    01234567;

    subroutine infect-executable :=
        {loop:
            file := get-random-executable-file;
        if (first-line-of-file = 01234567) then goto loop;
    (1)    compress file;
    (2)    prepend CV to file;
    }

main: main-program :=
            {if ask-permission then infect-executable;
    (3)    uncompress rest-of-file;
    (4)    run uncompressed file;}
    }
```

Figure 18.4 Logic for a Compression Virus

In this example, the virus does nothing other than propagate. As previously mentioned, the virus may include a logic bomb.

INITIAL INFECTION Once a virus has gained entry to a system by infecting a single program, it is in a position to potentially infect some or all other executable files on that system when the infected program executes. Thus, viral infection can be completely prevented by preventing the virus from gaining entry in the first place. Unfortunately, prevention is extraordinarily difficult because a virus can be part of any program outside a system. Thus, unless one is content to take an absolutely bare piece of iron and write all one's own system and application programs, one is vulnerable. Many forms of infection can also be blocked by denying normal users the right to modify programs on the system.

The lack of access controls on early PCs is a key reason why traditional machine code based viruses spread rapidly on these systems. By contrast, while it is easy enough to write a machine code virus for UNIX systems, they were almost never seen in practice because the existence of access controls on these systems prevented effective propagation of the virus. Traditional machine code based viruses are now less prevalent, because modern PC operating systems have more effective access controls. However, virus creators have found other avenues, such as macro and e-mail viruses, as discussed subsequently.

VIRUSES CLASSIFICATION There has been a continuous arms race between virus writers and writers of antivirus software since viruses first appeared. As effective countermeasures are developed for existing types of viruses, newer types are developed. There is no simple or universally agreed upon classification scheme for viruses. In this section, we classify viruses along two orthogonal axes: the type of target the virus tries to infect and the method the virus uses to conceal itself from detection by users and antivirus software.

A virus **classification by target** includes the following categories:

- **Boot sector infector:** Infects a master boot record or boot record and spreads when a system is booted from the disk containing the virus
- **File infector:** Infects files that the operating system or shell considers to be executable
- **Macro virus:** Infects files with macro code that is interpreted by an application

A virus **classification by concealment strategy** includes the following categories:

- **Encrypted virus:** A typical approach is as follows: A portion of the virus creates a random encryption key and encrypts the remainder of the virus. The key is stored with the virus. When an infected program is invoked, the virus uses the stored random key to decrypt the virus. When the virus replicates, a different random key is selected. Because the bulk of the virus is encrypted with a different key for each instance, there is no constant bit pattern to observe.
- **Stealth virus:** A form of virus explicitly designed to hide itself from detection by antivirus software. Thus, the entire virus, not just a payload, is hidden.
- **Polymorphic virus:** A virus that mutates with every infection, making detection by the "signature" of the virus impossible.
- **Metamorphic virus:** As with a polymorphic virus, a metamorphic virus mutates with every infection. The difference is that a metamorphic virus rewrites itself completely at each iteration, increasing the difficulty of detection. Metamorphic viruses may change their behavior as well as their appearance.

One example of a **stealth virus** was discussed earlier: a virus that uses compression so that the infected program is exactly of the same length as an uninfected version. Far more sophisticated techniques are possible. For example, a virus can place intercept logic in disk I/O routines, so that when there is an attempt to read suspected portions of the disk using these routines, the virus will present back the original, uninfected program. Thus, *stealth* is not a term that applies to a virus as such but, rather, refers to a technique used by a virus to evade detection.

A **polymorphic virus** creates copies during replication that are functionally equivalent but have distinctly different bit patterns. As with a stealth virus, the purpose is to defeat programs that scan for viruses. In this case, the "signature" of the virus will vary with each copy. To achieve this variation, the virus may randomly insert superfluous instructions or interchange the order of independent instructions. A more effective approach is to use encryption. The strategy of the encryption virus is followed. The portion of the virus that is responsible for generating keys and performing encryption/decryption is referred to as the *mutation engine*. The mutation engine itself is altered with each use.

VIRUS KITS   Another weapon in the virus writers' armory is the virus-creation toolkit. Such a toolkit enables a relative novice to quickly create a number of different viruses. Although viruses created with toolkits tend to be less sophisticated than viruses designed from scratch, the sheer number of new viruses that can be generated using a toolkit creates a problem for antivirus schemes.

MACRO VIRUSES   In the mid-1990s, macro viruses became by far the most prevalent type of virus. Macro viruses are particularly threatening for a number of reasons:

1. A macro virus is platform independent. Many macro viruses infect Microsoft Word documents or other Microsoft Office documents. Any hardware platform and operating system that supports these applications can be infected.

2. Macro viruses infect documents, not executable portions of code. Most of the information introduced onto a computer system is in the form of a document rather than a program.

3. Macro viruses are easily spread. A very common method is by electronic mail.

4. Because macro viruses infect user documents rather than system programs, traditional file system access controls are of limited use in preventing their spread.

Macro viruses take advantage of a feature found in Word and other office applications such as Microsoft Excel—namely, the macro. In essence, a macro is an executable program embedded in a word processing document or other type of file. Typically, users employ macros to automate repetitive tasks and thereby save keystrokes. The macro language is usually some form of the Basic programming language. A user might define a sequence of keystrokes in a macro and set it up so that the macro is invoked when a function key or special short combination of keys is input.

Successive releases of MS Office products provide increased protection against macro viruses. For example, Microsoft offers an optional Macro Virus Protection tool that detects suspicious Word files and alerts the customer to the potential risk of opening a file with macros. Various antivirus product vendors have also developed tools to detect and correct macro viruses. As in other types of viruses, the arms race continues in the field of macro viruses, but they no longer are the predominant virus threat.

E-MAIL VIRUSES   A more recent development in malicious software is the e-mail virus. The first rapidly spreading e-mail viruses, such as Melissa, made use of a Microsoft Word macro embedded in an attachment. If the recipient opens the e-mail attachment, the Word macro is activated. Then the virus performs the following two functions:

1. The e-mail virus sends itself to everyone on the mailing list in the user's e-mail package.

2. The virus does local damage on the user's system.

In 1999, a more powerful version of the e-mail virus appeared. This newer version can be activated merely by opening an e-mail that contains the virus rather than opening an attachment. The virus uses the Visual Basic scripting language supported by the e-mail package.

Thus we see a new generation of malware that arrives via e-mail and uses e-mail software features to replicate itself across the Internet. The virus propagates itself as soon as it is activated (either by opening an e-mail attachment or by opening the e-mail) to all of the e-mail addresses known to the infected host. As a result, whereas viruses used to take months or years to propagate, they now do so in hours. This makes it very difficult for antivirus software to respond before much damage is done. Ultimately, a greater degree of security must be built into Internet utility and application software on PCs to counter the growing threat.

Worms

A worm is a program that can replicate itself and send copies from computer to computer across network connections. Upon arrival, the worm may be activated to replicate and propagate again. In addition to propagation, the worm usually performs some unwanted function. An e-mail virus has some of the characteristics of a worm because it propagates itself from system to system. However, we can still classify it as a virus because it uses a document modified to contain viral macro content and requires human action. A worm actively seeks out more machines to infect and each machine that is infected serves as an automated launching pad for attacks on other machines.

Network worm programs use network connections to spread from system to system. Once active within a system, a network worm can behave as a computer virus or bacteria, or it could implant Trojan horse programs or perform any number of disruptive or destructive actions.

To replicate itself, a network worm uses some sort of network vehicle. Examples include the following:

- **Electronic mail facility:** A worm mails a copy of itself to other systems, so that its code is run when the e-mail or an attachment is received or viewed.

- **Remote execution capability:** A worm executes a copy of itself on another system, either by using an explicit remote execution facility or by exploiting a program flaw in a network service to subvert its operations.

- **Remote login capability:** A worm logs onto a remote system as a user and then uses commands to copy itself from one system to the other, where it then executes.

The new copy of the worm program is then run on the remote system, where, in addition to any functions that it performs at that system, it continues to spread in the same fashion.

A network worm exhibits the same characteristics as a computer virus: a dormant phase, a propagation phase, a triggering phase, and an execution phase. Typically, a worm performs the following functions during the propagation phase:

1. Search for other systems to infect by examining host tables or similar repositories of remote system addresses.
2. Establish a connection with a remote system.
3. Copy itself to the remote system and cause the copy to be run.

The network worm may also attempt to determine whether a system has previously been infected before copying itself to the system. In a multiprogramming system, it may also disguise its presence by naming itself as a system process or using some other name that may not be noticed by a system operator.

As with viruses, network worms are difficult to counter.

The state of the art in worm technology includes the following:

- **Multiplatform:** Newer worms are not limited to Windows machines but can attack a variety of platforms, especially the popular varieties of UNIX.
- **Multi-exploit:** New worms penetrate systems in a variety of ways, using exploits against Web servers, browsers, e-mail, file sharing, and other network-based applications.
- **Ultrafast spreading:** One technique to accelerate the spread of a worm is to conduct a prior Internet scan to accumulate Internet addresses of vulnerable machines.
- **Polymorphic:** To evade detection, skip past filters, and foil real-time analysis, worms adopt the virus polymorphic technique. Each copy of the worm has new code generated on the fly using functionally equivalent instructions and encryption techniques.
- **Metamorphic:** In addition to changing their appearance, metamorphic worms have a repertoire of behavior patterns that are unleashed at different stages of propagation.
- **Transport vehicles:** Because worms can rapidly compromise a large number of systems, they are ideal for spreading other distributed attack tools, such as distributed denial-of-service bots.
- **Zero-day exploit:** To achieve maximum surprise and distribution, a worm should exploit an unknown vulnerability that is only discovered by the general network community when the worm is launched.

Bots

A bot (robot), also known as a zombie or drone, is a program that secretly takes over another Internet-attached computer and then uses that computer to launch attacks that are difficult to trace to the bot's creator. The bot is typically planted on hundreds or thousands of computers belonging to unsuspecting third parties. The collection of bots often is capable of acting in a coordinated manner; such a collection is referred to as a **botnet**.

A botnet exhibits three characteristics: the bot functionality, a remote control facility, and a spreading mechanism to propagate the bots and construct the botnet. We examine each of these characteristics in turn.

USES OF BOTS The following are uses of bots:

- **Distributed denial-of-service attacks:** A DDoS attack is an attack on a computer system or network that causes a loss of service to users.
- **Spamming:** With the help of a botnet and thousands of bots, an attacker is able to send massive amounts of bulk e-mail (spam).
- **Sniffing traffic:** Bots can also use a packet sniffer to watch for interesting clear-text data passing by a compromised machine. The sniffers are mostly used to retrieve sensitive information like usernames and passwords.

- **Keylogging:** If the compromised machine uses encrypted communication channels (e.g., HTTPS or POP3S), then just sniffing the network packets on the victim's computer is useless because the appropriate key to decrypt the packets is missing. But by using a keylogger, which captures keystrokes on the infected machine, an attacker can retrieve sensitive information. An implemented filtering mechanism (e.g., "I am only interested in key sequences near the keyword 'paypal.com' ") further helps in stealing secret data.

- **Spreading new malware:** Botnets are used to spread new bots. This is very easy since all bots implement mechanisms to download and execute a file via HTTP or FTP. A botnet with 10,000 hosts that acts as the start base for a worm or mail virus allows very fast spreading and thus causes more harm.

- **Installing advertisement add-ons and browser helper objects (BHOs):** Botnets can also be used to gain financial advantages. This works by setting up a fake Web site with some advertisements: The operator of this Web site negotiates a deal with some hosting companies that pay for clicks on ads. With the help of a botnet, these clicks can be "automated" so that instantly a few thousand bots click on the pop-ups. This process can be further enhanced if the bot hijacks the start page of a compromised machine so that the "clicks" are executed each time the victim uses the browser.

- **Attacking IRC chat networks:** Botnets are also used for attacks against Internet Relay Chat (IRC) networks. Popular among attackers is especially the so-called clone attack: In this kind of attack, the controller orders each bot to connect a large number of clones to the victim IRC network. The victim is flooded by service requests from thousands of bots or thousands of channel-joins by these cloned bots. In this way, the victim IRC network is brought down, similar to a DDoS attack.

- **Manipulating online polls/games:** Online polls/games are getting more and more attention, and it is rather easy to manipulate them with botnets. Since every bot has a distinct IP address, every vote will have the same credibility as a vote cast by a real person. Online games can be manipulated in a similar way.

REMOTE CONTROL FACILITY   The remote control facility is what distinguishes a bot from a worm. A worm propagates itself and activates itself, whereas a bot is controlled from some central facility, at least initially.

A typical means of implementing the remote control facility is on an IRC server. All bots join a specific channel on this server and treat incoming messages as commands. More recent botnets tend to avoid IRC mechanisms and use covert communication channels via protocols such as HTTP. Distributed control mechanisms are also used, to avoid a single point of failure.

Once a communications path is established between a control module and the bots, the control module can activate the bots. In its simplest form, the control module simply issues command to the bot that causes the bot to execute routines that are already implemented in the bot. For greater flexibility, the control module can issue update commands that instruct the bots to download a file from some Internet location and execute it. The bot in this latter case becomes a more general-purpose tool that can be used for multiple attacks.

CONSTRUCTING THE ATTACK NETWORK   The first step in a botnet attack is for the attacker to infect a number of machines with bot software that will ultimately be used to carry out the attack. The essential ingredients in this phase of the attack are the following:

1. Software that can carry out the attack. The software must be able to run on a large number of machines, must be able to conceal its existence, must be able to communicate with the attacker or have some sort of time-triggered mechanism, and must be able to launch the intended attack toward the target.

2. A vulnerability in a large number of systems. The attacker must become aware of a vulnerability that many system administrators and individual users have failed to patch and that enables the attacker to install the bot software.

3. A strategy for locating and identifying vulnerable machines, a process known as **scanning** or **fingerprinting**.

In the scanning process, the attacker first seeks out a number of vulnerable machines and infects them. Then, typically, the bot software that is installed in the infected machines repeats the same scanning process, until a large distributed network of infected machines is created. The following are types of scanning strategies:

- **Random:** Each compromised host probes random addresses in the IP address space, using a different seed. This technique produces a high volume of Internet traffic, which may cause generalized disruption even before the actual attack is launched.

- **Hit list:** The attacker first compiles a long list of potential vulnerable machines. This can be a slow process done over a long period to avoid detection that an attack is underway. Once the list is compiled, the attacker begins infecting machines on the list. Each infected machine is provided with a portion of the list to scan. This strategy results in a very short scanning period, which may make it difficult to detect that infection is taking place.

- **Topological:** This method uses information contained on an infected victim machine to find more hosts to scan.

- **Local subnet:** If a host can be infected behind a firewall, that host then looks for targets in its own local network. The host uses the subnet address structure to find other hosts that would otherwise be protected by the firewall.

Spam (Unsolicited Bulk) E-Mail

With the explosive growth of the Internet over the last few decades, the widespread use of e-mail, and the extremely low cost required to send large volumes of e-mail, has come the rise of unsolicited bulk e-mail, commonly known as spam. A number of recent estimates suggest that spam e-mail may account for 90% or more of all e-mail sent. This imposes significant costs both on the network infrastructure needed to relay this traffic and on users who need to filter their legitimate e-mails out of this flood. In response to this explosive growth, there has been the equally rapid growth of the anti-spam industry that provides products to detect and filter spam e-mails. This has led to an arms race between the spammers devising techniques to sneak their content through and the defenders making efforts to block them.

While some spam is sent from legitimate mail servers, most recent spam is sent by botnets using compromised user systems. A significant portion of spam e-mail content is just advertising, trying to convince the recipient to purchase some product online, such as pharmaceuticals, or used in scams, such as stock scams or money mule job ads. But spam is also a significant carrier of malware. The e-mail may have an attached document, which if opened, may exploit a software vulnerability to install malware on the user's system, as we discussed in the previous section. Or, it may have an attached Trojan horse program or scripting code that, if run, also installs malware on the user's system. Some trojans avoid the need for user agreement by exploiting a software vulnerability in order to install themselves, as we discuss next. Finally the spam may be used in a phishing attack, typically directing the user either to a fake Web site that mirrors some legitimate service, such as an online banking site, where it attempts to capture the user's login and password details; or to complete some form with sufficient personal details to allow the attacker to impersonate the user in an identity theft. All of these uses make spam e-mails a significant security concern. However, in many cases it requires the user's active choice to view the e-mail and any attached document, or to permit the installation of some program, in order for the compromise to occur.

18.6 KEYLOGGERS, PHISHING, SPYWARE

We now consider payloads where the malware gathers data stored on the infected system for use by the attacker. A common target is the user's login and password credentials for banking, gaming, and related sites, which the attacker then uses to impersonate the user to access these sites for gain. Less commonly, the payload may target documents or system configuration details for the purpose of reconnaissance or espionage. These attacks target the confidentiality of this information.

Credential Theft, Keyloggers, and Spyware

Typically, users send their login and password credentials to banking, gaming, and related sites over encrypted communication channels (e.g., HTTPS or POP3S), which protects them from capture by monitoring network packets. To bypass this, an attacker can install a **keylogger**, which captures keystrokes on the infected machine to allow an attacker to monitor this sensitive information. Since this would result in the attacker receiving a copy of all text entered on the compromised machine, keyloggers typically implement some form of filtering mechanism that only returns information close to desired keywords (e.g., "login" or "password" or "paypal.com").

In response to the use of keyloggers, some banking and other sites switched to using a graphical applet to enter critical information, such as passwords. Since these do not use text entered via the keyboard, traditional keyloggers do not capture this information. In response attackers developed more general **spyware** payloads, which subvert the compromised machine to allow monitoring of a wide range of activity on the system. This may include monitoring the history and content of browsing activity, redirecting certain Web page requests to fake sites controlled by the attacker, and dynamically modifying data exchanged between the browser and certain Web sites of interest. All of which can result in significant compromise of the user's personal information.

The Zeus banking Trojan, created from its crimeware toolkit, is a prominent example of such spyware that has been widely deployed in recent years [BINS10]. It steals banking and financial credentials both by using a keylogger and by capturing and possibly altering form data for certain Web sites. It is typically deployed either using spam e-mails or via a compromised Web site in a "drive-by-download."

Phishing and Identity Theft

Another approach used to capture a user's login and password credentials is to include a URL in a spam e-mail that links to a fake Web site controlled by the attacker, but which mimics the login page of some banking, gaming, or similar site. This is normally included in some message suggesting that urgent action is required by the user to authenticate their account, to prevent it being locked. If users are careless, and don't realize that they are being conned, then following the link and supplying the requested details will certainly result in the attackers exploiting their account using the captured credentials.

More generally, such a spam e-mail may direct a user to a fake Web site controlled by the attacker, or to complete some enclosed form and return to an e-mail accessible to the attacker, which is used to gather a range of private, personal information on the user. Given sufficient details, the attacker can then "assume" the user's identity for the purpose of obtaining credit, or sensitive access to other resources. This is known as a **phishing** attack and exploits social engineering to leverage user's trust by masquerading as communications from a trusted source [GOLD10].

Such general spam e-mails are typically widely distributed to very large numbers of users, often via a botnet. While the content will not match appropriate trusted sources for a significant fraction of the recipients, the attackers rely on it reaching sufficient users of the named trusted source, a gullible portion of whom will respond, for it to be profitable.

A more dangerous variant of this is the **spear-phishing** attack. This again is an e-mail claiming to be from a trusted source. However, the recipients are carefully researched by the attacker, and each e-mail is carefully crafted to suit its recipient specifically, often quoting a range of information to convince them of its authenticity. This greatly increases the likelihood of the recipient responding as desired by the attacker.

Reconnaissance and Espionage

Credential theft and identity theft are special cases of a more general reconnaissance payload, which aims to obtain certain types of desired information and return this to the attacker. These special cases are certainly the most common; however other targets are known. Operation Aurora in 2009 used a Trojan to gain access to and potentially modify source code repositories at a range of high-tech, security, and defense contractor companies [SYMA11]. The Stuxnet worm discovered in 2010 included capture of hardware and software configuration details in order to determine whether it had compromised the specific desired target systems. Early versions of this worm returned this same information, which was then used to develop the attacks deployed in later versions [CHEN11].

18.7 COMPUTER SECURITY TRENDS

In order to assess the relative severity of various threats and the relative importance of various approaches to computer security, it is useful to look at the experience of organizations. A useful view is provided by the CSI Computer Crime and Security Survey for 2010/2011, conducted by the Computer Security Institute [CSI10]. The respondents consisted of over 350 U.S.-based companies, nonprofit organizations, and public sector organizations.

Figure 18.5 shows the types of attacks experienced by respondents in nine major categories.[2] Most noteworthy is the large and growing prevalence of malicious

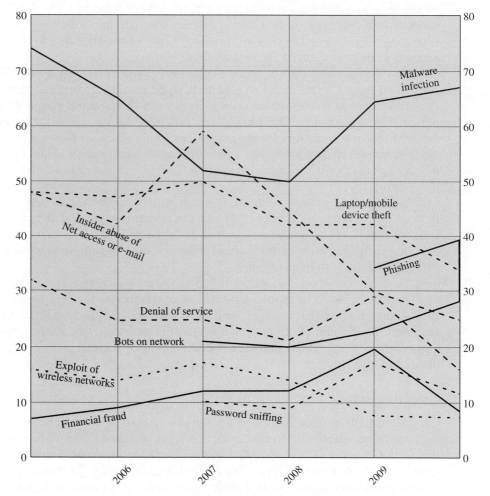

Figure 18.5   Types of Attacks Experienced (by percent of respondents)
Source: Computer Security Institute 2010/2011 Computer Crime and Security Survey

---

[2]A complete list, including low-incidence categories, is available as the file Types-of-Attacks.pdf in the Documents folder in the Premium Content site for this book.

software (malware) attacks. It is also worth noting that most categories of attack exhibit a somewhat downward trend. The CSI report speculates that this is due in large part to improved security techniques by organizations.

Figure 18.6 indicates the types of security technology used by organizations to counter threats. Both firewalls and antivirus software are used almost universally. This popularity reflects a number of factors:

- The maturity of these technologies means that security administrators are very familiar with the products and are confident of their effectiveness.

- Because these technologies are mature and there are a number of vendors, costs tend to be quite reasonable and user-friendly interfaces are available.

- The threats countered by these technologies are among the most significant facing security administrators.

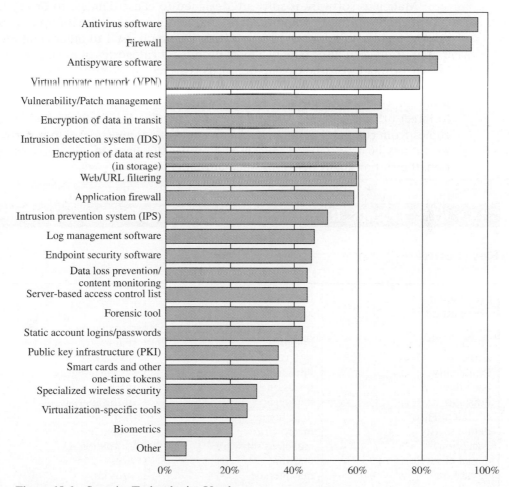

Figure 18.6 Security Technologies Used

Source: Computer Security Institute 2010/2011 Computer Crime and Security Survey

18.8 SUMMARY

The key objectives of any computer or network security system are confidentiality (assurance that data remain confidential and that privacy is maintained for individuals), integrity (assurance that data are not changed in an unauthorized manner and that systems perform as intended), and availability (assurance that system services are not denied to authorized users). Additional objectives are authenticity (assurance that the message and its source are valid) and accountability (requirement that actions of an entity be traced uniquely to that entity). With these objectives in mind, security threats can be classified based on how a given attack provides a threat to a given objective.

The two most critical types of security threats are intruders and malicious software. Intruders exhibit a variety of behavior patterns and use a variety of techniques to gain unauthorized access to system resources.

Malicious software is software designed to cause damage to or use up the resources of a target computer. It is frequently concealed within or masquerades as legitimate software. In some cases, it spreads itself to other computers via e-mail or infected discs. The two most prominent categories of malicious software are viruses and worms. A computer virus is a piece of software that can "infect" other programs by modifying them; the modification includes injecting the original program with a routine to make copies of the virus program, which can then go on to infect other programs. A worm is a program that can replicate itself and send copies from computer to computer across network connections. Upon arrival, the worm may be activated to replicate and propagate again. In addition to propagation, the worm usually performs some unwanted function.

18.9 KEY TERMS, REVIEW QUESTIONS, AND PROBLEMS

Key Terms

accountability	falsification	privacy
active attack	hacker	replay
asset	insider attack	repudiation
attack	integrity	spam
authenticity	interception	spyware
availability	intruder	system integrity
back door	intrusion	threat
bots	keylogger	traffic analysis
confidentiality	logic bomb	trap door
data integrity	macro virus	Trojan horse
deception	malicious software	usurpation
denial of service	malware	virus
disruption	masquerade	virus kit
e-mail virus	passive attack	worm
exposure	phishing	

Review Questions

18.1 Define *computer security*.

18.2 What are the fundamental requirements addressed by computer security?

18.3 What is the difference between passive and active security threats?

18.4 List and briefly define three classes of intruders.

18.5 List and briefly define three intruder behavior patterns.

18.6 What is the role of compression in the operation of a virus?

18.7 What is the role of encryption in the operation of a virus?

18.8 What are typical phases of operation of a virus or worm?

18.9 In general terms, how does a worm propagate?

Problems

18.1 Consider an automated tell machine (ATM) in which users provide a personal identification number (PIN) and a card for account access. Give examples of confidentiality, integrity, and availability requirements associated with the system and, in each case, indicate the degree of importance of the requirement.

18.2 Repeat Problem 18.1 for a telephone switching system that routes calls through a switching network based on the telephone number requested by the caller.

18.3 Consider a desktop publishing system used to produce documents for various organizations.
  a. Give an example of a type of publication for which confidentiality of the stored data is the most important requirement.
  b. Give an example of a type of publication in which data integrity is the most important requirement.
  c. Give an example in which system availability is the most important requirement.

18.4 For each of the following assets, assign a low, moderate, or high impact level for the loss of confidentiality, availability, and integrity, respectively. Justify your answers.
  a. An organization managing public information on its Web server.
  b. A law enforcement organization managing extremely sensitive investigative information.
  c. A financial organization managing routine administrative information (not privacy-related information).
  d. An information system used for large acquisitions in a contracting organization contains both sensitive, pre-solicitation phase contract information and routine administrative information. Assess the impact for the two data sets separately and the information system as a whole.
  e. A power plant contains a SCADA (supervisory control and data acquisition) system controlling the distribution of electric power for a large military installation. The SCADA system contains both real-time sensor data and routine administrative information. Assess the impact for the two data sets separately and the information system as a whole.

18.5 Assume that passwords are selected from four-character combinations of 26 alphabetic characters. Assume that an adversary is able to attempt passwords at a rate of one per second.
  a. Assuming no feedback to the adversary until each attempt has been completed, what is the expected time to discover the correct password?
  b. Assuming feedback to the adversary flagging an error as each incorrect character is entered, what is the expected time to discover the correct password?

18.6 There is a flaw in the virus program of Figure 18.3. What is it?

18.7   The question arises as to whether it is possible to develop a program that can analyze a piece of software to determine if it is a virus. Consider that we have a program D that is supposed to be able to do that. That is, for any program P, if we run D(P), the result returned is TRUE (P is a virus) or FALSE (P is not a virus). Now consider the following program:

```
Program CV :=
  {...
  main-program :=
    {if D(CV) then goto next:
        else infect-executable;
    }
next:
  }
```

In the preceding program, infect-executable is a module that scans memory for executable programs and replicates itself in those programs. Determine if D can correctly decide whether CV is a virus.

18.8   The point of this problem is to demonstrate the type of puzzles that must be solved in the design of malicious code and, therefore, the type of mindset that one wishing to counter such attacks must adopt.

a.   Consider the following C program:

```
begin
    print (*begin print (); end.*);
end
```

What do you think the program was intended to do? Does it work?

b.   Answer the same questions for the following program:

```
char [] = {'0', ' ', '}', ';', 'm', 'a', 'i', 'n', '(',
           ')', '{',
and so on... 't', ')', '0'};
main ()
  {
    int I;
    printf(*char t[] = (*);
    for (i=0; t[i]!=0; i=i+1)
            printf("%d, ", t[i]);
    printf("%s", t);
  }
```

c.   What is the specific relevance of this problem to this chapter?

18.9   Consider the following fragment:

```
legitimate code
if data is Friday the 13th;
  crash_computer();
legitimate code
```

What type of malicious software is this?

18.10   Consider the following fragment in an authentication program:

```
username = read_username();
password = read_password();
if username is "133t h4ck0r"
  return ALLOW_LOGIN;
if username and password are valid
  return ALLOW_LOGIN;
else return DENY_LOGIN
```

What type of malicious software is this?

18.11   The following code fragments show a sequence of virus instructions and a polymorphic version of the virus. Describe the effect produced by the metamorphic code.

Original Code	Metamorphic Code

mov eax, 5
add eax, ebx
call [eax]
	mov eax, 5
	push ecx
	pop ecx
	add eax, ebx
	swap eax, ebx
	swap ebx, eax
	call [eax]
	nop

COMPUTER AND NETWORK SECURITY TECHNIQUES

CHAPTER 19

Learning Objectives

After reading this chapter, you should be able to:

♦ Discuss the use of Internet Protocol security (IPsec) to create a virtual private network (VPN).

♦ Discuss the role of Secure Sockets Layer (SSL) in Web security and describe its basic functionality.

♦ Explain the use of Wi-Fi Protected Access (WPA) in an 802.11 network.

♦ Understand the basic principles and techniques of intrusion detection systems.

♦ Explain the characteristics and types of firewalls.

♦ Assess the approaches for defending against the various types of malicious software.

This chapter introduces common measures and protocols used to counter the security threats discussed in Chapter 18.

19.1 VIRTUAL PRIVATE NETWORKS AND IPSEC

Virtual private networks (VPNs) and IPsec (Internet Protocol security) were introduced in Chapter 8, where we looked at the applications and benefits of IPsec. This section provides some of the technical details.

IPsec Functions

IP-level security encompasses three functional areas: authentication, confidentiality, and key management. The authentication mechanism assures that a received packet was, in fact, transmitted by the party identified as the source in the packet header. In addition, this mechanism assures that the packet has not been altered in transit. The confidentiality facility enables communicating nodes to encrypt messages to prevent eavesdropping by third parties. The key management facility is concerned with the secure exchange of keys. The current version of IPsec, known as IPsecv3, encompasses authentication and confidentiality using a protocol known as Encapsulating Security Payload (ESP). Key management is provided by the Internet Key Exchange standard, IKEv2.

Transport and Tunnel Modes

ESP supports two modes of use: transport mode and tunnel mode.

Transport mode provides protection primarily for upper-layer protocols. That is, transport mode protection extends to the payload of an IP packet. Typically, transport mode is used for end-to-end communication between two hosts (e.g., a client and a server, or two workstations). ESP in transport mode encrypts and optionally authenticates the IP payload but not the IP header (Figure 19.1b). This configuration is useful for relatively small networks, in which each host and

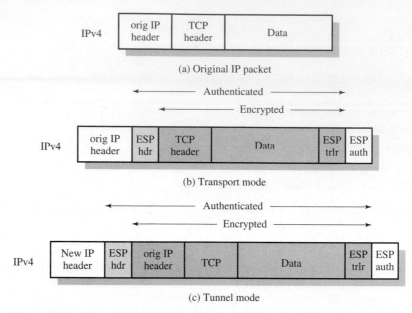

Figure 19.1 Scope of ESP Encryption and Authentication

server is equipped with IPsec. However, for a full-blown VPN, tunnel mode is far more efficient.

Tunnel mode provides protection to the entire IP packet. To achieve this, after the ESP fields are added to the IP packet, the entire packet plus security fields is treated as the payload of new "outer" IP packet with a new outer IP header. The entire original, or inner, packet travels through a "tunnel" from one point of an IP network to another; no routers along the way are able to examine the inner IP header. Because the original packet is encapsulated, the new, larger packet may have totally different source and destination addresses, adding to the security. Tunnel mode is used when at least one of the two ends is a security gateway, such as a firewall or router that implements IPsec. With tunnel mode, a number of hosts on networks behind firewalls may engage in secure communications without implementing IPsec. The unprotected packets generated by such hosts are tunneled through external networks by using tunnel mode, set up by the IPsec software in the firewall or secure router at the boundary of the local network.

Here is an example of how tunnel-mode IPsec operates. Host A on a network generates an IP packet with the destination address of host B on another network. This packet is routed from the originating host to a firewall or secure router at the boundary of A's network. The firewall filters all outgoing packets to determine the need for IPsec processing. If this packet from A to B requires IPsec, the firewall performs IPsec processing and encapsulates the packet in an outer IP header. The source IP address of this outer IP packet is this firewall, and the destination address may be a firewall that forms the boundary to B's local network. This packet is now routed to B's firewall, with intermediate routers examining only the outer IP header. At B's firewall, the outer IP header is stripped off, and the inner packet is delivered to B.

ESP in tunnel mode encrypts and optionally authenticates the entire inner IP packet, including the inner IP header.

Key Management

The key management portion of IPsec involves the determination and distribution of secret keys. The IPsec Architecture document mandates support for two types of key management:

- **Manual:** A system administrator (SA) manually configures each system with its own keys and with the keys of other communicating systems. This is practical for small, relatively static environments.

- **Automated:** An automated system enables the on-demand creation of keys and facilitates the use of keys in a large distributed system with an evolving configuration. An automated system is the most flexible but requires more effort to configure and requires more software, so smaller installations are likely to opt for manual key management.

IPsec and VPNs

The driving force for the acceptance and deployment of secure IP is the need for business and government users to connect their private WAN/LAN infrastructure to the Internet for (1) access to Internet services, and (2) use of the Internet as a component of the WAN transport system. Users need to secure their networks and at the same time send and receive traffic over the Internet. The authentication and privacy mechanisms of secure IP provide the basis for a security strategy.

Because IP security mechanisms have been defined independent of their use with either the current IP or IPv6, deployment of these mechanisms does not depend on deployment of IPv6. Indeed, it is likely that we will see widespread use of secure IP features long before IPv6 becomes popular, because the need for IP-level security is greater than the need for the added functions that IPv6 provides compared to the current IP.

With the arrival of IPsec, managers have a standardized means of implementing security for VPNs. Further, all of the encryption and authentication algorithms, and security protocols, used in IPsec are well studied and have survived years of scrutiny. As a result, the user can be confident that the IPsec facility indeed provides strong security.

IPsec can be implemented in routers or firewalls owned and operated by the organization. This gives the network manager complete control over security aspects of the VPN, which is much to be desired. However, IPsec is a complex set of functions and modules and the management and configuration responsibility is formidable. The alternative is to seek a solution from a service provider. A service provider can simplify the job of planning, implementing, and maintaining Internet-based VPNs for secure access to network resources and secure communication between sites.

19.2 SSL AND TLS

Chapter 10 introduced the Secure Sockets Layer (SSL) and the follow-on Internet standard known as Transport Layer Security (TLS). This section provides some of the technical details.

SSL Architecture

SSL is designed to make use of Transmission Control Protocol (TCP) to provide a reliable end-to-end secure service. SSL is not a single protocol but rather two layers of protocols, as illustrated in Figure 19.2.

The SSL Record Protocol provides basic security services to various higher-layer protocols. In particular, the Hypertext Transfer Protocol (HTTP), which provides the transfer service for Web client/server interaction, can operate on top of SSL. Three higher-layer protocols are defined as part of SSL: the Handshake Protocol, the Change Cipher Spec Protocol, and the Alert Protocol. These SSL-specific protocols are used in the management of SSL exchanges and are examined later in this section.

Two important SSL concepts are the SSL session and the SSL connection, which are defined in the specification as follows:

- **Connection:** A connection is a transport (in the Open Systems Interconnection (OSI) layering model definition) that provides a suitable type of service. For SSL, such connections are peer-to-peer relationships. The connections are transient. Every connection is associated with one session.

- **Session:** An SSL session is an association between a client and a server. Sessions are created by the Handshake Protocol. Sessions define a set of cryptographic security parameters, which can be shared among multiple connections. Sessions are used to avoid the expensive negotiation of new security parameters for each connection.

Between any pair of parties (applications such as HTTP on client and server), there may be multiple secure connections. In theory, there may also be multiple simultaneous sessions between parties, but this feature is not used in practice.

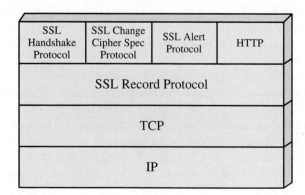

Figure 19.2   SSL Protocol Stack

SSL Record Protocol

The SSL Record Protocol provides two services for SSL connections:

- **Confidentiality:** The Handshake Protocol defines a shared secret key that is used for symmetric encryption of SSL payloads.
- **Message Integrity:** The Handshake Protocol also defines a shared secret key that is used to form a message authentication code (MAC).

Figure 19.3 indicates the overall operation of the SSL Record Protocol. The first step is **fragmentation**. Each upper-layer message is fragmented into blocks of 2^{14} bytes (16,384 bytes) or less. Next, **compression** is optionally applied. The next step in processing is to compute a **message authentication code** over the compressed data. Next, the compressed message plus the MAC are **encrypted** using symmetric encryption. (The cryptographic concepts referenced in this chapter are discussed in Appendix J.)

The final step of SSL Record Protocol processing is to prepend a header, which includes a length field and an indication of which higher-layer protocol (Figure 19.2) is used to process the enclosed fragment.

The Record Protocol then transmits the resulting unit in a TCP segment. Received data are decrypted, verified, decompressed, and reassembled, and then delivered to higher-level users.

Handshake Protocol

There are three SSL-specific protocols that use the SSL Record Protocol. The Change Cipher Spec Protocol updates the cipher suite to be used on this connection. The Alert Protocol is used to convey SSL related alerts to the peer entity.

The most complex part of SSL is the Handshake Protocol. This protocol allows the server and client to authenticate each other and to negotiate an encryption

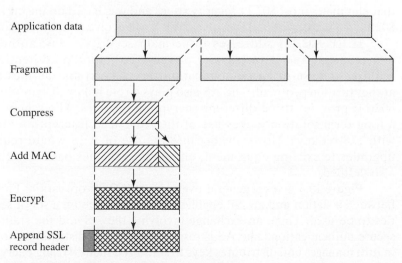

Figure 19.3   SSL Record Protocol Operation

and MAC algorithm and cryptographic keys to be used to protect data sent in an SSL record. The Handshake Protocol is used before any application data are transmitted.

The Handshake Protocol consists of a series of messages exchanged by client and server. The exchange can be viewed as having four phases.

Phase 1 is used to initiate a logical connection and to establish the security capabilities that will be associated with it. The exchange is initiated by the client, which sends a client_hello message that contains the combinations of cryptographic algorithms supported by the client, in decreasing order of preference. Each element of the list (each cipher suite) defines both a key exchange algorithm and a CipherSpec.

After sending the client_hello message, the client waits for the server_hello message, which contains the same parameters as the client_hello message.

The details of **phase 2** depend on the underlying public-key encryption scheme that is used. In some cases, the server passes a certificate to the client, possibly additional key information, and a request for a certificate from the client.

In **phase 3**, the client should verify that the server provided a valid certificate if required and check that the server_hello parameters are acceptable. If all is satisfactory, the client sends one or more messages back to the server, depending on the underlying public-key scheme.

Phase 4 completes the setting up of a secure connection by signaling to both parties that the exchange has been successful.

19.3 WI-FI PROTECTED ACCESS

As discussed in Chapter 14, the 802.11i task group has developed a set of capabilities to address wireless LAN (WLAN) security issues. In order to accelerate the introduction of strong security into WLANs, the Wi-Fi Alliance promulgated **Wi-Fi Protected Access (WPA)** as a Wi-Fi standard. WPA is a set of security mechanisms that eliminates most 802.11 security issues and was based on the current state of the 802.11i standard. As 802.11i evolves, WPA will evolve to maintain compatibility.

IEEE 802.11i addresses three main security areas: authentication, key management, and data transfer privacy. To improve authentication, 802.11i requires the use of an authentication server (AS) and defines a more robust authentication protocol. The AS also plays a role in key distribution. For privacy, 802.11i provides three different encryption schemes. The scheme that provides a long-term solution makes use of the Advanced Encryption Standard (AES) with 128-bit keys. However, because the use of AES would require expensive upgrades to existing equipment, alternative schemes based on 104-bit RC4 are also defined.

Figure 19.4 gives a general overview of 802.11i operation. First, an exchange between a station and an AP enables the two to agree on a set of security capabilities to be used. Then, an exchange involving the AS and the station provides for secure authentication. The AS is responsible for key distribution to the AP, which in turn manages and distributes keys to stations. Finally, strong encryption is used to protect data transfer between the station and the AP.

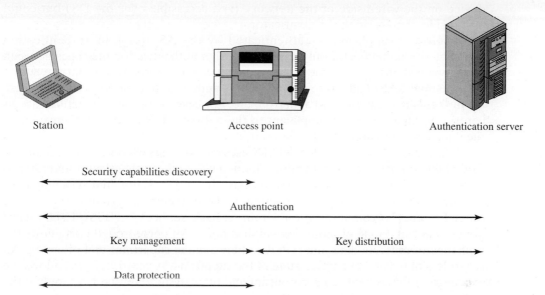

Figure 19.4   802.11i Operational Phases

The 802.11i architecture consists of three main ingredients:

- **Authentication:** A protocol is used to define an exchange between a user and an AS that provides mutual authentication and generates temporary keys to be used between the client and the AP over the wireless link.

- **Access control:** This function enforces the use of the authentication function, routes the messages properly, and facilitates key exchange. It can work with a variety of authentication protocols.

- **Privacy with message integrity:** MAC-level data (e.g., an LLC PDU) are encrypted, along with a message integrity code that ensures that the data have not been altered.

Authentication operates at a level above the LLC and MAC protocols and is considered beyond the scope of 802.11. There are a number of popular authentication protocols in use, including the Extensible Authentication Protocol (EAP) and the Remote Authentication Dial-In User Service (RADIUS). These are not covered in this book. The remainder of this section examines access control and privacy with message integrity.

Access Control

IEEE 802.11i makes use of another standard that was designed to provide access control functions for LANs. The standard is IEEE 802.1X, Port-Based Network Access Control. IEEE 802.1X uses the terms *supplicant, authenticator*, and *authentication server* (AS). In the context of an 802.11 WLAN, the first two terms correspond to the wireless station and the AP. The AS is typically a separate device on the wired side of the network (i.e., accessible over the DS) but could also reside directly on the authenticator.

Before a supplicant is authenticated by the AS, using an authentication protocol, the authenticator only passes control or authentication messages between the supplicant and the AS; the 802.1X control channel is unblocked but the 802.11 data channel is blocked. Once a supplicant is authenticated and keys are provided, the authenticator can forward data from the supplicant, subject to predefined access control limitations for the supplicant to the network. Under these circumstances, the data channel is unblocked.

As indicated in Figure 19.5, 802.1X uses the concepts of controlled and uncontrolled ports. Ports are logical entities defined within the authenticator and refer to physical network connections. For a WLAN, the authenticator (the AP) may have only two physical ports, one connecting to the distribution system (DS) and the other for wireless communication within its basic service set (BSS). Each logical port is mapped to one of these two physical ports. An uncontrolled port allows the exchange of protocol data units (PDUs) between the supplicant and other the AS regardless of the authentication state of the supplicant. A controlled port allows the exchange of PDUs between a supplicant and other systems on the LAN only if the current state of the supplicant authorizes such an exchange.

The 802.1X framework, with an upper-layer authentication protocol, fits nicely with a BSS architecture that includes a number of wireless stations and an AP. However, for an independent BSS (IBSS), there is no AP. For an IBSS, 802.11i provides a more complex solution that, in essence, involves pairwise authentication between stations on the IBSS.

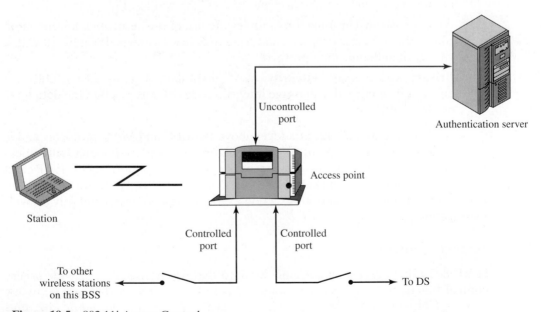

Figure 19.5   802.11i Access Control

19.4 INTRUSION DETECTION

The following definitions from RFC 4949 (Internet Security Glossary) are relevant to our discussion:

Security Intrusion: A security event, or a combination of multiple security events, that constitutes a security incident in which an intruder gains, or attempts to gain, access to a system (or system resource) without having authorization to do so.

Intrusion Detection: A security service that monitors and analyzes system events for the purpose of finding, and providing real-time or near-real-time warning of, attempts to access system resources in an unauthorized manner.

Intrusion detection systems (IDSs) can be classified as follows:

- **Host-based IDS:** Monitors the characteristics of a single host and the events occurring within that host for suspicious activity.
- **Network-based IDS:** Monitors network traffic for particular network segments or devices and analyzes network, transport, and application protocols to identify suspicious activity.

An IDS comprises three logical components:

- **Sensors:** Sensors are responsible for collecting data. The input for a sensor may be any part of a system that could contain evidence of an intrusion. Types of input to a sensor include network packets, log files, and system call traces. Sensors collect and forward this information to the analyzer.
- **Analyzers:** Analyzers receive input from one or more sensors or from other analyzers. The analyzer is responsible for determining if an intrusion has occurred. The output of this component is an indication that an intrusion has occurred. The output may include evidence supporting the conclusion that an intrusion occurred. The analyzer may provide guidance about what actions to take as a result of the intrusion.
- **User interface:** The user interface to an IDS enables a user to view output from the system or control the behavior of the system. In some systems, the user interface may equate to a manager, director, or console component.

Basic Principles

Authentication facilities, access control facilities, and firewalls all play a role in countering intrusions. Another line of defense is intrusion detection, and this has been the focus of much research in recent years. This interest is motivated by a number of considerations, including the following:

1. If an intrusion is detected quickly enough, the intruder can be identified and ejected from the system before any damage is done or any data are

compromised. Even if the detection is not sufficiently timely to preempt the intruder, the sooner that the intrusion is detected, the less the amount of damage and the more quickly that recovery can be achieved.

2. An effective IDS can serve as a deterrent, thus acting to prevent intrusions.
3. Intrusion detection enables the collection of information about intrusion techniques that can be used to strengthen intrusion prevention measures.

Intrusion detection is based on the assumption that the behavior of the intruder differs from that of a legitimate user in ways that can be quantified. Of course, we cannot expect that there will be a crisp, exact distinction between an attack by an intruder and the normal use of resources by an authorized user. Rather, we must expect that there will be some overlap.

Figure 19.6 suggests, in abstract terms, the nature of the task confronting the designer of an IDS. Although the typical behavior of an intruder differs from the typical behavior of an authorized user, there is an overlap in these behaviors. Thus, a loose interpretation of intruder behavior, which will catch more intruders, will also lead to a number of **false positives**, or authorized users identified as intruders. On the other hand, an attempt to limit false positives by a tight interpretation of intruder behavior will lead to an increase in **false negatives**, or intruders not identified as intruders. Thus, there is an element of compromise and art in the practice of intrusion detection.

In Anderson's study [ANDE80], it was postulated that one could, with reasonable confidence, distinguish between a masquerader and a legitimate user. Patterns

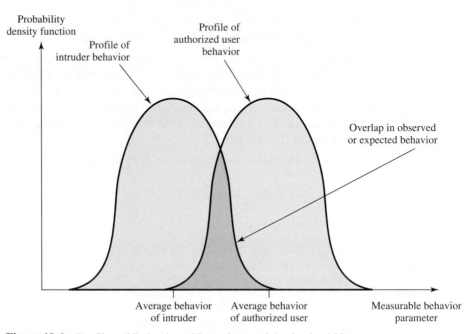

Figure 19.6   Profiles of Behavior of Intruders and Authorized Users

of legitimate user behavior can be established by observing past history, and significant deviation from such patterns can be detected. Anderson suggests that the task of detecting a misfeasor (legitimate user performing in an unauthorized fashion) is more difficult, in that the distinction between abnormal and normal behavior may be small. Anderson concluded that such violations would be undetectable solely through the search for anomalous behavior. However, misfeasor behavior might nevertheless be detectable by intelligent definition of the class of conditions that suggest unauthorized use. Finally, the detection of the clandestine user was felt to be beyond the scope of purely automated techniques. These observations, which were made in 1980, remain true today.

For the remainder of this section, we concentrate on host-based intrusion detection.

Host–Based Intrusion Detection Techniques

Host-based IDSs add a specialized layer of security software to vulnerable or sensitive systems; examples include database servers and administrative systems. The host-based IDS monitors activity on the system in a variety of ways to detect suspicious behavior. In some cases, an IDS can halt an attack before any damage is done, but its primary purpose is to detect intrusions, log suspicious events, and send alerts.

The primary benefit of a host-based IDS is that it can detect both external and internal intrusions, something that is not possible either with network-based IDSs or firewalls.

Host-based IDSs follow one of two general approaches to intrusion detection:

1. **Anomaly detection:** Involves the collection of data relating to the behavior of legitimate users over a period of time. Then statistical tests are applied to observed behavior to determine with a high level of confidence whether that behavior is not legitimate user behavior. The following are two approaches to statistical anomaly detection:

   a. *Threshold detection:* This approach involves defining thresholds, independent of user, for the frequency of occurrence of various events.

   b. *Profile based:* A profile of the activity of each user is developed and used to detect changes in the behavior of individual accounts.

2. **Signature detection:** Involves an attempt to define a set of rules or attack patterns that can be used to decide that a given behavior is that of an intruder.

In essence, anomaly approaches attempt to define normal, or expected, behavior, whereas signature-based approaches attempt to define proper behavior.

In terms of the types of attackers listed earlier, anomaly detection is effective against masqueraders, who are unlikely to mimic the behavior patterns of the accounts they appropriate. On the other hand, such techniques may be unable to deal with misfeasors. For such attacks, signature-based approaches may be able to recognize events and sequences that, in context, reveal penetration. In practice, a system may employ a combination of both approaches to be effective against a broad range of attacks.

19.5 FIREWALLS

The firewall is an important complement to host-based security services such as IDSs. Typically, a firewall is inserted between the premises network and the Internet to establish a controlled link and to erect an outer security wall or perimeter. The aim of this perimeter is to protect the premises network from Internet-based attacks and to provide a single choke point where security and auditing can be imposed.

The firewall provides an additional layer of defense, insulating the internal systems from external networks. This follows the classic military doctrine of "defense in depth," which is just as applicable to IT security.

Firewall Characteristics

[BELL94] lists the following design goals for a firewall:

1. All traffic from inside to outside, and vice versa, must pass through the firewall. This is achieved by physically blocking all access to the local network except via the firewall. Various configurations are possible, as explained later in this chapter.

2. Only authorized traffic, as defined by the local security policy, will be allowed to pass. Various types of firewalls are used, which implement various types of security policies, as explained later in this chapter.

3. The firewall itself is immune to penetration. This implies the use of a hardened system with a secured operating system. Trusted computer systems are suitable for hosting a firewall and often required in government applications.

[SMIT97] lists four general techniques that firewalls use to control access and enforce the site's security policy. Originally, firewalls focused primarily on service control, but they have since evolved to provide all four:

- **Service control:** Determines the types of Internet services that can be accessed, inbound or outbound. The firewall may filter traffic on the basis of IP address, protocol, or port number; may provide proxy software that receives and interprets each service request before passing it on; or may host the server software itself, such as a Web or mail service.

- **Direction control:** Determines the direction in which particular service requests may be initiated and allowed to flow through the firewall.

- **User control:** Controls access to a service according to which user is attempting to access it. This feature is typically applied to users inside the firewall perimeter (local users). It may also be applied to incoming traffic from external users; the latter requires some form of secure authentication technology, such as is provided in IPsec.

- **Behavior control:** Controls how particular services are used. For example, the firewall may filter e-mail to eliminate spam, or it may enable external access to only a portion of the information on a local Web server.

Before proceeding to the details of firewall types and configurations, it is best to summarize what one can expect from a firewall. The following capabilities are within the scope of a firewall:

1. A firewall defines a single choke point that keeps unauthorized users out of the protected network, prohibits potentially vulnerable services from entering or leaving the network, and provides protection from various kinds of IP spoofing and routing attacks. The use of a single choke point simplifies security management because security capabilities are consolidated on a single system or set of systems.

2. A firewall provides a location for monitoring security-related events. Audits and alarms can be implemented on the firewall system.

3. A firewall is a convenient platform for several Internet functions that are not security related. These include a network address translator, which maps local addresses to Internet addresses, and a network management function that audits or logs Internet usage.

4. A firewall can serve as the platform for IPsec. Using the tunnel mode capability described in Section 19.1, the firewall can be used to implement VPNs.

Firewalls have their limitations, including the following:

1. The firewall cannot protect against attacks that bypass the firewall. Internal systems may have dial-out capability to connect to an Internet service provider (ISP). An internal LAN may support a modem pool that provides dial-in capability for traveling employees and telecommuters.

2. The firewall may not protect fully against internal threats, such as a disgruntled employee or an employee who unwittingly cooperates with an external attacker.

3. An improperly secured WLAN may be accessed from outside the organization. An internal firewall that separates portions of an enterprise network cannot guard against wireless communications between local systems on different sides of the internal firewall.

4. A laptop, tablet, or portable storage device may be used and infected outside the corporate network, and then attached and used internally.

Types of Firewalls

A firewall may act as a packet filter. It can operate as a positive filter, allowing to pass only packets that meet specific criteria, or as a negative filter, rejecting any packet that meets certain criteria. Depending on the type of firewall, it may examine one or more protocol headers in each packet, the payload of each packet, or the pattern generated by a sequence of packets. In this section, we look at the principal types of firewalls.

PACKET FILTERING FIREWALL   A packet filtering firewall applies a set of rules to each incoming and outgoing IP packet and then forwards or discards the packet (Figure 19.7b). The firewall is typically configured to filter packets going in both directions (from and to the internal network). Filtering rules are based on information contained in a network packet, such as source and destination address.

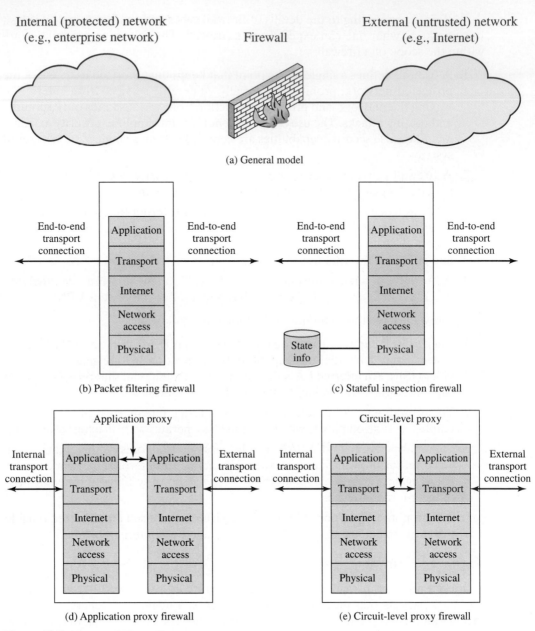

Figure 19.7 Types of Firewalls

The packet filter is typically set up as a list of rules based on matches to fields in the IP or TCP header. If there is a match to one of the rules, that rule is invoked to determine whether to forward or discard the packet. If there is no match to any rule, then a default action is taken. Two default policies are possible:

- **Default = discard:** That which is not expressly permitted is prohibited.
- **Default = forward:** That which is not expressly prohibited is permitted.

The default = discard policy is more conservative. Initially, everything is blocked, and services must be added on a case-by-case basis. This policy is more visible to users, who are more likely to see the firewall as a hindrance. However, this is the policy likely to be preferred by businesses and government organizations. Further, visibility to users diminishes as rules are created. The default = forward policy increases ease of use for end users but provides reduced security; the security administrator must, in essence, react to each new security threat as it becomes known. This policy may be used by generally more open organizations, such as universities.

One advantage of a packet filtering firewall is its simplicity. Also, packet filters typically are transparent to users and are very fast. [WACK02] lists the following weaknesses of packet filter firewalls:

- Because packet filter firewalls do not examine upper-layer data, they cannot prevent attacks that employ application-specific vulnerabilities or functions. For example, a packet filter firewall cannot block specific application commands; if a packet filter firewall allows a given application, all functions available within that application will be permitted.

- Because of the limited information available to the firewall, the logging functionality present in packet filter firewalls is limited. Packet filter logs normally contain the same information used to make access control decisions (source address, destination address, and traffic type).

- Most packet filter firewalls do not support advanced user authentication schemes. Once again, this limitation is mostly due to the lack of upper-layer functionality by the firewall.

- Packet filter firewalls are generally vulnerable to attacks and exploits that take advantage of problems within the TCP/IP specification and protocol stack, such as *network layer address spoofing*. Many packet filter firewalls cannot detect a network packet in which the OSI Layer 3 addressing information has been altered. Spoofing attacks are generally employed by intruders to bypass the security controls implemented in a firewall platform.

- Finally, due to the small number of variables used in access control decisions, packet filter firewalls are susceptible to security breaches caused by improper configurations. In other words, it is easy to accidentally configure a packet filter firewall to allow traffic types, sources, and destinations that should be denied based on an organization's information security policy.

STATEFUL INSPECTION FIREWALLS A traditional packet filter makes filtering decisions on an individual packet basis and does not take into consideration any higher-layer context. To understand what is meant by *context* and why a traditional packet filter is limited with regard to context, a little background is needed. Most standardized applications that run on top of TCP follow a client/server model. For example, for the Simple Mail Transfer Protocol (SMTP), e-mail is transmitted from a client system to a server system. The client system generates new e-mail messages, typically from user input. The server system accepts incoming e-mail messages and places them in the appropriate user mailboxes. SMTP operates by setting up a TCP connection between client and server, in which the TCP server port number, which identifies the SMTP server application, is 25. The TCP port number for the SMTP client is a number between 1024 and 65535 that is generated by the SMTP client.

In general, when an application that uses TCP creates a session with a remote host, it creates a TCP connection in which the TCP port number for the remote (server) application is a number less than 1024 and the TCP port number for the local (client) application is a number between 1024 and 65535. The numbers less than 1024 are the "well-known" port numbers and are assigned permanently to particular applications (e.g., 25 for server SMTP). The numbers between 1024 and 65535 are generated dynamically and have temporary significance only for the lifetime of a TCP connection.

A simple packet-filtering firewall must permit inbound network traffic on all these high-numbered ports for TCP-based traffic to occur. This creates a vulnerability that can be exploited by unauthorized users.

A stateful packet inspection firewall reviews the same packet information as a packet filtering firewall, but also records information about TCP connections (Figure 19.7c). Some stateful firewalls also keep track of TCP sequence numbers to prevent attacks that depend on the sequence number, such as session hijacking. Some even inspect limited amounts of application data for some well-known protocols like FTP, instant messaging (IM), and Session Initiation Protocol (SIP) commands, in order to identify and track related connections.

APPLICATION-LEVEL GATEWAY   An application-level gateway, also called an **application proxy**, acts as a relay of application-level traffic (Figure 19.7d). The user contacts the gateway using a TCP/IP application, such as Telnet or FTP, and the gateway asks the user for the name of the remote host to be accessed. When the user responds and provides a valid user ID and authentication information, the gateway contacts the application on the remote host and relays TCP segments containing the application data between the two endpoints. If the gateway does not implement the proxy code for a specific application, the service is not supported and cannot be forwarded across the firewall. Further, the gateway can be configured to support only specific features of an application that the network administrator considers acceptable while denying all other features.

Application-level gateways tend to be more secure than packet filters. Rather than trying to deal with the numerous possible combinations that are to be allowed or forbidden at the TCP and IP levels, the application-level gateway need only scrutinize a few allowable applications. In addition, it is easy to log and audit all incoming traffic at the application level.

A prime disadvantage of this type of gateway is the additional processing overhead on each connection. In effect, there are two spliced connections between the end users, with the gateway at the splice point, and the gateway must examine and forward all traffic in both directions.

CIRCUIT-LEVEL GATEWAY   A fourth type of firewall is the circuit-level gateway or **circuit-level proxy** (Figure 19.7e). This can be a standalone system or it can be a specialized function performed by an application-level gateway for certain applications. As with an application gateway, a circuit-level gateway does not permit an end-to-end TCP connection; rather, the gateway sets up two TCP connections, one between itself and a TCP user on an inner host and one between itself and a TCP user on an outside host. Once the two connections are established, the gateway typically relays TCP segments from one connection to the other without examining the contents. The security function consists of determining which connections will be allowed.

A typical use of circuit-level gateways is a situation in which the system administrator trusts the internal users. The gateway can be configured to support application-level or proxy service on inbound connections and circuit-level functions for outbound connections. In this configuration, the gateway can incur the processing overhead of examining incoming application data for forbidden functions but does not incur that overhead on outgoing data.

19.6 MALWARE DEFENSE

Antivirus Approaches

The ideal solution to the threat of viruses is prevention: Do not allow a virus to get into the system in the first place. This goal is, in general, impossible to achieve, although prevention can reduce the number of successful viral attacks. The next best approach is to be able to do the following:

- **Detection:** Once the infection has occurred, determine that it has occurred and locate the virus.
- **Identification:** Once detection has been achieved, identify the specific virus that has infected a program.
- **Removal:** Once the specific virus has been identified, remove all traces of the virus from the infected program and restore it to its original state. Remove the virus from all infected systems so that the disease cannot spread further.

If detection succeeds but either identification or removal is not possible, then the alternative is to discard the infected program and reload a clean backup version.

Advances in virus and antivirus technology go hand in hand. Early viruses were relatively simple code fragments and could be identified and purged with relatively simple antivirus software packages. As the virus arms race has evolved, both viruses and, necessarily, antivirus software have grown more complex and sophisticated. Increasingly sophisticated antivirus approaches and products continue to appear. In this subsection, we highlight one of the most important antivirus approaches, known as **behavior-blocking software**.

Behavior-blocking software integrates with the operating system of a host computer and monitors program behavior in real time for malicious actions. The behavior-blocking software then blocks potentially malicious actions before they have a chance to affect the system. Monitored behaviors can include

- Attempts to open, view, delete, and/or modify files;
- Attempts to format disk drives and other unrecoverable disk operations;

- Modifications to the logic of executable files or macros;
- Modification of critical system settings, such as start-up settings;
- Scripting of e-mail and instant messaging clients to send executable content; and
- Initiation of network communications.

Figure 19.8 illustrates the operation of a behavior blocker. Behavior-blocking software runs on server and desktop computers and is instructed through policies set by the network administrator to let benign actions take place but to intercede when unauthorized or suspicious actions occur. The module blocks any suspicious software from executing. A blocker isolates the code in a sandbox, which restricts the code's access to various OS resources and applications. The blocker then sends an alert.

Because a behavior blocker can block suspicious software in real time, it has an advantage over such established antivirus detection techniques as fingerprinting or heuristics. While there are literally trillions of different ways to obfuscate and rearrange the instructions of a virus or worm, many of which will evade detection by a fingerprint scanner or heuristic, eventually malicious code must make a well-defined request to the operating system. Given that the behavior blocker can intercept all such requests, it can identify and block malicious actions regardless of how obfuscated the program logic appears to be.

Behavior blocking alone has limitations. Because the malicious code must run on the target machine before all its behaviors can be identified, it can cause harm before it has been detected and blocked. For example, a new virus might shuffle a number of seemingly unimportant files around the hard drive before infecting a single file and being blocked. Even though the actual infection was blocked, the user may be unable to locate his or her files, causing a loss to productivity or possibly worse.

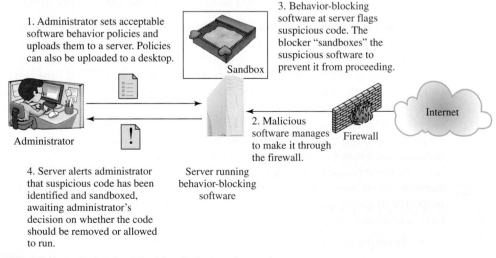

1. Administrator sets acceptable software behavior policies and uploads them to a server. Policies can also be uploaded to a desktop.

Sandbox

3. Behavior-blocking software at server flags suspicious code. The blocker "sandboxes" the suspicious software to prevent it from proceeding.

Administrator

2. Malicious software manages to make it through the firewall.

Firewall

Internet

4. Server alerts administrator that suspicious code has been identified and sandboxed, awaiting administrator's decision on whether the code should be removed or allowed to run.

Server running behavior-blocking software

Figure 19.8   Behavior-Blocking Software Operation

Worm Countermeasures

There is considerable overlap in techniques for dealing with viruses and worms. Once a worm is resident on a machine, antivirus software can be used to detect it. In addition, because worm propagation generates considerable network activity, network activity and usage monitoring can form the basis of a worm defense.

To begin, let us consider the requirements for an effective worm countermeasure scheme:

- **Generality:** The approach taken should be able to handle a wide variety of worm attacks, including polymorphic worms.
- **Timeliness:** The approach should respond quickly so as to limit the number of infected systems and the number of generated transmissions from infected systems.
- **Resiliency:** The approach should be resistant to evasion techniques employed by attackers to evade worm countermeasures.
- **Minimal denial-of-service costs:** The approach should result in minimal reduction in capacity or service due to the actions of the countermeasure software. That is, in an attempt to contain worm propagation, the countermeasure should not significantly disrupt normal operation.
- **Transparency:** The countermeasure software and devices should not require modification to existing (legacy) OSs, application software, and hardware.
- **Global and local coverage:** The approach should be able to deal with attack sources both from outside and inside the enterprise network.

No existing worm countermeasure scheme appears to satisfy all these requirements. Thus, administrators typically need to use multiple approaches in defending against worm attacks. In general, worm countermeasures focus either on identifying suspected worm content or on identifying traffic patterns that appear to conform to worm behavior.

Bot Countermeasures

A number of the countermeasures discussed in this chapter make sense against bots, including IDSs and behavior-blocking software. Once bots are activated and an attack is underway, these countermeasures can be used to detect the attack. But the primary objective is to try to detect and disable the botnet during its construction phase.

APPLICATION NOTE

Security Layers

Security regarding computers and networks can be very confusing. In addition to the large number of threats, the wide variety of systems and technologies that need to be protected can make the job of security guru seem all but impossible. It can be helpful to divide up the tasks or areas and find the best security approach. One method is to divide the domain

(Continued)

into system and network security groups. Another might be to secure different areas of the network perimeter.

Perhaps one of the first rules of security, no matter what area you are focusing on, is to understand the nature of the threat. Companies spend millions of dollars on equipment and personnel in order to protect things that don't need protection. Most organizations agree that their own users, whether accidentally or with intent, become their worst security problem. The range of difficulties can include downloaded viruses, improper use of company resources, and poor control of their own passwords and the passwords of others. One recent experiment showed that people were willing to give up their passwords for a free cup of coffee. But the cracker burrowing through corporate firewalls in order to steal valuable company research isn't the typical case. From the outside, the bad guys are usually trying to shut things down with some sort of denial-of-service attack or use company resources. Another common problem is simply that unauthorized computers are getting a free ride using your bandwidth.

When working with system security, the network administrators are usually focused on servers and end-user computers. These are the most common devices to be compromised. Examine any recent attack and you see that most problems end up being solved or blocked with a variety of upgrades, system patches, or personal firewalls. Every time a server or service is brought online, it must be up to date regarding the operating system and only the required communication ports opened. Other ports must be disabled.

With network security, we are trying to prevent unauthorized traffic. The problem is that there are dozens of protocols used today and there are a myriad of services open. Thus, blocking a certain type of traffic may cause a valid service to be disrupted. As a result, network administrators must have a deep understanding of not only initial configuration, but how protocols operate as well. It is also important to protect your network devices from attack just as you protect the servers.

Often we refer to the programs and techniques used in security as our toolbox. For the network security analyst, one of the easiest ways to think of this toolbox is as a series of layers that correspond to the layers of the TCP/IP or OSI networking models. A sample of the tools for TCP/IP layers follows:

1. **Physical:** The problem is with the actual signal and so the approaches are very straight forward—locking doors, minimizing access to ports, selecting antenna locations, and using low-level encryption such as AES, 3DES, or WPA. Encryption of this type includes protection for layer 2.

2. **Network:** Moving up the stack, we are now dealing with increased intelligence in the networking devices and can start to apply low-level firewalls such as MAC address based filters. Additional tools include VLANs and 802.1x.

3. **Internetwork:** At layer 3 the IP header is exposed and so filtering or firewalls can be applied to IP addresses. Other valuable methods include VPNs and network address translation (NAT).

4. **Transport:** The TCP and User Datagram Protocol (UDP) ports are the main focus and so our filters now target particular streams of communication such as HTTP or FTP. Filters are sometimes referred to as standard or extended access control lists.

5. **Application:** The tools available to us here are usually focused at the user with passwords and authentication. These can be combined with other tools mentioned earlier like 802.1x and VPNs. In addition, other forms of encryption exist like those used in secure shell (SSH) and SSL.

This is only a partial list, and no single approach can be said to work against all threats. In fact, most security techniques can be defeated if they are applied individually. However, taken together as a layered approach, they represent a formidable barrier to would-be interlopers.

Whatever your area of focus, system or network, of great importance is a policy regarding safe and acceptable use. Education for users is also very important. Many times users defeat security practices unintentionally by going around them; viruses provide an excellent example. Policies and some basic education for best practices can go a long way toward protecting the network and system assets.

19.7 SUMMARY

IPsec (IP security) is a set of protocols for providing encryption, authentication, and key management for IP. IPsec provides a standardized means of implementing security for virtual private networks (VPNs).

The Secure Sockets Layer (SSL) and the follow-on Internet standard known as Transport Layer Security (TLS) provide a reliable end-to-end secure transport service over TCP. SSL (and TLS) uses a two-level stack of protocols. These standards provide confidentiality, message integrity, and key management. A common use of SSL or TLS is to provide secure connection between a client computer and a Web site using HTTP on top of SSL or TLS.

For wireless local area networks (WLANs), the Wi-Fi Protected Access (WPA) standard consists of a set of mechanisms to provide secure communication across a WLAN. WPA provides confidentiality, authentication, and access control.

An intrusion detection system (IDS) is a security service that monitors and analyzes system events for the purpose of finding, and providing real-time or near-real-time warning of, attempts to access system resources in an unauthorized manner. An IDS includes a data collection component, to observe user behavior, an analyzer component to determine if an unauthorized intrusion has occurred, and a user interface. In general terms, an IDS looks for user behavior that differs from that expected from a legitimate user.

A firewall is a hardware or software entity inserted between a system or network to be protected and the Internet or other outside access network to control traffic in both directions to enforce a security policy. Firewalls monitor traffic content and/or traffic patterns to achieve their objectives.

Methods for defending against malicious software (malware) continue to evolve as the malware threat evolves. Malware defense can involve a combination of prevention, detection, and removal.

Case Study XI: Cloud Computing (In)Security

The major concepts addressed in this case study include Cloud computing, network security, and network design. **This case study and more are available at www.pearsoninternationaleditions.com/stallings**

19.8 KEY TERMS, REVIEW QUESTIONS, AND PROBLEMS

Key Terms

antivirus	intrusion detection system (IDS)	stateful inspection firewall
behavior-blocking software	IP security (IPsec)	Transport Layer Security (TLS)
bot	malware	Wi-Fi Protected Access (WPA)
firewall	packet-filtering firewall	Worm
host-based IDS	Secure Sockets Layer (SSL)	
intrusion detection		

Review Questions

19.1 What services are provided by IPsec?
19.2 What protocols comprise SSL?
19.3 What is the difference between an SSL connection and an SSL session?
19.4 What services are provided by the SSL Record Protocol?
19.5 What security areas are addressed by IEEE 802.11i?
19.6 Explain the difference between anomaly intrusion detection and signature intrusion detection.
19.7 List three design goals for a firewall.
19.8 List four techniques used by firewalls to control access and enforce a security policy.
19.9 What information is used by a typical packet-filtering router?
19.10 What are some weaknesses of a packet-filtering router?
19.11 What is the difference between a packet-filtering router and a stateful inspection firewall?
19.12 How does behavior-blocking software work?
19.13 Describe some worm countermeasures.

Problems

19.1 The ESP header in IPsec includes an Integrity Check Value (ICV), which is calculated over all of the fields of the IPsec packet except IP header fields that either do not change in transit (immutable) or are predictable in value upon arrival at the endpoint. Fields that may change in transit and whose values on arrival are unpredictable are set to zero for purposes of calculation at both source and destination.

    a. For each of the fields in the IPv4 header, indicate whether the field is immutable, mutable but predictable, or mutable.

    b. Do the same for the IPv6 header.

In each case, justify your decision for each field.

19.2 In SSL and TLS, why is there a separate Change Cipher Spec Protocol rather than including a change_cipher_spec message in the Handshake Protocol?

19.3 In the context of an IDS, we define a false positive to be an alarm generated by an IDS in which the IDS alerts to a condition that is actually benign. A false negative occurs when an IDS fails to generate an alarm when an alert-worthy condition is in effect. Using the following diagram, depict two curves that roughly indicate false positives and false negatives, respectively.

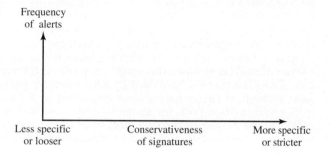

19.4 The overlapping area of the two probability density functions of Figure 19.6 represents the region in which there is the potential for false positives and false negatives. Further, Figure 19.6 is an idealized and not necessarily representative depiction of the relative shapes of the two density functions. Suppose there is 1 actual intrusion for every 1000 authorized users, and the overlapping area covers 1% of the authorized users and 50% of the intruders.

    a. Sketch such a set of density functions and argue that this is not an unreasonable depiction.

    b. What is the probability that an event that occurs in this region is that of an authorized user? Keep in mind that 50% of all intrusions fall in this region.

19.5 An example of a host-based intrusion detection tool is the tripwire program. This is a file integrity checking tool that scans files and directories on the system on a regular basis and notifies the administrator of any changes. It uses a protected database of cryptographic checksums for each file checked and compares this value with that recomputed on each file as it is scanned. It must be configured with a list of files and directories to check, and what changes, if any, are permissible to each. It can allow, for example, log files to have new entries appended, but not for existing entries to be changed. What are the advantages and disadvantages of using such a tool? Consider the problem of determining which files should only change rarely, which files may change more often and how, and which change frequently and hence cannot be checked. Consider the amount of work both in the configuration of the program and on the system administrator monitoring the responses generated.

19.6 Test the vulnerability of a machine at the following site: http://grc.com/default.htm. Follow the ShieldsUP! link for a series of free tests listed midway down the page.

19.7 The tiny fragment attack is a form of firewall attack. The intruder uses the IP fragmentation option to create extremely small fragments and force the TCP header information into a separate packet fragment. This attack is designed to circumvent filtering rules that depend on TCP header information. Typically, a packet filter will make a filtering decision on the first fragment of a packet. All subsequent fragments of that packet are filtered out solely on the basis that they are part of the packet whose first fragment was rejected. The attacker hopes that the filtering firewall examines only the first fragment and that the remaining fragments are passed through. A tiny fragment attack can be defeated by enforcing a rule that the first fragment of a packet must contain a predefined minimum amount of the transport header. If the first fragment is rejected, the filter can remember the packet and discard all subsequent fragments. However, the nature of IP is such that fragments may arrive out of order. Thus, an intermediate fragment may pass through the filter before the initial fragment is rejected. How can this situation be handled?

19.8   In an IPv4 packet, the size of the payload in the first fragment, in octets, is equal to Total Length $-$ $(4 \times$ IHL$)$. If this value is less than the required minimum (8 octets for TCP), then this fragment and the entire packet are rejected. Suggest an alternative method of achieving the same result using only the Fragment Offset field.

19.9   RFC 791, the IPv4 protocol specification, describes a reassembly algorithm that results in new fragments overwriting any overlapped portions of previously received fragments. Given such a reassembly implementation, an attacker could construct a series of packets in which the lowest (zero-offset) fragment would contain innocuous data (and thereby be passed by administrative packet filters), and in which some subsequent packet having a nonzero offset would overlap TCP header information (destination port, for instance) and cause it to be modified. The second packet would be passed through most filter implementations because it does not have a zero fragment offset. Suggest a method that could be used by a packet filter to counter this attack.

APPENDIX A

PROJECTS FOR TEACHING BUSINESS DATA COMMUNICATIONS

A.1 Animations and Animation Projects

A.2 Practical Exercises

A.3 Wireshark Projects

A.4 Research Projects

A.5 Security Case Studies

A.6 Reading/Report Assignments

A.7 Writing Assignments

Many instructors believe that research or implementation projects are crucial to the clear understanding of the concepts of data communications and networking. Without projects, it may be difficult for students to grasp some of the basic concepts and interactions among components. Projects reinforce the concepts introduced in the book, give the student a greater appreciation of how protocols and transmission schemes work, and can motivate students and give them confidence that they have mastered the material.

In this text, we have tried to present the concepts of business data communications as clearly as possible and have provided numerous homework problems to reinforce those concepts. Many instructors will wish to supplement this material with projects. This appendix provides some guidance in that regard and describes the support material available in the **Instructor's Resource Center (IRC)** for this book, accessible from Prentice Hall for instructors. The support material covers seven types of projects and other student exercises:

- Animations and animation projects
- Practical exercises
- Wireshark projects
- Research projects
- Security case studies
- Reading/report assignments
- Writing assignments

A.1 ANIMATIONS AND ANIMATION PROJECTS

Animations provide a powerful tool for understanding the complex mechanisms of network protocols. A total of 17 Web-based animations are used to illustrate protocol behavior. Each animation allows the users to step through the operation of the protocol by selecting the next step at each point in the protocol exchange. Table A.1 lists the animations by chapter. To access the animations, click on the rotating globe at this book's Companion Web site at http://williamstallings.com/ BusinessDataComm.

The animations can be used in two ways. In a **passive mode**, the student can click more or less randomly on the next step at each point in the animation and watch as the given concept or principle is illustrated. The **active mode** can be used for two types of assignments. First, the student can be given a specific set of steps to invoke and watch the animation, and then be asked to analyze and comment on the results. Second, the student can be given a specific endpoint and required to devise a sequence of steps that achieve the desired result. The IRC includes a set of assignments for each of the animations, plus suggested solutions so that instructors can assess the student's work.

These animations were developed at the University of Stirling in Scotland by Iain Robin and Ken Turner, with contributions from Paul Johnson and Kenneth Whyte. Larry Tan of the University of Stirling developed the animation assignments.

Table A.1   Business Data Communications Animations by Chapter

Chapter 6 - Data Link Control and Multiplexing	
Alternating Bit Protocol	A connection-less protocol for transferring messages in one direction between a pair of protocol entities. It is a simple form of the Sliding Window Protocol with a window size of 1.
Sliding Window Protocol (3-column)	Illustrates sliding-window operation without showing the end users.
Sliding Window Protocol (5-column)	Illustrates sliding-window operation showing the end users.
Abracadabra Protocol	A connection-oriented protocol that allows data to be sent in either direction using the Alternating Bit Protocol.
Multiplexing	Illustrates how data can be multiplexed among multiple sources and sinks via a shared communications channel.
Chapter 7 - The Internet	
Boot Protocol	A simple connection-less protocol, typically used by a diskless workstation to discover its Internet address and/or the name of its bootstrap file.
Chapter 8 - TCP/IP	
Protocol Stack	Illustrates how data flows through a typical protocol stack.
TCP Client/Server	The use of TCP to support client/server interaction.
TCP Peer-to-Peer	The use of TCP to support peer-to-peer interaction.
TCP Slow Start	Illustrates dynamic window management using Slow Start.
UDP	Demonstrates UDP Operation.
IP	Demonstrates IP Operation.
Trivial File Transfer Protocol	Demonstrates TFTP Operation.
Chapter 10 - Internet-Based Applications	
SMTP	Simulator deals with main commands: HELO, MAIL FROM, RCPT TO, DATA, QUIT.
HTTP	Simulator deals with main commands: GET, HEAD, POST, PUT.
Chapter 11 - Internet Operation	
Multicasting	Illustrates how data can be sent from a source to multiple destinations over a network.
Chapter 13 - Ethernet	
CSMA/CD	Illustrates how multiple systems can share a common communications medium using CSMA/CD.

A.2 PRACTICAL EXERCISES

The IRC includes Web pages that provide a set of practical exercises for an introduction to the use of IP over a LAN. The exercises naturally follow one another and build on the experience of the previous exercises. They do not, however, need to be attempted one after another. The four exercises may more easily be done on four separate occasions. The practical exercises are designed to help the student understand the operation of an Ethernet LAN and an IP network. The exercises involve using simple network commands available on most computers. About an hour is needed to perform all four exercises. The exercises cover the following topics: your own network connection, computers on your LAN, computers on remote networks, and the Internet.

A.3   WIRESHARK PROJECTS

Wireshark, formerly known as Ethereal, is used by network professionals around the world for troubleshooting, analysis, software and protocol development, and education. It has all of the standard features you would expect in a protocol analyzer and several features not seen in any other product. Its open-source license allows talented experts in the networking community to add enhancements. It runs on all popular computing platforms, including UNIX, Linux, Windows, and Mac OS X.

Wireshark is ideal for allowing students to study the behavior of protocols not only because of its many features and multiplatform capability but also because students may subsequently use Wireshark in their professional life.

The IRC includes a Student User's Manual and a set of project assignments for Wireshark created specifically for use with *Business Data Communications*. In addition, there is a very useful video tutorial that introduces the student to the use of Wireshark.

Michael Harris of Indiana University initially developed the Ethereal exercises and user's guide. Dave Bremer of Otago Polytechnic in New Zealand updated the material for the most recent Wireshark release; he also developed the online video tutorial.

A.4   RESEARCH PROJECTS

An effective way of reinforcing basic concepts from the course and for teaching students research skills is to assign a research project. Such a project could involve a literature search as well as a Web search of vendor products, research lab activities, and standardization efforts. Projects could be assigned to teams or, for smaller projects, to individuals. In any case, it is best to require some sort of project proposal early in the term, giving the instructor time to evaluate the proposal for appropriate topic and appropriate level of effort. Student handouts for research projects should include

- A format for the proposal
- A format for the final report
- A schedule with intermediate and final deadlines
- A list of possible project topics

The students can select one of the listed topics or devise their own comparable project. The IRC includes a suggested format for the proposal and final report plus a list of possible research topics.

A.5 SECURITY CASE STUDIES

Teaching with case studies engages students in active learning. The IRC includes case studies that deal with security issues in the following areas:

- Disaster recovery
- Incidence response
- Physical security
- Risk
- Security policy
- Virtualization

Each case study includes learning objectives, case description, and a series of case discussion questions. Each case study is based on real-world situations and includes papers or reports describing the case.

The case studies were developed at North Carolina A&T State University.

A.6 READING/REPORT ASSIGNMENTS

Another excellent way to reinforce concepts from the course and to give students research experience is to assign papers from the literature to be read and analyzed. The IRC site includes a suggested list of papers to be assigned, organized by chapter. The Premium Content Web site provides a copy of each of the papers. The IRC also includes a suggested assignment wording.

A.7 WRITING ASSIGNMENTS

Writing assignments can have a powerful multiplier effect on the learning process in a technical discipline such as data communications and networking. Adherents of the Writing Across the Curriculum (WAC) movement (http://wac.colostate.edu/) report substantial benefits of writing assignments in facilitating learning. Writing assignments lead to more detailed and complete thinking about a particular topic. In addition, writing assignments help to overcome the tendency of students to pursue a subject with a minimum of personal engagement, just learning facts and problem-solving techniques without obtaining a deep understanding of the subject matter.

The IRC contains a number of suggested writing assignments, organized by chapter. Instructors may ultimately find that this is the most important part of their approach to teaching the material. We would greatly appreciate any feedback on this area and any suggestions for additional writing assignments.

GLOSSARY

amplitude   The size or magnitude of a voltage or current waveform.

amplitude-shift keying   Modulation in which the two binary values are represented by two different amplitudes of the carrier frequency.

analog data   Data represented by a physical quantity that is considered to be continuously variable and whose magnitude is made directly proportional to the data or to a suitable function of the data.

analog signal   A continuously varying electromagnetic wave that may be propagated over a variety of media.

analog transmission   The transmission of analog signals without regard to content. The signal may be amplified, but there is no intermediate attempt to recover the data from the signal.

application layer   Layer 7 of the OSI model. This layer determines the interface of the system with the user and provides useful application-oriented services.

asynchronous transfer mode (ATM)   A form of packet switching in which fixed-size cells of 53 octets are used. There is no network layer and many of the basic functions have been streamlined or eliminated to provide for greater throughput.

asynchronous transmission   Transmission in which each information character is individually synchronized, usually by the use of start elements and stop elements.

attenuation   A decrease in magnitude of current, voltage, or power of a signal in transmission between points.

automatic repeat request (ARQ)   A feature that automatically initiates a request for retransmission when an error in transmission is detected.

availability   The percentage of time that a particular function or application is available for users.

bandwidth   The difference between the limiting frequencies of a continuous frequency band.

baud   A unit of signaling speed equal to the number of discrete conditions or signal events per second, or the reciprocal of the time of the shortest signal element.

best effort   A network or internet delivery technique that does not guarantee delivery of data and treats all packets equally. All packets are forwarded on a first-come-first-served basis. Preferential treatment based on priority or other concerns is not provided.

bit   Binary digit. A unit of information represented by either a zero or a one.

bridge   An internetworking device that connects two similar LANs that use the same LAN protocols.

byte   A binary bit string operated on as a unit and usually eight bits long and capable of holding one character in the local character set.

cellular network   A wireless communications network in which fixed antennas are arranged in a hexagonal pattern and mobile stations communicate through nearby fixed antennas.

central office (CO)   The place where telephone companies terminate customer lines and locate switching equipment to interconnect those lines with other networks.

checksum An error-detecting code based on a summation operation performed on the bits to be checked.

ciphertext The output of an encryption algorithm; the encrypted form of a message or data.

circuit switching A method of communicating in which a dedicated communications path is established between two devices through one or more intermediate switching nodes. Unlike with packet switching, digital data are sent as a continuous stream of bits. Data rate is guaranteed, and delay is essentially limited to propagation time.

client/server A common form of distributed system in which software is split between server tasks and client tasks. A client sends requests to a server, according to some protocol, asking for information or action, and the server responds.

cloud computing A loosely defined term for any system providing access via the Internet to processing power, storage, software, or other computing services, often via a Web browser. Typically these services will be rented from an external company that hosts and manages them.

coaxial cable A cable consisting of one conductor, usually a small copper tube or wire, within and insulated from another conductor of larger diameter, usually copper tubing or copper braid.

codec Coder–decoder. Transforms analog data into a digital bit stream (coder) and digital signals into analog data (decoder).

code division multiple access A multiplexing technique used with spread spectrum.

common channel signaling Technique in which network control signals (e.g., call request) are separated from the associated voice or data path by placing the signaling from a group of voice or data paths on a separate channel dedicated to signaling only.

customer premises equipment (CPE) Telecommunications equipment that is located on the customer's premises (physical location) rather than on the provider's premises or in between.

cyclic redundancy check (CRC) An error-detecting code in which the code is the remainder resulting from dividing the bits to be checked by a predetermined binary number.

database A collection of interrelated data, often with controlled redundancy, organized to serve multiple applications. The data are stored so that they can be used by different programs without concern for the internal data structure or organization.

datagram In packet switching, a self-contained packet, independent of other packets, that carries information sufficient for routing from the originating data terminal equipment (DTE) to the destination DTE without relying on earlier exchanges between the DTEs and the network.

data link layer Layer 2 of the OSI model. Converts an unreliable transmission channel into a reliable one.

decibel A measure of the relative strength of two signals. The number of decibels is 10 times the log of the ratio of the power of two signals, or 20 times the log of the ratio of the voltage of two signals.

decryption The translation of encrypted text or data (called ciphertext) into original text or data (called plaintext). Also called deciphering.

differentiated services Functionality in the Internet and private internets to support specific QoS requirements for a group of users, all of whom use the same service label in IP packets.

digital data Data represented by discrete values or conditions.

digital signal A discrete or discontinuous signal, such as a sequence of voltage pulses.

digital signature An authentication mechanism that enables the creator of a message to attach a code that acts as a signature. The signature guarantees the source and integrity of the message.

digital transmission The transmission of digital data or analog data that have been digitized, using either an analog or digital signal, in which the digital content is recovered and repeated at intermediate points to reduce the effects of impairments, such as noise, distortion, and attenuation.

direct sequence spread spectrum A form of spread spectrum in which each bit in the original signal is represented by multiple bits in the transmitted signal, using a spreading code.

distributed database A database that is not stored in a single location but is dispersed over a network of interconnected computers.

distributed data processing Data processing in which some or all of the processing, storage, and control functions, in addition to input/output functions, are dispersed among data processing stations.

domain A group of networks that are part of the Internet and that are under the administrative control of a single entity, such as a company or government agency.

Domain Name System (DNS) A directory lookup service that provides a mapping between the name of a host on the Internet and its numerical address.

downlink The communications link from satellite to earth station.

electronic mail Correspondence in the form of messages transmitted between workstations over a network. The most common protocol used to support electronic mail is the Simple Mail Transfer Protocol (SMTP).

encryption To convert plain text or data into unintelligible form by means of a reversible mathematical computation.

error control A technique for detecting and correcting errors.

error detecting code A code in which each data signal conforms to specific rules of construction, so that departures from this construction in the received signal can be automatically detected.

extranet The extension of a company's intranet out onto the Internet to allow selected customers, suppliers, and mobile workers to access the company's private data and applications via the World Wide Web. This is in contrast to, and usually in addition to, the company's public Web site, which is accessible to everyone. The difference can be somewhat blurred, but generally an extranet implies real-time access through a firewall of some kind.

frame A group of bits that includes data plus one or more addresses and other protocol control information. Generally refers to a link layer (OSI layer 2) protocol data unit.

frame check sequence (FCS) An error-detecting code inserted as a field in a block of data to be transmitted. The code serves to check for errors upon reception of the data.

frame relay A form of packet switching based on the use of variable-length link layer frames. There is no network layer, and many of the basic functions have been streamlined or eliminated to provide for greater throughput.

frequency Rate of signal oscillation in cycles per second (Hertz).

frequency-division multiplexing (FDM) Division of a transmission facility into two or more channels by splitting the frequency band transmitted by the facility into narrower bands, each of which is used to constitute a distinct channel.

frequency-shift keying Modulation in which the two binary values are represented by two different frequencies near the carrier frequency.

guided medium A transmission medium in which electromagnetic waves are guided along a solid medium, such as copper twisted pair, copper coaxial cable, or optical fiber.

header System-defined control information that precedes user data in a protocol data unit.

host Any end system, such as a PC, workstation, or server, that connects to the Internet.

Internet A worldwide internetwork based on TCP/IP that interconnects thousands of public and private networks and millions of users.

Internet Protocol (IP) A standardized protocol that executes in hosts and routers to interconnect a number of independent networks.

Internet service provider (ISP) A company that provides other companies or individuals with access to, or presence on, the Internet.

internetworking Communication among devices across multiple networks.

intranet A corporate internetwork that provides the key Internet applications, especially the World Wide Web. An intranet operates within the organization for internal purposes and can exist as an isolated, self-contained internet, or may have links to the Internet. The most common example is the use by a company of one or more World Wide Web servers on an internal TCP/IP network for distribution of information within the company.

local area network (LAN) A communications network that encompasses a small area, typically a single building or cluster of buildings, used to connect various data processing devices, including PCs, workstations, and servers.

local loop A transmission path, generally twisted pair, between the individual subscriber and the nearest switching center of a public telecommunications network. Also referred to as a subscriber loop.

medium access control (MAC) For a communications network, the method of determining which station has access to the transmission medium at any time.

modem Modulator/demodulator. A device that converts digital data to an analog signal that can be transmitted on a telecommunication line and converts the received analog signal to digital data.

multiplexing In data transmission, a function that permits two or more data sources to share a common transmission medium such that each data source has its own channel.

network access point (NAP) In the United States, a network access point (NAP) is one of several major Internet interconnection points that serve to tie all the ISPs together.

network layer Layer 3 of the OSI model. Responsible for routing data through a communication network.

network service provider (NSP) A company that provides backbone services to an Internet service provider (ISP), the company that most Web users use for access to the Internet.

noise Unwanted signals that combine with and hence distort the signal intended for transmission and reception.

octet A group of eight adjacent bits, usually operated upon as a unit.

Open Systems Interconnection (OSI) reference model A model of communications between cooperating devices. It defines a seven-layer architecture of communication functions.

optical fiber A thin filament of glass or other transparent material through which a signal-encoded light beam may be transmitted by means of total internal reflection.

packet A group of bits that includes data plus control information. Generally refers to a network layer (OSI layer 3) protocol data unit.

packet switching A method of transmitting messages through a communications network, in which long messages are subdivided into short packets. Each packet is passed from source to destination through intermediate nodes. At each node, the entire message is received, stored briefly, and then passed on to the next node.

parity bit A check bit appended to an array of binary digits to make the sum of all the binary digits, including the check bit, always odd or always even.

period The absolute value of the minimum interval after which the same characteristics of a periodic waveform recur.

periodic signal A signal $f(t)$ that satisfies $f(t) = f(t + nk)$ for all integers n, with k being a constant.

phase For a periodic signal $f(t)$, the fractional part t/P of the period P through which t has advanced relative to an arbitrary origin. The origin is usually taken at the last previous passage through zero from the negative to the positive direction.

phase-shift keying Modulation in which the phase of the carrier signal is shifted to represent digital data.

physical layer Layer 1 of the OSI model. Concerned with the electrical, mechanical, and timing aspects of signal transmission over a medium.

plaintext The input to an encryption function or the output of a decryption function.

point of presence (POP) A site that has a collection of telecommunications equipment, usually refers to ISP or telephone company sites. An ISP POP is the edge of the ISP's network; connections from users are accepted and authenticated here. An Internet access provider may operate several POPs distributed throughout their area of operation to increase the chance that its subscribers will be able to reach one with a local telephone call.

point-to-point A configuration in which two and only two stations share a transmission path.

port A transport-layer address that identifies a user of a transport-layer protocol.

presentation layer Layer 6 of the OSI model. Concerned with data format and display.

protocol A set of semantic and syntactic rules that describe how to transmit data, especially across a network. Low-level protocols define the electrical and physical standards to be observed, bit- and byte-ordering, and the transmission and error detection and correction of the bit stream. High-level protocols deal with the data formatting, including the syntax of messages, the semantics of messages, character sets, and sequencing of messages.

protocol architecture The software structure that implements the communications function. Typically, the protocol architecture consists of a layered set of protocols, with one or more protocols at each layer.

protocol data unit (PDU) Information that is delivered as a unit between peer entities of a network. A PDU typically contains control information and address information in a header. The PDU may also contain data.

public-key encryption A form of cryptosystem in which encryption and decryption are performed using two different keys, one of which is referred to as the public key and one of which is referred to as the private key.

pulse code modulation (PCM) A process in which a signal is sampled, and the magnitude of each sample with respect to a fixed reference is quantized and converted by coding to a digital signal.

quality of service (QoS) A set of parameters that describe the quality (e.g., data rate, timeliness, buffer usage, priority) of a specific stream of data. The minimum QoS is best effort, which treats all packets equally on a first-come-first-served basis. QoS may dictate the path chosen for delivery by a router, the network service requested by the router of the next network on that path, and the order in which waiting packets are forwarded from the router.

router An internetworking device that connects two computer networks. It makes use of an internet protocol and assumes that all attached devices on the networks use the same protocol architecture at the internet layer and above.

routing The determination of a path that a data unit (frame, packet, message) will traverse from source to destination.

service access point (SAP) A means of identifying a user of the services of a protocol entity. A protocol entity provides one or more SAPs, for use by higher-level entities.

service-oriented architecture (SOA) The modularization of business functions for greater flexibility and reusability. Instead of building monolithic applications for each department, an SOA organizes business software in a granular fashion so that common functions can be used interchangeably by different departments internally and by external business partners as well. The more granular the components (the more pieces), the more they can be reused.

session layer Layer 5 of the OSI model. Manages a logical connection (session) between two communicating processes or applications.

signal An electromagnetic wave used to convey information.

signaling The production of an electromagnetic signal that represents analog or digital data and its propagation along a transmission medium.

spectrum   Refers to an absolute, contiguous range of frequencies.

symmetric encryption   A form of cryptosystem in which encryption and decryption are performed using the same key. Also known as conventional encryption.

synchronous time-division multiplexing   A method of TDM in which time slots on a shared transmission line are assigned to devices on a fixed, predetermined basis.

synchronous transmission   Data transmission in which the time of occurrence of each signal representing a bit is related to a fixed time frame.

time-division multiplexing (TDM)   The division of a transmission facility into two or more channels by allotting the common channel to several different information channels, one at a time.

transmission   The communication of data by the propagation and processing of signals. In the case of digital signals or of analog signals that encode digital data, repeaters may be used. For analog signals, amplifiers may be used.

transmission medium   The physical medium that conveys data between data stations.

transport layer   Layer 4 of the OSI model. Provides reliable, sequenced transfer of data between endpoints.

twisted pair   A transmission medium that consists of two insulated conductors twisted together to reduce noise.

unguided medium   A transmission medium, such as the atmosphere or outer space, used for wireless transmission.

uplink   The communications link from earth station to satellite.

virtual circuit   A packet-switching mechanism in which a logical connection (virtual circuit) is established between two stations at the start of transmission. All packets follow the same route, need not carry a complete address, and arrive in sequence.

virtual private network (VPN)   The use of encryption and authentication in the lower protocol layers to provide a secure connection through an otherwise insecure network, typically the Internet. VPNs are generally cheaper than real private networks using private lines but rely on having the same encryption and authentication system at both ends. The encryption may be performed by firewall software or possibly by routers.

white noise   Noise that has a flat, or uniform, frequency spectrum in the frequency range of interest.

wireless transmission   Electromagnetic transmission through air, vacuum, or water by means of an antenna.

World Wide Web (WWW)   A networked, graphically oriented hypermedia system. Information is stored on servers, exchanged between servers and browsers, and displayed on browsers in the form of pages of text and images.

REFERENCES

ABBREVIATIONS

ACM — Association for Computing Machinery
IBM — International Business Machines Corporation
IEEE — Institute of Electrical and Electronics Engineers

ANDE80 Anderson, J. *Computer Security Threat Monitoring and Surveillance.* Fort Washington, PA: James P. Anderson Co., April 1980.

ANTE06 Ante, S., and Grow, B. "Meet the Hackers." *Business Week*, May 29, 2006.

BELL94 Bellovin, S., and Cheswick, W. "Network Firewalls." *IEEE Communications Magazine*, September 1994.

BIDG06 Bidgoli, H., editor. *Handbook of Information Security.* New York: Wiley, 2006.

BIDG08a Bidgoli, H., editor. *Handbook of Computer Networks.* New York: Wiley, 2008.

BIDG08b Bidgoli, H., editor. "The Internet Fundamentals." In [BIDG08a].

BIH06 Bih, J. "Service Oriented Architecture (SOA): A New Paradigm to Implement Dynamic E-Business Solutions." *ACM Ubiquity*, August 2006. acm.org/ubiquity/views/v7i30_soa.html

BINS10 Binsalleeh, H.; Ormerod, T.; Boukhtouta, V; Sinha, P.; Youssef, A.; Debbabi, M.; and Wang, L. "On the Analysis of the Zeus Botnet Crimeware Toolkit." *Proceedings of the 8th Annual International Conference on Privacy, Security and Trust*, IEEE, September 2010.

BRAG00 Bragg, A. "Which Network Design Tool Is Right for You?" *IT Pro*, September/October 2000.

CAHN98 Cahn, R. *Wide Area Network Design.* San Francisco: Morgan-Kaufmann, 1998.

CERF74 Cerf, V., and Kahn, R. "A Protocol for Packet Network Interconnection." *IEEE Transactions on Communications*, May 1974.

CHEN11 Chen, T. M., and Abu-Nimeh, S. "Lessons from Stuxnet." *IEEE Computer*, 44(4), pp. 91–93, April 2011.

CISC07 Cisco Systems, Inc. " 802.11n: The Next Generation of Wireless Performance." Cisco White Paper, 2007. cisco.com

CLAR03 Clark, E. "Dallas County Plugs into eGovernment." *Network Magazine*, April 2003.

COHE94 Cohen, F. *A Short Course on Computer Viruses.* New York: Wiley, 1994.

CONN99 Connor, D. "Data Replication Helps Prevent Potential Problems." *Network World*, December 13, 1999.

CORM10 Cormen, T.; Leiserson, C.; Rivest, R.; and Stein, C. *Introduction to Algorithms.* Cambridge, MA: MIT Press, 2010.

CSI10 Computer Security Institute. *2010/2011 Computer Crime and Security Survey.* New York, NY: Computer Security Institute, 2010.

DEBE07 Debeasi, P. "802.11n: Beyond the Hype." *Burton Group White Paper*, July 2007. www.burtongroup.com

DWYE92 Dwyer, S., et al. "Teleradiology Using Switched Dialup Networks." *IEEE Journal on Selected Areas in Communications*, September 1992.

ELSA02 El-Sayed, M., and Jaffe, J. "A View of Telecommunications Network Evolution." *IEEE Communications Magazine*, December 2002.

ENGE80 Enger, N., and Howerton, P. *Computer Security*. New York: Amacom, 1980.

GARF02 Garfinkel, S., and Spafford, G. *Web Security, Privacy & Commerce*. Sebastapol, CA: O'Reilly, 2002.

GAUD00 Gaudin, S. "The Omega Files." *Network World*, June 26, 2000.

GOLD10 Gold, S. "Social Engineering Today: Psychology, Strategies and Tricks." *Network Security*, November 2010.

GOLI99 Golick, J. "Distributed Data Replication." *Network Magazine*, December 1999.

GUYN88 Guynes, J. "Impact of System Response Time on State Anxiety." *Communications of the ACM*, March 1988.

HAFN96 Hafner, K., and Lyon, M. *Where Wizards Stay Up Late*. New York: Simon and Schuster, 1996.

HARB92 Harbison, R. "Frame Relay: Technology for Our Time." *LAN Technology*, December 1992.

HOFF02 Hoffer, J.; Prescott, M.; and McFadden, F. *Modern Database Management*. Upper Saddle River, NJ: Prentice Hall, 2002.

HUFF06 Huff, D. "Perspective on 100 Gb/s Ethernet." *100 Gb/s Ethernet Workshop*, Optoelectronics Industry Development Association, September 2006. www.ethernetalliance.org/technology/presentations

INSI12 Insight Research Corp. *Private Line and Wavelength Services 2011–2016*. Mountain Lakes, NJ: Insight Research Corp., January 2012.

JONE09 Jones, P. "Everything over IP Transitions to IP over Everything. *Defense*, September 2009. defensesystems.com/articles/2009/09/02/Industry-Perspective.aspx?p=1

KANA11 Kanaracus, C. "Forrester: SOA is Alive and Well." *Network World*, March 23, 2011.

KING06 King, N. "E-Mail and Internet Use Policy." In [BIDG06].

KLEI75 Kleinrock, L. *Queueing Systems, Vol. I: Theory*. New York: John Wiley, 1975.

KNAU05 Knauer, B. "Voice Goes Wireless." *Cisco Packet Magazine*, Third Quarter, 2005.

LAYL04 Layland, R. "Understanding Wi-Fi Performance." *Business Communications Review*, March 2004.

LAZA07 Laxar, I. *Unified Communications: What, Why, and How?* Issue Paper, Nemertes Research, 2007.

LELA94 Leland, W.; Taqqu, M.; Willinger, W.; and Wilson, D. "On the Self-Similar Nature of Ethernet Traffic (Extended Version)." *IEEE/ACM Transactions on Networking*, February 1994.

MART88 Martin, J., and Leban, J. *Principles of Data Communication*. Englewood Cliffs, NJ: Prentice Hall, 1988.

MILO00 Milonas, A. "Enterprise Networking for the New Millennium." *Bell Labs Technical Journal*, January–March 2000.

NG11 Ng, J. "Global Data Traffic to Hit 60,000 Petabytes by 2116." May 12, 2011. Retrieved online from http://www.zdnet.co.uk/news/networking/2011/05/12/global-data-traffic-to-hit-60000-petabytes-by-2016-40092753/

NIST95 National Institute of Standards and Technology. *An Introduction to Computer Security: The NIST Handbook*. Special Publication 800-12. Gaithersburg, MD: National Institute of Technology, October 1995.

NOWE07   Nowell, M.; Vusirikala, V.; and Hays, R. "Overview of Requirements and Applications for 40 Gigabit and 100 Gigabit Ethernet." *Ethernet Alliance White Paper.* Beaverton, OR: Ethernet Alliance, August 2007.

OU07   Ou, G. "The Role of 802.11n in the Enterprise." *White Paper*, zdnet.com, July 2007.

PARZ06   Parziale, L., et al. *TCP/IP Tutorial and Technical Overview.* IBM Redbook GG24-3376-07, 2006. http://www.redbooks.ibm.com/abstracts/gg243376.html

PAXS94   Paxson, V., and Floyd, S. "Wide-Area Traffic: The Failure of Poisson Modeling." *Proceedings of SIGCOMM '94*, 1994.

RADC04   Radcliff, D. "What Are They Thinking?" *Network World*, March 1, 2004.

ROTH93   Rothschild, M. "Coming Soon: Internal Markets." *Forbes ASAP*, June 7, 1993.

SENS02   Sens, T. "Next Generation of Unified Communications for Enterprises." *Alcatel Telecommunications Review*, Fourth Quarter 2002.

SEVC96   Sevcik, P. "Designing a High-Performance Web Site." *Business Communications Review*, March 1996.

SEVC03   Sevcik, P. "How Fast Is Fast Enough?" *Business Communications Review*, March 2003.

SHNE84   Shneiderman, B. "Response Time and Display Rate in Human Performance with Computers." *ACM Computing Surveys*, September 1984.

SMIT88   Smith, M. "A Model of Human Communication." *IEEE Communications Magazine*, February 1988.

SMIT97   Smith, R. *Internet Cryptography.* Reading, MA: Addison-Wesley, 1997.

SRIR88   Sriram, K., and Whitt, W. "Characterizing Superposition Arrival Processes in Packet Multiplexers for Voice and Data." *IEEE Journal on Selected Areas in Communications,* September 1988.

STAL11   Stallings, W. *Data and Computer Communications, Ninth Edition.* Upper Saddle River, NJ. Prentice Hall, 2011.

STAL12   Stallings, W., and Brown L. *Computer Security: Principles and Practice.* Upper Saddle River, NJ: Prentice Hall, 2012.

SYMA11   Symantec. "Internet Security Threat Report, Vol. 16." April 2011.

TEGE95   Teger, S. "Multimedia: From Vision to Reality." *AT&T Technical Journal*, September/October 1995.

THAD81   Thadhani, A. "Interactive User Productivity." *IBM Systems Journal*, No. 1, 1981.

TIME90   Time, Inc. *Computer Security, Understanding Computers Series.* Alexandria, VA: Time-Life Books, 1990.

VANS86   Van Slyke, R. "Computer Communication Networks." In *Handbook of Modern Electronics and Electrical Engineering*, Charles Belove, editor. New York: John Wiley and Sons, 1986.

WACK02   Wack, J.; Cutler, K.; and Pole, J. *Guidelines on Firewalls and Firewall Policy.* NIST Special Publication SP 800-41, January 2002.

WHET96   Whetzel, J. "Integrating the World Wide Web and Database Technology." *AT&T Technical Journal*, March/April 1996.

WELK11   Welke, R.; Hirschheim, R.; and Schwarz, A. "Service-Oriented Architecture Maturity." *Computer*, February 2011.

Index